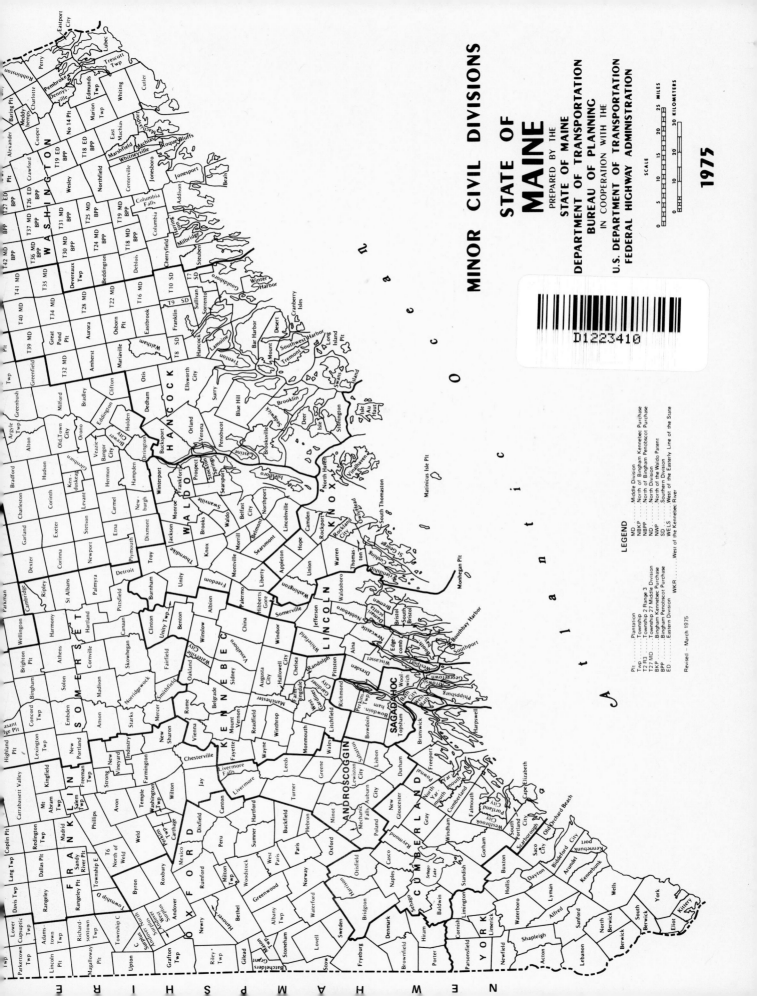

MINOR CIVIL DIVISIONS
STATE OF
MAINE

PREPARED BY THE
STATE OF MAINE
DEPARTMENT OF TRANSPORTATION
BUREAU OF PLANNING
IN COOPERATION WITH THE
U.S. DEPARTMENT OF TRANSPORTATION
FEDERAL HIGHWAY ADMINISTRATION

SCALE

0   5   10   15   20   25 MILES

0   10   20   30 KILOMETERS

1975

D1223410

LEGEND

MD	Middle Division
NBKP	North of Bingham Kennebec Purchase
NBPP	North of Bingham Penobscot Purchase
ND	North Division
NWP	North of the Waldo Patent
SD	Southern Division
WELS	West of the Easterly Line of the State
WKR	West of the Kennebec River

Plt	Plantation
Twp	Township
T2 R3	Township 2 Range 3
T27 MD	Township 27 Middle Division
BKP	Bingham Kennebec Purchase
BPP	Bingham Penobscot Purchase
ED	Eastern Division

Revised – March 1975

NEW HAMPSHIRE

ATLANTIC OCEAN

WASHINGTON
HANCOCK
KNOX
WALDO
LINCOLN
KENNEBEC
SOMERSET
FRANKLIN
OXFORD
ANDROSCOGGIN
SAGADAHOC
CUMBERLAND
YORK

Maine

A Bibliography of Its History

Maine

A Bibliography of Its History

Volume Two of Bibliographies of New England History

Prepared by the

COMMITTEE FOR A NEW ENGLAND BIBLIOGRAPHY

JOHN BORDEN ARMSTRONG
Boston University
Chairman

Edited by
JOHN D. HASKELL, JR.

G.K. HALL & CO. 70 LINCOLN ST. BOSTON, MASS.
1977

*This volume has been
made possible in part by a grant
from the Research Materials
Program of the National Endowment
for the Humanities*

Copyright © 1977 by The Committee for a New England
Bibliography, Inc.

Library of Congress Cataloging in Publication Data
Committee for a New England Bibliography
    Maine, a bibliography of its history.
    (Its Bibliographies of New England History; v. 2)
    Includes index.
    1. Maine—History—Bibliography. I. Haskell, John Duncan.
    II. Title.
Z1291.C65   1977   [F19]   016.9741   77-9072
ISBN 0-8161-8010-5

This publication is printed on permanent/durable acid-free paper
MANUFACTURED IN THE UNITED STATES OF AMERICA

Sponsors

American Antiquarian Society
Amherst College Library
Bangor Public Library
Bay State Historical League
Boston Athenaeum
Boston College
Boston Public Library
Boston University
Bowdoin College
Brown University Library
William L. Bryant Foundation
Helen P. Burns
Colonial Society of Massachusetts
Randolph P. Compton
Connecticut Historical Society
Connecticut Library Association
Fred Harris Daniels Foundation, Inc.
Dartmouth College Library
Essex Institute
Faust and Louisa Fiore Memorial
Historic Deerfield, Inc.
Janet Wilson James
Maine Historical Society
Maine State American Revolution
Bicentennial Commission
Maine State Archives
Maine State Museum
Massachusetts Historical Society
Mount Holyoke College
Museum of Our National Heritage
New England Historic Genealogical Society
New England Library Association
New Hampshire American Revolution
Bicentennial Commission

New Hampshire Historical Society
Old Sturbridge Village
Providence Public Library
Putnam Foundation
Rhode Island Historical Society
Smith College
Society of Colonial Wars in Massachusetts
Abbott and Dorothy H. Stevens Foundation
Stoddard Charitable Trust
Trinity College Library
University of Connecticut Foundation
University of Maine
University of Massachusetts
University of New Hampshire
University of Rhode Island Library
University of Vermont Library
UpCountry Magazine
Vermont Bicentennial Commission
Vermont Department of Libraries
Vermont Historical Society
Warren Brothers Company
Wellesley College Library
Wesleyan University
Williams College

Officers

Committee for a New England Bibliography

John Borden Armstrong Boston University	*Chairman*
Albert T. Klyberg Rhode Island Historical Society	*First Vice Chairman*
Edward T. James Radcliffe College	*Editorial Vice Chairman*
Marcus A. McCorison American Antiquarian Society	*Treasurer*
Bryant F. Tolles, Jr. Essex Institute	*Clerk*
Edwin A. Churchill Maine State Museum	*Vice Chairman for Maine*
Mary L. Fisher General Electric Co.	*Vice Chairman for Connecticut*
James L. Garvin New Hampshire Historical Society	*Vice Chairman for New Hampshire*
Gertrude R. Mallary Bradford, Vermont	*Vice Chairman for Vermont*
Nancy E. Peace Simmons College	*Vice Chairman for Massachusetts*
Stuart C. Sherman Brown University	*Vice Chairman for Rhode Island*

Contents

PREFACE xxxi

ACKNOWLEDGMENTS xxxiii

CITIES, TOWNS, AND OTHER CIVIL DIVISIONS WITHIN COUNTIES xxxv

SERIAL ABBREVIATIONS xliii

LOCATION SYMBOLS xlvii

INTRODUCTION xlix

MAINE 1-1421 1

COUNTIES

    Androscoggin County 1422-1436 51

    Aroostook County 1437-1479 51

    Cumberland County 1480-1536 53

    Franklin County 1537-1552 55

    Hancock County 1553-1622 56

    Kennebec County 1623-1650 58

    Knox County 1651-1676 59

    Lincoln County 1677-1712 60

    Oxford County 1713-1727 61

    Penobscot County 1728-1765 62

    Piscataquis County 1766-1801 63

    Sagadahoc County 1802-1810 65

    Somerset County 1811-1831 65

    Waldo County 1832-1838 66

Washington County 1839-1876 66

York County 1877-1913 67

CITIES, TOWNS, AND OTHER CIVIL DIVISIONS

Abbot (Piscataquis Co.) 1914 71

Acton (York Co.) 1915-1916 71

Adamstown Township (Oxford Co.) 1917 71

Addison (Washington Co.) 1918 71

Albany Township (Oxford Co.) 1919-1920 71

Albion (Kennebec Co.) 1921 71

Alder Brook Township (Somerset Co.) 1922 71

Alder Stream Township (Franklin Co.) 1923 71

Alexander (Washington Co.) 1924 71

Alfred (York Co.) 1925-1934 71

Allagash Plantation (Aroostook Co.) 1935-1935A 72

Alna (Lincoln Co.) 1936-1939 72

Alton (Penobscot Co.) 1940 72

Amherst (Hancock Co.) 1941 72

Amity (Aroostook Co.) 1942 72

Andover (Oxford Co.) 1943 72

Andover North Surplus (Oxford Co.) 1944 72

Andover West Surplus (Oxford Co.) 1945 72

Anson (Somerset Co.) 1946-1947 72

Appleton (Knox Co.) 1948 72

Appleton Township (Somerset Co.) 1949 72

Argyle Township (Penobscot Co.) 1950 72

Arrowsic (Sagadahoc Co.) 1951 72

Arundel (York Co.) 1952 72

Ashland (Aroostook Co.) 1953 72

Athens (Somerset Co.) 1954-1956 73

Atkinson (Piscataquis Co.) 1957 73

Attean Township (Somerset Co.) 1958 73

Auburn (Androscoggin Co.) 1959-1970 73

Augusta (Kennebec Co.) 1971-2035 73

Aurora (Hancock Co.) 2036 75

CONTENTS

Avon (Franklin Co.) 2037 76

Baileyville (Washington Co.) 2038-2040 76

Bald Mountain Township (Somerset Co.) 2041 76

Baldwin (Cumberland Co.) 2042 76

Bancroft (Aroostook Co.) 2043 76

Bangor (Penobscot Co.) 2044-2164 76

Bar Harbor (Hancock Co.) 2165-2194 80

Baring Plantation (Washington Co.) 2195 81

Barnard Plantation (Piscataquis Co.) 2196 81

Batchelders Grant (Oxford Co.) 2197 81

Bath (Sagadahoc Co.) 2198-2250 81

Beals (Washington Co.) 2251-2252 83

Beattie Township (Franklin Co.) 2253 83

Beddington (Washington Co.) 2254 83

Belfast (Waldo Co.) 2255-2273 83

Belgrade (Kennebec Co.) 2274-2276 84

Belmont (Waldo Co.) 2277 84

Benedicta (Aroostook Co.) 2278 84

Benton (Kennebec Co.) 2279 84

Berwick (York Co.) 2280-2284 84

Bethel (Oxford Co.) 2285-2291 84

Biddeford (York Co.) 2292-2311 85

Big Six Township (Somerset Co.) 2312 85

Big Squaw Township (Piscataquis Co.) 2313 85

Big Ten Township (Somerset Co.) 2314 85

Big Twenty Township (Aroostook Co.) 2315 85

Big W Township (Somerset Co.) 2316 85

Bigelow Township (Somerset Co.) 2317 86

Bingham (Somerset Co.) 2318-2319 86

Blaine (Aroostook Co.) 2320 86

Blake Gore (Somerset Co.) 2321 86

Blanchard Plantation (Piscataquis Co.) 2322-2323 86

Blue Hill (Hancock Co.) 2324-2345 86

Boothbay (Lincoln Co.) 2346-2350 87

Boothbay Harbor (Lincoln Co.) 2351-2354 87

Contents

Bowdoin (Sagadahoc Co.) 2355 87

Bowdoin College Grant East (Piscataquis Co.) 2356 87

Bowdoin College Grant West (Piscataquis Co.) 2357 87

Bowdoinham (Sagadahoc Co.) 2358-2361 87

Bowerbank (Piscataquis Co.) 2362 87

Bowmantown Township (Oxford Co.) 2363 87

Bowtown Township (Somerset Co.) 2364 87

Bradford (Penobscot Co.) 2365 87

Bradley (Penobscot Co.) 2366 87

Bradstreet Township (Somerset Co.) 2367 88

Brassua Township (Somerset Co.) 2368 88

Bremen (Lincoln Co.) 2369-2370 88

Brewer (Penobscot Co.) 2371-2375 88

Bridgewater (Aroostook Co.) 2376 88

Bridgton (Cumberland Co.) 2377-2391 88

Brighton Plantation (Somerset Co.) 2392 89

Bristol (Lincoln Co.) 2393-2438 89

Brooklin (Hancock Co.) 2439-2441 90

Brooks (Waldo Co.) 2442 90

Brooksville (Hancock Co.) 2443-2447 91

Brookton Township (Washington Co.) 2448 91

Brownfield (Oxford Co.) 2449-2451 91

Brownville (Piscataquis Co.) 2452-2462 91

Brunswick (Cumberland Co.) 2463-2582 91

Buckfield (Oxford Co.) 2583-2585 96

Bucksport (Hancock Co.) 2586-2598 96

Burlington (Penobscot Co.) 2599 96

Burnham (Waldo Co.) 2600 96

Buxton (York Co.) 2601-2610 96

Byron (Oxford Co.) 2611 97

C Surplus (Oxford Co.) 2612 97

Calais (Washington Co.) 2613-2630 97

Cambridge (Somerset Co.) 2631 98

Camden (Knox Co.) 2632-2650 98

Canaan (Somerset Co.) 2651-2653 98

Canton (Oxford Co.)   2654 98

Cape Elizabeth (Cumberland Co.)   2655-2666 99

Caratunk Plantation (Somerset Co.)   2667 99

Caribou (Aroostook Co.)   2668-2675 99

Carmel (Penobscot Co.)   2676 99

Carrabassett Valley (Franklin Co.)   2677 99

Carroll Plantation (Penobscot Co.)   2678 99

Carrying Place Town Township (Somerset Co.)   2679 99

Carrying Place Township (Somerset Co.)   2680 100

Carthage (Franklin Co.)   2681 100

Cary Plantation (Aroostook Co.)   2682 100

Casco (Cumberland Co.)   2683-2684 100

Castine (Hancock Co.)   2685-2748 100

Castle Hill (Aroostook Co.)   2749 102

Caswell Plantation (Aroostook Co.)   2750 102

Centerville (Washington Co.)   2751 102

Chain of Ponds Township (Franklin Co.)   2752 102

Chapman (Aroostook Co.)   2753 102

Charleston (Penobscot Co.)   2754 102

Charlotte (Washington Co.)   2755-2756 102

Chase Stream Township (Somerset Co.)   2757 102

Chelsea (Kennebec Co.)   2758-2759 102

Cherryfield (Washington Co.)   2760-2761 103

Chester (Penobscot Co.)   2762 103

Chesterville (Franklin Co.)   2763-2764 103

Chesuncook Township (Piscataquis Co.)   2765 103

China (Kennebec Co.)   2766-2768 103

Clifton (Penobscot Co.)   2769 103

Clinton (Kennebec Co.)   2770-2773 103

Coburn Gore (Franklin Co.)   2774 103

Codyville Plantation (Washington Co.)   2775 103

Columbia (Washington Co.)   2776-2780 103

Columbia Falls (Washington Co.)   2781-2786 104

Comstock Township (Somerset Co.)   2787 104

Concord Township (Somerset Co.)   2788 104

Connor Township (Aroostook Co.) 2789 104

Cooper (Washington Co.) 2790 104

Coplin Plantation (Franklin Co.) 2791 104

Corinna (Penobscot Co.) 2792 104

Corinth (Penobscot Co.) 2793 104

Cornish (York Co.) 2794-2798 104

Cornville (Somerset Co.) 2799 104

Cove Point Township (Piscataquis Co.) 2800 105

Cox Patent (Aroostook Co.) 2801 105

Cranberry Isles (Hancock Co.) 2802-2804 105

Crawford (Washington Co.) 2805 105

Crystal (Aroostook Co.) 2806 105

Cumberland (Cumberland Co.) 2807-2813 105

Cushing (Knox Co.) 2814 105

Cutler (Washington Co.) 2815 105

Cyr Plantation (Aroostook Co.) 2816 105

Dallas Plantation (Franklin Co.) 2817 105

Damariscotta (Lincoln Co.) 2818-2826 105

Danforth (Washington Co.) 2827 106

Davis Township (Franklin Co.) 2828 106

Days Academy Grant (Piscataquis Co.) 2829 106

Dayton (York Co.) 2830 106

Dead River Township (Somerset Co.) 2831 106

Deblois (Washington Co.) 2832 106

Dedham (Hancock Co.) 2833 106

Deer Isle (Hancock Co.) 2834-2844 106

Denmark (Oxford Co.) 2845-2848 107

Dennistown Plantation (Somerset Co.) 2849 107

Dennysville (Washington Co.) 2850-2854 107

Detroit (Somerset Co.) 2855 107

Devereaux Township (Washington Co.) 2856 107

Dexter (Penobscot Co.) 2857-2867 107

Dixfield (Oxford Co.) 2868 108

Dixmont (Penobscot Co.) 2869-2871 108

Dole Brook Township (Somerset Co.) 2872 108

Dover-Foxcroft (Piscataquis Co.) 2873-2884 108

Dresden (Lincoln Co.) 2885-2897 108

Drew Plantation (Penobscot Co.) 2898 109

Dudley Township (Aroostook Co.) 2899 109

Durham (Androscoggin Co.) 2900-2901 109

Dyer Brook (Aroostook Co.) 2902 109

Dyer Township (Washington Co.) 2903 109

E Plantation (Aroostook Co.) 2904 109

Eagle Lake (Aroostook Co.) 2905 109

Eagle Lake Township (Piscataquis Co.) 2906 109

East Machias (Washington Co.) 2907-2911 109

East Middlesex Canal Grant (Piscataquis Co.) 2912 109

East Millinocket (Penobscot Co.) 2913-2915 109

East Moxie Township (Somerset Co.) 2916 110

Eastbrook (Hancock Co.) 2917 110

Easton (Aroostook Co.) 2918 110

Eastport (Washington Co.) 2919-2938 110

Eddington (Penobscot Co.) 2939-2940 110

Edgecomb (Lincoln Co.) 2941-2951 111

Edinburg (Penobscot Co.) 2952 111

Edmunds Township (Washington Co.) 2953 111

Eliot (York Co.) 2954-2992 111

Elliottsville Plantation (Piscataquis Co.) 2993 112

Ellsworth (Hancock Co.) 2994-3022 112

Elm Stream Township (Somerset Co.) 3023 113

Embden (Somerset Co.) 3024 113

Enfield (Penobscot Co.) 3025 113

Etna (Penobscot Co.) 3026 114

Eustis (Franklin Co.) 3027 114

Exeter (Penobscot Co.) 3028 114

Fairfield (Somerset Co.) 3029-3036 114

Falmouth (Cumberland Co.) 3037-3043 114

Farmingdale (Kennebec Co.) 3044 114

Farmington (Franklin Co.) 3045-3071 114

Fayette (Kennebec Co.) 3072-3073 115

Flagstaff Township (Somerset Co.) 3074 115

Forest City Township (Washington Co.) 3075 115

Forest Township (Washington Co.) 3076 115

The Forks Plantation (Somerset Co.) 3077 116

Forkstown Township (Aroostook Co.) 3078 116

Forsyth Township (Somerset Co.) 3079 116

Fort Fairfield (Aroostook Co.) 3080-3085 116

Fort Kent (Aroostook Co.) 3086-3089 116

Fowler Township (Washington Co.) 3090 116

Frankfort (Waldo Co.) 3091 116

Franklin (Hancock Co.) 3092 116

Freedom (Waldo Co.) 3093 116

Freeman Township (Franklin Co.) 3094-3095 116

Freeport (Cumberland Co.) 3096-3113 116

Frenchtown Township (Piscataquis Co.) 3114 117

Frenchville (Aroostook Co.) 3115 117

Friendship (Knox Co.) 3116-3119 117

Fryeburg (Oxford Co.) 3120-3147 117

Gardiner (Kennebec Co.) 3148-3175 118

Garfield Plantation (Aroostook Co.) 3176 120

Garland (Penobscot Co.) 3177-3178 120

Georgetown (Sagadahoc Co.) 3179-3183 120

Gilead (Oxford Co.) 3183A-3184 120

Glenburn (Penobscot Co.) 3185 120

Glenwood Plantation (Aroostook Co.) 3186 120

Gore A2 (Piscataquis Co.) 3187 120

Gorham (Cumberland Co.) 3188-3210 121

Gorham Gore (Franklin Co.) 3211 121

Gouldsboro (Hancock Co.) 3212-3220 121

Grafton Township (Oxford Co.) 3221-3222 121

Grand Falls Plantation (Penobscot Co.) 3223 121

Grand Isle (Aroostook Co.) 3224 121

Grand Lake Stream Plantation (Washington Co.) 3225 122

Gray (Cumberland Co.) 3226-3228 122

Great Pond Plantation (Hancock Co.) 3229 122

CONTENTS

Greenbush (Penobscot Co.) 3230 122

Greene (Androscoggin Co.) 3231-3232 122

Greenfield (Penobscot Co.) 3233 122

Greenville (Piscataquis Co.) 3234-3241 122

Greenwood (Oxford Co.) 3242 122

Grindstone Township (Penobscot Co.) 3243 122

Guilford (Piscataquis Co.) 3244-3247 122

Hallowell (Kennebec Co.) 3248-3269 122

Hamlin Plantation (Aroostook Co.) 3270 123

Hammond Plantation (Aroostook Co.) 3271 123

Hammond Township (Somerset Co.) 3272 123

Hampden (Penobscot Co.) 3273-3279 123

Hancock (Hancock Co.) 3280-3282 124

Hanover (Oxford Co.) 3283 124

Harfords Point Township (Piscataquis Co.) 3284 124

Harmony (Somerset Co.) 3285 124

Harpswell (Cumberland Co.) 3286-3307 124

Harrington (Washington Co.) 3308 125

Harrison (Cumberland Co.) 3309-3311 125

Hartford (Oxford Co.) 3312 125

Hartland (Somerset Co.) 3313 125

Haynesville (Aroostook Co.) 3314 125

Hebron (Oxford Co.) 3315-3319 125

Hermon (Penobscot Co.) 3320-3321 125

Hersey (Aroostook Co.) 3322 126

Herseytown Township (Penobscot Co.) 3323 126

Hibberts Gore (Lincoln Co.) 3324 126

Highland Plantation (Somerset Co.) 3325 126

Hiram (Oxford Co.) 3326-3330 126

Hobbstown Township (Somerset Co.) 3331 126

Hodgdon (Aroostook Co.) 3332 126

Holden (Penobscot Co.) 3333 126

Holeb Township (Somerset Co.) 3334 126

Hollis (York Co.) 3335 126

Hope (Knox Co.) 3336 126

Hopkins Academy Grant (Penobscot Co.)   3337 126

Houlton (Aroostook Co.)   3338-3355 126

Howland (Penobscot Co.)   3356 127

Hudson (Penobscot Co.)   3357 127

Indian Island Penobscot Indian Reservation (Penobscot Co.)   3358 127

Indian Stream Township (Somerset Co.)   3359 127

Indian Township State Indian Reservation (Washington Co.)   3360 127

Industry (Franklin Co.)   3361-3362 127

Island Falls (Aroostook Co.)   3363 127

Isle au Haut (Knox Co.)   3364-3368 127

Islesboro (Waldo Co.)   3369-3377 128

Jackman (Somerset Co.)   3377A-3378 128

Jackson (Waldo Co.)   3379 128

Jay (Franklin Co.)   3380-3382 128

Jefferson (Lincoln Co.)   3383-3385 128

Jim Pond Township (Franklin Co.)   3386 128

Johnson Mountain Township (Somerset Co.)   3387 128

Jonesboro (Washington Co.)   3388 129

Jonesport (Washington Co.)   3389-3396A 129

Katahdin Iron Works Township (Piscataquis Co.)   3397-3401 129

Kenduskeag (Penobscot Co.)   3402 129

Kennebunk (York Co.)   3403-3425 129

Kennebunkport (York Co.)   3426-3446 130

Kibby Township (Franklin Co.)   3447 131

Kineo Township (Piscataquis Co.)   3448-3450 131

King & Bartlett Township (Somerset Co.)   3451 131

Kingfield (Franklin Co.)   3452-3455 131

Kingman Township (Penobscot Co.)   3456 131

Kingsbury Plantation (Piscataquis Co.)   3457 131

Kittery (York Co.)   3458-3506 131

Knox (Waldo Co.)   3507 133

Kossuth Township (Washington Co.)   3508 133

Lagrange (Penobscot Co.)   3509 133

Lake View Plantation (Piscataquis Co.)   3510 133

Lakeville Plantation (Penobscot Co.)   3511 133

Lambert Lake Township (Washington Co.) 3512 133

Lamoine (Hancock Co.) 3513-3516 133

Lang Township (Franklin Co.) 3517 133

Lebanon (York Co.) 3518-3523 133

Lee (Penobscot Co.) 3524-3525 134

Leeds (Androscoggin Co.) 3526 134

Levant (Penobscot Co.) 3527 134

Lewiston (Androscoggin Co.) 3528-3577 134

Lexington Township (Somerset Co.) 3578 136

Liberty (Waldo Co.) 3579-3582 136

Lily Bay Township (Piscataquis Co.) 3583 136

Limerick (York Co.) 3584-3587 136

Limestone (Aroostook Co.) 3588-3589 136

Limington (York Co.) 3590-3593 136

Lincoln (Penobscot Co.) 3594-3598 136

Lincoln Plantation (Oxford Co.) 3599 137

Lincolnville (Waldo Co.) 3600-3601 137

Linneus (Aroostook Co.) 3602 137

Lisbon (Androscoggin Co.) 3603-3606 137

Litchfield (Kennebec Co.) 3607-3611 137

Little Squaw Township (Piscataquis Co.) 3612 137

Little W Township (Somerset Co.) 3613 137

Littleton (Aroostook Co.) 3614 137

Livermore (Androscoggin Co.) 3615-3624 137

Livermore Falls (Androscoggin Co.) 3625-3627 138

Lobster Township (Piscataquis Co.) 3628 138

Long A Township (Penobscot Co.) 3629 138

Long Island Plantation (Hancock Co.) 3630 138

Long Pond Township (Somerset Co.) 3631 138

Lovell (Oxford Co.) 3632-3634 138

Lowell (Penobscot Co.) 3635 138

Lowelltown Township (Oxford Co.) 3636 138

Lower Cupsuptic Township (Oxford Co.) 3637 138

Lower Enchanted Township (Somerset Co.) 3638 138

Lubec (Washington Co.) 3639-3647 138

Ludlow (Aroostook Co.) 3648 139

Lyman (York Co.) 3649 139

Lynchtown Township (Oxford Co.) 3650-3651 139

Machias (Washington Co.) 3652-3683 139

Machiasport (Washington Co.) 3684 140

Macwahoc Plantation (Aroostook Co.) 3685 140

Madawaska (Aroostook Co.) 3686-3693 140

Madison (Somerset Co.) 3694-3696 141

Madrid (Franklin Co.) 3697 141

Magalloway Plantation (Oxford Co.) 3698 141

Manchester (Kennebec Co.) 3699-3700 141

Mapleton (Aroostook Co.) 3701 141

Mariaville (Hancock Co.) 3702 141

Marion Township (Washington Co.) 3703 141

Mars Hill (Aroostook Co.) 3704-3705 141

Marshfield (Washington Co.) 3706 141

Masardis (Aroostook Co.) 3707 141

Mason Township (Oxford Co.) 3708 141

Massachusetts Gore (Franklin Co.) 3709 141

Matinicus Isle Plantation (Knox Co.) 3710-3715 141

Mattamiscontis Township (Penobscot Co.) 3716 142

Mattawamkeag (Penobscot Co.) 3717-3719 142

Maxfield (Penobscot Co.) 3720 142

Mayfield Township (Somerset Co.) 3721 142

Mechanic Falls (Androscoggin Co.) 3722-3723 142

Meddybemps (Washington Co.) 3724 142

Medford (Piscataquis Co.) 3725 142

Medway (Penobscot Co.) 3726 142

Mercer (Somerset Co.) 3727 142

Merrill (Aroostook Co.) 3728 142

Merrill Strip (Franklin Co.) 3729 142

Mexico (Oxford Co.) 3730 142

Milbridge (Washington Co.) 3731-3735 142

Milford (Penobscot Co.) 3736 143

Millinocket (Penobscot Co.) 3737-3741 143

Milo (Piscataquis Co.) 3742-3743 143

Milton Township (Oxford Co.) 3744 143

Minot (Androscoggin Co.) 3745-3748 143

Misery Gore (Somerset Co.) 3749 143

Misery Township (Somerset Co.) 3750 143

Molunkus Township (Aroostook Co.) 3751 143

Monhegan Plantation (Lincoln Co.) 3752-3766 143

Monmouth (Kennebec Co.) 3767-3772 144

Monroe (Waldo Co.) 3773 144

Monson (Piscataquis Co.) 3773A-3780 144

Monticello (Aroostook Co.) 3781 144

Montville (Waldo Co.) 3782 144

Moose River (Somerset Co.) 3783 144

Moro Plantation (Aroostook Co.) 3784 145

Morrill (Waldo Co.) 3785-3786 145

Moscow (Somerset Co.) 3787 145

Mt. Abram Township (Franklin Co.) 3788 145

Mount Chase Plantation (Penobscot Co.) 3789 145

Mount Desert (Hancock Co.) 3790-3798 145

Mt. Katahdin Township (Piscataquis Co.) 3799-3817 145

Mount Vernon (Kennebec Co.) 3818 146

Moxie Gore (Somerset Co.) 3819 146

Naples (Cumberland Co.) 3820-3822 146

Nashville Plantation (Aroostook Co.) 3823 146

Nesourdnahunk Township (Piscataquis Co.) 3824 146

New Canada Plantation (Aroostook Co.) 3825 146

New Gloucester (Cumberland Co.) 3826-3850 146

New Limerick (Aroostook Co.) 3851 147

New Portland (Somerset Co.) 3852-3854 147

New Sharon (Franklin Co.) 3855 147

New Sweden (Aroostook Co.) 3856-3871 147

New Vineyard (Franklin Co.) 3872-3873 148

Newburgh (Penobscot Co.) 3874 148

Newcastle (Lincoln Co.) 3875-3882 148

Newfield (York Co.) 3883 149

Newport (Penobscot Co.) 3884-3886 149

Newry (Oxford Co.) 3887 149

Nobleboro (Lincoln Co.) 3888 149

Norridgewock (Somerset Co.) 3889-3902 149

North Berwick (York Co.) 3903-3910 149

North Haven (Knox Co.) 3911-3913 150

North Yarmouth (Cumberland Co.) 3914-3937 150

North Yarmouth Academy Grant (Aroostook Co.) 3938 151

Northeast Carry Township (Piscataquis Co.) 3939 151

Northfield (Washington Co.) 3940 151

Northport (Waldo Co.) 3941 151

Norway (Oxford Co.) 3942-3959 151

No. 14 Plantation (Washington Co.) 3960 152

No. 21 Plantation (Washington Co.) 3961 152

Oakfield (Aroostook Co.) 3962 152

Oakland (Kennebec Co.) 3963-3968 152

Old Orchard Beach (York Co.) 3969-3978 152

Old Town (Penobscot Co.) 3979-3985 152

Orient (Aroostook Co.) 3986 153

Orland (Hancock Co.) 3987-3989 153

Orneville Township (Piscataquis Co.) 3990 153

Orono (Penobscot Co.) 3991-4034 153

Orrington (Penobscot Co.) 4035 154

Osborn Plantation (Hancock Co.) 4036 155

Otis (Hancock Co.) 4037 155

Otisfield (Cumberland Co.) 4038-4041 155

Owls Head (Knox Co.) 4042-4045 155

Oxbow Plantation (Aroostook Co.) 4046 155

Oxbow Township (Oxford Co.) 4047 155

Oxford (Oxford Co.) 4048-4050 155

Palermo (Waldo Co.) 4051-4053 155

Palmyra (Somerset Co.) 4054 155

Paris (Oxford Co.) 4055-4066 155

Parkertown Township (Oxford Co.) 4067 156

Parkman (Piscataquis Co.) 4068-4069 156

Parlin Pond Township (Somerset Co.) 4070 156

Parmachenee Township (Oxford Co.) 4071 156

Parsonsfield (York Co.) 4072-4074 156

Passadumkeag (Penobscot Co.) 4075-4076 156

Patten (Penobscot Co.) 4077-4078 156

Pembroke (Washington Co.) 4079-4082 157

Penobscot (Hancock Co.) 4083-4089 157

Perham (Aroostook Co.) 4090 157

Perkins Township (Franklin Co.) 4091 157

Perkins Township (Sagadahoc Co.) 4092 157

Perry (Washington Co.) 4093-4095 157

Peru (Oxford Co.) 4096-4097 157

Phillips (Franklin Co.) 4098-4099 158

Phippsburg (Sagadahoc Co.) 4100-4137 158

Pierce Pond Township (Somerset Co.) 4138 159

Pittsfield (Somerset Co.) 4139-4142 159

Pittston (Kennebec Co.) 4143 159

Pittston Academy Grant (Somerset Co.) 4144 160

Pleasant Point State Indian Reservation (Washington Co.) 4145 160

Pleasant Ridge Plantation (Somerset Co.) 4146 160

Plymouth (Penobscot Co.) 4147 160

Plymouth Township (Somerset Co.) 4148 160

Poland (Androscoggin Co.) 4149-4159 160

Portage Lake (Aroostook Co.) 4160 160

Porter (Oxford Co.) 4161-4162 160

Portland (Cumberland Co.) 4163-4533 160

Pownal (Cumberland Co.) 4534-4538 174

Prentiss Plantation (Penobscot Co.) 4539 174

Prentiss Township (Somerset Co.) 4540 174

Presque Isle (Aroostook Co.) 4541-4551 174

Princeton (Washington Co.) 4552-4553 174

Prospect (Waldo Co.) 4554 174

Rainbow Township (Piscataquis Co.) 4555 175

Randolph (Kennebec Co.) 4556 175

Rangeley (Franklin Co.) 4557-4561 175

Rangeley Plantation (Franklin Co.) 4562 175

Raymond (Cumberland Co.) 4563-4566 175

Readfield (Kennebec Co.) 4567-4573 175

Redington Township (Franklin Co.) 4574 175

Reed Plantation (Aroostook Co.) 4575 175

Richardsontown Township (Oxford Co.) 4576 175

Richmond (Sagadahoc Co.) 4577-4583 175

Riley Township (Oxford Co.) 4584 176

Ripley (Somerset Co.) 4585 176

Robbinston (Washington Co.) 4586-4587 176

Rockland (Knox Co.) 4588-4611 176

Rockport (Knox Co.) 4612-4616 177

Rockwood Strip (Somerset Co.) 4617 177

Rome (Kennebec Co.) 4618 177

Roque Bluffs (Washington Co.) 4619 177

Roxbury (Oxford Co.) 4620 177

Rumford (Oxford Co.) 4621-4629 177

Russell Pond Township (Somerset Co.) 4630 177

Sabattus (Androscoggin Co.) 4631 178

Saco (York Co.) 4632-4651 178

St. Agatha (Aroostook Co.) 4652-4653 178

St. Albans (Somerset Co.) 4654 178

St. Croix Township (Aroostook Co.) 4655 178

St. Francis (Aroostook Co.) 4656 178

St. George (Knox Co.) 4657-4662 179

St. John Plantation (Aroostook Co.) 4663 179

St. John Township (Somerset Co.) 4664 179

Salem Township (Franklin Co.) 4665 179

Sandbar Tract (Somerset Co.) 4666 179

Sandwich Academy Grant (Somerset Co.) 4667 179

Sandy Bay Township (Somerset Co.) 4668 179

Sandy River Plantation (Franklin Co.) 4669 179

Sanford (York Co.) 4670-4692 179

Sangerville (Piscataquis Co.) 4693-4695 180

Sapling Township (Somerset Co.) 4696 180

Contents

Scarborough (Cumberland Co.) 4697-4716 180

Searsmont (Waldo Co.) 4717-4720 181

Searsport (Waldo Co.) 4721-4730 181

Sebago (Cumberland Co.) 4731-4732 181

Sebec (Piscataquis Co.) 4733 181

Seboeis Plantation (Penobscot Co.) 4734 182

Seboomook Township (Somerset Co.) 4735 182

Sedgwick (Hancock Co.) 4736-4745 182

Seven Ponds Township (Franklin Co.) 4746 182

Shapleigh (York Co.) 4747-4748 182

Shawtown Township (Piscataquis Co.) 4749 182

Sherman (Aroostook Co.) 4750 182

Shirley (Piscataquis Co.) 4751 182

Sidney (Kennebec Co.) 4752 182

Silver Ridge Township (Aroostook Co.) 4753 182

Skinner Township (Franklin Co.) 4754 182

Skowhegan (Somerset Co.) 4755-4771 182

Smithfield (Somerset Co.) 4772 183

Smyrna (Aroostook Co.) 4773 183

Soldiertown Township (Penobscot Co.) 4774 183

Soldiertown Township (Somerset Co.) 4775 183

Solon (Somerset Co.) 4776-4780 183

Somerville (Lincoln Co.) 4781 183

Soper Mountain Township (Piscataquis Co.) 4782 183

Sorrento (Hancock Co.) 4783-4784 183

South Berwick (York Co.) 4785-4809 184

South Bristol (Lincoln Co.) 4810 184

South Portland (Cumberland Co.) 4810A-4821 185

South Thomaston (Knox Co.) 4822-4823 185

Southport (Lincoln Co.) 4824-4830 185

Southwest Harbor (Hanock Co.) 4831-4834 186

Spencer Bay Township (Piscataquis Co.) 4835 186

Springfield (Penobscot Co.) 4836 186

Squapan Township (Aroostook Co.) 4837 186

Squaretown Township (Somerset Co.) 4838 186

CONTENTS

Stacyville (Penobscot Co.) 4839 186

Standish (Cumberland Co.) 4840-4843 186

Starks (Somerset Co.) 4844 186

Stetson (Penobscot Co.) 4845 186

Stetsontown Township (Franklin Co.) 4846 186

Steuben (Washington Co.) 4847-4848 186

Stockholm (Aroostook Co.) 4849 186

Stockton Springs (Waldo Co.) 4850-4854 186

Stoneham (Oxford Co.) 4855 187

Stonington (Hancock Co.) 4856-4857 187

Stow (Oxford Co.) 4858 187

Strong (Franklin Co.) 4859 187

Sugarloaf Township (Franklin Co.) 4860 187

Sullivan (Hancock Co.) 4861-4862 187

Summit Township (Penobscot Co.) 4863 187

Sumner (Oxford Co.) 4864 187

Surry (Hancock Co.) 4865-4866 187

Swans Island (Hancock Co.) 4867-4869 187

Swanville (Waldo Co.) 4870 187

Sweden (Oxford Co.) 4871 188

T3 Indian Purchase (Penobscot Co.) 4872 188

T4 Indian Purchase (Penobscot Co.) 4873 188

Talmadge (Washington Co.) 4874 188

Taunton & Raynham Academy Grant (Somerset Co.) 4875 188

Temple (Franklin Co.) 4876 188

Thomaston (Knox Co.) 4877-4907 188

Thorndike (Waldo Co.) 4908-4909 189

Thorndike Township (Somerset Co.) 4910 189

Tim Pond Township (Franklin Co.) 4911 189

Tomhegan Township (Somerset Co.) 4912 189

Topsfield (Washington Co.) 4913 189

Topsham (Sagadahoc Co.) 4914-4917 189

Township C (Oxford Co.) 4918 189

Township D (Franklin Co.) 4919 189

Township E (Franklin Co.) 4920 189

CONTENTS

Township 6 (Franklin Co.) 4921 190

Tremont (Hanock Co.) 4922-4926 190

Trenton (Hancock Co.) 4927 190

Trescott Township (Washington Co.) 4928 190

Trout Brook Township (Piscataquis Co.) 4929 190

Troy (Waldo Co.) 4930 190

Turner (Androscoggin Co.) 4931-4934 190

Union (Knox Co.) 4935-4940 190

Unity (Waldo Co.) 4941-4945 190

Unity Township (Kennebec Co.) 4946 191

Upper Cupsuptic Township (Oxford Co.) 4947 191

Upper Enchanted Township (Somerset Co.) 4948 191

Upper Molunkus Township (Aroostook Co.) 4949 191

Upton (Oxford Co.) 4950 191

Van Buren (Aroostook Co.) 4951-4953 191

Vanceboro (Washington Co.) 4954 191

Vassalboro (Kennebec Co.) 4955-4960 191

Veazie (Penobscot Co.) 4961 191

Veazie Gore (Penobscot Co.) 4962 191

Verona (Hancock Co.) 4963 191

Vienna (Kennebec Co.) 4964 191

Vinalhaven (Knox Co.) 4965-4973 192

Wade (Aroostook Co.) 4974 192

Waite (Washington Co.) 4975 192

Waldo (Waldo Co.) 4976 192

Waldoboro (Lincoln Co.) 4977-4999 192

Wales (Androscoggin Co.) 5000 193

Wallagrass Plantation (Aroostook Co.) 5001 193

Waltham (Hancock Co.) 5002 193

Warren (Knox Co.) 5003-5010 193

Washburn (Aroostook Co.) 5011 193

Washington (Knox Co.) 5012-5013 193

Washington Township (Franklin Co.) 5014 194

Waterboro (York Co.) 5015-5018 194

Waterford (Oxford Co.) 5019-5023 194

Waterville (Kennebec Co.) 5024-5117 194

Wayne (Kennebec Co.) 5118-5122 197

Webbertown Township (Aroostook Co.) 5123 197

Webster Plantation (Penobscot Co.) 5124 197

Weld (Franklin Co.) 5125-5128 197

Wellington (Piscataquis Co.) 5129 198

Wells (York Co.) 5130-5140 198

Wesley (Washington Co.) 5141 198

West Bath (Sagadahoc Co.) 5142 198

West Forks Plantation (Somerset Co.) 5143 198

West Gardiner (Kennebec Co.) 5144-5145 198

West Middlesex Canal Grant (Somerset Co.) 5146 198

West Paris (Oxford Co.) 5147-5149 198

Westbrook (Cumberland Co.) 5150-5171 198

Westfield (Aroostook Co.) 5172 199

Westmanland Plantation (Aroostook Co.) 5173 199

Weston (Aroostook Co.) 5174 199

Westport (Lincoln Co.) 5175 199

Whitefield (Lincoln Co.) 5176-5178 199

Whiting (Washington Co.) 5179 200

Whitneyville (Washington Co.) 5180 200

Williamsburg Township (Piscataquis Co.) 5181 200

Willimantic (Piscataquis Co.) 5182 200

Wilton (Franklin Co.) 5183-5191 200

Windham (Cumberland Co.) 5192-5211 200

Windsor (Kennebec Co.) 5212 201

Winn (Penobscot Co.) 5213-5215 201

Winslow (Kennebec Co.) 5216-5221 201

Winter Harbor (Hancock Co.) 5222-5226 201

Winterport (Waldo Co.) 5227-5234 202

Winterville Plantation (Aroostook Co.) 5235 202

Winthrop (Kennebec Co.) 5236-5245 202

Wiscasset (Lincoln Co.) 5246-5276 202

Woodland (Aroostook Co.) 5277 203

Woodstock (Oxford Co.) 5278-5282 204

Woodville (Penobscot Co.) 5283 204

Woolwich (Sagadahoc Co.) 5284-5285 204

Wyman Township (Franklin Co.) 5286 204

Yarmouth (Cumberland Co) 5287-5303 204

York (York Co.) 5304-5355 205

SUPPLEMENTARY BIBLIOGRAPHIES AND GUIDES 207

INDEX 209

Preface

Users of this volume who are interested in the origins and early history of the Bibliographies of New England History project will find an account in my preface to the first volume in the series, *Massachusetts: A Bibliography of Its History.* In brief, beginning in 1968 a group of college history teachers, librarians, and historical society and museum personnel concerned at the lack of bibliographical keys to the vast historical resources of the region formed a committee to compile and publish a multivolume bibliography of New England history. The committee formulated a publication plan, editorial guidelines, and a strategy for securing financial support. By 1972, the committee had acquired funding that enabled it to obtain an editor and commence work on the first volume. The complexity of the project, the absence of models, and the prevailing economic stringency made for slow progress on the road to publication.

In that same preface, I expressed the opinion that the publication of the first volume indicated that the committee had reached a turning point in the project. Now, less than two years later, the second volume in the series has been completed. Many individuals and institutions have contributed time and money to this end. They are too numerous to list, but their contributions should be acknowledged.

The committee itself, with a growing membership, has evolved an effective structure for administering and overseeing the project, and its members continue to give close attention to its many details. Working in close harmony with the committee, the editor and his assistants have developed an increasingly effective editorial process.

The favorable reception accorded the Massachusetts volume has been gratifying. Some reviewers have noted how the bibliography reveals the unevenness of historical coverage of subjects and locales in Massachusetts. This is a welcome observation, since one of the committee's goals has been to encourage research and writing by demonstrating the "needs and opportunities" in historical writing on New England. Reviewers and users have also made suggestions for improving the bibliographies. Those consistent with the committee's general plan and guidelines have been incorporated into this volume. I should like to emphasize the request made in the editor's introduction to this volume for corrections and such addenda as fall within the guidelines and terminal dates for inclusion in the volumes. The committee hopes to publish these corrections and addenda in a section of the New England volume, which will be the final volume in the series.

The committee continues to seek financial support from both individuals and institutions. A contribution of five hundred dollars or more qualifies the donor as a "sponsor" of the Bibliographies of New England History series. In the last two years, the number of our sponsors has risen from forty-three to fifty-eight; except for two who wish to remain anonymous, they are listed herein. Some contributors have given much more than the amount stipulated for a sponsorship, others have given less. All have helped to demonstrate a commitment to the project, and have thereby assisted the committee's efforts to secure major foundation support. The National Endowment for the Humanities has provided funding for the project since 1972 on the basis of the committee's continuing to raise matching funds. Once again, it is my pleasure to express the committee's gratitude to the Endowment for its aid, and for the guidance and encouragement provided by the Endowment's staff. I should also like to acknowledge the generous editorial assistance and financial support that has come from within the state of Maine, especially from the Maine State Archives and the Maine State American Revolution Bicentennial Commission.

Great efforts must still be made to complete the Bibliographies of New England History according to schedule in the next five or six years. The editor will continue to need editorial assistance. The matching funds must be raised for the grant from the National Endowment for the Humanities. Nonetheless, prospects for success are good, and they will become increasingly so with each volume. Work on New Hampshire and Vermont is now underway; when complete, it will take the project to its half-way point.

In the preface to the Massachusetts volume, I stated that this publication project contained a moral. The series should serve as an instructive example of how scholarly projects of merit but with no special allure or modishness can be accomplished even in difficult times by the voluntary, cooperative efforts of individuals and institutions. That moral, that larger value of the Bibliographies of New England History, is restated more emphatically with the appearance of this second volume in the series.

John Borden Armstrong
Associate Professor of History
Boston University

1 May 1977

Acknowledgments

The compilation of a bibliography is a rewarding experience because so many people are interested in its development and betterment. Many have proffered aid, others have responded wholeheartedly when asked for opinions, and all have given generously of their time.

Initially, work on this volume was undertaken in appropriate Boston area libraries. The greater part of the compilation process, however, was conducted in Maine, where detailed searches were made of the four most helpful collections for the study of Maine History: the Bangor Public Library, the Maine Historical Society, the Maine State Library, and the University of Maine at Orono. The following staff members of institutions visited by the editorial staff were most helpful and hospitable: James C. Agnew and Gary B. Roberts, New England Historic Genealogical Society; Helen Atchison, Cary Library, Houlton; Esta J. Astor, Thomas L. Gaffney, E. Virginia Gronberg, Julieanne B. Irving, and Gerald E. Morris, Maine Historical Society; Karen Berg, Bonnie Hunter, Steven Robbins, Hilda Russ, and Margaret Taylor, Maine State Library; Eric S. Flower and Frances C. Hartgen, Fogler Library, University of Maine at Orono; Edith L. Hary, Maine State Law Library; Robert W. Lovett, Baker Library, Harvard University; Edith H. McCauley, Portland Public Library; Arthur Monks, Bowdoin College Library; Peter C. Schmidt, Grand Lodge of Maine (Freemasons), Portland; Evelyn Vradenburgh, American Congregational Association, Boston; and Robert C. Woodward, Bangor Public Library. The collections of the Boston Public Library and Widener Library, Harvard University, were also utilized, particularly for the examination of runs of periodicals.

The following individuals were more than willing to meet with the editor in order that he might draw upon their specialized knowledge of Maine and its history: Ronald F. Banks and Alice R. Stewart, University of Maine at Orono; Edwin A. Churchill, Maine State Museum; Richard F. Dole, South Portland, Maine; Charlotte L. Melvin, Ricker College; James B. Vickery, III, Brewer, Maine; and Margaret A. Whalen, Maine State Archives.

For bibliographical contributions, gratitude is expressed to John Borden Armstrong, Boston University; John E. Frost, New York University; and Irene M. Simano, University of Maine at Orono.

The following individuals corresponded with the editor regarding particular bibliographical questions: Marjory Bryant, Wilton Free Public Library; Natalie S. Butler, Farmington Public Library; Geraldine Chasse, Madawaska Historical Society; Priscilla Harrman, Newagen Memorial Library; Mary B. Howard, Rice Public Library, Kittery; Claire Lambert, Jesup Memorial Library, Bar Harbor; Frances M. Parker, Colby College Library; Martha P. Perkins, Waldoboro Public Library; Marlene Pooler, Fort Kent Public Library; Mary Riley, Bates College Library; Michael J. Sheehy, University of Maine at Orono, and Anne D. Stimpson, Turner Memorial Library, Presque Isle.

Jonathan Randolph and Margaret M. Meehan, Editorial Assistants for this volume both made immeasurable contributions. Margaret Landy typed the final copy, Webb Dordick proofread it, and Neil H. Aronson assisted with preparation of the index.

Cities, Towns, and Other Civil Divisions within Counties*

Androscoggin County

AUBURN
Durham
Greene
Leeds
LEWISTON
Lisbon
Livermore
Livermore Falls
Mechanic Falls
Minot
Poland
Sabattus
Turner
Wales

Aroostook County

Allagash Plantation
Amity
Ashland
Bancroft
Benedicta
Big Twenty Township
Blaine
Bridgewater
CARIBOU
Cary Plantation
Castle Hill
Caswell Plantation
Chapman
Connor Township
Cox Patent
Crystal
Cyr Plantation
Dudley Township

Dyer Brook
E Plantation
Eagle Lake
Easton
Forkstown Township
Fort Fairfield
Fort Kent
Frenchville
Garfield Plantation
Glenwood Plantation
Grand Isle
Hamlin Plantation
Hammond Plantation
Haynesville
Hersey
Hodgdon
Houlton
Island Falls
Limestone
Linneus
Littleton
Ludlow
Macwahoc Plantation
Madawaska
Mapleton
Mars Hill
Masardis
Merrill
Molunkus Township
Monticello
Moro Plantation
Nashville Plantation
New Canada Plantation
New Limerick
New Sweden
North Yarmouth Academy Grant
Oakfield
Orient
Oxbow Plantation

---

*Cities are designated by capital letters.   xxxv

Perham
Portage Lake
PRESQUE ISLE
Reed Plantation
St. Agatha
St. Croix Township
St. Francis
St. John Plantation
Sherman
Silver Ridge Township
Smyrna
Squapan Township
Stockholm
Upper Molunkus Township
Van Buren
Wade
Wallagrass Plantation
Washburn
Webbertown Township
Westfield
Westmanland Plantation
Weston
Winterville Plantation
Woodland

Cumberland County

Baldwin
Bridgton
Brunswick
Cape Elizabeth
Casco
Cumberland
Falmouth
Freeport
Gorham
Gray
Harpswell
Harrison
Naples
New Gloucester
North Yarmouth
Otisfield
PORTLAND
Pownal
Raymond
Scarborough
Sebago
SOUTH PORTLAND
Standish
WESTBROOK

Windham
Yarmouth

Franklin County

Alder Stream Township
Avon
Beattie Township
Carrabassett Valley
Carthage
Chain of Ponds Township
Chesterville
Coburn Gore
Coplin Plantation
Dallas Plantation
Davis Township
Eustis
Farmington
Freeman Township
Gorham Gore
Industry
Jay
Jim Pond Township
Kibby Township
Kingfield
Lang Township
Lowelltown Township
Madrid
Massachusetts Gore
Merrill Strip
Mt. Abram Township
New Sharon
New Vineyard
Perkins Township
Phillips
Rangeley
Rangeley Plantation
Redington Township
Salem Township
Sandy River Plantation
Seven Ponds Township
Skinner Township
Stetsontown Township
Strong
Sugarloaf Township
Temple
Tim Pond Township
Township D
Township E
Township 6
Washington Township

Weld
Wilton
Wyman Township

Hancock County

Amherst
Aurora
Bar Harbor
Blue Hill
Brooklin
Brooksville
Bucksport
Castine
Cranberry Isles
Dedham
Deer Isle
Eastbrook
ELLSWORTH
Franklin
Gouldsboro
Great Pond Plantation
Hancock
Lamoine
Long Island Plantation
Mariaville
Mount Desert
Orland
Osborn Plantation
Otis
Penobscot
Sedgwick
Sorrento
Southwest Harbor
Stonington
Sullivan
Surry
Swans Island
Tremont
Trenton
Verona
Waltham
Winter Harbor

Kennebec County

Albion
AUGUSTA
Belgrade
Benton

Chelsea
China
Clinton
Farmingdale
Fayette
GARDINER
HALLOWELL
Litchfield
Manchester
Monmouth
Mount Vernon
Oakland
Pittston
Randolph
Readfield
Rome
Sidney
Unity Township
Vassalboro
Vienna
WATERVILLE
Wayne
West Gardiner
Windsor
Winslow
Winthrop

Knox County

Appleton
Camden
Cushing
Friendship
Hope
Isle au Haut
Matinicus Isle Plantation
North Haven
Owls Head
ROCKLAND
Rockport
St. George
South Thomaston
Thomaston
Union
Vinalhaven
Warren
Washington

Lincoln County

Alna
Boothbay
Boothbay Harbor
Bremen
Bristol
Damariscotta
Dresden
Edgecomb
Hibberts Gore
Jefferson
Monhegan Plantation
Newcastle
Nobleboro
Somerville
South Bristol
Southport
Waldoboro
Westport
Whitefield
Wiscasset

Oxford County

Adamstown Township
Albany Township
Andover
Andover North Surplus
Andover West Surplus
Batchelders Grant
Bethel
Bowmantown Township
Brownfield
Buckfield
Byron
C Surplus
Canton
Denmark
Dixfield
Fryeburg
Gilead
Grafton Township
Greenwood
Hanover
Hartford
Hebron
Hiram
Lincoln Plantation
Lovell
Lower Cupsuptic Township

Lynchtown Township
Magalloway Plantation
Mason Township
Mexico
Milton Township
Newry
Norway
Oxbow Township
Oxford
Paris
Parkertown Township
Parmachenee Township
Peru
Porter
Richardsontown Township
Riley Township
Roxbury
Rumford
Stoneham
Stow
Sumner
Sweden
Township C
Upper Cupsuptic Township
Upton
Waterford
West Paris
Woodstock

Penobscot County

Alton
Argyle Township
BANGOR
Bradford
Bradley
BREWER
Burlington
Carmel
Carroll Plantation
Charleston
Chester
Clifton
Corinna
Corinth
Dexter
Dixmont
Drew Plantation
East Millinocket
Eddington

Edinburg
Enfield
Etna
Exeter
Garland
Glenburn
Grand Falls Plantation
Greenbush
Greenfield
Grindstone Township
Hampden
Hermon
Herseytown Township
Holden
Hopkins Academy Grant
Howland
Hudson
Indian Island Penobscot Indian Reservation
Kenduskeag
Kingman Township
Lagrange
Lakeville Plantation
Lee
Levant
Lincoln
Long A Township
Lowell
Mattamiscontis Township
Mattawamkeag
Maxfield
Medway
Milford
Millinocket
Mount Chase Plantation
Newburg
Newport
OLD TOWN
Orono
Orrington
Passadumkeag
Patten
Plymouth
Prentiss Plantation
Seboeis Plantation
Soldiertown Township
Springfield
Stacyville
Stetson
Summit Township
T3 Indian Purchase
T4 Indian Purchase
Veazie

Veazie Gore
Webster Plantation
Winn
Woodville

Piscataquis County

Abbot
Atkinson
Barnard Plantation
Big Squaw Township
Blanchard Plantation
Bowdoin College Grant East
Bowdoin College Grant West
Bowerbank
Brownville
Chesuncook Township
Cove Point Township
Days Academy Grant
Dover-Foxcroft
Eagle Lake Township
East Middlesex Canal Grant
Elliottsville Plantation
Frenchtown Township
Gore A2
Greenville
Guilford
Harfords Point Township
Katahdin Iron Works Township
Kineo Township
Kingsbury Plantation
Lake View Plantation
Lily Bay Township
Little Squaw Township
Lobster Township
Medford
Milo
Monson
Mt. Katahdin Township
Nesourdnahunk Township
Northeast Carry Township
Orneville Township
Parkman
Rainbow Township
Sangerville
Sebec
Shawtown Township
Shirley
Soper Mountain Township
Spencer Bay Township

Trout Brook Township
Wellington
Williamsburg Township
Willimantic

Sagadahoc County

Arrowsic
BATH
Bowdoin
Bowdoinham
Georgetown
Perkins Township
Phippsburg
Richmond
Topsham
West Bath
Woolwich

Somerset County

Alder Brook Township
Anson
Appleton Township
Athens
Attean Township
Bald Mountain Township (2)
Big Six Township
Big Ten Township
Big W Township
Bigelow Township
Bingham
Blake Gore
Bowtown Township
Bradstreet Township
Brassua Township
Brighton Plantation
Cambridge
Canaan
Caratunk Plantation
Carrying Place Town Township
Carrying Place Township
Chase Stream Township
Comstock Township
Concord Township
Cornville
Dead River Township
Dennistown Township
Detroit

Dole Brook Township
East Moxie Township
Elm Stream Township
Embden
Fairfield
Flagstaff Township
The Forks Plantation
Forsyth Township
Hammond Township
Harmony
Hartland
Highland Plantation
Hobbstown Township
Holeb Township
Indian Stream Township
Jackman
Johnson Mountain Township
King & Bartlett Township
Lexington Township
Little W Township
Long Pond Township
Lower Enchanted Township
Madison
Mayfield Township
Mercer
Misery Gore
Misery Township
Moose River
Moscow
Moxie Gore
New Portland
Norridgewock
Palmyra
Parlin Pond Township
Pierce Pond Township
Pittsfield
Pittston Academy Grant
Pleasant Ridge Plantation
Plymouth Township
Prentiss Township
Ripley
Rockwood Strip
Russell Pond Township
St. Albans
St. John Township
Sandbar Tract
Sandwich Academy Grant
Sandy Bay Township
Sapling Township
Seboomook Township
Skowhegan
Smithfield

Soldiertown Township
Solon
Squaretown Township
Starks
Taunton & Raynham Academy Grant
Thorndike Township
Tomhegan Township
Upper Enchanted Township
West Forks Plantation
West Middlesex Canal Grant

Waldo County

BELFAST
Belmont
Brooks
Burnham
Frankfort
Freedom
Islesboro
Jackson
Knox
Liberty
Lincolnville
Monroe
Montville
Morrill
Northport
Palermo
Prospect
Searsmont
Searsport
Stockton Springs
Swanville
Thorndike
Troy
Unity
Waldo
Winterport

Washington County

Addison
Alexander
Baileyville
Baring Plantation
Beals
Beddington
Brookton Township

CALAIS
Centerville
Charlotte
Cherryfield
Codyville Plantation
Columbia
Columbia Falls
Cooper
Crawford
Cutler
Danforth
Deblois
Dennysville
Devereaux Township
Dyer Township
East Machias
EASTPORT
Edmunds Township
Forest City Township
Forest Township
Fowler Township
Grand Lake Stream Plantation
Harrington
Indian Township State Indian Reservation
Jonesboro
Jonesport
Kossuth Township
Lambert Lake Township
Lubec
Machias
Machiasport
Marion Township
Marshfield
Meddybemps
Milbridge
Northfield
No. 14 Plantation
No. 21 Plantation
Pembroke
Perry
Pleasant Point State Indian Reservation
Princeton
Robbinston
Roque Bluffs
Steuben
Talmadge
Topsfield
Trescott Township
Vanceboro
Waite
Wesley
Whiting
Whitneyville

York County
Acton
Alfred
Arundel
Berwick
BIDDEFORD
Buxton
Cornish
Dayton
Eliot
Hollis
Kennebunk
Kennebunkport
Kittery
Lebanon

Limerick
Limington
Lyman
Newfield
North Berwick
Old Orchard Beach
Parsonsfield
SACO
Sanford
Shapleigh
South Berwick
Waterboro
Wells
York

Serial Abbreviations

AASP	American Antiquarian Society. Proceedings
AgricHist	Agricultural History
AHR	American Historical Review
AIrHSJ	American-Irish Historical Society. Journal
AJHQ	American Jewish Historical Quarterly
Am Heritage	American Heritage
AmJLegalHist	American Journal of Legal History
AmJSoc	American Journal of Sociology
AmNep	American Neptune
AmPolSciRev	American Political Science Review
AmQ	American Quarterly
AmSocRev	American Sociological Review
Atlantic	Atlantic Monthly
BA	Bowdoin Alumnus
BBHS	Bulletin of the Business Historical Society
BHistMag	Bangor Historical Magazine
BHistMed	Bulletin of the History of Medicine
BHSSC	Berkshire Historical and Scientific Society. Collections
BSM	Bay State Monthly
BTJ	Board of Trade Journal (Portland)
BULRev	Boston University Law Review
CanHistRev	Canadian Historical Review
CanJHist	Canadian Journal of History
CathHistRev	Catholic Historical Review
CCJM	Chamber of Commerce Journal of Maine
CEAIA	Chronicle of the Early American Industries Association

ColbLibQ	Colby Library Quarterly
CongQ	Congregational Quarterly
CSMP	Colonial Society of Massachusetts. Publications
DARMag	Daughters of the American Revolution Magazine
EconHistRev	Economic History Review
EEH	Explorations in Entrepreneurial History (became Explorations in Economic Histor with second series, volume seven)
EIHC	Essex Institute. Historical Collections
FR	Freemason's Repository
GeogRev	Geographical Review
Granite Mo	Granite Monthly
HistEdQ	History of Education Quarterly
HistMag	Historical Magazine
HMPEC	Historical Magazine of the Protestant Episcopal Church
HPHR	Hyde Park Historical Record
JAH	Journal of American History, (1964-)
JAmHist	Journal of American History, (1907-1935)
JEconHist	Journal of Economic History
JHistMed	Journal of the History of Medicine and Allied Sciences
JLibHist	Journal of Library History
JMS	Journal of Medicine and Science
JNegroHist	Journal of Negro History
LabHist	Labor History
LJ	Library Journal
MagAmHist	Magazine of American History
MagHist	Magazine of History
Maine Dig	Maine Digest
MASB	Massachusetts Archaeological Society. Bulletin
MassLQ	Massachusetts Law Quarterly
MassMag	Massachusetts Magazine
MeArchSocB	Maine Archaeological Society. Bulletin
MeCathHM	Maine Catholic Historical Magazine
MeCP	Maine Christian Pilgrim
MeHistMag	Maine Historical Magazine
MeHSC	Maine Historical Society. Collections

MeHSN	Maine Historical Society Newsletter
MeHSP	Maine Historical Society. Proceedings
MeHSQ	Maine Historical Society Quarterly
MeLAB	Maine Library Association Bulletin
MeLB	Maine Library Bulletin
MHGR	Maine Historical and Genealogical Recorder
MHSC	Massachusetts Historical Society. Collections
MHSP	Massachusetts Historical Society. Proceedings
MNEH	Magazine of New England History
Moravian HST	Moravian Historical Society. Transactions
MPAP	Maine Press Association. Proceedings
MVHR	Mississippi Valley Historical Review
NEG	New England Galaxy
NEHGR	New England Historical and Genealogical Register
NEJMed	New England Journal of Medicine
NEM	New England Magazine
NEQ	New England Quarterly
OTNE	Old-Time New England
PCHSC	Piscataquis County Historical Society. Collections
PejHSC	Pejepscot Historical Society. Collections
PolSciQ	Political Science Quarterly
Potter's AmMo	Potter's American Monthly
Putnam's HM	Putnam's Historical Magazine
PVMA	Pocumtuck Valley Memorial Association. History and Proceedings
QH	Quaker History
RLHSB	Railway and Locomotive Historical Society. Bulletin
SJMH	Sprague's Journal of Maine History
SocArchHistJ	Society of Architectural Historians. Journal
UHSP	Unitarian Historical Society. Proceedings
WMHJ	Worcester Magazine and Historical Journal
WMQ	William and Mary Quarterly
Worcester HsProc	Worcester Historical Society. Proceedings of the Worcester Society of Antiquity
WPSAM	White Pine Series of Architectural Monographs

Location Symbols

MB	Boston Public Library
MBC	American Congregational Association, Boston
MBNEH	New England Historic Genealogical Society, Boston
Me	Maine State Library, Augusta
MeB	Bowdoin College, Brunswick
MeBa	Bangor Public Library
MeFarP	Farmington Public Library
MeForK	Fort Kent Public Library
MeForF	Fort Fairfield Public Library
MeHi	Maine Historical Society, Portland
MeHoC	Cary Library, Houlton
MeHoR	Ricker College, Houlton
MeMaHi	Madawaska Historical Society
MeP	Portland Public Library
MePGLM	Grand Lodge of Maine, Ancient Free and Accepted Masons, Portland
MePriT	Turner Memorial Library, Presque Isle
MeU	University of Maine, Orono
MH	Harvard University, Cambridge
MH-BA	Baker Library, Harvard University
MWA	American Antiquarian Society, Worcester

Introduction

In keeping with the guidelines established by the Committee for a New England Bibliography, the entries in this volume are arranged by geographical units. Subject access is provided by means of the index. The initial section of the bibliography contains works relating to the state as a whole, or to more than one of its counties. Sections then follow for the individual counties and, after these, for the subordinate political units, which in Maine are known collectively as minor civil divisions. Within each section, entries are arranged alphabetically.

For the purposes of this bibliography, Maine has been considered in terms of its present boundaries. Although Maine was part of Massachusetts until 1820, writings relating to Maine appear in the present volume regardless of the period of time to which they pertain. Works relating to the separation of Maine from Massachusetts appear both in the present volume and in the Massachusetts volume, which was published in 1976.

Maine's civil divisions below the county level comprise four types: cities, towns, plantations, and unorganized townships. All told, there are 909 such civil divisions, but of these only 666 are named. The remainder are designated by township and range numbers, e.g., T15 R10, and generally have little or no population. In the preparation of this volume, the search was limited to materials relating to named civil divisions. For many of these, particularly plantations and unorganized townships, it will be noted that no items were located. This is not surprising when one considers the meager population of much of the state. According to the 1970 census, there were only forty-two civil divisions with a population of over 5,000, and only fifteen with more than 10,000 inhabitants. In population density, Maine ranked thirty-eighth among the fifty states, with thirty persons per square mile. Information on some of the civil divisions for which no items were located can be gleaned from county histories (where they exist), gazetteers, and guidebooks.

Works that deal explicitly with more than one civil division are treated in the following manner. If the divisions are all within the same county, the work is listed under that county, with SEE ALSO cross-references under the particular civil divisions. The entry is also indexed under the names of the civil divisions treated. Works pertaining to civil divisions in more than one county are entered under the first-named civil division, with cross-references under the others and, again, full indexing. Thus a reader who wishes to locate all of the entries pertaining to a particular county or civil division is urged to consult not only the entries listed under that heading but in addition the SEE ALSO references at the end of the section. All of the entries pertaining to a particular county or civil division may also be located by means of the index. The index also provides access to materials pertaining to centers of population within civil divisions, such as villages, hamlets, and localities. It should be noted, however, that no attempt has been made to list or index the material on particular civil divisions that may be found within county histories.

The general terminal date established for listings in this volume is December 1975. Some later titles, however, have been included when they have come to the editor's attention. Spelling of place names follows the *Standard Geographic Code for Minor Civil Divisions by County and Planning Development District*, a 1974 publication of the Maine State Planning Office.

One general rule for this bibliography series should be mentioned. Works that deal with more than one New England state, as, for example, an article on a boundary dispute between two states, will appear in the final volume on New England as a whole rather than in the volumes for the particular states involved.

In coverage, as in arrangement, this volume follows the guidelines established by the Committee for a New England Bibliography. It is confined to published works—principally books and magazine articles—written in whole or in part with a conscious historical purpose. These may be scholarly monographs or a more informal review of the history of a local church or business firm. Within these listings may be found material on political, economic, social, and intellectual history, along with natural history, literary history, historical archaeology, folklore, and military history. Practical and budgetary considerations made it necessary for the committee to set some limits to the types of material covered. Government documents are exluded, except for edited series of published archival and vital records; but published diaries, personal papers, journals, account books, and travel narratives that are significant for the history of a locale are listed. Works of collected biography have been included, but not biographies of individuals. Books and periodical articles, however, on aspects of an individual career related to the state or to a locality within it are included. Examples are a periodical article on Oscar Wilde's visit to Bangor, or a book on the governorship of Kenneth Curtis. Other categories left out, sometimes regretfully, are unpublished doctoral dissertations, works of genealogy, maps and atlases, guidebooks, fiction, and works that are primarily pictorial. Although the editorial search has been limited to American libraries and catalogs, foreign-language titles have been included when found.

Birth and death dates of authors are given only when necessary to distinguish those persons from others of the same name who appear as authors or subjects in this bibliography. Pseudonymous works are entered under the author's autonym, with a cross reference from the pseudonym in the index. Authorships attributed by individuals or libraries other than the Library of Congress are noted.

Writings by the same author which appear consecutively are arranged alphabetically, regardless of whether they were written by the author alone or jointly. In those few entries where a multivolume work was written by several authors who did not write contemporaneously, this distinction has been noted. Title changes are indicated in a note. For works of more than one edition, the latest edition is cited, with the date of the first edition, if known, indicated in parentheses immediately following the title. Place of publication and dates supplied by the editor appear in square brackets. Variant imprints for multivolume works appear in a note. For broadsides, dimensions are given in inches, height before width.

A location is given only for those works which do not appear in the published catalogs of the Library of Congress or in the *National Union Catalog*. The symbols are those used in the *National Union Catalog*, except for those supplied by the editor, in square brackets, for works in libraries which do not have an assigned symbol. See page xlvii for location symbols. No locations are given for periodicals. Users should refer to the *Union List of Serials, New Serial Titles*, or regional lists as available. For a union list of serials in Maine libraries, see entry 173.

Index listings are given for authors, editors, compilers, subjects, and geographical places, including earlier names of localities. Histories of institutions are indexed both under collective subjects, such as railroads and insurance companies, and under the institution's proper name. Entry numbers for bibliographies relating to a particular place or subject appear in the index immediately after the heading for that place or subject; they are set off by a semicolon from the other entry numbers for that place or subject.

The reader should make particular note of the fact that since index references are to entry numbers, the reader can choose those entries under a subject which refer to a particular place by first referring to the inclusive numbers for that place in the table of contents.

The committee will welcome both corrections and such addenda as fall within the guidelines for inclusion and within the terminal date for a particular volume. The terminal date for the Massachusetts volume was 1972, and for the present volume, as noted, 1975.

Beyond the published material which these volumes bring to notice, the serious student of a locale is urged to make a personal visit to the local library and/or historical society, since, by their very nature, many local history materials are not widely distributed beyond the place to which they pertain. Often these institutions also have collections of mounted newspaper clippings, prints and photographs, scrapbooks, and typescripts prepared by members of the community. Inquiry should also be made about possible materials which may be yet uncataloged.

Maine

1 ABBOT, EDWARD. "The Androscoggin lakes." Harper's New Monthly Magazine, 55 (1877), 23-38.

2 ABBOTT, JOHN STEVENS CABOT. The history of Maine. (1875) Revised throughout and five chapters of new matter added by Edward H. Elwell. 2d ed. Portland: Brown Thurston, 1892. Pp. 608.

3 "THE ABENAQUIS Indians." MeHistMag, 9 (1894-1895), 147-148.

4 ADAMS, EPHRAIM DOUGLASS. "Lord Ashburton and the Treaty of Washington." AHR, 17 (1912), 764-782.

5 ADAMS, WILLIAM CUSHING. Jonathan Edwards Adams, D.D., and Maine Congregationalism. Portland: Southworth Pr., 1933. Pp. xvi, 164.

6 AHLIN, JOHN HOWARD. Maine Rubicon: Downeast settlers during the American Revolution. Calais: Calais Advertiser Pr., 1966. Pp. xi, 224.

7 ALBION, ROBERT GREENHALGH. "Suggested readings in Maine history: the forest." MeHSN, 1 (January, 1962), 6-8.

8 _____. "Suggested readings in Maine history: the sea." MeHSN, 1 (September, 1961), 7-8.

9 ALDRICH, PELEG EMORY. "Massachusetts and Maine, their union and separation." AASP, No. 71 (April 24, 1878), 43-64.

10 ALEXANDER, DE ALVA STANWOOD. The Alexanders of Maine. Buffalo, N.Y.: Peter Paul Book Co., 1898. Pp. 129.
   Alexander family.

11 ALLEN, C. F. H. "The end of steam on the Maine Central." RLHSB, No. 108 (1963), 39-48.

12 _____. "The ten wheeler on the Maine Central Railroad." RLHSB, No. 66 (1945), 51-52.

13 ALLEN, CHARLES EDWIN. "Huguenot settlers in the Kennebec Valley, Maine." MNEH, 3 (1893), 17-30.

14 _____. "Loyalists of the Kennebec." NEM, New Ser., 37 (1907-1908), 623-629.

15 _____. "A short romance of Arnold's Kennebec Expedition of 1775." MNEH, 3 (1893), 227-232.

16 ALLEN, FREDERIC. "The early lawyers of Lincoln and Kennebec counties." MeHSC, 6 (1859), 39-81.

17 ALLEN, JAMES P. "Franco-Americans in Maine: a geographical perspective." Acadiensis, 4 (Autumn, 1974), 32-66.

18 _____. "Migration fields of French Canadian immigrants to southern Maine." GeogRev, 62 (1972), 366-383.

19 _____. "Variations in Catholic-Protestant proportions among Maine towns." Association of American Geographers. Proceedings, 3 (1971), 15-18.

20 ALLEN, JOSEPH, JR. "The steamer J. T. Morse--her history and adventures." OTNE, 27 (1936-1937), 79-98, 129-147.
   Rockland to Bar Harbor.

21 ALLEN, STEPHEN and WILLIAM HACKET PILSBURY. History of Methodism in Maine, 1793-1886. Augusta: C. E. Nash, 1887. 2 v. in 1.
   Pilsbury is the author of volume two which has the title: History of Methodism in East Maine....

22 ALLEN, WILLIAM, 1780-1873. "Bingham land." MeHSC, 7 (1876), 351-360.

23 _____. "Sandy River." MeHSC, 4 (1856), 31-40.
   Economic conditions along the river.

24 ALLEN, WILLIAM, 1784-1868. "Account of Arnold's Expedition." MeHSC, 1 (1831), 387-416.

25 ALLIS, FREDERICK SCOULLER, ed. William Bingham's Maine lands, 1790-1820. Boston: The [Colonial] Society [of Massachusetts], 1954. 2v.

26 MAINE

26 "AMERICAN Home pilgrimages, No. 4--Maine."
American Home, 20 (August, 1938), 8-11,
54-56.
    1750-1890.

27 AMORY, THOMAS COFFIN. Life of James Sullivan: with selections from his writings.
Boston: Phillips, Sampson, 1859. 2v.

28 ANASTAS, PETER. Glooskap's children: encounters with the Penobscot Indians of
Maine. Boston: Beacon Pr., 1973. Pp. 216.

29 "ANCIENT land grants east of Penobscot
River." BHistMag, 1 (1885-1886), 29-31,
33-39.

30 ANDERSON, MIRIAM SYLVIA. The history of
secondary education in Waldo and Piscataquis
counties in Maine. Orono: University Pr.,
1939. Pp. viii, 111.

31 ANDREWS, L. A. "Squeaker Guzzle." The Rudder, 63 (November, 1947), 18-19, 68.
    Place names.

32 "THE ANTI-SLAVERY movement in Maine." SJMH,
1 (1913-1914), 38-39.

33 APPLETON, DANIEL FULLER, ed. The origin of
the Maine law and of prohibitory legislation,
with a brief memoir of James Appleton. N.Y.:
The National Temperance Society and Publication House, 1886. Pp. 52.

34 ARCHER, GLEASON LEONARD. "Maine's place in
early colonial history." Maine State Bar
Association. Proceedings, 30 (1936-1937),
26-50.

35 _____. "Pioneers of the rock-bound coast."
Americana, 32 (1938), 239-283, 486-524,
653-697; 33 (1939), 42-88, 349-414, 488-547.

36 "ARE Maine's Indians a disappearing race?"
Yankee, 17 (March, 1953), 38-40.

37 ARMSTRONG, LEBBEUS. The temperance reforma-
tion: its history, from the organization of
the first temperance society to the adoption
of the liquor law of Maine, 1851; and the
consequent influence of the promulgation of
that law on the political interest of the
State of New York, 1852. (1853) 2d ed.,
enlarged and improved. N.Y.: Fowlers and
Wells, 1853. Pp. xvi, 465.

38 "THE AROOSTOOK War and the volunteer troops
therein." BHistMag, 2 (1886-1887), 121-124.

39 ARSENAULT, BONA. History of the Acadians.
Québec: Conseil de la vie française en
Amérique, 1966. Pp. 265.
    A translation and revision of the author's
Histoire et généalogie des Acadiens.

40 "ART in Maine." Colby Alumnus, 52 (Fall,
1962), 1-5.

41 ARTHUR, ROBERT. "Coast forts in colonial
Maine." Coast Artillery Journal, 57 (1922),
217-238.

42 "ARTISTS born in Maine." MeLB, 13 (1927-
1928), 3-17.

43 "ARTISTS not born in Maine but having defi-
nite residence in this state." MeLB, 13
(1927-1928), 17-23.

44 "ASSOCIATION history." MeLAB, 20 (November,
1959), 21-22.
    Maine Library Association.

45 "THE ATLANTIC and St. Lawrence Railway."
Pine Tree Magazine, 6 (1906-1907), 127-134.

46 ATTWOOD, STANLEY BEARCE. The length and
breadth of Maine. Orono: Univ. of Maine,
1973. Pp. 279, 12, 30.

47 AUSTIN, HARRY B. "Salmon, shad and alewives,
rivers of Maine in olden days." SJMH, 6
(1918-1919), 158-160.

48 AVILA, LILIAN and ALICE ROSE STEWART. "French
in Maine." French Review, 27 (1953-1954),
460-466.
    French language, 1785-1954.

49 BABB, CYRUS CATES. Bibliography of Maine
geology. Waterville: Sentinel Publishing,
1913. Pp. 68.

50 BACON, GEORGE FOX. Northern Maine, its points
of interest, and its representative business
men, embracing Houlton, Presque Isle, Caribou,
Ft. Fairfield, Danforth, Lincoln, Mattawamkeag, Winn and Kingman. Newark, N.J.: Glenwood Publishing, 1891. Pp. 87.

51 BAGLEY, MARION MILLER. Maine history. [Port-
land]: J. Weston Walch, 1964. Pp. vi, 106.
MeBa.

52 _____. Maine history can be fun: an activity
text.... Portland: J. Weston Walch, 1956.
Pp. 81. MeBa.

53 _____. Maine history can be fun. Supplement.
Teacher's guide. Portland: J. Weston Walch,
1956. Pp. 16. MeBa.

54 BAILEY, DUDLEY PERKINS. "The Maine savings
banks and the late crisis." Banker's Magazine, (October, 1880), 257-268.

55 BAKER, ORVILLE DEWEY. Addresses and memorials
of Orville Dewey Baker (1847-1908). Manley H.
Pike, ed. Augusta: Kennebec Journal, 1909.
Pp. vii, 172.

56 BAKER, WILLIAM AVERY. "The Boston boats from
sail to steam." MeHSN, 9 (1969-1970), 5-16,
39-44.
    Steam navigation between the Kennebec River
and Boston.

57 _____. Maine shipbuilding: a bibliographical guide. Portland: Maine Historical Society, 1974. Pp. 22.

58 BALDWIN, J. R. "Ashburton-Webster boundary settlement." Canadian Historical Association. Report, (1938), 121-133.

59 BALLARD, EDWARD. "The early history of the Protestant Episcopal Church in the Diocese of Maine." MeHSC, 6 (1859), 171-202.

60 _____. "Geographical names on the coast of Maine." U.S. Coast Survey. Report, (1868), 243-259.
Also issued as a separate in 1871.

61 BANASIAK, CHESTER F. Deer in Maine. Augusta: Department of Inland Fisheries and Game, 1961. Pp. 159.
Includes history, 1623-1959.

61A BANGOR, ME. PUBLIC LIBRARY. Bibliography of the State of Maine; compiled in the Bangor Public Library. Boston: G. K. Hall, 1962. Pp. v, 803.

61B BANGOR AND AROOSTOOK RAILROAD COMPANY. History of the strike of engineers, firemen and hostlers on the Bangor & Aroostook Railroad, winter of 1913. n.p., [1913]. Pp. 36.
MeBa.

61C _____. 75 years: the Bangor and Aroostook, 1891-1966.... n.p., 1966. Pp. 48.

62 BANKS, CHARLES EDWARD. "The administration of William Gorges, 1636 to 1637." MeHSC, 2 Ser., 1 (1890), 125-131.

63 _____. "The early settlements in Maine, prior to 1620." MHGR, 2 (1885), 207-216.

64 _____. "Martha's Vineyard and the Province of Maine." MeHSC, 2 Ser., 9 (1898), 123-127.
1641-1664.

65 _____. "Sir Robert Carr in Maine." MagAmHist, 8 (1882), 623-626.
1665.

66 BANKS, RONALD FILLMORE. "The great and the good: a course that explores Maine's oft neglected history." Maine Alumnus, 58 (Fall, 1976), 9-11.

67 _____, comp. A history of Maine: a collection of readings on the history of Maine, 1600-1976. (1969) 4th ed. Dubuque, Iowa: Kendall/Hunt, 1976. Pp. vii, 460.

68 _____. Maine becomes a state; the movement to separate Maine from Massachusetts, 1785-1820. (1970) 2d ed. Somersworth: New Hampshire Publishing, 1973. Pp. xx, 266.

69 _____. Maine during the Federal and Jeffersonian period: a bibliographical guide.

Portland: Maine Historical Society, 1974. Pp. 49.

70 _____. "The Maine economy: 1820-1860." Thomas Business Review, 3 (Fall, 1975), 6-10.

71 BARKER, LEWIS A. "Great Maine conspiracy." NEM, New Ser., 37 (1907-1908), 371-382.
Gubernatorial election of 1879.

72 BARLOW, MRS. JAMES E. "The activities and a brief history of the Josselyn Botanical Society." Josselyn Botanical Society of Maine. Bulletin, No. 9 (1957), 34-39.

73 BARNES, CHARLES P. "A glimpse at Maine." SJMH, 12 (1924), 141-147.

74 BARR, ANNIE L. "Some who served." MeLAB, 3 (November, 1941), 5-6.
Maine librarians.

75 BARROWS, HAROLD KILBRITH. Water resources of the Kennebec river basin, Maine. Washington: Govt. Print. Off., 1907. Pp. vi, 235, iii.
Includes historical statistics.

76 _____ and CYRUS CATES BABB. Water resources of the Penobscot river basin, Maine. Washington: Govt. Print. Off., 1912. Pp. 285.

77 BARRY, PHILLIPS, FANNIE HARDY ECKSTORM and MARY WINSLOW SMYTH. British ballads from Maine: the development of popular songs with texts and airs. New Haven: Yale Univ. Pr., 1929. Pp. xlvi, 535.
Contains music.

78 BARTER, J. MALCOLM. "Spring freshet." Down East, 15 (April, 1969), 48-51.
Floods.

79 BARTLETT, ARTHUR. "Cruising Down East." Holiday, 14 (August, 1953), 48-53, 104-105.
Yachting.

80 BARTLETT, ARTHUR C. "The cradle of prohibition." Outlook and Independent, 156 (1930), 48-50, 76-77.

81 BATEMAN, LUTHER C. "The Indians of Maine: history and present condition." Red Man, 5 (1913), 443-447.

82 BATES MANUFACTURING COMPANY, LEWISTON, ME. Do you know Maine? Vol. I. How Maine became a state. Vol. II. Maine holidays by Robert P. T. Coffin. Augusta: Kennebec Journal, 1948. 2v. Me.

83 BAXTER, JAMES PHINNEY. "The Abnakis and their ethnic relations." MeHSC, 2 Ser., 3 (1892), 13-40.
Indians.

84 _____, ed. The Baxter manuscripts. Portland: Maine Historical Society, 1889-1916. 19v.
Documents relating to the early history

85 MAINE

of Maine gathered from the Massachusetts Archives; the Public Record Office, London; and the Bureau of Marine and Colonies, Paris.

85 _____. "The beginnings of Maine." MeHSC, 2 Ser., 2 (1891), 273-300.

86 _____. "The campaign against the Pequakets: its causes and results." MeHSC, 2 Ser., 1 (1890), 353-371.
1703-1713.

87 _____. "Reminiscences of a great enterprise." MeHSC, 2 Ser., 3 (1892), 247-263.
John A. Poor and the Atlantic and St. Lawrence Railway.

88 _____, ed. Sir Ferdinando Gorges and his Province of Maine, including the Brief Relation, the Brief Narration, his defence, the charter granted to him, his will, and his letters. Boston: The Prince Society, 1890. 3v.

89 _____, ed. The Trelawny papers, ed. and illustrated with historical notes and an appendix. Portland: Hoyt, Fogg and Donham, 1884. Pp. xxxi, 520.
Correspondence and other papers of Robert Trelawny, of Plymouth, England, relating to his Maine grants.

90 BAXTER, SYLVESTER. "The redevelopment of an old state." American Monthly Review of Reviews, 33 (1906), 55-61.

91 BAYLEY, WILLIAM SHIRLEY and FRANCIS PLAISTED KING. Catalogue of the Maine Geological Collection with a brief outline history of the two surveys of the state. Waterville: Geological Department, Colby Univ., 1890. Pp. 32.

92 BEARD, FRANK A. 200 years of Maine housing. [Augusta]: Maine Historic Preservation Commission, [1976]. Pp. 15. MeU.
Architecture.

93 BECK, HORACE PALMER. The folklore of Maine. Philadelphia: Lippincott, 1957. Pp. 284.

94 _____. "Folksong affiliations of Maine." Midwest Folklore, 6 (Fall, 1956), 159-166.
Since the eighteenth century.

95 _____. Gluskap the liar, & other Indian tales. Freeport: Bond Wheelwright, 1966. Pp. ix, 182.

96 BEEDY, HELEN COFFIN. Mothers of Maine. Portland: The Thurston Print, 1895. Pp. 451.

96A "BELFAST & Moosehead Lake." Trains, 4 (April, 1944), 4-5.
Railroad.

97 BENNETT, RANDY L. "The Rumford Falls and Rangeley Lakes Railroad." Down East, 21 (March, 1975), 48-51.

98 BERCHEN, WILLIAM. Maine. Boston: Houghton Mifflin, 1973. Pp. 112.

99 BESTON, HENRY. Northern farm, a chronicle of Maine. N.Y.: Rinehart, 1948. Pp. viii, 246.

100 _____, ed. White pine and blue water, a State of Maine reader. N.Y.: Farrar, Straus, 1950. Pp. xxii, 410.

101 "BIBLIOGRAPHY of eastern Maine." BHistMag, 5 (1889-1890), 221-225.

102 BIBLIOGRAPHY of studies of the Maine economy, 1945-1973, as found in Fogler Library, University of Maine at Orono, summer 1973. Prepared by Wayne M. O'Leary and David L. Bridgham, under the supervision of Arthur M. Johnson. Orono: Balanced Growth Project, Univ. of Maine at Orono, 1974. Pp. ix, 107 leaves.

103 BICKNELL, HENRY S. "Along the Kennebec." NEM, 4 (1886), 197-207.

104 BILLIAS, GEORGE ATHAN. "Misadventures of a Maine slaver." AmNep, 19 (1959), 114-119.
Samuel Patterson.

105 "BIOGRAPHIC glimpses of some Maine men." SJMH, 6 (1918-1919), 79-104.

106 BIOGRAPHICAL encyclopaedia of Maine of the nineteenth century. Henry Clay Williams, ed. Boston: Metropolitan Publishing, 1885. Pp. 441.

107 BIOGRAPHICAL review ... containing life sketches of leading citizens of Sagadaboc, Lincoln, Knox, and Waldo counties, Maine.... Boston: Biographical Review Publishing, 1897. Pp. 422.

108 BIOGRAPHICAL review ... containing life sketches of leading citizens of Somerset, Piscataquis, Hancock, Washington, and Aroostook counties, Maine. Boston: Biographical Review Publishing, 1898. Pp. 738.

109 BIOGRAPHICAL review; this volume contains biographical sketches of leading citizens of Oxford and Franklin counties, Maine.... Boston: Biographical Review Publishing, 1897. Pp. 639.

110 "BIOGRAPHICAL sketches of deceased members of the Maine bar." Maine State Bar Association. Proceedings, 15 (1906-1907), 120-160; 16 (1908-1909), 81-89.

111 BIOGRAPHICAL sketches of representative citizens of the State of Maine.... Boston: New England Historical Publishing, 1903. Pp. 452.

112 BIONDI, ARNOLD S. and FREDERICK W. LYMAN. Abandoned railroads in Maine: their potential

for trail use. [Augusta: Department of Parks & Recreation], 1973. Pp. 108.

113 BIRD, HARRISON. Attack on Quebec: the American invasion of Canada, 1775-1776. N.Y.: Oxford Univ. Pr., 1968. Pp. 255. Arnold's Expedition.

114 BISBEE, ERNEST EMERSON. The State o' Maine scrap book of stories and legends of "Way Down East." Lancaster, N.H.: The Bisbee Pr., 1940. Unpaged.

115 BISHOP, WILLIAM HENRY. "Fish and men in the Maine islands." Harper's Magazine, 61 (1881), 336-352, 496-510.

116 _____. "The lobster at home." Scribner's Monthly Magazine, 22 (1881), 209-218. Lobstermen.

117 BLANDING, EDWARD MITCHELL. Maine State Board of Trade, historical sketch ... delivered ... at Waterville, Me., September 24th, 1913. n.p., [1913]. Pp. 32. Me.

118 BOARDMAN, SAMUEL LANE. Agricultural bibliography of Maine: a list of Maine writers on agriculture, with biographical sketches and a catalogue of their works. Also an index to the volumes on the Agriculture of Maine from 1850 to 1892. Augusta: Burleigh & Flynt, 1893. Pp. 117.

119 _____. "A family of printers--George V. Edes." Maine Genealogist and Biographer, 1 (1875-1876), 56-60.

120 _____. Maine cattle: some materials for a history of the cattle of Maine; with facts concerning early breeders, and notices of the thoroughbred herds at present kept in the state. Augusta, 1875. Pp. 48. MeBa.

121 BOLTON, CHARLES KNOWLES, ed. "A journey to Maine in 1859: a diary of Charles Edward Bolton." NEQ, 9 (1936), 119-130.

122 A BOOK for the children of Maine, for the use of families and schools. Portland: Samuel Colman, 1831. Pp. 118.

123 BORNS, HAROLD W., JR. "Late Wisconsin fluctuations in the Lawrentide ice sheet in southern and eastern New England." Geological Society of America. Memoir 136, (1973), 37-45.

124 "THE BOSTON and Mt. Desert Limited." RLHSB, No. 82 (1951), 72-73.

125 BOURQUE, BRUCE J. "Aboriginal settlement and subsistence on the Maine Coast." Man in the Northeast, 6 (1973), 3-20.

126 BOWLER, ERNEST C. An album of the attorneys of Maine, with a portrait and brief record of the life of each. Bethel: News Publishing, 1902. Pp. vii, 316.

127 _____. An album of the executive and legislative departments of Maine. Bethel: News Publishing, 1901. Pp. 196. MeHi.

128 _____. An album of the legislative departments and seventy-first Legislature of Maine, with portrait and brief record of the life of each. Bethel: News Publishing, 1903. Pp. 209.

129 BOYLE, JAMES. "Review of legislation in Maine from 1820-1915, relating to the exemption of wages." Maine Law Review, 8 (1914-1915), 100-113.

130 [BRACKETT, GEORGE EMERSON.] "The school master fifty years ago." Maine Teacher and School Officer, 3 (1860-1861), 265-269; 4 (1861-1862), 39-42. Author attribution by the editor.

131 BRADBURY, JAMES WARE. "Railroad reminiscences." MeHSC, 2 Ser., 7 (1896), 379-390.

132 BRADFORD, CHARLES. "Arnold's march to Quebec through the State of Maine." Maine Trucking News, (March, 1964), 12-15, 26.

133 BRADFORD, PETER AMORY. Fragile structures: a story of oil refineries, national security, and the coast of Maine. N.Y.: Harper's Magazine Pr., 1975. Pp. xiii, 392.

134 BRADMAN, ARTHUR. A narrative of the extraordinary sufferings of Mr. Robert Forbes, his wife, and five children, during an unfortunate journey through the wilderness--from Canada to Kennebeck River, in the year 1784 ... taken partly from their own mouths, and partly from an imperfect journal; and compiled at their request. Portland: Thomas Baker Wait's Office, 1791. Pp. 23. See also entry 916.

135 BRAULT, GÉRARD J. "The Franco-Americans of Maine." MeHSN, 12 (1972-1973), 3-28.

136 BRAZER, ESTHER STEVENS. "Zachariah Brackett Stevens: founder of the japanned tinware industry in Maine." Antiques, 29 (1936), 98-102. Author's name appears incorrectly as Fraser.

136 BRICKETT, GEORGE EDMUND. History of ovariotomy in Maine. Portland: S. Berry, 1877. Pp. 26.

138 BRIEF biographies, Maine: a biographical dictionary of who's who in Maine. Vol. I, 1926-1927. Lewiston: Lewiston Journal, [1926]. Pp. 284. No more published.

139 "BRIEF history [of the Maine Department of Health and Welfare."] Maine. Department of Health and Welfare. Report, (1942-1944), 6-7.

140 "BRIEF history of the wild lands of Maine."
The Northern, 2 (April, 1922), 9-10, (May,
1922), 12, (June, 1922), 6.

141 BROWN, EVERETT S. "Maine's election date."
AmPolSciRev, 29 (1935), 437-441.
History of the legislation establishing the
date.

142 BROWN, JOHN MARSHALL. "Coasting voyages in
the Gulf of Maine, made in the years 1604, 5,
and 6, by Samuel Champlain." MeHSC, 7 (1876),
243-266.

143 _____. "The Mission of the Assumption on the
River Kennebec, 1646-1652." MeHSC, 2 Ser., 1
(1890), 87-99.
Mission of the Jesuit priest Gabriel Druil-
letes located at various points along the
Kennebec including the Augusta vicinity and
Moosehead Lake vicinity.

144 BROWN, PHILIP GREELY. First editions of
American authors, Americana, historical,
biographical and genealogical works, books
about Maine, exploration and sports; the
library of the late Philip Greely Brown,
Portland, Maine, sold by order of the National Bank of Commerce of Portland, executor.
Public sale ... October 15 and 16....
N.Y.: American Art Association, Anderson Gal-
leries, Inc., 1935. Pp. 99.

145 BRYANT, H. W., FIRM, BOOKSELLER, PORTLAND, ME.
A check list of Maine town histories, for the
use of librarians and collectors. (1902).
[Portland], 1904. Pp. 4.

146 BURGESS, GEORGE. "A discourse delivered before the Maine Historical Society, at Brunswick, August 2, 1854." MeHSC, 4 (1856),
67-91.
Church history.

147 BURNHAM, HORACE M. "Pharmacy of the red
man." SJMH, 6 (1918-1919), 69-71.
Medical practices among Indians.

148 BURRAGE, HENRY SWEETSER. "The attitude of
Maine in the Northeastern Boundary controversy." MeHSC, 3 Ser., 1 (1904), 353-368.

149 _____. The beginnings of colonial Maine,
1602-1658. Portland: Marks Printing House,
1914. Pp. xv, 412.

150 _____. "Capt. John Wilson and some military
matters in Maine in the War of 1812-15."
MeHSC, 2 Ser., 10 (1899), 403-429.

151 _____. Centennial discourse, one hundredth
anniversary of the Maine Baptist Missionary
Convention, Waterville, Oct. 5, 1904. Portland: Marks Printing House, 1904. Pp. 21.

152 _____. "Charter rights of Massachusetts in
Maine in the early part of the eighteenth
century." MeHSC, 2 Ser., 6 (1895), 392-414.

153 _____. George Folsom, John A. Poor and a
century of historical research with reference
to early colonial Maine.... n.p., 1926.
Pp. 62.

154 _____. Gorges and the grant of the Province
of Maine, 1622; a tercentenary memorial.
[Portland?]: Printed for the State, 1923.
Pp. xv, 178.

155 _____. History of the Baptists in Maine.
Portland: Marks Printing House, 1904.
Pp. viii, 497.

156 _____. Maine at Louisbourg in 1745. Augusta:
Burleigh & Flynt, 1910. Pp. viii, 143.

157 _____. Maine in the Northeastern Boundary
controversy. [Portland]: Printed for the
State, 1919. Pp. xiv, 398.

158 _____. "The Plymouth colonists in Maine."
MeHSC, 3 Ser., 1 (1904), 116-146.
Kennebec Patent.

159 _____. "The St. Croix Commission, 1796-98."
MeHSC, 2 Ser., 6 (1895), 225-251.
Northeast Boundary.

160 _____. "Waymouth's voyage to the coast of
Maine in 1605." MeHSC, 2 Ser., 2 (1891),
225-250.

161 BUTLER, EVA L. and WENDELL STANWOOD HADLOCK.
A preliminary survey of the Munsangan-Alla-
gash waterways. Bar Harbor: Robert Abbé
Museum, 1962. Pp. 31. MeHi.

162 BUXTON, HENRY [JAMES]. Assignment Down East.
Brattleboro, Vt.: Stephen Daye Pr., 1938.
Pp. 204.

163 BYERS, DOUGLAS S. "'Red Paint tombs' in
Maine." MASB, 15 (1953-1954), 2-8.

164 BYRNE, FRANK LOYOLA. Prophet of prohibition:
Neal Dow and his crusade. Madison: State
Historical Society of Wisconsin for Depart-
ment of History, Univ. of Wisconsin, 1961.
Pp. vii, 184.

165 "THE CABOT expedition." SJMH, 3 (1915-1916),
123.
1497.

166 CALHOUN, JOHN C., JR. "Yachts of the golden
era." Down East, 6 (August, 1959), 42-46.

167 CALHOUN, PHILO. "Charles Dickens in Maine."
ColbLibQ, 6 (1962-1964), 137-158.
1868.

168 CAMMETT, STEPHEN. "Early homes of Longfellow." Century, 73 (1907), 647-657.
In Portland and Hiram.

169 CAMPBELL, FREDERIC L. "A legend of Jefferson
Davis." Sun Up, 9 (January, 1931), 9.
His visits to Maine.

170 _____. "With Arnold in Maine." Sun Up, 9 (May, 1931), 16, 29, (July, 1931), 6, 26.
"To be continued," but no more appeared.

171 CAMPBELL, THOMAS JOSEPH. Three historical events in Maine. N.Y.: America Pr., 1910. Pp. 46.
Golden jubilee of St. John's, Bangor; laying of cornerstone of Church of Our Holy Redeemer, Bar Harbor; reconsecration of the Rasle Monument.

172 CAMPBELL, W. E. "Seventy-five years of waterworks progress in Maine." New England Water Works Association. Journal, 72 (June, 1958), 98-105.
1830-1957.

173 CAMPO, CHARLES A., comp. and ed. Maine union list of periodicals, 1974. Orono: Univ. of Maine, 1974. 456 columns. MeU.

174 CANAVAN, FRANCES EBBS. "The Catholic Indians of Maine." Catholic World, 135 (1932), 81-84.

175 "CAPT. George Weymouth's pond, discovered on coast of Maine, 1605." BHistMag, 4 (1888-1889), 201-202.
Controversy as to the location.

176 "THE CAPUCHINS in Maine." HistMag, 8 (1864), 301-304.

177 CARLES, REGINALD E. "Governors of Maine, 1860-1900." Pine Cone, 5 (Autumn, 1949), 11-15.
Biographical sketches.

178 _____. "Governors of Maine, 1900-1948." Pine Cone, 4 (Autumn, 1948), 34-37.
Biographical sketches.

179 CARR, JOSEPH WILLIAM and GEORGE DAVIS CHASE. "A word list from eastern Maine." Dialect Notes, 3 (1907), 239-251.

180 CARTER, ROBERT GOLDTHWAITE. "Col. Thomas Goldthwait--was he a Tory?" MeHSC, 2 Ser., 7 (1896), 23-44, 185-200, 254-274, 362-379; 8 (1897), 31-53.

181 CARY, AUSTIN. "The forests of Maine." Paper Trade Journal, (April 25, May 9, and May 16, 1896).

182 _____. "Forty years of forest use in Maine." Journal of Forestry, 33 (1935), 366-372.

183 _____. "Maine forestry in retrospect and in prospect." Maine Naturalist, 2 (1922), 148-154.

184 _____. "Notes on timber history of the Kennebec River." Maine. Forest Commissioner. Biennial Report, 12 (1933-1934), 133-147.
1896-1933.

185 "THE CATHOLIC Church in Maine." MeCathHM, 1 (July, 1913), 39-54, (August, 1913), 29-40, (September, 1913), 5-12, (October, 1913), 49-54, (November, 1913), 37-45, (December, 1913), 52-57; 2 (January, 1914), 40-45, (February, 1914), 38-43, (March, 1914), 33-42, (April, 1914), 50-54, (May, 1914), 32-39; 3 (July, 1914), 36-46, (August, 1914), 39-43, (September, 1914), 43-48, (October, 1914), 39-48, (November, 1914), 42-48; 4 (January, 1915), 25-28, 43-48, (February, 1915), 46-50, (March, 1915), 45-48, (April, 1915), 27-30, (May, 1915), 32-39, (June, 1915), 46-51; 5 (August, 1915), 45-48, (September, 1915), 40-48, (October, 1915), 42-47, (November, 1915), 19-23, (December, 1915), 38-41; 6 (January, 1916), 41-47, (February, 1916), 49-52, (March, 1916), 46-48, (April, 1916), 42-48, (May, 1916), 50-56; 7 (1916-1917), 79-88, 158-166, 272-278, 339-350.

186 "CATHOLIC footprints in Maine." MeCathHM, 7 (1916-1917), 97-101.

187 "THE CATHOLIC Indians of Maine in the Revolution." MeCathHM, 2 (May, 1914), 11-16.

188 "CATHOLIC landmarks in Maine." MeCathHM, 7 (1916-1917), 72-74.

189 CHADBOURNE, AVA HARRIET. The beginnings of education in Maine.... N.Y.: Columbia Univ., 1928. Pp. vi, 135.

190 _____. "Early social libraries in Maine." MeLAB, 31 (February, 1970), 3-16.

191 _____. A history of education in Maine, a study of a section of American educational history. Orono, 1936. Pp. xiii, 544.

192 _____. "Indian names in Maine." The Northern, 2 (September, 1922), 7.

193 _____. "Indian names in Maine towns." Pine Cone, 5 (Spring, 1949), 21-24.

194 _____. Maine place names and the peopling of its towns. Portland: Bond Wheelwright, 1955. Pp. 530.

195 _____. "Names of Maine cities." Pine Cone, 3 (Autumn, 1947), 16-19.

196 _____, comp. Readings in the history of education in Maine: a collection of sources and readings concerning the history of Maine and the development of educational theory and practice. Bangor: Burr Pr., 1932. Pp. 104.

197 CHADBOURNE, WALTER WHITMORE. A history of banking in Maine, 1799-1930. Orono: Univ. Pr., 1936. Pp. ix, 211.

198 CHADWICK, JOSEPH. "An account of a journey from Fort Pownal--now Fort Point--up the

199 MAINE

Penobscot River to Quebec, in 1764." BHist Mag, 4 (1888-1889), 141-148.
Notes by Joseph W. Porter.

199 CHAMBERLAIN, JOSHUA LAWRENCE. Maine. Boston: Little, Brown, 1882. Pp. 22.

200 _____. Maine: her place in history, address delivered at the Centennial Exhibition, Philadelphia, Nov. 4, 1876, and in convention of the Legislature of Maine, February 6, 1877.... Augusta: Sprague, Owen & Nash, 1877. Pp. v, 129.

201 CHAMPLIN, JAMES TIFT. "Educational institutions in Maine, while a district of Massachusetts." MeHSC, 8 (1881), 157-180.

202 CHAPMAN, J. K. "The mid-nineteenth-century temperance movement in New Brunswick and Maine." CanHistRev, 35 (1954), 42-60.
1830-1856.

203 CHAPMAN, LEONARD BOND. "Rev. Caleb Bradley on the Madawaska War." MeHSC, 2 Ser., 9 (1898), 418-425.
Northeast Boundary, 1839.

204 CHASE, EDWARD EVERETT. Maine railroads, a history of the development of the Maine railroad system. Portland: A. J. Huston, 1926. Pp. 145.

205 CHASE, GEORGE DAVIS. "Further word lists-- Maine." Dialect Notes, 4 (1914), 151-153.

206 CHASE, HENRY, ed. Representative men of Maine, a collection of portraits with biographical sketches of residents of the state, who have achieved success ... to which is added the portraits and sketches of all the governors since the formation of the state.... Portland: Lakeside Pr., 1893. Pp. 250, liii.

207 CHASE, MARY ELLEN. A goodly heritage. N.Y.: Henry Holt, 1932. Pp. 298.
Social life and customs.

208 _____. "My novels about Maine." ColbLibQ, 6 (1962-1964), 14-20.

209 CHASE, VIRGINIA. "Shipwreck ... the 'Portland' disaster." Down East, 4 (January, 1958), 16-18, 39-40, 42-43.

210 "CHIEF Justices of Maine." MeLB, 16 (1930-1931), 54-64.

211 CHISHOLM, HUGH JOSEPH, 1847-1912. "History of papermaking in Maine, and the future of the industry." Maine. Bureau of Industrial and Labor Statistics. Annual Report, 20 (1906), 161-169.

212 CHITTENDEN, ALBERT D. The story of the early years of the State of Maine Board of Osteopathic Examination & Registration. Bangor: Maine Osteopathic Association, [1964]. Pp. 15.

213 "CHRONOLOGY of the Sisters of Mercy in the Diocese of Portland." MeCathHM, 4 (June, 1915), 5-6.

214 CHURCH, BENJAMIN. The history of the eastern expeditions of 1689, 1690, 1692, 1696, and 1704, against the Indians and French. Henry Martyn Dexter, ed. Boston: J. K. Wiggin and W. P. Lunt, 1867. Pp. xxxii, 203.

215 CHURCHILL, EDWIN A. Maine communities and the War for Independence: a guide for the study of local Maine history as related to the American Revolution. Augusta: Maine State Museum, 1976. Pp. vi, 110.

216 _____ and JAMES S. LEAMON. "Maine in the Revolution, a reader's guide." MeHSQ, 15 (1975-1976), 145-195.

217 "CHURCH'S expeditions into Maine, 1689-1690-1692-1696-1704." BHistMag, 6 (1890-1891), 252-256.
Benjamin Church.

218 CILLEY, JONATHAN PRINCE. "Regimental histories." Maine Bugle, 1 (1894), 175-178.
Includes a bibliography of histories of Maine Civil War regiments.

219 CLARK, CALVIN MONTAGUE. American slavery and Maine Congregationalists: a chapter in the history of the development of anti-slavery sentiment in the Protestant churches of the North. Bangor, 1940. Pp. ix, 198.

220 _____. History of the Congregational churches in Maine.... Portland: Southworth Pr., 1926-1935. 2v.

221 CLARK, CHARLES E. Maine during the colonial period: a bibliographical guide. Portland: Maine Historical Society, 1974. Pp. 38.

222 _____. "The wonderful world of John Josselyn, Gent., a glimpse of seventeenth-century Maine." Bates College Bulletin, 73 (April, 1976), 28-30.

223 CLARK, CORNELIUS EDWARDS. "Provincial conditions in Maine in 1807." MeCP, 45 (January 15, 1958), 6-8, (February 15, 1958), 4-6.
Maine Missionary Society.

224 CLARK, LEWIS E. Trends in Maine agriculture, 1954-1964. Orono, [1966]. Pp. 20.

225 CLASSEN, H. GEORGE. Thrust and counter-thrust: the genesis of the Canada-United States boundary. Toronto: Longmans, 1965. Pp. 386.

226 CLEVELAND, GEORGE ARTHUR. Maine in verse and story. Boston: R. G. Badger, 1915. Pp. 275.

227 CLIFFORD, HAROLD BURTON. Maine and her people. (1957) With a supplement by Charlotte L. Melvin on The Story of Aroostook, Maine's last frontier. 2d ed. Freeport: Bond Wheelwright, 1963. Pp. iv, 346.

228 CLOUDMAN, S. B. "Early recollections of the Cumberland and Oxford Canal." MeHSC, 3 Ser., 1 (1904), 397-405.

229 _____. "Recollections of the old time militia and the general muster." MeHSC, 3 Ser., 2 (1906), 331-341.

230 CLOUGH, BLANCHE COLE. Grandma spins Down-East yarns. Portland: Fred L. Tower, 1953. Pp. 214. MH.

231 _____. More Down-East yarns by grandma. Book 2. Portland: House of Falmouth, 1956. Pp. 187.
Sequel to previous entry.

232 CLUBB, HENRY STEPHEN. The Maine liquor law: its origin, history, and results, including a life of Hon. Neal Dow. N.Y.: Fowler and Wells, 1856. Pp. 430.

233 CLUFF, DOHN A. "Lobster fishing on the Maine coast past and present." AmNep, 14 (1954), 203-208.

234 COATSWORTH, ELIZABETH JANE. Country neighborhood. N.Y.: Macmillan, 1944. Pp. 181.
Social life and customs.

235 _____. Maine memories. Brattleboro, Vt.: Stephen Greene Pr., 1968. Pp. ix, 165.
Social life and customs.

236 _____. Maine ways. N.Y., Macmillan, 1947. Pp. 213.
Social life and customs.

237 COBURN, LOUISE HELEN. Canal projects for the Kennebec, 1825 to 1832. [Skowhegan?, 1927?]. Pp. 21.

238 _____. "The Josselyn Botanical Society of Maine." Maine Naturalist, 1 (1921), 18-21.

239 CODMAN, JOHN. Arnold's Expedition to Quebec. (1901) 2d ed. N.Y.: Macmillan, 1902. Pp. ix, 340.

240 COE, HARRIE BADGER, ed. Maine, resources, attractions, and its people: a history. N.Y.: Lewis Historical Publishing, 1928. 4v.
Volumes 3 and 4 contain biographical material.

241 COFFIN, HAROLD WILHELM. Assignment in military intelligence. Old Town: Penobscot Pr. Associates, 1972. Pp. v, 210.
World War II.

242 COFFIN, ROBERT PETER TRISTRAM. Coast calendar. Decorations by the author. Indianapolis: Bobbs-Merrill, 1949. Unpaged.

243 _____. Kennebec, cradle of Americans. N.Y.: Farrar & Rinehart, 1937. Pp. x, 292.
Kennebec River.

244 _____. Maine, a state of grace; commencement address delivered at the University of Maine, June 14, 1937. Orono, 1937. Pp. 10.

245 _____. Maine doings. Indianapolis: Bobbs-Merrill, 1950. Pp. 266.
Social life and customs.

246 _____. "The State of Maine." American Mercury, 66 (January, 1948), 66-73.
1608-1947.

247 _____. Yankee coast. N.Y.: Macmillan, 1947. Pp. 333.
Social life and customs.

248 COLBY, (GEORGE N.) & CO. Atlas of the State of Maine including statistics and descriptions of its history.... 4th ed. Houlton, 1888. Pp. 111. MeU.

249 COLBY COLLEGE, WATERVILLE, ME. Artists active in Maine in the twentieth century. Waterville: Archives of Maine Art at Colby College, 1963. Pp. 12. Me.

250 _____. Exhibition of Maine art ... April 22-May 21, 1944. Waterville: Colby College, 1944. Unpaged.

251 COLBY COLLEGE, WATERVILLE, ME. ART DEPARTMENT. Exhibition of Maine architecture, from the 17th century to the Civil War, arranged by the Art Department of Colby College, Waterville, Maine. [Waterville, 1945]. Unpaged.

252 COLBY COLLEGE, WATERVILLE, ME. ART MUSEUM. Maine and its artists, 1710-1963, an exhibition in celebration of the sesquicentennial of Colby College, 1813-1963. Colby College Art Museum, Waterville, Maine, May 4-August 31, 1963.... [Waterville, 1963]. Pp. 31.

253 COLE, JOHN N. In Maine: "Of all the winds that blow I like the northwest best...." N.Y.: Dutton, 1974. Pp. 143.

254 COLE, WILLIAM I. "Maine in literature." NEM, New Ser., 22 (1900), 726-743.

255 COLE'S EXPRESS, BANGOR ME. Connecting Maine with the nation. 40th anniversary, 1917-1957. n.p., [1957]. Pp. 44.
A history of Cole's Express.

256 COLLIER, SARGENT F. Down East: Maine, Prince Edward Island, Nova Scotia, and the Gaspé. Boston: Houghton Mifflin, 1953. Pp. 148.

257 COLLINS, W. E. "Arnold's Expedition to Quebec." BHSSC, 2 (1894-1897), 59-67.

258 "COLONEL Thomas Westbrook's expedition to Penobscot River, 1722-23." BHistMag, 5 (1889-1890), 101-103.

259 CONGDON, ISABELLE. Indian tribes of Maine. Brunswick: Brunswick Publishing, 1961. Pp. 22. MeU.

260 CONNOLLY, DONALD F. X. "A chronicle of New England Catholicism before the Mayflower landing." American Catholic Historical Society of Philadelphia. Records, 70 (March-December, 1959), 3-17, 88-108.
Voyages of explorers and fishermen and their attempted settlements in Maine, 1497-1620.

261 CONSERVATIVE BAPTIST ASSOCIATION OF MAINE. The Conservative Baptist Association of Maine, 1955-1957. n.p., [1957?]. Pp. 28. MeU.

262 COOK, JULIA ANNA. "Maine's forest fires of twenty years ago." Down East, 14 (October, 1967), 34-36, 44-47.

263 COOK, WALTER LEONARD. The story of Maine Baptists, 1904-1954. Waterville: City Job Print, 1954. Pp. 163.

264 COOLIDGE, AUSTIN JACOBS and JOHN BRAINARD MANSFIELD. History and description of New England. Maine. Boston, 1860. Pp. iv, 406.

265 COOLIDGE, PHILIP TRIPP and W. C. WHEELER. "Growth of pulpwood in Maine." Journal of Forestry, 29 (1931), 907-914.
1917-1927.

266 COOLIDGE, PHILIP TRIPP. History of the Maine woods. Bangor: Furbush-Roberts, 1963. Pp. 805.

267 COREY, ALBERT BICKMORE. The crisis of 1830-1842 in Canadian-American relations. New Haven: Yale Univ. Pr., 1941. Pp. xi, 203.
Northeast Boundary.

268 CORLISS, CARLTON JONATHAN. Railway developments in Maine; an address at Ricker Classical Institute and Ricker College Alumni Association banquet, Houlton, Maine, June 8, 1953. n.p., [1953 or 4]. 19 leaves.

269 CORNISH, LESLIE C. "A century of the Supreme Judicial Court of Maine." Maine State Bar Association. Proceedings, 22 (1920-1921), 109-144, 242-251.

270 COSTRELL, EDWIN. How Maine viewed the war, 1914-1917. Orono: Univ. Pr., 1940. Pp. v, 101.

271 CRAM, HAL. "Horses, horses, horses." Sun Up, 3 (August, 1926), 30, 76.
Horseracing since 1850.

272 _____. "The long trail of transportation in Maine." Sun Up, 2 (February, 1926), 6, 16-17.

273 _____. "The why, when, and where of Maine names." Sun Up, 3 (June, 1926), 14, 19-21.
Geographical names.

274 CRANE, ABIJAH ROBINSON. The Baptist ministers in Maine from 1804 to 1904; paper read at Waterville, October 5, 1904, at the centennial of the Maine Baptist Missionary Convention. Portland: Marks Printing House, 1904. Pp. 20.

275 CRANE, J. R. "Ships and sawmills." American Forests, 63 (August, 1957), 24-26, 54-56.
Colonial period to 1955.

276 CRITTENDEN, HENRY TEMPLE. "Wiscasset, Waterville & Farmington Railway." RLHSB, No. 57 (1942), 114-135.

277 CROWELL, MARNIE REED. "Maine Indian baskets." Down East, 21 (October, 1974), 40-43.

278 CRUMB, LAWRENCE N. "The Anglican Church in colonial Maine." HMPEC, 33 (1964), 251-260.
1605-1820.

279 CUMMINGS, EPHRAIM CHAMBERLAIN. "The Rasles Dictionary." MeHSC, 2 Ser., 6 (1895), 144-152.
A manuscript Abnaki dictionary presently in the Houghton Library, Harvard University.

280 CUMMINGS, OSMOND RICHARD. "A history of the Atlantic Shore Line Railways." Transportation, 4 (June, 1950), 1-37.
Street railroad.

281 _____. "Portland - Lewiston Interurban." Transportation, 10 (May, 1956), 1-28.
Street railroad.

282 _____. Toonervilles of Maine, the Pine Tree State. Newburyport, Mass., 1955. Pp. 52. MeBa.

283 CURRENT, RICHARD N. "Webster's propaganda and the Ashburton Treaty." MVHR, 34 (1947), 187-200.

284 CURRIER, ISABEL. "The Belfast and Moosehead Lake RR." Down East, 10 (October, 1963), 36-44.

285 CUSHMAN, DAVID QUIMBY. "Weymouth's voyage." MeHSC, 6 (1859), 307-318.
     George Waymouth.

286 CUTLER, ALEXANDER MUNRO. Bent sails, a sail-making saga written in the words of a New England craftsman of square rigger days. Cincinnati: Mail It, 1962. Pp. 81.

287 DAGGETT, WINDSOR PRATT. A Down-East Yankee from the District of Maine. Portland: A. J. Huston, 1920. Pp. 80.

288 DALE, THOMAS NELSON. The granites of Maine. Washington: Govt. Print. Off., 1907. Pp. iv, 202.

289 DANA, SAMUEL TRASK. Forest fires in Maine 1916-1925. Augusta: Maine Forest Service, [1926?]. Pp. 73.

290 DANIELS, L. R. "Early Maine Conference of Unitarian Churches." Maine Unitarian, (1947), [12-14].

291 DARRAH, WILLIAM C. "A checklist of Maine photographers who issued stereographs." MeHSN, 6 (May, 1967), special supplement.
     1863-1890; alphabetical and geographical listings.

292 DAUGHTERS OF THE AMERICAN REVOLUTION. MAINE. A brief history of the Maine Daughters of the American Revolution, to March 1, 1925.... Mabel Goodwin Hall, ed. [Waterville, Me.? 1925]. Pp. 60.

293 _____. History of the Maine society, Daughters of the American Revolution.... Farmington: Knowlton & McLeary, 1946. Pp. 147. MeBa.

294 DAVIAU, JEROME G. Maine's life blood. Portland: House of Falmouth, 1958. Pp. 139.
     Industrial uses of water resources, 1820-1957.

295 DAVIDSON, JACQUELINE. "Maine and American artists, 1710-1963." American Artist, 27 (December, 1963), 32-39, 63-67.

296 DAVIS, GHERARDI. Alice and I go Down East again.... N.Y.: Gillis Pr., 1924. Pp. 48.
     Yachting.

297 DAY, CLARENCE ALBERT. Farming in Maine, 1860-1940. Orono: Univ. of Maine Pr., 1963. Pp. v, 306.
     A continuation of the next entry.

298 _____. A history of Maine agriculture, 1604-1860. Orono: Univ. Pr., 1954. Pp. ix, 318.

299 _____. How extension work in Maine began. Orono: Univ. of Maine, 1937. Pp. 23. MeBa.

300 _____. "Suggested readings in Maine history: agriculture." MeHSN, 1 (May, 1962), 4-5.

301 DAY, HOLMAN FRANCIS. "The queer folks of the Maine coast." Harper's Monthly Magazine, 119 (1909), 521-530.
     Social life and customs.

302 DEANE, CHARLES. "Indians kidnapped from Maine in 1605." MHSP, 2 Ser., 2 (1885-1886), 35-38.
     George Waymouth.

303 DEARBORN, VANCE E. and RONALD J. DAIGLE. A data file; Maine: population, natural increase, and migration trends, 1940-1970; births, deaths, migration, 1960-1969 (for counties and towns). Orono: Maine Cooperative Extension Service, 1971. Unpaged. MeU.

304 DE COSTA, BENJAMIN FRANKLIN. Ancient Norombega, or The voyages of Simon Ferdinando and John Walker to the Penobscot River, 1579-1580. Albany: J. Munsell's Sons, 1890. Pp. 12.
     A revision of the author's "Simon Ferdinando and John Walker in Maine, 1579-1580." NEHGR, 44 (1890), 149-158.

305 _____. "Champdoré in New England, 1608." NEHGR, 45 (1891), 137-141.
     Pierre Angibaut.

306 _____. The Northmen in Maine: a critical examination of views expressed in connection with the subject, by Dr. J. H. [i.e. G.] Kohl, in Volume 1 of the New Series of the Maine Historical Society, to which are added criticisms on other portions of the work, and a chapter on the discovery of Massachusetts Bay. Albany: J. Munsell, 1870. Pp. 146.
     See also entry 656.

307 _____. Sketches of the coast of Maine and Isles of Shoals, with historical notes. New York, 1869. Pp. 221.

308 DECROW, GERTRUDE. "Folklore from Maine." Journal of American Folklore, 5 (1892), 318-320.

309 DEEMS, MERVIN MONROE. Maine--first of conferences: a history of the Maine Conference-United Church of Christ. Bangor: Furbush-Roberts, 1974. Pp. vii, 168.

310 _____. The Maine Missionary Society, 1807-1957. Portland: Marks Printing House, [1957]. Pp. 31.

311 MAINE

311 DE LASKI, JOHN. "Glacial action about Penobscot Bay." American Journal of Science, 87 (1864), 335-344.

312 DEMERITT, DWIGHT BURGESS. Maine made guns and their makers. Hallowell: Published for the Maine State Museum by P. S. Plumer, Jr., 1973. Pp. vii, 209.

313 DENIS, MICHAEL J. Maine towns and counties: what was what, where and when. n.p., 1973. 63 leaves. MeHi.

314 DE PEYSTER, JOHN WATTS. The Dutch at the North Pole and the Dutch in Maine. A paper read before the New-York Historical Society, 3d March, 1857. N.Y.: Printed for the Society, 1857. Pp. 80.

315 [_____]. Proofs considered of the early settlement of Acadie by the Dutch; being an appendix to The Dutch in Maine. Poughkeepsie, N.Y.: Platt & Schram, 1858. Pp. 19.

316 DESJARDINS, PHILLIPPE E. "French Canadians, central and southern Maine." Church World, 21 (June 1, 1951), 4, 8-10.

317 "THE DEVELOPMENT of our telephone system." The Northern, 5 (June, 1925), 3-5.
Great Northern Paper Co.

318 DIBNER, MARTIN. Seacoast Maine: people and places. Garden City, N.Y.: Doubleday, 1973. Pp. 208.
Social life and customs.

319 DIETZ, LEW. "The character of Maine." Down East, 21 (August, 1974), 78-80, 85, 93-94.
Social life and customs.

320 _____. "Kennebec log drive." Down East, 15 (August, 1968), 52-56, 61.
Kennebec Log Driving Company.

321 _____. "Man on the Maine frontier--the Maine Finn." Down East, 19 (January, 1973), 36-39, 66, 68.

322 _____. "The unabashed apostles of the Allagash." Yankee, 31 (March, 1967), 88-93, 110-112, 114-115.

323 DILLINGHAM, CHARLES A., comp. The Penobscots. Bangor: Record Print, [1900?]. Unpaged. MeBa.
Indians.

324 DINGLEY, EDWARD N., JR. "The ship, the man, and the lady." Steamboat Bill, 28 (1971), 200-203.
S.S. Governor Dingley named after Nelson Dingley, Jr. and christened by Mrs. Edward N. Dingley.

325 DINGLEY, NELSON, JR. "The State of Maine." NEM, New Ser., 4 (1891), 547-570.

326 DINGLEY, ROBERT JORDAN. "Maine's pioneer automobile men." Down East, 13 (March, 1967), 52-55.

327 DIXON, JOSEPH H. "The Aroostook War." Old Eliot, 8 (1908), 192-195.

328 DOCUMENTARY history of the Maine Law: comprising the original Maine Law, the New-York Prohibitory Liquor Law, legislative debates, arguments, judicial decisions, statistics, important correspondence; "inquisition" and prohibition versus "freedom" and anti-prohibition.... N.Y.: Hall & Brother, 1855. Pp. vi, 126.

329 DODD, MARION E. "Along New England's book trails: I. Maine." Yankee, 4 (October, 1938), 19-21, 32-34.
Sketches of several Maine authors.

330 DODGE, STANLEY D. "Depopulation of Maine from 1840-1890." Association of American Geographers. Annals, 30 (1943), 86-87.

331 DOLE, NATHAN HASKELL and IRWIN LESLIE GORDON. Maine of the sea and pines; a description of its scenic beauty, its rugged coastline, its mountains, lakes and rivers; an account of its settlement, its Indians and their legends, and its appeal to the sportsman and vacationist; a survey of its commercial resources and industries, and its possibilities for water power development. Boston: L. C. Page, 1928. Pp. x, 375.

332 DOLE, RICHARD F. "Mother Hubbards, Mallet Compounds and Hudsons, a history of Maine Central steam power." Railroad Enthusiast, 9 (Winter and Spring, 1972), 20-32.

333 DOLE, SAMUEL THOMAS. "The Cumberland and Oxford Canal." MeHSC, 2 Ser., 9 (1898), 264-271.

334 DONOVAN, MICHAEL C. The St. Croix boundary question.... [Nashville, Tenn., 19--]. Pp. 15.

335 DOOLITTLE, DUANE, comp. Only in Maine: selections from Down East Magazine. Barre, Mass.: Barre Publishers, 1969. Pp. ix, 274.

336 DORSETT, E. LEE. "The Maine whalers." Down East, 2 (April, 1956), 14-15, 38-39.

337 DOW, FRED M. "History of prohibition in Maine." Americana, 23 (1929), 182-189.

338 DOW, ROBERT L. "Commercial fisheries of Maine." Maine Townsman, 16 (February, 1954), 8-9, 16, 18.

339 _____. The Maine blackback flounder: resource and fishery, 1925-1965. Augusta: Maine Department of Sea and Shore Fisheries, 1967. 4 leaves. MeU.

340 _____. "Some characteristics of Maine coastal kitchen middens." MeArchSocB, 11 (Summer, 1971), 6-13.

341 DOW, STERLING THAYER. Maine postal history and postmarks. (1943) Lawrence, Mass.: Quarterman Publications, 1976. Pp. 235. MeHi.

342 DOWNEAST politics: the government of the State of Maine. James F. Horan, comp. Dubuque, Iowa: Kendall/Hunt, 1975. Pp. x, 189.

343 DRAKE, SAMUEL ADAMS. The Pine-tree coast. Boston: Estes & Lauriat, 1891. Pp. 393.

344 DRUILLETTES, GABRIEL. "Journal of an embassy from Canada to the United Colonies of New England, in 1650." New-York Historical Society. Collections, 2 Ser., 3 Pt. 1, (1857), 303-328.
    Translated, with notes, by John Gilmary Shea.

345 DRUMMOND, JOSIAH HAYDEN. "Bibliographic memorandum of the laws of Maine." MeHSC, 2 Ser., 2 (1891), 391-402.

346 _____. The Maine Central Railroad system, an uncompleted historical sketch. n.p., 1902. Pp. 84.

347 DUBROS times: selected depositions of Maine Revolutionary War veterans. Sylvia J. Sherman, ed. Augusta: Maine State Archives, 1975. Pp. viii, 20.

348 DUNNACK, HENRY ERNEST. The Maine book. Augusta, 1920. Pp. xiii, 338.

349 _____. Rural life in Maine. Augusta: C. E. Nash & Son, 1928. Pp. 165.

350 DUREN, ELNATHAN FREEMAN. General Conference of the Congregational Churches in Maine; churches and ministers from 1672 to 1867, with the minutes of the forty-first annual meeting ... June 25, 26, 27, 1867. Portland: Brown Thurston, 1867. Pp. 157. MBC.
    A continuation for the period 1867 to 1876 appears in the "Minutes" of the Conference for 1876 on pp. 147-184. A further continuation for the period 1877 to 1886 appears in the "Minutes" for 1886 on pp. 169-208.

351 DURIN, DEA. "Statistics of the Maine General Conference of Churches, from its organization." CongQ, 8 (1866), 309-310.

352 DURNIN, RICHARD GERRY. "For piety, virtue and useful knowledge: Maine's eighteenth-century academies." MeHSN, 11 (1971-1972), 43-50, 54-63.

353 DUROST, LILLIAN MILLS and GRACE E. FITZ. History, Federation of Business and Professional Women's Clubs of Maine. n.p. [1944?]. Pp. 87. MeHi.

354 DYER, ISAAC WATSON. "The Cumberland and Oxford Canal." SJMH, 12 (1924), 94-113.

355 DYER, RICHARD NYE. "253 years of Maine art." Down East, 9 (May, 1963), 20-25.

356 DYER, WALTER A. "Historical and documented antiques from Maine." The Antiquarian, 14 (1930), 60-62, 80, 88.
    Furniture.

357 "EARLY Indian tribes in Maine and Nova Scotia." MeHistMag, 8 (1893), 89.

358 "EARLY mills on Penobscot River." BHistMag, 5 (1889-1890), 82-86.

359 "EARLY post offices in eastern Maine." BHistMag, 1 (1885-1886), 12-13.

360 "EARTHQUAKE history of Maine." Earthquake Information Bulletin, 5 (May-June, 1973), 26-29.

361 EATON, LOUIS WOODBURY. Pork, molasses, and timber; stories of bygone days in the logging camps of Maine. N.Y.: Exposition Pr., [1954]. Pp. 75.

362 ECKSTORM, FANNIE HARDY. "Champlain's visit to the Penobscot." SJMH, 1 (1913-1914), 56-65.

363 _____. The handicrafts of the modern Indians of Maine. Bar Harbor, 1932. Pp. 72.

364 _____. "History of the Chadwick Survey from Fort Pownal in the District of Maine to the province of Quebec in Canada in 1764." SJMH, 14 (1926), 63-89.
    Survey of a feasible route for a highway from the Penobscot River to Canada.

365 _____. Indian place-names of the Penobscot Valley and the Maine coast. Orono: Univ. Pr., 1941. Pp. xxix, 272.

366 _____ and MARY WINSLOW SMYTH. Minstrelsy of Maine: folk-songs and ballads of the woods and the coast. Boston: Houghton Mifflin, 1927. Pp. xvi, 390.

367 ECKSTORM, FANNIE HARDY. Old John Neptune and other Maine Indian shamans. Portland: Southworth-Anthoensen Pr., 1945. Pp. xii, 209.

368 "EDUCATIONAL legislation in Maine." Maine Journal of Education, 6 (1872), 218-223, 253-257.
    Signed: Theta.

369 MAINE

369 EDWARDS, GEORGE THORNTON. Music and musicians of Maine, being a history of the progress of music in the territory which has come to be known as the State of Maine, from 1604 to 1928. Portland: Southworth Pr., 1928. Pp. xxv, 542.

370 EDWARDS, LLEWELLYN NATHANIEL. The evolution of early American bridges ... with a brief discussion of the geology of Maine rivers and streams and a history of six early Maine bridges. Orono, 1934. Pp. 30.

371 ELKINS, L. WHITNEY. "Maine's lime industry." Sun Up, 2 (October, 1925), 7, 56.

372 _____. The story of Maine: coastal Maine. Bangor: Hillsborough Company, 1924. Pp. 392.

373 ELWELL, EDWARD HENRY. "The newspaper press in Maine." MPAP, 22 (1885), 14-32.

374 EMERSON, WALTER CRANE. The latchstring [to] Maine woods and waters. Boston: Houghton Mifflin, 1916. Pp. xi, 228.

375 _____. When north winds blow. Lewiston: Journal Printshop and Bindery, 1922. Pp. 229.

376 EMERY, GEORGE FREEMAN. "Our state christening: its name." MeHSC, 2 Ser., 4 (1893), 337-350.

377 _____. "Reminiscences of bench and bar." MeHSC, 2 Ser., 8 (1897), 113-143.

378 _____. "The voice of Maine as heard in the genesis of our nationality." MeHSC, 2 Ser., 2 (1891), 51-82.
Delegates to the Philadelphia Constitutional Convention.

379 EMERY, LUCILIUS ALONZO. "Changes in equity procedure in Maine." Maine Law Review, 9 (1915-1916), 29-34.
1820-1915.

380 _____. "Changes in the judicial system of Maine." Maine Law Review, 9 (1915-1916), 89-97.

381 _____. "The growth of equity powers of the Maine courts." Maine Law Review, 9 (1915-1916), 1-7.
1821-1891.

382 _____. "Maine and the federal Constitution." SJMH, 5 (1917-1918), 32-33.
Maine's part in the Constitutional Convention of 1788.

383 _____. "Some changes in the procedure in actions at law in Maine." Maine Law Review, 9 (1915-1916), 219-224.
1821-1879.

384 ENGLISH, THOMAS DUNN. Prohibition in Maine, a scathing exposure of the result of thirty years' effort.... Newark, N.J., 1882. Pp. 12. MeHi.

385 ENO, JOEL N. "The expansion of Maine--chronological--based on official records." Americana, 25 (1931), 380-410.

386 EVERSON, JENNIE G. Tidewater ice of the Kennebec River. Freeport: Published for the Maine State Museum, by Bond Wheelwright, 1970. Pp. xiii, 241.

387 THE EXCITER Magazine, electric railroad edition. Augusta: Central Maine Power Co., 1960. Pp. 28. Me.
Street railroads.

388 EXPLORATIONS in Maine history: miscellaneous papers. Proceedings of the sesquicentennial colloquium of the University of Maine, Orono, March 30, 1970. Orono: Univ. of Maine, 1970. Pp. 64. MeHi.

389 EXPRESSIONS from Maine, 1976. Hobe Sound, Fla.: Hobe Sound Gallery, [1976]. Unpaged. MeU.
A catalog of works by Maine artists with accompanying biographical sketches.

390 FAIRFIELD, JOHN. The letters of John Fairfield; a representative in Congress from 1835 to 1837; a member of the Senate of the United States from 1843 to 1847, and a governor of Maine in 1839, 1840, 1842 and a part of 1843. Arthur G. Staples, ed. Lewiston: Lewiston Journal, 1922. Pp. xxxiv, 475.

391 FARNHAM, MARY FRANCES, comp. The Farnham papers.... Portland: Thurston Print, 1901-1902. 2v.
Documents relating to the territorial history of Maine, 1603-1871; volume two has the imprint Portland: Lefavor-Tower, 1902.

392 FARRER, HIRAM P. "Maine historical anecdotes." SJMH, 13 (1925), 242-244.

393 FARRINGTON, INEZ. Maine is forever. Manchester: Falmouth Publishing House, 1954. Pp. 164.
Social life and customs.

394 _____. My Maine folks. Portland: Bond Wheelwright, 1956. Pp. 96.
Social life and customs.

395 FASSETT, FREDERICK GARDINER. A history of newspapers in the District of Maine, 1785-1820. Orono: Univ. Pr., 1932. Pp. 242.

396 FAVOUR, EDITH. Indian games, toys, and pastimes of Maine and the Maritimes. Bar Harbor: Robert Abbe Museum, 1974. Pp. 21.

397 FEDERAL WRITERS' PROJECT. MAINE. Maine: a guide to the Vacation State. Ray Bearse, ed. 2d ed. rev. Boston: Houghton Mifflin, 1969. Pp. xii, 460.
First edition of 1937 has the title: Maine, a guide 'Down East.'

398 FELLOWS, DANA WILLIS. History of dentistry in Maine; being a history of the Maine Dental Society.... Portland: Maine Dental Society, 1924. Pp. 126. MeBa.

399 FELT, JOSEPH BARLOW. Statistics of towns, Maine territory. American Statistical Association. Collections, 1 (1847), 57-99.

400 FENN, WILLIAM HENRY. The hope of Maine, a discourse delivered Thanksgiving Day, Nov. 26, 1868. Portland: Hoyt & Fogg, 1868. Pp. 23.

401 FEWKES, JESSE WALTER. "A contribution to Passamaquoddy folk-lore." Journal of American Folklore, 3 (1890), 257-280.

402 "THE FIRST English settlements in that part of Acadia now eastern Maine." MeHistMag, 8 (1893), 1-4.

403 "THE FIRST European settlement in New England." BHistMag, 2 (1886-1887), 225-228.
Pierre du Gast, Sieur de Mont, 1604.

404 FISHER, CHARLES E. "Locomotives of the Maine Central R.R." RLHSB, No. 55 (1941), 64-72; No. 56 (1941), 87-97.

405 FISHER, ELIJAH. Elijah Fisher's journal while in the War for Independence, and continued two years after he came to Maine, 1775-1784. William Berry Lapham, ed. Augusta: Badger & Manley, 1880. Pp. 29.

406 FISHER, J. ALVIN. "Maine coast Christmas." Down East, 8 (January, 1962), 33-34, 42-43.

407 "FISHERIES on the coast of Maine and Acadia." MeHistMag, 9 (1894-1895), 210-211.

408 FLETCHER, LUCILLE. "Indian legends of Maine's magnificent mountains." Sun Up, 3 (November, 1926), 12, 18-20.

409 _____. "Romance and history in Maine trees." Sun Up, 5 (February, 1928), 5, 21, 23, 26.

410 FOBES, CHARLES BARTLETT. "Historic forest fires in Maine." Economic Geography, 24 (1948), 269-273.

411 _____. "The ice clearing dates of the Maine lakes." American Meteorological Society. Bulletin, 26 (1945), 331-333.
1880-1944.

412 _____. "Indian names for Maine mountains." Appalachia, 34 (1962-1963), 521-529.

413 _____. "Lightning fires in the forests of northern Maine, 1926-1940." Journal of Forestry, 42 (1944), 291-293.

414 _____. "Maine winters--are they getting warmer or colder?" Down East, 22 (January, 1976), 28-33, 63.

415 _____. "Path of the settlement and distribution of population of Maine." Economic Geography, 20 (1944), 65-69.

416 _____. "Snowfall in Maine." GeogRev, 32 (1942), 245-251.
1895-1935.

417 FOGG, W. FRED P. The Republican Party in American politics, with a brief account of the movements to which the present great organization can trace its origin, together with the history of its formation in Maine on the recurrence of the thirtieth anniversary. Lewiston, 1884. Pp. 57.

418 FOLSOM, GEORGE. A catalogue of original documents in the English archives, relating to the early history of the State of Maine.... N.Y.: G. B. Teubner, 1858. Pp. iv, 135.

419 _____. "Discourse before the [Maine Historical] Society at its annual meeting, Sept. 6, 1846." MeHSC, 2 (1847), 3-79.
Discovery and settlement.

420 FOSTER, BENJAMIN BROWNE. Down East diary. Charles H. Foster, ed. [Orono]: Univ. of Maine at Orono Pr., 1975. Pp. 377.

421 FOSTER, ELIZABETH. The islanders. Boston: Houghton Mifflin, 1946. Pp. 348.
Rangeley Lakes.

422 FRANKLIN, LYNN. Profiles of Maine. Waldoboro: Maine Antique Digest, 1976. Pp. 160. MeU.
Biographies.

423 FREDYMA, JAMES P. A directory of Maine silversmiths and watch and clockmakers. Hanover, N.H., 1972. Pp. v, 26.
1636-1904.

424 FREEMAN, CHARLES. "Historical sketch of Presbyterianism in the State of Maine, with some account of Presbyterianism in New England." New Hampshire Repository, 1 (1846), 253-263.

425 _____. "History of the General Conference of Maine." American Quarterly Register, 10 (1837), 154-158.
Includes list of Congregational ministers by county.

426 FREEMASONS. MAINE. GRAND LODGE. Exercises at the seventy-fifth anniversary of the Grand Lodge of Maine, Free and Accepted Masons,

427 MAINE

May 8, 1895. Portland: Stephen Berry, 1895.
Pp. 44.
Includes historical address by Edward P.
Burnham.

427 _____. Proceedings at the centennial cele-
bration of the Grand Lodge of Maine, Ancient
Free and Accepted Masons, held at Masonic
Temple. Portland, Maine, Wednesday, May 5,
1920. Charles B. Davis, comp. Portland:
Tucker, 1920. Pp. 194.

428 FROST, JOHN ELDRIDGE. Maine genealogy: a
bibliographical guide. Portland: Maine
Historical Society, 1977. Pp. 46.

429 FULLER, HENRY MORRILL. Sir Ferdinando Gorges, 1566-1647, naval and military commander,
father of English colonization in America.
N.Y., Newcomen Society in North America,
1952. Pp. 24.

430 FULLER, NATHAN. "Maine Christmas, 1655."
Down East, 2 (November, 1955-January, 1956),
34-35.

431 FURBUSH, MRS. C. G. "Baker family." MHGR,
8 (1895), 154-167.

432 GALLATIN, ALBERT. "A memoir on the North
Eastern Boundary." New-York Historical Society. Proceedings, (1843), Appendix.

433 GANONG, WILLIAM FRANCIS. "The Ashburton
Treaty." New Brunswick Magazine, 1 (1898),
297-305.

434 _____. "A monograph of the evolution of the
boundaries of the Province of New Brunswick."
Royal Society of Canada. Proceedings and
Transactions, 2 Ser., 7 Pt. 2 (1901), 139-
449.

435 _____. "The St. Croix of the Northeastern
Boundary." MagAmHist, 26 (1891), 261-265.
Treaty of 1873.

436 GARDINER, HENRY. New England's vindication.
Charles Edward Banks, ed. Portland: The
Gorges Society, 1884. Pp. 83.
The editor believed the author to be Edward
Godfrey.

437 GARDINER, ROBERT HALLOWELL, 1782-1864. Early
recollections of Robert Hallowell Gardiner,
1782-1864. Hallowell: White & Horne, 1936.
Pp. 226.

438 _____. "History of the Kennebec Purchase."
MeHSC, 2 (1847), 269-294.

439 _____. "Observations on the opening and closing of the Kennebec River, Maine." Smithsonian Institution. Annual Report, (1858),
434-436.
1785-1803.

440 GARNISS, GEORGE W. Historical beginnings.
[Yarmouth: Yarmouth Historical Society],
1970. Unpaged. Me.

441 GAUVIN, MARIE ANNE. Linguistic and cultural
heritage of the Acadians of Maine and New
Brunswick. Madawaska: Priv. Print, 1969.
Pp. 56.

442 GEAGAN, BILL. The good trail. N.Y.: Coward-
McCann, 1954. Pp. 237.

443 "GENERAL Knox and the Bingham Purchase, 1791."
BHistMag, 5 (1889-1890), 164-165.

444 GETCHELL, IRA E. Tables showing the magnetic
declination in the State of Maine from 1609
to 1880, with notes on the variation of the
compass; the secular, the annual and the
diurnal change. North Vassalboro, 1880. Unpaged.

445 GILL, GEORGE J. "Edward Everett and the
Northeastern Boundary controversy." NEQ, 42
(1969), 201-213.

446 GILLETT, ELIPHALET. "Complete list of the
Congregational ministers, pastors of churches,
in the State of Maine, from the settlement of
the country to the present time, (September,
1841)." American Quarterly Register, 13
(1840-1841), 144-162, 253-269; 14 (1841-1842),
269-284.

447 GILMAN, STANWOOD CUSHING and MARGARET COOK
GILMAN. Land of the Kennebec; 'ye great and
beneficial river,' 1604-1965. Boston:
Branden Pr., 1966. Pp. 173.

448 GIVEN, CHARLES S. "Early locomotive[s] of
the Maine Central Railroad." RLHSB, No. 12
(1926), 34-38.

449 _____. "The first locomotives in the State of
Maine." RLHSB, No. 15 (1927), 34-37.

450 _____. "The Maine Central Railroad and its
leased lines." RLHSB, No. 3 (1922), 45-53.

451 GODFREY, JOHN EDWARDS. "The ancient Penobscot." MeHSC, 7 (1876), 1-22, 103-105.
River.

452 _____. "The ancient Penobscot, or Panawan-
skek." HistMag, 3 Ser., 1 (1872), 84-92.
River.

453 _____. Bashaba and the Tarratines. MeHSC,
7 (1876), 93-102.
Indians.

454 _____. "Castine the younger." HistMag,
3 Ser., 2 (1873), 121-127.
Baron Anselm de Saint Castin.

455 _____. "Norambega." MeHSC, 8 (1881), 317-
332.

456 GOLDEN era of logging on the Penobscot.
[Bangor]: Penobscot Heritage, 1970.
Pp. 12. MeBa.

457 GOODWIN, EMMA R. "Old school days on the
Maine coast." NEM, 48 (1912-1913), 474-480.

458 GOODWIN, WILLIAM FREDERIC, ed. "Thatcher
Papers." HistMag, 2 Ser., 6 (1869), 257-271.
George Thatcher.

459 GOOLD, WILLIAM. "Governor Christopher Gore
and his visit to Maine." MeHSC, 2 Ser., 5
(1894), 71-80.
In 1809; Governor of Massachusetts.

460 GORDON, ADELBERT W. "Schooling in unorganized territory in Maine." SJMH, 12 (1924),
173-175.

461 GORDON, HUGH TAYLOR. The Treaty of Washing-
ton, concluded August 9, 1842, by Daniel
Webster and Lord Ashburton. Berkeley,
Calif: Univ. Pr., 1908. Pp. 85.
Also paged [173]-257.

462 GORGES, RAYMOND. The story of a family
through eleven centuries, illustrated by
portraits and pedigrees, being a history of
the family of Gorges. Boston: Merrymount
Pr., 1944. Pp. xxiv, 289.

463 GORHAM STATE COLLEGE. A manual of Maine
history; a guide for the teaching of Maine
history ... by the class of 1933 in history
methods. [Gorham, 1933?]. Variously leaved.
Me.

464 GOSS, LEROY E. Afterglow: a Maine narrative
of Penobscot Bay islanders. Portland: House
of Falmouth, 1966. Pp. 158.
Social life and customs.

465 GOULD, EDWARD KALLOCH. British and Tory
marauders on the Penobscot. Rockland, 1932.
Pp. 41.

466 GOULD, JOHN. And one to grow on: recollections of a Maine boyhood. N.Y.: William
Morrow, 1949. Pp. 253.

467 _____. The Jonesport raffle, and numerous
other Maine veracities. Boston: Little,
Brown, 1969. Pp. 191.

468 _____ and LILLIAN ROSS. Maine lingo: boiled
owls, billdads & wazzats. Camden: Down East
Magazine, 1975. Pp. xiv, 342.

469 GOULD, JOHN. "Railroading the Maine mail."
Down East, 16 (November, 1969), 24-27.

470 _____. "Who owns off-shore Maine?" Yankee,
34 (March, 1970), 64-69, 102-107.

471 GOULD, RALPH ERNEST. Yankee drummer. N.Y.:
Whittlesey House, 1947. Pp. 236.
Commercial travelers.

472 _____. Yankee storekeeper. N.Y.: Whittlesey House, 1946. Pp. vi, 195.

473 GOVE, WILLIAM G. "Rough logging on the Wild
River Railroad." Down East, 17 (November,
1970), 30-33, 64-65, 68, 73-75, 77-79, 81-82.

474 "GOVERNORS of Maine, 1820 to 1892."
MeHistMag, 7 (1891-1892), 121-130.
Biographical sketches.

475 GOWER, CALVIN W. "The CCC: the forest service and politics in Maine, 1933-1936." New
England Social Studies Bulletin, 30 (Spring,
1973), 15-21.
Civilian Conservation Corps.

476 GRACE, PATRICK W. "The octagonals." Down
East, 23 (October, 1976), 40-43.
Houses.

477 GRAHAM, ELINOR MISH. Maine charm string.
N.Y.: Macmillan, 1946. Pp. 231.
Social life and customs.

478 _____. My window looks Down East. N.Y.:
Macmillan, 1951. Pp. 218.
Social life and customs.

479 _____. Our way Down East. N.Y.: Macmillan,
1943. Pp. 173.
Social life and customs.

480 GRAHAM, FRANK. Where the place called morn-
ing lies. N.Y.: Viking Pr., 1973.
Pp. xvi, 238.
Petroleum industry and the environment.

481 GRAND ARMY OF THE REPUBLIC. DEPARTMENT OF
MAINE. Historical journal, 1867-1948....
Portland, 1948. Pp. 69. Me.

482 GRANT, PHILIP A., JR. "The campaign of 1834
and the bank question." MeHSN, 12 (1972-
1973), 72-83.

483 GRAY, ROLAND PALMER, ed. Songs and ballads
of the Maine lumberjacks, with other songs
from Maine. Cambridge: Harvard Univ. Pr.,
1924. Pp. xxi, 191.

484 GREAT NORTHERN PAPER COMPANY. A greater
Great Northern. Wood, water, power, and
people, making paper in a completely inte-
grated operation, from forest to consumer.
Bangor, [1953?]. Pp. 52.

485 GREEN, SAMUEL M. "Maine's architectural
heritage." Colby Alumnus, 35 (October, 1945),
7-9.

486 [GREENE, CHARLES WARREN]. Maine. Philadelphia: J. B. Lippincott, 1890. Pp. 7.

487 GREENE, MARC T. "The old home ship." Ships
and the Sea, 7 (Fall, 1957), 38-39.
'Kennebec'; sidewheeler steamer operating
between Bath and Boston.

488 GREENING, W. E. "The historic Kennebec Road." Canadian Geographical Journal, 75 (1967), 162-167.

489 GREENLEAF, JONATHAN. Sketches of the ecclesiastical history of the State of Maine, from the earliest settlement to the present time. Portsmouth, N.H.: Harrison Gray, 1821. Pp. vi, 293.
Copy at the Maine Historical Society contains manuscript additions and corrections by the author.

490 GREENLEAF, MOSES. A statistical view of the District of Maine; more especially with reference to the value and importance of its interior. Boston: Cummings and Hilliard, 1816. Pp. viii, 154.

491 ____. A survey of the State of Maine, in reference to its geographical features, statistics and political economy; illustrated by maps. Portland: Shirley and Hyde, 1829. Pp. viii, 468.

492 GRIFFIN, JOSEPH. History of the press of Maine. Brunswick: The Press, [1872]. Pp. 284 [i.e. 276].
Includes a "Bibliography of Maine," on pp. [215]-272.

493 ____. Supplement to the history of the press of Maine, with complete indexes.... Brunswick, [1874]. Pp. 289-320.
Pagination continued from previous entry.

494 GRIFFIN, RALPH H., comp. Letters of a New England coaster, 1868-1872. n.p., [1968]. Pp. 284.
Seafaring life.

495 GRIFFITH, FRANK CARLOS, comp. Maine's hall of fame; Griffith's list of men and women born in Maine who have risen to distinction. [South Poland?], 1905. Pp. 12.

496 GRIFFITH, GEORGE BANCROFT, comp. The poets of Maine; a collection of specimen poems from over four hundred verse-makers of the Pine-Tree State, with biographical sketches. Portland: Elwell, Pickard, 1888. Pp. viii, 856.

497 GRIFFITHS, THOMAS MORGAN. Maine sources in 'The house of the seven gables.' Waterville, 1945. Pp. viii, 49.

498 ____ and ARTHUR MORGAN GRIFFITHS, eds. A pictorial history of the State of Maine on the occasion of its 150th birthday, 1970. Lewiston: Twin City Printery, 1970. Unpaged.

499 GRINDLE, ROGER LEE. Quarry and kiln: the story of Maine's lime industry. Rockland: Courier-Gazette, 1971. Pp. 331.

500 GROVER, ARCHER LEWIS. Historical graph showing senators and representatives from the State of Maine to the United States Congress, 1820-1946. Hallowell, 1946. Broadside, 22 1/2 x 15 1/4 inches. MeU.

501 GRUENING, ERNEST. "Maine as a political barometer." Current History, 37 (1932-1933), 420-424.
Elections.

502 GUIGNARD, MICHAEL. "Maine's Corporation Sole controversy." MeHSN, 12 (1972-1973), 111-130.
An 1887 law which made the Bishop of Portland sole owner of all parish property in his diocese.

503 GYLES, JOHN. Memoirs of odd adventures, strange deliverances, &c. in the captivity of John Gyles, Esq; commander of the garrison on St. George's River. Boston: S. Kneeland & T. Green, 1736. Pp. 40.
Manuscript note on flyleaf of a copy in the Boston Public Library states that this work was actually written by Joseph Seccombe.

504 HAAG, JAMES J. A study of plantation government in Maine. Orono: Bureau of Public Administration, Univ. of Maine, 1973. Pp. 20.

505 HADLOCK, WENDELL STANWOOD and ERNEST STANLEY DODGE. "A canoe from the Penobscot River." AmNep, 8 (1948), 289-301.

506 HADLOCK, WENDELL STANWOOD. "Indian relics in the Maine woods." In the Maine Woods, (1941), 55-59.

507 ____. "Observations concerning the 'Red Paint culture.'" American Antiquity, 7 (1941), 156-161.

508 HAGGERTY, MICHAEL. "Maine's big ditch: the Cumberland-Oxford Canal." Down East, 19 (August, 1972), 66-69, 101, 104.

509 [HAIG, GEORGE CANTERBURY]. Land of enchantment: the Penobscot Bay, Mount Desert region of Maine. Concord, N.H.: Sugar Ball Pr., 1945. Pp. 181.

510 HALE, CLARENCE. "A century of the Federal courts in Maine." Maine Bar Association. Proceedings, 22 (1920-1921), 72-108.

511 ____. "The State of Maine." SJMH, 9 (1921), 3-8.

512 HALE, HORATIO EMMONS. Remarks on the language of the St. John's or Wlastukweek Indians, with a Penobscot vocabulary. Boston, 1834. Pp. 8.

513 HALE, NATHAN. "North Eastern and Northern Boundary." North American Review, 33 (1831), 261-286.

514 _____. "The North Eastern Boundary." North American Review, 26 (1828), 421-444.

515 HALE, RICHARD WALDEN, JR. "The forgotten Maine Boundary Commission." MHSP, 71 (1953-1957), 147-155.
Northeast Boundary.

516 HALE, ROBERT. Early days of church and state in Maine. Brunswick: [Bowdoin] College, 1910. Pp. 52.

517 HALL, CHARLES B. "The National Guard of the State of Maine." Outing, 29 (1896-1897), 77-80, 181-184, 285-288, 388-391, 493-496, 597-600; 30 (1897), 77-80, 182-184, 281-284.
History to 1895.

518 HALL, DREW BERT. "Reference list on Maine local history." New York State Library. Bibliography Bulletin, No. 28 (June, 1901), 775-917.
Supplemented by entry 933.

519 HALL, EDWARD WINSLOW. History of higher education in Maine. Washington: Govt. Print. Off., 1903. Pp. 241.

520 HALL, ROBERT E. "Maine's admission to the Union." SJMH, 8 (1920), 8-18.

521 HALLET, RICHARD. "All finished with the engines." Down East, 8 (June, 1962), 44-47.
Steamboats.

522 _____. "When prohibiton came to Maine." Yankee, 25 (February, 1961), 38-41.

523 HALLOCK, LEAVITT HOMAN. Discourse delivered at the 75th anniversary of the Bible Society of Maine at Williston Church, Portland, Maine, May 24, 1885. Portland: William M. Marks, 1885. Pp. 16. MeB.

524 HAMLIN, CHARLES. "The Supreme Court of Maine." Green Bag, 7 (1895), 457-475, 504-523, 553-576; 8 (1896), 14-27, 61-82, 111-127.

525 HAMLIN, HELEN. Nine mile bridge: three years in the Maine woods. N.Y.: W. W. Norton, 1945. Pp. 233.

526 HAMM, MARGHERITA ARLINA. "The last settlement of a race." Peterson Magazine, New Ser., 7 (1897), 640-647.
Penobscot Indians.

527 HANCE, HELEN R. "The discovery of Maine: Vinland-Norumbega." Maine Dig, 2 (Spring, 1968), 69-73.

528 A HANDFUL of spice: a miscellany of Maine literature and history. Richard S. Sprague, ed. Orono: Univ. of Maine Pr., 1968. Pp. v, 205.

529 HARDING, ANNE BORDEN. "The 'eastern lands' of New Plymouth and Massachusetts Bay." NEHGR, 119 (1965), 15-22.

530 HARDING, R. BREWSTER. Greetings from Maine: celebrating America's bicentennial, 1975-1976. Portland: Old Port Publishing, 1975. Pp. 80.
Postal cards.

531 HARKNESS, O. A. "Log haulers twenty years ago." The Northern, 7 (December, 1927), 5, 15.

532 HARRINGTON, JOHN M. "Orono--Catholic Indian chief." SJMH, 5 (1917-1918), 9-16.

533 HARRIS, MAY PASHLEY. Twenty-five years of progress, a pageant of the Argicultural Extension Service. Orono: Univ. Pr., [1938?]. Pp. 31. MeU.

534 HASELTON, WALLACE M. Busy building Maine: the story of Depositors Corporation. N.Y.: Newcomen Society in North America, 1971. Pp. 24.

535 HASENFUS, NATHANIEL JOHN. More vacation days in Maine. West Roxbury, Mass.: Sagadahoc Publishing, 1949. Pp. 245.
Social life and customs; sequel to the following entry.

536 _____. We summer in Maine. West Roxbury, Mass.: Sagadahoc Publishing, 1946. Pp. 165.
Social life and customs.

537 HASENFUS, ROBERT. Maine Driver Education Association, history, 1955-1965. n.p., 1965. Pp. 30. Me.

538 HASKELL, CALEB. Caleb Haskell's diary, May 5, 1775-May 30, 1776, a Revolutionary soldier's record before Boston and with Arnold's Quebec Expedition. Lothrop Withington, ed. Newburyport, Mass.: W. H. Huse, 1881. Pp. 23.

539 HASKELL, JESSICA J. "State arms of Maine." DARMag, 50 (1917), 14-16.

540 HASKELL, LOREN E. "The great fore and afters." Yankee, 22 (February, 1958), 28-31.
Sailing ships built in Maine.

541 HASKELL, WILLIAM EDWIN. The International Paper Company, 1898-1924, its origin and growth in a quarter of a century, with a brief description of the manufacture of paper from the harvesting of pulpwood to the finished roll. N.Y.: International Paper Company, [1924]. Pp. 41.

542 MAINE

542 HASKINS, DAVID GREENE, JR. Biographical sketches of Captain Ebenezer Davis, and his son, the Hon. Charles Stewart Daveis, of Portland, Maine, members of the Massachusetts Society of the Cincinnati. Cambridge, Mass.: J. Wilson and Son, 1873. Pp. 17.

543 HASSE, ADELAIDE ROSALIA. Index of economic material in documents of the states of the United States: Maine, 1820-1904. [Washington]: Carnegie Institution of Washington, 1907. Pp. 95.

544 _____. "The North Eastern Boundary." Bulletin of the New York Public Library, 4 (1900), 391-411.
    A bibliography, 1609-1871.

545 HATCH, BENTON LE ROY. "Lucius Lee Hubbard's map of northern Maine, 1879-1929, a checklist." Appalachia, 28 (1950-1951), 453-464.
    History of the map with a descriptive bibliography of all editions.

546 HATCH, LOUIS CLINTON. Maine: a history: a facsimile of the 1919 edition ... with a new introduction and bibliography by William B. Jordan, Jr. Somersworth, N.H.: New Hampshire Publishing, 1974. Pp. 946.

547 HAVEN, HERBERT M. W. Tales of a homemade naturalist: the Maine diaries of Herbert M. W. Haven. Philip Morrill, ed. Winthrop: Winthrop Mineral Shop, 1966. Pp. 153.

548 HAWES, HILDRETH GILMAN. Early Maine cabinetmakers. [Augusta]: Maine State Museum, 1971. Variously leaved. Me.

549 HAY, DONALD GORDON, et al. Rural organization in three Maine towns. [Orono]: Agricultural Extension Service, 1949. Pp. 56. MeU.
    Addison, Easton, and Turner.

550 HAYDEN, RALPH HENRY. "How the Church came to Maine." The Northeast, 85 (October, 1958), 8-9.
    Episcopal Church.

551 HAYFORD, ELBERT D. "The District of Maine in Congress, 1789-1820." SJMH, 12 (1924), 34-38.

552 HAYNES, GEORGE HENRY. The State of Maine, in 1893. N.Y.: Moss Engraving, 1893. Pp. 98.

553 HAYWARD, JOHN. A gazetteer of the United States, comprising a series of gazetters of the several states and territories. Maine. Portland: S. H. Colesworthy, 1843. Pp. 92.

554 HAZELTON, LOUISE. Special subject resources in Maine, 1972. Augusta: Maine State Library, 1972. Pp. 63. MeP.

555 HEALY, RICHARD WYMAN. The history of secondary education in Androscoggin and Franklin counties in Maine. Orono: Univ. Pr., 1949. Pp. vii, 165.

556 HEBERT, RICHARD A. "The making of Maine: Bates Manufacturing Company." Pine Cone, 2 (Summer, 1946), 31-36.
    In Augusta, Lewiston, and Saco; textiles.

557 _____. Modern Maine: its historic background, people, and resources. N.Y.: Lewis Historical, 1951. 4v.

558 HECHT, ARTHUR and PAUL HANNEMANN. The post-offices of the District of Maine; a historical and geographical arrangement of the early Main [sic] offices. Jamaica, N.Y.: F. Billig, 1960. Pp. 22. MeBa.

559 HECHT, ARTHUR. "Postal history of the District of Maine in 1795." Collectors Club Philatelist, 36 (November, 1957), 305-308.

560 HEFFERNAN, JOHN PAUL. "A Maine family of Smiths." Down East, 21 (April, 1975), 36-41, 66-68, 70.

561 _____. "War clouds over Maine." NEG, 10 (Fall, 1968), 3-8.
    Gubernatorial election of 1879.

562 HELMREICH, ERNST CHRISTIAN. Religion and the Maine schools, an historical approach. Brunswick: Bureau for Research in Municipal Government, 1960. Pp. 83.

563 HEMPSTEAD, ALFRED GEER. "Getting Penobscot logs into Kennebec waters." The Northern, 7 (January, 1928), 5-6.
    1839-1893.

564 _____. The Penobscot boom and the development of the west branch of the Penobscot river for log driving. Orono: Univ. Pr., 1931. Pp. 187.

565 HENDERSON, KENNETH A., ed. "Penobscot East Branch in 1861: from the diary and letters of Alpheus Spring Packard." Appalachia, 28 (1950-1951), 414-426.

566 HENRY, JOHN JOSEPH. Campaign against Quebec: being an accurate and interesting account of the hardships and sufferings of that band of heroes who traversed the wilderness, by the route of the Kennebec, and Chaudiere River, to Quebec in 1775. (1812) Rev. ed. with corrections and alterations. Watertown, N.Y.: Knowlton & Rice, 1844.
    First edition has the title: "An accurate and interesting account..."; an 1877 printing has the title: "Account of Arnold's campaign against Quebec...."

567 HERRICK, ROBERT. "The State of Maine--'Down East.'" Nation, 115 (August 23, 1922), 182-183.

568 HESELTINE, CHARLES DANA. "Maine narrow gauge railroads." Narrow Gauge Society Newsletter, 2, No. 1 (1972), entire issue.

569 HILL, WINFIELD SCOTT. "Early Kennebec taverns." SJMH, 9 (1921), 21-23.
At points along the river.

570 HILTON, CECIL MAX. Rough pulpwood operating in northwestern Maine, 1935-1940. Orono: Univ. Pr., 1942. Pp. viii, 197.

571 HILTON, SEAVERNS W. Arnold's march to Quebec: an account in pictures. [Augusta?, 1968]. Unpaged.

572 HINCKS, FRANCIS. The boundaries formerly in dispute between Great Britain and the United States, a lecture ... 9th June, 1885. Montreal: John Lovell & Son, 1885. Pp. 29.

573 HISTORIC AMERICAN BUILDINGS SURVEY. Maine catalog: a list of measured drawings, photographs, and written documentation in the survey, 1974. Denys Peter Myers, comp. [Augusta]: Maine State Museum, 1974. Pp. vii, 254.

574 "HISTORIC forest fires of Maine." The Northern, 7 (May, 1927), 3-5.

575 HISTORIC Maine and Indian mythology. N.Y.: Consolidated Steamship Lines, [1906?]. Unpaged. Me.

576 "AN HISTORICAL note on the Association's early growth." New England Townsman, 1 (January, 1939), 9.
Maine Municipal Association.

577 HISTORICAL RECORDS SURVEY. MAINE. Counties, cities, towns and plantations of Maine: a handbook of incorporations, dissolutions and boundary changes. Portland, 1940. 165 leaves.

578 _____. Directory of churches and religious organizations in Maine. Portland, 1940. iii, 166 leaves.

579 _____. Inventory of federal archives in the states ... series IX, Department of Agriculture, No. 18, Maine. Rockland: National Archives Project, 1938. 86 leaves.

580 _____. Inventory of the town and city archives of Maine. Portland, 1938-1940. 7v.

581 _____. Town government in Maine. (Preliminary ed.) Portland, 1940. Pp. ii, 206.
No other edition appeared.

582 "HISTORICAL sketch of the Baptist denomination in Maine." Baptist Memorial and Chronicle, 3 (1843), 353-363.

583 "HISTORICAL sketch of the Maine Educational Association." Maine Pedagogical Society. Proceedings, (1880-1881), 1-44.

584 "HISTORY of state general relief." Maine Townsman, 13 (January, 1951), 11-12.

585 HOLMES, HERBERT EDGAR. The makers of Maine: essays and tales of early Maine history, from the first explorations to the fall of Louisberg, including the story of the Norse expeditions. Lewiston: Haswell Pr., 1912. Pp. 251.

586 HOOPES, DONELSON F. "Regional accent: Maine, a faith in nature." Art in America, 51, No. 3 (1963), 70-79.
American artists' reliance on Maine subject matter.

587 HOPKINS, JAMES DEAN. "Members of the bar in the District, now State, of Maine, from its first settlement to the year 1760, during which period it constituted only one county, viz. York." American Quarterly Register, 12 (1839-1840), 274-284.
Includes Cumberland County 1700-1838.

588 HORMELL, ORREN CHALMER. Maine towns. Brunswick: Bowdoin College, 1932. Pp. 101.

589 HOUGHTON, LLOYD E. "Arnold's march through Maine." The Northern, 4 (March, 1925), 3-5, 14-15; 5 (April, 1925), 6-7.

590 HOUGHTON, MRS. WILLIAM ADDISON. Maine's colonial claims. n.p.: National Society of Colonial Dames of America in Maine, [1900?]. Unpaged. MeHi.

591 HOWARD, PRESCOTT L. "The era of the Lombard log hauler." Forest History, 6 (1962-1963), 2-8.
Half-track log hauler invented by Alvin O. Lombard and used by Taylor Brothers Lumber Company of Maine in 1908.

592 HUBBARD, LUCIUS LEE. Woods and lakes of Maine: a trip from Moosehead Lake to New Brunswick in a birch-bark canoe, to which are added some Indian place-names and their meanings, now first published. Boston: J. R. Osgood, 1884. Pp. xvi, 223.

593 HUESTON, ETHEL POWELSON. Coasting Down East. N.Y.: Dodd, Mead, 1924. Pp. 304.

594 HUMISTON, FRED S. Blue water men--and women. Portland: G. Gannett, 1965. Pp. 172.
Seafaring life.

595 MAINE

595 _____. Windjammers and walking beams. Portland: Blue Water Books, 1968. Pp. 199.

596 NO ENTRY.

597 HUNT, HARMON C. "Keep Maine's village clocks
running." Down East, 21 (November, 1974),
40-43.

598 HUSSEY, ARTHUR M., II. Bibliography of Maine
geology, 1672-1972. Augusta: Department of
Conservation, 1974. Pp. v, 269. MeU.

599 HUSTON, A. J., BOOKSELLER, PORTLAND. A check
list of Maine local histories.... [Portland],
1915. Pp. 44.

600 HUSTON, JAMES A. "The logistics of Arnold's
march to Quebec." Military Affairs, 32
(1968-1969), 110-124.

601 HUTCHINS, ARTHUR E. and DANA A. LITTLE.
Progress in Maine municipal planning, 1956-
1966; a report of municipal planning activity
in the state. [Augusta]: Maine Dept. of
Economic Development, Division of Research
and Planning, 1967. Pp. iv, 24.

602 HYLAN, JOHN COFFEY. The history of secondary education in York and Oxford counties in
Maine. Orono: Univ. Pr., 1933. Pp. 78.

603 ILLUSTRATED souvenir 1908. [Lewiston]: R. J.
Lawton, 1908. Pp. 62. MeU.

604 "INDEX to Maine public documents, 1834-1867."
Maine State Library, 32d Biennial Report,
(1905-1906), 26-90.

605 "THE INDIAN Bashaba." SJMH, 1 (1913-1914),
47-52.

606 "INDIAN names in Maine." Journal of American
Folklore, 18 (1905), 316-317.

607 "INDIANS of Maine in the American Revolution."
MeCathHM, 4 (April, 1915), 16-24.

608 INTERNATIONAL BOUNDARY COMMISSION (U.S.,
ALASKA AND CANADA). Joint report upon the
survey and demarcation of the boundary between the United States and Canada from the
source of the St. Croix River to the Atlantic
Ocean, in accordance with the provisions of
articles I and II of the treaty signed at
Washington, April 11, 1908, articles I and II
of the treaty signed at Washington, May 21,
1910, and article III of the treaty signed at
Washington, February 24, 1925.... Washington: Govt. Print. Off., 1934. Pp. xiv, 318.

609 _____. Joint report upon the survey and demarcation of the boundary between the United
States and Canada from the source of the St.
Croix River to the St. Lawrence River, in
accordance with the provisions of article III
of the treaty signed at Washington, April 11,
1908.... Washington: Govt. Print. Off.,
1925. Pp. xv, 512.

610 IRISH, MARIA M. "The Northeastern Boundary
of Maine." JAmHist, 16 (1922), 311-322.

611 "ISLANDS and Gulf of Maine." Oceans, 7 (May-
June, 1974), 8-47.
Social life and customs.

612 JEWELL, MARGARET H. "Country life in Maine
a century ago." OTNE, 23 (1932-1933), 28-38.

613 _____. "Notes on Maine potteries." OTNE,
22 (1931-1932), 184-187.

614 JEWETT, FRED EUGENE. A financial history of
Maine. N.Y.: Columbia Univ. Pr., 1937.
Pp. 235.

615 JOHNSON, ALLEN. "Report on the archives of
the State of Maine." American Historical
Association. Annual Report, (1908), I, 257-
318.

616 JOHNSON, THEODORE ELLIOT. Hands to work and
hearts to God: the Shaker tradition in Maine.
[Brunswick]: Bowdoin College Museum of Art,
1969. Unpaged.

617 JOHNSTON, JOHN. "Abraham Shurt and John
Earthy: two interesting characters in the
early history of the State of Maine." NEHGR,
25 (1871), 131-137,

618 JONES, CARMITA DE SOLMS. "Acadia in Maine."
American Catholic Historical Society of
Philadelphia. Records, 36 (1925), 359-371.
Catholics.

619 _____. "The blackgowns among the Abnakis."
American Catholic Historical Society of
Philadelphia. Records, 33 (1922), 275-299.
Capuchins and Jesuits.

620 JONES, HERBERT GRANVILLE. I discover Maine:
little-known stories about a well-known state.
Portland: Machigonne Pr., 1937. Pp. vii, 99.
A two-volume braille edition was published by
the WPA Braille Project in Portland in 1940.

621 _____. The King's Highway from Portland to Kittery: stagecoach & tavern days on the old post
road. Portland: Longfellow Pr., 1953.
Pp. 226.

622 _____. Maine memories: little-known stories
about a well-known state. Portland: Harmon
Publishing, 1940. Pp. 223.

623 JONES, HOWARD. "Anglophobia and the Aroostook
War." NEQ, 48 (1975), 519-539.

624 JONES, WILBUR DEVEREUX. "The influence of slavery on the Webster-Ashburton negotiations."
Journal of Southern History, 22 (1956), 48-58.

625 _____. "Lord Ashburton and the Maine boundary
negotiations." MVHR, 40 (1953), 477-490.

626 JORDAN, NELLIE WOODBURY. "The Cumberland and
Oxford Canal." SJMH, 10 (1922), 23-26.

627 JORDAN, WILLIAM BARNES, JR., comp. A bibliography of Maine bibliography. n.p., 1952.
4 leaves.

628 _____. Episodes from the Unitarian Universalist experience in Maine. Norway: Oxford
Hills Pr., 1974. Pp. 12. MeHi.

629 _____. Maine in the Civil War: a bibliographical guide. Portland: Maine Historical
Society, 1976. Pp. 74.

630 _____. Maine in the War of the Rebellion,
1861-1865: check list and bibliography.
Portland: Bosworth Memorial Civil War Museum, 1962. 35 leaves.

631 JORGENSEN, FREDERICK E. 25 years a game
warden. Brattleboro, Vt.: Stephen Daye Pr.,
1937. Pp. 161.

632 JULIAN, GEORGE WASHINGTON. "Webster and
Blaine: historic justice." Magazine of
Western History, 8 (1888), 466-472.

633 KAHN, RICHARD. "An historical sketch of
medical education in Maine." Maine Medical
Association. Journal, 62 (1971), 212-216.

634 [KALER, JAMES OTIS]. Geography of Maine.
Portland: The Eagle Pr., 1910. Pp. 23.

635 KEARNEY, W. D. The open hand: an epic poem
dealing with the early settlement of Maine
and New Brunswick, founded on tradition.
Hartland, N.B.: Observer, Ltd., 1926.
Pp. 58.

636 KEENE, CARTER B. "The evolution of the American postal service: something about its
history in Maine." SJMH, 7 (1919-1920),
123-131.

637 NO ENTRY.

638 KELLIHER, JOHN T. "The Red Paint Indian
culture of Maine." Maine Naturalist, 10
(1930), 45-48.

639 KENDE, BERTHOLD. "History of life insurance
in Maine." BTJ, 17 (1904-1905), 535-542.

640 KENNEBEC AND WISCASSET RAILROAD COMPANY.
Narrow gauge railroads: their history and
progress, the Kennebec and Wiscasset rail-
road, the first narrow gauge enterprise in
Maine. Augusta: Sprague, Owen & Nash, 1872.
Pp. 31.

641 KERSHAW, GORDON E. "John Wentworth vs. Kennebeck proprietors: the formation of Royal
mast policy 1769-1778." AmNep, 33 (1973),
95-119.

642 _____. The Kennebeck proprietors, 1749-1775:
"gentlemen of large property & judicious men."
Somersworth, N.H.: New Hampshire Publishing,
1975. Pp. xvi, 343.

643 _____. "A question of orthodoxy: religious
controversy in a speculative land company:
1759-1775." NEQ, 46 (1973), 205-235.
Kennebec Purchase Company.

644 KEUNE, RUSSELL V. and JAMES REPLOGLE. "Two
Maine farmhouses." SocArchHistJ, 20 (1961),
38-39.
Miles Cobb Farm in Hinckley's Corner and
Perkins Homestead in Newcastle.

645 KIDDER, FREDERIC. "Colonel John Allan and
his operations in Maine and Nova Scotia, in
the Revolution." HistMag, 2 Ser., 4 (1868),
263-264.

646 _____. Military operations in eastern Maine
and Nova Scotia during the Revolution,
chiefly comp. from the journals and letters
of Col. John Allan, with notes and a memoir
of Col. John Allan. Albany: J. Munsell,
1867. Pp. x, 336.

647 KILBY, CYRUS HAMLIN. Binding of the links:
a story of forty years in Odd Fellowship.
Portland, [1889]. Pp. 125.

648 KILBY, WILLIAM HENRY. "Benedict Arnold on
the eastern frontier." BHistMag, 2 (1886-
1887), 188-190.

649 KING, MARQUIS FAYETTE, comp. Changes in
names by special acts of the Legislature of
Maine, 1820-1895. [Portland?, Priv. Print.],
1901. Pp. 67.

650 KIRTLEY, BASIL F. "On the origin of the
Maine-Maritimes legend of the plucked gorbey."
Journal of American Folklore, 87 (1974), 364-
365.

651 KLEIN, ELSA. The story of the State of Maine
Division of the American Association of University Women in its first five years.
n.p., [1952?]. Pp. 19. MeBa.

652 KNIGHT, ENOCH. The new story of the State of
Maine. Portland: Dresser, McLellan, 1876.
Pp. 26.

653 KNOWLTON, CLARENCE H. "History of the Josselyn Botanical Society of Maine." Josselyn
Botanical Society of Maine. Bulletin, No. 10
(1975), 21-24.

654 KNOWLTON, NEWELL R. A history of Odd Fellowship in the tenth district of Maine. Farmington: Knowlton & McLeary, 1898. Pp. 236.
MeU.

655 KNOWLTON, WILLIAM SMITH. The old schoolmas-
ter; or forty-five years with the girls and
boys. Augusta: Burleigh & Flynt, 1905.
Pp. 269.

656 MAINE

656 KOHL, JOHANN GEORG. A history of the discovery of Maine. With an appendix on the voyages of the Cabots, by M. d'Avezac.... Portland: Bailey and Noyes, 1869. Pp. viii, 535.
See also entry 306.

657 KURT, FRANKLIN T. "The little white steamers of Penobscot Bay." Down East, 18 (June, 1972), 56-59, 92, 97-98, 105.
Eastern Steamship Company.

658 KYPER, FRANK. "Maine Central perspective." Railroad Enthusiast, 9 (Winter and Spring, 1972), 3-6.

659 LACOGNATA, ANGELO A. We the Italians of Maine. [Portland?], 1975. Pp. 20. MeHi.

660 LADD, VAUGHN. "Adaptation of diesel locomotives by the Bangor & Aroostook Railroad." Maine Association of Engineers. Journal, No. 21 (April, 1950), 47-52.

661 LAMB, FRANCES A. "Shipwrecked shoppers." DARMag, 93 (February, 1959), 88.
Wreck of the 'Trial' at mouth of Kennebec in November, 1820.

662 LANCASTER, LANE W. "The Democratic Party in Maine." National Municipal Review, 18 (1929), 744-749.

663 LAPHAM, WILLIAM BERRY. "Notes on the Skillings family." MHGR, 2 (1885), 45-49.

664 LARSON, EDWIN VAN HORN. The forest wealth of Maine. Portland: Maine Forest Service, 1961. Pp. 29.
Includes history.

665 LAWRANCE, WILLIAM A. A twenty-five year review of Androscoggin River pollution control activities. Lewiston, 1967. Pp. 28. MeU.

666 LAWTON, R. J., comp. Franco-Americans of the State of Maine, U.S.A., and their achievements; historical, descriptive and biographical. J. H. Burgess, ed. Lewiston: H. F. Roy, 1915. Pp. 211.

667 "LEADING events in the colonial history of Maine." SJMH, 3 (1915-1916), 32-34.

668 LEAMON, JAMES S. "Maine's Swedish pioneers." Swedish Pioneer Historical Quarterly, 26 (1975), 73-91.

669 _____. "The Revolution comes to Maine." The Bates College Bulletin, 73 (April, 1976), 2-5.

670 LEAVITT, HAROLD WALTER. "Some interesting phases of the development of transportation in Maine." Maine Association of Engineers. Journal, No. 16 Pt. 2 (April, 1940), entire issue.

671 LE BLANT, ROBERT. Une figure légendaire de l'histoire acadienne: le baron de St-Castin. Dax, France: Editions P. Pradeu, [1934]. Pp. 175.

672 LE DUC, THOMAS HAROLD ANDRÉ. "The Maine frontier and the Northeastern Boundary controversy." AHR, 53 (1947-1948), 30-41.

673 LEE, RICHARD H. "Old railroad days on the Newport line." Down East, 18 (November, 1971), 42-45.

674 LEE, WILLIAM STORRS, comp. Maine: a literary chronicle. N.Y.: Funk & Wagnalls, 1968. Pp. xv, 487.

675 _____. "Maine, a literary chronicle." Maine Dig, 3 (Winter, 1969), 92-111.

676 LEGER, MARY CELESTE. The Catholic Indian missions in Maine (1611-1820). Washington: The Catholic Univ. of America, 1929. Pp. x, 184.

677 LEGER, PAUL A. "Hasey's Maine stages." Bus History, 1 (Fall, 1974), 3-6.
Buses.

678 LELAND, CHARLES GODFREY. The Algonquin legends of New England, or myths and folk lore of the Micmac, Passamaquoddy, and Penobscot tribes. (1884) 2d ed. Boston: Houghton, Mifflin, 1885. Pp. xv, 379.

679 _____. "Legends of the Passamaquoddy." Century, 28 (1884), 668-677.

680 LENHART, JOHN M. The Capuchins in Acadia and northern Maine (1632-1638). American Catholic Historical Society. Records, 27 (1916), 191-229, 300-327; 28 (1917), 47-63.

681 LERMOND, NORMAN WALLACE and ARTHUR HERBERT NORTON. Bibliography of mollusca of Maine, 1605-1930. Maine Naturalist, 10 (1930), 49-73, 100-121.

682 LEWIS, GERALD E. Up here in Maine. Garland: Lewis, 1974. Pp. 134.

683 LIBBY, RICHARD J. "A decade in elementary education in Maine." Maine Teachers' Digest, 1 (1940-1941), 141, 174-175.
1931-1940.

684 LIBBY, STEVE. "Nothing like the trolleys." Down East, 12 (January, 1966), 35-38.

685 LINCOLN, J. J. "The Revere bells of Maine." Down East, 17 (January, 1971), 34-37, 63-64, 66.
Bells made by Paul Revere.

686 LINSCOTT, EDWARD LYON. The history of secondary education in Washington and Hancock counties in Maine. Orono: Univ. Pr., 1937. Pp. viii, 171.

687 "LIST of books and documents in the State Library relating to the discovery, settlement, and growth of Maine." Maine State Library. Annual Report, (1891-1892), 19-33.

688 LITOFF, JUDY BARRETT and HAL LITOFF. "Working women in Maine: a note on sources." LabHist, 17 (1976), 88-95.

689 LITTLE, GEORGE BARKER. The kingdom of God not in externals: sermon delivered at Bath, June 24, 1857, before the Maine Missionary Society, at its fiftieth anniversary. Augusta: Elias G. Hodge, 1857. Pp. 64.
     Includes a history of the Society.

690 LITTLE, GEORGE THOMAS, ed. Genealogical and family history of the State of Maine ... and including among other local contributors Rev. Henry S. Burrage ... and Albert Roscoe Stubbs.... N.Y.: Lewis Historical Publishing, 1909. 4v.
     Paged continuously.

691 "LOCAL rimes and quatrains of the northeast." Folksong Society of the Northeast. Bulletin, No. 3 (1931), 17-20.

692 LOCKE, HERBERT E. "Right of access to great ponds by the Colonial Ordinance." Maine Law Review, 12 (1918-1919), 148-164.

693 LOHNES, BARRY J. "A new look at the invasion of eastern Maine, 1814." MeHSQ, 15 (1975-1976), 5-25.
     War of 1812; a comment by Ronald F. Banks follows on pages 26-29.

694 LOMBARD, LUCINA HAYNES. "The antiquarians: a sketch of the history of antique collecting in Maine." Maine's Own Magazine, 8 (April, 1930), 11-16, 29.

695 _____. "The covered bridges of Maine." Maine's Own Magazine, 7 (October, 1929), 11, 26.

696 _____. "The growth of Maine's granite industry." Sun Up, 9 (April, 1931), 4-5, 12, 26.

697 _____. "How springs helped make Maine history." Sun Up, 8 (July, 1930), 17, 44.

698 _____. "John Greenleaf Whittier and Lucy Larcom in Maine." Sun Up, 9 (June, 1931), 4-5, 28, 30.

699 _____. "The latchstring of Maine: some interesting facts about the history of commerce in the Pine Tree State. Sun Up, 9 (January, 1931), 7, 28-29, 31.

700 _____. "The lure of historic Maine houses." Sun Up, 2 (April, 1926), 10, 25, 31.

701 _____. "Maine roads are rich in romantic legend and history." Maine's Own Magazine, 7 (January, 1929), 4, 27.

702 _____. "Maine sea captains and their homes." Sun Up, 3 (February, 1927), 7, 27.

703 _____. "Maine's Paul Revere bells." Sun Up, 9 (July, 1931), 18, 29-31.

704 _____. "Mystic Indian water trails." Sun Up, 5 (August, 1928), 4-5, 24-25.

705 _____. "Post roads and taverns of old Maine." Sun Up, 3 (January, 1927), 12, 14, 37.

706 LOOMIS, ALFRED FULLERTON. Ranging the Maine coast. N.Y.: W. W. Norton, 1939. Pp. 274.

707 LOOMIS, CHARLES DANA. An architectural monograph on port towns of Penobscot Bay. St. Paul: White Pine Bureau, 1922. Pp. 16.
     Belfast, Camden, and Castine.

708 LORD, ARTHUR. "The sale of Matchebiguatus, 1644." MHSP, 49 (1915-1916), 357-360.
     Trading settlement at mouth of Penobscot River.

709 LORING, PHILIP QUINCY. "Outline history of Maine." Sun Up, 2 (October, 1925), 12, 25, 49-50, 52.

710 LOVEJOY, SCOTT K. "Small stream bridges of Maine." Down East, 4 (September, 1957), 18-20.

711 LOVERING, FRANK W. "The railroad that survived on chicken feed." Railroad Enthusiast, 4 (Winter and Spring, 1967), 3-7.
     Belfast & Moosehead Lake Railroad.

712 _____. "Watering places of the gay nineties." Down East, 6 (September, 1959), 16-19.
     Resorts.

713 LOWENTHAL, DAVID. "The Maine press and the Aroostook War." CanHistRev, 32 (1951), 315-336.

714 LUBBOCK, ALFRED BASIL. The Down Easters, American deep-water sailing ships, 1869-1929. Boston: C. E. Lauriat, 1929. Pp. xvi, 285.

715 LUCEY, WILLIAM LEO. The Catholic Church in Maine. Francestown, N.H.: M. Jones, 1957. Pp. 372.

716 _____. "Some correspondence of the Maine commissioners regarding the Webster-Ashburton Treaty." NEQ, 15 (1942), 332-348.
     Northeast Boundary dispute.

717 MAINE

717   LUND, MORTEN. Cruising the Maine coast. N.Y.: Walker, 1967. Pp. 224.

718   LUNT, DUDLEY CAMMETT. The woods and the sea: wilderness and seacoast adventures in the State of Maine. N.Y.: Knopf, 1965. Pp. ix, 304.

719   LYFORD, ELMORE B. "By way of the Kennebec." Yankee, 33 (November, 1969), 46-50, 52-54, 57-58, 63.
      Arnold's Expedition.

720   McALEER, NEIL. "Maine's meteorites." Down East, 21 (November, 1974), 61-63.

721   McCARTHY, MARCIA. "Maine breeds the best." Pine Cone, 3 (Spring, 1947), 22-28.
      Trotting horses.

722   MacDONALD, WILLIAM. "French Canadians in Maine." Nation, 63 (October 15, 1896), 285-286.

723   _____. The government of Maine: its history and administration. N.Y.: Macmillan, 1902. Pp. ix, 263.

724   MacDOUGALL, WALTER M. "Arnold's Expediton to Quebec, 1775." Down East, 22 (September, 1975), 36-41, 74, 77.

725   _____. "Lombard's iron monster." Yankee, 29 (March, 1965), 72, 77, 132, 135, 137.
      Steam powered log hauler.

726   _____. "The lower lakes." Down East, 13 (April, 1966), 22-26, 59.

727   _____. "Seboomook and Northeast Carry." Down East, 11 (April, 1965), 26-29, 38-41, 44.
      Overland transportation connecting two waterways.

728   MacDUFFIE, MALCOLM. "The old Vinal, gone but not forgotten." Steamboat Bill, 27 (1970), 214-216.
      Steamer 'Vinal Haven,' 1892-1945.

729   McKEEN, JOHN. "Remarks on the voyage of George Waymouth, to the coast of Maine, 1605." MeHSC, 5 (1857), 309-338.

730   McKENNEY, LEWIS TIMOTHY. Memories of Maine. Boston: Meador Publishing, 1934. Pp. 210.

731   MacKENZIE, GERTRUDE. My love affair with the State of Maine. N.Y.: Simon and Schuster, 1955. Pp. 311.
      Social life and customs.

732   McKUSICK, VINCENT L. [History of the Maine Supreme Judicial Court.] Maine State Bar Association. Report, 57 (1968), 142-153.

733   McLEAN, JAMES A. "Thumbnail sketch of militia history." MeLAB, 28 (February, 1967), 3-4.

734   McLIN, WILLIAM HELLEN. "The Maine Central and the 'off-beat' gauges." Railroad Enthusiast, 9 (Winter and Spring, 1972), 7-11.

735   McMURTRIE, DOUGLAS CRAWFORD. Maine imprints, 1792-1820; an open letter to R. Webb Noyes. Chicago: Priv. Print., 1935. 12 leaves.

736   _____. "Pioneer printing in Maine." National Printer Journalist, 50 (March, 1932), 18-19, 94-95.

737   MacWILLIAMS, JAMES DONALD. Yours in sports, a history: baseball, basketball, boxing, and bowling in Maine. Volume one. [Monmouth]: Monmouth Pr., 1969. Pp. 301A. MeHi.
      No more published.

738   MAINE (COLONY). Province and court records of Maine. Portland: Maine Historical Society, 1928-.
      Six volumes published as of 1977 covering 1636-1727.

739   MAINE (DISTRICT). CONSTITUTIONAL CONVENTION, 1819. The debates and journal of the Constitutional Convention of the State of Maine 1819-'20, and amendments subsequently made to the Constitution. Charles E. Nash, ed. Augusta: Maine Farmers' Almanac Press, 1894. Various pagings.

740   _____. The debates, resolutions, and other proceedings, of the convention of delegates, assembled at Portland on the 11th, and continued until the 29th day of October, 1819, for the purpose of forming a constitution for the State of Maine, to which is prefixed the constitution taken in convention. Jeremiah Perley, ed. Portland: A. Shirley, 1820. Pp. iv, 300.

741   MAINE. ADJUTANT GENERAL'S OFFICE. History, Maine State Guard, from its inception to 30 June 1946. [Augusta, 1946?]. Pp. 126. MeBa.

742   _____. Roster of Maine in the military service of the United States and allies in the World War, 1917-1919.... Augusta, 1929. 2v.

743   MAINE. AGRICULTURAL EXPERIMENT STATION, ORONO. Teamwork in the blueberry industry by the growers, processors, research and extension personnel, a 10-year history, 1945-1954. Orono, 1954. 36 leaves. MeU.

744   MAINE. ATTORNEY GENERAL. Index to the private and special laws enacted by the legislatures of the State of Maine from 1820-1944, inclusive. Augusta, 1944. Pp. 557. Me.

745   _____. Index to the private and special laws enacted by the legislatures of the State of Maine from 1944 to 1957. [Augusta, 1958]. Pp. 58. Me.

746 MAINE. BUREAU OF LABOR AND INDUSTRY. History of the Bureau of Labor and Industry. (1965) 2d revision. C. Wilder Smith and Madge E. Ames, comps. [Augusta]: Maine Dept. of Manpower Affairs, 1974. 119 leaves.
First edition has title: History of the Department of Labor and Industry.

747 MAINE. CENTENNIAL COMMITTEE. One hundredth anniversary of Maine's entrance into the Union; official program of state celebration, Portland, June 26th to July 5th, 1920, including list of towns to hold local observances and all other information regarding the event.... Augusta: C. E. Nash & Son, 1920. Pp. 36.

748 MAINE. CIVILIAN DEFENSE CORPS. The official history of the Maine Civilian Defense Corps. ... [Augusta, 1945?]. Pp. 218.

749 MAINE. COUNCIL. Aroostook War: historical sketch and roster of commissioned officers and enlisted men called into service for the protection of the northeastern frontier of Maine, from February to May, 1839. Augusta: Kennebec Journal Print, 1904. Pp. 95.

750 MAINE. DEPARTMENT OF EDUCATION. 150 years of education in Maine: sesqui-centennial history of Maine's educational system and the growth and development of the Maine State Department of Education. Kermit S. Nickerson, comp. Augusta, 1970. Pp. 58.

751 _____. A study of the history of education in Maine and the evolution of our present school system. [Augusta, 1901?]. Pp. 104.

752 _____. Through Maine on printed paths: a list of Maine books for teachers and pupils. Augusta, 1956. Pp. 58.

753 MAINE. DEPARTMENT OF EDUCATION AND CULTURAL SERVICES. History of Maine vocational rehabilitation program, 1921-1972. [Augusta?, 1973?]. 43 leaves. Me.

754 MAINE. DEPARTMENT OF HEALTH AND WELFARE. Condensed history of the State of Maine Department of Health and Welfare. [Augusta, 1961?]. 3 leaves. Me.

755 MAINE. DEPARTMENT OF SEA AND SHORE FISHERIES. Commercial fisheries of Maine.... (1957) George H. Taylor, ed. Rev. ed. [Augusta], 1963. Pp. 43.

756 MAINE. DEVELOPMENT COMMISSION. AGRICULTURAL SURVEY COMMITTEE. Report of the Agricultural Survey Committee of the Maine Development Commission on progress in Maine agriculture 1850 to 1920. [Augusta, 1929?]. Pp. 24.

757 MAINE. FOREST COMMISSIONER. Brief history and present organization. [Augusta?], 1929. Pp. 23.

758 _____. Report on public reserved lots: chapter 76, Resolves of 1961. [Augusta], 1963. Pp. 75.
History of public lands.

759 MAINE. FORESTRY DEPARTMENT. Maine forest fire record, 1903-1970. [Augusta, 1971?]. Broadside. 11 x 8 3/8 inches. MeU.

760 MAINE. GEOLOGICAL SURVEY. Bibliography on Maine geology, 1836-1957. Augusta: Department of Economic Development, 1958. Pp. 143.

761 MAINE. GOVERNOR, 1967-1974 (KENNETH M. CURTIS). The Curtis years: 1967-1974. Allen G. Pease ed. Augusta: Office of the Governor/New England Regional Commission, 1974. Pp. 203. MeBa.

762 MAINE. HYDROGRAPHIC SURVEY. The water-power of Maine. Augusta: Sprague, Owen & Nash, 1869. Pp. vii, 526.

763 MAINE. LAWS, STATUTES, ETC. Digest of the resolves of Maine, having the force of law, from 1820 to 1862 inclusive. Joseph B. Hall, comp. Augusta: Stevens and Sayward, 1862. Pp. xiii, 175, xii.

764 MAINE. NATIONAL GUARD. A brief history of the National Guard and the Maine National Guard. 2d. ed. Augusta, 1963. Pp. 12. Me.

765 _____. Historical and pictorial review, National Guard of the State of Maine. Baton Rouge, La.: Army and Navy Publishing, 1939. Pp. xxxvi, 152.

766 MAINE. OFFICE OF STATE COMMISSIONER OF EDUCATION. One hundred years of statehood, centennial studies, celebrations in the public schools of Maine, 1920, one hundred leading facts. Augusta, 1920. Pp. 38.

767 _____. The work of a decade in the schools of Maine. [Augusta, 1906?]. Pp. 14.

768 MAINE. STATE ARCHIVES. Agencies of government, State of Maine, 1820-1971. Augusta, [1972]. Pp. viii, 235.

769 _____. Microfilm list: Maine town records and Maine census records. Augusta, 1976. Pp. 32. MeP.

770 MAINE. STATE CHAMBER OF COMMERCE AND AGRICULTURAL LEAGUE. History of the public or school lots. Portland, [1923]. Unpaged. MeHi.

771 _____. History of the wild lands of Maine. Portland, [1923]. Pp. 11. MeHi.

772 MAINE

772   MAINE. STATE HIGHWAY COMMISSION. A history
of Maine roads, 1600-1970. Augusta, 1970.
Pp. 39.

773   MAINE. STATE LIBRARY, AUGUSTA. Bibliography
on Maine history. [Augusta], 1931. 7
leaves. Me.

774   _____. Maine forts. Augusta: Charles E.
Nash & Son, 1924. Pp. 252.

775   _____. Maine in the Civil War: a list of
material in the Maine State Library. [Augus-
ta], 1961. Pp. 13.

776   MAINE. STATE MUSEUM. Artists listed in city
directories in Maine, 1850-1899. [Augusta,
1976]. Unpaged. MeU.

777   _____. Maine furniture makers. [Augusta,
1976]. Unpaged. MeU.
   From colonial to the early Victorian
period.

778   MAINE. STATE PLANNING OFFICE. Maine population trends, 1960-1970. [Augusta], 1972.
Pp. 25.

779   MAINE. STATE POLICE. History and functions
of Maine State Police. (1968) 3d. revision.
[Augusta], 1974. 28 leaves. Me.

780   MAINE. STATE WATER STORAGE COMMISSION.
Gazetteer of the rivers and lakes of Maine.
Waterville: Sentinel Publishing, 1914.
Pp. 323.
   Arranged alphabetically by drainage basins.

781   MAINE. UNIVERSITY. Survey of higher education in Maine, by the University of Maine,
in cooperation with Bates, Bowdoin and Colby
Colleges. [Orono?, 1932?]. Pp. x, 430.

782   MAINE. UNIVERSITY. COLLEGE OF AGRICULTURE.
DEPARTMENT OF ANIMAL PATHOLOGY. Forty years
of pullorum disease eradication in poultry for
the State of Maine. Orono, [1962?]. Pp. 19.

783   MAINE. UNIVERSITY. COLLEGE OF AGRICULTURE.
EXTENSION DEPARTMENT. Fifty years of dairy
extension work in Maine. Ralph Corbett, ed.
Orono, 1962. Pp. 19. Me.

784   MAINE. UNIVERSITY. DEPARTMENT OF HISTORY
AND GOVERNMENT. A reference list of manuscripts relating to the history of Maine.
Elizabeth Ring, comp. Orono: Univ. Pr.,
1938-1941. 3v.

785   MAINE. UNIVERSITY. FORESTRY DEPARTMENT.
Golden anniversary, 1903-1953. Orono, 1954.
Pp. 92.

786   ["MAINE."] Holiday, 2 (August, 1947), 43-57,
97-100.

787   "MAINE artists." MeLB, 16 (1930-1931), 29-
30.

788   "THE MAINE boundary controversy." The Northern, 5 (July, 1925), 3-6, (August, 1925),
3-5.

789   MAINE BROADCASTING SYSTEM. The first 40 years,
1925-1965. n.p., [1965]. Unpaged.

790   MAINE CENTRAL RAILROAD COMPANY. A century of
service to the State of Maine, 1862-1962....
[Waterville?, 1963?]. Pp. 20.

791   _____. An historical account of the Maine
Central Railroad Company.... [Portland?],
1879. Pp. 16. MeHi.

792   _____. History of the capitalization of the
Maine Central Railroad Company during the
period June 30, 1911, to June 30, 1914. n.p.,
[1915]. Pp. 31.

793   "THE MAINE Central Railroad Company and its
system." BHistMag, 1 (1885-1886), 192-194.

794   "MAINE churches are historical landmarks."
Sun Up, 5 (December, 1927), 9, 21-23.

795   "MAINE covered bridges." MeLB, 17 (1931-
1932), 86-90.

796   MAINE FEDERATION OF MUSIC CLUBS. 25th anni-
versary [of the] Maine Federation of Music
Clubs, Lewiston-Auburn, May 13-14, 1948.
[Lewiston?, 1948]. Unpaged.

797   MAINE FEDERATION OF WOMEN'S CLUBS. Histori-
cal sketches, 1892-1924. Georgia Pulsifer
Porter, comp. Lewiston: Lewiston Journal
Printshop, 1925. Pp. 165.

798   _____. History of the Maine Federation of
Women's Clubs.... Lewiston, 1898. Pp. 52.

799   _____. Maine in history and romance. Lewiston: Lewiston Journal, 1915. Pp. 242.

800   _____. Prominent personalities in the Maine
Federation of Women's Clubs. West Boothbay
Harbor: James F. Waugh, 1962. Pp. iv, 217.

801   _____. The trail of the Maine pioneer.
Lewiston: Lewiston Journal, 1916. Pp. 340.

802   MAINE HISTORIC PRESERVATION COMMISSION. Historic preservation plan: the historic background. [Portland], 1973. Pp. 64. MeHi.

803   MAINE historical memorials.... [Augusta?]:
Printed for the State, 1922. Pp. xi, 199.

804   MAINE HISTORICAL SOCIETY. Indians of Maine:
a preliminary inventory of material on the
history of the Indians of Maine in the Society Library. Roger B. Ray, ed. Portland,
1969. Pp. ii, 11.

805 _____. Tercentenary of Martin Pring's first voyage to the coast of Maine, 1603-1903. Portland, [1905?]. Pp. 73.
　　Includes a bibliography.

806 _____. Waymouth tercentenary: an account of the celebration of the landing of George Waymouth on the coast of Maine. Portland, [1905?]. Pp. 53.

807 MAINE HISTORICAL SOCIETY. LIBRARY. The Indians of Maine: a bibliographical guide, being largely a selected inventory of material on the subject in the Society's library. Roger B. Ray, comp. Portland, 1972. Unpaged.

808 "MAINE history day by day--December." Sun Up, 2 (December, 1925), 16, 20.

809 "MAINE history day by day--February." Sun Up, 2 (February, 1926), 17.

810 "MAINE history day by day--January." Sun Up, 2 (January, 1926), 13, 45.

811 "MAINE history day by day--June." Sun Up, 3 (June, 1926), 36.

812 "MAINE history day by day--July." Sun Up, 3 (July, 1926), 55.

813 "MAINE history day by day--March." Sun Up, 2 (April, 1926), 25.

814 "MAINE history day by day--May." Sun Up, 2 (May, 1926), 31.

815 MAINE in review, 1776-1876. [Brunswick], 1976. Pp. 96. MeHi.

816 "MAINE: its early history--physical aspect--agricultural and mineral resources--commerce--manufactures--government--finances--population--schools, colleges, &c., &c." De Bow's Review, 12 (1852), 603-610.

817 "MAINE, its No. 1 industry--shoes." Leather and Shoes, 130 (December 3, 1955), 11-12, 14-16, 24.

818 "THE MAINE law, its history and results." Tait's Edinburgh Magazine, New Ser., 20 (1853), 666-670.
　　Prohibition; signed: S. P.

819 MAINE LEAGUE OF HISTORICAL SOCIETIES AND MUSEUMS. Maine, a guide "Down East." (1937) 2d ed. Dorris A. Isaacson, ed. Rockland: Courier-Gazette, 1970. Pp. xxiv, 510.
　　First edition written by the staff of the Federal Writers' Project.

820 "MAINE libraries." MeLAB, 2 (July, 1941), 2.

821 MAINE LIBRARY ASSOCIATION. BICENTENNIAL COMMITTEE. Bibliography of Maine, 1960-1975. Eric S. Flower, comp. Orono, 1976. 109 leaves.

822 MAINE OSTEOPATHIC ASSOCIATION. Golden Jubilee, 1904-1954. n.p., [1954]. Pp. 30. Me.

823 MAINE PEDAGOGICAL SOCIETY. Proceedings of the Maine Pedagogical Society for 1880-81, with a historical sketch of the Maine Educational Association, and journal of proceedings of the Maine Teachers' Association, 1875-80. Farmington: Knowlton, McLeary, 1883. Pp. 159.

824 "MAINE savings banks." Sun Up, 2 (November, 1925), 32-33, 38.

825 MAINE STATE BAR ASSOCIATION. Report ... for 1920 and 1921. Augusta: Charles E. Nash & Son, 1921. Pp. 328.
　　Includes celebration of the first century of jurisprudence in the state which was held in Augusta, January 12, 1921.

826 MAINE STATE BICENTENNIAL COMMISSION. Maine bicentennial atlas: an historical survey. Gerald E. Morris and Richard D. Kelly, Jr., eds. Portland: Maine Historical Society, 1976. Pp. 20.
　　Sixty-nine plates and accompanying historical notes.

827 MAINE STATE FEDERATED LABOR COUNCIL, AFL-CIO. Six decades of history, 1904-1963. [Augusta? 1964]. Pp. 15.

828 MAINE through the eyes of her artists. Portland: Hem Publishing, 1965. Unpaged.
　　Includes biographies of the artists.

829 "MAINE Turnpike story." The Maine Trail, (December, 1955), entire issue.
　　Includes a history of the turnpike by Lucius D. Barrows.

830 MAINE WRITERS RESEARCH CLUB. Historic churches and homes of Maine. Portland: Falmouth Book House, 1937. Pp. x, 289.

831 _____. Just Maine folks. Lewiston: Journal Printshop, 1924. Pp. 331.
　　Biographies.

832 _____. Maine Indians in history and legends. Portland: Severn-Wylie-Jewett, [1952]. Pp. 180.

833 _____. Maine, my state. Lewiston: Journal Printshop, 1919. Pp. 350.

834 _____. Maine, past & present. Boston: D. C. Heath, 1929. Pp. x, 321.

835 MAINE

835 _____. Maine writers of fiction for juve-
niles. Orono: Univ. of Maine, 1965. Pp. v,
69.

836 "MAINE'S early history." BTJ, 4 (1891-1892),
331.

837 "MAINE'S early Irish colonists." MeCathHM,
2 (February, 1914), 17-21, (March, 1914),
48-51.

838 "MAINE'S library background." MeLAB, 2
(April, 1941), 4-5.

839 "MAINE's railroad covered bridges." Down
East, 14 (August, 1967), 60-63.

840 "MALECITE and Passamaquoddy tales." Northeast Folklore, 6 (1964), entire issue.

841 MANTOR, AGNES P. Our State of Maine: its
story briefly told. Farmington: Knowlton &
McLeary, 1933. Pp. 43.

842 MARBLE, ALBERT PRESCOTT. "Geography and history of Maine." Worcester HSProc, 6 (1883),
29-47.

843 _____. Geography of Maine. Cincinnati: Van
Antwerp, Bragg, 1880. Pp. 10.

844 "THE MARCH of Benedict Arnold through the
District of Maine." SJMH, 11 (1923), 144-150,
195-208.

845 MARKS, ARTHUR E. "Indian relics in Maine."
MHGR, 8 (1895), 183-184.

846 MARRINER, ERNEST CUMMINGS. "Maine doctors of
long ago." Maine Medical Association. Journal, 32 (1941), 161-167.

847 _____. "The Maine economy: before 1820."
Thomas Business Review, 3 (Fall, 1975), 2-5.

848 _____. Remembered Maine. Waterville: Colby
College Pr., 1957. Pp. 149.

849 MARSHALL, ROBERT BRADFORD. Spirit leveling
in Maine, 1899-1915. Washington: Govt.
Print. Off., 1916. Pp. 64.

850 MARTIN, FREDERIC THURMAN. The first fifty
years of the Maine Section of the American
Chemical Society. [Orono]: Univ. Pr.,
[1962?]. Pp. 7. MeU.

851 MARTIN, GEORGE CASTOR. "Indian burial in New
Jersey, Maine and Maryland." Archaeological
Bulletin, 2 (March, 1910), 33-38.

852 MARTIN, KENNETH R. "The folk art of Maine's
whalemen." The Quarterdeck, 2 (Spring-Sum-
mer, 1972), 10-11.

853 MASSACHUSETTS. GENERAL COURT. Documents re-
lating to the North Eastern Boundary of
Maine. Boston: Dutton & Wentworth, 1828.
Pp. 275.

854 MASSACHUSETTS BAR ASSOCIATION. Some accounts
of early Maine history, presented at the regional meeting of the American Bar Association.... n.p., [1957]. Pp. 31.

855 MASTA, HENRY LORNE. Abenaki Indian legends,
grammar and place names. Victoriaville,
P.Q.: La Voix des bois-francs, 1932.
Pp. 110.

856 MATTHEWS, ALBERT. "Edward Goddard's journal
of the peace commission to the eastern Indians." CSMP, 20 (1917-1919), 129-147.

857 _____. "Origin of the name of Maine." CSMP,
12 (1908-1909), 366-382.

858 MAUNDER, ELWOOD R. and AMELIA FRY. "Samuel
Trask Dana, the early years." Forest History,
10 (July, 1966), 2-13.
Maine Forest Commissioner.

859 MAURAULT, JOSEPH PIERRE ANSELME. Histoire
des Abenakis, depuis 1605 jusqu' à nos jours.
[Sorel, Quebec]: Imprimé à l'atelier typo-
graphique de la "Gazette de Sorel," 1866.
Pp. iii, x, 631.

860 MAXFIELD, EZRA KEMPTON. "Maine dialect."
American Speech, 2 (1927), 76-83.

861 _____. "Maine list." Dialect Notes, 5
(1926), 385-390.

862 MEAD, EDGAR THORN, JR. "Bridgton and Saco
River R.R.: riding the narrow gauge to
Bridgton." Down East, 15 (October, 1968),
30-33.

863 "MEANING of the Indian names Penobscot and
Kennebec." Ladies' Repository, 24 (1864),
631.
Signed: H. Y. W.

864 MEIGS, RETURN JONATHAN. Journal of the ex-
pedition against Quebec under command of Col.
Benedict Arnold in the year 1775. Charles
Ira Bushnell, ed. N.Y.: Priv. Print., 1864.
Pp. vi, 57.

865 MELLON, GERTRUD A. and ELIZABETH F. WILDER,
eds. Maine and its role in American art,
1740-1963. N.Y.: Viking Pr., 1963.
Pp. 178.

866 MELVIN, JAMES. The journal of James Melvin,
private soldier in Arnold's Expedition against
Quebec in the year 1775. Andrew A. Melvin,
ed. Portland: H. W. Bryant, 1902. Pp. 90.

867 MEN of progress: biographical sketches and portraits of leaders in business and professional life in and of the State of Maine. Richard Herndon, comp. Boston: New England Magazine, 1897. Pp. 626.

868 MENDENHALL, THOMAS CORWIN. "Twenty unsettled mules in the Northeast Boundary." AASP, New Ser., 11 (1896-1897), 188-210.

869 MERCHANT, CHARLES HENRY. "Changes in the apple industry in Maine." Maine Agricultural Experiment Station. Report, 62 (1945-1946), 35-63.
    1924-1944.

870 _____. "Maine farm prices during world war periods." Maine Agricultural Experiment Station. Report, 61 (1944-1945), 293-399.

871 _____. Prices on farm products in Maine. Orono: Maine Agricultural Experiment Station, 1933. Pp. 179. MH-BA.
    1852-1932.

872 MERK, FREDERICK. Fruits of propaganda in the Tyler administration. Cambridge: Harvard Univ. Pr., 1971. Pp. x, 259.
    Northeast Boundary.

873 MERRILL, DAPHNE WINSLOW. The lakes of Maine: a compilation of fact and legend. Rockland: Courier-Gazette, 1973. Pp. 263.

874 METZGER, HOMER B. and VANCE E. DEARBORN. Commercial farming in Maine, 1960-70: income, production, location, prices. Orono: Maine Cooperative Extension Service, 1971. Pp. 32. MeU.

875 MILIKEN, HENRY. "Old-time logging camp clerk." Down East, 19 (March, 1973), 48-51.

876 MILITARY ORDER OF THE LOYAL LEGION OF THE UNITED STATES. MAINE COMMANDERY. Historical address at the fiftieth anniversary of the Maine Commandery, December 7, 1916, by Henry S. Burrage. Portland: Fred. L. Tower, 1917. Pp. 20. Me.

876A MILLER, ALAN R. "America's first political satirist, Seba Smith of Maine." Journalism Quarterly, 47 (1970), 488-492.

877 MILLER, C. S. S. "The story of the states No. 6: Maine." Pearson's Magazine, 12 (August, 1901), 216.

878 MILLET, JOSHUA. A history of the Baptists in Maine; together with brief notices of societies and institutions, and a dictionary of the labors of each minister. Portland: C. Day, 1845. Pp. xii, 472.

879 MILLIKEN, PHILIP I. Notes on the Cumberland and Oxford Canal and the origin of the Canal Bank. Portland: Bradford Pr., 1935. Pp. 40.

880 MILLS, DUDLEY A. "British diplomacy in Canada: the Ashburton Treaty." United Empire, New Ser., 2 (1911), 683-712.

881 MILLS, HIRAM FRANCIS. Natural resources and their development. Memorial ... to the Governor and Council of Maine.... Augusta: Stevens & Sayward, 1867. Pp. 23.

882 MILLS, WILLIAM HOWARD. "Benedict Arnold's march to Canada." MagAmHist, 13 (1885), 143-154.

883 "MILLS at the eastward prior to 1800." BHist Mag, 6 (1890-1891), 18-21.
    East of the Penobscot River.

884 ["MINERALS of Maine."] Rocks and Minerals, 5 (June, 1932), entire issue.

885 MINOT, JOHN CLAIR. "Maine's contribution to literature." MeLB, 8 (1918-1919), 104-106; 9 (1919-1920), 6-8, 31-34, 57-61.

886 "MISSIONS in Maine from 1603 to 1854." Catholic World, 22 (1875-1876), 666-677.

887 MITCHELL, DOROTHY. Along the Maine coast. N.Y.: McGraw-Hill, 1947. Pp. 97.

888 MITCHELL, EDWIN VALENTINE. Anchor to windward. N.Y.: Coward-McCann, 1949. Pp. 270.

889 _____. It's an old State of Maine custom. N.Y.: Vanguard Pr., 1949. Pp. 248.

890 _____. Maine summer. N.Y.: Coward-McCann, 1939. Pp. 210.

891 MOFFETT, ROSS. "Some samples of red ochre." MASB, 15 (1953-1954), 58.
    Red Paint People.

892 MONTAGUE, HENRY BURT. "Some legal incidents in the separation of Maine from Massachusetts." Maine Law Review, 3 (1909-1910), 126-138.

893 MONTGOMERY, JOB HERRICK. "The judiciary of Maine." Maine Law Review, 7 (1913-1914), 222-235.

894 MOODY, LINWOOD W. The Maine two-footers: the story of the two-foot gauge railroads of Maine. Berkeley, Calif.: Howell-North, 1959. Pp. xv, 203.

895 _____. "Two foot gage." Railroad Magazine, 67 (December, 1955), 22-33.
    Ten two-foot lines in Maine.

896 MOODY, RALPH. The fields of home. N.Y.:
Norton, 1953. Pp. 335.
Country life.

897 MOODY, ROBERT EARLE. "A letter from Thomas
Gorges' letterbook." MeHSN, 12 (1972-1973),
45-50.

898 _____. A proprietary experiment in early
New England history: Thomas Gorges and the
Province of Maine. [Boston]: Boston Univer-
sity Pr., 1963. Pp. 33.

899 MOORE, GLOVER. The Missouri controversy
1819-1821. Lexington: Univ. of Kentucky
Pr., 1953. Pp. vii, 383.

900 MOORE, MARJORIE ANN. Literary landmarks of
Maine. Veazie, 1969. Unpaged. Me.
Homes of Maine authors.

901 MOOREHEAD, WARREN KING. "The Red-Paint People of Maine." American Anthropologist, New
Ser., 15 (1913), 33-47.
A comment on this article by D. I. Bushnell, Jr. in American Anthropologist, New
Ser., 15 (1913), 707 was answered by Moorehead in his "'The Red-Paint People'--a reply." American Anthropologist, New Ser., 16
(1914), 358-361.

902 _____. A report on the archaeology of Maine;
being a narrative of explorations in that
state, 1912-1920, together with work at Lake
Champlain, 1917. Andover, Mass.: Andover
Pr., 1922. Pp. 272.

903 MORISON, SAMUEL ELIOT. "Notes from Maine."
American Speech, 4 (1929), 356.

904 MORRELL, JENNIE MAY. Reminiscences of early
meetings of the Josselyn Botanical Society.
Josselyn Botanical Society of Maine. Bulletin,
No. 10 (1955), 18-19.

905 MORRIS, EDWARD PARMELEE. "Along the Maine
coast." Yale Review, New Ser., 5 (1916),
843-855.
Social life and customs.

906 MORRIS, GERALD E. ["Maine state seal."]
MeHSN, 10 (1970-1971), 35-42, 70.

907 MORSE, FRANK LEANDER STAPLES. The history of
secondary education in Knox and Lincoln
counties in Maine. Orono: Univ. Pr., 1939.
Pp. vii, 86.

908 MOSELEY, EMMA. "Maine's prima donnas." Sun
Up, 3 (June, 1927), 7, 47-48.
Singers.

909 MOULTON, AUGUSTUS FREEDOM. Maine historical
sketches. Lewiston: Lewiston Journal Printshop, 1929. Pp. 293.

910 _____, ed. Memorials of Maine: a life record of men and women of the past, whose
sterling character and energy and industry
have made them preeminent in their own and
many other states. N.Y.: American Historical Society, 1916. Pp. 415.

911 _____. Sir Fernando Gorges and his palati-
nate of Maine: an address delivered before
the Society of the Colonial Dames of America
resident in the State of Maine, November 2,
1903. Portland: Printed for the Society,
1903. Pp. 28.

912 MUNSON, GORHAM BERT. "First Penobscot cruise:
Champlain in 1604." Down East, 5 (April,
1959), 26-28, 33, 38-39.

913 _____. "Maine's first vacationist." Down
East, 5 (January, 1959), 27-35.
Henry David Thoreau.

914 _____. Penobscot: Down East paradise.
Philadelphia: Lippincott, 1959. Pp. 399.
Penobscot Valley.

915 MYERS, EDWARD A. "The law of the lobster."
NEG, 4 (Spring, 1963), 13-20.

916 "NARRATIVE of the sufferings of Robert Forbes
& family: their journey in 1784 from Canada
to the Kennebec River." Down East, 3 (April,
1957), 20-23, 36-37.
A variation of an earlier account by Arthur
Bradman; see entry 134.

917 NASON, EMMA HUNTINGTON. Old colonial houses
in Maine built prior to 1776. Augusta: Kennebec Journal, 1908. Pp. x, 106.

918 _____. "The Pilgrim Fathers on the Kennebec."
NEM, New Ser., 30 (1904), 309-320.
Kennebec Patent.

919 "NATIVE poets of Maine." MeLB, 13 (1927-
1928), 101-114.

920 "NEGRO folk-songs from Maine." Folksong Society of the Northeast. Bulletin, No. 8
(1934), 13-16; No. 9 (1935), 10-15; No. 10
(1935), 21-24.

921 NETT, BRUCE OWEN. "44 miles of memories."
Down East, 7 (April, 1961), 36-40.
Wiscasset, Waterville and Farmington Rail-
road.

922 NO ENTRY.

923 NEWELL, WILLIAM STARK. Shipbuilding in Maine:
a brief history. Princeton, N.J.: Princeton
Univ. Pr., 1938. Pp. 24.

924 NICHOLS, CHARLES JOSEPH. "Completion of Arnold's march through Maine." SJMH, 13 (1925),
69-78.

925 NICHOLS, GEORGE E. "Raised bogs in eastern Maine." GeogRev, 7 (1919), 159-167.
Peat moss for surgical dressings.

926 NICHOLS, L. NELSON. "Studies in early American title pages--Maine." American Printer, 80 (March 20, 1925), 44-45.

927 NITKIN, NATHANIEL. "The lumberers." NEG, 11 (Winter, 1970), 28-36.

928 NIXON, MILTON A. "Supreme court of judicature." Maine Law Review, 14 (1962), 58-65.
Supreme Judicial Court.

929 NOBLE, JOHN. "Land controversies in Maine--1736-1770." CSMP, 8 (1902-1904), 104-117.

930 "NORTH Eastern Boundary of the U. States." Boston Monthly Magazine, 1 (1825), 571-584.

931 NORWOOD, LESLIE E. "Colony Ordinance of 1641-47 and its effect on Maine law." Peabody Law Review, 3 (1939), 77-83.

932 NOYES, REGINALD WEBB. A bibliography of Maine imprints to 1820. Stonington, 1930. Pp. ix, 22.
Supplemented by entry 934.

933 _____. A guide to the study of Maine local history. [Ann Arbor? Mich.], 1936. v, 87 leaves.
Supplement to entry 518.

934 _____. Supplement to "A bibliography of Maine imprints to 1820." Stonington, 1934. Pp. 11. MeBa.
See entry 932.

935 NUTTING, WALLACE. Maine beautiful: a pictorial record covering all the counties of Maine, with text between. Framingham, Mass.: Old America, 1924. Pp. 302.

936 O'BRIEN, FRANCIS MASSEY. "Selected readings in Maine history: local history." MeHSN, 5 (May, 1966), 5-9.

937 O'BRIEN, MICHAEL J. "The early Irish in Maine." AIrHSJ, 10 (1911), 162-170.

938 NO ENTRY.

939 ODD FELLOWS. INDEPENDENT ORDER OF. MAINE. GRAND LODGE. I.O.O.F., history of Odd Fellowship in Maine. Portland: F. G. Rich, 1878. Pp. iv, 356.

940 O'DWYER, GEORGE FRANCIS. "Captain James Howard, Col. William Lithgow, Col. Arthur Noble, and other Irish pioneers of Maine." AIrHSJ, 19 (1920), 71-88.

941 OGDEN, MARGUERITE. "How our church came to Maine." Spirit of Missions, 83 (1918), 135-142.
Episcopal Church.

942 OLIVER, VELMA K. A history, State of Maine Division, American Association of University Women, 1946-1974. n.p., [1974?]. Pp. 36. MeBa.

943 OLMSTED, CAROLYN and MARGARET OLMSTED. Penobscot Bay treasures. Portland: Falmouth Publishing, 1950. Pp. 118.

944 ORCHARD, WILLIAM C. "Notes on Penobscot houses." American Anthropologist, New Ser., 11 (1909), 601-606.
Penobscot Indian tepees.

945 "ORIGIN of the name of some of our Maine towns." MeLB, 13 (1927-1928), 25-27.

946 OSBORN, WILLIAM C. The paper plantation: Ralph Nader's study group report on the pulp and paper industry in Maine. N.Y.: Grossman Publishers, 1974. Pp. xx, 300.

947 O'TOOLE, FRANCIS J. and THOMAS N. TUREEN. "State power and the Passamaquoddy tribe: 'a gross national hypocrisy.'" Maine Law Review, 23 (1971), 1-39.

948 OWEN, HOWARD, comp. Biographical sketches of the members of the Senate and House of Representatives of Maine.... Augusta, 1872-1967. 53v.

949 OWEN, M. B. Story of Benedict Arnold's march on Quebec. n.p., [197-?]. Pp. 12. MeP.

950 PACKARD, ALPHEUS SPRING. "Discourse of Rev. Prof. Alpheus S. Packard, D.D., of Bowdoin College, at the semi-centennial anniversary of the General Conference of Congregational Churches in Maine, delivered in Portland, June 28, 1876." General Conference of Congregational Churches in Maine. Minutes, (1875), 111-133.

951 PACKARD, LEONARD O. "The decrease of population along the Maine coast." GeogRev, 2 (1916), 334-341.

952 PARK, FRANCIS E. "Eastward with No. 71." Down East, 9 (September, 1962), 34-36, 52.
Maine Central Railroad.

953 PARKER, LESTER WARD. "Diary of a young man, 1807-1808." NEG, 7 (Summer, 1965), 31-42.
Everett Howard, silhouette maker.

954 PARKER, WILLIAM J. "The Seguin: the little tugboat that has served Maine shipping since 1884." Down East, 6 (November, 1959), 38-40.

955 MAINE

955 PARSONS, USHER. "Memoir of Charles Frost."
NEHGR, 3 (1849), 249-262.
Seventeenth-century Maine.

956 PARSONS, VESTA M. "Thoreau's 'The Maine
Woods'; an essay in appreciation." Husson
Review, 1 (1967-1968), 17-27.

957 PATRONS OF HUSBANDRY. MAINE STATE GRANGE.
Golden jubilee, Maine State Grange, 1873-
1923. n.p., [1923?]. Pp. 64. MeU.
Includes history by E. H. Libby.

958 PATTANGALL, WILLIAM ROBINSON. The Meddybemps
letters, reproduced from the Machias Union of
1903-1904; Maine's hall of fame, reproduced
from the Maine Democrat of 1909-1910; memorial addresses. Lewiston: Lewiston Journal,
1924. Pp. 359.

959 PATTERSHALL, MARGARET S. "One hundred books
about Maine." Maine Teacher, 13 (December,
1952), 103-105.

960 PATTERSON, WILLIAM DAVIS. "Dunning family of
Maine." BHistMag, 6 (1890-1891), 35-42.

961 PAYNE, WILLIAM ELISHA. "History of homeopathy
in Maine." North American Journal of Homeopathy, 16 (1867-1868), 210-226.

962 PEABODY, HENRY GREENWOOD, comp. The coast of
Maine, Campobello to the Isles of Shoals.
Boston, 1889. Pp. 71.

963 PEAKS, JOSEPH B. "Maine's railroad growth."
BTJ, 16 (1903-1904), 14-15.

964 PEARL, CYRIL. "Maine, as a field for moral
and religious enterprise." American Quarterly
Register, 10 (1837), 185-192.

965 PECK, HENRY AUSTIN. Seaports in Maine: an
economic study. Orono: Univ. Pr., 1955.
Pp. v, 70.

966 PEIRCE, CHARLES. The unmasked nabob of Hancock County; or, the scales dropt from the
eyes of the people. Portsmouth, N.H., 1796.
Pp. 24.
A satire referring to the Kennebec Patent.

967 PÉLADEAU, MARIUS B. "Maine: preservation
Yankee style." Historic Preservation, 25
(October-December, 1973), 4-11.
Architecture.

968 PELLETIER, LAWRENCE LEE. The initiative and
referendum in Maine. Brunswick, 1951.
Pp. 35.

969 "PENOBSCOT Bay in 1556." BHistMag, 5 (1889-
1890), 61.

970 PERHAM, HAROLD C., ed. The Maine book on
Universalism. Norway: Advertiser-Democrat,
1953. Pp. 220.

971 PERKINS, ANNE E. "More notes on Maine dialect." American Speech, 5 (1929), 118-131.

972 _____. "Vanishing expressions of the Maine
coast." American Speech, 3 (1927), 134-141.

973 PERKINS, EDWARD H. "The evolution of Maine
scenery." Maine Naturalist, 9 (1929), 47-52.

974 PERKINS, VIRGINIA CHASE. "A mining boom in
Maine." NEQ, 14 (1941), 437-456.
1870s.

975 PERRY, TRUEMAN SUMMERFIELD. A sermon delivered before the Union Conference, at the
semi-centennial session, South Bridgton,
Maine, June 14, 1886. Portland: B. Thurston, 1886. Pp. 23. MB.
Formed from Congregational churches in Cumberland and Oxford counties.

976 PETERS, BRADLEY L. Maine Central Railroad
Company, a story of success and independence.
[Portland]: Maine Central Railroad Company,
1976. Pp. 16. MeHi.

977 PHILOON, JAMES E. The Maine Universalist
Convention: a brief history. Boston: Universalist Publishing, [1929]. Pp. 62.

978 PIERCE, WILLIAM C. "The rise and fall of the
York and Cumberland Rail Road." MeHSQ, 15
(1975-1976), 106-128.

979 PILSBURY, CHARLES ALBERT. "Some early Maine
journalists." SJMH, 3 (1915-1916), 41-43.

980 POLLARD, J. A. Polluted paradise: the story
of the Maine rape. Lewiston: Twin City
Printing, 1973. Pp. 328. MeP.
Environmental policy.

981 POLLARD, RALPH J. Freemasonry in Maine,
1762-1945. Portland: Tucker, [1945?].
Pp. 310. MeBa.

982 POOR, JOHN ALFRED. English colonization in
America: a vindication of Sir Ferdinando
Gorges, as the father of English colonization
in America. (Delivered before the Historical
Societies of Maine, and New York.) N.Y.:
D. Appleton, 1862. Pp. 144.

983 _____. The first international railway and
the colonization of New England. Laura E.
Poor, ed. N.Y.: G. P. Putnam's Sons, 1892.
Pp. 400.

984 _____. "Railroads in Maine." American Railroad Journal, 2 Ser., 4 (November 18, 1848),
737-738.

985 _____. The railway: remarks at Belfast,
Maine, July 4, 1867. Boston: Little, Brown,
1867. Pp. 61.

986 PORTER, FLORENCE COLLINS and HELEN BROWN TRASK, eds. Maine men and women in southern California: a volume regarding the lives of Maine men and women of note and substantial achievement, as well as those of a younger generation whose careers are certain, yet still in the making. Los Angeles: Kingsley, Mason & Collins, 1913. Pp. 144.

987 PORTER, FREDERIC HUTCHINSON. A survey of existing colonial architecture in Maine. Architectural Review, 7 (1918), 29-32, 47-51, 94-96; 11 (1920), 13-15, 45-48, 83-88, 119-120, 155-156, 183-186; 12 (1921), 41-46, 64, 73-76, 179-184. American Architect, 120 (1921), 149-151.

988 [PORTER, JOSEPH WHITCOMB.] "The Aroostook War." SJMH, 1 (1913-1914), 142-143.
Author attribution by the editor.

989 [_____.] "Notes on the early history of the Catholic Church in eastern Maine." SJMH, 1 (1913-1914), 66-68.
Author attribution by the editor.

990 [_____.] "Owners of Maine lands when Maine became a state." SJMH, 2 (1914-1915), 16-25.
Author attribution by the editor.

991 _____. "Porter families in Maine." Maine Genealogist and Biographer, 1 (1875-1867), 45-49.

992 POTTLE, GEORGE. "The growth of Maine in the last decade." BTJ, 16 (1903-1904), 44-46.

993 POWERS, W. A. "Maine." Town and Country, 108 (June, 1954), 42-45, 89-90, 93.
Social life and customs.

994 PREHISTORIC peoples of Maine: a Maine State Museum teacher's resource unit. (1970) Rev. William H. Soule, ed. Augusta: Maine State Museum, 1975. Pp. 55. Me.

995 PRENTISS, THOMAS MELLEN. The Maine spelling book: containing rules and examples for spelling and pronouncing the English language ... to which is annexed a concise geographical description of Maine, its boundaries, bays, islands, counties, capital towns, mountains, rivers, character, etc; designed for the use of schools in the District of Maine. Leominster, Mass.: Charles & John Prentiss, 1799. Pp. vii, 123.

996 "PRESBYTERIANISM in Maine, prior to 1870." BHistMag, 3 (1887-1888), 205-207.

997 "PRESIDENTIAL electors in the District of Maine when it was part of Massachusetts." BHistMag, 4 (1888-1889), 127-128.
1789-1816.

998 PRINCE, GEORGE. "The voyage of Capt. Geo. Weymouth to the coast of Maine in 1605." MeHSC, 6 (1859), 291-306.

999 PRINCE, J. DYNELEY. "Notes on Passamaquoddy literature." New York Academy of Sciences. Annals, 13 (1900-1901), 381-386.

1000 _____. "A Passamaquoddy tobacco famine." International Journal of American Linguistics, 1 (1917), 58-63.

1001 _____. "The Passamaquoddy wampum records." American Philosophical Society. Proceedings, 36 (1897), 479-495.

1002 _____. "The Penobscot language of Maine." American Anthropologist, 12 (1910), 183-208.

1003 _____. "Some Passamaquoddy witchcraft tales." American Philosophical Society. Proceedings, 38 (1899), 181-189.

1004 PROMINENT men of Maine: individual biographic studies with character portraits. N.Y.: Historical Records, 1940. Unpaged.
Morrill Goddard and Charles William Goddard; no more published.

1005 PROSSER, ALBERT L. "History of the Josselyn Botanical Society." Josselyn Botanical Society of Maine. Bulletin, No. 10 (1975), 6-17.

1006 PROTESTANT EPISCOPAL CHURCH IN THE U.S.A. MAINE (DIOCESE). One hundredth anniversary of the Diocese of Maine, 1820-1920, Christ Church, Gardiner, Maine, May thirtieth to June third. Gardiner, 1920. Pp. xi, 159.

1007 PROVOST, HONORIUS. "Un chapitre d'histoire religieuse dans le Maine." La Revue de l'Université Laval, 2 (June, 1948), 853-860.
Services of l'Abbé Moyse Fortier to Canadian immigrants in Maine, 1838-1845.

1008 "PUBLISHERS and journalists of Maine." MeLB, 14 (1928-1929), 55-75.

1009 PULLEN, JOHN J. A shower of stars: the Medal of Honor and the 27th Maine. Philadelphia: Lippincott, 1966. Pp. 269.
An historical mystery of the disappearance of a barrelful of medals and the showering of medals on members of the 27th Maine Regiment, less than half of whom were qualified to receive them.

1010 PURCELL, RICHARD J. "Maine: early schools and Irish teachers." Catholic Educational Review, 33 (1935), 211-225.

1011 PUTNAM, FRANK ARTHUR. "Maine: a study in land-grabbing, tax-dodging, and isolation." NEM, New Ser., 36 (1907), 515-540.

1012 MAINE

1012 PUTNAM, FREDERICK WARD. "The kitchen-middings of Maine." Kansas City Review, 6 (1882-1883), 523-526."

1013 [RADCLIFFE, JANE E.] 150 years of Maine governors. Augusta: Maine State Museum, 1972. Unpaged. Me.

1014 RAHILL, PETER JAMES. "A new trail is blazed in Maine." Social Justice Review, 51 (December, 1958), 264-267.
Catholics in Maine since 1780.

1015 RAND, EDWIN HOLMES. "Maine privateers in the Revolution." NEQ, 11 (1938), 826-834.

1016 RANDALL, DANIEL BOODY. A statistical history of the Maine Conference of the M. E. Church from 1793 to 1893. Portland: Lakeside Pr., 1893. Pp. 233.

1017 RANLETT, CHARLES EVERETT. Master mariner of Maine, being the reminiscences of Charles Everett Ranlett, 1816-1917, as told to his son Frederick Jordan Ranlett, with additional chapters by his daughter Susan Alice Ranlett; an introduction and notes by his grandson L. Felix Ranlett and notes by Lincoln Colcord. Portland: Southworth-Anthoensen Pr., 1942. Pp. xi, 145.

1018 [RATTERMANN, HEINRICH ARMIN.] "Geschichte des deutschen Elements in Staate Maine: dessen Ursprung, Entwickelung und Verfall, vom Jahre 1739 bis Gegenwart." Der Deutsche Pionier, 14 (1882-1883), 7-13, 53-62, 90-98, 141-150, 174-188, 217-233, 266-276, 292-303, 338-361, 425-434, 464-468; 15 (1883-1884), 74-82, 104-114, 201-210, 226-235, 267-283, 358-375; 16 (1884-1885), 11-18, 71-77, 98-102, 195-204, 227-238, 276-281, 302-311, 349-359.

1019 RAWLINGS, CHARLES. "The secret of Maine cider." Saturday Evening Post, 231 (October 25, 1958), 44-15, 106-108.
Social life and customs.

1020 RAY, ROGER BRAY. "Maine Indians' concept of land tenure." MeHSQ, 13 (1973-1974), 28-51, 178-179.

1021 _____. "The Norsemen and the Indians of Maine." MeHSN, 9 (1969-1970), 61-62.

1022 READE, JOHN. "Some Wabanaki songs." Royal Society of Canada. Proceedings and Transactions, 5 Pt. 2 (1887), 1-8.

1023 "RECORD of big game shipments, 1895-1908." In the Maine Woods, (1909), 83.

1024 REDDEN, JOHN. "The beginnings of Catholic education in Maine." Catholic Educational Review, 37 (1939), 509-516.
1612-1864.

1025 REDDINGTON, ASA. "Complete list of attorneys at law in the counties of Franklin and Somerset, Maine." American Quarterly Register, 13 (1840-1841), 293-295.

1026 REED, DONALD WINSLOW. Tax trends in Maine towns.... Orono: Maine Agricultural Experiment Station, 1939. Pp. 12. MeBa.

1027 REED, PARKER McCOBB. History of the lower Kennebec, 1602-1889. Bath: Sentinel & Times Print, 1889. Pp. 72.

1028 "REGARDING soldiers of the American Revolution: Maine Indians in the Revolution." SJMH, 6 (1918-1919), 105-111.

1029 REID, JOHN G. "Styles of colonisation and social disorders in early Acadia and Maine: a comparative approach." Société Historique Acadienne. Cahiers, 7 (1976), 105-117.

1030 "REMARKS on the Indian languages." MeHSC, 1 (1831), 310-323.
Abenaqui and Norridgewock Indians.

1031 REYHER, REBECCA. "Maine ship carvings of the nineteenth century." Down East, 21 (November, 1974), 44-47.

1032 REYNOLDS, HORACE. "Down East dialects." Yankee, 19 (January, 1955), 68-69.

1033 RICE, MARSHALL. "Indian history." MeArch SocB, No. 7 (October, 1967), 14-17.

1034 RICE, W. A. and ISAAC R. CLARK. Objects and history of United Fellowship in Maine. Bangor: O. F. Knowles, 1883. Pp. 32. MeHi.
Fraternal organization.

1035 RICE, WILLIAM B. "Sidewheelers and propellers, 1823-1860." The Quarterdeck, 1 (Summer, 1971), 6-7, 14-15; 2 (Winter, 1972), 12-14.
Steamships.

1036 RICH, LOUISE DICKINSON. The coast of Maine, an informal history. (1956) Updated ed. N.Y.: Crowell, 1975. Pp. xiv, 385.

1037 _____. Happy the land. Philadelphia: J. B. Lippincott, 1946. Pp. 259.

1038 _____. The natural world of Louise Dickinson Rich. N.Y.: Dodd, Mead, 1962. Pp. xxvi, 195.

1039 _____. State o' Maine. N.Y.: Harper & Row, 1964. Pp. xvi, 302.

1040 _____. We took to the woods. Philadelphia: J. B. Lippincott, 1942. Pp. 322.

1041 RICHARDS, JOSEPHINE. "The descendants of Rev. John Lovejoy in Maine, and reminiscences of early Maine times." SJMH, 3 (1915-1916), 112-114.

1042 RICHARDSON, HOBART WOOD. "The Pemaquid country under the Stuarts." MeHSC, 8 (1881), 183-195.
   Land given to the Duke of York by his brother, King Charles II, in 1664.

1043 RICHARDSON, JOHN MITCHELL. Steamboat lore of the Penobscot: an informal story of steamboating in Maine's Penobscot region. (1941) 5th ed. Rockland: Courier Gazette, 1971. Pp. 207. MeP.

1044 RICKER, JOSEPH. Personal recollections: a contribution to Baptist history and biography. Augusta: Burleigh & Flynt, 1894. Pp. x, 434.

1045 RIDLON, GIDEON TIBBETTS. Saco Valley settlements and families: historical, biographical, genealogical, traditional and legendary.... Portland, 1895. Pp. xiv, 1250.

1046 RINEHART, JONATHAN. "Down East." USA *1, 1 (June, 1962), 76-84.

1047 RING, ELIZABETH. Maine bibliographies: a bibliographical guide. Portland: Maine Historical Society, 1973. Pp. 34.

1048 _____. The progressive movement of 1912 and third party movements of 1924 in Maine. Orono: Univ. Pr., 1933. Pp. 68.

1049 _____. A unit of study in Maine history and government based on the "Maine Register." Portland: Fred L. Tower, 1945. Pp. 24. MeBa.

1050 ROBERTS, KENNETH LEWIS. "Don't say that about Maine." Saturday Evening Post, 221 (November 6, 1948), 30-31, 126, 130, 132, 135-136.
   Social life and customs; a reply to uncomplimentary remarks in Arnold J. Toynbee's "Study of History."

1051 _____, ed. March to Quebec: journals of the members of Arnold's Expedition. N.Y.: Doubleday, Doran, 1938. Pp. xiv, 657.

1052 _____. Trending into Maine. (1938) Rev. ed. N.Y.: Doubleday, Doran, 1944. Pp. 421.

1053 ROBINSON, CLARENCE CROMWELL. A study of the background and work experience of war production trainees in Maine, 1940-1943. Augusta: Vocational Training for War Production Workers, 1943. 25 leaves.

1054 ROBINSON, CLAUDE E. "Maine--political barometer." PolSciQ, 47 (1932), 161-184.

1055 ROBINSON, WILLIAM A. "Maine's century of statehood." Granite Mo, 52 (1920), 170-171.

1056 RODGER, WILLIAM. "Maine's folk art." Down East, 22 (November, 1974), 44-47.

1057 ROGERS, DONALD. "Capture of the rumrunner 'Grey Ghost.'" Down East, 18 (June, 1972), 60-61, 113-114, 119-120.
   1920s.

1058 ROGERS, LORE ALFRED and CALEB WARREN SCRIBNER. "The log haulers." The Northern Logger and Timber Processer, 16 (August, 1967), 8-9, 34-38.

1059 ROGERS, LORE ALFRED. "The old pine days." Down East, 8 (March, 1962), 28-32, 44-45.
   Logging and log drives.

1060 _____ and CALEB WARREN SCRIBNER. "The peavey cant-dog." CEAIA, 20 (June, 1967), 17-21.
   Lumbering tools.

1061 ROSIER, JAMES. Rosier's relation of Waymouth's voyage to the coast of Maine, 1605. Henry S. Burrage, ed. Portland: Gorges Society, 1887. Pp. xi, 176.

1062 ROSS, LINWOOD. "The adoption of an archival program for Maine." American Archivist, 29 (1966), 395-402.
   History of archival legislation.

1063 ROUNDY, CHARLES G. "Some geographic aspects of civilian defense during World War II." Maine Geographer, No. 4 (November, 1969), 1-7.

1064 ROUNDY, RODNEY W. Cooperation, a record of Christian service, the Interdenominational Commission of Maine. n.p., 1950. Pp. 35. MBC.

1065 _____. "Sesquicentennial." MeCP, 44 (February 15, 1957), 8-9, (March 15, 1957), 3-4.
   Maine Missionary Society.

1066 ROWE, JOHN HOWLAND. "Archaeology and history in eastern Maine." MASB, 2 (July, 1941), 7-13.

1067 ROWE, WILLIAM HUTCHINSON. The maritime history of Maine, three centuries of shipbuilding and seafaring. N.Y.: W. W. Norton, 1948. Pp. 333.

1068 RUSH, NIXON ORWIN. The history of college libraries in Maine. Worcester, Mass.: Clark Univ. Library, 1946. Pp. 53.

1069 RUSSELL, WALTER E. "Evolution of the Maine Teachers' Association." Maine Teachers' Digest, 3 (1942-1943), 9-10.

1070 RUTHERFORD, PHILLIP R. The dictionary of Maine place-names. Freeport: Bond Wheelwright, 1971. Pp. xx, 283.

1071 MAINE

1071 RYAN, ALLIE. Penobscot Bay, Mount Desert and Eastport steamboat album. Camden: Down East Enterprise, 1972. Pp. 72.

1072 SABINE, LORENZO. "Forest lands and timber trade of Maine." North American Review, 58 (1844), 299-335.

1073 _____. "Indian tribes of New England." Christian Examiner, 52 (1852), 96-117; 62 (1857), 27-54, 210-237.

1074 SALTONSTALL, RICHARD. Maine pilgrimage: the search for an American way of life. Boston: Little, Brown, 1974. Pp. x, 353.

1075 SANBORN, V. C. "Stephen Bachiler and the Plough Company of 1630." MeHSC, 3 Ser., 2 (1906), 342-369.

1076 SANDS, DONALD B. "The nature of the generics in island, ledge, and rock names of the Maine coast." Names, 7 (December, 1959), 193-202.

1077 SANGER, DAVID and ROBERT G. MacKAY. Maine prehistory: a selection of short papers. Orono: Univ. of Maine, 1973. Variously leaved. Me.

1078 SANGER, DAVID. "Who were the Red Paints?" MeArchSocB, 13 (Spring, 1973), 3-12.

1079 SARGENT, PAUL. "Maine highways and their history...." Sun Up, 3 (January, 1927), 10-11, 18, 20, 22, 39.

1080 SARGENT, WILLIAM MITCHELL. "Bearing of Captain John Mason's titles upon Maine history." MeHSC, 2 Ser., 8 (1897), 53-66, 175-193.
    Land titles.

1081 _____. Maine wills, 1640-1760. Portland: Brown, Thurston, 1887. Pp. xii, 953.

1082 SAVAGE, ALBERT RUSSELL. An index-digest of the reports of cases decided by the Supreme Judicial Court of Maine, volumes 1 to 88, Maine Reports, inclusive. 1820-1896. Portland: Loring, Short & Harmon, 1897. Pp. 1180.

1083 _____. A supplemental index-digest of the reports of cases decided by the Supreme Judicial Court of Maine, volumes 89 to 103, Maine Reports, inclusive. 1896-1908. Portland: Loring, Short & Harmon, 1909. Pp. 404.

1084 SAVAGE, RICHARD A. "Maine steamboating, 1818-1868." Steamboat Bill, 27 (1970), 196-203.

1085 SAWTELLE, WILLIAM OTIS. Historic trails and waterways of Maine. Augusta: Maine Development Commission, 1932. Pp. 108.

1086 SAWYER, ALDEN H. History of trust business in Maine. New Brunswick, N.J.: Rutgers Univ., 1949. 92 leaves. MeP.

1087 SCAMMON, E. PARKER. "An interesting chapter of the early history of Maine." Catholic World, 56 (1892-1893), 181-190.

1088 _____. "Maine of a later day." Catholic World, 56 (1892-1893), 549-559.
    Father Rasles and Maine in the Revolution.

1089 _____. "The settlement of Maine." Catholic World, 56 (1892-1893), 365-375.

1090 SCAMMON, JONATHAN YOUNG. An address delivered before the Society of the Sons of the State of Maine in Illinois, at its second annual meeting, at the Palmer House, Chicago, March 15, 1882; together with a sketch of its organization and proceedings, constitution, by-laws, list of officers, and roll of members. Chicago: Fergus Printing, 1882. Pp. 39.

1091 SCHMECKEBIER, L. F. "How Maine became a state." MeHSC, 2 Ser., 9 (1898), 146-171.

1092 SCHRIVER, EDWARD OSWALD. "Abolitionists organize: the Maine Antislavery Society." MeHSN, 9 (1969-1970), 33-38, 73-78.

1093 _____. "Antislavery: the Free Soil and Free Democratic parties in Maine." NEQ, 42 (1969), 82-94.

1094 _____. "Black politics without blacks: Maine 1841-1848." Phylon, 31 (1970), 194-201.

1095 _____. Go free: the antislavery impulse in Maine, 1833-1855. Orono: Univ. of Maine Pr., 1970. Pp. xvi, 154.

1096 _____. "Maine: a bibliographical review." Acadiensis, 5 (Spring, 1976), 154-162.

1097 _____. Maine newspapers in the smaller Maine public libraries. Orono, n.d. 17 leaves. MeU.

1098 _____. "Select list of unpublished master's theses from the University of Maine." MeHSN, 8 (May, 1969), 8-15; 9 (1969-1970), 17-19.
    All on Maine subjects.

1099 SCOFIELD, JOHN. "Character marks the coast of Maine." National Geographic Magazine, 133 (1968), 799-843.

1100 SCONTRAS, CHARLES ANDREW. Two decades of labor politics in Maine, 1880-1900. Orono: Bureau of Labor Education, Univ. of Maine, 1969. Pp. 202.
    A shorter version of this work was published in 1966 with the title "Organized labor and labor politics in Maine 1880-1890."

1101   SCULL, GIDEON DELAPLAINE, ed. "The Montrésor Journals." New-York Historical Society. Collections, 14 (1881), xi-xiv, 3-578.
        Includes expedition across Maine from Canada, 1760.

1102   "THE SEAL of the State of Maine." MeLB, 15 (1929-1930), 114-116.

1103   SEWALL, RUFUS KING. Ancient dominions of Maine, embracing the earliest facts, the recent discoveries of the remains of aboriginal towns, the voyages, settlements, battle scenes, and incidents of Indian warfare, and other incidents of history, together with the religious developments of society within the ancient Sagadahoc, Sheepscot and Pemaquid precincts and dependencies. Bath: E. Clark, 1859. Pp. x, 366.

1104   _____. Ancient voyages to the western continent: three phases of history on the coast of Maine. N.Y.: Knickerbocker Pr., 1895. Pp. ix, 79.

1105   SHAILER, WILLIAM HOSMER. A historical discourse delivered in Winthrop, June 16, 1874 before the Maine Baptist Missionary Convention. Portland: B. Thurston, 1874. Pp. 68. MeHi.
        Baptists; Pages [37]-67 have a separate title page: A memorial paper read at the semi-centennial meeting of the Maine Baptist Missionary Convention, held at East Winthrop, June 16, 17, 18, 1874. By Charles Greenleaf Porter. Portland: B. Thurston, 1874.

1106   SHARF, FREDERIC ALAN. "Fitz Hugh Lane: visits to the Maine coast, 1848-1855." EIHC, 98 (1962), 111-120.

1107   SHAUGHNESSY, JIM. "Ghost train in the Maine woods." Down East, 13 (July, 1966), 40-43, 79.
        Transportation routes in northern Maine.

1108   SHAY, FLORENCE NICOLA. History of the Penobscot tribe of Indians. n.p., Priv. Print., 1941. Pp. 15. Me.

1109   SHEA, JOHN GILMARY. "Early missions in Acadia." Catholic World, 12 (1870-1871), 629-643, 826-837.

1110   SHELDON, EDWARD STEVENS. "Some specimens of Canadian French dialect spoken in Maine." Modern Language Association of America. Transactions and Proceedings, 3 (1887), 210-218.

1111   SHENTON, EDWARD H. Historical review of oil spills along the Maine coast, 1953-1973. [Portland?]: Research Institute of the Gulf of Maine, 1973. v.p. MeU.

1112   SHERWOOD, MARY P. "Thoreau's Penobscot Indians." Thoreau Journal, 1 (January 15, 1969), 1-13.

1113   SHERWOOD, R. H. "Missions in Maine from 1613 to 1854." Catholic World, 22 (1876), 666-678.

1114   SHETTLEWORTH, EARLE G., JR. Maine historic resources inventory. Augusta: Maine Historic Preservation Commission, 1975. 128 leaves.

1115   SHORT, VINCENT. Sail and steam along the Maine coast. Portland: Bond Wheelwright, 1955. Pp. 203.

1116   SHUTE, ALBERTA VAN HORN. "Or ever the silver cord." n.p., 1957. Pp. 71.
        Social life and customs.

1117   SIEBERT, WILBUR HENRY. "The exodus of the loyalists from Penobscot and the loyalist settlements at Passamaquoddy." New Brunswick Historical Society. Collections, 3 (1914), 485-529.

1118   SIEUR de Monts commission. De Monts and Acadia, an appreciation. George B. Dorr, ed. Bar Harbor: Wild Gardens of Acadia, [1917?] Pp. 12.

1119   SILBER, MARK, comp. The family album: photographs of the 1890s & 1900s, by Gilbert Wight Tilton and Fred W. Record. Boston: D. R. Godine, 1973. Pp. 93.

1120   NO ENTRY.

1121   SILSBY, HERBERT T., II. "A secret emissary from Down East." MeHSN, 11 (1971-1972), 106-126.
        George Herbert in the War of 1812.

1122   SILSBY, SAMUEL SCHOPPEE. History of statutory law in the State of Maine. [St. Paul, Minn.: West, 1964.] Pp. 225. Me.
        Reprinted from volume one of Maine Revised Statutes Annotated.

1123   _____. Materials in collected public documents of Maine on state constitutional amendments, 1833-1963. Augusta, 1963. 58 leaves. Me.

1124   SIMMONS, MILDRED. "They're off ... harness racing past and present." Down East, 2 (September, 1955), 16-20.

1125   SIMPSON, DOROTHY. The Maine islands, in story and legend. Philadelphia: Lippincott, 1960. Pp. 256.

1126   SIMPSON, SUELLEN, ed. ["Bicentennial Maine."] Salt, 3 (June, 1976), entire issue.

1127 MAINE

1127 SINCOCK, W. E. "In Maine, looking back 50 years." Maine Medical Association. Journal, 33 (1942), 31-33.

1128 "SKETCH of the life of General Lafayette, with an account of his visit to Maine." MeHSC, 2 Ser., 3 (1892), 57-78.
Visited in 1825.

1129 SLAFTER, EDMUND FARWELL. "The discovery of America by Northmen in the early part of the eleventh century." BHistMag, 5 (1889-1890), 78-80.

1130 SMALL, ALBION KEITH PARRIS. Memorial sermon ... East Brunswick Baptist Church ... 75th anniversary of the Cumberland Association.... Portland: B. Thurston, 1885. Pp. 14. MeHi.

1131 SMALL, CARLETON POTTER. "Unitarianism in Maine." UHSP, 8 Pt. 2 (1950), 18-33.

1132 SMALL, EDWIN SUMNER. A centennial review of the Bowdoinham Association of Baptist Churches in Maine delivered at the one hundredth anniversary meeting, at Bowdoinham, September 13, 1887. Portland: B. Thurston & Co., 1887. Pp. 54. Me.

1133 SMALL, WILLIAM A. "Schooling in the unorganized territory of Maine." Elementary School Journal, 56 (November, 1956), 117-120.
1895-1945.

1134 SMILLIE, WILSON GEORGE and JEAN ALONZO CURRAN. Medical care in the State of Maine, 1956-1962. Bethel: Bingham Associates Fund, [1962]. Pp. 156.

1135 SMITH, BENJAMIN L. "An analysis of the Maine cemetery complex." MASB, 9 (1947-1948), 21-71.
Notes on forty-four cemeteries in Maine.

1136 _____. "Some aspects of the use of red ochre in prehistoric burials." MASB, 11 (1949-1950), 22-28.

1137 SMITH, CHARLES W. A history of clockmaking in Maine. National Association of Watch and Clock Collectors. Bulletin, 15 (April, 1973).

1138 SMITH, DAVID CLAYTON. A history of lumbering in Maine, 1861-1960. Orono: Univ. of Maine Pr., 1972. Pp. xvi, 468.

1139 _____. "The logging frontier." Forest History, 18 (1974), 96-106.

1140 _____. Lumbering and the Maine woods: a bibliographical guide. Portland: Maine Historical Society, 1971. Pp. 34.

1141 _____. "Wood pulp paper comes to the northeast, 1865-1900." Forest History, 10 (April, 1966), 12-25.

1142 SMITH, DOROTHY, ed. Union list of serials in Maine libraries. Orono: Univ. Pr., 1937. Pp. x, 257.

1143 SMITH, EDGAR CROSBY. "Maine map-makers and their maps: Osgood Carleton." SJMH, 2 (1914-1915), 3-9.

1144 _____. Maps of the State of Maine: a bibliography of the maps of the State of Maine. Bangor, 1903. Pp. 29.

1145 _____. Moses Greenleaf, Maine's first map-maker; a biography, with letters, unpublished manuscripts and a reprint of Mr. Greenleaf's rare paper on Indian place-names; also a bibliography of the maps of Maine. Bangor: C. H. Glass, 1902. Pp. xviii, 165.

1146 _____. "Short biographies of the members of the first Maine Senate." SJMH, 8 (1920), 22-26.

1147 SMITH, ELIZABETH OAKES PRINCE. "Maine: an historical sketch." Potter's AmMo, 13 (1879), 198-202.

1148 SMITH, GEORGE OTIS. "Maine, the outpost state: some forgotten incidents in the life of an old stout-hearted commonwealth." National Geographic Magazine, 67 (1935), 533-592.

1149 SMITH, JOSEPH COBURN. "The life of the Maine woodsmen in 1926." CEAIA, 26 (1973), 45-48.

1150 _____. "Maine and her trees." Maine Naturalist, 7 (1927), 3-14.
Forest history.

1151 _____. "The tools of the Maine woodsmen in 1926." CEAIA, 25 (1972), 49-54.

1152 _____. "The work of the woodsmen in the Maine woods." CEAIA, 26 (1973), 28-29.

1153 SMITH, JOSEPH S. "How two Maine parishes started." The North East, 35 (December, 1907), 8-10.
Grace Church, Bath and the first Episcopal service in Wiscasset.

1154 SMITH, JUSTIN HARVEY. Arnold's march from Cambridge to Quebec: a critical study, together with a reprint from Arnold's journal. N.Y.: G. P. Putnam's Sons, 1903. Pp. xix, 498.

1155 _____. Our struggle for the fourteenth colony: Canada and the American Revolution. N.Y.: G. P. Putnam's Sons, 1907. 2v.
Arnold's Expedition.

1156 SMITH, LINCOLN. "The Great Pond Ordinance--collectivism in northern New England." BULRev, 30 (1950), 178-190.
1641.

1157 _____. "Maine's power embargo--how it may be terminated." Cornell Law Quarterly, 36 (1951), 342-354.
Fernald Law (1909), prohibiting export of electrical power from Maine.

1158 _____. The power policy of Maine. Berkeley: Univ. of California Pr., 1951. Pp. vi, 344.

1159 SMITH, MARION JAQUES. A history of Maine, from wilderness to statehood. Portland: Falmouth Publishing, 1949. Pp. 348.

1160 SMITH, MARION WHITNEY. Algonquian and Abenaki Indian myths and legends. Lewiston: Central Maine Pr., 1962. Unpaged.

1161 _____. Strange tales of Abenaki shamanism. Lewiston: Central Maine Pr., 1963. Pp. 47.

1162 SMITH, NICHOLAS N. "The challenge of Maine archaeology." MeArchSocB, No. 1, (Spring, 1964), [3-4].

1163 _____. Penobscot traditions: Penobscot life in prehistoric times. n.p., n.d. Unpaged. MeHi.

1164 _____. "Smoking habits of the Wabanaki." MASB, 18 (1956-1957), 76-77.
Indians.

1165 _____. "The survival of the Red Paint complex in Maine." MASB, 17 (1955-1956), 4-6.

1166 SMITH, OSCAR S. The lumber industry on Penobscot waters. The Northern, 4 (April, 1924), 5-10, (May, 1924), 2-3, 5-10, (June, 1924), 2-4, 13-15, (July, 1924), 2-9, (August, 1924), 3-4, 14, (September, 1924), 5-6, 9, 15.

1167 SMITH, ROLAND. "Maine beginnings." Sun Up, 9 (June, 1931), 1.

1168 SMITH, WALTER BROWN. "Aboriginal axes of the Penobscot." Bangor Historical Society. Proceedings, (1914-1915), 34-41.

1169 _____. Indian remains of the Penobscot Valley and their significance. Orono: Univ. Pr., 1926. Pp. 90.

1170 _____. The lost Red Paint People of Maine, a few things we think we know about them and more that we know we don't. Bar Harbor, 1930. Pp. 43.

1171 SMITH, WILLIAM H. "The King family of Maine." MHGR, 1 (1884), 1-8, 33-40.

1172 _____. "Reminiscences of the Grand Lodge of Maine." FR, 13 (1883-1884), 381-382.
Freemasons.

1173 "SMUGGLING in Maine during the War of 1812." BHistMag, 3 (1887-1888), 201-203.

1174 "SMUGGLING in Maine in 1813." BHistMag, 3 (1887-1888), 105-108.

1175 SMYTH, LAWRENCE T. "The lumber industry in Maine." NEM, New Ser., 25 (1901-1902), 629-648.

1176 SNOW, CHARLES AUGUSTUS. The history of the development of public school supervision in the State of Maine. Orono: Univ. Pr., 1939. Pp. vii, 99.

1177 SNOW, DEAN R. "A century of Maine archaeology." MeArchSocB, No. 8 (1968), 8-25.

1178 _____. "The changing prey of Maine's early hunters." Natural History, 83 (November, 1974), 15-16, 18, 22, 24.

1179 _____. The Penobscot Indians in Thoreau's time." Thoreau Journal, 2 (January 15, 1970), 7-11.

1180 _____. "Rising sea level and prehistoric cultural ecology in northern New England." American Antiquity, 37 (1972), 211-221; 39 (1974), 136-137.
Second part is a comment by Walter S. Newman.

1181 _____. A summary of prehistoric sites in the State of Maine. [Orono]: Department of Anthropology, Univ. of Maine, 1969. Pp. v, 142.

1182 _____. "Wabanaki family hunting territories." American Anthropologist, 70 (1968), 1143, 1151.

1183 SOCIETY OF COLONIAL WARS. MAINE. History of Society of Colonial Wars in the State of Maine, 1898-1946, and roll of members. Charles J. Nichols, comp. [Portland?], 1947. Pp. x, 81.

1184 _____. Register of the officers and members of the Society of Colonial Wars in the State of Maine; also history, roster and record of Colonel Jedidiah Preble's regiment, campaign of 1758; together with Capt. Samuel Cobb's journal. Portland: Marks Printing, 1905. Pp. 180.

1185 "SOLON Chase and 'them steers' back in Maine days in 1878." Sun Up, 3 (February, 1927), 26.
Greenback Party and the election of 1878.

1186 "SOME account of the Catholic missions in Maine." MeHSC, 1 (1831), 323-340.
Seventeenth century.

1187 MAINE

1187 "SOME representative Maine men of yesterday and today." SJMH, 8 (1920), 50-78, 117-118.

1188 SONS OF THE AMERICAN REVOLUTION. MAINE SOCIETY. What the Society in Maine has done, organization and officers of the Society, constitution of the Society, roll of members, officers of National Society, constitution of the National Society. Portland: LeFavor-Tower, 1903. Pp. 259.

1189 SOULE, ALFRED MORTON GILMORE. "The Maine Department of Agriculture." Maine. Commissioner of Agriculture. Biennial Report, (1948-1950), 79-92.
A departmental history.

1190 SOULE, PHELPS. "The Hampton Boat." AmNep, 3 (1943), 141-147.
Shipbuilding.

1191 SOULE, WILLIAM H., ed. European exploration, discovery, and early settlement of Maine. Augusta: Maine State Museum, 1975. Pp. v, 113. Me.

1192 "SOURCES for a maritime history of Maine." MeLB, 17 (1931-1932), 34-40.
Bibliography.

1193 SOUTHARD, EUGENIA M. and CHARLES E. CAMPBELL. "Books by Maine authors and books about Maine, 1950-1951." Pine Cone, 7 (Spring, 1951), 30-33.

1194 SPALDING, JAMES ALFRED. "Lowell vs. Faxon and Hawkes, a celebrated malpractice suit in Maine." American Academy of Medicine. Bulletin, 11 (1910), 4-31.
1821-1826.

1195 _____. Maine physicians of 1820: a record of the members of the Massachusetts Medical Society practicing in the District of Maine at the date of separation. Lewiston: Lewiston Journal Printshop, 1928. Pp. 179.

1196 SPANOGLE, JOHN A., JR. "Changes in the present Maine law created by the Maine Consumer Credit Code." Maine Law Review, 26 (1974), 173-215.
Legislative history of the code.

1197 SPECK, FRANK GOULDSMITH. Penobscot man: the life history of a forest tribe in Maine. Philadelphia: Univ. of Pennsylvania Pr., 1940. Pp. xx, 325.

1198 _____. "Penobscot shamanism." American Anthropological Association. Memoirs, 6 (1919), 239-288.

1199 _____. "Penobscot tales and religious beliefs." Journal of American Folklore, 48 (1935), 1-107.

1200 _____. "Penobscot transformer tales." International Journal of American Linguistics, 1 (1918), 187-244.

1201 _____. "Symbolism in Penobscot Art." American Museum of Natural History. Anthropological Papers, 29 Pt. 2 (1927), 25-80.

1202 _____. "A visit to the Penobscot Indians." University of Pennsylvania Museum Journal, 2 (1911), 21-26.

1203 _____. Wawenock myth texts from Maine. U.S. Bureau of American Ethnology. Annual Report, 43 (1925-1926), 165-197.

1204 SPENCER, WILBUR DANIEL. Maine immortals, including many unique characters in early Maine history. Augusta: Northeastern Pr., 1932. Pp. viii, 316.

1205 _____. The Maine Spencers: a history and genealogy, with mention of many associated families, 1596-1898. Concord, N.H.: Rumford Pr., 1898. Pp. 247.

1206 _____. Pioneers on Maine rivers, with lists to 1651, compiled from the original sources. ... Portland: Lakeside Printing, 1930. Pp. 414.

1207 SPERRY, WILLARD LEAROYD. Summer yesterdays in Maine: memories of boyhood vacation days. N.Y.: Harper & Bros., 1941. Pp. xi, 263.

1208 SPRAGUE, JOHN FRANCIS. "Aroostook War documents." SJMH, 2 (1914-1915), 31-34.

1209 _____. Backwoods sketches. Augusta: Kennebec Journal Shop, 1912. Pp. 154.

1210 _____. "Brief notes on ancient Kennebec." SJMH, 3 (1915-1916), 83-88.
Kennebec Valley.

1211 _____. "Canadian refugees in Maine and New England during the Revolution." SJMH, 12 (1924), 16-20.

1212 _____. "A century of the bar in Maine." Maine State Bar Association. Proceedings, 22 (1920-1921), 21-68.

1213 _____. "The counties of Maine--town government in Maine." SJMH, 8 (1920), 205-207.

1214 _____. "Indian treaties in Maine." SJMH, 8 (1920), 183-195.

1215 _____. "Maine." SJMH, 8 (1920), 3-7.

1216 _____. "Maine as a district and as a state has had two successful immigration enterprises." SJMH, 8 (1920), 38-41.
Attempts at promoting foreign immigration; Germans to Waldoboro and Swedes to New Sweden.

1217 _____. "Making history in the Maine woods-- culture for the lumberjack." SJMH, 9 (1921), 126-130.

1218 _____. "A Massachusetts colonial ordnance that is the law of Maine." SJMH, 1 (1913-1914), 201-205.
Great Pond Ordinance, 1641.

1219 _____. "The Millerites in Maine." SJMH, 10 (1922), 3-6.

1220 _____. The North Eastern Boundary controversy and the Aroostook War. Dover: Observer Pr., 1910. Pp. 116.

1221 _____. Three men from Maine: Sir William Pepperrell, Sir William Phips, James Sullivan; and, A bit of old England in New England, by Bertram E. Packard. Dover-Foxcroft: Sprague's Journal of Maine History, 1924. Pp. 89.

1222 _____. "William Bingham and the million acre tract." PCHSC, 1 (1910), 434-441.
Bingham Purchase.

1223 _____. "Your river in history." Good Will Record, 29 (November, 1916), 292-298.
Kennebec.

1224 SPRAGUE, RICHARD. "Carl Sprinchorn in the Maine woods." Forest History, 14 (1970), 6-15.
Art.

1225 SPRINGER, JOHN S. Forest life and forest trees; comprising winter camp-life among the loggers, and wild-wood adventure; with descriptions of lumbering operations on the various rivers of Maine, and New Brunswick. N.Y.: Harper and Bros., 1851. Pp. xii, 259.
Includes lumbering statistics.

1226 STAACK, F. "A journey into Maine, 1786." Down East, 6 (January, 1960), 22-25, 41, 43-46.
Luigi Castiglioni's trip from Portsmouth, N.H. to Old Town, Me. to study plants and trees for the Italian government.

1227 STACKPOLE, EVERETT BIRNEY. "State banking in Maine." Sound Currency, 7 (May, 1900), 57-88.

1228 STACKPOLE, EVERETT SCHERMERHORN, ed. "An old journal." MeHSC, 3 Ser., 2 (1906), 241-244.
Lieut. John Stackpole.

1229 STANLEY, GEORGE FRANCIS GILMAN. "British operations on the Penobscot in 1814." Society for Army Historical Research Journal, 19 (1940), 168-178.
War of 1812.

1230 _____. Canada invaded, 1775-1776. Toronto: Hakkert, 1973. Pp. xiv, 186.
Arnold's Expedition.

1231 STANLEY, RUEL H. and GEORGE O. HALL. Eastern Maine and the rebellion; being an account of the principal local events in eastern Maine during the war, and brief histories of eastern Maine regiments; contains accounts of mobs, riots, destruction of newspapers, war meetings, drafts, Confederate raids, peace meetings, celebrations, soldiers' letters, and scenes and incidents at the front, never before in print. Bangor, 1887. Pp. 392.

1232 STANTON, DON C. A history of the white-tailed deer in Maine. Augusta, 1963. Pp. viii, 75.

1233 STANWOOD, EDWARD. "The separation of Maine from Massachusetts." MHSP, 3 Ser., 1 (1907-1908), 125-164.

1234 STAPLES, ARTHUR GRAY. "Conservation problems of central Maine." SJMH, 12 (1924), 128-135, 191-197.
Water power.

1235 _____. The inner man; or, some contemporary portraits of prominent men of Maine. Lewiston: Lewiston Journal, 1923. Pp. 248.

1236 _____. The passing age: a collection of familiar essays as published in the newspaper of which the writer is editor-in-chief. Augusta: Katahdin Publishing, 1924. Pp. 416.
Social life and customs.

1237 STAPLES, FRANKLIN. "Reminiscences of Maine medical schools and physicians." JMS, 3 (1896-1897), 86-89.

1238 STARBIRD, CHARLES MILLARD. The Indians of the Androscoggin Valley: tribal history, and their relations with the early English settlers of Maine. [Lewiston]: Lewiston Journal Printshop, 1928. Pp. 108.

1239 STARKEY, GLENN WENDELL. Maine, its history, resources, and government. (1920) 4th ed. N.Y.: Silver Burdett, 1947. Pp. x, 263.

1240 STARR, JOHN T. My Maine islands. American Forests, 73 (February, 1967), 38-41, 60.

1241 START, EDWIN A. "Penobscot Bay." NEM, New Ser., 14 (1896), 579-600.

1242 "THE STATE of Maine, now with us more than 100 years." Literary Digest, 65 (May 8, 1920), 69-70.

1243 STERLING, ROBERT THAYER. Lighthouses of the Maine coast and the men who keep them. Brattleboro, Vt.: Stephen Daye Pr., 1935. Pp. 223.

1244 STETSON, WILLIAM WALLACE. History and civil government of Maine ... and, The government of the United States by B. A. Hinsdale. Chicago: Werner, 1898. Pp. 340.

1245 MAINE

1245 _____. "History of education and the evolution of the present school system in Maine." Maine. State Superintendent of Public Schools. Report, (1900), 56-156.

1246 STEVENS, SUSAN MacCULLOCH. Passamaquoddy economic development in cultural and historical perspective. Mount Vernon, 1973. Pp. 162. Me.
Passamaquoddy Indians.

1247 STEWART, ALICE ROSE. "The State of Maine and Canadian Confederation." CanHistRev, 33 (1952), 148-164.

1247A _____. "Suggested readings in Maine history: the Northeastern Boundary dispute." MeHSN, 2 (May, 1963), 8.

1248 STEWART, JOHN C. "Biographical sketches of natives of Maine who have served in the Congress of the United States." SJMH, 10 (1922), 85-96, 140-154, 196-208; 11 (1923), 35-42, 61-71, 150-160.

1249 STOKESBURY, JAMES L. "Jonathan Eddy and the fourteenth colony." Down East, 22 (April, 1976), 18-22, 25, 27.

1250 STOLLE, JOHN WILLIAM. Maine stories. Bangor: H. P. Snowman, 1953. Pp. 148. MB.
Social life and customs.

1251 STORMS, ROGER C. A history of three corners. Lee: Lee Academy, 1971. 168 leaves.
Twenty-four towns in the vicinity of the adjacent corners of Aroostook, Penobscot and Washington counties.

1252 A STRANGE account of the rising and breaking of a great bubble. [Boston], 1767. Pp. 22.
An attack on the Kennebec proprietors.

1253 STUART, RICHARD KENNETH. Financing public improvements by the State of Maine. Orono: Univ. Pr., 1957. Pp. viii, 188.
1820-1957.

1254 "A STUDY of the schools of northeastern Maine." Maine. State Superintendent of Public Schools. Report, (1897), 45-78.

1255 STUIVER, MINZE and HAROLD W. BORNS, JR. "Late quarternary marine invasion in Maine: its chronology and associated crustal movement." Geological Society of America. Bulletin, 86 (1975), 99-104.

1256 NO ENTRY.

1257 SULLIVAN, JAMES. The history of the District of Maine. Boston: I. Thomas and E. T. Andrews, 1795. Pp. vii, 421.

1258 _____. "The history of the Penobscot Indians." MHSC, 9 (1804), 207-232.

1259 _____. Index of names and places in Sullivan's District of Maine; the manuscript of this index was found in a copy of the above work formerly the property of John Wingate Thornton. Portland: A. J. Huston, [1914?]. Unpaged.

1260 SWEETSER, MOSES FOSTER. Summer days Down East. Portland: Chisholm Bros., 1883 Pp. 160. MeU.

1261 SWETT, CLYDE W. and MARY L. HASKELL. All about Maine: print and film materials to enrich the study of Maine history in grade eight. Augusta: Maine State Department of Education, 1969. Pp. 90. Me.

1262 SWETT, SOPHIA MIRIAM. Stories of Maine. N.Y.: American Book Co., 1899. Pp. 278.

1263 SWITZER, DAVID C. "Down-East ships of the Union navy." United States Naval Institute. Proceedings, 90 (November, 1964), 82-88.

1264 SYLVESTER, HERBERT MILTON. The land of St. Castin. Boston: W. B. Clarke, 1909. Pp. 380.
Also published the same year as volume five of the author's "Maine pioneer settlements."

1265 _____. The Sokoki trail. Boston: Stanhope Pr., 1907. Pp. 465.
Also published in 1909 as volume three of the author's "Maine pioneer settlements."

1266 TALBOT, ARCHIE LEE. "A new Plymouth Colony at Kennebeck": John Carver, the first governor of Plymouth Colony, the Moses of the Pilgrims, a symbol of America; an earnest appeal for the erection of a Pilgrim memorial monument, in Maine, by the State, and a statue of John Carver at Plymouth, by the Commonwealth of Massachusetts; Hubbard Hall, Bowdoin College, Brunswick, Maine, Thursday, January 9, 1930.... [Brunswick?, 1930]. Pp. 14.

1267 TALLMAN, RONALD D. and JULIE I. TALLMAN. "The diplomatic search for the St. Croix River, 1796-1798." Acadiensis, 1 (Spring, 1972), 59-71.

1268 TAYLOR, CLYDE C. A review of lobster rearing in Maine. Augusta: Maine Department of Sea and Shore Fisheries, 1950. Pp. 16. Me.

1269 TEBBETTS, LEON HAROLD. The amazing story of Maine. Portland: Falmouth Book House, 1935. Pp. ix, 104.

1270 "TEN years of bookmobile service in Maine." MeLAB, 24 (November, 1963), 3-5.

1271 THAYER, HENRY OTIS. "Early ministry on the Kennebec." MeHSC, 2 Ser., 8 (1897), 289-312; 9 (1888), 113-123.
Robert Gutch and Ichabod Wiswall.

1272 _____. "The Lithgow immigrants." SJMH, 10 (1922), 70-85.

1273 _____. "Loyalists of the Kennebec and one of them--John Carleton." SJMH, 5 (1917-1918), 241-262.

1274 _____. "Ministry on the Kennebec: period of the Indian Wars." MeHSC, 2 Ser., 10 (1899), 263-281.

1275 _____. "The problem of Hammond's Fort: Richard Hammond, his home and death." MeHSC, 2 Ser., 1 (1890), 261-294.

1276 THAYER, SIMEON. The invasion of Canada: including the journal of Captain Simeon Thayer, describing the perils and sufferings of the army under Colonel Benedict Arnold, in its march ... to Quebec. Edwin Martin Stone, ed. Providence: Knowles, Anthony, 1867. Pp. xxiv, 104.

1277 THIELEN, BENEDICT. "The wild and beautiful coast of Maine." Holiday, 32 (July, 1962), 45-57.

1278 THOMAS, ELMER ERWIN. In the north woods of Maine: the story of a winter in the wilderness fifty years ago. Yonkers-on-Hudson, N.Y.: World Book, 1923. Pp. vii, 109.

1279 THOMAS, MIRIAM STOVER. Come hell or high water. n.p., 1970. Pp. 138. MeU. Essays.

1280 _____. Flotsam and jetsam. n.p., 1973. Pp. 121.

1281 THOMPSON, DEBORAH, ed. Maine forms of American architecture. Waterville: Colby Museum of Art, 1976. Pp. xxxii, 362. Me.

1282 THOMPSON, GARRETT W. "The Germans in Maine." The Pennsylvania German, 12 (1911), 595-602, 684-691, 724-735. Penn Germania, New Ser., 1 (1912), 36-44, 106-113, 161-169.

1283 THOMPSON, JOHN WALLACE. Sketches, historical and descriptive, of noted Maine horses, past and present, their ancestors and descendants; with an alphabetical index, a list of Maine 2.30 horses, alphabetically arranged.... Portland: Hoyt & Fogg, 1874-1877. 2v.

1284 THURLOW, CLINTON F. Over the rails by steam: a railroad scrapbook. Weeks Mills, 1965. Pp. 104.

1285 _____. The W W & F two footer, hail and farewell. (1964) 2d ed. Weeks Mills, 1965. Pp. 116. Wiscasset, Waterville & Farmington Railroad.

1286 THURSTON, BROWN. "The mechanical condition and improvements in the art of printing in Maine for the past one hundred years." MPAP, 22 (1885), 32-41.

1287 TITUS, ANSON. "Reminiscences of early American Universalism: Universalism in Maine prior to 1820." The Universalist Quarterly, 42 (1885), 430-453.

1288 TITUS, EDWARD KIRK. "Prehistoric Maine--a glimpse of aboriginal life." MagHist, 12 (1910), 105-108.

1289 TOD, GILES M. S. The last sail Down East. Barre, Mass.: Barre Publishers, 1965. Pp. xii, 281.

1290 TODD, ALAN. "Memories of Maine." Railroad Magazine, 50 (1949), 80-95. Reminiscences of an engineer on the Bangor and Aroostook Railroad.

1291 TRASK, WILLIAM BLAKE, ed. Letters of Colonel Thomas Westbrook and others relating to Indian affairs in Maine 1722-1726. Boston: G. E. Littlefield, 1901. Pp. 196. Indexed.

1292 TRAVIS, HAROLD G. "Maine's pre-1850 law offices." Maine History News, 9 (April, 1974), 4-5, 10, (October, 1974), 10; 10 (January, 1975), 14, 16.

1293 TRUE, NATHANIEL TUCKERMAN. "Indian names on the Androscoggin." HistMag, 8 (1864), 237-238.

1294 _____. "The Indians." Old Times, 3 (1879), 351-354.

1295 _____. "Mineralogy among the aborigines of Maine." Portland Society of Natural History. Proceedings, 1 Pt. 2 (1869), 165-168.

1296 _____. "Names and location of the tribes on the Androscoggin." HistMag, 8 (1864), 150-151.

1297 TRUEMAN, STUART. The ordeal of John Gyles; being an account of his odd adventures, strange deliverances, etc., as a slave of the Maliseets. Toronto: McClelland and Stewart, 1966. Pp. ix, 155.

1298 TUNLEY, ROUL. "Maine and her artists." Woman's Day, (August, 1964), 62-66, 68.

1299 THE TWO banner prohibition states; being a careful review of conditions in Maine and Kansas under prohibition legislation. Prohibition at its best in Maine, by Cyrus W. Davis .... Facts about Kansas "on the water wagon," by Hon. Royal E. Cabell.... Cincinnati: National Home Rule Association, 1914. Pp. 31.

1300 TYZZER, E. E. "Animal tooth implements from shell heaps of Maine." American Antiquity, 8 (1943), 354-360.

1301 MAINE

1301   UNITED STATES. COMMISSION ON CIVIL RIGHTS. MAINE ADVISORY COMMITTEE. Federal and state services and the Maine Indian: a report. Washington, 1974. Pp. ix, 108.

1302   U. S. DISTRICT COURT. MAINE. Reports of cases argued and determined in the District Court of the United States for the District of Maine; 1822-[1866].... Portland: Colman & Chisholm, 1839-1874. 3v.

1303   U. S. LIBRARY OF CONGRESS. Maine: the sesquicentennial of statehood; an exhibition in the Library of Congress, Washington, D.C., December 21, 1970 to September 6, 1971. Washington: Govt. Print. Off., 1970 [i.e. 1971]. Pp. 86.

1304   VARNEY, GEORGE JONES. A brief history of Maine. (1880) 2d ed. Portland: McLellan, Mosher, 1890. Pp. 336. MeHi.

1305   _____. A gazetteer of the State of Maine. Boston: B. B. Russell, 1881. Pp. 611.
        A typescript index by Genevieve R. Ireland is at the Maine Historical Society.

1306   _____. The young people's history of Maine; from its earliest discovery to the final settlement of its boundaries in 1842. (1873) 3d ed., rev. Portland: Dresser, McLellan, 1877. Pp. xviii, 289. MeHi.

1307   VEAZIE, CARL E. "The Maine economy, 1940-1975." Thomas Business Review, 3 (Fall, 1975), 32-42.

1308   VERRILL, ALPHEUS HYATT. Romantic and historic Maine. N.Y.: Dodd, Mead, 1933. Pp. xx, 277.

1309   VETROMILE, EUGENE. "The Abnaki Indians." MeHSC, 6 (1859), 203-244.

1310   _____. The Abnakis and their history; or, historical notices of the aborigines of Acadia. N.Y.: J. B. Kirker, 1866. Pp. xi, 171.

1311   VICKERY, JAMES BERRY, III. "A bibliography of local history--the town registers of Maine." MeHSN, 5 (November, 1965), 7-11.

1312   _____. "Some magazines of Maine." MeLAB, 29 (November, 1968), 3-14; 30 (February, 1969), 3-11, 14-21.

1313   "VIEW of the history and present condition of the Commonwealth of Maine." American Quarterly Register, 5 (1832-1833), 105-121.

1314   VIGNERAS, LOUIS-ANDRÉ. "Letters of an Acadian trader, 1674-1676." NEQ, 13 (1940), 98-110.
        Henri Brunet.

1315   VINTON, JOHN ADAMS. "Thomas Gyles, and his neighbors." NEHGR, 21 (1867), 352-363.

1316   VIRGIN, WILLIAM WIRT. Digest of the decisions of the Supreme Judicial Court, of the State of Maine, contained in volumes twenty-seven to forty-three, (both inclusive), of the Maine Reports, [1847-1857]. Hallowell: Masters, Smith, 1859. Pp. lxxx, 604.

1317   VOSE, CLEMENT E. Political party platforms, State of Maine, 1952-1958. Brunswick: Bowdoin College, 1958. Variously leaved. MeU.

1318   "THE VOYAGE of Captain George Waymouth to the coast of Maine in 1605." BHistMag, 2 (1886-1887), 205-208.

1319   VROOM, JAMES. "Penobscot loyalists." Acadiensis, 3 (1903), 172-182.

1320   WADSWORTH, R. C. "The men in medicine in eastern Maine during the early days." Maine Medical Association. Journal, 44 (1953), 150-155.

1321   WALDRON, C. W. "The Northeastern Boundary." Pine Tree Magazine, 5 (1906), 557-560.

1322   WALKER, CHARLES HOWARD. "Some old houses on the southern coast of Maine." WPSAM, 4 (April, 1918), 3-14.
        Wiscasset, York, Kennebunk, South Berwick, and Wells.

1323   WALKER, DAVID BRADSTREET. A Maine profile: some conditioners of her political system. Brunswick: Bowdoin College, Bureau for Research in Municipal Government, 1964. Pp. 55.

1324   _____. Politics and ethnocentrism: the case of the Franco-Americans. Brunswick: Bowdoin College, Bureau for Research in Municipal Government, 1961. Pp. 48.

1325   WALKER, ELINOR STEVENS. More about Maine. Rumford: Rumford Publishing, 1974. Pp. 199.

1326   WALKER, WILLARD. The Indians of Maine. n.p., [196-]. v.p. MeBa.

1327   _____. The pre-history of the Maine-Maritime area. [Middletown, Conn.?], 1970. 42 leaves. MeU.

1328   WALSH, LOUIS SEBASTIAN. "Sermon on the tercentenary of [the] Catholic Church in Maine." MeCathHM, 1 (August, 1913), 10-23.

1329   WARE, JOSEPH. "Expedition against Quebec." NEHGR, 6 (1852), 129-145.
        An edited journal with notes by Justin Winsor; Arnold's Expedition.

1330 WARNER, MAURICE J. Civil War memorials erected in the State of Maine. [Augusta]: Maine Civil War Centennial Commission, 1965. Pp. 79.

1331 WARREN, JULIET MARION STANLEY. Maine centennial, 1820-1920, historical souvenir poem. Portland, 1920. Pp. 7.

1332 WASHBURN, FREMONT E. Flinches and other strange birds: the history and humor of Maine trapshooting since 1874. South Berwick: Chronicle Print Shop, 1971. Pp. 58. MeU.

1333 WASHBURN, ISRAEL, 1813-1883. "The North-Eastern Boundary." MeHSC, 8 (1881), 1-106.

1334 WASSON, GEORGE SAVARY. Sailing days on the Penobscot: the story of the river and the bay in the old days. (1932) New ed. N.Y.: W. W. Norton, 1949. Pp. 246.

1335 WATERMAN, CHARLES ELMER. "Shaker communities of Maine." SJMH, 6 (1918-1919), 139-146.

1336 _____. "Some knights of the road." SJMH, 6 (1918-1919), 10-17.
Postal delivery and the development of roads and other forms of transportation.

1337 WATTS, GEORGE B. "Catholic missionaries in Maine, the Middle West, Louisiana: colonial days." French Review, 37 (1963), 11-35.

1338 WAYNE, JOHN LAKMORD. "Odd names of early Down East periodicals." Hobbies, 47 (November, 1942), 103.

1339 WEBBER, SAMUEL R. "Early days in Maine surgery." NEJMed, 260 (January, 1959), 167-169.

1340 WEBSTER, DANIEL. Mr. Webster's vindication of the Treaty of Washington of 1842; in a speech delivered in the Senate of the United States, on the 6th and 7th of April, 1846. Washington: J. & G. S. Gideon, 1846. Pp. 88.
Two other printings of 1846 contain 64 and 85 pages respectively.

1341 WEBSTER, DONALD B., JR. "The Penobscot Expedition of 1814." Tradition, 4 (January, 1961), 45-58.

1342 WEBSTER, HENRY SEWALL. History of Maine Commandery, No. 1, of Knights Templar, from its organization as King Darius's Council of Knights of the Red Cross, May 29, 1806, to December 1, 1893. Gardiner: Reporter-Journal Pr., 1893. Pp. 110. MeBa.

1343 WELSH, DAVID. "The Passamaquoddy Indians." Ramparts, 5 (March, 1967), 40-45.

1344 WENTWORTH, BERTRAND HEBRON. A chart of Maine winters--1785 to 1913--from Kennebec River records, and daily observations at Gardiner, Maine. Portland: Southworth Print, 1914. Broadside, 14 1/2 x 11 1/2 inches.

1345 WESTON, ISAAC. "Law and lawyers." Northern Monthly, 1 (1864), 173-176.

1346 WETHERBE, R. L. "The Acadian boundary disputes and the Ashburton Treaty." Nova Scotia Historical Society. Collections, 6 (1887-1888), 17-51.

1347 WETHERELL, ALICE M. "Two pioneers from Maine." MeLAB, 13 (May, 1952), 14-16.
Alice M. Jordan and Anne Carroll Moore; librarians.

1348 WHEATLAND, STEPHEN. "History of Pingree heir timberland ownership." Maine. Biennial Report of the Forest Commissioner, 38 (1969-1970), 119-121.

1349 WHILE Maine grew. By the pen of a Maine writer. n.p., 1971. Pp. 34. MeU.

1350 WHIPPLE, JOSEPH. The history of Acadie, Penobscot Bay and River, with a more particular geographical and statistical view of the District of Maine than has ever before been published, also, statistical tables, shewing at one view the comparative progress of the population of Maine with each other individual state in the Union, with an alphabetical list of all the towns with their date of incorporation, census in 1810, polls and valuation in 1812, counties, and distances from Boston. Bangor: Peter Edes, 1816. Pp. 102.
Pub. also at Bangor, 1816, under title: A geographical view of the District of Maine ... including the history of Acadie, Penobscot Bay....

1351 WHITE, JOHN W. "The Burleigh scheme: an idea that became a railroad." New England Social Studies Bulletin, 15 (March, 1958), 5-11.
Albert A. Burleigh and the Bangor and Aroostook Railroad.

1352 WHITESIDE, WILLIAM B. "The Maine economy: 1860-1900." Thomas Business Review, 3 (Fall, 1975), 11-20.

1353 WHITIN, ERNEST STAGG. Factory legislation in Maine. N.Y.: Columbia Univ., 1908. Pp. 145.

1354 MAINE

1354 WHITMAN, WILLIAM EDWARD SEAVER and CHARLES HENRY TRUE. Maine in the war for the Union: a history of the part borne by Maine troops in the suppression of the American rebellion. Lewiston: N. Dingley, Jr., 1865. Pp. viii, 637.

1355 WHITNEY, CLINTON. "Bangor and Aroostook Railroad." Railroad Enthusiast, 3 (March-August, 1966), 10-14.

1356 _____ and DICK MURRAY. "The Maine Central Railroad." Railroad Enthusiast, 2 (March-August, 1965), 14-16.

1357 WHITNEY, SETH HARDING. The Kennebec Valley: this work is devoted to the early history of the valley; also relating many incidents and adventures of the early settlers, including a brief sketch of the Kennebec Indians. Augusta: Sprague, Burleigh & Flynt, 1887. Pp. 122.

1358 _____. New Somersetshire or a sketch of Kennebec and Somerset counties. Waterville: W. M. Ladd, 1900. Pp. 23. MeHi.

1359 WHO'S who in Maine. Lewiston: Twin City Printery, [1947]. Pp. 147. MeBa.

1360 WIGGIN, FRANCES TURGEON. Maine composers and their music: a biographical dictionary. [Rockland?]: Maine Federation of Music Clubs, 1959-1976. 2v.
Volume two was published by the Maine Historical Society.

1361 WIGGIN, RUBY CROSBY. Big dreams and little wheels. Clinton, 1971. Pp. 103.
Wiscasset, Waterville & Farmington Railroad.

1362 WILKINS, AUSTIN HORATIO. The forests of Maine, their extent, character, ownership, and products. Augusta: Maine Forest Service, 1932. Pp. 107.

1363 _____. [History of Maine forests and forestry. Augusta: Maine Forest Service, 1969?]. 26 unnumbered leaves. MeU.

1364 WILKINS, RAYMOND S. "The state appelate court now and forty years ago." Maine State Bar Association. Proceedings, 41 (1952), 75-83.

1365 WILLEY, AUSTIN. The history of the antislavery cause in state and nation. Portland: B. Thurston, 1886. Pp. xii, 503.

1366 WILLIAMSON, JOSEPH. A bibliography of the State of Maine from the earliest period to 1891. Portland: Thurston Print, 1896. 2v.

1367 _____. "Capital trials in Maine before the separation." MeHSC, 2 Ser., 1 (1890), 159-172.

1368 _____. "Condition of the religious denominations of Maine, at the close of the Revolution." MeHSC, 7 (1876), 217-229.

1369 _____. "Daniel Webster's visit to Maine, in 1835." HistMag, 2 Ser., 9 (1871), 11-13.

1369A _____. "Historical review of literature in Maine." MeHSC, 2 Ser., 2 (1891), 113-127. Intellectual life.

1370 _____. "The Northmen in Maine." HistMag, 2 Ser., 5 (1869), 30-31.

1371 _____. "Presidential visits to Maine." Hist Mag, 22 (1873), 340-345.
John Adams, James Monroe, James K. Polk, Ulysses S. Grant.

1372 _____. "The professional tours of John Adams in Maine." MeHSC, 2 Ser., 1 (1890), 301-308. 1765-1774.

1373 _____. "Slavery in Maine." MeHSC, 7 (1876), 207-216.

1374 _____. "Smuggling on the Penobscot, 1814." BHistMag, 3 (1887-1888), 167.

1375 WILLIAMSON, ROBERT B. "The convention of 1819." MeHSN, 9 (1969-1970), 64-72.
Held to consider separation from Massachusetts.

1376 WILLIAMSON, WILLIAM DURKEE. The history of the State of Maine; from its first discovery, A.D. 1602, to the separation, A.D. 1820, inclusive; with an appendix and general index. (1832) A new impression.... Hallowell: Glazier, Masters & Smith, 1839. 2v.

1377 _____. "Sketches of the lives of early Maine ministers." MeHSC, 2 Ser., 3 (1892), 41-55, 191-208, 293-315; 4 (1893), 62-82, 186-208, 320-327, 410-424; 5 (1894), 99-103, 211-214, 320-328, 427-434; 6 (1895), 85-93, 184-196, 306-320, 441-445; 7 (1896), 45-52, 204-212, 313-326.

1378 WILLIS, JOHN LEMUEL MURRAY. "Early history of medicine in Maine." Old Eliot, 6 (1903), 109-119.

1379 _____. "Submission of Maine to Massachusetts." Old Eliot, 7 (1906), 53-64. 1652.

1380 _____. "The submission of Maine to Massachusetts." Old Eliot, 9 (1909), 123-150. Differs from above entry.

1381 WILLIS, WILLIAM. A business directory of the subscribers to the new map of Maine, with a brief history and description of the state; also valuable statistics and advertisements. Portland: J. Chace, Jr., 1862. Pp. 344.

1382 _____. "A descriptive catalogue of books and pamphlets relating to the history and statistics of Maine, or portions of it." HistMag, 17 (1870), 145-182.

1383 _____. A history of the law, the courts, and the lawyers of Maine, from its first colonization to the early part of the present century. Portland: Bailey & Noyes, 1863. Pp. viii, 712.

1384 _____. "Inaugural address containing biographical notices of former presidents [of the Maine Historical Society."] MeHSC, 5 (1857), xvii-lxviii.
    Also published the same year as a book with title: "An address delivered before the Maine Historical Society, at Augusta, March 5, 1857...."

1385 [_____.] "Judicial changes in Maine." Monthly Law Reporter, 11 (1848), 429-431.
    Changes in the Maine Supreme Judicial Court: author attribution by Joseph Williamson.

1386 _____. "Language of the Abnaquies." MeHSC, 4 (1856), 95-117.
    Brief history of tribe and excerpts from Father Rasles' dictionary.

1387 [_____.] "Notes on the early jurisprudence of Maine." Law Reporter, 3 (1840-1841), 31-35, 41-51, 121-127.
    Signed "W"; author attribution by Joseph Williamson.

1388 _____. "The Scotch-Irish immigration to Maine, and Presbyterianism in New England." MeHSC, 6 (1859), 1-37.

1389 WILLOUGHBY, CHARLES CLARK. Prehistoric burial places in Maine. Cambridge, Mass.: Peabody Museum, 1898. Pp. 52.

1390 WILSON, CHARLES MORROW. "Gateway to the north." Railroad Magazine, 69 (December, 1957), 19-26.
    Bangor and Aroostook Railroad since 1892.

1391 WILSON, JAMES and ROBERT WATKINS CROWE. Managers in Maine. Brunswick: Bowdoin College, Bureau for Research in Municipal Government, 1962. Pp. 40.
    City managers.

1392 WING, HENRY A. Maine's war upon the liquor traffic: a series of historical articles, ... published in the Portland Evening Express. [Portland, 1909?] Pp. 89.

1393 WINSOR, JUSTIN. "The settlement of the Northeastern Boundary." MHSP, 2 Ser., 3 (1886-1887), 349-368.

1394 WISCASSET AND QUEBEC RAILROAD. Wiscasset and Quebec Railroad. Wiscasset: Charles E. Emerson, 1877. Pp. 15. MH.
    Includes brief history of the railroad.

1395 "WITCHCRAFT in Maine." NEHGR, 13 (1859), 193-196.

1396 WOHLFARTH, J. B. "Evolution of Maine water powers." SJMH, 12 (1924), 64-65.

1397 "WOMEN fiction writers of Maine." MeLB, 14 (1928-1929), 8-24.
    Biobibliographies.

1398 WOOD, CHARLES DAYTON and E. R. MANSFIELD. Studies of the food of Maine lumberman. Washington: Govt. Print. Off., 1904. Pp. 60. MeBa.

1399 WOOD, ETHEL M. "The Maine Indians, and their relations with the white settlers." SJMH, 9 (1921), 61-69, 120-125, 170-174; 10 (1922), 6-17.

1400 WOOD, RICHARD GEORGE. "A bibliography of travel in Maine, 1783-1861." NEQ, 6 (1933), 426-439.

1401 _____. A history of lumbering in Maine, 1820-1861. Orono: Univ. Pr., 1935. Pp. 267.

1402 WOODBURY, KENNETH B., JR. "An incident between the French Canadians and the Irish in the Diocese of Maine in 1906." NEQ, 40 (1967), 260-269.
    Opposition of French Canadians to assimilation into American culture.

1403 WOODBURY, NATHAN FRANKLIN. Prohibition in Maine: history of its origin, results, political nullification and final ratification, from 1837 to 1920. Lewiston: Journal Printshop and Bindery, 1920. Pp. 30.

1404 _____, comp. The prohibition law of Maine, from the revised statutes of 1883, with amendments of 1885 and 1887, revised to 1888; also some decisions thereon by the Supreme Judicial Court; the prohibitory constitutional amendment, adopted in 1884; brief history of the law; amendments desired, etc.; important decision on prohibition by United States Supreme Court. Auburn: Prohibition Club, 1888. Pp. 36.

1405 WOODS, JOHN B. "The forests of Maine." American Forests, 54 (June, 1948), 266-268, 285, 287.

1406 WOODSIDE, CHARLES L. and LURA WOODSIDE WATKINS. "Three Maine pewterers." Antiques, 22 (1932), 8-10.
    Allen Porter, Freeman Porter, and Rufus Dunham.

1407 WOOLLEY, DION E. "Amateur journalism in Maine." Sun Up, 9 (May, 1931), 4-5, 25, 29-30.

1408   MAINE

1408   WORTHEY, MARY G. Liquor sales in Maine,
        1936-1960. Waterville: Civic League Publi-
        cations, [1962?]. Unpaged. MeU.
           Statistical tables.

1409   WRAY, RUTH ARLINE. The history of secondary
        education in Cumberland and Sagadahoc coun-
        ties in Maine. Orono: Univ. Pr., 1940.
        Pp. vii, 158.

1410   WRIGHT, HAROLD W. "Designating our wild land
        townships." The Northern, 5 (December, 1925),
        3-4, 14.

1410A   WYMAN, MARY ALICE. Two American pioneers,
        Seba Smith and Elizabeth Oakes Smith. N.Y.:
        Columbia Univ. Pr., 1927. Pp. viii, 249.

1411   YEARBOOK and church directory with historical
        sketches; churches of Saco Valley and vicin-
        ity, 1932-1933. n.p., [1933?]. Pp. 33.
        MeHi.

1412   YERXA, DONALD A. "The State of Maine and the
        new navy, 1889-1893." MeHSQ, 14 (1974-1975),
        183-205.

1413   YORK, DICK. "The man who brough music to
        Maine." Down East, 21 (January, 1975), 54-
        56, 61.
           William Rogers Chapman and the Maine Music
        Festival.

1414   YORK, ROBERT M. "Down-East Yankees in na-
        tional politics." New England Social Studies
        Bulletin, 10 (December, 1952), 3-10.

1415   _____. "The Maine economy: 1900-1940."
        Thomas Business Review, 3 (Fall, 1975), 21-31.

1416   _____. "A quick trip through historical
        Maine." Maine Alumnus, 38 (February, 1957),
        14-16.

1417   _____. "Suggested reading in Maine history:
        a bibliography of religious history." MeHSN,
        4 (February, 1965), 7-10.

1418   _____. "The three R's in early Maine." The
        Bates College Bulletin, 73 (April, 1976),
        13-15.

1419   YORK, VINCENT. The Sandy River & its valley.
        Farmington: Knowlton & McLeary, 1976.
        Pp. 251. MeHi.

1420   YORKE, DANE. "The Florida of the north."
        American Mercury, 20 (1930), 275-280.
           Maine tourist trade.

1421   YOUNG, HAROLD H. "Trolley days in central
        Maine." Down East, 21 (October, 1974), 49-
        53.

Counties

ANDROSCOGGIN COUNTY

1422 BATEMAN, LUTHER C. "The industrial heart of
Maine." National Magazine, 25 (1906-1907),
[113-119].
Lewiston and Auburn.

1423 DINGLEY, NELSON, JR. ["History of the press
in Androscoggin County."] MPAP, 24 (1887),
25-27.

1424 KIWANIS CLUB, AUBURN-LEWISTON, ME. 25th an-
niversary history, Auburn-Lewiston Kiwanis
Club ... 1922-1947. n.p., [1947?]. Unpaged.
MeU.

1425 LADD, WILLIAM. "Annals of Bakerstown, Poland,
and Minot." MeHSC, 2 (1847), 111-130.
Poland and Minot were formerly a tract
known as Barkerstown.

1426 THE LEWISTON and Auburn directory, containing
the names of the inhabitants, their occupation
and place of business, etc., the officers of
the various societies, together with a history of Lewiston and Auburn. Lewiston:
W. F. Stanwood, 1864. Pp. 179.

1427 LOMBARD, LUCINA HAYNES. "Lewiston and Auburn: historical and industrial centers."
Sun Up, 5 (February, 1928), 12-15, 18-19.

1428 MERRILL, GEORGIA DREW, ed. History of Androscoggin County, Maine. Boston: W. A. Fer-
gusson, 1891. Pp. xiv, 879.
Pages 432a-432f follow page 432 and pages
690a-690b follow page 690.

1429 OWEN, HOWARD. ["History of the press in Androscoggin County."] MPAP, 26 (1889), 34.

1430 PIDGIN, WILLIAM ABNER. ["History of the press
in Androscoggin County."] MPAP, 43 (1906),
25.

1431 RAND, JOHN A. The peoples Lewiston-Auburn,
Maine, 1875-1975. Freeport: Bond Wheel-
wright, 1975. Pp. xi, 116.
Introduction in English and French.

1432 ST. JOHN, FREDERIC. "Lewiston-Auburn." Sun
Up, 8 (October, 1930), 15, 27.
Author's name is a pseudonym.

1433 SANFORD, EVERTS & CO. Atlas and history of
Androscoggin County, Maine.... Philadelphia,
1873. Pp. 120. MeHi.

1434 SKINNER, RALPH BURGESS. Historically speak-
ing on Lewiston-Auburn, Maine, churches: an
historical study of the origin and development of religious organizations in a two-city
community from its date of settlement to and
including the ecumenical year 1964. Lewiston:
Twin City Printery, 1965. Pp. v, 176.

1435 SMITH, EDGAR CROSBY. "Androscoggin notes."
SJMH, 3 (1915-1916), 39-40.

1436 WATERMAN, CHARLES ELMER. ["History of the
press in Androscoggin County."] MPAP, 31
(1894), 20-22; 32 (1895), 27-28; 33 (1896),
35-36; 34 (1897), 27; 35 (1898), 19-20; 36
(1899), 33-34; 37 (1900), 33-34; 38 (1901),
34; 39 (1902), 36-37; 40 (1903), 36-37; 44
(1907), 47; 46 (1909), 28-29; 47 (1910), 10-
11; 48 (1911), 29; 49 (1913), 24-26; 50
(1913), 24-25; 51 (1914), 27-28.

SEE ALSO entry 555.

AROOSTOOK COUNTY

1437 ALBERT, JULIE A. "The Madawaska and Fort
Kent centennials." Down East, 15 (July,
1969), 66-67.

1438 ART work of Aroostook County, Maine. Chicago:
W. H. Parish, 1895. Unpaged. MeHi.
Includes an historical sketch of the county.

1439 BAILEY, JACOB WHITMAN. The St. John River in
Maine, Quebec, and New Brunswick. Cambridge,
Mass.: Riverside Pr., 1894. Pp. iv, 178.

1439A BANGOR AND AROOSTOOK RAILROAD COMPANY. Inside northern Maine. [Bangor?, 1949].
Pp. 45.

1440 AROOSTOOK COUNTY

1440 BARNES, ANNA. The pageant of Aroostook and Major Dickey, the Duke of Fort Kent, by Beulah Sylvester Oxton. [Lewiston]: Lewiston Journal Co., 1916. Pp. 40. [MeHoC.]

1441 BRASSARD, FRANCIS. The origin of certain public schools in the St. John River Valley of Aroostook County, Maine. Cassadaga, N.Y., 1967. 174 leaves. MeU.

1442 CARY, THEODORE. "Record of newspapers in Aroostook County." MPAP, [5] (1868), 31-35; 31 (1894), 22; 32 (1895), 27-28.

1443 CHOUINARD, EVA. Notre heritage vivant. n.p., 1973. Pp. 66. [MeMaHi.]

1444 DAY, CLARENCE ALBERT. A history of the M P G, Inc., 1932-1952. n.p., [1952?]. Pp. 88, 4. [MePriT.]
Maine Potato Growers.

1445 DAY, RICHARD L. Aroostook Valley Railroad Company. Chicago: Central Electric Railfans' Association, 1946. Pp. 11. MeBa.

1446 DIETZ, LEW. The Allagash. N.Y.: Holt, Rinehart, Winston, 1968. Pp. xxiv, 264.
Allagash River.

1447 ____. "The Allagash." Down East, 13 (October, 1966), 20-23, 50-52.

1448 ELWELL, EDWARD HENRY. Aroostook: with some accounts of the excursions thither of the editors of Maine, in the years 1858 and 1878, and of the colony of Swedes, settled in the town of New Sweden. Portland: Transcript Printing, 1878. Pp. 50.

1449 FACES of Aroostook: a bicentennial portrait of Aroostook County. Presque Isle: Polar Star Associates, [1976]. Pp. 72. MeU.

1450 FOGG, CHARLES H. ["History of the press in Aroostook County."] MPAP, 47 (1910), 11; 49 (1912), 26-27; 50 (1913), 25-26.

1451 GILMAN, GEORGE H. ["History of the press in Aroostook County."] MPAP, 24 (1887), 25; 26 (1889), 34-35; 30 (1893), 29-30; 35 (1898), 20-21; 36 (1899), 34-35; 38 (1901), 34-35; 39 (1902), 37.

1452 GILMAN, WILLIAM S. ["History of the press in Aroostook County."] MPAP, 17 (1880), 11; 19 (1882), 25.

1453 GRANT, RENA V. Three men from Aroostook: the story of the Hardison family. Berkeley, Calif.: Brazelton-Hanscom, 1963. Pp. 172.

1454 HAMLIN, HELEN. Pine, potatoes and people: the story of Aroostook. N.Y.: W. W. Norton, 1948. Pp. 238.

1455 HANNAN, ANNE. "Aroostook yesterdays." Down East, 3 (November, 1956-January, 1957), 18-20.

1456 HEDE, RICHARD, comp. and ed. Centennial history of Maine's Swedish colony: New Sweden, Westmanland, Stockholm, and adjoining areas, 1870-1970. [Stockholm?]: Thayer's, [1970?]. v.p. Me.

1457 HUFF, JEAN KEIRSTEAD. The history of secondary education in Aroostook County in Maine. Orono: Univ. Pr., 1946. Pp. vii, 138.

1458 JACKSON, ANNETTE. My life in the Maine woods: a game warden's wife in the Allagash country. N.Y.: W. W. Norton, 1954. Pp. 236.

1459 KIDNEY, DOROTHY BOONE. Away from it all. South Brunswick, N.J.: A. S. Barnes, 1969. Pp. 200.
Allagash River.

1460 MICHAUD, A. J. An Acadian heritage: from the Saint John River Valley. Madawaska: Valley Publishing, [1972]. Pp. 87.

1461 "THE POTATO industry in Aroostook County." The Northern, 3 (February, 1924), 8-13.

1462 PULLEN, CLARENCE. In fair Aroostook, where Acadia and Scandinavia's subtle touch turned a wilderness into a land of plenty. Bangor: Bangor & Aroostook Railroad, 1902. Pp. 94.

1463 PUTNAM, BEECHER. "History of Aroostook County probate office and records." SJMH, 4 (1916-1917), 255-259.

1464 RAYMOND, WILLIAM ODBER. The river St. John, its physical features, legends and history, from 1604 to 1784. St. John, N.B.: J. A. Bowes, 1910. Pp. 552.

1465 ROGERS, MARY ELIZABETH BARKER. "Aroostook pioneers." Down East, 12 (April, 1966), 32-36, 49-50, 53, 56, 58, 60.

1466 RULE, GLENN K. "Aroostook--its people and hospitality." In the Maine Woods, (1934), 117-120.
Social life and customs.

1467 SPRAGUE, RICHARD W. "The face of Aroostook." Down East, 4 (October, 1957), 14-17.

1468 ____. "Potato, king of Aroostook." Down East, 2 (October, 1955), 22-25.

1469 STICKNEY, DANIEL. ["History of the press in Aroostook County."] MPAP, 13 (1876), 23-24; 15 (1878), 23-30.

1470 VALLEAU, STEVEN L. Lumbering history of the Allagash. [Orono]: Univ. of Maine Environmental Studies Center, [1975]. Pp. 187. MeBa.

1471 VIOLETTE, LAWRENCE A. How the Acadians came to Maine. n.p., 1951. Pp. 79. Me.

1472 WALKER, HOWELL. "Aroostook County, Maine, source of potatoes." National Geographic, 94 (1948), 459-478.

1473 WALKER, RAYMOND J. "Early newspapers in Aroostook County." Hobbies, 60 (December, 1955), 119, 125.
    1857-1872.

1474 WATSON, ANDREW ELWELL. "A study of land use in thirty-one towns in Aroostook County, Maine." Maine Agricultural Experiment Station. Report, 59 (1942-1943), 53-106.

1475 WHITE, JOHN W. "Early transportation in northernmost New England, 1820-1870." New England Social Studies Bulletin, 12 (March, 1955), 18-24.

1476 WIGGIN, EDWARD. Aroostook: extracts from address ... delivered before the Farmer's Club, at Boothbay, Dec. 14, 1885; also, opinions of others with reference to that county. Portland: Tucker Printing, 1887. Pp. 26.

1477 _____. History of Aroostook. Vol. 1. Presque Isle: Star-Herald Pr., 1922. 2 pts. in 1 v.
    Part two is by George H. Collins; Part one was also issued separately; no more published.

1478 WILSON, CHARLES MORROW. Aroostook: our last frontier; Maine's picturesque potato empire. Brattleboro, Vt.: Stephen Daye Pr., 1937. Pp. 240.

1479 WILSON, ELLA M. "The Aroostook Valley: a study in potatoes." GeogRev, 16 (1926), 196-205.

    SEE ALSO entries 108, 207, 1251, and 2673.

CUMBERLAND COUNTY

1480 BACHELDER, PETER DOW. Lighthouses of Casco Bay. Portland: Breakwater Pr., 1975. Pp. x, 88.

1481 BAXTER, JAMES PHINNEY. George Cleeve of Casco Bay, 1630-1667, with collateral documents.... Portland: Gorges Society, 1885. Pp. 339.

1482 BIOGRAPHICAL review: this volume contains biographical sketches of leading citizens of Cumberland County, Maine.... Boston: Biographical Review Publishing, 1896. Pp. 706.

1483 CHAPMAN, LEONARD BOND. "Block and garrison houses of ancient Falmouth." MeHSC, 2 Ser., 6 (1895), 37-53.
    Ancient Falmouth included Falmouth, Cape Elizabeth, Portland, Deering, and Westbrook.

1484 CHASE, ALBRO ELMORE. ["History of the press in Cumberland County."] MPAP, 21 (1884), 23.

1485 CLAYTON, W. WOODFORD. History of Cumberland Co., Maine; with illustrations and biographical sketches of its prominent men and pioneers.... Philadelphia: Everts & Peck, 1880. Pp. 456.

1486 COLESWORTHY, DANIEL CLEMENT. Chronicles of Casco Bay. Portland: Sanborn and Carter, 1850. Pp. 56.

1487 COUNCIL OF SOCIAL AGENCIES, PORTLAND, ME. Greater Portland's, Portland, South Portland, Cape Elizabeth, Falmouth, provisions for health, education, safety, welfare. Margaret B. Hodges, ed. Portland, 1941. Pp. 284.

1488 CRITTENDEN, HENRY TEMPLE. "Bridgton & Harrison Railway." RLHSB, No. 57 (1942), 73-86.

1489 CUMBERLAND ASSOCIATION OF CONGREGATIONAL MINISTERS. The centennial of the Cumberland Association of Congregational Ministers, at the Second Parish Church in Portland, Maine ... May 28 and 29, 1888. Portland: B. Thurston, 1888. Pp. 75.
    Historical address by Abiel H. Wright.

1490 CUMBERLAND COUNTY, ME. 200TH ANNIVERSARY COMMITTEE. Cumberland County, 1760, bicentennial, 1960. [Portland?], 1960. Pp. 132. Me.

1491 DINGLEY, ROBERT JORDAN. "Songo River steamers." Down East, 21 (July, 1975), 82-85, 94.

1492 DIRECTORY of the city of Portland, and of the towns of Cape Elizabeth, Deering, Westbrook and Falmouth, for A.D. 1882, being the 250th anniversary of the settlement of those towns which comprised the territory of "Ancient Falmouth," containing the names, occupations, and residence of each adult inhabitant of the city; a street directory, showing the occupant of each building in the city, designated by street and number; a business directory; lists of copartnerships with the members comprising them; corporations with their officers; societies, institutions, etc., historical and statistical matters relating thereto. John T. Hull, comp. Portland: Dresser, McLellan, 1882. Pp. 720, 150.

1493 DOLE, SAMUEL THOMAS. "Gambo, old and new." MeHSC, 2 Ser., 8 (1897), 255-262.
    Gunpowder manufacture at Gambo Falls on the Presumpscot River between Gorham and Windham.

1494 _____. "White's Bridge." MeHSC, 2 Ser., 6 (1895), 252-255.
    Between towns of Windham and Standish.

1495 DUNN, WILLIAM WARREN. Casco Bay steamboat album. Camden: Down East Enterprise, 1969. Pp. 42. MeHi.

1496 ELDEN, ALFRED OWEN. "Beacons that shine in Casco Bay." Pine Tree Magazine, 6 (1906-1907), 38-44.

1497 ELWELL, EDWARD HENRY. "History of the press in Cumberland County." MPAP, 12 (1875), 4-7; 13 (1876), 25-27; 14 (1877), 22-31; 15 (1878), 31.

1498 FOBES, CHARLES S. "The story of the Presumpscot." MeHSC, 2 Ser., 5 (1894), 360-386.
    River.

1499 GARDNER, FRANK A. "Colonel Edmund Phinney's 26th Regiment." MassMag, 11 (1918), 12-36.

1500 GILBERT, FRANK Y. "Hospitals in Cumberland County." Sun Up, 3 (September, 1926), 52-53.

1501 GOOLD, NATHAN. Col. Edmund Phinney's 18th Continental Regiment; one year's service, commencing January 1, 1776. MeHSC, 2 Ser., 9 (1898), 45-106.

1502 _____. "History of Col. Edmund Phinney's 31st Regiment of Foot." MeHSC, 2 Ser., 7 (1896), 85-102, 151-185.
    Raised in Cumberland County.

1503 HAYNES, WILLIAMS. Casco Bay yarns. N.Y.: D. O. Haynes, 1916. Pp. 189.

1504 HOLDEN, CHARLES. "The origin and history of the newspaper press of Cumberland County." MPAP, [6] (1869), 29-56.

1505 HOLDEN, THEODORE L. and RUSSELL W. KNIGHT. "The Songo River steamboats." AmNep, 24 (1964), 233-246.
    1847-1930.

1506 HOPKINS, JAMES DEAN. An address to the members of the Cumberland bar, delivered during the sitting of the Court of Common Pleas, at Portland, June term, 1833. Portland: C. Day, 1833. Pp. 79.

1507 "A HUNDRED years ago Sebago Lake was connected with the sea: the history of an old canal." Sun Up, 2 (May, 1926), 15, 36.
    Sebago Lake to Portland.

1508 JEPSON, ADA F. "Presumpscot Union Parish 20th anniversary." MeCP, 145 (January, 1949), 27-29.

1509 JOHNSON, THEODORE ELLIOT, ed. "Elder Otis Sawyer's 'A complete register of all the deaths that have occurred in the United Societies of Gorham and New Gloucester, Maine.'" Shaker Quarterly, 1 (1961), 32-42.

1510 JONES, HERBERT GRANVILLE. The isles of Casco Bay in fact & fancy. Portland: Jones Book Shop, 1946. Pp. 141.

1511 _____. Sebago Lake land in history, legend and romance. Portland: Bowker Pr., 1949. Pp. 130.

1512 [KALER, JAMES OTIS]. The story of old Falmouth. By James Otis, pseud. N.Y.: Thomas Y. Crowell, 1901. Pp. 127.

1513 KENNEDY, BEN F. Buried treasure of Casco Bay, Maine: a guide to locations for the modern hunter. Falmouth: Grace Pr., 1963. Pp. 79.

1514 LOWRY, LOIS. "The Maine boyhoods of Longfellow and Hawthorne." Down East, 22 (March, 1976), 32-35, 58.
    In Portland and Raymond respectively.

1515 [McLAUGHLIN, PETER J.] Casco Bay Islands, Casco Bay, Maine. By Carthwheel Baxtree, pseud. Portland: Casco Bay Line, [1964?]. Pp. 10. MeP.

1516 MEAD, EDGAR THORN, JR. "In behalf of a railroad." Yankee, 6 (July, 1940), 25-26.
    Bridgton & Harrison Railway.

1517 MUNN, HENRY. "The shell heaps of Casco Bay." Maine Field Naturalist, 12 (April, 1956), 34-40.

1518 OLIPHANT, DUNCAN. Maine's Cumberland County. [Portland]: Maine Printing, [1961?]. Pp. 56. Me.

1519 "PAPERS in Mass. archives relating to settlements in Casco Bay." Putnam's HM, 2 (1893-1894), 227-228.

1520 PICKARD, SAMUEL THOMAS. ["History of the press in Cumberland County."] MPAP, 20 (1883), 18.

1521 ROWE, WILLIAM HUTCHINSON. Ancient North Yarmouth and Yarmouth, Maine, 1636-1936: a history. Yarmouth, 1937. Pp. xiii, 427.

1522 _____. Shipbuilding days and tales of the sea, in old North Yarmouth and Yarmouth, Maine. Portland: Marks Printing, 1924. Pp. 145.

1523 _____. Shipbuilding days in Casco Bay, 1727-1890; being footnotes to the maritime history of Maine. Yarmouth, 1929. Pp. xii, 222.

1524 ____. Yarmouth personages, an introduction: an attempt to revive the memory of individuals whose names were once household words in old North Yarmouth and Yarmouth. [Yarmouth?, 1916]. Unpaged.

1525 SALE, THOMAS D. ["History of the press in Cumberland County."] MPAP, 49 (1903), 37-38; 41 (1904), 45; 42 (1905), 32-33; 43 (1906), 25; 44 (1907), 47-48; 45 (1908), 30-31; 46 (1909), 29; 47 (1910), 11-12; 48 (1911), 29-30; 52 (1915), 13.

1526 SCHNEIDER, STEWART P. "Casco Bay steamboats." Down East, 12 (June, 1966), 30-33, 64-66, 68-70.

1527 SHOREY, HENRY A. ["History of the press in Cumberland County."] MPAP, 34 (1897), 27-30.

1528 SNOW, EDWARD ROWE. The romance of Casco Bay. N.Y.: Dodd, Mead, 1975. Pp. x, 228.

1529 SYLVESTER, HERBERT MILTON. Ye romance of Casco Bay. Boston: Stanhope Pr., 1904. Pp. 348.
Also published in 1909 as volume one of the author's "Maine pioneer settlements."

1530 ____. "Ye romance of Casco Bay." NEM, New Ser., 6 (1892), 379-390, 500-512, 756-766; 7 (1892-1893), 728-735; 8 (1893), 62-70.

1531 THURSTON, BROWN. ["History of the press in Cumberland County."] MPAP, 16 (1879), 29; 17 (1880), 12-15; 18 (1881), 27-28; 19 (1882), 25-27; 23 (1886), 19-20; 24 (1887), 27-28; 25 (1888), 27; 27 (1890), 29; 28 (1891), 28-29; 29 (1892), 23-24; 30 (1893), 30-32.

1532 WALDRON, HOLMAN DOUGLAS. "Casco Bay." NEM, New Ser., 14 (1896), 355-374.

1533 WESTON, ISAAC. "History of the Association of Ministers of Cumberland County, Maine, from 1788 to 1867." CongQ, 9 (1867), 334-347.

1534 WILLIS, WILLIAM. "Remarks on coins found at Portland in 1849, and Richmond's Island in 1855, with a general notice of coins and coinage." MeHSC, 6 (1859), 127-151.

1535 WISH, OSCAR R. ["History of the press in Cumberland County."] MPAP, 39 (1902), 38.

1536 WYMAN, DREW T. A brief sketch of the history of the Cumberland Association, 1811-1892. Portland: Brown Thurston, 1892. Pp. 16. Me.
Baptists.

SEE ALSO entries 228, 333, 354, 508, 587, 626, 879, 975, 978, 1045, 1409, 2709, and 4386.

FRANKLIN COUNTY

1537 AUSTIN, HARRY B. "The Sandy River and Rangeley Lakes Railroad." Sun Up, 5 (June, 1928), 13-15.

1538 BRACKETT, LUCY B. ["History of the press in Franklin County."] MPAP, 50 (1913), 26-28.

1539 CORNWALL, L. PETER and JACK W. FARRELL. Ride the Sandy River: a trip into the past on what was America's largest two-foot gauge railroad. Edmonds, Wash.: Pacific Fast Mail, 1973. Pp. 248.

1540 CRITTENDEN, HENRY TEMPLE. The Maine scenic route: a history of the Sandy River & Rangeley Lakes Railroad. Parsons, W. Va.: McClain Printing, 1966. Pp. 229.

1541 ____. "The Sandy River & Rangeley Lakes Railroad." RLHSB, No. 57 (1942), 15-72.

1542 ____. "Sandy River & Rangeley Lakes R.R. System." RLHSB, No. 37 (1935), 15-32.

1543 ____. Supplement--the Maine scenic route. n.p., 1966. Pp. 8, 16. MeHi.
Sandy River & Rangeley Lakes Railroad.

1544 DURRELL, JANICE. Franklin County, Maine. Portland: Gross & Allen, [1973?]. Pp. 72. MeU.

1545 FRANKLIN COUNTY AGRICULTURAL SOCIETY. Historical sketch, by-laws, and list of members of the Franklin County Agricultural Society, incorporated March 13, 1840. Farmington: Knowlton, McLeary, 1888. Pp. 26. MeHi.
Historical sketch is by Edward A. Hall.

1546 HOAR, JAY S. Small-town motion pictures, and other sketches of Franklin County, Maine. Farmington: Knowlton & McLeary, 1969. Pp. 92.

1547 HUNTER, JOHN M. S. ["History of the press in Franklin County."] MPAP, 31 (1894), 22-23; 32 (1895), 28; 33 (1897), 30.

1548 KEYES, CHARLES WESLEY. ["History of the press in Franklin County."] MPAP, 14 (1877), 31-37; 16 (1879), 29-30; 18 (1881), 29; 19 (1882), 27-28; 20 (1883), 18-19; 21 (1884), 23-26; 22 (1885), 43; 23 (1886), 20-21; 24 (1887), 28-29.

1549 KNOWLTON, DAVID HUNTER. ["History of the press in Franklin County."] MPAP, 25 (1888), 27-29; 35 (1898), 21-23; 36 (1899), 35; 37 (1900), 34; 38 (1901), 35; 39 (1902), 38-39; 40 (1903), 38-39; 43 (1906), 26; 44 (1907), 48-49; 46 (1909), 29-30.

1550 MOODY, LINWOOD W. "Mighty midgets of the old F & M." Down East, 11 (March, 1965), 28-32.
Franklin and Megantic Railroad.

1551   ____. "Shadow of the Sandy River." Trains, (August, 1946), 10-16.
    Sandy River and Rangeley Lakes Railroad.

1551A   NETT, BRUCE OWEN. "The old narrow gauge." Down East, 1 (October, 1954), 19-22.
    Sandy River and Rangeley Lakes Railroad.

1552   WILSON, CHARLES G. "Rolling into Kingfield on the Sandy River line." Down East, 9 (January, 1963), 8-21.
    Sandy River and Rangeley Lakes Railroad.

SEE ALSO entries 109, 555, and 1025.

HANCOCK COUNTY

1553   BARTER, J. MALCOLM. "Deer Isle and Stonington." Down East, 22 (April, 1976), 54-60.

1554   BROOKES, GEORGE S. These hundred years: history of the Hancock Association of Congregational Churches and Ministers, 1825-1925. n.p., [1923?]. Pp. 56. MeHi.

1555   BROWN, LENARD E. Acadia National Park, Maine: history basic data. Washington: Office of History and Historic Architecture, Eastern Service Center, 1971. Pp. iii, 191.

1556   ____. Significance of St. Sauveur Mission, established 1613, Mount Desert Island. Washington: Office of History and Historic Architecture, Eastern Service Center, 1970. iv, 57 leaves.

1557   BURT, FRANK H. "Mount Desert's mountain railway." Appalachia, 24 (1942-1943), 435-440.
    Green Mountain Railway.

1558   BUTCHER, RUSSELL D. Maine paradise: Mount Desert Island and Acadia National Park. N.Y.: Viking Pr., 1973. Pp. 94.

1559   CHADWICK, JOSEPH. "Journal through part of Mount Desart, 1768." MeHistMag, 9 (1894-1895), 123-129.
    Edited.

1560   CHAPMAN, CARLETON ABRAMSON. The geology of Acadia National Park. [Chatham, Mass.]: Chatham Pr., 1970. Pp. 128.

1561   CHATTO, CLARENCE I. and CLAIR E. TURNER. Register of the towns of Sedgwick, Brooklin, Deer Isle, Stonington, and Isle au Haut, 1910. Brooklin: Friend Memorial Public Library, 1972. Pp. 243.
    Includes historical sketches of the towns.

1562   CHILCOTT, JAMES C. ["History of the press in Hancock County."] MPAP, 26 (1889), 35; 27 (1890), 29-30; 28 (1891), 29; 29 (1892), 24; 30 (1893), 32.

1563   COLLIER, SARGENT F. Acadia National Park: George B. Dorr's triumph, with map and the illustrated story of "Mt. Desert, the most beautiful island in the world." Farmington: Knowlton & McLeary, 1965. Pp. 96.

1564   ____ and THOMAS PATRICK HORGAN. Mount Desert, the most beautiful island in the world. Boston: Houghton Miflin, 1952. Pp. ii, 106.

1565   CUMMINGS, EPHRAIM CHAMBERLAIN. "Father Biard's relation of 1616 and Saint Sauveur." MeHSC, 2 Ser., 5 (1894), 81-99.
    Saint Sauveur was Biard's early settlement on Mount Desert Island.

1566   DE COSTA, BENJAMIN FRANKLIN. The hand-book of Mount Desert, coast of Maine, with all the routes thither, descriptions of the scenery and topography, sketches of the history, with illustrations and a map of Mount Desert, and Penobscot and Frenchman's Bay, from the United States Coast Survey.... (1868) Boston: A. Williams, 1878. Pp. xiii, 161.
    First edition, 1868, has title: Scenes in the isle of Mount Desert.

1567   ____. "Mount Desert." National Repository, 4 (1878), 97-110.

1568   ____. Rambles in Mount Desert; with sketches of travel on the New England coast, from Isles of Shoals to Grand Menan. N.Y.: A. D. F. Randolph, 1871. Pp. 280.

1569   "THE DE GREGOIRE Grant of Mount Desert Island and what is now Ellsworth, Hancock, Trenton and Lamoine." BHistMag, 2 (1886-1887), 81-83.

1570   DODGE, E. H. Mount Desert Island, and the Cranberry Isles.... Ellsworth: N. K. Sawyer, 1871. Pp. 64.

1571   DORR, GEORGE BUCKNAM. Acadia National Park. Bangor: Burr Print, 1942-1948. 2v.

1572   ____. "Acadia National Park." Nature Magazine, 13 (1929), 315-318, 345-348.

1573   ____. The Sieur de Monts National Monument as commemorating Acadia and early French influences of race and settlement in the United States. Bar Harbor: Wild Gardens of Acadia, [1917?]. Pp. 15.

1574   ____, ERNEST HOWE FORBUSH and MERRITT CALDWELL FERNALD. "The unique island of Mount Desert." National Geographic, 26 (1914), 75-89.

1575   EDWARDS, HERBERT. "Mt. Desert writers." Down East, 11 (August, 1964), 42-45, 72-74, 76.

1576 ELIOT, CHARLES WILLIAM. "The forgotten millions: a study of the common American mode of life." Century, 40 (1890), 556-564.
Economic conditions on Mt. Desert Island, 1880s.

1577 ELIOT, SAMUEL ATKINS. "The romance of Mount Desert." NEM, New Ser., 20 (1899), 682-697.
French exploration.

1578 FISHER, JONATHAN. "Origin of the name of Union River between Surry and Ellsworth." BHistMag, 6 (1890-1891), 48.
Written in 1827 and contributed by Joseph Williamson.

1579 FOSS, THOMAS. A brief account of the early settlements along the shores of Skilling's River, including West Sullivan, West Gouldsborough, Trenton Point and North Hancock; also reminescences [sic] and anecdotes of old times and old folks. [Ellsworth]: N. K. Sawyer, 1870. Pp. 25.

1580 GRAZIER, JOHN S. "Prologue." NEG, 9 (Spring, 1968), 31-39.
A confrontation in Frenchman's Bay in 1613 between the French vessel "Jonas" from Nova Scotia and English vessel "Treasurer" from Jamestown, which was the prologue to Anglo-French rivalry.

1581 GREEN, SAMUEL M. "Thomas Lord, joiner and housewright." Magazine of Art, 40 (1947), 230-235.

1582 HADLOCK, WENDELL STANWOOD. "Bone implements from shell heaps around Frenchman's Bay." American Antiquity, 8 (1943), 341-353.

1583 _____. The three shell heaps on Frenchman's Bay. [Bar Harbor], 1941. Pp. 23.

1584 "HANCOCK County lawyers." BHistMag, 2 (1886-1887), 173-176.
Brief biographies.

1585 HIGGINS, ALBERT L. Notes from the early history of Mt. Desert Island. [Bar Harbor?], 1929. Unpaged. MeBa.

1586 HILTON, FLORA A. "Historical sketch of Old Point." American Monthly Magazine, 36 (1910), 398-404.
Hancock and Lamoine.

1587 THE ISLAND of Mount Desert register, with the Cranberry Isles, 1909-1910. Auburn: Lawton-Jordan, 1910. Pp. 334.
Includes history of Mount Desert, Bar Harbor, Tremont, Southwest Harbor, and Cranberry Isles.

1588 JOHNSON, LELIA ARDELL CLARK. Sullivan and Sorrento since 1760. Ellsworth: Hancock County Publishing, 1953. Pp. 410.

1589 LAPHAM, WILLIAM BERRY. Bar Harbor and Mount Desert Island.... (1886) 3d ed., rev. and enl. Augusta: Maine Farmer Job Print, 1888. Pp. 72.

1590 MAINE. STATE PLANNING OFFICE. A bibliography of Mount Desert Island. Augusta, 1974. 20 leaves. MeU.

1591 MARTIN, CLARA BARNES. Mount Desert, on the coast of Maine ... (1867) 6th ed. Portland: Loring, Short & Harmon, 1885. Pp. 115.

1592 MORISON, SAMUEL ELIOT. The story of Mount Desert Island, Maine. Boston: Little, Brown, 1960. Pp. 81.

1593 "MOUNT Desert." MeHistMag, 8 (1893), 19-23.

1594 "MOUNT Desert Island." BHistMag, 1 (1885-1886), 179-192.

1595 THE MOUNT Desert Larger Parish, historic and descriptive manual of the first seven years of the organization, 1925-1932. n.p., [1932]. Pp. 32. Me.

1596 "MOUNT Desert Rock: Maine's outermost light." Down East, 8 (October, 1961), 38-41.

1597 "PENOBSCOT, Castine and Brooksville." MeHist Mag, 8 (1893), 6-12.
Biographies of early settlers.

1598 PERRY, ADELAIDE E. This is Maine's Hancock County. Portland: Gross and Allen, [1971?]. Pp. 100. MeU.

1599 POHL, FREDERICK J. "The adventure of the hasty grave." American-Scandinavian Review, 40 (March, 1952), 15-24.
Alleged battle between Leif Ericsson and Indians on Mt. Desert Island.

1600 RAISZ, ERWIN JOSEPHUS. "The scenery of Mt. Desert Island: its origin and development." New York Academy of Sciences. Annals, 31 (1929), 121-186.

1601 "REPRESENTATIVES to General Court, from what is now Hancock County, prior to 1820." BHistMag, 3 (1887-1888), 138.
Chronological within each locale.

1602 [ROBINSON, BERNICE NELKE]. Our island lighthouse. By Bernice Richmond, pseud. N.Y.: Random House, 1947. Pp. 275.

1603 ROLLINS, FRANK W. ["History of the press in Hancock County."] MPAP, 44 (1907), 49.

1604 SAVAGE, RICHARD A. "The collectors of old Frenchman's Bay." NEG, 14 (1973), 21-29.
Collectors of customs, 19th century.

1605   SAWTELLE, WILLIAM OTIS. Acadia National Park: random notes of the significance of the name. [Bar Harbor?], 1929. Unpaged. MeBa.

1606   _____. "Father Pierre Biard, superior of the Mount Desert Jesuit Mission of Saint Sauveur." SJMH, 10 (1922), 179-191.

1607   _____. "The island of Mount Desert: the romantic story of Charles Maurice de Talleyrand-Perigord, one of the world's most famous diplomats, and its connection with Maine's early history." SJMH, 11 (1923), 127-143.

1608   _____. "Mount Desert: Champlain to Bernard." SJMH, 13 (1925), 131-186.
     Samuel de Champlain and John Bernard.

1609   _____. "Mount Desert: the story of Saint Sauveur." SJMH, 9 (1921), 101-120.

1610   _____. "Pioneers of Mount Desert, 1763." SJMH, 14 (1926), 179-187.

1611   _____. "Sir Francis Bernard and his grant of Mount Desert." CSMP, 24 (1920-1922), 197-238.

1612   SAWYER, NATHANIEL KNIGHT. "Record of newspapers in Hancock County." MPAP, 3 (1866), 5-10.

1613   SCHAUFFLER, ROBERT HAVEN. "Unique Mount Desert." Century, 82 (1911), 477-490.
     Mount Desert Island.

1614   "THE SECOND settlement in Acadia, now Maine, 1611-13." BHistMag, 6 (1890-1891), 1-3.
     Saint Sauveur.

1615   SELIGMANN, HERBERT J. "Acadia National Park: mountain playground by the sea." Down East, 6 (August, 1959), 36-41, 60.

1616   STREET, GEORGE EDWARD. Mount Desert: a history. (1905) Samuel A. Eliot, ed. New ed. Boston: Houghton, Mifflin, 1926. Pp. x, 339.

1617   THORNTON, NELLIE C. Traditions and records of Southwest Harbor and Somesville, Mount Desert Island, Maine. Auburn: Merrill & Webber, 1938. Pp. vi, 346.

1618   TRUAX, C. V. "The pink granite of Somes Sound." Down East, 19 (October, 1972), 34-37, 67-69, 71.

1619   WASSON, SAMUEL. A survey of Hancock County, Maine. Augusta: Sprague, Owen & Nash, 1878. Pp. 91.

1620   WEBSTER, ARTHUR GORDON. "Evolution of Mount Desert." Nation, 99 (September 17, 1914), 347-348.

1621   WHEELER, GEORGE AUGUSTUS. History of Castine, Penobscot, and Brooksville, Maine; including the ancient settlement of Pentagöet. Bangor: Burr & Robinson, 1875. Pp. x, 401.

1622   WOOD, JOSEPH. ["History of the press in Hancock County."] MPAP, 22 (1885), 45-47; 23 (1886), 21-22; 24 (1887), 29; 25 (1888), 29; 33 (1896), 36-37; 34 (1897), 30-31; 35 (1898), 23; 37 (1900), 34; 39 (1902), 39; 41 (1904), 45-46; 42 (1905), 33-34; 43 (1906), 26-27.

    SEE ALSO entries 108, 686, and 966.

KENNEBEC COUNTY

1623   ADAMS, SARAH B. Reminiscences of the churches and pastors of Kennebec County, read at the Kennebec Conference in Waterville, Oct. 17, 1894. Hallowell: Register Job Print, 1894. Pp. 24. MBC.
     Limited to Congregational churches and pastors.

1624   ANDREWS, RICHARD L. "From Randolph to Togus on the Kennebec Central." Trains, 11 (September, 1951), 24-26.
     Kennebec Central Railroad Company, 1889-1929.

1625   BOARDMAN, SAMUEL LANE. The agriculture and industry of the county of Kennebec, Maine, with notes upon its history and natural history. Augusta: Kennebec Journal, 1867. Pp. 199. MH.

1626   _____. History of the agriculture of Kennebec County, Maine. N.Y.: Blake, 1892. Pp. 40.

1627   BOWDITCH, HORACE E. ["History of the press in Kennebec County."] MPAP, 48 (1911), 30; 49 (1912), 27.

1628   BRANIN, M. LELYN. "The early stoneware potteries in Gardiner-Farmingdale, Maine." National Antiques Review, 4 (January, 1973), 24-26.

1629   CRITTENDEN, HENRY TEMPLE. "The Kennebec Central Railroad." RLHSB, No. 57 (1942), 103-111.
     Randolph to Togus.

1630   DUNBAR, KENDALL M. ["History of the press in Kennebec County."] MPAP, 27 (1890), 30-31.

1631   FINLEY, RAYMOND STEVENS. The history of secondary education in Kennebec County in Maine. Orono: Univ. Pr., 1941. Pp. vii, 119.

1632   FLYNT, CHARLES F. ["History of the press in Kennebec County."] MPAP, 36 (1899), 36.

1633 HANSON, JOHN WESLEY. History of Gardiner, Pittston and West Gardiner, with a sketch of the Kennebec Indians; and New Plymouth purchase, comprising historical matter from 1602 to 1852; with genealogical sketches of many families. Gardiner: W. Palmer, 1852. Pp. xi, 343.

1634 KINGSBURY, HENRY D. and SIMEON L. DEYO, eds. Illustrated history of Kennebec County, Maine: 1625-1799-1892. N.Y.: H. W. Blake, 1892. 2v.

1635 LAPHAM, WILLIAM BERRY. ["History of the press in Kennebec County."] MPAP, 15 (1878), 31-32; 24 (1887) 30; 25 (1888), 30; 26 (1889), 35-36; 30 (1893), 32.

1636 MARRINER, ERNEST CUMMINGS. Kennebec yesterdays. Waterville: Colby College Pr., 1954. Pp. 320.

1637 "NEW England manufacturing towns." New England Magazine of Industry and Trade, 1 (1859), 72-75.
   Gardiner, Hallowell, and Augusta.

1638 OWEN, HOWARD. "History of the press in Kennebec County." MPAP, 12 (1875), 7.

1639 POPE, ALTON S. and RAYMOND S. PATTERSON. "M. Appleton, 1800, chronicler of colonial medicine." Harvard Medical Alumni Bulletin, 36 (Spring, 1962), 17-23.
   His journal in Waterville and Winslow in early 1800s.

1640 QUINBY, GEORGE WASHINGTON. ["History of the press in Kennebec County."] MPAP, 18 (1881), 29-32; 19 (1882), 28.

1641 REDDINGTON, ASA. "Attorneys at law in Kennebec County, Maine." American Quarterly Register, 15 (1842-1843), 501.

1642 RICHARDS, ROSALIND. A northern countryside. N.Y.: Henry Holt, 1916. Pp. vi, 210.

1643 SANBORN, FRED W. ["History of the press in Kennebec County."] MPAP, 49 (1912), 27.

1644 SHAILER, WILLIAM HOSMER. A discourse delivered at the fiftieth anniversary of the Kennebec Association, at Norridgewock, September 2, 1879. Portland: B. Thurston, 1879. Pp. 24. MB.
   Baptists.

1645 SIDNEY, ME. The town register: Sidney, Vassalboro, China, Albion. Augusta: Mitchell-Cony, 1908. Pp. 160, 216, 51. MB.
   Includes histories of the four towns.

1646 SMITH, CAROLYN B. Union list of periodicals in the libraries of the Kennebec Valley region. Waterville: Kennebec Valley Library Service Area Council, 1972. Pp. 33. MeP.

1647 SPRAGUE, CHARLES A. ["History of the press in Kennebec County."] MPAP, 20 (1883), 19.

1648 THURLOW, CLINTON F. "The Kennebec Central Railroad." Down East, 15 (May, 1969), 50-55.

1649 WEBSTER, HENRY SEWALL. Land titles in old Pittston. Gardiner: Reporter-Journal Pr., 1912. Pp. 55.
   By "Old Pittston" is here meant the town as it existed at the time of its incorporation. It comprised the territory now lying in Pittston, Randolph, Gardiner, most of West Gardiner, and part of Farmingdale.

1650 WRITERS' PROGRAM. MAINE. Augusta-Hallowell on the Kennebec. [Augusta]: Kennebec Journal Print Shop, 1940. Pp. 123.

   SEE ALSO entries 16 and 1358.

KNOX COUNTY

1651 ART work of Knox County, Maine.... [Chicago]: W. H. Parish Publishing, 1895. 15 leaves.
   Includes an historical sketch of the county by True P. Pierce.

1652 BEVERIDGE, NORWOOD P. "Yankees from Finland." Down East, 3 (February-March, 1957), 20-21, 28.

1653 CAMDEN HERALD PUBLISHING COMPANY. Camden-Rockport bicentennial 1769-1969: commemorative book. Camden, 1969. Pp. 68.

1654 CHRONICLES of Cushing and Friendship, containing historical, statistical, and miscellaneous information of the two towns.... Rockland: Maine Home Journal, 1892. Pp. 80.

1655 CILLEY, JONATHAN PRINCE. ["History of the press in Knox County."] MPAP, 34 (1897), 31-34; 35 (1898), 23-24; 37 (1900), 34-35; 38 (1901), 35.

1656 CRONE, ALTON H. The Fox Islands, Vinalhaven-North Haven, sesquicentennial celebration, 1789-1939. Camden: Megunticook Pr., [1939]. Pp. 64.

1657 CUMMINGS, OSMOND RICHARD. "Rockland, Thomaston and Camden Street Railroad." Transportation, 6 (January, 1952), 1-18.
   1892-1931.

1658 _____. "Rockland, Thomaston & Camden Street Railway." Down East, 18 (October, 1971), 46-49, 87-88, 91-92.

1659 DIETZ, LEW. "A special place--the Oyster River Bog." Down East, 22 (November, 1975), 24-27, 58.
   Rockland, Rockport, Warren, and Thomaston.

1660 EATON, CYRUS. History of Thomaston, Rockland, and South Thomaston, Maine, from their first exploration, A.D. 1605; with family genealogies. Hallowell: Masters, Smith, 1865. 2v.

1661 FILLMORE, ROBERT B., comp. Chronicles of Knox County. [Rockland?], 1922. Pp. 106.

1662 _____. Chronicles of Knox County. n.p., 1923. Pp. 20.

1663 GOULD, ALBERT TROWBRIDGE. The St. George's River. [Beverly Farms?, Mass.], 1950. Pp. xii, 188.

1664 HESELTINE, CHARLES DANA. "Maine's 'Toonerville Trolley.'" Down East, 20 (October, 1973), 64-65.
Rockland, South Thomaston & St. George Railway.

1665 JONES, ARNOLD H. ["History of the press in Knox County."] MPAP, 50 (1913), 28.

1666 THE MAINE magazine. Special ed. Rockland, Camden and environs, 1907. n.p., [1907?]. Pp. 56.
Camden, Rockland, Rockport, Thomaston, and Warren.

1667 MOODY, LINWOOD W. "The doodlebug railroad." Down East, 15 (January, 1969), 50-53, 60, 63-64, 66.
George's Valley Railroad.

1668 _____. "The Rockport Railroad." Down East, 14 (July, 1968), 44-45, 81-82, 85, 88.

1669 OGIER, JESSE H. ["History of the press in Knox County."] MPAP, 41 (1904), 56; 46 (1909), 30.

1670 PERRY, WILDER WASHINGTON. ["History of the press in Knox County."] MPAP, 20 (1883), 19-20.

1671 ROBINSON, REUEL. History of Camden and Rockport, Maine. Camden: Camden Publishing, 1907. Pp. xiii, 644.

1672 SPRAGUE, EDWIN. "Record of newspapers in Knox County." MPAP, 3 (1866), 10-13; 15 (1878), 32-34.

1673 STIMPSON, MARY STOYELL. "Rockland, Rockport and Camden." NEM, New Ser., 31 (1904-1905), 3-15.

1674 TENNEY, HELEN. Ship's Timbers: a cottage on the coast of Maine. N.Y.: Exposition Pr., 1971. Pp. 71.
Social life and customs.

1675 VOSE, Z. POPE. ["History of the press in Knox County."] MPAP, 16 (1879), 30-31; 18 (1881), 32.

1676 WALKER, HAROLD S. "Knox Railroad, formerly Georges Valley R.R." RLHSB, No. 41 (1936), 44-46.

SEE ALSO entries 107 and 907.

LINCOLN COUNTY

1677 ALLEN, CHARLES EDWIN. "Ancient Pownalboro and her daughters." NEM, New Ser., 24 (1901), 516-534.
Pownalboro, Wiscasset, Dresden, Alna and Perkins.

1678 CASTNER, HAROLD WEBBER. The story of the Great Salt Bay and Vaughn's Pond. (1950) 2d ed. Boothbay Harbor: Boothbay Register, 1956. Pp. 34.

1679 _____. A story of the mystifying, prehistoric oyster shell heaps of the Damariscotta River; containing records of explorations by scientists and all known data on this man-made wonder of antiquity, together with pictures of the excavation, 1886. (1930) 3rd ed. Boothbay Harbor, 1956. Pp. 20.

1680 CHRISTIAN, SHELDON. "How the Enterprise beat the Boxer." Down East, 10 (September, 1963), 29-31, 50.
War of 1812.

1681 "THE CHRONOLOGICAL history of the Boothbay region." Sun Up, 3 (September, 1926), 60-62.
1000-1926.

1682 CLIFFORD, HAROLD BURTON. The Boothbay region, 1906 to 1960. Freeport: Bond Wheelwright, 1961. Pp. 354.

1683 CUSHMAN, DAVID QUIMBY. The history of ancient Sheepscot and Newcastle including early Pemaquid, Damariscotta, and other contiguous places, from earliest discovery to the present time, together with the genealogy of more than four hundred families. Bath: E. Upton & Son, 1882. Pp. xvii, 458.

1684 DAMARISCOTTA, ME. Centennial celebration at Damariscotta and Newcastle, July 4th, 1876, together with the historical address delivered by Gen. James A. Hall. Waldoboro: Miller & Atwood, 1876. Pp. 18.

1685 DUNBAR, KENDALL M. ["History of the press in Lincoln County."] MPAP, 27 (1890), 31-32; 29 (1892), 25.

1686 FERTIG, ILONKA. Eighteenth-century meeting houses, Lincoln County, Maine. [Pemaquid]: Pemaquid Historical Association, 1970. Pp. 11. MeHi.

1687 FILLMORE, ROBERT B., comp. Chronicles of Lincoln County. Augusta: Kennebec Journal Print Shop, 1924. Pp. 152.

1688 FREDERICKS, KATHERINE M. E. Bar-bits from old court records in Lincoln County, Maine. [Wiscasset], County Commissioners of Lincoln County, 1970. Pp. 74. Me.

1689 GREENE, FRANCIS BYRON. History of Boothbay, Southport and Boothbay Harbor, Maine, 1623-1905; with family genealogies. Portland: Loring, Short & Harmon, 1906. Pp. vi, 693.

1690 HALLET, RICHARD. Boothbay region story, 1764-1964, 200th anniversary. n.p., 1964. Pp. 47. Me.
    Boothbay, Boothbay Harbor, and Southport.

1691 HANKS, CARLOS C. "Gun brigs off Pemaquid." United States Naval Institute. Proceedings, 62 (1936), 371-372.
    'Enterprise' and 'Boxer' in War of 1812.

1692 HOLMAN, W. O. Centennial of the Lincoln Baptist Association: historical discourse at the hundredth anniversary held in the First Baptist Church, St. George, September 5 and 6, 1904. n.p., [1904]. Pp. 18.

1693 JOHNSTON, JOHN. A history of the towns of Bristol and Bremen in the State of Maine, including the Pemaquid settlement. Albany, N.Y.: Joel Munsell, 1873. Pp. v, 524.

1694 JONES, CARMITA DE SOLMS. "Missions in Lincoln County, Maine." American Catholic Historical Society of Philadelphia. Records, 36 (1925), 396-400.

1695 LANG, CONSTANCE ROWE. Kennebec, Boothbay Harbor steamboat album, including Monhegan Island, Sheepscot and Damariscotta Rivers. Camden: Down East Enterprise, 1971. Pp. 51.

1696 LINCOLN COUNTY BICENTENARY COMMITTEE. The Lincoln County pilgrimage. n.p., [1960]. Unpaged. MeHi.
    Historic houses.

1697 MARPLE, HOWARD A., ed. Lincoln County, Maine, 1760-1960. Rockland: Seth Low Pr., [1960]. Unpaged. MeHi.

1698 MILLER, SAMUEL LLEWELLYN. ["History of the press in Lincoln County."] MPAP, 18 (1881), 32-33; 19 (1882), 29; 20 (1883), 20; 21 (1884), 26; 23 (1886), 22; 24 (1887), 30-31; 26 (1889), 36; 44 (1907), 49; 45 (1908), 31.

1699 MOUNTFORT, JULIA ANN DYKE. Drogeo land. Damariscotta: Lincoln County News, [1936?]. Pp. 18.

1700 OGIER, JESSE H. ["History of the press in Lincoln County."] MPAP, 32 (1895), 28; 34 (1897), 34-35; 35 (1898), 24.

1701 PATTERSON, WILLIAM DAVIS. "Old mansion houses in Lincoln County." BHistMag, 5 (1889-1890), 231.

1702 _____, ed. The probate records of Lincoln County, Maine, 1760 to 1800; compiled and edited for the Maine Genealogical Society. Portland: Printed for the Society, 1895. Pp. xxi, 368.
    Index of names and places.

1703 PICKING, SHERWOOD. Sea fight off Monhegan: Enterprise and Boxer. Portland: Machigonne Pr., 1941. Pp. x, 195.

1704 "POWNALBOROUGH and Lincoln County." BHistMag, 3 (1887-1888), 121-125.

1705 PREBLE, GEORGE HENRY. "Three historic flags and three September victories." NEHGR, 28 (1874), 17-41.
    Bon Homme Richard, 1779; Enterprise (Boxer vs. Enterprise), and Fort McHenry.

1706 SAWYER, EDITH A. "Three old meeting-houses in Maine." NEM, New Ser., 24 (1901), 594-604.
    Alna, Waldoborough, and Walpole.

1707 SEWALL, RUFUS KING. Memorials of the bar of Lincoln County, Maine, 1760-1900. [2d ed.] Wiscasset: Sheepscot Echo Print, 1900. Pp. 40.

1708 SIDELINGER, LOWELL H. List of vessels built in Newcastle, Damariscotta, Nobleboro and Bristol ... with historical sketches of some of the old vessels and builders. n.p., [1896?]. Pp. 25. MeHi.

1709 STURGES, FLORENCE M. High points in the history of the Newcastle-Damariscotta area. [Damariscotta?]: Newcastle-Damariscotta Woman's Club, 1976. Pp. 46. Me.

1710 THAYER, HENRY OTIS. "Centenary of [the] War [of] 1812-15: naval combat of Enterprise and Boxer, September 5, 1813." SJMH, 2 (1914-1915), 63-73.

1711 WOOD, JOSEPH. "History of the press in Lincoln County." MPAP, 12 (1875), 10-11; 14 (1877), 37-39; 15 (1878), 34-35; 17 (1886), 15; 18 (1881), 39.

1712 WOODBURY, CHARLES LEVI. "Pemaquid and Monhegan." HPHR, 1 (1891-1892), 5-8, 20-26, 46-50, 61-64.

SEE ALSO entries 16, 107, 907, and 966.

OXFORD COUNTY

1713 BARKER, FRED COSHIN and JOHN S. DANFORTH. Hunting and trapping on the Upper Magalloway

1714 OXFORD COUNTY

River and Parmachenee Lake: a winter in the wilderness. (1882) Rev. ed. Boston: Lothrop, Lee & Shepard, 1929. Pp. 238.
1876.

1714 BOWLER, ERNEST C. ["History of the press in Oxford County."] MPAP, 41 (1904), 56-57.

1715 CLEPPER, HENRY EDWARD. "The Parmachenee Belle." American Forests, 62 (March, 1956), 12-13, 56-57.
Fishing in Parmachenee Lake, 1876-1956.

1716 CROCKETT, GEORGE B., comp. Consolidated history of the churches of the Oxford Baptist Association, State of Maine; and a historical sketch of the Association. Bryant's Pond: A. M. Chase, 1905. Pp. 138.

1717 FORBES, ARTHUR ELBRIDGE. ["History of the press in Oxford County."] MPAP, 24 (1887), 31; 25 (1888), 30-31; 26 (1889), 36; 27 (1890), 32-33; 28 (1891), 30; 29 (1892), 25; 30 (1893), 33; 31 (1894), 23; 33 (1896), 38; 34 (1897), 35; 35 (1898), 24; 36 (1899), 36; 37 (1900), 36; 38 (1901), 36; 40 (1903), 39.

1718 HEBERT, RICHARD A. "Norway and South Paris." Pine Cone, 1 (Winter, 1945-1946), 25-28.

1719 MOULTON, AUGUSTUS FREEDOM. "The county of Lincoln." SJMH, 13 (1925), 3-28.

1720 SANBORN, FRED W. ["History of the press in Oxford County."] MPAP, 50 (1913), 28.

1721 STEVENS, JANE PERHAM. Maine's treasure chest: gems and minerals of Oxford County. West Paris: Perham's Maine Mineral Store, 1972. Pp. 216.

1722 STONE, THOMAS TREADWELL. Sketches of Oxford County. Portland: Shirley and Hyde, 1830. Pp. 111.

1723 TIDD, MARSHALL, M. "Up the Magalloway River in 1861." Appalachia, 31 (1956-1957), 457-471; 32 (1955-1959), 45-65.
Edited by Benton L. Hatch and Louis Felix Ranlett from Tidd's manuscript journal in the Bangor Public Library.

1724 WATERMAN, CHARLES ELMER. The Oxford Hills and other papers. Auburn: Merrill & Webber, [1929?]. Pp. 90.

1725 WATKINS, GEORGE HENRY. ["History of the press in Oxford County."] MPAP, 14 (1877), 39; 16 (1879), 31-32; 18 (1881), 33; 21 (1884), 29-30; 22 (1885), 47; 23 (1886), 23.

1726 WIGHT, DENHAM BARTLETT. The Androscoggin River Valley, a gateway to the White Mountains. Rutland, Vt.: Charles E. Tuttle, 1967. Pp. 561.

1727 WOOD, JACOB. A sermon delivered at the dedication of the New Universalist Meeting House in Norway Village, September 30, 1829, to which is added an appendix containing a short sketch of the history of the Universalist Society and Church in Norway and Paris. Norway: Goodnow & Phelps, 1829. Pp. 20. MeHi.

SEE ALSO entries 109, 228, 333, 354, 508, 602, 626, 879, 975, and 1045.

PENOBSCOT COUNTY

1728 "ANCIENT Norumbega." BHistMag, 2 (1886-1887), 134-135.
Supposedly the Penobscot River.

1729 BAKER, RICHARD W. Penobscot County, Maine. Portland: Gross and Allen, 1973. Pp. 75.

1730 BARTLETT, CHARLES H. "Reminiscences of the Penobscot Bar." SJMH, 13 (1925), 30-34.

1731 BARTLETT, EDMUND HOBART. Local government in Penobscot County. Orono: Univ. Pr., 1932. Pp. 82.

1732 DOLE, RICHARD F. "Maine's first steam railroad--Bangor to Old Town." Down East, 18 (May, 1972), 52-54, 59, 62, 64.
Bangor and Piscataquis Canal and Railroad Company.

1733 "EARLY settlements on Penobscot River, now Orono, Milford, Argyle, [and] Bradford." BHistMag, 1 (1885-1886), 206-210.

1734 "THE FIRST steam railroad built in Maine and probably New England." MeHistMag, 7 (1891-1892), 29-30.
Bangor and Piscataquis Canal and Railroad Company.

1735 FISHER, CHARLES E. "The Bangor and Piscataquis R.R." RLHSB, No. 55 (1941), 73-75.

1736 FLOOD, ERNEST CECIL. History of Methodism in Bangor and Brewer, 1814-1964. n.p., 1964. Pp. 17.

1737 GANONG, WILLIAM FRANCIS. "The origin and place-names Acadia and Norumbega." Royal Society of Canada. Proceedings and Transactions, 3 Ser., 11 Pt. 2 (1917), 105-111.
Norumbega as the Penobscot River.

1738 HAYNES, AARON. "Reminiscences of [the] Penobscot River." BHistMag, 2 (1886-1887), 100-102.

1739 HEMPSTEAD, ALFRED GEER. "Improvements on the West Branch of the Penobscot River: the Penobscot Log Driving Company, 1856-1903." The Northern, 8 (May, 1928), 3-4.

1740 ____. "The Penobscot boom." The Northern, 8 (June, 1928), 5-6.
Lumbering.

1741 HISTORY of Penobscot County, Maine, with illustrations and biographical sketches. Cleveland: Williams, Chase, 1882. Pp. 922.
Williamson's "Bibliography of the State of Maine" states that "the putative author or compiler of the work was Henry A. Ford of Detroit;" chapter seventeen is a bibliography.

1742 "JAILS of Penobscot County." BHistMag, 5 (1889-1890), 112.

1743 KEITH, PHILIP EDWARD. The history of secondary education in Penobscot County in Maine. Orono: Univ. Pr., 1948. Pp. v, 249.

1744 KIMBALL, MARION REED. "Steamboating on the upper Penobscot." Down East, 20 (April, 1974), 58-59, 77-78.

1745 "LAWYERS admitted to practice in courts of Penobscot County." BHistMag, 3 (1887-1888), 228-229.
Chronological listing for the period 1824-1847.

1746 "THE LUMBERMAN." Eastern Magazine, 1 (1835-1836), 33-43.

1747 LYNN, JOHN A. "Samuel de Champlain in the Penobscot wilderness." Down East, 23 (March, 1975), 40-42.

1748 MASON, WILLIAM CASTEIN, JERRIE K. PHILLIPS and THOMAS U. COE. History of the Penobscot County Medical Association.... Bangor, 1898. Pp. 79. MeBa.

1749 NILE, LE ROY. Tales of the Rangeley Lakes. Farmington: Knowlton & McLeary, 1948. Pp. 128. Me.

1750 NORTON, DAVID. "Sketches of Old Town and Orono." MHGR, 9 (1898), 183-191.

1751 PAINE, ALBERT WARE. "The territorial history of Bangor and vicinity." MeHSC, 9 (1887), 223-234.

1752 PERHAM, DAVID. "Early history of Orrington and Brewer." BHistMag, 1 (1885-1886), 17-20.

1753 "ROADS on the Penobscot River above Bangor." BHistMag, 5 (1889-1890), 77-78.

1754 ROBBINS, CHESTER W. ["History of the press in Penobscot County."] MPAP, 29 (1892), 26; 30 (1893), 33; 35 (1898), 24-25.

1755 ROWE, HERBERT W. ["History of the press in Penobscot County."] MPAP, 44 (1907), 49-50.

1756 "SENATORS from Penobscot County from 1820 to the incorporation of Piscataquis County, March 23, 1838." BHistMag, 5 (1889-1890), 21-23.
Senators and representatives arranged chronologically.

1757 SMITH, FRANK K. ["History of the press in Penobscot County."] MPAP, 13 (1876), 28-32.

1758 "SOME pioneer settlers on upper Penobscot River." BHistMag, 6 (1890-1891), 28-34.

1759 SPRAGUE, JOHN FRANCIS. "Norombega." SJMH, 8 (1920), 91-96.

1760 "THE STORY OF the Penobscot bar." BHistMag, 6 (1890-1891), 25-26.

1761 THAYER, MILDRED N. "The Bon Ton ferries." Down East, 13 (March, 1967), 49, 72.
Bangor to Brewer.

1762 ____ and AGNES H. AMES. Brewer, Orrington, Holden, Eddington, history and families. [Brewer?], 1962. Pp. 285, ccvii.

1763 WALKER, HAROLD S. "The Bangor, Oldtown & Milford Railroad, 1836-1869." RLHSB, No. 106 (1962), 40-48.

1764 WARD, KENT. Penobscot County, Maine. Portland: Gross & Allen, [1971?]. Pp. 96. MeU.

1765 WILLIAMSON, WILLIAM DURKEE. "Sketches of early lawyers in Penobscot County." BHistMag, 4 (1888-1889), 24-25.
Pelatiah Hitchcock, Samuel Upham, Andrew Morton, and Peleg Chandler.

SEE ALSO entry 1251.

PISCATAQUIS COUNTY

1766 "ALONG the old Savage Road." SJMH, 1 (1913-1914), 145-147.

1767 NO ENTRY.

1768 AVERY, MYRON HALBURTON. "The story of the Wassataquoik, a Maine epic." Maine Naturalist, 9 (1929), 83-96.
Lumbering.

1769 BEARD, GEORGE MILLER. "Experiments with the 'Jumper of Maine.'" Popular Science Monthly, 18 (1880-1881), 170-178.
"Jumping" is a disease similar to epilepsy; experiments conducted in the Moosehead Lake region.

1770 BOARDMAN, SAMUEL LANE. "Moosehead Lake." In the Maine Woods, (1907), 115-121.

1771 PISCATAQUIS COUNTY

1771   NO ENTRY.

1772   EARLE, A. GERTRUDE. "Universalism in Piscataquis County." PCHSC, 1 (1910), 86-99.

1773   ECKSTORM, FANNIE HARDY. "Is Kokadjo Indian?"
SJMH, 13 (1925), 95-97.
        Indian names for lakes and mountains in
Moosehead Lake region.

1774   EVANS, LISTON P. ["History of the press in
Piscataquis County."] MPAP, 36 (1899), 37;
37 (1900), 36; 29 (1902), 39; 40 (1903), 39;
43 (1906), 27; 44 (1907), 50; 45 (1908), 31;
46 (1909), 30; 47 (1910), 13; 48 (1911), 30;
51 (1914), 28; 52 (1915), 14.

1775   GAGNON, LANA. Chesuncook memories. Greenville: Oscar Gagnon, 1974. Pp. 67. MeU.
        Chesuncook Lake region.

1776   HASKELL, CHARLES B. ["History of the press
in Piscataquis County."] MPAP, 31 (1894),
23.

1777   HAYES, CHARLES WELLS. "Early navigation on
Sebec Lake." PCHSC, 1 (1910), 127-137.

1778   HEMPSTEAD, ALFRED GEER. "The Sourdnahunk
Dam and Improvement Company, 1878-1900."
The Northern, 7 (June, 1927), 3-4, 8-9.
        Sourdnahunk Stream.

1779   _____. "Sourdnahunk Dam and Improvement
Company, 1900-1927." The Northern, 7 (August, 1927), 5-6.
        Sourdnahunk Stream.

1780   HERRING, CHARLES MACOMBER. Historical discourse at the semi-centennial of the Piscataquis Baptist Association at Dexter, August 27, 1889. Portland: B. Thurston,
1889. Pp. 15.

1781   JACKSON, HERBERT G., JR. "Boat rides, blueberries, and band concerts: steamboat days
on Sebec Lake." Down East, 21 (September,
1974), 60-63, 96.

1782   KENISTON, FRANK WALTER. Biographies of
Guilford, Sangerville, Abbot, and Parkman,
Maine. Auburn: Merrill & Webber, 1942.
Pp. 109.

1783   LORING, AMASA. History of Piscataquis County, Maine, from its earliest settlement to
1880. Portland: Hoyt, Fogg & Donham, 1880.
Pp. 304.

1784   MacDOUGALL, WALTER M. "Moosehead Lake steamboats." Down East, 9 (May, 1963), 40-43, 45.

1785   McGUIRE, JOSEPH DEAKINS. "Ethnological and
archeological notes on Moosehead Lake, Maine."
American Anthropologist, New Ser., 10 (1908),
549-557.

1786   MOOSEHEAD souvenir booklet, a collection of
articles, 1776, 1836, 1976. n.p., [1976].
Unpaged. MeU.

1787   "NAVIGATION on Moosehead Lake: a brief account of the activities of the Coburn Steamboat Company activities and its predecessors."
The Northern, 6 (May, 1926), 3-4, 15.

1788   PARSONS, WILLIS E. "Odd Fellowship in Piscataquis County." SJMH, 1 (1913-1914), 85-117.

1789   PISCATAQUIS COUNTY HISTORICAL SOCIETY, DOVER,
ME. Piscataquis County Historical Society,
its by-laws and membership, etc., and a bibliography of Piscataquis County. Dover: Observer Publishing, 1916.

1790   PRATT, F. H. "History of the Baptist churches
in Piscataquis County." PCHSC, 1 (1910), 66-
85.

1791   RED EAGLE, HENRY. "Historic Moosehead Lake,
early explorers and pioneers." In the Maine
Woods, (1936), 37-42.

1792   ROGERS, LORE ALFRED. "The Telos Cut."
Northern Logger, 14 (May, 1966), 26-27, 40-
45.
        Lumbering.

1793   "RONCO'S Camp and Mud Pond carry." The Northern, 6 (November, 1926), 6-7, (January,
1927), 5.

1794   SMITH, EDGAR CROSBY. "Sketches of some revolutionary soldiers of Piscataquis County."
PCHSC, 1 (1910), 154-203.

1795   SMITH, FRANK K. ["History of the press in
Piscataquis County."] MPAP, 13 (1876), 32-
33.

1796   SPRAGUE, JOHN FRANCIS. Address delivered
before the Piscataquis County Historical Society,... July 23, 1908. n.p., 1908.
Pp. 9. Me.

1797   _____. Piscataquis biography and fragments.
Bangor: C. H. Glass, 1899. Pp. 102.

1798   STEELE, THOMAS SEDGWICK. Canoe and camera:
a two hundred mile tour through the Maine
forests. N.Y.: O. Judd, 1880. Pp. 139.

1799   THOMPSON, WINFIELD MARTIN. Debsconeag. Boston: Barta Pr., 1902. Pp. 16.
        Debsconeag Lakes.

1800   THOREAU, HENRY DAVID. The Maine woods.
(1864) Joseph J. Moldenhauer, ed. Princeton:
Princeton Univ. Pr., 1972. Pp. 485.

1801   WARD, JULIUS HAMMOND. "Moosehead Lake."
Harper's New Monthly Magazine, 51 (1875), 350-
365.

SEE ALSO entries 30 and 108.

SAGADAHOC COUNTY

1802 BALLARD, EDWARD. "Location of Sasanoa's River, in Maine." HistMag, 2 Ser., 3 (1868), 164-166.

1803 BARKER, FEN. G. "History of the press in Sagadahoc County." MPAP, 15 (1878), 36.

1804 DUNBAR, KENDALL M. ["History of the press in Sagadahoc County."] MPAP, 26 (1889), 37.

1805 GARDINER, ROBERT HALLOWELL, 1782-1864. "Jones's Eddy." MeHSC, 4 (1856), 45-48.
    On Kennebec River below Bath; established to rival Wiscasset but never attracted trade.

1806 LEMONT, LEVI P. 1400 historical dates of the town and city of Bath, and town of Georgetown, from 1604 to 1874, together with the address of Francis Winter delivered at Bath ... July 4, 1825. Bath: E. Upton & Son, 1874. Pp. 104.

1807 MAYERS, CLAYTON W. "Duck hunting on Merrymeeting Bay 60 years ago." Down East, 7 (October, 1960), 31-33, 40-41.

1807A O'BRIEN, MICHAEL J. "The lost town of Cork, Maine: an early attempt by Robert Temple and emigrants from Ireland to establish a settlement in the Kennebec wilderness." AIrHSJ, 12 (1913), 175-184.
    Controversy as to location.

1808 PURINGTON, WILLIAM C. "The Bath and Woolwich railroad ferries." Down East, 22 (April, 1976), 61-64.

1809 THAYER, HENRY OTIS. "The transient town of Cork." MeHSC, 2 Ser., 4 (1893), 240-265.

1810 UPTON, JOSHUA FOY. ["History of the press in Sagadahoc County."] MPAP, 18 (1881), 34-38; 37 (1900), 36-39; 43 (1906), 27-29.

    SEE ALSO entries 107 and 1409.

SOMERSET COUNTY

1811 BOWEN, HOWARD LANCASTER. The history of secondary education in Somerset County in Maine. Orono: Univ. Pr., 1935. Pp. 85.

1812 CHATTO, CLARENCE I. East Somerset County register, 1911-12. Auburn: Chatto and Turner, [1911?]. Pp. 539. Me.

1813 DANFORTH, FLORENCE WAUGH. Somerset County in the World War. Lewiston: Journal Printshop, [1920?]. Pp. 330.

1814 DOLE, RICHARD F. Sebasticook and Moosehead Railroad Company. n.p., 1961. 5 leaves. MeU.
    1886-1911.

1815 GOVE, WILLIAM G. "The railroad that went nowhere." Down East, 19 (May, 1973), 21-22, 25-26, 29-32, 34, 36.
    Seboomook Lake and St. John Railroad; carried pulpwood to paper mills at Millinocket.

1816 HANSON, JOHN WESLEY. History of the old towns, Norridgewock and Canaan, comprising Norridgewock, Canaan, Starks, Skowhegan, and Bloomfield, from their early settlement to the year 1849; including a sketch of the Abnakis Indians. Boston, 1849. Pp. 371.
    Williamson's "Bibliography of the State of Maine" notes that the first part, comprising 120 pages, was issued with a separate title page as "Historical sketch of the Norridgewock Indians," perhaps without the author's knowledge.

1817 HASKELL, CHARLES B. ["History of the press in Somerset County."] MPAP, 33 (1896), 38-39; 36 (1899), 37; 37 (1900), 39.

1818 HASKELL, LOUIS O. ["History of the press in Somerset County."] MPAP, 50 (1913), 28-29.

1819 NO ENTRY.

1820 KILBY, CYRUS HAMLIN. ["History of the press in Somerset County."] MPAP, 13 (1876), 34; 14 (1877), 40; 15 (1878), 36-37; 16 (1879), 32-33; 17 (1880), 15-16.

1821 MacDONALD, THOMAS L. Scenes of Flagstaff and Dead River. Flagstaff: Flagstaff Cemetery Association, 1974. Pp. 76.

1822 MacDOUGALL, WALTER M. "Gulf Stream trestle." Down East, 22 (November, 1975), 36-39, 61.
    Somerset Railroad.

1823 _____. "The old Somerset Railroad." Down East, 8 (November, 1961), 32-37.

1824 _____. "Wooden spans of the Somerset Railroad." Down East, 16 (June, 1970), 66, 87, 90, 94-95, 99-100, 102.

1825 MERRIMAN, EDWARD A. ["The story of the press in Somerset County."] MPAP, 43 (1906), 30.

1826 PORTER, ALBERT O. "When all was not harmony on the Harmony line." Down East, 14 (January, 1968), 32-33, 48-49.
    Sebasticook and Moosehead Railroad.

1827 PRINCE, HENRY C. ["History of the press in Somerset County."] MPAP, 44 (1907), 50-51; 48 (1911), 30-31.

1828 SMITH, JOSEPH OTIS. ["History of the press in Somerset County."] MPAP, 23 (1886), 23-24; 24 (1887), 31; 25 (1888), 31; 26 (1889), 38; 28 (1891), 30; 30 (1893), 34; 31 (1894), 23-24.

1829 SOMERSET COUNTY FARM BUREAU. Ten years of extension and farm bureau work in Somerset County, 1918-1928. n.p., [1929?]. Unpaged. Me.

1830 SOMERSET County, Maine. Portland: Gross & Morris, [1962]. Pp. 88. MeHi.

1831 WOOD, JOSEPH. ["History of the press in Somerset County."] MPAP, 19 (1882), 29-30.

SEE ALSO entries 108, 1025, and 1358.

WALDO COUNTY

1832 BRACKETT, GEORGE EMERSON. ["History of the press in Waldo County."] MPAP, 29 (1892), 26-27; 31 (1894), 24.

1833 DAKIN, MOSES. Monterey, or the mountain city: containing a description of the boundaries, situation, mountains, lakes, rivers, soil and climate ... of the southern part of the county of Waldo, Maine; to which is added an appendix, giving a brief account of some of the islands of Penobscot Bay. Boston: Mead's Pr., 1847. Pp. 26.
    Camden, Hope, Lincolnville, and Northport.

1834 LANG, JOHN WILSON. A survey of Waldo County, Maine: historical, physical, agricultural. Augusta: Sprague, Owen & Nash, 1873. Pp. 131. MeHi.

1835 MURCH, LUCIUS H. ["History of the press in Waldo County."] MPAP, 32 (1895), 28-29; 33 (1896), 39; 34 (1897), 35; 35 (1898), 25-26; 36 (1899), 37-38; 37 (1900), 39-40.

1836 PILSBURY, CHARLES ALBERT. ["History of the press in Waldo County."] MPAP, 21 (1884), 26-28; 23 (1886), 24; 24 (1887), 31; 26 (1889), 37-39.

1837 "REPRESENTATIVES to General Court, prior to 1820, from what is now Waldo County." BHist Mag, 3 (1887-1888), 155.
    Arranged chronologically within each locale.

1838 WATSON, ANDREW ELWELL. Land classification in Waldo County, Maine. Orono: Maine Agricultural Experiment Station, 1943. Pp. 313. MeP.
    Includes brief agricultural history.

SEE ALSO entries 30 and 107.

WASHINGTON COUNTY

1839 "ANCIENT Machias Bay and River." BHistMag, 6 (1890-1891), 75.

1840 BACON, GEORGE FOX. Calais, Eastport and vicinity, their representative business men, and points of interest, embracing Calais, Eastport, Machias, Machiasport, Milltown, Jonesport, Princeton, Millbridge, Cherryfield and Lubec. Newark, N.J.: Glenwood Publishing, 1892. Pp. 119.

1841 BORDER cities souvenir. [Lewiston]: R. J. Lawton, 1908. Pp. 77. MeHi.
    Includes Calais and Eastport.

1842 BOYD, CHARLES H. "An incident on the coast of Maine in 1861." MagHist, 15 (1912), 38-41.
    First Confederate flag captured by U.S. forces in Passamaquoddy Bay.

1843 COMAN, DALE REX. Pleasant River. N.Y.: W. W. Norton, 1966. Pp. 169.

1844 DAVIS, HAROLD ARTHUR. "The Fenian raid on New Brunswick." CanHistRev, 36 (1955), 316-334.
    Launched from Calais/Eastport region.

1845 _____. An international community on the St. Croix, 1604-1930. Orono: Univ. Pr., 1950. Pp. 412.

1846 _____. "Shipbuilding on the St. Croix. Am Nep, 15 (1955), 173-190.
    1784-1870s.

1847 DAY, CLARENCE ALBERT. A history of the blueberry industry in Washington County. Orono, [1954?]. 22 leaves. MeU.

1848 _____. Title deeds to land in the Pleasant River Valley. n.p., n.d. 7 leaves. MBNEH.

1849 "'DOWN East' fifty years ago." BTJ, 1 (1888-1889), 271.

1850 DRISKO, GEORGE WASHINGTON. "Record of newspapers in Washington County." MPAP, [4] (1867), 27-35; 21 (1884), 28; 24 (1887), 32-33; 27 (1890), 33; 34 (1897), 36; 36 (1899), 38; 38 (1901), 36; 40 (1903), 40; 42 (1905), 39-40.

1851 _____. The revolution: life of Hannah Weston, with a brief history of her ancestry, also a condensed history of the first settlement of Jonesborough, Machias and other neighboring towns. (1857) 2d ed. Machias: G. A. Parlin, 1902. Pp. 140.

1852 DU WORS, RICHARD E. "Persistence and change in local values of two New England communities." Rural Sociology, 17 (September, 1952), 207-217.
    Eastport and Lubec; based on historical data for 1798-1924 and interviews during 1938-1949.

1853 GATSCHET, ALBERT SAMUEL. "All around the Bay of Passamaquoddy." National Geographic Magazine, 8 (1897), 16-24.
Includes origin of Indian place names; supplemented by an article in the "Eastport Sentinel," September 15, 1897.

1854 GLUEK, ALVIN C., JR. "The Passamaquoddy Bay Treaty, 1910: a diplomatic sideshow in Canadian-American relations." CanHistRev, 47 (1966), 1-21.

1855 GREENAN, JOHN THOMAS, ed. Way Down East in Maine: the story of a pioneer family, as told by themselves. Morristown, N.J.: Compton Pr., 1958. Pp. 210.

1856 GREENE, NANCY H. and CLARENCE H. DRISKO. A history of Columbia and Columbia Falls in honor of the American bicentennial, 1776-1976. Cherryfield: Narraguagus Printing, [1976]. Pp. 65. MeHi.

1857 GRINNELL, ART. "Quoddy power." Down East, 22 (May, 1976), 70-73, 99-100, 103.

1858 HAMMOND, ROBERT B. An era to remember: a historical sketch of the shipbuilding industry in West Washington County. [Harrington?], 1972. Pp. 102. Me.

1859 HEBERT, RICHARD A. "Eastport and Lubec." Pine Cone, 2 (Spring, 1946), 15-18.

1860 KEELER, SETH HARRISON. A semi-centennial discourse delivered in Calais, Maine, June 3, 1879, in memory of the organization of the Washington County Conference of Congregational Churches organized at Eastport, February 13, 1829. Calais: J. A. Sears, [1879]. Pp. 24. MeHi.

1861 KILBY, CYRUS HAMLIN. "Incidents at the settlement of Dennysville and Edmunds in Washington County." MHGR, 8 (1895), 218-223; 9 (1898), 11-18.

1862 THE LOGGERS: or six months in the forests of Maine. Boston: H. B. Fuller, 1870. Pp. 75.

1863 MACHIASPORT HISTORICAL SOCIETY. The Whitneyville and Machiasport Railroad. [Machiasport, 1976?]. Pp. 20. MeHi.

1864 MILLIKEN, JAMES ALPHONSO. The Narraguagus Valley: some account of its early settlement and settlers. Machias: C. O. Furbush, [1886]. Pp. 24.

1865 MITCHELL, HARRY EDWARD and EDWARD MELVIN CAMPBELL, comps. The Addison and Harrington register, 1905. Brunswick: H. E. Mitchell, 1905. Pp. 126.
Contains sketches of the early history of both towns.

1866 MURCHIE, GUY. Saint Croix, the sentinel river: historical sketches of its discovery, early conflicts and final occupation by English and American settlers, with some comments on Indian life. N.Y.: Duell, Sloan and Pearce, 1947. Pp. 281.

1867 NEAL, BEN. "Early days in the wildcat district." Down East, 18 (November, 1971), 13-14, 17-20.
Hunting.

1868 "REPRESENTATIVES from Washington County, 1820-1851." BHistMag, 4 (1888-1889), 105-109.
A chronological listing.

1869 SAYLOR, JOHN P. "Passamaquoddy boondoggle." Public Utilities Fortnightly, 74 (January 17, 1963), 15-22.

1870 "SENATORS from Washington County, 1820-1852." BHistMag, 4 (1888-1889), 16.
A chronological listing.

1871 "SETTLEMENT of the Maine border." Americana, 6 (1911), 27-31.

1872 SMITH, LINCOLN. "Tidal power in Maine." Land Economics, 24 (1948), 239-252.
Passamaquoddy Tidal Project, 1920-1947.

1873 TODD, WILLIAM. Todds of the St. Croix valley. Mount Carmel, Conn., 1943. Pp. 24.

1874 VROOM, JAMES. "The Fenians on the St. Croix." Canadian Magazine, 10 (1897-1898), 411-413.
In vicinity of Eastport and Calais.

1875 WILLEY, A. S. Historical sketch of Cherryfield and Harrington.... Machias: C. O. Furbush, 1893. Pp. 49. Me.

1876 WINTER, CARL GEORGE. "A note on the Passamaquoddy boundary affair." CanHistRev, 34 (1953), 46-53.
Line through the Bay, 1908-1910.

SEE ALSO entries 108, 686, and 1251.

YORK COUNTY

1877 ANDREWS, RALPH. Index to the probate records of the county of York, Maine, from January 1, 1917 to January 1, 1949. Saco: Reny Bros., 1950. Pp. 497.
A copy is in the York County Probate Office, Alfred, Maine.

1878 BAER, ANNIE WENTWORTH. "Early farming." Old Eliot, 8 (1908), 33-42.

1879 YORK COUNTY

1879 BARTLETT, RALPH SYLVESTER. The history of York County, Maine, and a rambling narrative about the town of Eliot and its mother-town old Kittery, with personal reminiscences: an address delivered by Ralph Sylvester Bartlett at exercised held in Eliot, Maine, August 29, 1936, in commemoration of the 300th anniversary of the founding of York County in the Province of Maine. Boston: Jerome Pr., 1938. Pp. 21.

1880 BECKFORD, WILLIAM HALE. Leading business men of Kennebunkport, Kennebunk and Old Orchard Beach, with an historical sketch of each place. Boston: Mercantile Publishing, 1888. Pp. 62.

1881 "BIDDEFORD and Saco." Sun Up, 19 (March, 1931), 10-13.

1882 BIOGRAPHICAL review: this volume contains biographical sketches of leading citizens of York County, Maine.... Boston: Biographical Review Publishing, 1896. Pp. 619.

1883 BOURNE, EDWARD EMERSON, 1797-1873. "Garrison houses, York County." MeHSC, 7 (1876), 107-120.

1884 _____. The history of Wells and Kennebunk from the earliest settlement to the year 1820, at which time Kennebunk was set off, and and incorporated; with biographical sketches. Edward E. Bourne, Jr., ed. Portland: B. Thurston, 1875. Pp. xxiii, 797.

1885 BUTLER, JOYCE. "Canoes on the Kennebec." Down East, 20 (July, 1974), 72-75.

1886 CLAYTON, W. WOODFORD. History of York County, Maine: with illustrations and biographical sketches of its prominent men and pioneers.... Philadelphia: Everts & Peck, 1880. Pp. 442.
    Includes a roster of Civil War soldiers from York County.

1887 CONGREGATIONAL CHURCHES IN MAINE. YORK COUNTY CONFERENCE. Semi-centennial of York County Conference, Buxton, Maine, June 4 and 5, 1872; papers there read, and sketches of the Congregational churches in the county, with notes appended down to the present time, June, 1876. John D. Emerson and Benjamin P. Snow, eds. Portland: Hoyt, Fogg & Donham, 1876. Pp. 119.

1888 COOK, JULIA ANNA. "Black Thursday." Yankee, 31 (October, 1967), 102-103, 128-130, 133-137.
    Forest fire of October 23, 1947.

1889 CREDIFORD, ANNIE JOYCE. ["History of the press in York County."] MPAP, 47 (1910), 13; 48 (1911), 31; 49 (1912), 27-28; 50 (1913) 29-30; 51 (1914), 28; 52 (1915), 14-15.

1890 CUMMINGS, OSMOND RICHARD. The Biddeford and Saco Railroad. Chicago: Electric Railway Historical Society, 1956. Pp. 35. MeBa.

1891 DEXTER, FRANK HENRY ["History of the press in York County."] MPAP, 27 (1890), 34; 28 (1891), 30-31; 29 (1892), 27; 30 (1893), 34; 31 (1894), 24-25; 33 (1896), 39-40; 34 (1897), 36-37; 35 (1898), 26; 37 (1900), 40; 39 (1902), 39-40; 40 (1903), 40-41.

1892 ELWELL, EDWARD HENRY. ["History of the press in York County."] MPAP, 25 (1888), 31-33; 26 (1889), 39.

1893 FOLSOM, GEORGE. History of Saco and Biddeford.... (1830) Somersworth, N.H.: New Hampshire Publishing, 1975. Pp. 331.
    This reprint contains a new foreword by Robert E. Moody and an index prepared in 1922 by Frank C. Deering.

1894 GOULD, NATHAN. "Col. James Scamman's 30th Regiment of foot, 1775." MeHSC, 2 Ser., 10 (1899), 337-402.

1895 "HOSPITALS in York County." Sun Up, 3 (August, 1927), 68.

1896 JOY, KENNETH. The Kennebunks: out of the past. Freeport: Bond Wheelwright, 1967. Pp. xvi, 135.
    Kennebunk and Kennebunkport.

1897 KEEFE, FRANCIS. "Some of the earlier dwellers on the long reach of the Piscataqua River." Old Eliot, 1 (1897), 45-61.

1898 MORANG, BRUCE. Journal of the Kennebunks. [Kennebunk]: Kennebunk Journal, [1952?]. Unpaged. Me.
    Kennebunk and Kennebunkport.

1898A MORGAN, CHARLES S. Shipbuilding on the Kennebunk, the closing chapter; adapted from an address ... to the [Historical] Society [of Kennebunkport] on the occasion of its first public meeting, February 15, 1952. Kennebunkport, [1952]. Pp. 40.

1899 MOUNTFORT, JULIA ANN DYKE and KATHERINE EASTMAN MARSHALL. Witch trot land; being a bit about the mother of Maine, York County, or Yorkshire, or New Somersetshire, from which all Maine counties came, of her hopes and dreams and heartbreaks, and of the first incorporated English city in America.... Damariscotta: Lincoln County News, 1937. Pp. 43.

1900 MURRAY, JOHN CHICK. History of the Grange in York County.... Sanford: Averill Pr., 1922. Pp. 154.

1901 PEPPERELL MANUFACTURING COMPANY. The romance of Pepperell, being a brief account of the career of Sir William Pepperell, soldier, pioneer, American merchant and developer of New England industry, for whom the Pepperell Manufacturing Company was named, and of the towns of Saco and Biddeford in the State of Maine, wherein the first manufacturing unit of the Pepperell Company was established. Boston, 1943. Pp. 48.

1902 PERKINS, ESSELYN GILMAN. Billowing sails. Portland: House of Falmouth, 1947. Pp. 90.
   Shipbuilding.

1903 PERRY, ADELAIDE E. York County. Portland: Gross and Allen, [1971]. Pp. 72. MeU.

1904 PEVERLY, ELAINE M. and WILLIAM H. McLIN. "The Old Orchard 'dummy line.'" Down East, 19 (September, 1972), 74-75.
   Orchard Beach Railroad; Old Orchard to Camp Ellis.

1905 RANDEL, WILLIAM PEIRCE. "Town names of York County, Maine." NEQ, 11 (1938), 565-575.

1906 REMICK, OLIVER PHILBRICK. "Piscataqua Pioneers." Old Eliot, 9 (1909), 1-8.
   An historical society.

1907 _____. A record of the services of the commissioned officers and enlisted men of Kittery and Eliot, Maine, who served their country on land and sea in the American Revolution, from 1775 to 1783. Boston: A. Mudge & Son, 1901. Pp. 223.

1908 SAMUELS, HARRIET BROCKMAN. A Maine county, rich in beauty and historic lore. [Princeton?, N.J.], 1961. Pp. 39.

1909 SHAPLEIGH, CHARLES A. "Glances at people and localities." Old Eliot, 9 (1909), 30-33.

1910 TAYLOR, HELEN V. A time to recall: the delights of a Maine childhood. N.Y.: Norton, 1963. Pp. 224.

1911 THOMPSON, RALPH E. and MATTHEW R. THOMPSON. Pascataway: de facto capital of New England, 1623-1630. Monmouth, Oregon, 1973. Pp. 58.
   Berwick, Eliot, Kittery, and South Berwick.

1912 TITCOMB, EDWARD S. Index to the probate records of the county of York, Maine, from January 1, 1901, to January 1, 1917. [Biddeford]: Biddeford Journal, 1918. Pp. 220.
   A copy is in the York County Probate Office, Alfred, Maine.

1913 YORK CO., ME. REGISTER OF DEEDS. York deeds. Portland: John T. Hull, 1887-1896; Bethel, 1903-1910. 18 v. in 19.
   Covers 1642-1737; detailed indexes of grantors, grantees, and other persons; imprint varies.

   SEE ALSO entries 602, 978, and 1045.

Cities, Towns, and Other Civil Divisions

ABBOT (PISCATAQUIS CO.)

1914   "THE MOOSE horn sign in Abbot, Maine." SJMH,
2 (1914-1913), 194-201.
      Town history.

SEE ALSO entry 1782.

ACTON (YORK CO.)

1915   BRACKETT, MURIEL. Pine cones and forget me
nots. n.p., [1951?]. 4v. MeHi.

1916   FULLONTON, JOSEPH. The history of Acton,
Me. Dover, N.H.: William Burr, 1847.
Pp. iv, 36.

ADAMSTOWN TOWNSHIP (OXFORD CO.)

1917   No items located.

ADDISON (WASHINGTON CO.)

1918   SEE entries 549 and 1865.

ALBANY TOWNSHIP (OXFORD CO.)

1919   BALL, WILBUR I. "The Albany sesquicentennial." MeCP, 40 (October 15, 1953), 8.
      Congregational church.

1920   PERRY, TRUEMAN SUMMERFIELD. A hundred years:
historical address delivered at the centennial of the Congregational Church in Albany,
Maine. Bethel: E. C. Bowler, 1903. Pp. 14.
MBC.

ALBION (KENNEBEC CO.)

1921   WIGGIN, RUBY CROSBY. Albion on the Narrow
Gauge. [Clinton?], 1964. Pp. 282.
      Wiscasset, Waterville & Farmington Railroad.

SEE ALSO entry 1645.

ALDER BROOK TOWNSHIP (SOMERSET CO.)

1922   No items located.

ALDER STREAM TOWNSHIP (FRANKLIN CO.)

1923   No items located.

ALEXANDER (WASHINGTON CO.)

1924   No items located.

ALFRED (YORK CO.)

1925   "THE ALFRED Shakers." MeLB, 16 (1930-1931),
111-112 [i.e. 17 (1931-1932), 3-4].

1926   BARKER, R. MILDRED. "A history of 'Holy
Land'--Alfred, Maine." Shaker Quarterly, 3
(1963), 75-95, 107-127.

1927   BRADLEE, CHARLES W. Historical sermon, delivered at the semi-centennial celebration of
Methodism at Alfred, Maine, December 14th,
1879. Bridgton: H. S. Shorey, 1880. Pp. 16.
MeBa.

1928   DANE, MARY ELIZABETH. Alfred. n.p., [191-?].
Pp. 7.

1929   JOHNSON, THEODORE ELLIOT, comp. "A complete
register of deaths which have occurred in the
United Society of Believers, Alfred, Maine
1790-1931." Shaker Quarterly, 1 (1961), 168-
178.

1930   KELLEY, MARY CARPENTER. "When the Shaker
sisters made soap." Down East, 11 (May, 1965),
26-29.

1931   PARSONS, USHER. A centennial history of Alfred, York County, Maine, with a supplement by
Samuel M. Came. Philadelphia: Sanford, Everts, 1872. Pp. 36.

1932   PARSONS MEMORIAL LIBRARY, ALFRED, ME. Par-
        sons Memorial Library, Alfred, Maine. [Al-
        fred, 1905?]. Pp. 46.

1933   PERKINS, LUCIUS M. "How the town of Alfred
        disposed of its share of the U.S. revenue
        surplus, 1836-7." SJMH, 6 (1918-1919), 72-
        73.

1934   ST. JOHN, FREDERIC. "Alfred." Maine's Own
        Magazine 8 (May and June, 1930), 16, 29.
        Author's name is a pseudonym.

ALLAGASH PLANTATION (AROOSTOOK CO.)

1935   DIETZ, LEW. "The 'lost' settlement of the
        Allagash." Down East, 14 (October, 1967),
        26-29, 56, 58.

1935A   KELLEY, EDITH. Bits and pieces of Allagash
        history. Madawaska: St. John Valley Print-
        ers, 1976. Pp. 28. [MeMaHi.]

ALNA (LINCOLN CO.)

1936   BROWN, FRANK CHOUTEAU. "The Congregational
        Church at Head Tide, Maine." OTNE, 30 (1939-
        1940), 95-100.

1937   CUMMINGS, RANDALL FREDERICK. Elementary
        school history of Alna, Dresden, Edgecomb,
        Pittston, Wiscasset, State of Maine. [North
        Edgecomb, 1933]. Pp. 86.

1938   MERRY, EDWIN D. "Captain Jote Jones--scowman
        out of Puddle Dock." Down East, 21 (June,
        1975), 60-61, 79-81.

1939   SEWALL, RUFUS KING. Centennial memorial serv-
        ices of old Alna meetinghouse, Alna, Maine,
        September 11, 1889. Wiscasset: Emerson,
        1896. Pp. 24.

        SEE ALSO entries 1677, 1704, and 1706.

ALTON (PENOBSCOT CO.)

1940   No items located.

AMHERSET (HANCOCK CO.)

1941   JELLISON, CONSTANCE HANSCOM. Amherst, Maine,
        her settlement and her people, 1790-1975.
        [Bar Harbor]: Bar Harbor Times, 1975.
        Pp. 116. Me.

AMITY (AROOSTOOK CO.)

1942   No items located.

ANDOVER (OXFORD CO.)

1943   No items located.

ANDOVER NORTH SURPLUS (OXFORD CO.)

1944   No items located.

ANDOVER WEST SURPLUS (OXFORD CO.)

1945   No items located.

ANSON (SOMERSET CO.)

1946   ANSON ACADEMY. Anson Academy centennial,
        1823-1923. Lewiston: Journal Printshop
        and Bindery, [1923]. Pp. 72. MeHi.

1947   MOORE, ALBERT. History of Northern Star
        Lodge, No. 28, of Free and Accepted Masons,
        North Anson, Me. North Anson, 1875. Pp. 35.
        MeBa.

        SEE ALSO entry 3362.

APPLETON (KNOX CO.)

1948   No items located.

APPLETON TOWNSHIP (SOMERSET CO.)

1949   No items located.

ARGYLE TOWNSHIP (PENOBSCOT CO.)

1950   SEE entry 1733.

ARROWSIC (SAGADAHOC CO.)

1951   "ARROWSIC Island." BHistMag, 3 (1887-1888),
        41-44.

ARUNDEL (YORK CO.)

1952   No items located.

ASHLAND (AROOSTOOK CO.)

1953   No items located.

ATHENS (SOMERSET CO.)

1954   ATHENS VICTORY CLUB. A historical sketch of Athens, Maine commemorative of its sesquicentennial, July 2-5, 1804-1954. Skowhegan: Skowhegan Pr., 1954. Pp. 44. Me.

1955   JONES, MRS. C. H. Brief historical sketch of Athens, Maine, commemorative of its centennial observance on Wednesday, June 22nd, 1904. Skowhegan: J. O. Smith, [1904]. Pp. 19. MBNEH.

1956   SOMERSET ACADEMY, ATHENS, ME. Somerset Academy, a brief statement of its history, condition and need. n.p., [1933]. Pp. 11. MeHi.

ATKINSON (PISCATAQUIS CO.)

1957   CROSBY, S. P. "Notes on the Crosby family and a sketch of the life of Josiah Crosby." PCHSC, 1 (1910), 204-215.

ATTEAN TOWNSHIP (SOMERSET CO.)

1958   No items located.

AUBURN (ANDROSCOGGIN CO.)

1959   AUBURN, ME. ELM STREET UNIVERSALIST PARISH. Semi-centennial exercises of the Elm Street Universalist Parish, Auburn, Maine, February 11th, 12th and 13th, 1879, historical address by Rev. William R. French, poem by Mrs. Mary Salina Read. Lewiston: Geo. A. Callahan, 1879. Pp. 14.

1960   "AUBURN, the shire town of Androscoggin County." BTJ, 25 (1912-1913), 523, 525, 527.

1961   BANKS, ELIAS. "Historical sketch of Danville, Me." MHGR, 5 (1888), 12-16.

1962   BARRON, EARL T. "St. Michael's Church, Auburn." The Northeast, 71 (Pentecost, 1944), 2-4.

1963   BLOUNT, EDWARD F. Historical notes on the construction of the First Universalist Church, Auburn, Maine, one hundred years ago. Auburn: First Universalist Church, 1976. Pp. 23. MeHi.

1964   KELLY, FRANCIS R. "Seventy-fifth anniversary of [the] Sixth Street Congregational Church." MeCP, 146 (October, 1950), 28.

1965   LEPAGE, REGIS A. Seventy years of quality: the F. R. Lepage Bakery, Inc. N.Y.: Newcomen Society in North America, 1973. Pp. 20.

1966   MARTIN, ROBERT. History of Tranquil Lodge, No. 29, F. & A. M., Auburn, Maine. Lewiston: Geo. A. Callahan, 1876. Pp. 40.

1967   MORRILL, JOHN ADAMS. Historical address on the occasion of the one hundredth anniversary of the High Street Congregational Church, Auburn, Maine, Sunday, June 13, 1926. n.p., [1926]. Pp. 57. MeHi.

1968   [NORRIS, JANE P.] Mechanic Savings Bank, one hundred years of growth, 1875-1975. n.p., [1975]. Unpaged. MeHi.
   Author attribution by the Maine Historical Society.

1969   SKINNER, RALPH BURGESS, JOHN E. LIBBY and DAPHNE WINSLOW MERRILL. 1869--Auburn--1969: 100 years a city; a study in community growth. Lewiston: Twin City Printery, 1968. Pp. 410.

1970   WING, GEORGE CURTIS. Auburn, Maine, "Fifty years a city," address delivered ... September 12, 1919. [Auburn]: Auburn Chamber of Commerce, [1919]. Unpaged. MB.

   SEE ALSO entries 1422, 1424, 1426-1427, 1431-1432, 1434, and 3532.

AUGUSTA (KENNEBEC CO.)

1971   ALLEN, JOSHUA. "Mortality in Augusta, Maine, 1852-1855." MeHSC, 5 (1857), 431-435.

1972   AUGUSTA, ME. ALL SOULS CHURCH (UNITARIAN). Centennial services, 1826-1926, combined with "The first seventy-five years," by Hon. Leslie C. Cornish, Augusta, Maine, January 10, 1926. Augusta, [1926]. Pp. 30.

1973   AUGUSTA, ME. SESQUICENTENNIAL COMMITTEE. The romance of Augusta, 1797-1947. [Augusta]: Augusta Pr., [1947]. Unpaged. Me.

1974   AUGUSTA, ME. SOUTH PARISH CONGREGATIONAL CHURCH. The articles of faith and covenant of the South Congregational Church in Augusta, adopted January, 1874, with a list of the members from 1794 to 1874. Augusta: Sprague, Owen & Nash, 1874. Pp. 72.
   Includes a brief historical sketch.

1975   _____. Dedicatory exercises of the chapel and church home of the Congregational Church and Society, Dec. 17, 1890. Augusta: Maine Farmers' Almanac, 1891. Pp. 48.
   Includes history by Charles E. Nash.

1976   AUGUSTA SAVINGS BANK. 1848. 1898. Fiftieth anniversary of the Augusta Savings Bank, September 29, 1898.... Augusta: Maine Farmer Publishing, 1898. Pp. 30.

1977   _____. Seventy-fifth anniversary 1848-1923 ... September 29, 1923. [Augusta, 1923]. Unpaged.

1978 AUGUSTA

1978 "THE AWAKENING of an old parish." MeCathHM, 3 (November, 1914), 37-42.
St. Mary's Church.

1979 BALLARD, EDWARD. "Augusta: at Small Point Harbor." Northern Monthly, 1 (1864), 475-478.

1980 BASSETT, NORMAN L. "History of the Blaine Mansion." SJMH, 8 (1920), 196-201.

1981 BECK, JOSEPH T. Historical notes on Augusta, Maine. Farmington: Knowlton & McLeary, 1962-1963. 2v.

1982 "BLAINE House." MeLB, 15 (1929-1930), 79-82.

1983 BOARDMAN, SAMUEL LANE. "A chapter in the history of ancient Cushnoc--now Augusta." MeHSC, 3 Ser., 2 (1906), 310-330.

1984 BOWLES, ELLA SHANNON. "Augusta, city of personalities." Yankee, 2 (January, 1936), 19-23.

1985 BUTLER, BENJAMIN and NATALIE STURGES BUTLER. "Pilgrim traders on the Kennebec." Mayflower Quarterly, 41 (1975), 117-120.

1986 CHURCHILL, EDWIN A. "Fort Western: a reading bibliography." Friends of Fort Western Newsletter, 2 (May, 1976), 1.

1987 LE CLUB CALUMET, INC. Semicentennial celebration history, 1922-1972, fifty years of progress. Augusta: K. J. Litho, 1972. Pp. 70. Me.

1988 CUMMINGS, OSMOND RICHARD. "Trolleys to Augusta, Maine." Transportation Bulletin, No. 76 (January-August, 1969), 1-52.

1989 CURTIS, SILAS. Sermon preached at the dedication of the Free Will Baptist Meeting House, Augusta, Maine, Thursday, November 3, 1853. Augusta: Russell Eaton, 1853. Pp. 46.
Includes a brief history of the Free Will Baptists in Augusta.

1990 DEMERS, MABEL GOULD. "Doorways and beyond." Pine Cone, 3 (Autumn, 1947), 33-37.
Reuel Williams House.

1991 DOW, GEORGE FRANCIS. Fort Western on the Kennebec: the story of its construction in 1754 and what has happened there. Augusta: Gannett, 1922. Pp. 59.

1992 DOW, STERLING THAYER. "Hallowell Court House post office--Maine." Mekeel's Weekly Stamp News, 67 (July 15, 1946), 51.

1993 DROWN, EDWARD S. "There was war in heaven." NEQ, 4 (1931), 30-53.
1840, South Parish Congregational Church.

1994 FEDERAL WRITERS' PROJECT. MAINE. Maine's capitol. Augusta: Kennebec Journal Print Shop, 1939. Pp. 60.

1995 FISH, JOHN L. "Side-light on ancient local history and modern spiritualism in the Kennebec region." SJMH, 14 (1926), 146-151.
Execution of Joseph Sanger, convicted of murdering his wife Phoebe, 1836.

1996 "FORT Western." Down East, 7 (September, 1960), 42-45.

1997 HAMLEN, EWING W. "Augusta, the capital of Maine." NEM, New Ser., 14 (1896), 195-213.

1998 HAWES, HILDRETH GILMAN. "Augusta--past and present." Maine's Own Magazine, 7 (July, 1929), 9.

1999 HENDERSON, RUTH. "Augusta--Maine's executive city and a beautifully located community." Sun Up, 3 (June, 1927), 11-27.

2000 HILL, HENRY FRANCIS, JR. Augusta's city hall and city government, 1797-1968. Augusta, 1968. 6 leaves. Me.

2001 _____. Remembrances, etc., of Gannett's Woods, Augusta, Maine. Augusta, 1966. 14 leaves. Me.

2002 "HISTORY of the State House." MeLB, 6 (1916-1917), 115.

2003 HUNT, HARRY DRAPER. The Blaine House: home of Maine's governors. Somersworth, N.H.: New Hampshire Publishing, 1974. Pp. 136.

2004 HUNT, ISAAC H. Astounding disclosures! Three years in a mad house. By a victim. Written by himself. A true account of the barbarous, inhuman and cruel treatment of Isaac H. Hunt, in the Maine Insane Hospital, in the years 1844, '45, '46, and '47, by Drs. Isaac Ray, James Bates, and their assistants and attendants.... Skowhegan: Amos Angier Mann, 1851. Pp. 84.

2005 JONES, HERBERT GRANVILLE. Koussinoc, the Indian trading post, address given for Daughters of Colonial Wars, Portland, Maine, August, 1928. [Portland, 1938.] Pp. 12.

2006 KENNEBEC JOURNAL. Augusta centennial souvenir, June 9, 1897. [Augusta, 1897.] Pp. 63. Me.

2007 "LIBRARY service in Maine." Sun Up, 3 (February, 1927), 4, 28, 30.
Maine State Library.

2008 LITHGOW LIBRARY AND READING ROOM, AUGUSTA, ME. The Lithgow Library and Reading Room, Augusta, Maine. Augusta: Maine Farmers' Almanac Pr., 1897. Pp. 174.

2009 LOVETT, ROBERT WOODBERRY. "Publisher and advertiser extraordinary: the E. C. Allen Collection." BBHS, 24 (1950), 210-215.
E. C. Allen Co., 1871-1895; collection is at Baker Library, Harvard University.

2010 McLANATHAN, RICHARD B. K. "Bulfinch's drawings for the Maine State House." SocArch HistJ, 14 (May, 1955), 12-17.

2011 MAINE. STATE HOSPITAL, AUGUSTA. Augusta State Hospital, established October 14, 1840. [Augusta?, 1965]. Pp. 55.

2012 _____. With the years. Thorndike: Hutchins Bros., [1938?]. Pp. 77. MeHi.
History of the hospital, nursing school, and Nurses' Alumni Association.

2013 "THE MAINE State Library, 1839/1970." Maine. State Library. Biennial Report, 60 (1968-1970), entire issue.

2014 MASON, EDWARD G. "The presidential campaign of 1884 in Mr. Blaine's home city." NEM, New Ser., 24 (1901), 248-257.

2015 MOORE, KATRINA. "Blaine House." Down East, 5 (May, 1959), 24-25, 36, 39.

2016 NASH, CHARLES ELVENTON. The history of Augusta: first settlements and early days as a town, including the diary of Mrs. Martha Moore Ballard, 1785 to 1812. Augusta: Charles E. Nash & Son, 1904 [i.e. 1961]. Pp. vii, 612.
Signatures printed in 1904, first published in 1961.

2017 NEWBERT, E. E. "Outline history of the Unitarian Church of Augusta." The Church Exchange, 4 (1896-1897), 34-35.

2018 NORTH, JAMES WILLIAM. The history of Augusta, from the earliest settlement to the present time; with notices of the Plymouth Company, and settlements on the Kennebec; together with biographical sketches and genealogical register. Augusta: Clapp and North, 1870. Pp. xii, 990.

2019 PARTRIDGE, CORA PRESSON. "Maine state capitol." DARMag, 69 (1935), 390.

2020 PÉLADEAU, MARIUS B. "Guardian of the northern frontier: the Kennebec Arsenal." Down East, 23 (September, 1976), 60-63, 82.

2021 [PIERCE, HARRY H.] A short history of Augusta. Augusta: J. Frank Pierce Store, [1931]. Pp. 20. Me.

2022 ST. JOHN, FREDERIC. "Fort Western." Sun Up, 8 (December, 1930), 18.
Author's name is a pseudonym.

2023 SANFORD, LEWIS W. "Brief history of the All Souls Church (Unitarian) of Augusta." The Maine Church Exchange, No. 20 (September, 1944), Inside of front cover and page 1.

2024 SAYWARD, DOROTHY STEWARD. Comfort Magazine, 1888-1942: a history and critical study. Orono: Univ. of Maine, 1960. Pp. 108.

2025 SHUTE, ALBERTA VAN HORN. A year and a day along Bond Brook. South Windham: Living Word Pr., 1954. Pp. 80.

2026 _____. A year and a day in the park. Litchfield: Living Word Pr., 1956. Pp. 40. MeP.

2027 SMITH, EDGAR CROSBY. "The State of Maine burying ground." SJMH, 8 (1920), 30-33.

2028 "THE SOUTH Parish Congregational Church of Augusta." MeCP, 52 (April, 1965), 3.

2029 "THE STATE House, Augusta." BHistMag, 2 (1886-1887), 145-150.

2030 STUBBS, MARION BRAINERD. Centennial anniversary program and historical sketch of Green Street Methodist Episcopal Church, Augusta, Maine, November 11-14, 1928. n.p., 1928. Pp. 12. Me.

2031 TRUE, MRS. HILTON W. Quarto-centenary history, Unity Club, Augusta, Maine. Augusta: Journal Print, [1905]. Unpaged. Me.

2032 UPJOHN, SAMUEL. A sermon preached in St. Mark's Church, Augusta, Me., on the Sunday Next Before Advent, November 25, 1883. Augusta: Sprague & Son, 1883. Pp. 15. Me.
Relates to the church.

2033 WESTON, NATHAN. Oration at the centennial celebration of the erection of Fort Western, on the anniversary of American independence, July 4, 1854. Augusta: William H. Simpson, 1854. Pp. 23.

2034 WILLIAMSON, JOSEPH. "The first Democratic State Convention in Maine during the Rebellion." MeHSC, 3 Ser., 2 (1906), 279-284. 1861.

2035 "YACHTING on the Kennebec." BTJ, 24 (1911-1912), 574-575.
Augusta Yacht Club.

SEE ALSO entries 143, 556, 1637, 1650, and 3532.

AURORA (HANCOCK CO.)

2036 SILSBY, HERBERT T., II. A history of Aurora, Maine.... Ellsworth: Hancock Publishing, 1958. Pp. 159.

AVON (FRANKLIN CO.)

2037   SEE entry 1419.

BAILEYVILLE (WASHINGTON CO.)

2038   BAILEY, ALBERT W. History: early Bailey-
        ville, Maine, and its pioneers.... Calais:
        Calais Advertiser Pr., 1972. Pp. 100.

2039   BRUMMITT, HOWARD. "Love and labor serve the
        Lord: thirty-five years in Eastern Maine."
        The Northeast, 78 (May, 1951), 5-7.
           St. Luke's Church.

2040   OBER, GRACE M. Some history of Woodland:
        the village in Baileyville. Calais: Adver-
        tiser Publishing, 1975. Pp. 108. MeU.

BALD MOUNTAIN TOWNSHIP (SOMERSET CO.)

2041   No items located; there are two unorganized
        townships by this name in Somerset County.

BALDWIN (CUMBERLAND CO.)

2042   BALDWIN, ME. Souvenir of Baldwin, Maine,
        1912. Brunswick: Maine Map & Register,
        1912. Pp. 39. Me.
           Includes historical sketch.

BANCROFT (AROOSTOOK CO.)

2043   No items located.

BANGOR (PENOBSCOT CO.)

2044   ADAMS, WILLIAM CUSHING. "Memories and appre-
        ciations of Bangor Theological Seminary pro-
        fessors, 1886-1936." The Alumni Bulletin of
        Bangor Theological Seminary, 11 (January,
        1937), 1-3, 7-8.

2045   "ANCIENT Norombega." BHistMag, 6 (1890-1891),
        49.
           Supposedly Bangor.

2046   ART work of Bangor, Maine. Chicago: W. H.
        Parish, 1895. Unpaged. MeU.

2047   BACON, GEORGE FOX. Bangor: its points of
        interest and its representative business men;
        including an historical sketch of Brewer.
        Newark, N.J.: Glenwood Publishing, 1891.
        Pp. 95.

2048   BANGOR, ME. The centennial celebration of
        the settlement of Bangor, September 30, 1869.
        Bangor: Benjamin A. Burr, 1870. Pp. 182.
           Historical address by John Edwards Godfrey.

2049   _____. City councils and mayors, from incor-
        poration of the city, in 1834 to 1881....
        Bangor: B. A. Burr, 1881. Pp. 50. MeBa.

2050   BANGOR, ME. BOARD OF TRADE. The city of
        Bangor, "Queen City of the East," a condensed
        historical and descriptive review, together
        with a brief statement of facts relating to
        her commercial and manufacturing advantage
        ... for the year 1882. Bangor, 1883. Pp. 36.

2051   BANGOR, ME. CENTRAL CONGREGATIONAL CHURCH.
        Central Congregational Church, Bangor, Maine,
        1847-1912: historical address delivered
        January 24, 1912, by Edward Mitchell Bland-
        ing.... Bangor, 1912. Pp. 31. MeBa.

2052   BANGOR, ME. CHAMBER OF COMMERCE. Historic
        Bangor.... Bangor, 1940. Pp. 13. MeBa.

2053   BANGOR, ME. CONGREGATION BETH ISRAEL. Dia-
        mond jubilee, 1888-1963. Henry H. Segal,
        ed. Bangor: Furbush-Roberts, [1963].
        Pp. 163.

2054   BANGOR, ME. FIRST BAPTIST CHURCH. Semicen-
        tennial anniversary of the First Baptist
        Church, Bangor, January 25, 1868. Bangor:
        Wheeler & Lynde, 1868. Pp. 34. MeBa.
           Historical discourse by Albion K. P. Small.

2055   BANGOR, ME. FIRST CONGREGATIONAL CHURCH.
        Historical sketch of the First Congregational
        Church, Bangor, Maine, 1811-1911. Bangor:
        Ira H. Joy, 1911. Pp. 46.

2056   BANGOR, ME. FIRST METHODIST EPISCOPAL CHURCH.
        Centennial anniversary, First Methodist Epis-
        copal Church, Bangor, Maine, 1837-1937....
        n.p., [1937]. Pp. 28. MeBa.

2057   BANGOR, ME. FIRST UNIVERSALIST CHURCH. High-
        lights of the history of the First Universal-
        ist Church and Society. n.p., 1961. Unpaged.

2058   BANGOR, ME. HAMMOND STREET CONGREGATIONAL
        CHURCH. Seventy-fifth anniversary, December 6,
        8, 9, 1908. n.p., 1908. Unpaged.

2059   NO ENTRY.

2060   BANGOR, ME. ST. GEORGE GREEK ORTHODOX CHURCH.
        Fortieth anniversary and history. n.p., 1967.
        Unpaged.

2061   BANGOR, ME. ST. JOHN'S CATHOLIC CHURCH. The
        story of St. John's, 1856-1906. [Bangor,
        1906]. Unpaged. MeBa.

2062 BANGOR, ME. ST. MARY'S CATHOLIC CHURCH. The bells of St. Mary's.... n.p., 1967. Unpaged.

2063 _____. St. Mary's Church, Bangor, Me., 1872-1972, 100 years of faith. n.p., 1972. Unpaged. MeBa.

2064 BANGOR, ME. SECOND BAPTIST CHURCH. Jubilee of the Second Baptist Church, of Bangor; historical discourse by the pastor, George B. Ilsley and poem by Ellen Hamlin Butler, Thursday eve, Sept. 12, at the First Baptist's house of worship. Bangor, 1895. Pp. 12. MeBa.

2065 BANGOR, ME. WATER DEPARTMENT. History of the Bangor Water Works, from its commencement, while under the charge of the first board of water commissioners. Bangor: Burr & Robinson, 1877. Pp. 64. MeBa.

2066 NO ENTRY.

2067 NO ENTRY.

2068 NO ENTRY.

2069 BANGOR CHILDREN'S HOME. Historical sketch of the Bangor Female Orphan Asylum, 1868. Bangor: Smith & Hill, 1868. Pp. 23. MeBa.

2070 BANGOR DAILY NEWS. A bicentennial look at bygone Bangor. Bangor, 1976. Pp. 52. Me.

2071 BANGOR HEBREW COMMUNITY CENTER. Dedication of the Bangor Hebrew Community Center at the Liss Memorial Building, September 18, 1938. Bangor, [1938]. Pp. 24. MeBa.
      Includes a history of the settlement of the Jews in Bangor by Catherine Epstein and Lucille Epstein.

2072 BANGOR HEBREW SCHOOL. Fortieth anniversary, 1907-1947.... n.p., [1947]. Pp. 36. MeBa.
      Includes history by Mrs. Lawrence Cutler.

2073 BANGOR HISTORICAL SOCIETY. Fiftieth anniversary of the Bangor Historical Society: proceedings at the Bangor Public Library, Wednesday, April 8th, 1914. Bangor, 1914. Pp. 88.
      Historical address by Edward Mitchell Blanding.

2074 "THE BANGOR House." BTJ, 25 (1912-1913), 253.
      Hotel.

2075 BANGOR, Maine, a city of progress. Bangor: C. H. Glass, [1912?]. Pp. 32.

2076 BANGOR MECHANIC ASSOCIATION. [Historical sketch]. n.p., 1929. Unpaged. MeBa.

2077 BANGOR SAVINGS BANK. Rounding out a century, 1852-1952. Bangor, [1952?]. Pp. 32. MeBa.

2078 "BANGOR: the lumber trade." Merchant's Magazine and Commercial Review, 18 (1848), 517-520.
      Includes chronological table of output.

2079 BANGOR THEOLOGICAL SEMINARY. Historical catalogue of Bangor Theological Seminary.... [Bangor], 1928. 2 v. in 1.

2080 NO ENTRY.

2081 BARWISE, MARK A. "Sources of land title in Bangor." Maine Law Review, 10 (1916-1917), 201-209.

2082 BECKFORD, WILLIAM HALE and GEORGE W. RICHARDSON. Leading business men of Bangor, Rockland and vicinity; embracing Ellsworth, Bucksport, Belfast, Camden, Rockport, Thomaston, Old Town, Orono, Brewer.... Boston: Mercantile Publishing, 1888. Pp. 260.

2083 BLANCHARD, DOUGLAS. "Great days at the Bangor salmon pool." Down East, 13 (April, 1966), 36-38.

2084 BLANDING, EDWARD MITCHELL. "Bangor, Maine." National Magazine, 17 (1902-1903), 800-805.

2085 _____. "Bangor, Maine." NEM, New Ser., 16 (1897), 225-244.
      Differs from above article.

2086 _____. Central Congregational Church, Bangor, Maine, 1847-1912: historical address delivered January 24, 1912. Bangor, 1912. Pp. 31.

2087 _____, comp. The city of Bangor: the industries, resources, attractions and business life of Bangor and its environs.... Bangor: Industrial Journal, 1899. Pp. 256.

2088 BLANDING, INA POTTER, comp. History of the Bangor District Nursing Association, Inc.... 1913-1941, inclusive. [Bangor, 1941]. 19 leaves. MeBa.

2089 BOARDMAN, SAMUEL LANE. Descriptive sketches of six private libraries of Bangor, Maine. Bangor, 1900. Pp. 161.

2090 BOSTON AND BANGOR STEAMSHIP COMPANY. History of the Boston and Bangor Steamship Company, formerly known as Sanford's Independent Line, (1823-1882). Boston: T. R. Marvin & Son, 1882. Pp. 26.

2091 CHAPMAN, HARRY J. "The first Bangor city hall." Bangor Historical Society. Proceedings, (1914-1915), 51-56.

2092 CLARK, CALVIN MONTAGUE. History of Bangor Theological Seminary. Boston: Pilgrim Pr., 1916. Pp. xix, 408.

2093 BANGOR

2093 CLIFFORD, ANGELA GODFREY. Cliff Cottage,
1847-1947. Bangor, 1947. Pp. 37. MeBa.
Clifford and Godfrey families.

2094 COFFIN, HAROLD WILHELM. A brief history of
Dow Field. n.p., [1946?]. 15 leaves. MeU.

2095 COLLAMORE, CHARLES I. "History of Rising
Virtue Lodge of F. & A. M. of Bangor, and of
other lodges growing out of it." MeHistMag,
7 (1891-1892), 1-13.

2096 COOK, WALTER LEONARD. Bangor Theological
Seminary: a sesquicentennial history. Orono:
Univ. of Maine Pr., 1971. Pp. x, 217.

2097 CROSBY, JAMES HENRY. "A bell." Bangor Historical Society. Proceedings, (1914-1915),
42-44.
A Paul Revere bell.

2098 DOUCETTE, EARL. "Something special about fly
rods." Yankee, 6 (April, 1940), 16-17.
Thomas Rod Company.

2099 "EARLY settlement of Bangor." BHistMag, 1
(1885-1886), 2-4.

2100 FELLOWS, RAYMOND. "Daniel Webster and Maine."
Portland University Law Review, 4 (1955-1956),
28-34.
Visits in 1804 and 1835.

2101 FIELD, GEORGE WARREN. Fiftieth anniversary of
the Central Congregational Church: historical
address ... delivered April 1, 1897. [Bang-
or], 1897. Unpaged.

2102 "THE FIRST Congregational Church and Society
in Bangor, Me." BHistMag, 3 (1887-1888),
101-103.

2103 "THE FIRST printer in Bangor." BHistMag, 4
(1888-1889), 235-236.
Peter Edes.

2104 "FIRST settlers in Bangor, and their lots."
BHistMag, 1 (1885-1886), 119-124."

2105 FLAGG, CHARLES ALLCOTT. "The Bangor Public
Library." CCJM, 28 (1915-1916), 203-204.

2106 GILMAN, CHARLES. "Bangor." American Magazine
of Useful and Entertaining Knowledge, 3
(1837), 329-332.

2107 GODFREY, GEORGE FREDERICK. A sketch of Bangor
.... Boston: James R. Osgood, 1882. Pp. 68.

2108 GRAHAM, EDWARD MONTROSE. John R. Graham
(1847-1915) and the Bangor Railway & Electric
Co. N.Y.: Newcomen Society in North America,
1950. Pp. 24.

2109 HEBERT, RICHARD A. "Bangor." Pine Cone, 2
(Winter, 1946-1947), 13-17.

2110 HENNESSEY, WILFRID A. "Peter Edes and the De
Burians." Bangor Historical Society. Proceedings, (1914-1915), 45-50.
The De Burians was a club of bibliophiles
founded in 1900.

2111 HESELTINE, CHARLES DANA. "Bangor Street Railway." Transportation Bulletin, No. 81 (1974),
entire issue.

2112 "HISTORY of postal affairs in Bangor." Bangor
Local Postal Guide, 1 (September, 1899), 1-12.

2113 ["HISTORY of the Girls' High School, Bangor."]
Burr's Fifty Cent Monthly, (October, 1873),
1-3.

2114 HOLBROOK, STEWART H. "Bangor, Maine." American Forests, 44 (1938), 69-71, 94.
Lumbering.

2115 _____. "The flowering of a lumbertown." Down
East, 21 (January, 1975), 36-39, 64-65, 67-69.

2116 HUTCHINS, CURTIS MARSHALL and RUSSELL H.
PETERS. Dead River Co.: a history, 1907-
1972. Farmington: Knowlton & McLeary,
[1973?]. Unpaged. MeU.
Lumber.

2117 NO ENTRY.

2118 JOHNSTON, DONALD P. "History and problems of
the Bangor Water Department." New England Water Works Association. Journal, 67 (1953),
212-229.
1875-1952.

2119 KNICKERBOCKER, FRANCES WENTWORTH CUTLER. The
minister's daughter: a time-exposure photo-
graph of the years 1903-1904. Charles H.
Knickerbocker, ed. Philadelphia: Dorrance,
1974. Pp. 148.

2120 KNOWLES' Bangor business almanac for 1875,
with historical sketches of Bangor, and its
business enterprises. Charles Phelps Roberts,
ed. Bangor: O. F. Knowles, 1875. Pp. 84.
MeBa.
Includes biographies of business men.

2121 LEAGUE OF WOMEN VOTERS OF BANGOR. Bangor,
Maine. (1960) Rev. ed. Bangor, 1968. Pp. 24.

2122 LINDQUIST, VERNON R. "Emerson in Bangor: the
disenchantment of a Transcendental intruder."
The Alumni Bulletin [of Bangor Theological
Seminary], 44 (Winter, 1969), 3-12.
Visits of 1834 and 1846.

2123 NO ENTRY.

2124 McGOVERN, JAMES R. Yankee family. New Or-
leans: Polyanthos, 1975. Pp. iv, 191.
Poor and Pierce families.

2125 MELITA CLUB, BANGOR, ME. Annals of Melita
from 1884 to 1900. Bangor, [1900?]. Pp. 40.
MeU.

2126 MOULTON, WARREN J. "What the Hammond Street Church has meant to Maine." MeCP, 31 (May, 1944), 5-7.

2127 "MUNICIPAL history of Bangor." BHistMag, 1 (1885-1886), 4-8.

2128 NEW ENGLAND TELEPHONE AND TELEGRAPH COMPANY. The story of the telephone in Bangor. n.p., [1954]. Unpaged. MeBa.

2129 PAINE, ALBERT WARE. "The graveyards of Bangor." BHistMag, 4 (1888-1889), 84-86.

2130 _____. History of Mt. Hope Cemetery, Bangor, Maine. Bangor: O. F. Knowles, 1907. Pp. iv, 103.

2131 _____. "Residences of early settlers and prominent citizens of Bangor." BHistMag, 3 (1887-1888), 169-174, 233-235.

2132 _____. "The streets of Bangor." BHistMag, 3 (1887-1888), 213-216.

2133 PENOBSCOT SAVINGS BANK. 100 years, Penobscot Savings Bank, Bangor, and the world, 1869-1969. L. Felix Ranlett, ed. Bangor, [1969]. Pp. 23.

2134 PERRY, GEORGE SESSIONS. "The cities of America: Bangor, Maine." Saturday Evening Post, 223 (March 10, 1951), 24, 89-90, 92, 94, 97.

2135 PHILIPS, DAVID E. "Bangor--Queen City." Down East, 4 (April, 1958), 16-20, 35-37.

2136 POND, ENOCH. "Bangor Theological Seminary." CongQ, 12 (1870), 484-497.

2137 _____. An historical address delivered at the semi-centennial anniversary of the Theological Seminary at Bangor, July 27th, 1870.... Cambridge, Mass.: Welch, Bigelow, 1870. Pp. 16.

2138 _____. "Historical sketch of the Theological Seminary at Bangor." American Quarterly Register, 14 (1842), 27-33.

2139 PORTER, J. B. "Early history of Bangor, Maine." MNEH, 1 (1891), 1-7.

2140 [PORTER, JOSEPH WHITCOMB.] "The Bangor Theological Seminary." SJMH, 1 (1913-1914), 68-72, 136-140, 185-187.
     Author attribution by the editor.

2141 POTTER, EDWARD WESLEY. "Bangor, the consequences of industrial change." Talos, 2 (Summer, 1970), 31-39.

2142 POTTER, MARK L. "First saw mill on the Kenduskeag in Bangor, and Joseph Potter." Me HistMag, 8 (1893), 44-45.

2143 RANLETT, LOUIS FELIX. All Souls Congregational Church (United Church of Christ), Bangor, Maine. [Bangor]: Furbush-Roberts, 1962. Pp. 69.
     Fiftieth anniversary.

2144 _____. The Samuel Hersey Fund and the Bangor Public Library. Bangor, 1956. Unpaged.

2145 REYNOLDS, HARRIS WALTER. The beginnings of St. John's Church, Bangor, Maine. Brookline, Mass.: Priv. Print., 1934. Pp. 24. MBNEH.

2146 ROBERTS, CHARLOTTE. The first forty years of the Shakespeare Club of Bangor, 1896-1936. Mary-Louise Rowe, ed. n.p., [1936]. Pp. 32. MeBa.

2147 ROBINSON, D. A. "The schools of Bangor." BTJ, 25 (1912-1913), 243, 245, 247, 249.

2148 ROTARY INTERNATIONAL, BANGOR, ME. Twenty-fifth anniversary of the Rotary Club, Bangor, Maine. n.p., [1942]. Unpaged. MeBa.
     Includes brief history.

2149 ROWE, HERBERT W. ["The earliest Bangor newspaper."] MPAP, 41 (1904), 57-61; 42 (1905), 34-39.

2150 [ROWE, JAMES SWETT.] Fire service of Bangor. [Bangor]: Firemen's Relief Association, 1890. Pp. 62. MeHi.
     Author attribution by Maine Historical Society.

2151 "ST. JOHN'S Church, Bangor, 1835-1945." The Northeast, 72 (Christmas, 1945), 1-4.
     Signed: J. A. F.

2152 [SANDFORD, WILLIAM.] Historical sketch, articles of faith, covenant and catalogue of the First Congregational Church, Bangor, Me., from 1811 to 1856. Bangor: Samuel S. Smith, 1856. Pp. 55. MeBa.
     Author attribution by Joseph Williamson.

2153 SHETTLEWORTH, EARLE G., JR. Bangor historical resources inventory, 1975. Augusta: Maine Historic Preservation Commission, 1975. 94 leaves. Me.

2154 SIMPSON, CORELLI C. W. Leaflets of artists. Bangor: John H. Bacon, 1893. Pp. 59.
     Biographical sketches of Bangor artists.

2155 "SKETCH of Bangor." Maine Monthly Magazine, 1 (1836-1837), 529-533.

2156 SMITH, EDGAR CROSBY. "Brief notes on the early settlement of Bangor." SJMH, 1 (1913-1914), 33-36.

2157 SNIDER, ROSE. "Oscar Wilde's progress Down East." NEQ, 13 (1940), 7-23.
     Visit in 1882.

2158 BANGOR

2158 SPRAGUE, JOHN FRANCIS. "An old Maine newspaper." SJMH, 14 (1926), 17-18.
Bangor Jeffersonian.

2159 TROWBRIDGE, MASON, JR., CARL E. BLAISDELL and GEORGE R. WALKER. "125 years of Bangor medicine." Maine Medical Association. Journal, 50 (1959), 441, 444-446.

2160 VETERANS OF FOREIGN WARS OF THE UNITED STATES. MAINE. NORMAN N. DOW POST, BANGOR. Comrades of all wars: Bangor--its people and history. [Bangor]: Hugh V. Knox, 1936. Unpaged.

2161 VICKERY, JAMES BERRY, III. An illustrated history of the city of Bangor, Maine. (1969) Rev. ed. Bangor: Bangor Bicentennial Committee, 1976. Pp. 118. MeBa.

2162 WHITTAKER, FREDERICK W. "Sesquicentennial perspective." The Alumni Bulletin of Bangor Theological Seminary, 41 (October, 1966), 1-7.
Bangor Theological Seminary.

2163 WILLIAMSON, WILLIAM DURKEE. "Annals of the city of Bangor, Maine." MeHistMag, 9 (1894-1895), 1-16.

2164 WOMAN'S CHRISTIAN TEMPERANCE CRUSADE. A partial history of the Woman's Christian Temperance Crusade of Bangor, Maine. Mrs. L. B. Wheelden, comp. Bangor: Industrial Journal, [1897]. Pp. 28. MeBa.
1874-1897.

SEE ALSO entries 171, 1736, 1751, 1761, and 4510.

BAR HARBOR (HANCOCK CO.)

2165 "BAR Harbor." The New Englander, No. 400 (July, 1957), 19, 38-40.

2166 BAR HARBOR VILLAGE LIBRARY. [History of the Library], 1875-1905. n.p., [1905]. Pp. 12.

2167 BLANK, JOHN S., III. "Bar Harbor." Ships and the Sea, 2 (August, 1952), 42-45.
Shipping since 1900.

2168 BUETTELL, ROGER B. "The Bar Harbor Express." Yankee, 31 (August, 1967), 138-147.

2169 CHILMAN, C. WILLIAM. "'Baymeath' and the Bar Harbor that was." NEG, 14 (Summer, 1972), 10-20.
Home of Mrs. Joseph T. Bowen.

2170 _____. "I'm sorry, Miss Lona...." Yankee, 37 (January, 1973), 150-156.
Hull's Cove Grammar School.

2171 "THE CHURCH of Our Father, Hull's Cove." The Northeast, 75 (May, 1948), 3-6.

2172 CLAYTON, CATHLEEN SHERMAN. "Memories of old Bar Harbor." Down East, 22 (July, 1976), 68-73.

2173 COLE, NAN. "A native's memories of old Bar Harbor." Down East, 17 (September, 1970), 60-62, 67, 90, 95-98.

2174 _____. "Personal glimpses of Bar Harbor's lush era." Down East, 15 (July, 1969), 42-47, 81-83, 87-89, 92.
1890s-1900s.

2175 COLLIER, SARGENT F. Green grows Bar Harbor: reflections from Kebo Valley, including profiles of the town that refused to die. [Bar Harbor?], 1964. Pp. 107.

2176 "EARLY settlements on Mount Desert at Town Hill, now West Eden." MeHistMag, 7 (1891-1892), 57-58.

2177 FREEMASONS. BAR HARBOR, ME. BAR HARBOR LODGE NO. 185. History of Bar Harbor Lodge, No. 185, Free and Accepted Masons, at Bar Harbor, Maine, from date of precedence, April 19th, 1882, to January 1st, 1890. Benjamin L. Hadley, comp. Bar Harbor: Bar Harbor Pr., 1890. Pp. 27.

2178 [GRANT, A. J.]. Directory of Bar Harbor ... also a historical sketch and guide.... Ellsworth: W. F. Stanwood & W. H. Perry, 1886. Pp. 62.

2179 GRANT, ROBERT. "A plea for Bar Harbor." Outing, 6 (1885), 515-524.
Social life and customs.

2180 HALE, RICHARD WALDEN, JR. "Cadillac's old Green Mountain Railway." Down East, 3 (July, 1957), 40-43.

2181 _____. The story of Bar Harbor: an informal history recording one hundred and fifty years in the life of a community. N.Y.: I. Washburn, 1949. Pp. 259.

2182 HAMMEL, MARGARET F. "Bar Harbor's great cottages." Down East, 19 (June, 1973), 58-63.

2183 HAMOR, H. E. "First meeting house at Hull's Cove, Eden, Me." BHistMag, 6 (1890-1891), 50.

2184 HARRISON, CONSTANCE CARY. "Bar Harbor." Independent, 55 (June 4, 1903), 1308-1313.

2185 HAYDEN, RALPH HENRY. "'I want these things to endure': an historical sketch of St. Saviour's, Bar Harbor." The Northeast, 81 (May, 1954), 12-19.

2186 OPDYCKE, LEONARD. Naval visits to Bar Harbor. Bar Harbor: Bar Harbor Times, 1952. Pp. 31.

2187 PEABODY, MARIAN L. "Old Bar Harbor days." Down East, 11 (July, 1965), 34-35, 64, 67-68, 72, 74-76.

2188 RINEHART, MARY ROBERTS. "Phoenix in New England: Bar Harbor, yesterday and tomorrow." Town and Country, 103 (July, 1949), 32-33, 90-92.

2189 SAVAGE, RICHARD A. "The Bar Harbor auto war." Down East, 22 (August, 1975), 66-69, 84, 87.
    1903-1913.

2190 _____. "Bar Harbor: the hotel era, 1868-1880." MeHSN, 10 (1970-1971), 101-121.

2191 SELIGMANN, HERBERT J. "Bar Harbor--from Eden to tourism." Down East, 4 (August, 1957), 24-29, 45-46.

2192 SPIKER, LA RUE. "Equestrian extravaganza." Down East, 14 (August, 1967), 40-43.
    Horse racing.

2193 _____. "Maine's sea coast mission." Down East, 20 (January, 1974), 40-45, 64-66.
    Maine Seacoast Missionary Society.

2194 WILLIAMS, ANSON R. and MARGARET WILLIAMS. "The big fire: thousands flee as raging blaze sweeps Bar Harbor, October, 1947." Down East, 9 (October, 1962), 14-19, 40-41.
    As told to Mary Wilkes Haley.

SEE ALSO entries 20, 171, 603, 1587, and 1589.

BARING PLANTATION (WASHINGTON CO.)

2195 CHASE, CLIFFORD G. A history of Baring, compiled for the centenary celebration, July 4, 1925, and revised to July 1, 1950. n.p., [1950?]. Pp. 28. Me.

BARNARD PLANTATION (PISCATAQUIS CO.)

2196 TRUE, MABEL L. "Some early settlers of Barnard, Maine." SJMH, 13 (1915-1916), 220.

BATCHELDERS GRANT (OXFORD CO.)

2197 "THE MOST unique village in Maine." BTJ, 18 (1905-1906), 207-208.
    Hastings.

BATH (SAGADAHOC CO.)

2198 APPLEBEE, ROBERT B. "Notes on the Palmer schooners." AmNep, 5 (1945), 79-81.
    Palmer family.

2199 BAILEY, LOUISE C. "The little brick town of Bath." Yankee, 35 (May, 1971), 102-107, 166-169.
    Domestic architecture.

2200 BAKER, WILLIAM AVERY. A maritime history of Bath, Maine, and the Kennebec River region. Bath: Marine Research Society of Bath, 1973. 2v.

2201 BARTLET, WILLIAM STOODLEY. "A contribution to the history of Bath." MeHSC, 3 (1853), 273-277.

2202 BATH, ME. CENTENNIAL COMMITTEE. Bath, Maine, centennial, 1847-1947. Bath, 1947. Pp. 52. Me.

2203 BATH, ME. CENTRAL CONGREGATIONAL CHURCH. The 125th anniversary of Central Congregational Church, Bath, Maine. [Bath?, 1960?]. Pp. 8. MBC.
    Historical sketch is by Jane Stevens.

2204 BATH, ME. WINTER STREET CONGREGATIONAL CHURCH. A century of church history: celebration of the one hundredth anniversary of the Winter Street Congregational Church at Bath, Maine, Sunday and Monday, December 8 and 9, 1895. Bath: Times Company Print, 1896. Pp. 72.

2205 _____. Manual of the Winter Street Church, of Bath, Maine, containing its articles of faith, covenant, standing rules, list of members, and history. [Bath]: Geo. E. Newman, 1888. Pp. 25. MeHi.

2206 BATH HISTORY CLUB OF 1935. Brief history of early Bath. [Bath?, 1936?]. 59 leaves. Me.

2207 BATH IRON WORKS. Bath Iron Works Corporation: condensed history. Bath, 1971. Pp. 23. MeU.
    Shipbuilding.

2208 BATH NATIONAL BANK. Our first hundred years: the story of the Bath National Bank, 1855-1955. Bath, 1955. Pp. 89.

2209 "BATH, past and present." Maine Magazine, 1 (November, 1906), 81-120.

2210 BRAGDON, ROGER. "Last of the Bath-built square riggers." Down East, 22 (March, 1976), 44-45.
    "Astral," "Acme," and "Atlas."

2211 DOUGLAS, ALICE MAY. "Bath's oldest schoolhouse." SJMH, 10 (1922), 26-28.

2212 BATH

2212 ESKEW, GARNETT LAIDLAW. Cradle of ships. N.Y.: Putnam, 1958. Pp. 279.
Bath Iron Works.

2213 NO ENTRY.

2214 GAULD, JOSEPH W. The courage to grow. [Bath?, 1974?]. Pp. 91. MeU.
Hyde School.

2215 GLIDDEN, WALTER S. A history of Montgomery and St. Bernard Royal Arch Chapter No. 2, Bath, Maine. Bath: Times Co., 1912. Pp. 48. MeB.

2216 GRANT, MANLEY. "Boy, I'd love to have a big yacht." Yankee, 37 (September, 1973), 76-82, 174-178, 180-181.
Yachts built at the Bath Iron Works.

2217 GREENE, MARC T. "Bath, Maine." Yankee, 20 (August, 1956), 27-35.

2218 HEFFERNAN, JOHN PAUL. "Charles W. Morse: Bath's king of ice and steam." Down East, 22 (January, 1976), 38-43.

2219 HENNESSY, MARK WILLIAM. The Sewall ships of steel. Augusta: Kennebec Journal Pr., 1937. Pp. xxx, 686.
Arthur Sewall & Co.

2220 HUNTER, MICHAEL REED. "Maine's largest family." New Hampshire Profiles, 5 (June, 1959), 40-43.
State Military and Naval Children's Home, 1866-1959.

2221 JONES, CLIF. "The Bath-built Down Easter 'Challenger.'" Down East, 21 (March, 1975), 23-24, 26-28, 30.

2222 KING, WILLIAM and MARK LANGDON HILL. Remarks upon a pamphlet published at Bath, Me., relating to alleged infractions of the laws during the embargo, non-intercourse and war. Bath: T. Eaton, 1825. Pp. 25.

2223 LYMAN, JOHN, ed. "Maine shipbuilding." Nautical Research Journal, 3 (February, 1951), 15-16, 21.
Methods employed by William Rogers, 1847-1902.

2224 MAINE. STATE MILITARY AND NAVAL CHILDREN'S HOME. State Military and Naval Children's Home, 1868-1946. n.p., [1946?]. Unpaged. Me.

2225 OWEN, HENRY WILSON. "Bath, Maine." National Magazine, 24 (1906), [668-673].

2226 _____. The Edward Clarence Plummer history of Bath, Maine. Bath: Times Co., 1936. Pp. 547, xxviii.

2227 PATTEN FREE LIBRARY, BATH, ME. Historical sketch, deed of gift, by-laws and corporate members. Bath, 1907. Unpaged. MeB.

2228 _____. Patten Free Library, 1889-1930. Bath, [1930]. Pp. 20. MeBa.

2229 _____. Patten Free Library, 1847-1952: a handbook containing brief historical data.... [Bath, 1952]. Pp. 24. MeBa.

2230 "PATTEN Library Association of Bath started in 1847." SJMH, 9 (1921), 76-77.

2231 PLUMMER, EDWARD CLARENCE. "Bath, the city of ships." NEM, New Ser., 15 (1896-1897), 353-374.

2232 PORTER, JOSEPH WHITCOMB. "A famous lawsuit relating to Bath and the Kennebec River." SJMH, 3 (1915-1916), 15-18, 98-100.
David Jeffries vs. Joseph Sergeant, 1765.

2233 PREBLE, GEORGE A. and F. S. PARTRIDGE, comps. Complete schedule of vessels built and registered in the District of Bath, Maine, commencing at 1783.... Bath: Fen. G. Barker, 1878. Pp. 48. MeHi.
See also entry 2235.

2234 QUINN, WILLIAM P. "The 90 year wonder--Seguin." Steamboat Bill, 31 (1974), 221-222.
Tugboat.

2235 RAYMOND, JOHN H. Complete schedule of vessels built and enrolled in the District of Bath, Maine commencing at 1781. Bath: Fen. G. Barker, 1878. Pp. 49-75. MeHi.
Paging continued from 1878 work by Preble and Partridge; see entry 2233.

2236 REED, PARKER McCOBB. History of Bath and environs, Sagadahoc County, Maine, 1607-1894.... Portland: Lakeside Pr., 1894. Pp. 526.

2237 ROSS, FRANK D. A personal memento of destroyers built for victory in World War II. Lewiston: Twin City Printers, 1946. Unpaged. MeHi.
Bath Iron Works.

2238 ST. JOHN, FREDERIC. "Old landmarks of Bath." Maine's Own Magazine, 8 (March, 1930), 15.
Author's name is a pseudonym.

2239 SEWALL, FRANK. "Beginnings and founders of the New Church in America--the Church in Bath, Maine." New-Church Messenger, 86 (May 11, 1904), 270-273, (May 18, 1904), 287-289, (May 25, 1904), 299-301.
New Jerusalem Church.

2240 SEWALL, JOSEPH. "History of Bath." MeHSC, 2 (1847), 189-228.

2241 "SHIPBUILDING in Bath, Maine." Maine's Own Magazine, 8 (March, 1930), 12, 14.
Bath Iron Works.

2242 SMITH, MARION JAQUES. Brief history of education in Bath, Maine. Bath: Adams Pr., [1957]. Pp. 20. Me.

2243 SNOW, RALPH L. "Percy and Small shipyard." Maine History News, 9 (April, 1974), 11.

2244 SOUVENIR of the three hundredth anniversary of American shipbuilding, Bath, Maine, August 5-9, 1907. Bath: Times Co., 1907. Unpaged. MeHi.
Shipbuilding in Bath.

2245 TANNER, VIRGINIA. A pageant of the State of Maine in celebration of the official dedication of the Carlton Bridge, Bath, Maine ... June 30, July 2, 3, 4 ... 1928. [Augusta], 1928. Pp. 136.

2246 THAYER, HENRY OTIS. "The last tragedy of the Indian Wars: the Preble Massacre at the Kennebec." MeHSC, 3 Ser., 1 (1904), 406-420.
June 9, 1758.

2247 TROTT, RAYMOND H. "A Down East merchant fleet." AmNep, 4 (1944), 45-52.
Built, owned, and operated by the Houghton family.

2248 TURNER, WALTER FRYE. Illustrated historical souvenir of the city of Bath, Maine, containing half-tone engravings of the mayors, ship-builders, business and professional men of 1800-1899. [Bath], 1899. Pp. 320.

2249 WESLEY METHODIST-EPISCOPAL CHURCH, BATH, ME. Wesley Methodist-Episcopal Church, Bath, Maine, 1884-85. Bath: H. W. Howard, [1885?]. Pp. 24. MeU.
Includes historical sketch.

2250 "WINTER Street Church, Bath." MeCP, 39 (April 15, 1952), 15.

SEE ALSO entries 259, 286, 923, 1153, 1806, 1808, and 3532.

BEALS (WASHINGTON CO.)

2251 CURRIER, ISABEL. "Beals--Maine's 'tight little island.'" Down East, 15 (September, 1968), 40-43, 72-77, 80, 83.

2252 JONESPORT-BEALS HIGH SCHOOL. AMERICAN HISTORY DEPARTMENT. Pictorial history of the town of Beals, Maine. Jonesport, [1975?]. Pp. iii, 140. MeU.

BEATTIE TOWNSHIP (FRANKLIN CO.)

2253 No items located.

BEDDINGTON (WASHINGTON CO.)

2254 "JEFF Davis on Mt. Humpback." Yankee, 17 (November, 1953), 20-24.
1858.

BELFAST (WALDO CO.)

2255 ABBOT, HERMAN. History of Belfast, Maine, to 1825. Belfast: Grace E. Burgess, 1900. Pp. 18.

2256 BELFAST, ME. City of Belfast, Maine, 1853-1953. n.p., [1953]. Unpaged. MeHi.

2257 BELFAST, ME. CONGREGATIONAL CHURCH. LADIES' CIRCLE. Footnotes of Belfast history. [Belfast]: Waldo County Herald Job Print, 1913. Pp. 26. MeU.

2258 BELFAST, ME. NORTH CHURCH. Celebration of the one hundredth anniversary of the organization of the First Congregational Church (now called the North Church) at Belfast, Maine, Tuesday ... December 29, 1896. Belfast: Belfast Age Publishing, 1897. Pp. 68.

2259 NO ENTRY.

2260 "THE BELFAST Free Library, an historical sketch." LJ, 13 (1888), 250-251.

2261 "BELFAST, Maine." BTJ, 3 (1890-1891), 297-300.
Signed: Winkle.

2262 BENNETT, WELLS. "Doric interlude." Journal of the American Institute of Architects, 11 (1949), 33-39, 69-75.
Historic houses.

2263 "THE CATHOLIC church in Belfast." MeCathHM, 7 (1916-1917), 222-237.
St. Francis of Assisi Church.

2264 [CLARK, CORNELIUS EDWARDS]. "Sesquicentennial in Belfast." MeCP, 143 (February, 1947), 26-27.
First Congregational Church; author attribution by the editor.

2265 DURHAM, MRS. J. C. Old houses of Belfast. [Belfast]: Waldo County Herald Job Printing Department, 1911. Pp. 11. MBNEH.

2266 DYER, RUSSELL GLOVER. History of Corinthian Chapter, No. 7, of Royal Arch Masons, Belfast, Maine, from 1848 to 1880. Belfast: G. W. Burgess, 1880. Pp. 80. MeHi.

2267 BELFAST

2267 [_____]. "Masonic temple, Belfast, Maine."
FR, 15 (1885-1886), 253-256.
Author attribution by the editor; signed
R. G. D.

2268 KUHNERT, DALE WILLIAM. "The Belfast fire of
1873." Down East, 20 (August, 1973), 52-55.

2269 LOCKE, JOHN LYMBURNER. History of Phoenix
Lodge, No. 24, of Belfast, Maine. Belfast:
Belfast Printing, 1900. Pp. 112. MeHi.
Freemasons, 1817-1900.

2270 WALSH, LOUIS SEBASTIAN. "St. Francis of
Assisi, Belfast, silver jubilee sermon."
MeCathHM, 7 (1916-1917), 245-253.

2271 WHITE, WILLIAM. A history of Belfast, with
introductory remarks on Acadia. Belfast:
E. Fellowes, 1827. Pp. 119.

2272 WILLIAMSON, JOSEPH. Belfast Academy fifty
years ago. Belfast: Geo. W. Burgess, 1888.
Pp. 7. MeBa.

2273 _____. History of the city of Belfast in the
State of Maine.... Portland: Loring, Short
and Harmon, 1877-1913. 2v.
Includes a bibliography, 1875-1900; volume
two, completed and edited by Alfred Johnson,
was published in Boston by Houghton Mifflin.

SEE ALSO entries 707, 2082, and 4589.

BELGRADE (KENNEBEC CO.)

2274 "BELGRADE, Maine." Sun Up, 3 (June, 1926),
42-44, 46-47, 49.

2275 GUPTILL, ROBERT A., CAROL F. NYE, and H.
PAULINE PLOURDE. Past & present pictures and
people of Belgrade, Maine, 1774-1976. [Bel-
grade]: Heritage Committee of Belgrade Bicentennial Observance, [1976]. Pp. 64. MeU.
Includes errata slip.

2276 PENNEY, WILL and MINNIE PENNEY. Eighty-eight
years on a Maine farm. Lawrence M. Sturtevant, ed. Farmington: Knowlton & McLeary,
1970. Pp. 144. MeHi.

BELMONT (WALDO CO.)

2277 No items located.

BENEDICTA (AROOSTOOK CO.)

2278 BENEDICTA, ME. Souvenir program of the cen-
tenary of Benedicta, 1834-1934. n.p., [1934?].
Pp. 16.
A copy is at the Aroostook Historical and
Art Museum, Houlton.

BENTON (KENNEBEC CO.)

2279 BENTON, ME. 100TH YEAR HISTORICAL SURVEY
COMMITTEE. Town of Sebasticook-Benton,
Maine, 1842-1942. Chester E. Basford, ed.
Fairfield: Galahad Pr., 1942. Pp. 54.

SEE ALSO entry 1421.

BERWICK (YORK CO.)

2280 BERWICK, ME. The story of Berwick, published
on the occasion of the town of Berwick's
250th anniversary, June 30-July, 1963. J.
Wilfrid Albert, comp. Berwick, 1963.
Pp. 166.

2281 DAVIS, ANDREW McFARLAND. "The case of Frost
vs. Leighton." AHR, 2 (1897), 229-240.
1739.

2282 JEWETT, SARAH ORNE. "The old town of Berwick." NEM, New Ser., 10 (1894), 585-609.

2283 SPENCER, WILBUR DANIEL, comp. A list of
Revolutionary soldiers of Berwick, compiled
from the records of the town. [Berwick],
1898. Pp. 18.

2284 WEBSTER, MILLARD D. Highlights of Berwick
history. Berwick, 1939. Unpaged. MeU.

SEE ALSO entry 1911.

BETHEL (OXFORD CO.)

2285 BEAN, EVA MARION. East Bethel Road. Bethel:
Citizen Print Shop, 1959. Pp. 452.

2286 BETHEL, ME. Report of the centennial cele-
bration at Bethel, August 26, 1874. Portland:
B. Thurston, 1874. Pp. 78.
Historical address by Nathaniel Tuckerman
True.

2287 BETHEL SAVINGS BANK. Bethel Savings Bank,
1872-1972. n.p., [1972]. Unpaged. Me.

2288 CROSBY, RUTH. I was a summer boarder. Boston: Christopher Publishing, 1966. Pp. 142.
Social life and customs.

2289 LAPHAM, WILLIAM BERRY. History of Bethel,
formerly Sudbury, Canada, Oxford County,
Maine, 1768-1890; with a brief sketch of
Hanover and family statistics. Augusta:
Maine Farmer, 1891. Pp. xv, 688.

2290 PARKMAN, FRANCIS. The Gould Academy story,
1836-1976. Bethel: Gould Academy, 1976.
Pp. x, 226. MeHi.

2291 TIBBETTS, MRS. RAYMOND R. "A brief history of the West Parish Congregational Church of Bethel." MeCP, 143 (October, 1947), 38-39.

BIDDEFORD (YORK CO.)

2292 ABENAKEE CLUB, BIDDEFORD, ME. The Abenakee Club of Biddeford Pool, Maine. [Biddeford, 1911]. Pp. 18.

2293 BIDDEFORD, ME. FIRST UNIVERSALIST CHURCH. First Universalist Church, Saco and Biddeford, Maine. n.p. [1898?]. Pp. 23. MeHi.
   Includes a history of the church.

2294 BIDDEFORD, ME. PAROISSE ST. JOSEPH. Paroisse St. Joseph, 75e anniversaire, programme-souvenir, 6-7 Mai, 1945. [Saco]: Reny Frères, 1945. Pp. 89. MBC.

2295 BIDDEFORD, ME. PUBLIC LIBRARY. An introduction to Biddeford's history and a chronological outline of events. [Biddeford], 1944. 57 leaves.

2296 _____. Stories and legends of old Biddeford. Biddeford, 1945-1946. 2v. Me.
   1600-1800.

2297 BIDDEFORD, ME. SECOND CONGREGATIONAL CHURCH. Order of exercises for the celebration of the one hundredth anniversary of the organization, 1805-1905, with historical notes. Biddeford: Biddeford Journal Print, 1905. Pp. 16.

2298 DAY, BENJAMIN F. and NAHUM S. DROWN. History of Dunlap Lodge No. 47, F. and A. M., commencing with organization of Buxton Lodge in 1826, located at Buxton, and continuing its history after its removal to Biddeford in 1854, and reorganization as Dunlap Lodge, up to A.D. 1890. Biddeford: Standard Publishing, 1890. Pp. 99. [MePGLM].

2299 EMERY, GEORGE ADDISON. "The old Thornton Academy." MeHSC, 2 Ser., 10 (1899), 1-51.

2300 "FORT St. George, or the ancient dominion of New England." Knickerbocker Magazine, 16 (1840), 308-316.
   Signed: P. S.

2301 GUIGNARD, MICHAEL. "Maine's Franco-Americans: Biddeford." Maine History News, 7 (July, 1972), 8-9, 12, 14.

2302 HALEY, ADELAIDE. "The Haley House and Farm, 763 Pool Road, Biddeford, Maine." OTNE, 35 (1944-1945), 3-9.

2303 HERRICK, MARY DARRAH. "The oldest public library in Maine." MeLAB, 3 (February, 1942), 8-9.
   Established in 1863; McArthur Public Library.

2304 LAWRENCE, CHARLES K. C. "A sketch of Christ Church, Biddeford, Maine." The Northeast, 73 (May, 1946), 8-9.

2305 MEEDS, MELVIL F. "Fort Mary." SJMH, 14 (1926), 7-8.

2306 PEPPERELL MANUFACTURING COMPANY. Biddeford, the home of Pepperell. Biddeford, [1937?]. Unpaged. MeHi.

2307 "RAVAGES of fire erased in summer community; S. Philip's by the Sea, Fortune's Rocks rebuilt." The Northeast, 78 (July, 1951), 12-14.
   Includes history.

2308 "THE SECOND Church, Biddeford, Maine." CongQ, 11 (1869), 241-248.

2309 TATTERSON, ESTELLE MORRIS. Three centuries of Biddeford: an historical sketch. n.p., [1916]. Unpaged. MeBa.

2310 WEYMOUTH, GORHAM N. and CORA BELLE BICKFORD. The city of Biddeford and vicinity [and] local landmarks. Biddeford: Riverside Pr., 1900. Pp. 38. MeHi.

2311 YORKE, DANE. The men and times of Pepperell, an account of the first one hundred years of the Pepperell Manufacturing Company, incorporated February 16, 1844. Boston, 1945. Pp. 107.

   SEE ALSO entries 799, 1265, 1881, 1890, 1893, 1901, 4181, and 4465.

BIG SIX TOWNSHIP (SOMERSET CO.)

2312 No items located.

BIG SQUAW TOWNSHIP (PISCATAQUIS CO.)

2313 No items located.

BIG TEN TOWNSHIP (SOMERSET CO.)

2314 No items located.

BIG TWENTY TOWNSHIP (AROOSTOOK CO.)

2315 No items located.

BIG W TOWNSHIP (SOMERSET CO.)

2316 No items located.

BIGELOW TOWNSHIP (SOMERSET CO.)

2317   No items located.

BINGHAM (SOMERSET CO.)

2318   ELDEN, ALFRED OWEN. "Bingham's first banquet." The Northern, 8 (June, 1928), 14.
Following the presidential election of 1828.

2319   HISTORY COMMITTEE OF THE BINGHAM SESQUICENTENNIAL. Bingham sesquicentennial history, 1812-1962. Skowhegan: Skowhegan Pr., 1962. Pp. 110.

BLAINE (AROOSTOOK CO.)

2320   No items located.

BLAKE GORE (SOMERSET CO.)

2321   No items located.

BLANCHARD PLANTATION (PISCATAQUIS CO.)

2322   BLANCHARD, EDWARD P. "The Blanchard family of Blanchard." PCHSC, 1 (1910), 442-445.

2323   _____. "Charles Blanchard, proprietor of the town of Blanchard, Maine." SJMH, 2 (1914-1915), 89-91.

BLUE HILL (HANCOCK CO.)

2324   THE ACADEMIES of Blue Hill, Maine, 1802-1952. Blue Hill, 1952. Pp. 19. MeU.
Blue Hill Academy and George Stevens Academy.

2325   BLUE HILL, ME. CONGREGATIONAL CHURCH. Centennial, Congregational Church, Blue Hill, Maine. Bangor: Samuel S. Smith & Son, 1874. Pp. 34. MeBa.
Historical address by Stephen Thurston.

2326   "BLUE Hill and settlers." MeHistMag, 8 (1893), 17-19.
Includes ecclesiastical history of the town.

2327   BLUE HILL TROUPE, NEW YORK. The Blue Hill Troupe, 25th anniversary. N.Y., 1949. Pp. 95.
Community theater.

2328   CANDAGE, RUFUS GEORGE FREDERICK. The centennial of Blue Hill Academy: a paper ... read at the meeting of the [Brookline Historical] Society, December 23, 1903. [Brookline, Mass.]: The [Brookline Historical] Society, 1904. Pp. 15.

2329   _____. Dedication of bowlders and tablets to John Roundy and James Candage, a founder and an early settler of Bluehill, Maine, with memorial addresses ... at Blue Hill Neck, August 22, 1905. Ellsworth: Hancock County Publishing, 1905. Pp. 21.

2330   _____. Historical sketches of Bluehill, Maine. Ellsworth: Hancock County Publishing, 1905. Pp. 83.

2331   _____. Settlement and progress of the town of Bluehill, Maine, an historical address ... at Bluehill Falls, September 7, 1886. Blue Hill: Ladies' Social Library, 1886. Pp. 43.

2332   _____. "Sketches of the representatives to the [General] Court of Massachusetts from Blue Hill, Me., prior to 1820." BHistMag, 3 (1887-1888), 191-193.

2333   CLOUGH, ANNIE L. Head of the bay: sketch and pictures of Blue Hill, Maine, 1762-1952.... Blue Hill: Shoreacre Pr., 1953. Pp. 52. MeBa.

2334   CUMMINGS, ABBOTT LOWELL. "The house the parson built." OTNE, 56 (1955-1956), 91-107.
Jonathan Fisher House.

2335   DODGE, REUBEN GEORGE WASHINGTON. "The Congregational Church at Bluehill." BHistMag, 2 (1886-1887), 113-117.
From notes prepared by Jonathan Fisher in 1810 with additions by Dodge.

2336   FISHER, JONATHAN. "Sketches of Bluehill." BHistMag, 1 (1885-1886), 148-153.

2337   FOBES, CHARLES BARTLETT. "Blue Hill in Maine." Appalachia, 29 (1952-1953), 531-533.

2338   LITTLEFIELD, OTIS. History of Ira Berry Lodge, No. 187, Free and Accepted Masons, Blue Hill, Me., from its organization, Nov. 12, 1883, to Jan. 1, 1902. Portland: Stephen Berry, 1902. Pp. 30. MeBa.

2339   NEVIN, DORIS. "Summer days in old Blue Hill." Down East, 21 (September, 1974), 54-57, 83-84.
Social life and customs.

2340   STANWOOD, CORDELIA J. "Glimpses of old Bluehill." House Beautiful, 45 (April, 1919), 222-223.

2341   WINCHESTER, ALICE. "Rediscovery: Parson Jonathan Fisher." Art in America, 58 (November-December, 1970), 92-99.
Fisher as an artist.

2342 WOOD, ESTHER E. "Blue Hill rusticators." Down East, 2 (September, 1955), 35-36, 39. Social life and customs.

2343 _____. Country fare. Somersworth, N.H.: New Hampshire Publishing, 1976. Pp. ix, x, 157.

2344 _____. "Historic Maine parsonage--the Jonathan Fisher House, Blue Hill, Maine." DARMag, 95 (1961), 537-538, 540, 572.

2345 _____. "The Jonathan Fisher House." Down East, 13 (August, 1966), 40-43.

SEE ALSO entries 207 and 1581.

BOOTHBAY (LINCOLN CO.)

2346 COAN, LEANDER SAMUEL. A century in one of the early New England churches: a sermon delivered in the First Congregational Church, Boothbay, Maine, September 23, 1866. Boston: T. R. Marvin & Son, 1866. Pp. 26.

2347 DIETZ, LEW. The story of Boothbay. n.p., 1937. Unpaged. MBNEH.

2348 RICE, GEORGE WHARTON. The shipping days of old Boothbay from the Revolution to the World War, with mention of adjacent towns. Boothbay Harbor, 1938. Pp. xv, 419.

2349 STEVENS, JAMES P., JR. "Boothbay schooners." Down East, 15 (September, 1968), 34-39, 68-70.

2350 THOMPSON, WINFIELD MARTIN. "Damariscove." NEM, New Ser., 11 (1894-1895), 34-41.

SEE ALSO entries 1681-1682 and 1689-1690.

BOOTHBAY HARBOR (LINCOLN CO.)

2351 BALDWIN, SIDNEY. Casting off from Boothbay Harbor, Maine. Boothbay Harbor: George M. Lowden, 1948. Pp. 127. Me.

2352 HALLET, RICHARD. "The deep roots of Boothbay Harbor." Down East, 5 (August, 1958), 36-41, 55.

2353 KYNETT, HAROLD HAVELOCK. Maine harbor, adventures in relaxation. [Philadelphia], 1940. Pp. 132.

2354 LARKIN, ALICE T. Our growing years. Boothbay Harbor: Harbor Print Shop, 1975. Pp. 63. MeU.

SEE ALSO entries 1681-1682 and 1689-1690.

BOWDOIN (SAGADAHOC CO.)

2355 No items located.

BOWDOIN COLLEGE GRANT EAST (PISCATAQUIS CO.)

2356 No items located.

BOWDOIN COLLEGE GRANT WEST (PISCATAQUIS CO.)

2357 No items located.

BOWDOINHAM (SAGADAHOC CO.)

2358 ADAMS, SILAS. The history of the town of Bowdoinham, 1762-1912. Fairfield: Fairfield Publishing, 1912. Pp. 295.

2359 AMES, JOHN WALLACE. Bowdoinham was my home. Kennebunk: Star Pr., 1975. Pp. 167. MeBa.

2360 BOWDOINHAM, ME. BICENTENNIAL HISTORICAL BOOKLET COMMITTEE. Bowdoinham: the seventeenth town in Maine, 1762-1962, bicentennial. Brunswick: Brunswick Publishing, 1962. Pp. 61. Me.

2361 CUMMINS, ROBERT. "Vessels built in Bowdoinham." MeHSN, 6 (November, 1966), an unpaged supplement at end of the issue. 1768-1877.

BOWERBANK (PISCATAQUIS CO.)

2362 No items located.

BOWMANTOWN TOWNSHIP (OXFORD CO.)

2363 No items located.

BOWTOWN TOWNSHIP (SOMERSET CO.)

2364 No items located.

BRADFORD (PENOBSCOT CO.)

2365 SEE entry 1733.

BRADLEY (PENOBSCOT CO.)

2366 "THE TOWN of Bradley, Maine." BHistMag, 3 (1887-1888), 79.

BRADSTREET TOWNSHIP (SOMERSET CO.)

2367   No items located.

BRASSUA TOWNSHIP (SOMERSET CO.)

2368   No items located.

BREMEN (LINCOLN CO.)

2369   BINGHAM, MILLICENT TODD. "Rescuing an is-
        land." Natural History, 39 (1937), 318-328.
        Hog Island.

2370   GIBBS, IRIS and ALONZO GIBBS. Bremen by-
        gones: 1876-1976. Bremen: Bremen Bicenten-
        nial Committee, 1976. Pp. 80. MeU.

        SEE ALSO entry 1693.

BREWER (PENOBSCOT CO.)

2371   BREWER, ME. FIRST CONGREGATIONAL CHURCH.
        Historical sketch of the First Congregational
        Church, Brewer, Maine, 1800-1928. Basil C.
        Gleason, comp. n.p., [1928?]. Pp. 36.
        MeU.

2372   "THE FIRST Congregational church and minis-
        ters on the Penobscot River." BHistMag, 1
        (1885-1886), 139-144.
        Brewer Church, formerly the Orrington
        Church.

2373   GARDINER, HARRY NORMAN. "Investigation of
        clairvoyance in a drowning accident at Brew-
        er, Maine." American Society for Psychical
        Research. Journal, 4 (1910), 447-464.
        Accident occurred in 1906; investigated
        for the author by Fannie H. Eckstorm.

2374   "150TH anniversary of [the] First Congrega-
        tional Church in Brewer." MeCP, 146 (June,
        1950), 20.

2375   VICKERY, JAMES BERRY, III. A pictorial his-
        tory of Brewer, Maine. [Brewer]: Brewer
        Bicentennial Committee, 1976. Pp. 59. Me.

        SEE ALSO entries 1736, 1752, 1761-1762, 2047,
        and 2082.

BRIDGEWATER (AROOSTOOK CO.)

2376   RIDEOUT, ANNIE E. History of Bridgewater,
        Maine. Manchester: Falmouth Publishing,
        1953. Pp. 153.

BRIDGTON (CUMBERLAND CO.)

2377   BRIDGTON, ME. FIRST CONGREGATIONAL CHURCH.
        Manual and history of the First Congregational
        Church, Bridgton, Maine. Minnie Gertrude
        Lewis, comp. n.p., 1929. Pp. 24. MBC.

2378   _____. Rules and regulations of the First
        Congregational Church, Bridgton, Me., togeth-
        er with the confession of faith, covenant,
        and a brief history of the church. Bridgton:
        Bridgton News Print, 1876. Pp. 16. MeHi.

2379   BRIDGTON ACADEMY, NORTH BRIDGTON, ME. Pro-
        ceedings at the re-union of the alumni of
        Bridgton Academy held at North Bridgton, Me.,
        on July 12th, 1882. Bridgton: Bridgton News
        Print, 1883. Pp. 69.
        History by A. S. Kimball.

2380   BRIDGTON, Maine 1768-1968. Eula M. Shorey
        and Cara Cook, eds. Bridgton: Bridgton
        Historical Society, 1968. Pp. 627. Me.

2381   CORLISS, LEWIS H. History of Oriental Lodge,
        No. 13, Free and Accepted Masons, Bridgton,
        Me., 1804-1894. [Bridgton]: Bridgton News
        Print, 1895. Pp. 111. MeU.

2382   CRAM, MARSHALL. An address delivered ... at
        the dedication of the town house in Bridgton,
        January 8, 1852. Portland: Brown Thurston,
        1852. Pp. 44.
        Town history.

2383   DAVIS, BLYNN EDWIN. Moody Bridges, Pondi-
        cherry, and the beginnings of Bridgton.
        Bridgton, 1959. Pp. 70.

2384   _____. The Ridge. Bridgton, 1971. 95
        leaves.

2385   McINTYRE, PHILIP WILLIS. An account of the
        ceremonies at the dedication of the soldiers'
        monument, Bridgton, Maine, July 21, 1910,
        containing also the addresses delivered on
        that occasion and biographical sketches.
        [Bridgton?, 1910]. Pp. 48.

2386   McLIN, WILLIAM HELLEN, ROBERT JORDAN DINGLEY,
        and EDGAR THORN MEAD, JR. The twenty-four-
        inch gauge railroad at Bridgton, Maine.
        Bridgton: Bridgton News, 1941. Pp. 36.
        Bridgton & Harrison Railway.

2387   MEAD, EDGAR THORN, JR. "Busted and still
        running:" the famous two-foot gauge railroad
        of Bridgton, Maine. Brattleboro, Vt.:
        Stephen Greene Pr., 1968. Pp. vi, 58.
        Bridgton and Saco River Railroad Company.

2388   MONK, GUY MAXWELL. The story of North Bridg-
        ton, Maine, 1761-1958: a little history, a
        little legend, and some recollections. [North
        Bridgton?], 1958. Pp. 70.

2389 ODD FELLOWS, INDEPENDENT ORDER OF. BRIDGTON, ME., CUMBERLAND LODGE NO. 30. Anniversary address ... Sunday afternoon, April 21, '07. Bridgton: News Print, 1907. Pp. 31. MeHi.
Address is by Henry A. Shorey.

2390 STEVENS, ERNEST N. A brief history of Bridgton Academy, 1808-1957. Cambridge, Mass.: Cuneo Pr., 1958. Pp. 194.

2391 WOOD, SOLOMON. "Journal of a survey of Bridgeton, Me., in 1776." NEHGR, 28 (1874), 63-67.
Edited by Isaac B. Choate.

BRIGHTON PLANTATION (SOMERSET CO.)

2392 No items located.

BRISTOL (LINCOLN CO.)

2393 "ANCIENT Pemaquid, Maine--occupied by whites before Plymouth." BTJ, 13 (1900-1901), 271-272.

2394 BANKS, CHARLES EDWARD. "The pirate of Pemaquid." MHGR, 1 (1884), 57-61.
Dixey Bull.

2395 BRISTOL HIGH SCHOOL. Inside Bristol. Damariscotta: Twin Village Printing, [1951]. Pp. 68. Me.

2396 BURRAGE, HENRY SWEETSER. "The first mention of Pemaquid in history." MeHSC, 2 Ser., 6 (1895), 53-62.

2397 _____. "Military operations at Pemaquid, in the second war with Great Britain." MeHSC, 2 Ser., 3 (1892), 187-190.
War of 1812.

2398 CAMP, HELEN B. Archaeological excavations at Pemaquid, Maine, 1965-1974. Augusta: Maine State Museum, 1975. Pp. xx, 89. Me.

2399 _____. Pemaquid lost and found. Arlington, Mass.: Ancient Pemaquid Restoration, 1967. Pp. 44.

2400 CARTLAND, JOHN HENRY. Ancient pavings of Pemaquid. Pemaquid Beach, 1899. Pp. 11.

2401 _____. Ten years at Pemaquid: sketches of its history and its ruins. Pemaquid Beach, 1899. Pp. vi, 196.

2402 _____. Twenty years at Pemaquid: sketches of its history and its remains, ancient and modern. Pemaquid Beach, 1914. Pp. 224.

2403 CASTNER, HAROLD WEBBER. The story of ancient Pemaquid, "Metropolis of the New World." (1950) 3d ed. Boothbay Harbor, 1956. Pp. 23.

2404 DANFORTH POINT TRUST. A brief description of Danforth Point, New Harbor, Maine, with an account of the Danforth Point Trust. Exeter, N.H.: Academy Pr., 1924. Unpaged.

2405 DUNBAR, ROBERT E. "The fort that wouldn't stay built." Down East, 23 (August, 1976), 82-85.
Fort William Henry.

2406 FOGG, CLARA NEWHALL. "Maine's most historic spot." DARMag, 64 (1931), 91-92.
Pemaquid.

2407 FULLER, G. SPENCER. "The old fort at Pemaquid." PVMA, 5 (1905-1911), 432-447.
Fort William Henry.

2408 HACKELTON, MARIA W. Jamestown of Pemaquid: a poem, read on the site of Fort Frederic, on the reception of the committee of the Maine Historical Society by the citizens of Bristol, August 26, 1869. N.Y.: Hurd and Houghton, 1869. Pp. 40.

2409 HAWES, HILDRETH GILMAN. "Maine's first pirate sacked Fort Pemaquid." Sun Up, 10 (May, 1932), 27, 32.
Dixey Bull, 1632.

2410 HOUGH, FRANKLIN BENJAMIN. Papers relating to Pemaquid and parts adjacent in the present State of Maine, known as Cornwall County, when under the colony of New-York, compiled from official records in the office of the Secretary of State at Albany, N.Y. Albany: Weed, Parsons, 1856. Pp. vii, 136.

2411 _____. "Pemaquid in its relation to our colonial history." MeHSC, 7 (1876), 127-164.

2412 JOHN, TIMOTHY. "Restoration of the Harrington Meeting House." Down East, 22 (April, 1976), 48-51.

2413 JOHNSON, ALFRED. "Some recent impressions of the forts and other evidences of early occupancy at Pemaquid, and elsewhere, in Maine." CSMP, 25 (1922-1924), 427-430.

2414 [KALER, JAMES OTIS]. The story of Pemaquid. By James Otis, pseud. N.Y.: T. Y. Crowell, 1902. Pp. 181.

2415 LABRIE, ROSE CUSHING. The story of Pemaquid Light. Hampton, N.H.: Hampton Publishing, 1961. Pp. 19. Me.

2416 LIBBY, HILDA. The story of the Pemaquid Point lighthouse. n.p., [1975?]. Pp. 27. Me.

2417 BRISTOL

2417 LOWELL, W. L. "Historical Pemaquid." BTJ, 9 (1896-1897), 17.

2418 McCRILLIS, HERBERT O. "Ancient Pemaquid: Jamestown of New England." NEM, New Ser., 34 (1906), 278-288.

2419 _____ and JOHN HENRY CARTLAND. A brief sketch of Pemaquid. Boothbay Harbor: Register Book and Job Print, 1917. Pp. 38.

2420 McCRILLIS, HERBERT O. "Pemaquid, the Jamestown of the North." Pine Tree Magazine, 7 (1907), 311-326.

2421 MOOREHEAD, WARREN KING. "The ancient remains at Pemaquid, Maine: some observations." OTNE, 14 (1923-1924), 133-141.
    Discusses possibility of pre-Plymouth settlement at Pemaquid.

2422 NELSON, G. J. "Historic Pemaquid." BTJ, 15 (1902-1903), 143-144.

2423 NOBLE, JOHN. "Land controversies in Maine--1769-1772." CSMP, 6 (1899-1900), 11-57.
    Pemaquid Patent.

2424 PALTSITS, VICTOR HUGO. "The depredation at Pemaquid in August, 1698." MeHSC, 3 Ser., 2 (1906), 261-274.

2425 PARKER, ARLITA DODGE. A history of Pemaquid, with sketches of Monhegan, Popham and Castine. Boston: MacDonald & Evans, 1925. Pp. 226.

2426 _____. "Traces of probable Norse relics--and mysterious stone pavements uncovered at historic Pemaquid." Sun Up, 3 (August, 1927), 30-32.

2427 ROBINSON, GRACE LOUISE. "St. George's at Popham: forerunner of all American forts." JAmHist, 14 (1920), 233-235.

2428 SEWALL, RUFUS KING. Pemaquid, its genesis, discovery, name and colonial relations to New England. Read before the Lincoln County Historical Society, May 22, 1896. [Wiscasset]: The [Lincoln County Historical] Society, 1896. Pp. 21.

2429 SYLVESTER, HERBERT MILTON. Ye romance of olde Pemaquid. Boston: Stanhope Pr., 1908. Pp. 431.
    Also published in 1909 as volume four of the author's "Maine pioneer settlements."

2430 TAFT, LEWIS A. "The republic of Muscongus." Yankee, 28 (September, 1964), 64-69, 138.
    Election of 1860.

2431 THAYER, HENRY OTIS. "Ancient Pemaquid." MeHSC, 3 Ser., 2 (1906), 374-388.

2432 _____. "Beginnings at Pemaquid." MeHSC, 2 Ser., 6 (1895), 62-84.

2433 THOMPSON, ERNEST. "Louds Island." Down East, 8 (April, 1962), 20-24.

2434 THORNTON, JOHN WINGATE. "Ancient Pemaquid: an historical review." MeHSC, 5 (1857), 141-299.

2435 VINTON, JOHN ADAMS. The Giles memorial ... with a history of Pemaquid, ancient and modern; some account of early settlements in Maine, and some details of Indian warfare.... Boston: H. W. Dutton & Son, 1864. Pp. viii, 600.

2436 VONDEL, JOSEPH LEMAN. "The restoration of Pemaquid." MagHist, 11 (1909), 139-144.

2437 YOUNG, ARTHUR H. "The big dig at Pemaquid." Yankee, 31 (September, 1967), 82-85, 170, 173.

2438 _____. Pemaquid, New England's first city.... n.p., 1969. Pp. 22.

SEE ALSO entries 286, 799, 1683, 1693, 1708, 1712, and 4100.

BROOKLIN (HANCOCK CO.)

2439 BROOKLIN CENTENNIAL COMMITTEE. Centennial celebration, Brooklin, Me., July 29-31, 1949. George M. Murray, ed. [Brooklin?, 1949]. Pp. 51. Me.

2440 FISH, E. S. History of Brooklin: an address delivered at Brooklin, Maine, July 4, 1876. Bangor: Burr & Robinson, 1876. Pp. 32.

2441 FREEMASONS. BROOKLIN, ME. NASKEAG LODGE, NO. 171. History of Naskeag Lodge, No. 171, of F. and A. Masons, June, 1873 to 1890. Portland: Stephen Berry, 1890. Pp. 27. MeBa.

SEE ALSO entries 1561 and 1589.

BROOKS (WALDO CO.)

2442 NORWOOD, SETH WADEMERE, comp. Sketches of Brooks history. Dover, N.H.: J. B. Page, 1935. Pp. 454.
    Includes short biographies and genealogies.

BROOKSVILLE (HANCOCK CO.)

2443 BROOKSVILLE HISTORICAL SOCIETY. Traditions and records of Brooksville, Maine, collected by the Brooksville Historical Society, 1935-1936. Grace Limeburner, et al., eds. Auburn: Merrill & Webber, 1936. Pp. 152.

2444 CARBERG, WARREN C. "The amazing Tapley brothers." Yankee, 33 (January, 1969), 122-123, 125.

2445 LIMEBURNER, GRACE M. GRINDLE. Stories of Brooksville. Bangor: Seely, 1924. Pp. 81.
   History, not literature.

2446 SNOW, WALTER A., comp. Brooksville, Maine, "A town of the Bagaduce." Blue Hill: Blue Hill Packet, 1967. Pp. 136.

2447 _____. Brooksville, Maine, a town in the Revolution. [Brooksville: Brooksville] Bicentennial Committee, 1976. Pp. iii, 75. MeU.

   SEE ALSO entries 1581, 1597, and 1621.

BROOKTON TOWNSHIP (WASHINGTON CO.)

2448 No items located.

BROWNFIELD (OXFORD CO.)

2449 BROWNFIELD, ME. CONGREGATIONAL CHURCH. Service at the Congregational Church ..., sermon by Rev. Samuel Tyler; Brownfield centennial, 1802-1902, commemorative service, Sunday, August 24, 1902. Brownfield, 1902. Pp. 24.

2450 STICKNEY, ELIZA ANN GIBSON. Reminiscences of Brownfield: short sketches from the history of the town. East Brownfield, 1901. Pp. 69.

2451 TEG, WILLIAM. History of Brownfield, Maine. Cornish: Carbrook Pr., 1966. Pp. 202.
   Includes errata slip.

BROWNVILLE (PISCATAQUIS CO.)

2452 BROWNVILLE, ME. A handbook of Brownville history, with records of its centennial celebration.... Susan M. Lewis, comp. Bangor: Jordan-Frost, 1935. Pp. 122. MeBa.

2453 "THE CALLIOPEAN baseball team." The Pioneer, 1 (February, 1912), [3-5].

2454 "COMING of the Welch people and the slate quarries." The Pioneer, 1 (July, 1911), [1-2].

2455 GERRISH, JUDSON C. and HENRY GERRISH. History of Brownville, 1824-1924. Dover-Foxcroft: F. D. Barrows, 1924. Pp. 59.

2456 JENKINS, SUE PERRIGO. Memories of Ebeeme: the delights of nature and living at a summer camp in Maine. N.Y.: Exposition Pr., 1959. Pp. 43.

2457 JENKS, E. A. "The lotting of Brownville." The Pioneer, 1 (July, 1911), [5].
   Land.

2458 MacDOUGALL, WALTER M. "Brownville slate and slaters." Down East, 15 (September, 1968), 58-61, 90.

2459 "REMINISCENCES." The Pioneer, 1 (June, 1911), [5-6].

2460 RUSSELL, CARRIE PAGE. "In the early days." The Pioneer, 1 (April, 1912), [4].

2461 TIBBETTS, R. G. "Brick-making in North Brownville." The Pioneer, 1 ([August], 1911), [4].

2462 _____. "Sketch of some of the early settlers of Brownville." The Pioneer, 1 (May, 1911), [1-3].

BRUNSWICK (CUMBERLAND CO.)

2463 ACHORN, EDGAR OAKES, ed. Bowdoin in the World War: the story of the cooperation of the college with the government and the record of Bowdoin men who served with the colors. [Brunswick: Bowdoin] College, 1929. Pp. xv, 225.

2464 ALLEN, WILLIAM, 1780-1873. "Brunswick Convention of 1816." MeHSC, 2 Ser., 2 (1891), 129-142.
   Convention to count votes cast by Maine towns regarding separation from Massachusetts.

2465 ASHBY, THOMPSON ELDRIDGE. A history of the First Parish Church in Brunswick, Maine. Louise R. Helmreich, ed. Brunswick: J. H. French, 1969. Pp. xv, 414.

2466 _____. "'Uncle Tom's Cabin' and the Brunswick Church." MeCP, 28 (February, 1941), 3-6.

2467 BEREAN BAPTIST CHURCH, BRUNSWICK, ME. Centennial anniversary of the Berean Baptist Church, October 28, 1940. n.p., [1940?]. Pp. 12. MeU.
   Includes history by Evelyn E. Langford.

2468 "BIRTHPLACE of a national industry." Sun Up, 9 (October, 1931), 14, 48.
   Dennison paper boxes.

2469   BLISS, FRANCIS R.   "The rise of music at Bowdoin." BA, 14 (1939-1940), 107-111.

2470   BOWDOIN COLLEGE. Addresses and poem on the occasion of the one hundredth anniversary of the incorporation of Bowdoin College, June 27 and 28, 1894. Brunswick, 1894. Pp. 86.
        This work and entry 2477 were also bound together and published in the same year with the title: Memorial of the one hundredth anniversary of the incorporation of Bowdoin College.

2471   _____. Addresses at the centennial exercises of the Bowdoin Medical School, June 23, 1920. Brunswick, 1920. Pp. 18.
        Addresses by Kenneth Charles Morton Sills and Addison Sanford Thayer.

2472   _____. Bowdoin College, 1802-1952: the commemoration of the opening of the college. Brunswick, 1952. Pp. 79.
        Includes historical address by Herbert Ross Brown.

2473   _____. Bowdoin College, 1794-1944: exercises of the sesquicentennial of the college charter. June 24: the convocation, the sesquicentennial dinner. June 25: the service of thanksgiving and remembrance. Brunswick, 1944. Pp. v, 87.

2474   _____. Bowdoin College, 1794-1949: an historical sketch. [Brunswick], 1950. Pp. 46. MeHi.

2475   _____. A decade of progress, 1952-1962. Brunswick, 1962. Pp. 35. Me.

2476   _____. General catalogue of Bowdoin College and the Medical School of Maine: a biographical record of alumni and officers, 1794-1950. Brunswick, 1950. Pp. xv, 670.

2477   _____. General catalogue of Bowdoin College and the Medical School of Maine 1794-1894; including a historical sketch of the institution during its first century prepared by George Thomas Little. Brunswick, 1894. Pp. cxii, 216.
        This work and entry 2470 were also bound together and published in the same year with the title: Memorial of the one hundredth anniversary of the incorporation of Bowdoin College.

2478   _____. Named professorships at Bowdoin College. Brunswick, 1976. Pp. vi, 99. MeHi.

2479   BOWDOIN COLLEGE. ATHENAEAN SOCIETY. Catalogue of the Athenaean Society, Bowdoin College. [Brunswick: J. Griffin], 1856. Pp. 68. MH.
        Prefaced by an historical sketch of the society.

2480   BOWDOIN COLLEGE. BOWDOIN ALUMNI ASSOCIATION OF BOSTON. History of the Bowdoin Alumni Association of Boston and vicinity, 1868-1887. Frank V. Wright, Arthur T. Parker, and Frank R. Kimball, comps. Salem, Mass.: Salem Pr., 1888. Pp. 128.

2481   BOWDOIN COLLEGE. MASQUE AND GOWN. The Masque and Gown of Bowdoin College presents. Brunswick, 1939. Pp. 20. Me.
        A history with a list of plays produced from 1903/04-1939/40.

2482   BOWDOIN COLLEGE. MUSIC DEPARTMENT. Ten years of music at Bowdoin, 1936-1946. Brunswick: Bowdoin College, [1946]. Pp. 16.

2483   "BOWDOIN College." Old and New, 4 (1871), 112-115.

2484   "A BOWDOIN journal of 1850." BA, 3 (1928-1929), 35-36.
        Kept by John Glidden Stetson.

2485   "BOWDOIN'S intercollegiate track beginnings." BA, 8 (1933-1934), 63-64.

2486   BOYER, KENNETH J. "The college library--past, present, future." BA, 15 (1940-1941), 73-76.
        Bowdoin College.

2487   _____. "Library facilities at Bowdoin College 1802-1960." BA, 34 (December, 1959), 2-7.

2488   BRAULT, GÉRARD J. "The earliest painting of the Bowdoin College campus." OTNE, 51 (1960-1961), 101-103.

2489   _____. "On the name 'Bowdoin.'" BA, 34 (June, 1960), 6-7.

2490   BRUNEAU, CHARLES G. E. M. "A Frenchman looks at Brunswick." BA, 6 (1931-1932), 33-37.
        In French.

2491   BRUNSWICK, ME. Brunswick, 200 years a town, 1739-1939. Brunswick: The Town, 1939. Pp. 80. MBNEH.

2492   _____. Celebration of the one hundred and fiftieth anniversary of the incorporation of the town of Brunswick, June 13, 1899. Brunswick: Pejepscot Historical Society, 1889. Pp. 92.
        Oration by Charles Carroll Everett.

2493   BRUNSWICK, ME. BICENTENNIAL COMMITTEE. Bicentennial commemoration of American independence, Brunswick, Maine, July 3rd, 4th, & 5th, 1976. Brunswick: Brunswick Publishing, 1976. Unpaged. MeHi.
        Includes historical sketch of Brunswick by Philip S. Wilder.

2494 BRUNSWICK, ME. CHURCH OF ST. JOHN THE BAP-
TIST. Souvenir of the 50th anniversary of
St. John the Baptist Parish, Brunswick, Maine.
Brunswick: Brunswick Publishing, 1927.
Pp. 80.
In French and English.

2495 BRUNSWICK, ME. FIRST PARISH CONGREGATIONAL
CHURCH. First Congregational Church in Brunswick, Me.; historical sketch, confession of
faith, covenant rules of the church, and catalogue of members, to January 15, 1872. Brunswick: Joseph Griffin, 1872. Pp. 72.

2496 _____. The First Parish in Brunswick, Maine.
n.p., [1953?]. Unpaged. MBC.

2497 _____. Manual of the First Parish Congregational Church, Brunswick, Maine, June 15,
1909. Brunswick: Record Pr., 1909. Pp. 52.
MBNEH.
Includes chronology by George T. Little.

2498 "THE BRUNSWICK bicentennial." MeCP, 25
(April, 1938), 8-9, 16-17.
First Parish Church.

2499 BURNHAM, PHILIP E. "Hawthorne's 'Fanshawe'
and Bowdoin College." EIHC, 80 (1944), 131-
138.

2500 BURTON, ALFRED E. "The engineering school at
Bowdoin." BA, 4 (1929-1930), 33-35.
1871-1881.

2501 CAMPBELL, HELEN A. "Housed in historic
Brunswick mansion." Sun Up, 10 (February,
1932), 12, 32.
Gilman Mansion.

2502 CHAPMAN, HENRY LELAND. "Early movements to
separate the District of Maine from Massachusetts; and the Brunswick Convention of 1816."
PejHSC, 1 Pt. 1 (1889), 1-20.

2503 _____. "History of Bowdoin College." BTJ,
17 (1904-1905), 344-347.

2504 CHASE, F. HALCYON. Brunswick, a brief history
of the growth and development of the town....
Brunswick: Brunswick Record, 1903. Pp. 32.
Me.

2505 CHRISTIAN, SHELDON. One hundred and twenty-
five years of religious pioneering; being the
history of the First Universalist Church in
Brunswick, Maine. [Brunswick?], 1937.
Pp. 18.

2506 CLEAVELAND, NEHEMIAH. History of Bowdoin College; with biographical sketches of its graduates, from 1806 to 1879, inclusive. Boston:
J. R. Osgood, 1882. Pp. iv, 905.
Edited and completed by Alpheus Spring Packard; for additions and corrections see entry
2526.

2507 CLEAVELAND, PARKER. Results of meteorological
observations made at Brunswick, Maine, between
1807 and 1859. Reduced and discussed at the
expense of the Smithsonian Institution by
Charles A. Schott.... Washington: Smithsonian Institution, 1867. Pp. v, 53.

2508 CUMMINGS, OSMOND RICHARD. "Trolleys to Brunswick, Maine, 1896-1937." Transportation Bulletin, No. 73 (1966), 1-42.

2509 DAGGETT, ATHERN P. "The Chapel." BA, 20
(November, 1945), 3-4.
Bowdoin College Chapel, built in 1845.

2510 DOLE, FREDERICK HOWARD, ed. A history of the
Alpha-Rho Chapter of Kappa Sigma, Bowdoin Col-
lege, March 22, 1895-1945. n.p., [1945].
Pp. 126.

2511 EATON, THOMAS H. "Memories of Chi Phi." BA,
5 (1930-1931), 78-79.
Bowdoin College.

2512 ELLIOTT, VAN COURTLANDT. "Hellenism in the
20th century at Bowdoin." BA, 10 (1935-1936),
81-83.
Teaching of Greek.

2513 FLETCHER, EDWARD GARLAND. Bowdoin, 1794-1944:
occasional stanzas. Portland: Machigonne Pr.,
1944. Pp. 11.

2514 FURBISH, JOHN. Facts about Brunswick, Maine.
[Brunswick: Pejepscot Historical Society],
1976. Pp. 62. Me.
1862-1879.

2515 HAMMOND, ANNE W. "Skolfield: shipbuilders &
seafarers." Down East, 21 (April, 1975), 52-
55, 71.

2516 HASTINGS, CHARLES H. "The eight-oared crews
of fifty years ago." BA, 15 (1940-1941), 107-
111.
Bowdoin College.

2517 HATCH, LOUIS CLINTON. The history of Bowdoin
College. Portland: Loring, Short & Harmon,
1927. Pp. xii, 500.

2518 HAWES, CHARLES T. "The first twenty years of
football at Bowdoin." BA, 13 (1938-1939),
9-12, 56-60.

2519 "HAWTHORNE'S 'Pot-8-O Club' at Bowdoin College." EIHC, 67 (1931), 225-232.

2520 HELMREICH, LOUISE ROBERTS, ed. Our town:
reminiscences and historical studies of Brunswick, Maine. Brunswick, 1967. Pp. 93. Me.

2521 HERRING, CHARLES MACOMBER. Historical discourse at the semi-centennial of the Berean
Baptist Church of Brunswick, at Brunswick,
September 2, 1890.... Brunswick: H. C. Upton, 1890. Pp. 15.

2522 BRUNSWICK

2522 KIRKLAND, EDWARD CHASE. Brunswick's golden age. Lewiston: C. P. Loring, 1941. Pp. 45.

2523 LADD, HORATIO O. "Life at Bowdoin, 1855-1859." BA, 5 (1930-1931), 110-114.

2524 LINCOLN, CHARLES STUART FESSENDEN. "Close bond between St. Paul's Church and Bowdoin faculty and students." The Northeast, 71 (October, 1944), 8-14.
Includes history of the parish.

2525 _____. The story of the first hundred years of St. Paul's Episcopal Church in Brunswick, Maine, 1844-1944. [Brunswick]: The Church, 1944. Pp. 45.

2526 [LITTLE, GEORGE THOMAS]. Additions and corrections to [the] history of Bowdoin College. n.p., 1887. Pp. [909]-933. MH.
Pagination continued from Nehemiah Cleaveland's history of the college, entry 2506; authorship attributed by Joseph Williamson.

2527 LOCKE, WILLIAM NASH. "The French colony at Brunswick, Maine, a historical sketch." Archives de Folklore, 1 (1946), 97-111.

2528 _____. "Notes on the vocabulary of the French Canadian dialect spoken in Brunswick, Maine." French Review, 19 (1945-1946), 416-422.

2529 _____. Pronunciation of the French spoken at Brunswick, Maine. Greensboro, N.C.: American Dialect Society, 1949. Pp. 201.

2530 LUNT, ROBERT H. "Bowdoin's Graeco-Roman war." BA, 16 (1941-1942), 14-15.
Literary societies.

2531 McINTIRE, GLENN R. "Chi Psi centennial." BA, 19 (November, 1944), 7-8.
Bowdoin College.

2532 "THE MAKING of Maine: H. C. Baxter & Bro." Pine Cone, 2 (Autumn, 1946), 32-38.
Canners.

2533 MALLETT, RICHARD PURINGTON. "Bowdoin leisure, 1840-1846." BA, 21 (May, 1947), 2-3.

2534 MEANS, EDGAR L. "Some baseball recollections of the eighties." BA, 10 (1935-1936), 76-78.
Bowdoin College.

2535 MEDEIROS, JOHN. "'The Orient': the early years." BA, 45 (March, 1971), 6-9.
Student newspaper at Bowdoin College.

2536 MICHENER, ROGER. "Rivals and partners: early literary societies at Bowdoin College." JLibHist, 10 (1975), 215-230.
Philomathian Society (became Peucinian Society in 1807) and the Athenaean Society.

2537 MINOT, JOHN CLAIR and DONALD FRANCIS SNOW, eds. Tales of Bowdoin: some gathered fragments and fancies of undergraduate life in the past and present told by Bowdoin men. Augusta: Kennebec Journal, 1901. Pp. 377.

2538 MINOT, JOHN CLAIR. Theta of Delta Kappa Epsilon: the story of sixty years, 1844-1904; being a historical sketch of ΔKE Fraternity at Bowdoin College, and brief biographies of its members, from its establishment to date. Augusta: Kennebec Journal Print, 1904. Pp. 272.

2539 _____, ed. Under the Bowdoin pines: a second collection of short stories of the life at Bowdoin College written by Bowdoin men. Augusta: Kennebec Journal Print, 1907. Pp. vi, 157.

2540 MITCHELL, WILMOT BROOKINGS. A remarkable Bowdoin decade, 1820-1830: a paper read at a meeting of the Town and College Club, Brunswick, Maine, December, 1950. Brunswick: Bowdoin College, 1952. Pp. 34.

2541 _____. Three score and ten: the Town and College Club, 1884-1954, and historical essay. Brunswick: [Bowdoin College], 1954. Unpaged.

2542 NIXON, PAUL. "Phi Beta Kappa at Bowdoin, 1910-1939." BA, 14 (1939-1940), 74-75.

2543 NORTH, JAMES WILLIAM. "The establishment of a college in the District of Maine." Maine Genealogist and Biographer, 1 (1875-1876), 113-116.
Bowdoin College.

2544 [PACKARD, ALPHEUS SPRING]. "Historical sketch of Bowdoin College." American Quarterly Register, 8 (1835-1836), 105-117.
Author attribution by Joseph Williamson in his "Bibliography of the State of Maine."

2545 _____. Our alma mater: an address delivered before the association of the alumni of Bowdoin College. Brunswick: J. Griffin, 1858. Pp. 49.

2546 PACKARD, CHARLOTTE MELLEN. "A New England college town." American Home Magazine, (1896), 191-199.

2547 PACKARD, GEORGE THOMAS. "Sketch of Bowdoin College." Scribner's Monthly Magazine, 12 (1876), 47-61.

2548 PARSONS, LOUIS A. "St. Paul's Parish, Brunswick, fifty years ago." The North East, 39 (December, 1911), 6-10.

2549 PHI BETA KAPPA. MAINE ALPHA, BOWDOIN COL-
LEGE. Catalogue of the fraternity of Phi
Beta Kappa, Alpha of Maine, Bowdoin College,
Brunswick. Lewiston: Journal Office, 1888.
Pp. 77. MeB.
Prefaced by an historical sketch by Henry
Leland Chapman.

2550 PRINCE, KATHERINE H. "Bowdoin and medicine
since 1921." BA, 8 (1933-1934), 42-43.

2551 [PUTNAM, HENRY]. A description of Brunswick,
Me. in letters, by a Gentleman from South
Carolina, to a friend in that state. (1820)
2d ed. Brunswick, 1823. Pp. 39. MB.

2552 REED, THOMAS BRACKETT. "May training." University Quarterly, 1 (1860), 264-268.
Military display at Bowdoin College in
1836.

2553 RICHARDS, HELEN M. "The 'bad book' which
made good." Yankee, 20 (March, 1956), 41-46.
Harriet Beecher Stowe in Brunswick.

2554 SCHUYLER, MONTGOMERY. "Bowdoin, 1794." Architectural Record, 29 (1911), 151-156.

2555 SEARS, GEORGE B. "The beginning of football
at Bowdoin." BA, 9 (1934-1935), 39-40.

2556 SHIPMAN, WILLIAM D. The early architecture
of Bowdoin College and Brunswick, Maine.
[Brunswick]: Brunswick Publishing, 1973.
Pp. 65.

2557 NO ENTRY.

2558 SILLS, KENNETH CHARLES MORTON. "Bowdoin College." Pine Cone, 3 (Spring, 1947), 18-21.

2559 _____. Joseph McKeen (1757-1807) and the beginnings of Bowdoin College, 1802. N.Y.:
Newcomen Society, 1945. Pp. 28.

2560 "SKETCH of Bowdoin College." HistMag, 2 Ser.,
8 (1870), 371-373.
From the Salem Gazette under the signature
of "Gris."

2561 SLATTERY, CHARLES LEWIS. "Brunswick and Bowdoin College." NEM, New Ser., 5 (1891-1892),
449-469.

2562 SMITH, LINCOLN. "Political leadership in a
New England community." Review of Politics,
17 (1955), 392-409.
1902-1954.

2563 _____. "Power politics in Brunswick: a case
study." Human Organization, 22 (Summer,
1963), 152-158.

2564 _____. "This may happen in Brunswick, Maine."
Social Science, 38 (June, 1963), 140-144.
Town meeting.

2565 _____. "Town manager government--a case
study." Social Science, 33 (January, 1958),
27-35.
1929-1957.

2566 _____. "Town meeting government." Social
Science, 30 (June, 1955), 174-185.

2567 _____. "Unrequited quest for city status--
a case study of 100 years." Rural Sociology,
26 (1961), 170-186.

2568 SMYTH, EGBERT COFFIN. Three discourses upon
the religious history of Bowdoin College,
during the administrations of presidents
M'Keen, Appleton and Allen. Brunswick: J.
Griffin, 1858. Pp. 80.

2569 TILLSON, GEORGE W. "Freshman recollections
of the seventies." BA, 14 (1939-1940), 77-
80.
Bowdoin College.

2570 TITCOMB, JOSEPH, JOHN MARSHALL BROWN and
JOTHAM BRADBURY SEWALL. The Memorial Hall of
Bowdoin College: its history and present
advancement. n.p., [1873]. Pp. 3. MeB.

2571 TOBIE, WALTER E. "Old-fashioned medical
school." Maine Medical Association. Journal,
33 (August, 1942), 175-179.
Bowdoin College.

2572 WEED, ERNEST H. "The river." Down East, 16
(April, 1970), 53-55.
Androscoggin River; reminiscences of a paper
mill worker.

2573 WHEELER, GEORGE AUGUSTUS and HENRY WARREN
WHEELER. History of Brunswick, Topsham and
Harpswell, Maine, including the ancient ter-
ritory known as Pejepscot. Boston: Alfred
Mudge & Son, 1878. Pp. viii, 959.

2574 WHEELER, HENRY WARREN. "Brunswick at the
time of its incorporation." PejHSC, 1 Pt. 1
(1889), 21-45.

2575 _____. "Brunswick wharf." PejHSC, 1 Pt. 1
(1889), 65-66.

2576 WHEELER, WILLIAM A. Brunswick yesterdays, a
boy's eye view of the old town in the early
'80s. Gorham, 1944. Pp. 30. Me.

2577 WHITE, BRUCE H. M. "Delta Kappa Epsilon centennial." BA, 19 (February, 1945), 3-4.
Bowdoin College.

2578 WHITTIER, ISABEL MARY SKOLFIELD. Captain Alfred Skolfield's home, a Victorian mansion.
Brunswick: Brunswick Publishing, 1956. Unpaged. MeHi.

2579 WILDER, GERALD G. "Twenty-five years in Hubbard Hall." BA, 2 (1927-1928), 104-105.
Bowdoin College Library.

2580 WILDER, PHILIP S. "The beginnings of hockey at Bowdoin." BA, 8 (1933-1934), 33-34.

2581 _____. "Bowdoin College." Maine's Own Magazine, 7 (April, 1929), 7, 28, 36.

2582 _____. "The President's House." BA, 27 (February, 1953), 2-3.
Bowdoin College.

SEE ALSO entries 259, 516, and 3532.

BUCKFIELD (OXFORD CO.)

2583 BUCKFIELD, ME. A pictorial history of Buckfield, Maine, 1776-1976. Dixfield: Coburn Farm Pr., 1976. Pp. 55. MeU.

2584 COLE, ALFRED and CHARLES FOSTER WHITMAN. A history of Buckfield, Oxford County, Maine, from the earliest explorations to the close of the year 1900. Buckfield, 1915. Pp. 758.

2585 LONG, ZADOC. From the journal of Zadoc Long, 1800-73. Peirce Long, ed. Caldwell, Id.: Caxton Printers, 1943. Pp. 316.

SEE ALSO entry 3532.

BUCKSPORT (HANCOCK CO.)

2586 BUCK, RUFUS. "Buck family of Bucksport." BHistMag, 2 (1886-1887), 19-22.

2587 _____. "A history of Bucksport, up to 1857." BHistMag, 1 (1885-1886), 65-72, 85-89, 103-108.

2588 BUCKSPORT, ME. The 150th anniversary of Bucksport, Maine, June 25, 1942. Bucksport: Bucksport Free Pr., 1942. Pp. 51. Me.

2589 BUCKSPORT, ME. ELM STREET CONGREGATIONAL CHURCH. 150th anniversary booklet ... 1803-1953. n.p., [1953]. Pp. 13. MBC.

2590 "BUCKSPORT is out on a limb." Yankee, 17 (August, 1953), 14-17.
Monument to Jonathan Buck.

2591 BUCKSPORT, past and present. n.p., 1951. Pp. 54.

2592 BUXTON, PHILIP W. "The Jed Prouty Tavern." Down East, 1 (Winter, 1955), 41-44.

2593 HATCH, FRANCIS WHITING. "Down East western." Yankee, 22 (October, 1958), 30-31.
An 1898 fracas.

2594 _____. "From Bucksport to Broadway: Dustin and William Farnum." Down East, 19 (July, 1973), 72-75, 91-93.

2595 LITTLE, HENRY. "An account of Bucksport in 1827." BHistMag, 6 (1890-1891), 42-45.

2596 MITCHELL, GEORGE O. History of Felicity Lodge, No. 19, Free and Accepted Masons, Bucksport, Maine, from March 14, 1809 to Dec. 1, 1890. Portland: Stephen Berry, 1892. Pp. 118. MeBa.

2597 WEBB, NATHAN B. East Maine Conference Seminary war record. Boston: Albert J. Wright, 1877. Pp. 54.

2598 WHITTEMORE, JAMES O. "The witch's curse, a legend of an old Maine town." NEM, New Ser., 27 (1902-1903), 111-113.

SEE ALSO entries 2082 and 4589.

BURLINGTON (PENOBSCOT CO.)

2599 No items located.

BURNHAM (WALDO CO.)

2600 No items located.

BUXTON (YORK CO.)

2601 BUXTON, ME. Bicentennial, 1772-1972, historical souvenir book, Buxton, Maine, August 10, 11, 12, and 13, 1972. n.p., 1972. Pp. 96. Me.

2602 _____. The one hundred and fiftieth anniversary of the incorporation of the town of Buxton, Maine, held at Buxton Lower Corner, August 16, 1922; with additional history. Portland: Southworth Pr., 1926. Pp. 200.

2603 _____. A report of the proceedings at the celebration of the first centennial anniversary of the incorporation of the town of Buxton, Maine, held at Buxton, August 14, 1872; being a full account of the exercise of the day--historical address ... and a list of the Revolutionary soldiers from Buxton.... Joel M. Marshall, ed. Portland: Dresser, McLellan, 1874. Pp. 288.

2604 BUXTON, ME. PROPRIETORS. Records of the proprietors of Narraganset Township, No. 1, now the town of Buxton, York County, Maine, from August 1, 1733 to January 4, 1811. William F. Goodwin, ed. Concord, N.H.: Priv. Print., 1871. Pp. xx, 400.

2605 COFFIN, CHARLES. "Narraganset Number One, now the town of Buxton, Maine." HistMag, 2 Ser., 4 (1868), 202-204.

2606 COUSENS, ALICE C. and OLIVE W. HANNAFORD. Recollections of Old Buxton, Maine. Farmington: Knowlton & McLeary, 1972. Pp. 173.

2607 LOMBARD, LUCINA HAYNES. "The Garland Tavern." Pine Tree Magazine, 7 (1907), 266-271.

2608 SARGENT, CHARLES F. Pastoral reminiscences. East Brookfield, Mass.: Sargent Holm Pr., [1918?]. Pp. 27. Me.
Buxton Congregational Church.

2609 WILLIAMS, NATHANIEL WEST. An address, delivered at Buxton, Maine, in the Congregational meeting-house, being the first centennial celebration of the settlement of this town ... 1850. Portland: Thurston, 1850. Pp. 34.

2610 WOODMAN, CYRUS. A sermon by Rev. Paul Coffin, D.D. preached August 15, 1762 in Narraganset No. 1, now Buxton, Maine and an address delivered there August 15, 1886 by Cyrus Woodman. Cambridge, Mass.: J. Wilson and Son, 1888. Pp. 95.
Woodman's address is historical; includes a bibliography of works relating to the town.

SEE ALSO entry 2298.

BYRON (OXFORD CO.)

2611 No items located.

C SURPLUS (OXFORD CO.)

2612 No items located.

CALAIS (WASHINGTON CO.)

2613 BOONE, FLORENCE E. Calais schools yesterday and today. Calais: Calais Advertiser, 1948. Pp. 46. Me.

2614 BRUMMITT, HOWARD. "An Episcopalian outpost in northeastern Maine: St. Anne's Church, Calais." The Northeast, 74 (September, 1947), 15-17.

2615 CALAIS, ME. FIRST CONGREGATIONAL CHURCH. A brief history of the First Congregational Church, Calais, Maine; their articles of faith, church covenant, standing rules, questions for self-examination and catalogue of church members. Boston: Printed for the Church, 1855. Pp. 19. MBC.

2616 _____. Historical sketch of the First Congregational Church, Calais, Maine, with confession of faith, rules, and catalogue of members to May, 1877. Boston: Thomas Todd, 1877. Pp. 35. MeHi.

2617 CALAIS, ME. ORDINANCES, ETC. The charter, ordinances, and a brief history of the city of Calais, Maine, together with other matter relating to city affairs. William J. Fowler, comp. Calais: Advertiser Publishing, 1901. Pp. 165.

2618 "THE CENTENARY of St. Anne's." The Northeast, 80 (July, 1953), 2-3.
St. Anne's Church.

2619 CHURCHILL, LAURIE. "The Gregory House." Roots, 1 (Spring, 1975), 26-31.

2620 COLE, SHARON. "Memories of Calais." Roots, 1 (Spring, 1975), 39-42.

2621 GANONG, WILLIAM FRANCIS. Ste. Croix (Dochet) Island. (1902) Susan Brittain Ganong, ed. [2d ed.]. Saint John, N.B., 1945. Pp. xix, 125.

2622 GARDNER, OLIVE. "Retrospective glances." Pine Tree Magazine, 6 (1906-1907), 426-432.

2623 HADLOCK, WENDELL STANWOOD. "Recent excavations at De Monts' Colony, St. Croix Island, Maine." OTNE, 44 (1953-1954), 93-99.

2624 KNOWLTON, ISAAC CASE. Annals of Calais, Maine, and St. Stephen, New Brunswick; including the village of Milltown, Me., and the present town of Milltown, N.B. Calais: J. A. Sears, 1875. Pp. 208.

2625 MAINE HISTORICAL SOCIETY. Tercentenary of De Mont's settlement at St. Croix Island, June 25, 1904. Portland, 1905. Pp. 78.
Includes address by Joshua Lawrence Chamberlain.

2626 MILLIGAN, D. WINFIELD. History of the First Methodist Episcopal Church of Calais, Maine. ... [Calais]: Calais Advertiser Pr., [1935?]. Pp. 19. MBNEH.

2627 PARKER, BARRETT. Saint Croix Island, 1604-1942. Cambridge, Mass.: Crimson Printing, 1942. Pp. 19.

2628 ROGERS, C. TALBOT. "America's first Christmas." Yankee, 25 (December, 1961), 32-33, 100, 102.

2629 SHAW, DONALD E. "Calais Street Railway." Transportation, 3 (January, 1949), 1-4.

2630 SMITH, MASON PHILIP. "Confederate raid on Calais." Down East, 13 (October, 1966), 30-33, 43-45, 48-49.
1864.

2631 CAMBRIDGE

SEE ALSO entries 1840-1841, 1844, and 1874.

CAMBRIDGE (SOMERSET CO.)

2631   No items located.

CAMDEN (KNOX CO.)

2632   "A BRIEF historical sketch of the Camden Public Library." MeLB, 16 (1930-1931), 99-100.

2633   CAMDEN, ME. CHESTNUT STREET BAPTIST CHURCH. The 150th anniversary of the Chestnut Street Baptist Church, Camden, Maine, 1808-1958. n.p., [1958]. Pp. 8. MeHi.

2634   CAMDEN, ME. FIRST CONGREGATIONAL CHURCH. Services in celebration of the 100th anniversary of the First Congregational Church, Camden, Maine, Sept. 10-11-12, 1905. Camden: Camden Publishing, 1905. Pp. 80. MBC.

2635   ["CAMDEN, Maine."]   BTJ, 22 (1909-1910), 321-364.

2636   CAMPBELL, LEROY A. History of the Chestnut Street Baptist Church of Camden, Me. [Camden]: Camden Pub., 1934. Pp. 28. MeHi.

2637   CHASE, BENJAMIN CHAPMAN. An address ... delivered at Camden, Maine, September 11, 1855, at the expiration of half a century, from the organization of the First Congregational Church in that town; also a brief sketch of the revival there in the year 1836, names of church members.... Boston: T. R. Marvin, 1855. Pp. 28.

2638   CROCKETT, FRED E. "The yachts 'Robador' of Camden." Down East, 22 (September, 1975), 42-45, 70-71.
        Several vessels of the same name owned by members of the Law family.

2639   CULLER, R. D. Skiffs and schooners. Camden: International Marine Publishing, 1974. Pp. 199.

2640   CUMMINGS, MILDRED H. "The golden turrets of Norumbega." Down East, 21 (August, 1974), 56-59, 88, 92.
        A stone castle built in the 1880s by Joseph B. Stearns.

2641   DIETZ, LEW. Camden Hills: an informal history of the Camden-Rockport region. Camden: Camden Herald Pr., 1947. Pp. 93.

2642   LOCKE, JOHN LYMBURNER. Sketches of the history of the town of Camden, Maine; including incidental references to the neighboring places and adjacent waters. Hallowell: Masters, Smith, 1859. Pp. xii, 267.

2643   "A LOVELY English church on the green in Camden town." The Northeast, 73 (September, 1946), 10-12.
        St. Thomas' Church.

2644   MALCOLM, JOHN. "Maine's historic Conway House." Down East, 12 (August, 1965), 39-41.

2645   MUNSON, GORHAM BERT. "Parnassus on Penobscot." NEQ, 41 (1968), 264-273.

2646   ROBINSON, REUEL. History of Amity Lodge, No. 6, Free and Accepted Masons, Camden, Maine. Camden: Camden Publishing, 1897. Pp. 103.

2647   "THE SACRIFICE, a tale of the War of 1814." Eastern Magazine, 1 (1835-1836), 1-13.

2648   "SAINT Thomas' Church, Camden, 1855-1955." The Northeast, 82 (July, 1955), 10-19.

2649   TEWKSBURY, JOHN LESLIE. History of Camden Commandery, No. 23, Knights Templar, Camden, Maine, chartered February 10, 1905. Camden: Camden Herald Print, 1930. Pp. 95. Me.

2650   WEBBER, JOHN W. "The high mountains of Penobscot: notes on the Camden Hills." Appalachia, 27 (1948-1949), 131-148.

        SEE ALSO entries 707, 1653, 1666, 1671, 1673, 1833, 2082, 4589, and 4612.

CANAAN (SOMERSET CO.)

2651   JOHNSON, GEORGE W. History of Carrabasett Lodge, No. 161, Free and Accepted Masons, Canaan, Me., from March 2, 1871 to October, 1891. Portland: Stephen Berry, 1892. Pp. 27. MeBa.

2652   LEWIS, JULIA TUTTLE. "Canaan, Maine." SJMH, 10 (1922), 33-34.

2653   SMITH, LILLIAN CLAYTON. Old Canaan during the Revolution, by Lillian Clayton Smith; Grandmother's grandmother, by Louise Helen Coburn. Skowhegan: Independent Reporter, 1910. Unpaged.

        SEE ALSO entry 1816.

CANTON (OXFORD CO.)

2654   FREEMASONS. CANTON, ME. WHITNEY LODGE. No. 167. History of Whitney Lodge, Canton, from March 21, A.D. 1872, to December 31, A.D. 1880. Canton: J. W. Bicknell, 1880. Pp. 23. [MePGLM].
        Signed by committee of W. H. H. Washburn, Dana Bradford, and T. C. Wright.

SEE ALSO entry 3532.

CAPE ELIZABETH (CUMBERLAND CO.)

2655 BAXTER, JAMES PHINNEY. "Richmond's Island." MeHSC, 3 Ser., 1 (1904), 66-87.

2656 CAPE ELIZABETH, ME. FIRST CHURCH OF CHRIST. Address and poem delivered at Cape Elizabeth, Maine, September 10, 1884, at the 150th anniversary of the First Church of Christ (North Congregational). Portland: Southworth Bros., 1884. Pp. 27. MeHi.
    Address by Edwin A. Harlow; poem by Louisa E. Harris.

2657 DELANO PARK AND ANNEX ASSOCIATION, CAPE ELIZABETH, ME. History and by-laws of the Delano Park and Annex Association, 1885-1965. n.p., [1965?]. Pp. 21. MeHi.

2658 NO ENTRY.

2659 JORDAN, WILLIAM BARNES, JR. A history of Cape Elizabeth, Maine. Portland: House of Falmouth, 1965. Pp. 385.

2660 NORWOOD, LESLIE E. "The port of Richmond's Island." SJMH, 13 (1925), 100-101.

2661 OGDEN, MARGUERITE. "A visit to an historical island." SJMH, 7 (1919-1920), 154-155.
    Richmond's Island.

2662 RAY, ROGER BRAY. Cape Elizabeth and the American Revolution. Cape Elizabeth, 1975. Unpaged.

2663 REYNOLDS, EDWARD CLAYTON, comp. The Cape Elizabeth High School, a history. Portland: Stevens & Jones, 1892. Pp. 76.

2664 ROERDEN, HAROLD H. Collections from Cape Elizabeth, Maine. Cape Elizabeth: Published by the Town, 1965. Pp. 144.

2665 TRYON, SYLVIA. "Maine's leading light-house." Maine's Own Magazine, 8 (April, 1930), 6.
    Cape Elizabeth Light.

2666 WILLIS, WILLIAM. "Treasure trove in Maine." Bankers Magazine, 10 (1855), 9-12.

    SEE ALSO entries 1265, 1483, 1487, 1492, 1512, 1534, 4202, 4287, and 4820.

CARATUNK PLANTATION (SOMERSET CO.)

2667 CARATUNK, ME. CONGREGATIONAL CHURCH OF CHRIST. The seventy-fifth anniversary service ... August 12, 1962. n.p., [1962]. Pp. 4. MBC.
    Includes a history of the church.

CARIBOU (AROOSTOOK CO.)

2668 CARIBOU, ME. Caribou centennial 1859-1959, week of July 19-25, historical program. [Caribou]: Caribou Publishing, 1959. Pp. 56. Me.

2669 CARIBOU, ME. FIRST UNIVERSALIST CHURCH. Addresses delivered Sunday, January 19, 1975 celebrating the Society's 80th anniversary. n.p., 1975. Unpaged. MeHi.
    Historical addresses by Clara C. Piper, Marjorie A. Crockett, and Earle T. McKinney.

2670 CARTER, GEORGE M. "Caribou--the potato town." Sun Up, 5 (October, 1927), 14-17.

2671 COLLINS, (S. W.) CO., CARIBOU, ME. Lumber than and now: S. W. Collins Co., 1844-1959. Caribou, 1960. Unpaged. MeU.

2672 COLLINS, SAMUEL WILSON, JR. 100 years of lumbering by the Collins family of Caribou, Maine. [Caribou], 1944. Unpaged. Me.

2673 HARDISON, GROVER M. and FRANK W. LOVERING. Romance of the Eaton Grant--part of Caribou Township and early land surveys in Aroostook County. Caribou, 1947. Pp. 22. MeHi.

2674 SINCOCK, LORA K. A history of the First Universalist Church of Caribou, Maine, 1895-1935. n.p., [1935?]. Unpaged. MBC.

2675 WHITE, STELLA KING. Early history of Caribou, Maine, 1843-1895. [Houlton?], 1945. Pp. 147.

    SEE ALSO entry 50.

CARMEL (PENOBSCOT CO.)

2676 No items located.

CARRABASSETT VALLEY (FRANKLIN CO.)

2677 No items located.

CARROLL PLANTATION (PENOBSCOT CO.)

2678 No items located.

CARRYING PLACE TOWN TOWNSHIP (SOMERSET CO.)

2679 No items located.

CARRYING PLACE TOWNSHIP (SOMERSET CO.)

2680   No items located.

CARTHAGE (FRANKLIN CO.)

2681   No items located.

CARY PLANTATION (AROOSTOOK CO.)

2682   No items located.

CASCO (CUMBERLAND CO.)

2683   HOLDEN, WILLIAM CROSS. The story and history of Casco, Maine. Casco, 1941. Pp. 60. Me.

2684   "RATTLESNAKE Mountain has moved." Yankee, 17 (June, 1953), 19-21.

CASTINE (HANCOCK CO.)

2685   ADAMS, GEORGE MOULTON. Castine sixty years ago, a historical address delivered in connection with old home week in Castine, Maine, Sunday evening, August 12, 1900. Boston: Samuel Usher, 1900. Pp. 17.

2686   BALLARD, WILLIAM. "Castine, October 1, 1815 [i.e. 1814]." BHistMag, 2 (1886-1887), 45-51.

2687   BATCHELDER, SAMUEL FRANCIS. "Adventures of John Nutting, Cambridge loyalist." Cambridge [Massachusetts] Historical Society. Publications, 5 (1910), 56-98.

2688   BOURNE, MIRIAM ANNE and RUSSELL BOURNE. "A man for Castine." Yankee, 33 (October, 1969), 76-81, 126-127, 129-131.
        John Perkins.

2689   BOURNE, RUSSELL. "The Penobscot fiasco." Am Heritage, 25 (October, 1974), 28-33.
        Ill-starred attempt to eject British in 1779.

2690   BROOKS, NOAH. "An old town with a history." Century, 24 (1882), 695-708.

2691   [CALEF, JOHN]. The siege of Penobscot by the rebels; containing a journal of the proceedings of His Majesty's forces, detached from the 74th and 82d regiments, consisting of about 700 rank and file, under the command of Captain Brigadier General Francis M'Lean, and of three of His Majesty's sloops of war, of 16 guns each, under the command of Captain Henry Mowat, senior officer; when besieged by three thousand three hundred (rebels) land forces, under the command of Brigadier-General Solomon Lovell, and seventeen rebel ships and vessels of war, under the command of G. Saltonstall, commodore; to which is annexed a Proclamation issued June 15, 1779, by General M'Lean and Captain Barclay to the inhabitants; also Brigadier-General Lovell's proclamation to the inhabitants; and his letter to Commodore Saltonstall, found on board the rebel ship Hunter; together with the names, force, and commanders, of the rebel ships destroyed in Penobscot Bay and River, August 14 and 15, 1779. With a chart of the peninsula of Majabigwaduce, and of Penobscot River. To which is subjoined a postscript, wherein a short account of the country of Penobscot is given. Nathan Goold, ed. N.Y.: W. Abbatt, 1910. Pp. 55.
        Originally published in London in 1781.

2692   CAMPBELL, THOMAS JOSEPH. "A link with the past." CathHistRev, New Ser., 2 (1922), 283-284.
        Early Catholic mission.

2693   CASTINE, ME. The centennial of Castine: an account of the exercises at the celebration of the one hundredth anniversary of the incorporation of the town, July 9, 1896. Castine, 1896. Pp. 67.

2694   "THE CASTINE centennial." The Church Exchange, 6 (1898-1899), 17-21.
        Unitarian Society.

2695   "CASTINE-1814." Wilson Museum Bulletin, 1 (Winter, 1972-73), [1-3].

2696   "A CASTINE summer, 1779." Wilson Museum Bulletin, 2 (Fall, 1975), [1-3].

2697   CAYFORD, JOHN E. The Penobscot Expedition, being an account of the largest American naval engagement of the Revolutionary War. Orrington: C & H Publishing, 1976. Pp. xi, 132. Me.

2698   CLARK, GEORGE FABER. "Military operations at Castine, Maine." Worcester HSProc, 9 (1889), 18-38.
        1525 through the Civil War.

2699   CLAYTON, TOM. "Maine Maritime Academy." Down East, 5 (October, 1958), 16-18.

2700   CUMMINGS, EPHRAIM CHAMBERLAIN. "Capuchin and Jesuit Fathers at Pentagoët." MeHSC, 2 Ser., 5 (1894), 161-188.

2701   DEVEREUX, CHARLENE. Castine then's and now's. n.p., [1966?]. Pp. 24. MeHi.

2702   DRAKE, SAMUEL ADAMS. "The Plymouth trading-house at Penobscot: where was it?" MeHSC, 2 Ser., 3 (1892), 409-418.
        Drake claims it was at Castine.

°2703 "EASTERN State Normal School." Maine Teachers' Digest, 1 (1940-1941), 64-65, 75.

2704 EVANS, ELIZABETH EDSON GIBSON. "A new watering place." Harper's New Monthly Magazine, 55 (1877), 345-356.

2705 FELLOWS, RAYMOND. "The trial of Ebenezer Ball." Peabody Law Review, 2 (1937-1938), 43-46, 70-75.
    Murder of John Tileston Downes in Robbinston in 1811.

2706 FREEMASONS. CASTINE, ME. HANCOCK LODGE, NO. 4. History of Hancock Lodge, No. 4, Free and Accepted Masons, Castine. Portland: S. Berry, 1872-1911. 5v.
    Volume 5 has imprint: Ellsworth: Hancock County Publishing Company.

2707 GODFREY, JOHN EDWARDS. "Pilgrims at Penobscot." American Historical Record, 3 (1874), 366-371.

2708 "'THE GOOD old days,' a hundred years ago in Castine." Wilson Museum Bulletin, 1 (Summer, 1969), [1-2].

2709 GOOLD, NATHAN. "Colonel Jonathan Mitchell's Cumberland County Regiment: Bagaduce Expedition, 1779." MeHSC, 2 Ser., 10 (1899), 52-80, 143-174.

2710 GOULD, EDWARD KALLOCH. Storming of the heights: Maine's embattled farmers at Castine in the Revolution. Rockland: Courier-Gazette Pr., 1932. Pp. 59.

2711 GREENBIE, SYDNEY and MARJORIE LATTA BARSTOW GREENBIE. Castine, a dramatized biography of a town, in three parts. n.p., Traversity Pr., 1948. Pp. 95.

2712 HARVEY, D. C. "The Halifax-Castine Expedition." Dalhousie Review, 18 (1938), 207-213.
    War of 1812.

2713 HATCH, FRANCIS WHITING. "Castine--historic gem of Penobscot Bay." Down East, 17 (July, 1971), 66-69, 88, 91.

2714 _____. "Dennett's Wharf." Yankee, 24 (April, 1960), 52-53, 100-102.

2715 _____. "Seagoing bank notes with denominational masts." AmNep, 15 (1955), 213-216.

2716 HATCH, FRIEDA. "Facts of interest concerning Fort George." SJMH, 12 (1924), 47-52.

2717 "HISTORICAL geology of Maine." Wilson Museum Bulletin, 1 (Winter, 1968), [1].

2718 "IN old Castine." MeCathHM, 5 (July, 1915), 38-53.

2719 JACK, EDWARD. "Loyalists at Penobscot." BHistMag, 1 (1885-1886), 97-101.

2720 MUNSON, GORHAM BERT. "St. Castin: a legend revised." Dalhousie Review, 45 (1965), 339-360.

2721 NASH, GILBERT. The original journal of General Solomon Lovell, kept during the Penobscot Expedition, 1779; with a sketch of his life, together with the proceedings of the [Weymouth Historical] Society for 1879-1880. [Weymouth, Mass.]: Weymouth Historical Society, 1881. Pp. 127.

2722 NOE, SYDNEY PHILIP. The Castine deposit: an American hoard. N.Y.: American Numismatic Society, 1942. Pp. 37.

2723 "NOTES on colonial Penobscot." SJMH, 1 (1913-1914), 17-21.

2724 "ONCE upon a time on Perkins Street." Wilson Museum Bulletin, 1 (Winter, 1968), [2-3].

2725 "'QUALITY avenue'--Upper Main Street, Castine." Wilson Museum Bulletin, 1 (Summer, 1974), entire issue.

2726 ROY, LUCIENNE C. "Castine." Women's Canadian Historical Society of Ottawa. Transactions, 9 (1925), 48-54.
    Castine as an outpost of New France.

2727 "ROYALISTS at Penobscot, Fort George now Castine, 1777, 1782." BHistMag, 5 (1889-1890), 89-91.

2728 SCOTT, KENNETH. "New Hampshire's part in the Penobscot Expedition." AmNep, 7 (1947), 200-212.

2729 SEWALL, RUFUS KING. "Field day of the Maine Historical Society at Castine, Sept. 21, 1880." MeHistMag, 8 (1893), 60-64.
    Relates to Castine.

2730 SHAW, HENRY I., JR. "Penobscot assault--1779." Military Affairs, 17 (Summer, 1953), 83-94.

2731 SPRAGUE, JOHN FRANCIS. "The proposed province of New Ireland." SJMH, 2 (1914-1915), 219-220.
    A new British province to be colonized by American loyalists, 1780.

2732 STANWOOD, CORDELIA J. "Castine, a village by the sea." House Beautiful, 48 (1920), 92-94, 126, 128.
    Historic houses.

2733 STEVENSON, EDWARD IRENAEUS. "The story of Castine, Maine." MagAmHist, 29 (1893), 21-31.

2734 CASTINE

2734 STORM, COLTON. "The relief of Fort George." ColbLibQ, 1 (1943), 60-64.
Penobscot Expedition, 1779.

2735 SYLVESTER, TORREY A. "Down East naval defeat." Down East, 12 (September, 1965), 32-33, 46-49, 51, 53, 55.
Penobscot Expedition, 1779.

2736 UPHAM, FRANK KIDDER. Genealogy and family history of the Uphams, of Castine, Maine, and Dixon, Illinois.... Newark, N.J.: Advertiser Printing, 1887. Pp. iv, 68.

2737 WALSH, LOUIS SEBASTIAN. "Old mission site regained by Church." MeCathHM, 8 (1919-1928), 206-211.

2738 WHEELER, GEORGE AUGUSTUS. Castine past and present: the ancient settlement of Pentagöet and the modern town. Boston: Rockwell and Churchill, 1896. Pp. ix, 112.

2739 _____. "Fort Pentagöet and the French occupation of Castine." MeHSC, 2 Ser., 4 (1893), 113-123.

2740 WILLIAMSON, JOSEPH. "The British occupation of Penobscot during the Revolution." MeHSC, 2 Ser., 1 (1890), 389-400.

2741 _____. "Castine, and the old coins found there." MeHSC, 6 (1859), 105-126.

2742 _____. "The conduct of Paul Revere in the Penobscot Expedition." MeHSC, 2 Ser., 3 (1892), 379-392.

2743 _____. "The proposed province of New Ireland." MeHSC, 7 (1876), 199-206.
A new British province to be colonized by American loyalists, 1780.

2744 _____. "The proposed province of New Ireland." MeHSC, 3 Ser., 1 (1904), 147-157.
Differs from earlier article above.

2745 _____. "The trial of Ebenezer Ball, at Castine, 1811." BHistMag, 3 (1887-1888), 61-65.
Accused of killing John Tileston Downes in Robbinston in 1811.

2746 WILSON MUSEUM, CASTINE, ME. Castine. Castine, 1958. Unpaged.

2747 "THE WILSON Museum--on its 50th birthday." Wilson Museum Bulletin, 1 (Spring, 1971), entire issue.

2748 "WINTERS in old Castine." Wilson Museum Bulletin, 1 (Winter, 1973-1974), [1-2].

SEE ALSO entries 707, 962, 1264, 1597, 1621, 2425, and 4587.

CASTLE HILL (AROOSTOOK CO.)

2749 No items located.

CASWELL PLANTATION (AROOSTOOK CO.)

2750 No items located.

CENTERVILLE (WASHINGTON CO.)

2751 No items located.

CHAIN OF PONDS TOWNSHIP (FRANKLIN CO.)

2752 No items located.

CHAPMAN (AROOSTOOK CO.)

2753 No items located.

CHARLESTON (PENOBSCOT CO.)

2754 SMITH, OSCAR L. History of Olive Branch Lodge, No. 124, of Free and Accepted Masons, Charleston, Me., from A.D. 1864 to A.D. 1881. Portland: Stephen Berry, 1881. Pp. 24. MeBa.

CHARLOTTE (WASHINGTON CO.)

2755 CHARLOTTE, ME. SESQUICENTENNIAL COMMITTEE. Charlotte, Maine, sesquicentennial, 1825-1975, historical souvenir book. n.p., 1975. Pp. 80. Me.

2756 FISHER, LEWIS BEALS. The story of a Down East plantation: facts and fancies about the Pine Tree State. Chicago, 1914. Pp. 219.

CHASE STREAM TOWNSHIP (SOMERSET CO.)

2757 No items located.

CHELSEA (KENNEBEC CO.)

2758 BARTER, J. MALCOLM. "A century at Togus, 1866-1966." Down East, 12 (June, 1966), 34-35, 54-55, 60-61.
National Home for Disabled Volunteer Soldiers.

2759 WHITMAN, WILLIAM EDWARD SEAVER. History and description of the eastern branch of the National Home for Disabled Volunteer Soldiers, near Augusta, Maine: a complete guide book for visitors. Augusta: Sprague, Owen & Nash, 1879. Pp. viii, 79.

SEE ALSO entries 1624, 1629, and 1648.

CHERRYFIELD (WASHINGTON CO.)

2760 MILLIKEN, JAMES ALPHONSO. "Ancient Narraguagus." MeHistMag, 7 (1891-1892), 162-164.

2761 "125TH anniversary at Cherryfield." MeCP, 45 (December 15, 1958), 10.
First Congregational Church.

SEE ALSO entries 1840, 1864, and 1875.

CHESTER (PENOBSCOT CO.)

2762 BOOKER, MABEL LIBBY. History and genealogy of Chester, Maine.... n.p., [1949?]. Pp. 180.

CHESTERVILLE (FRANKLIN CO.)

2763 BUTLER, BENJAMIN and NATALIE STURGES BUTLER. Father Sewall and his Zion's Hill neighborhood, Chester (Chesterville), Maine, c. 1800. [Chester], 1967. Pp. 65.

2764 SEWALL, OLIVER. History of Chesterville, Maine. Farmington: J. S. Swift, 1875. Pp. 96.

SEE ALSO entry 1419.

CHESUNCOOK TOWNSHIP (PISCATAQUIS CO.)

2765 GETCHELL, DAVID R. "Ghost town--Chesuncook." Down East, 4 (June, 1958), 32-34.

CHINA (KENNEBEC CO.)

2766 CHINA, Maine: a bicentennial history. Weeks Mills: Marion T. Van Strien, 1975. Pp. xi, 290, iii, 121.

2767 JONES, RUFUS M. Reminiscences of South China. [South China]: South China Library Association, 1955. 46 leaves. MeU.

2768 THURLOW, CLINTON F. The Weeks Mills "Y" of the two-footer. [Weeks Mills?], 1964. Pp. 63.
Railroad.

SEE ALSO entry 1645.

CLIFTON (PENOBSCOT CO.)

2769 No items located.

CLINTON (KENNEBEC CO.)

2770 DODGE, A. D. History of Sebasticook Lodge, No. 146, of Free and Accepted Masons, Clinton, Maine, from A.D. 1881 to A.D. 1891. Clinton: B. T. Foster, [1891?]. Pp. 23. MeHi.

2771 FISHER, CARLETON EDWARD. History of Clinton, Maine. Augusta: K. J. Printing, 1970. Pp. x, 409.

2772 HAMMONS, EVERETT. History of Sebasticook Lodge, No. 146, of Free and Accepted Masons, Clinton, Maine, from 1874 to 1881. Clinton: B. T. Foster, 1881. MeHi.

2773 HATCH, M. P. History of Sebasticook Lodge, No. 146, of Free and Accepted Masons, Clinton, Maine, from A.D. 1868, to A.D. 1874. Portland: Stephen Berry, 1875. Pp. 19. MeBa.

SEE ALSO entry 799.

COBURN GORE (FRANKLIN CO.)

2774 No items located.

CODYVILLE PLANTATION (WASHINGTON CO.)

2775 No items located.

COLUMBIA (WASHINGTON CO.)

2776 DAY, CLARENCE ALBERT. Leighton's Store at Epping Lower Corner. n.p., n.d. 6 leaves. MBNEH.

2777 _____. Town affairs in old Columbia. n.p., n.d. 10 leaves. MBNEH.

2778 COLUMBIA

2778 HARRIS, HERBERT. History of the Tuscan Lodge, Free and Accepted Masons, Columbia, Maine, from its organization in 1798, to its close in 1817. Portland: The Grand Lodge, 1894. Pp. 36.

2779 LEIGHTON, LEVI. Centennial historical sketch of the town of Columbia as gathered from the town records, family records and traditional history from the memory of its aged citizens; from 1796 to 1896. Machias: The Republican, 1896. Pp. 31.

2780 _____. "Sketches in Columbia, Maine." MHGR, 9 (1898), 84-94.
Biographies.

SEE ALSO entry 1856.

COLUMBIA FALLS (WASHINGTON CO.)

2781 BUCKNAM, SAMUEL. "The town of Columbia Falls." BHistMag, 1 (1885-1886), 136-137.

2782 CHAMBERLAIN, SAMUEL. "The Thomas Ruggles House in Columbia Falls, Maine." Antiques, 101 (1972), 367-373.

2783 CRANE, J. R. "Priceless example of a lost art." Yankee, 18 (January, 1954), 60-63.
Woodcarving in the Ruggles House.

2784 DONWORTH, C. B. "The Thomas Ruggles House at Columbia Falls, Maine." SJMH, 10 (1922), 138-139.

2785 GOLDSMITH, MARGARET O. "The Ruggles House at Columbia Falls, Maine." OTNE, 15 (1924-1925), 68-76.

2786 SELIGMANN, HERBERT J. "First flower of the wilderness, the Ruggles House." Down East, 6 (June, 1960), 47-50.

SEE ALSO entry 1856.

COMSTOCK TOWNSHIP (SOMERSET CO.)

2787 No items located.

CONCORD TOWNSHIP (SOMERSET CO.)

2788 No items located.

CONNOR TOWNSHIP (AROOSTOOK CO.)

2789 No items located.

COOPER (WASHINGTON CO.)

2790 No items located.

COPLIN PLANTATION (FRANKLIN CO.)

2791 No items located.

CORINNA (PENOBSCOT CO.)

2792 WOOD, LILLA EVA. A brief history of Corinna, Maine, from its purchase in 1804 to 1916. Bangor: J. P. Bass, 1916. Pp. 55.

CORINTH (PENOBSCOT CO.)

2793 PALMER, MASON SKINNER. Early gleamings and random recollections of the town of Corinth, Maine, from 1792 to 1883. Bangor: B. A. Burr, 1883. Pp. 34.

CORNISH (YORK CO.)

2794 ELLIS, LEOLA CHAPLIN and KERA C. MILLARD. Early Cornish, 1616-1916. n.p., [1972?]. Pp. 135. MBNEH.

2795 _____. More about early Cornish. [Cornish?, 1975]. Pp. 217. MeHi.

2796 FREEMASONS. CORNISH, ME. GREENLEAF LODGE, NO. 117. History of Greenleaf Lodge, No. 117, Cornish, Maine, instituted May 4, A. L. 6863. Portland: Stephen Berry, 1873. Pp. 14. MeBa.

2797 HILLSIDE CONGREGATIONAL CHURCH, CORNISH, ME. Hillside Congregational Church, sixty-fifth anniversary in memory of the Reverend Albert Cole, M.A. ... record of exercises and historical address.... Portland: Southworth, 1905. Pp. 51. MeHi.

2798 SMALL, LAURISTON WARD. The old Baptist Church in Cornish, Maine. Kezar Falls: R. Fult: Wormwood, 1887. Pp. 55. MeHi.

CORNVILLE (SOMERSET CO.)

2799 FOLSOM, EMMA B. "Cornville's old church." Sun Up, 10 (March, 1932), 17, 56.
Built in 1825.

COVE POINT TOWNSHIP (PISCATAQUIS CO.)

2800   No items located.

COX PATENT (AROOSTOOK CO.)

2801   No items located.

CRANBERRY ISLES (HANCOCK CO.)

2802   "THE CRANBERRY Islands." BHistMag, 4 (1888-1889), 22-23.

2803   GROSSINGER, RICHARD. Book of the Cranberry Islands. Los Angeles: Black Sparrow Pr., 1974. Pp. ix, 308.

2804   SPIKER, LA RUE. "The Cranberry Islands." Down East, 13 (May, 1966), 30-35.

SEE ALSO entries 1570, 1587, and 1617.

CRAWFORD (WASHINGTON CO.)

2805   McKEOWN, JUDY. "The common school." Roots, 1 (Spring, 1975), 52-54.

CRYSTAL (AROOSTOOK CO.)

2806   No items located.

CUMBERLAND (CUMBERLAND CO.)

2807   CHEBEAGUE ISLAND METHODIST HISTORICAL SOCIETY. The church on Chebeague, 1802-1960. n.p., [1960]. Pp. 54. MeHi.

2808   CUMBERLAND CENTRE, ME. CONGREGATIONAL CHURCH. One hundredth anniversary of the Congregational Church, Cumberland Centre, Me., September 21, 1893. Portland: Southworth Bros., 1893. Pp. 64.
Includes historical addresses by Trueman Summerfield Perry and B. B. Merrill.

2809   HAUK, ZARAH WILLIAM. The stone sloops of Chebeauge and the men who sailed them; also some Chebeague miscellany. (1949) 2d ed. rev. Boston: Alden-Hauk, 1953. Pp. 167. MeHi.

2810   PERRY, TRUEMAN SUMMERFIELD. A sermon, preached on the eighty-fifth anniversary of the Congregational Church, at Cumberland, Maine, September 1, 1878. Portland: Globe Publishing, 1879. Pp. 20.

2811   SWEETSER, MARY E. History of the town of Cumberland, Maine for the centennial celebration, July 2-4, 1921. Yarmouth: A. F. Tilton, [1921?]. Pp. 36. Me.

2812   SWEETSER, PHYLLIS STURDIVANT. Cumberland, Maine in four centuries. Cumberland, 1976. Pp. viii, 351. Me.

2813   WESTON, ISAAC. A history of the Congregational Church and Society in Cumberland, Me. Portland: Brown Thurston, 1861. Pp. 55. MeBa.

CUSHING (KNOX CO.)

2814   SEE entries 1654 and 4660.

CUTLER (WASHINGTON CO.)

2815   CUTLER, Maine. Boston: E. H. Pierce, n.d. Pp. 15. MeHi.

SEE ALSO entry 962.

CYR PLANTATION (AROOSTOOK CO.)

2816   CYR Plantation centennial, 1870-1970. n.p., [1970?]. Pp. 312.

DALLAS PLANTATION (FRANKLIN CO.)

2817   No items located.

DAMARISCOTTA (LINCOLN CO.)

2818   BERRY, GEORGE STILLMAN. "The great shell mounds of Damariscotta." NEM, New Ser., 19 (1898-1899), 178-188.

2819   CHADBOURNE, PAUL ANSEL. "Oyster shell deposit in Damariscotta." MeHSC, 6 (1859), 347-351.

2820   DUNBAR, ROBERT E. "Lord of the mills: the James Kavanagh House, 1803." Down East, 23 (September, 1976), 40-43, 79.

2821   GOLDTHWAIT, RICHARD P. "The Damariscotta shell heaps and coastal stability." American Journal of Science, 5 Ser., 30 (1935), 1-13.

2822   HILTON, WILLIAM H. History of Alna Lodge, No. 43, Damariscotta, from its institution to April, 1874. Portland: Stephen Berry, 1874. Pp. 24.
Freemasons; continued by entries 2824 and 2825.

2823 LINCOLN, EDWARD JOSHUA. The Blackstones and their Indian's paradise (old Damariscotta). Damariscotta: News Print Shop, 1952. Pp. 52.
Blackstone family.

2824 MERRY, CHARLES GLIDDEN. History of Alna Lodge, No. 43, Free and Accepted Masons, Damariscotta, Me., from April, 1874 to December, 1880. Portland: Stephen Berry, 1883. Pp. 25-40. MeBa.
Pagination continued from a history covering 1823 to April, 1874 by William H. Hilton; entry 2822.

2825 _____. History of Alna Lodge, No. 43, Free and Accepted Masons, Damariscotta, Maine, from 1880 to 1881 ... Part III. Portland: Stephen Berry, 1891. Pp. 41-68. MeBa.
Pagination continued from previous entry.

2826 WEYGANDT, CORNELIUS. "Red swarms." Yankee, 1 (December, 1935), 28-30.
Shell heaps.

SEE ALSO entries 1678, 1683-1684, 1708-1709, and 4589.

DANFORTH (WASHINGTON CO.)

2827 LOVE, WILBUR J. A history of Danforth, Maine. n.p., [1936]. Pp. 64. Me.

SEE ALSO entry 50.

DAVIS TOWNSHIP (FRANKLIN CO.)

2828 NILE, LE ROY. Kennebago summer. Farmington: Knowlton & McLeary, 1947. Pp. 107.
Social life and customs; Kennebago Lake.

DAYS ACADEMY GRANT (PISCATAQUIS CO.)

2829 No items located.

DAYTON (YORK CO.)

2830 DAYTON, ME. HISTORICAL COMMITTEE. 100th anniversary, Dayton, Maine, 1854-1954. Gorham: H. F. Brent, [1954]. Unpaged. Me.

DEAD RIVER TOWNSHIP (SOMERSET CO.)

2831 SEE entry 1821.

DEBLOIS (WASHINGTON CO.)

2832 No items located.

DEDHAM (HANCOCK CO.)

2833 EMERY, MARTHA. History of Dedham, Maine. [Dedham]: Dedham Bicentennial Committee, [1976]. Pp. 69. MeU.

DEER ISLE (HANCOCK CO.)

2834 ALLEN, MILDRED SELLERS. Deer Isle's history, comprising that territory now the towns of Deer Isle, Stonington and Isle au Haut. Rockland: Courier-Gazette, 1934. Pp. 44.

2835 ALLISON, ROLAND. "Shell heaps around Deer Isle." MeArchSocB, No. 2 ([October, 1964]), [3-5, 7].

2836 DEER ISLE, ME. Bicentennial, 1762-1962. [Deer Isle]: Deer Isle-Stonington Historical Society, [1962]. Unpaged. Me.
Includes a brief history of the town.

2837 "DEER Isle and settlers." MeHistMag, 8 (1893), 13-16.

2838 ENK, JOHN C. A family island in Penobscot Bay: the story of Eagle Island. Rockland: Courier-Gazette, 1973. Pp. vii, 350.

2839 HOSMER, GEORGE LAWRENCE. An historical sketch of the town of Deer Isle, Maine; with notices of its settlers and early inhabitants. Boston: Fort Hill Pr., 1905. Pp. 289.

2840 HUTCHINSON, VERNAL R. Deer Isle in the Revolution. Ellsworth: Hancock County Publishing, 1949. Unpaged.

2841 _____. A Maine town in the Civil War: a chronicle of the vanished town of Old Deer Isle, Maine, during the crucial years 1861-1865, as found in town, state and national records, and as retained in the memories of the last survivors of that generation. Freeport: Bond Wheelwright, 1967. Pp. 114.
First published in 1957 with title: A Yankee town in the Civil War.

2842 _____. When revolution came: the story of Old Deer Isle in the Province of Maine during the War for American Independence. Ellsworth: Ellsworth American, 1972. Pp. x, 186.

2843 NOYES, BENJAMIN LAKE. Deer Isle pioneers (including Stonington) Maine, plus an appendix, Caleb Haskell's war diary. Stonington, 1901 [i.e. 1928]. 104, xxi leaves.

2844 SMALL, HERMAN WESLEY. History of Marine Lodge, No. 122, Free and Accepted Masons, Deer Isle, Me. from its institution March 29, 1864, to January 5, 1914. Portland: Stephen Berry, 1914. Pp. 191. MeHi.

SEE ALSO entries 1553 and 1561.

DENMARK (OXFORD CO.)

2845 DENMARK CONGREGATIONAL CHURCH. The Denmark Congregational Church, Denmark, Maine, centennial anniversary, 1829-1929. n.p., [1929]. Unpaged. Me.

2846 McMULLAN, JEAN G. "Fifty years in Maine." Pine Cone, 7 (Spring, 1951), 3-6.
Camp Wyonegonic.

2847 SANBORN, EVELYN. This way to Denmark: a vignette (somewhat enlarged) of a Maine town. ... Denmark: Cardinal Printing, 1957. Unpaged.

2848 SCRIBNER, FRED C., JR. Remarks by Under Secretary of the Treasury Fred C. Scribner, Jr., on the occasion of the 150th anniversary of the founding of the town of Denmark, Maine, August 10, 1957, 2:30 p.m. n.p., [1957?]. 6 leaves. MeU.

DENNISTOWN PLANTATION (SOMERSET CO.)

2849 SEE entry 3377A.

DENNYSVILLE (WASHINGTON CO.)

2850 DENNYSVILLE, ME. Memorial of the 100th anniversary of the settlement of Dennysville, Maine, 1886. Portland: B. Thurston, 1886. Pp. 115.

2851 DENNYSVILLE, ME. CONGREGATIONAL CHURCH. Exercises in commemoration of the one hundredth anniversary of the Congregational Church, Dennysville, Maine, October 25, 1905. Bangor: O. F. Knowles, [1905]. Pp. 42.
Historical address by Charles Whittier.

2852 DRAPER, RUTH L. W. "Old days--old ways." Down East, 19 (March, 1973), 40-41.
Reminiscences.

2853 _____. "Through the stereoscope." Down East, 15 (June, 1969), 44-47.
Lincoln family and their home.

2854 "HISTORY of Dennysville and vicinity with an account of some of the first settlers there." BHistMag, 6 (1890-1891), 269-272.

SEE ALSO entry 1861.

DETRIOT (SOMERSET CO.)

2855 No items located.

DEVEREAUX TOWNSHIP (WASHINGTON CO.)

2856 No items located.

DEXTER (PENOBSCOT CO.)

2857 BARRON MEMORIAL CONGREGATIONAL CHURCH, DEXTER, ME. Manual of the Barron Memorial Congregational Church, Dexter, Maine. Dexter: Eastern State Publishing, 1889. Pp. 23. MeHi.
Includes an historical sketch.

2858 BRADFORD, E. ALICE. Interesting bits of local history. n.p., [1929]. Pp. 20. Me.

2859 CHASE, HALCYON. The early history of the town of Dexter. Dexter, 1904. Pp. 32.

2860 DEXTER, ME. HIGH SCHOOL. CLASS OF 1916. Brief history of Dexter, prepared by members of the Class of 1916, Dexter High School, as a part of their graduation exercises on the one hundredth anniversary of the incorporation of the town, 1816-1916. Dexter: Eastern Gazette, 1916. Pp. 19.

2861 DEXTER, ME. UNIVERSALIST CHURCH. Souvenir booklet and history of the one hundredth anniversary of the Universalist Church of Dexter, Maine, September 20, 21, 22, 1929. n.p., [1929]. Unpaged. Me.

2862 DEXTER GRAMMAR SCHOOL. CLASS of 1937. Facts and incidents about our town. [Dexter?], 1937. Unpaged. Me.

2863 EASTERN GAZETTE, DEXTER, ME. Dexter, Maine, our town for 150 years, 1801-1951. [Dexter], 1951. Pp. 52. Me.

2864 HAYNES, GEORGE HENRY. The scenic beauties, industries, and resources of Dexter, Maine. Dexter: W. S. Ladd, [189-]. Unpaged. MeHi.

2865 KEENE, HIRAM A. History of the Methodist Episcopal Church, Dexter, Maine, 1822-1900. Dexter: Eastern Gazette, 1900. Unpaged. MeU.

2866 MOWER, ELLA J., comp. History of Dexter. Dexter: Gazette Book and Job Print, 1908. Pp. 14.

2867 ROSS, LELAND A. and FRANK B. ARNOLD. One hundred years of Masonry, history of Penobscot Lodge, No. 39. Dexter: Eastern Gazette, 1922. Pp. 111. Me.

SEE ALSO entry 3532.

DIXFIELD (OXFORD CO.)

2868 DIXFIELD BICENTENNIAL COMMITTEE. The early history of Dixfield, Maine including the section of Mexico near Webb's River. Dixfield: Coburn Farm Pr., 1976. Pp. 92. MeHi.

DIXMONT (PENOBSCOT CO.)

2869 CHADBOURNE, SUMNER J. Recollections of the old meeting house and history of the new Union Church. n.p., [1900?]. Pp. 33. MeBa.

2870 KIMBALL, AMOS. 100th anniversary history of Archon Lodge, A.F. and A.M., East Dixmont, Me., 1866-1966. n.p., [1966]. Pp. 52. MeU.

2871 TOOTHAKER, LLEWELLYN P. and ELEANOR A. TOOTHAKER. The history of Dixmont, Maine. [Dixmont]: Bi-centennial Committee, [1976]. Pp. 77. MeU.
    Latter portion, by Eleanor Toothaker, updates original work which was delivered as a speech in 1907.

DOLE BROOK TOWNSHIP (SOMERSET CO.)

2872 No items located.

DOVER-FOXCROFT (PISCATAQUIS CO.)

2873 BEASLEY, KATHERINE A. and THOMPSON L. GUERNSEY. Thompson Free Library, fiftieth anniversary, 1898-1948, Dover-Foxcroft, Maine. n.p., 1948. Unpaged.

2874 DAVIS, B. H. "Reminiscences of the old towns of Dover and Foxcroft." SJMH, 11 (1923), 163-166.

2875 "DOVER, Maine." MeHistMag, 9 (1894-1895), 208-210."

2876 EVANS, LISTON P. and ORA L. EVANS. History of Dover-Foxcroft Congregational Church (United Church of Christ), 150th anniversary observance, December 31, 1972. Farmington: Knowlton, McLeary, 1972. Pp. 34. MBC.
    History for 1822 through 1922 was written in the latter year by Liston P. Evans.

2877 "FAVOR Tavern, Dover." SJMH, 8 (1920), 47-49.

2878 "FOXCROFT centennial." SJMH, 5 (1917-1918), 51-134.

2879 HAYES, CHARLES WELLS. "Joseph Ellery Foxcroft, the original proprietor of the town of Foxcroft, Maine." SJMH, 1 (1913-1914), 150-156.

2880 KENISTON, FRANK WALTER. Biographies of Dover-Foxcroft. Bangor: Furbush-Roberts, 1948. Pp. 154.

2881 KOHN, CLYDE FREDERICK. The history of land use in old Foxcroft, Maine. Orono: University of Maine Pr., 1944. Pp. 32.

2882 LOWELL, MARY CHANDLER, comp. Old Foxcroft, Maine: traditions and memories, with family records. Concord, N.H.: Rumford Pr., 1935. Pp. x, 262.

2883 PARSONS, WILLIS E. "Foxcroft Academy." PCHSC, 1 (1910), 100-117.

2884 PISCATAQUIS OBSERVER, DOVER, ME. The Piscataquis Observer, sixty-fifth anniversary, October, 1902, Dover, Maine. [Dover, 1902]. Pp. 59.

DRESDEN (LINCOLN CO.)

2885 ALLEN, CHARLES EDWIN. History of Dresden, Maine, formerly part of the old town of Pownalborough, from its earliest settlement to the year 1900.... Augusta: Kennebec Journal Print Shop, 1931. Pp. 894.

2886 _____. "Leaves from the early history of Dresden." MeHSC, 2 Ser., 1 (1890), 313-320.

2887 _____. "The old Gardiner Mills now standing at Dresden, Maine." SJMH, 11 (1923), 18-19. Grist and saw mills.

2888 _____. "Rev. Freeman Parker and the church in Dresden." MeHSC, 3 Ser., 1 (1904), 212-220.

2889 _____. "Some Huguenot and other early settlers on the Kennebec in the present town of Dresden." MeHSC, 2 Ser., 3 (1892), 351-379.

2890 BOLTÉ, MARY. "1761 courthouse on the Kennebec." Down East, 22 (July, 1976), 63-67, 90. Pownalborough Court House.

2891 "DEDICATION exercises, memorial boulder and tablet, Dresden, Maine, July 19, 1925." SJMH, 13 (1925), 209-227.

2892 DRESDEN FREE HIGH SCHOOL. A history of Dresden Free High School or Dresden Academy. Wiscasset: Chas. E. Emerson, [1889]. Pp. 40. MeBa.

2893 GARDINER, ROBERT HALLOWELL, b. 1882. "An early settlement on the Kennebec." SJMH, 9 (1921), 83-85.

2894 HALLET, RICHARD. "A frontier courthouse." Down East, 1 (November-December, 1954), 17-19.
Pownalborough Court House.

2895 KERSHAW, GORDON E. "Settling in the district called Frankfort." MeHSN, 10 (1970-1971), 73-83.

2896 MAYERS, CLAYTON W. "The oddest ship ever built in Maine." Down East, 9 (March, 1963), 45, 67-68.
'Experiment' built by James Tupper.

2897 WEST, ALBERT. "A frontier of Massachusetts justice." MassLQ, 42 (July, 1957), 70-74.
Pownalborough Court House.

SEE ALSO entries 1677, 1704, and 1937.

DREW PLANTATION (PENOBSCOT CO.)

2898 No items located.

DUDLEY TOWNSHIP (AROOSTOOK CO.)

2899 No items located.

DURHAM (ANDROSCOGGIN CO.)

2900 ST. JOHN, FREDERIC. "The church on the hill." Maine's Own Magazine, 8 (February, 1930), 16.
South Durham Friends' Meeting House; author's name is a pseudonym.

2901 STACKPOLE, EVERETT SCHERMERHORN. History of Durham, Maine; with genealogical notes. Lewiston: Lewiston Journal, 1899. Pp. vii, 314.

DYER BROOK (AROOSTOOK CO.)

2902 No items located.

DYER TOWNSHIP (WASHINGTON CO.)

2903 No items located.

E PLANTATION (AROOSTOOK CO.)

2904 No items located.

EAGLE LAKE (AROOSTOOK CO.)

2905 No items located.

EAGLE LAKE TOWNSHIP (PISCATAQUIS CO.)

2906 No items located.

EAST MACHIAS (WASHINGTON CO.)

2907 FREEMASONS. EAST MACHIAS, ME. WARREN LODGE, NO. 2. History of Warren Lodge, No. 2, Free and Accepted Masons, East Machias, Me., from its organization to June, 1896. By Herbert Harris.... Machias: The Republican, 1898. Pp. 245.

2908 _____. A history of Warren Lodge, No. 2, Free and Accepted Masons, East Machias, Maine, from September, 1778 to July, 1886. Machias: C. O. Furbish, 1886. Pp. 22.

2909 WASHINGTON ACADEMY, EAST MACHIAS, ME. Memorial of the centennial celebration, at East Machias, Me., August 7th, 8th and 9th, 1892, commemorative of the founding of Washington Academy. n.p., [1892]. Pp. viii, 149.
Historical address by George F. Talbot.

2910 _____. Washington Academy alumni book; containing brief biographies of the students attending Washington Academy between the years 1823 and 1906. May Pierce, Emily F. Sanborn, Maud Elma Kingsley, comps. [East Machias, 1906?]. Pp. 126.

2911 WHITTIER, HENRY SMITH. East Machias, 1765-1926. Machias: Univ. of Maine, 1975. 2v. MeU.

SEE ALSO entry 603.

EAST MIDDLESEX CANAL GRANT (PISCATAQUIS CO.)

2912 No items located.

EAST MILLINOCKET (PENOBSCOT CO.)

2913 EAST MILLINOCKET, ME. FIRST CONGREGATIONAL CHURCH. The First Congregational Church of East Millinocket, Me. In observance of its fiftieth anniversary, June 17, 1959. n.p., [1959]. Unpaged. MBC.
Includes a history of the church.

2914 MACK, JAMES H. Early history of East Millinocket. n.p., [1951?]. 6 leaves. Me.

2915   TURNER, DANIEL. "Ten years of dramatics in a small high school." The High School Thespian, 9 (January-February, 1938), 8-9.
      Schenck High School.

EAST MOXIE TOWNSHIP (SOMERSET CO.)

2916   No items located.

EASTBROOK (HANCOCK CO.)

2917   No items located.

EASTON (AROOSTOOK CO.)

2918   EASTON, ME. Centennial celebration, town of Easton, County of Aroostook, State of Maine, July 9 and 10, 1965. n.p., [1965?]. Unpaged. [MePriT].

    SEE ALSO entry 549.

EASTPORT (WASHINGTON CO.)

2919   BROWN, C. DONALD. "Eastport: a maritime history." AmNep, 28 (1968), 113-127.

2920   BUTTERFIELD, CHESTER F. "One hundred years of Methodism in Eastport, Maine." Zion's Herald, (September 4, 1940), 857.

2921   BUTWIN, DAVID. "Portrait of a declining town." Saturday Review, 51 (October 5, 1968), 17-19, 40, 42.

2922   DONNELL, ALBERT. Historical address delivered at the seventieth anniversary of the formation of the Central Congregational Church, of Eastport, Friday, February 8, 1899. Eastport: Sentinel Office, 1889. Pp. 20.

2923   "EASTPORT, farthest east parish in U.S.; has history linked with sea and pearls." The Northeast, 84 (June, 1957), 12-14.
      Christ Church.

2924   KILBY, WILLIAM HENRY, comp. Eastport and Passamaquoddy: a collection of historical and biographical sketches. Eastport: Edward E. Shead, 1888. Pp. 505.

2925   _____. The Eastport Sentinel: a historical sketch, 1818-1893. Eastport: Sentinel Pr., 1893. 20 leaves.
      Newspaper.

2926   _____. "A New England town under foreign martial law." NEM, New Ser., 14 (1896), 685-698.
      British military rule, 1814-1818.

2927   KINGSBURY, ISAAC W. and WENDELL S. HADLOCK. "An early occupation site, Eastport, Maine." MASB, 12 (1950-1951), 22-26.
      Shell heap.

2928   LOWRY, LOIS. "Eastport, Maine: the same salty whiff." Yankee, 39 (May, 1975), 66-71.

2929   McINNIS, A. E. "Thunder on Middle Street." Down East, 14 (May, 1968), 36-38, 43, 55-56.
      Fire department.

2930   MILLIKEN, FRED G. "Eastport, Maine." Pine Tree Magazine, 6 (1906-1907), 359-366.

2931   "THE PASSING of Fort Sullivan." BTJ, 14 (1901-1902), 75.

2932   SABINE, LORENZO. "Early settlers of Eastport." BHistMag, 1 (1885-1886), 115-118.

2933   _____. "Moose Island and its dependencies, four years under martial law." HistMag, 2 Ser., 7 (1870), 220-229, 317-324.
      War of 1812.

2934   TAKACH, STEVE. "Birth of a Maine newspaper: 'The Quoddy Times.'" Down East, 17 (May, 1971), 44-45, 68-74.

2935   VARNEY, MARIANNE. "The easternmost parish in America: the story of Christ Church, Eastport." The Northeast, 74 (July, 1947), 5-6, 9.

2936   VESEY, MAXWELL. "A strange interlude in border history." Dalhousie Review, 30 (1941), 417-424.
      British occupation, 1814-1818.

2937   WESTON, JONATHAN DELESDERNIER. The history of Eastport, and vicinity: a lecture, delivered April, 1834, before the Eastport Lyceum. Boston: Marsh, Capen and Lyon, 1834. Pp. 61.

2938   YOUNG, NORMA. "Eastport--the Sunrise City." Down East, 9 (June, 1963), 30-35, 67-69.

    SEE ALSO entries 1071, 1840-1841, 1844, 1852, 1859, and 1874.

EDDINGTON (PENOBSCOT CO.)

2939   [HARRISON, O. M.]. Historical sketch of East Eddington area: a review of the early settlement from Meadow Brook to Clifton and the Holden lines. By Burdock Rube, pseud. [Bangor]: Morse-Norris Press, 1942. Pp. 40. Me.

2940 PORTER, JOSEPH WHITCOMB. Memoir of Col. Jonathan Eddy of Eddington, Me.; with some account of the Eddy family, and of the early settlers on Penobscot River. Augusta: Sprague, Owen & Nash, 1877. Pp. 72.

SEE ALSO entry 1762.

EDGECOMB (LINCOLN CO.)

2941 AVERILL, ESTHER C. "Furnished in days gone by for a long dead queen: The Marie Antoinette House in Edgecomb, Maine." Sun Up, 5 (November, 1927), 6, 27, 32.

2942 CHASE, VIRGINIA. "Fanny Stone." Down East, 5 (April, 1959), 22-25.
Her general store and tenure as postmistress.

2943 _____. "Fort Edgecomb on the Sheepscot." Down East, 4 (July, 1958), 36-39.

2944 _____. "Village library." Down East, 5 (March, 1959), 28, 53-56.

2945 _____. "Village school." Down East, 5 (September, 1958), 30-31, 40-41.

2946 DOGGETT, MARGARET F. "Doggett Castle." Down East, 20 (May, 1974), 13-14, 17-18, 21-22, 24, 28.

2947 LOWELL, W. L. "Fort Edgecomb." MHGR, 8 (1895), 33-34.

2947A PATTERSON, WILLIAM DAVIS. "Old Fort Edgecomb." SJMH, 14 (1926), 165-179.

2948 PITCHER, DONALD T. "A queen's asylum at Wiscasset." Down East, 19 (May, 1973), 66-69.
Clough House; it was moved to Edgecomb in 1838.

2949 ST. JOHN, FREDERIC. "The house that was built for a queen." Maine's Own Magazine, 8 (January, 1930), 11.
Marie Antoinette House; author's name is a pseudonym.

2950 SEWALL, RUFUS. History of the Congregational Church, Edgecomb, embracing articles of faith and covenant and a full schedule of members. Portland: Stephen Berry, 1871. Pp. 20. MBNEH.

2951 SEWALL, RUFUS KING. "A refuge for Marie Antoinette in Maine." MeHSC, 2 Ser., 5 (1894), 284-305.
Clough House.

SEE ALSO entry 1937.

EDINBURG (PENOBSCOT CO.)

2952 No items located.

EDMUNDS TOWNSHIP (WASHINGTON CO.)

2953 HOBART, ISAAC. "A sketch of No. 10, now Edmunds, Washington County, Maine." BHistMag, 1 (1885-1886), 49-52.
Edited by Peter E. Vose.

SEE ALSO entry 1861.

ELIOT (YORK CO.)

2954 "ALL aboard for Eliot! The history of a depot." Shoreliner, 3 (November, 1952), 43-45.

2955 BUTLER, MARY A. "East Eliot M. E. Church." Old Eliot, 9 (1909), 105-107.

2956 CALDWELL, AUGUSTINE. "The first minister of the First Church, Eliot, Maine, the Rev. John Rogers, and Mrs. Susannah (Whipple) Rogers, his wife." Old Eliot, 7 (1906), 1-14.

2957 CHASE, A. L. "The Eliot Meeting House of 1715 and early religious customs." Old Eliot, 3 (1899), 97-103.

2958 CHASE, EDITH F. "The growth of a grange." Shoreliner, 3 (October, 1952), 41-47.
John F. Hill Grange.

2959 COLE, AARON BURR and JOHN LEMUEL MURRAY WILLIS, eds. History of the centennial of the incorporation of the town of Eliot, Maine, August 7th-13th, 1910. Eliot: A. Caldwell, 1912. Pp. 133.

2960 COLE, ICHABOD. "Shipbuilders and shipbuilding in Eliot." Old Eliot, 2 (1898), 9-11.

2961 DIXON, JOSEPH H. "Eliot in the Rebellion." Old Eliot, 7 (1906), 157-175.

2962 _____. "Town meetings and current events: Eliot, 1810-1880." Old Eliot, 2 (1898), 109-117.

2963 ELIOT, ME. CONGREGATIONAL CHURCH. Twenty-fifth anniversary of the dedication of the meeting house of the Congregational Church and Society, Eliot, Maine; commemorative services. Eliot: J. A. Coleman, 1906. Pp. 40.

2964 ELIOT HISTORICAL SOCIETY. Twice told tales of old Eliot. Eliot, [1968]. Pp. 42. Me.

2965 ELIOT

2965 ELIOT miscellany: bits of forgotten history. [Eliot?, 1876?]. Pp. 10.

2966 "THE ELIOT Second Advent Church." Old Eliot, 9 (1909), 41-43.

2967 FERNALD, FRANK L. "The naval constructors of Eliot." Old Eliot, 8 (1908), 167-179.
Biographies.

2968 FERNALD, WILLIAM LINWOOD. "The Hanscoms: a family of shipbuilders." Old Eliot, 2 (1898), 1-9.

2969 FROSST, GEORGE W. "The old Fields Meeting Houses." Old Eliot, 2 (1898), 103-108.

2970 GOOLD, NATHAN. "The Furbush or Furbish family." Old Eliot, 3 (1899), 1-4.

2971 _____. "The old Shapleigh House." Old Eliot, 3 (1899), 13-14.

2972 HAYES, ADA. "A church of their own." Shore-liner, 2 (October, 1951), 61-63.
East Eliot Methodist Episcopal Church.

2973 "INDIAN mound near the Eliot B. and M. station." Old Eliot, 9 (1909), 39-40.

2974 INGERSOLL, ANNA JOSEPHINE. Greenacre on the Piscataqua. N.Y.: Alliance Publishing, 1900. Pp. 22.

2975 KEEFE, FRANCIS. "The early Hills of Eliot." Old Eliot, 5 (1902), 62-76.
Hill family.

2976 _____. "Eliot incorporation papers." Old Eliot, 1 (1897), 127-164.

2977 _____. "Eliot Social Library." Old Eliot, 1 (1897), 189-197.

2978 "'THE OLD road.'" Old Eliot, 9 (1909), 28-30.

2979 REEVE, SAMUEL H. "South Eliot M. E. Church." Old Eliot, 9 (1909), 109-111.

2980 "THE SCHOOL house of 1804, school district no. V, Eliot." Old Eliot, 7 (1906), 46-52.

2981 SHAPLEIGH, CHARLES A. "Items of Eliot history." Old Eliot, 7 (1906), 29-33.
Eliot Academy, the Town House, and the Third Congregational Church.

2982 "SOME facts in the ministry of John Rogers and in the early history of the Congregational Church of Eliot." Old Eliot, 3 (1899), 81-95.

2983 "SOME well known men of the past generation." Old Eliot, 8 (1908), 179-191; 9 (1909), 217-220.

2984 SPINNEY, MARY L. "Witch days in long ago Eliot." Old Eliot, 8 (1908), 139-140.

2985 STACKPOLE, EVERETT SCHERMERHORN. "Josselyn's Point." Old Eliot, 5 (1902), 30-34.

2986 STAPLES, CHARLES J. "The Staples family." Old Eliot, 6 (1903), 37-43.

2987 WILLIS, JOHN LEMUEL MURRAY. "Eliot in the olden time." Old Eliot, 6 (1903), 145-147.

2988 _____. "Eliot in the Revolution." Old Eliot, 7 (1906), 101-156.

2989 _____. "Notes on Eliot." Old Eliot, 1 (1897), 1-6, 9-13.

2990 _____. "The old houses of Eliot." Old Eliot, 1 (1897), 33-34.
"To be continued," but no more published.

2991 _____. "The physicians of Eliot." Old Eliot, 7 (1906), 176-196.

2992 _____. "Story of Eliot Academy." Old Eliot, 6 (1903), 125-133.

SEE ALSO entries 987, 1879, 1907, and 1911.

ELLIOTTSVILLE PLANTATION (PISCATAQUIS CO.)

2993 MacDOUGALL, WALTER M. "The Onawa wreck." Down East, 19 (November, 1972), 36-39, 63-65, 68.
A train wreck on December 20, 1919.

ELLESWORTH (HANCOCK CO.)

2994 BLACK Mansion, Ellsworth, Maine. n.p., n.d. Pp. 24. MeU.

2995 CHILCOTT, JAMES C. and JAMES E. PARSONS. History of Lygonia Lodge, No. 40, Free and Accepted Masons, Ellsworth, Maine, from January 1, 1874 to January 1, 1890. Ellsworth: Hancock County Publishing, 1891. Pp. 45.

2996 CUNNINGHAM, AGNES H. History of Ellsworth, 1763 to 1910. n.p., [1936?]. Unpaged. Me.

2997 DAVIS, ALBERT H. "Early history of Ellsworth, Maine." SJMH, 13 (1925), 228-234.

2998 _____. History of Ellsworth, Maine. Lewiston: Lewiston Journal Printshop, 1927. Pp. 244.

2999 DEANE, JOSEPH AUGUSTUS. History of Lygonia Lodge, No. 40, Free and Accepted Masons, at Ellsworth, Maine, from 1822 to 1874. Revised by John B. Redman. Ellsworth: Hancock County Publishing, 1874. Pp. 57. MeBa.

3000 DEMERS, MABEL GOULD. "Doorways and beyond." Pine Cone, 3 (Summer, 1947), 29-32.
Black Mansion.

3001 DURNBAUGH, JERRY L. "The Black House." Down East, 2 (July, 1956), 28-31.

3002 ELLSWORTH, ME. Historical record and program, bicentennial celebration, July 20-27, 1963. Bangor: Furbush-Roberts, 1963. Unpaged. Me.
Includes history by Herbert T. Silsby, II.

3003 _____. Souvenir program, historical sketches, of Ellsworth, Me. n.p., [1925?]. Pp. 44. MeU.
Includes history by Albert H. Davis.

3004 ELLSWORTH, ME. FIRST CONGREGATIONAL CHURCH. Centennial exercises of the founding of the First Congregational Church and Society in Ellsworth, Maine, September 12, 1912. Ellsworth: Hancock County Publishing, 1913. Pp. 61. Me.

3005 "ELLSWORTH, one of the most pleasant spots on the coast of Maine." Sun Up, 3 (April, 1927), 51-55.

3006 GREEN, FRED C. "Last of the Ellsworth fleet." Down East, 2 (August, 1955), 22-25.
Schooner "Lavolta."

3007 HADLOCK, WENDELL STANWOOD and DOUGLAS S. BYERS. "Radio carbon dates from Ellsworth Falls, Maine." American Antiquity, 21 (1956), 419-420.

3008 HALE, CLARENCE. "An address delivered by the honorable Clarence Hale at the centennial celebration of the First Congregational Church at Ellsworth, Maine, September 12, 1912." SJMH, 1 (1913-1914), 3-13.

3009 LORD, TRUEMAN C. History of Esoteric Lodge, No. 159, of Free and Accepted Masons, at Ellsworth, Maine, from its organization, Sept. 3, 1870 to Jan. 1, 1891. Ellsworth: Hancock County Publishing, 1891. Pp. 37. [MePGLM].

3010 "MATERIALS for a history of Ellsworth, Me." MeHistMag, 8 (1893), 181-218.

3011 MILES, CARLTON E. "Ellsworth's treasure from historic days." Sun Up, 10 (April, 1932), 12-13, 20.
Black Mansion.

3012 MILLER, ALICE M. "Back to yesterday: old Black House, Ellsworth, Maine." National Historical Magazine, 72 (1938), 28-29.

3013 MOOR, JOHN LOUDER. "An account of the first settlement of what is now Ellsworth--Union River." BHistMag, 3 (1887-1888), 125-127.

3014 PECK, CALVIN. "History of Ellsworth." BHist Mag, 5 (1889-1890), 106-108.

3015 SILSBY, HERBERT T., II. A church has been gathered: history of the First Congregational Church in Ellsworth, Maine. Ellsworth: Hancock County Publishing, 1962. Pp. 97. MBC.

3016 _____. "Maine river town: Ellsworth." Maine Dig, 2 (Spring, 1968), 74-76, 78.

3017 STANWOOD, CORDELIA J. "The story of Ellsworth, Maine." House Beautiful, 46 (1919), 373-375.
Historic houses.

3018 STURGES, WALTER KNIGHT. "The Black House, Ellsworth--an Asher Benjamin house in Maine." Antiques, 65 (1954), 398-400.

3019 TREACY, GERALD C. "Father John Bapst, S.J., and the Ellsworth outrage." U.S. Catholic Historical Society. Records and Studies, 14 (1920), 7-19.
Anti-Catholic sentiment in 1850s and 1860s.

3020 UNION TRUST COMPANY, ELLSWORTH, ME. Seventy-five years of service, 1887-1962. n.p., [1962]. Unpaged.

3021 WASSON, MILDRED. "Up the road to yesterday." Country Life in America, 58 (May, 1930), 65-66, 96, 108.
Black Mansion.

3021A WHITMORE, ALLAN R. "Portrait of a Maine 'Know-Nothing': William H. Chaney (1821-1903); his early years and his role in the Ellsworth nativist controversy, 1853-1854." MeHSQ, 14 (1974-1975), 1-57.

3022 YALLALEE, BUD. "The doll house." Down East, 18 (April, 1972), 42-43, 81, 86-87.
Doll museum.

SEE ALSO entries 603, 1569, 1578, 2082, and 4589.

ELM STREAM TOWNSHIP (SOMERSET CO.)

3023 No items located.

EMBDEN (SOMERSET CO.)

3024 WALKER, ERNEST GEORGE. Embden town of yore: olden times and families there and in adjacent towns. Skowhegan: Independent-Reporter, 1929. Pp. xiv, 760.

ENFIELD (PENOBSCOT CO.)

3025 No items located.

ETNA (PENOBSCOT CO.)

3026 CARTER, BERTHA WHEELER. Etna sesquicentennial program, June 13-14, 1970. [Etna?], 1970. Pp. 15. Me.

EUSTIS (FRANKLIN CO.)

3027 No items located.

EXETER (PENOBSCOT CO.)

3028 No items located.

FAIRFIELD (SOMERSET CO.)

3029 DUREN, GLADYS, RAY TOBEY and CLIFTON HORNE. Gleanings of the past and present of Fairfield, Maine. n.p., [1963?]. Pp. 46. MeU.
Cover title: 175th anniversary and history of the town of Fairfield, 1788-1963.

3030 "GOOD Will." Sun Up, 5 (November, 1927), 8, 25-27.
Charity.

3031 "GOOD Will Home Association." SJMH, 9 (1921), 196-197.

3032 HINCKLEY, GEORGE WALTER. Fifty years with the Good Will Record. Hinckley: Good Will Publishing, 1937. Pp. 149.
Newspaper.

3033 _____. The Good Will idea. Hinckley: Good Will Publishing, 1929. Pp. 105.

3034 MARTIN, ELEANOR DUTTON. "A living monument." Pine Cone, 3 (Winter, 1947-1948), 7-13.
Good Will Home Association.

3035 SHETTLEWORTH, EARLE G., JR. "A mark upon the land: the life and work of Charles D. Lawrence, a mid-nineteenth-century Fairfield, Maine builder." OTNE, 58 (1967-1968), 31-48.

3036 WINSLOW, WILL P. Early history of Larone. n.p., 1918. Pp. 26. MeP.

SEE ALSO entries 1421, 3532, and 5041.

FALMOUTH (CUMBERLAND CO.)

3037 NO ENTRY.

3038 BROWN, DAVID A. and EDGAR P. LUND. "Old Falmouth is modern." Maine Townsman, 18 (August, 1956), 14-15, 25-26, (September, 1956), 12-13, 25, (October, 1956), 10-11.

3039 DOW, STERLING THAYER. "Pennyweights and grains." Mekeel's Weekly Stamp News, 66 (February 25, 1946), 163-164.
Eighteenth-century postal rates.

3040 FALMOUTH, ME. Falmouth, Maine, 250th anniversary, 1718-1968. [Falmouth: Grace Pr., 1968?]. Pp. 32.

3041 HOLT, ANNE CARROLL PAYSON. "A memorial to the dead for the benefit of the living: Church of Saint Mary the Virgin, Falmouth Foreside." The Northeast, 75 (January, 1948), 17-20.

3042 WALLACE, CHARLOTTE and DONALD WALLACE. E Pluribus Unum, a story of Falmouth, Maine. [Falmouth]: Falmouth Historical Society, 1976. Pp. 56. MeHi.

3043 WINSLOW, HOWARD L. A history of Congregationalism in Falmouth, 1754-1954.... Portland: Grace Pr., 1954. Unpaged. MBC.
A history of the Falmouth Congregational Church.

SEE ALSO entries 1483, 1487, 1492, and 1512.

FARMINGDALE (KENNEBEC CO.)

3044 [WHITE, JESSIE WING], ed. History of town of Farmingdale, Maine ... 1852-1952. n.p., [1952?]. Pp. 85. Me.

SEE ALSO entries 1628 and 1649.

FARMINGTON (FRANKLIN CO.)

3045 ABBOTT, MORETON. "Farmington's August 17th." Yankee, 31 (August, 1967), 76-77, 118-123.
Concert by Lillian Nordica, August 17, 1911.

3046 ABBOTT SCHOOL, FARMINGTON, ME. The Abbott School: the Little Blue School founded by Rev. Samuel Abbot [in] 1844 on [the] estate of Jacob Abbott. [Farmington?], 1926. Pp. 48. MeU.

3047 BUTLER, BENJAMIN and NATALIE STURGES BUTLER. "Early meeting-houses in Farmington, Maine." Pioneer America, 1 (January, 1969), 27-32.

3048 _____. The Falls: where Farmington, Maine began in 1776. Farmington: Knowlton & McLeary, 1976. Pp. 131. Me.

3049 _____. Farmington's musical heritage from Belcher to 'TDX.' Farmington: Knowlton & McLeary, 1975. Pp. 48. MeU.

3050 _____. History of the Old South Church, United Church of Christ, Farmington, Maine, 1814-1965. Farmington: Knowlton & McLeary, 1966. Pp. 258.

3051 _____. Porter and Russell lived on a hill (Farmington, Maine) c. 1800. [Farmington?: Farmington Historical Society?], 1969. Pp. 83.

3052 _____. The Red Schoolhouse neighborhood (Farmington, Maine). Farmington: Farmington Historical Society, 1973. Pp. 79.
   Historic houses.

3053 _____. Thomas Wendell moves to Fairbanks (Farmington, Maine) c. 1794. n.p., 1966. Pp. 89.

3054 BUTLER, FRANCIS GOULD. A history of Farmington, Franklin County, Maine, from the earliest explorations to the present time, 1776-1885. Farmington: Knowlton, McLeary, 1885. Pp. 683.

3055 "A CHAPTER of biography, the Solomon Adams family." Franklin Historical Magazine, 1 (April, 1881), 9-26.

3056 DEMERS, MABEL GOULD. "Doorways and beyond." Pine Cone, 4 (Autumn, 1948), 19-21.
   Lillian Nordica's birthplace.

3057 FARMINGTON, ME. FIRST CONGREGATIONAL CHURCH. Historical sketch and principles and regulations.... Farmington: Knowlton & McLeary, 1915. Pp. 67. MBC.

3058 _____. Manual of the First Congregational Church in Farmington, Maine, containing a brief sketch of its history, a list of those formerly connected with it, the creed, covenant, and rules, and a list of its officers. Farmington: Knowlton, McLeary, 1884. Pp. 31. [MeFarP].

3059 "FARMINGTON." Pine Cone, 2 (Summer, 1946), 9-13.

3060 FARMINGTON HISTORICAL SOCIETY. Pilgrimage, October 3, 1965, to some homes of "William Allen's new world." Sandy River Township (Farmington) c. 1792. Benjamin and Natalie Sturges Butler, comps. n.p., [1965]. Pp. 23.

3061 "FARMINGTON State Normal School." Maine Teachers' Digest, 1 (1940-1941), 96-97, 110.

3062 "THE FIRST Unitarian Society of Farmington, Maine." The Church Exchange, 4 (1896-1897), 49-50.

3063 FLINT, J. P. "Farmington's banking institutions." BTJ, 23 (1910-1911), 685, 687.

3064 "HISTORICAL notes about Farmington, Maine." SJMH, 14 (1926), 97-99.

3065 MALLETT, RICHARD PURINGTON. University of Maine at Farmington: a study in educational change, 1864-1974. Freeport: Bond Wheelwright, 1974. Pp. xiv, 288.

3066 MALLETT, WILBERT GRANT. "Farmington, a school town." BTJ, 23 (1910-1911), 674-677.

3067 MARCH, HELEN SEARLES. "Let's go back to the farm." OTNE, 25 (1934-1935), 141-144.
   Social life and customs.

3068 PARKER, THOMAS. History of Farmington, Maine, from its settlement to the year 1846. (1846) 2d ed. Farmington: J. S. Swift, 1875. Pp. 120.

3069 PURINGTON, GEORGE COLBY. History of the State Normal School, Farmington, Maine; with sketches of the teachers and graduates. Farmington: Knowlton, McLeary, 1899. Pp. v, 204.

3070 STIMPSON, MARY STOYELL. "Farmington, Maine." NEM, New Ser., 30 (1904), 387-403.

3071 YEATON, POLLY. War paint: a historical and pictorial revue of the Old Crow Indian Band. Farmington: Heritage Printing, 1975. Pp. 120. MeU.

   SEE ALSO entries 1419 and 3532.

FAYETTE (KENNEBEC CO.)

3072 STURTEVANT, REGINALD H. The Fayette Baptist Church, 1792-1967. [Livermore Falls?, 1967?]. Pp. 64. MeHi.

3073 UNDERWOOD, JOSEPH H. History of Fayette; Russell C. Tuck, ed. Augusta: C. E. Nash, 1956. Pp. 174.
   The manuscript of this work is in the Maine State Library.

FLAGSTAFF TOWNSHIP (SOMERSET CO.)

3074 ROUNDY, RODNEY W. "Our Flagstaff Church." MeCP, 39 (January 15, 1952), 8-9.

   SEE ALSO entry 1821.

FOREST CITY TOWNSHIP (WASHINGTON CO.)

3075 No items located.

FOREST TOWNSHIP (WASHINGTON CO.)

3076 No items located.

THE FORKS PLANTATION (SOMERSET CO.)

3077   No items located.

FORKSTOWN TOWNSHIP (AROOSTOOK CO.)

3078   No items located.

FORSYTH TOWNSHIP (SOMERSET CO.)

3079   No items located.

FORT FAIRFIELD (AROOSTOOK CO.)

3080   "CHRISTIAN pioneers establish the Apostolic Church: the story of Saint Paul's, Fort Fairfield." The Northeast, 74 (March, 1947), 10-11.

3081   ELLIS, CALEB HOLT. History of Fort Fairfield and biographical sketches. Fort Fairfield: Fort Fairfield Printing, 1894. Pp. 382.

3082   FORT FAIRFIELD, ME. Sesquicentennial observance of the first settlement of Fort Fairfield, Maine, July 22, 23, 24, 1966. n.p., [1966?]. Unpaged. [MeForF].
        Includes brief history by Mrs. Roger L. Durepo.

3083   THE HISTORIC pageant of Fort Fairfield and the Aroostook Valley, produced at the celebration of the centennial of the first settlement of Fort Fairfield, Maine, August 8, 9, and 10, 1916; Eva Winnifred Scates, director.... Fort Fairfield: "Review" Pr., 1916. Pp. 55.

3084   HOPKINS, RUTH. "Fort Fairfield." Sun Up, 5 (October, 1927), 20-21, 23.

3085   TRAFTON, JOHN B. and BENONI T. DURGIN. History of Eastern Frontier Lodge, No. 112, of Free and Accepted Masons, Fort Fairfield, Maine, from A.D. 1862 to 1871. Portland: Stephen Berry, 1871. Pp. 18. MeBa.

        SEE ALSO entry 50.

FORT KENT (AROOSTOOK CO.)

3086   DUBAY, GUY. With justice for all. n.p., 1976. Pp. iii, 73. [MeForK].
        Egery et al. vs. Berube, land title case, 1876.

3087   FIRST NATIONAL BANK, FORT KENT, ME. Fort Kent, 1829-1929. Fort Kent, 1930. Pp. 55. Me.

3088   FORT KENT, ME. CENTENNIAL BOOK COMMITTEE. Fort Kent centennial, 1869-1969. n.p., n.d. Pp. 159.

3089   "MADAWASKA Training School--Fort Kent." Maine Teachers' Digest, 2 (1941-1942), 14-15, 49.
        Now the University of Maine at Fort Kent.

        SEE ALSO entry 1437.

FOWLER TOWNSHIP (WASHINGTON CO.)

3090   No items located.

FRANKFORT (WALDO CO.)

3091   JONES, ERASMUS ARCHIBALD. History of the town of Frankfort. Winterport: Advertiser Job Print, 1897. Pp. 57.
        Includes the early history of Winterport.

        SEE ALSO entry 1282.

FRANKLIN (HANCOCK CO.)

3092   OBERMANN, HENRY B. Franklin, Maine, a history. Franklin: Franklin Historical Society, 1975. Pp. 103.

FREEDOM (WALDO CO.)

3093   No items located.

FREEMAN TOWNSHIP (FRANKLIN CO.)

3094   "OLDEST house in Franklin County." SJMH, 11 (1923), 33-35.
        Dodge Farm.

3095   SEDGLEY, GEORGE BURBANK. The Wellcome family of Freeman, Maine. Israel Riggs Bray, 1808-1890. Henry Solomon Wellcome, 1853-1936. Phillips: Phillips Print Shop, 1939. Pp. 26.

FREEPORT (CUMBERLAND CO.)

3096   "BAPTIST Church in Freeport, Me." American Baptist Memorial, 13 (1854), 335-336.

3097 BARTLETT, ARTHUR. "The discovery of L. L. Bean." Saturday Evening Post, 219 (December 14, 1946), 30-31, 92, 95-97, 99.

3098 BEAN, LEON LEONWOOD. My story: the autobiography of a Down-East merchant. Freeport, 1960. Pp. 163.
L. L. Bean, sporting goods.

3099 BENSEN, RICHARD A. "Where students go at daybreak's glow." BA, 47 (November, 1973), 24-25.
L. L. Bean, sporting goods.

3100 DIETZ, LEW. "Bean, Maine, U.S.A." Down East, 16 (March, 1970), 38-41.
L. L. Bean, sporting goods.

3101 FREEPORT, ME. FIRST PARISH CHURCH, CONGREGATIONAL. A history of the First Parish Church, Congregational, Freeport, Maine, 1774-1959. [Portland]: Fred. L. Tower, 1959. Pp. 29. MeHi.

3102 FREEPORT HISTORICAL SOCIETY AND FREEPORT SESQUICENTENNIAL COMMITTEE. Freeport yesterdays. Freeport, 1970. Unpaged. Me.

3103 "FREEPORT, Maine, past and present." BTJ, 17 (1904-1905), 237-244.

3104 GOULD, JOHN. "Let's go to the old sand farm." Yankee, 32 (October, 1968), 84-85, 152, 155-156.
"The Desert of Maine."

3105 HAYNES, GEORGE HENRY. Wolf's Neck, the gem of Casco Bay, the charming suburb of Freeport, Maine, with its many important industries, and superior granite productions. Portland, 1890. Pp. 31.

3106 HENDERSON, RUTH. "Casco Castle." Down East, 10 (July, 1964), 42-43.
A hotel destroyed by fire in 1914.

3107 HOSMER, MIRIAM. "Old days on Bustins Island." Down East, 15 (June, 1969), 60-61.

3108 "L. L. Bean's bonanza: how a Maine man improved the hunting boot and founded the firm that made Freeport famous." Down East, 1 (April, 1955), 38-40.

3109 NASON, REUBEN. "A topographical and historical sketch of Freeport, county of Cumberland, and District of Maine." MHSC, 2 Ser., 4 (1816), 176-184.

3110 RICHARDSON, MRS. EDWIN A. "The birthplace of the State of Maine." SJMH, 3 (1915-1916), 169-171.
Papers separating Maine from Massachusetts were signed in Jameson's Tavern, March 15, 1820.

3111 RICHARDSON, GEORGE B. History of Bustins Island, Casco Bay, 1660-1960. Bustins Island, 1960. Pp. 84.

3112 TALBOT, LOUISA. South Freeport notes. n.p., [1972?]. Unpaged. Me.

3113 THURSTON, FLORENCE G. and HARMON S. CROSS. Three centuries of Freeport, Maine. Freeport, 1940. Pp. x, 254.

SEE ALSO entry 3532.

FRENCHTOWN TOWNSHIP (PISCATAQUIS CO.)

3114 No items located.

FRENCHVILLE (AROOSTOOK CO.)

3115 FRENCHVILLE, ME. ST. LUCE PARISH. Livre d'or de la Paroisse Ste. Luce, 1843-1943. n.p., [1943?]. Unpaged.

FRIENDSHIP (KNOX CO.)

3116 ENDURING friendships, by Roger F. Duncan et al. Al Roberts, ed. Camden: International Marine Publishing, 1970. Pp. 74.
Friendship sloops.

3117 JONES, HERALD A., ed. It's a Friendship. Friendship: Friendship Sloop Society, 1965. Pp. 95.

3118 MORSE, IVAN. Friendship Long Island. Middletown, N.Y.: Whitlock Pr., 1974. Pp. v, 140. MeU.

3119 VOGEL, C. WILLIAM. Friendship: 150 years. Orono, 1957. 12 leaves. Me.

SEE ALSO entry 1654.

FRYEBURG (OXFORD CO.)

3120 AMES, NATHANIEL P. Story of Lovewell's fight. [Medford, Mass., 190-?]. Pp. 14.

3121 BARROWS, JOHN STUART. "Fryeburg." NEM, New Ser., 9 (1893-1894), 33-45.

3122 _____. Fryeburg, Maine, an historical sketch. Fryeburg: Pequawket Pr., 1938. Pp. 309.

3123 BEEBE, RICHARD W. The first 200 years: the history of the First Congregational Church, Fryeburg, Maine. Center Conway, N.H.: Walker's Pond Pr., 1975. Pp. 118.

3124 BICKFORD, GAIL H. "Lovewell's fight, 1725-1958." AmQ, 10 (1958), 358-366.

3125 _____. "Lovewell's fight, 1725-1975." Down East, 21 (April, 1975), 50-51, 72.

3126 CHAMBERLAIN, GEORGE WALTER. "John Chamberlain, the Indian fighter at Pigwacket." MeHSC, 2 Ser., 9 (1898), 1-14.
1725.

3127 DAVEIS, CHARLES STEWART. An address delivered on the commemoration at Fryeburg, May 19, 1825. Portland: James Adams, Jr., 1825. Pp. 64.
Centennial of the Pigwacket fight.

3128 ECKSTORM, FANNIE HARDY. "Pigwacket and Parson Symmes." NEQ, 9 (1936), 378-402.
New evidence to refute Thomas Symmes, chronicler of the Pigwacket fight.

3129 ENGLISH, J. S. "Captain Lovewell's fight with Paugus." Pine Tree Magazine, 5 (1906), 456-458.
Pigwacket fight.

3130 EVANS, GEORGE HILL. Pigwacket: Part I, old Indian days in the valley of the Saco. [Conway, N.H.:], Conway, N.H. Historical Society, 1939. Pp. 135.
No more published.

3131 FRYEBURG, ME. The centennial celebration of the settlement of Fryeburg, Me., with the historical address, by Rev. Samuel Souther. ... Worcester, Mass.: Tyler & Seagrave, [1864]. Pp. 79.

3132 FRYEBURG Webster centennial, celebrating the coming of Daniel Webster to Fryeburg, 100 years ago, to take the principalship of Fryeburg Academy; Fryeburg, January 1st, 1902. Fryeburg: A. F. Lewis, 1902. Pp. 83.

3133 HARVEY, GEORGE A. The First Congregational Church, Fryeburg, Maine, a brief history, 1775-1963. [Fryeburg?], 1963. Pp. 22. MBC.

3134 THE ILLUSTRATED Fryeburg Webster memorial. Fryeburg: A. F. & C. W. Lewis, 1882. Pp. 39.

3135 KIDDER, FREDERIC. The expeditions of Capt. John Lovewell, and his encounters with the Indians; including a particular account of the Pequauket battle, with a history of that tribe, and a reprint of Rev. Thomas Symmes's sermon. Boston: Bartlett & Halliday, 1865. Pp. 138.

3136 LEWIS, ALONZO FREEMAN. Festival of the Fryeburg septuagenarians born in 1834; held at Fryeburg, Maine, August 9th, 1904. Fryeburg, 1904. Pp. 143.

3137 [LINCOLN, ENOCH]. The village: a poem. Portland: Edward Little, 1816. Pp. 180.

3138 LOVEJOY, DAVID SHERMAN. "Lovewell's fight and Hawthorne's 'Roger Malvin's Burial.'" NEQ, 27 (1954), 527-531.
Pigwacket fight as the source for a Hawthorne tale.

3139 "LOVEWELL'S fight." WMHJ, 1 (1825-1826), 20-26.

3140 McCLINTOCK, JOHN NORRIS. "Lovewell's War." BSM, 1 (1884), 80-83.

3141 "175TH anniversary of [the] Fryeburg Church." MeCP, 146 (June, 1950), 18.

3142 RIEDEL, WESLEY U. "Fryeburg Academy." MeCP, 29 (May, 1942), 5-6, 46.

3143 "THE SEVEN covered bridges of Fryeburg." Down East, 13 (August, 1966), 52-55.

3144 SMITH, SEBA. "Lovewell's fight." The Ladies' Companion, 13 (1840), 199-201.

3145 SYMMES, THOMAS. The original account of Capt. John Lovewell's "great fight" with the Indians, at Pequawket, May 8, 1725. (1725) A new edition with notes by Nathaniel Bouton. Concord, N.H.: P. B. Cogswell, 1861. Pp. vi, 48.
First edition has title: Lovewell lamented.

3146 WHITE, JOHN. Scout journals, 1725: journal of Capt. John White, one of the scouts during Lovewell's War in northern New England. G. Waldo Browne, ed. Manchester, N.H.: Priv. Print., 1907. Pp. 11.

3147 WINSOR, JUSTIN. "Lovewell's fight with the Indians." MHSP, 2 Ser., 3 (1886-1887), 259-260.

GARDINER (KENNEBEC CO.)

3148 BARSTOW, JAMES S. My Tilbury town. [N.Y.?], 1939. Pp. 11.
Author's memories of Gardiner during his youth and that of Edwin Arlington Robinson.

3149 BEANE, C. H. Souvenir of the flood of March 2, 1896 with an historical sketch of Gardiner. n.p., [1896]. Unpaged. Me.

3150 "THE CATHOLIC Church in Gardiner: notes on her early history." MeCathHM, 6 (1916), 45-48.

3151 CHADWICK, EDMUND ALEXANDER and J. N. STODDARD. History of Hermon Lodge, No. 32, of Free and Accepted Masons, Gardiner, Maine, from January 23, 1820, to January, 1870. Gardiner: G. O. Bailey, 1870. Pp. 58. [MePGLM].

3152 CLASON, O. B. "Wide awake Gardiner." BTJ, 20 (1907-1908), 561-568.

3153 COOPER, JOHN H. "An account of the Gardiner Lyceum, the first trade school established in the United States." Journal of the Franklin Institute, 140 (1895), 275-287.

3154 DUNN, CHARLES, JR. "Oaklands." Pine Tree Magazine, 7 (1907), 158-166.
Home of the Gardiner family.

3155 DUNN, GERALD C. and WILLIAM S. FOWLER. "An Indian campsite on Cobbosecontee Stream." MASB, 12 (1950-1951), 1-8.

3156 ERSKINE, ROBERT J., LAUREN M. SANBORN and ELMER D. COLCORD. The Gardiner story, 1849-1949: historical sketches of the plantation, town, city, and noted people. Gardiner: The City, 1949. Unpaged.

3157 FOSSETT, MILDRED B. "For over 125 years, a sentinel of the Episcopal Church: Christ Parish, Gardiner, Maine." The Northeast, 74 (May, 1947), 3-6.

3158 GARDINER, ME. The centennial of Gardiner: an account of the exercises at the celebration of the one hundredth anniversary of the incorporation of the town, June 25, 1903. Gardiner, 1903. Pp. 79.
Includes a sketch of Gardiner's early history by Josiah S. Maxcy.

3159 GARDINER, ME. BOARD OF TRADE. The city of Gardiner, Maine, U.S.A.; its water power, industries, water front, picturesque avenues, attractions and surroundings.... [Gardiner], 1896. Pp. 112.

3160 _____. Gardiner and Bostonians: 55 years of progress. [Gardiner, 1951?]. Unpaged. MB.
Commonwealth Shoe and Leather Company; Bostonian shoes.

3161 GARDINER, ME. FIRST CONGREGATIONAL CHURCH. Semi-centennial of the Congregational Church in Gardiner, July 28, 1885; historical address by Rev. Richard W. Jenkins. Gardiner: E. W. Morrell, 1885. Pp. 29. MBC.

3162 GARDINER, ME. FIRST UNIVERSALIST CHURCH. One hundredth anniversary of the First Universalist Church of Gardiner, Maine, observed on Sunday, February 7, 1943, celebration on Tuesday, May 18, 1943. n.p., [1943]. Unpaged. Me.

3163 GARDINER SAVINGS INSTITUTION. Seventy-fifth anniversary of the Gardiner Savings Institution, June 26th, 1909. [Gardiner], 1909. Pp. 48. MeHi.

3164 GILMORE, EVELYN LANGDON. Christ Church, Gardiner, Maine: antecedents and history. Gardiner: Reporter-Journal Pr., 1893. Pp. 157.
A 1962 reprint published by the Kennebec Journal includes "A continuation of the story of Christ Church," by John Richards (70 pp.).

3165 HALE, ENOCH. History and description of an epidemic fever, commonly called spotted fever, which prevailed at Gardiner, Maine, in the spring of 1814. Boston: Wells and Lilly, 1818. Pp. xvi, 246.

3166 HATHAWAY, GEORGE E. "Gardiner post-offices past and present." SJMH, 10 (1922), 100-101.

3167 LEANE, JOHN J. "When mummies made paper in Maine." Yankee, 35 (February, 1971), 64-65, 112, 115.
Importation of rags from Egypt by I. Augustus Stanwood.

3168 MAXCY, JOSIAH SMITH. Centenary of Christ Church, Gardiner, Maine; historical address, May 31, 1920. n.p., [1920?]. Unpaged.

3169 MORRELL, HIRAM KELLY. "The newspapers and serials of Gardiner, with sketches of men connected with them." MPAP, 41 (1904), 46-56.

3170 "REMINISCENCES of Gardiner." MeCathHM, 6 (1916), 37-41.
Catholics.

3171 RICHARDS, LAURA ELIZABETH HOWE. Laura E. Richards and Gardiner. Augusta: Gannett Publishing, 1940. Pp. 152.

3172 ROBBINS, LINVILLE W. Annals of the people called Methodists in the city of Gardiner, Me. Augusta: Kennebec Journal, 1900. Pp. 93. MeHi.

3173 SMITH, DAVID CLAYTON. "Coastal shipping trade on the eve of the railroad: Gardiner, Maine in the early 1830's." MeHSQ, 13 (1974-1975), 148-177.

3174 STEVENS, NEIL E. "America's first agricultural school." The Scientific Monthly, 13 (1921), 531-540.
Gardiner Lyceum.

3175 WEBSTER, HENRY SEWALL. History of Hermon Lodge, No. 32, of Free and Accepted Masons, Gardiner, Maine, from January 1st, 1870 to April 1st, 1880. Gardiner: R. B. Caldwell, 1880. Pp. 35. Me.

SEE ALSO entries 1221, 1628, 1633, 1637, 1642, 1649, and 3532.

GARFIELD PLANTATION (AROOSTOOK CO.)

3176   No items located.

GARLAND (PENOBSCOT CO.)

3177   GARLAND, ME. CONGREGATIONAL CHURCH. One hundredth anniversary of the Congregational Church, Garland, Maine, June 13, 1911. Dexter: Gazette Book and Job Print, 1912. Pp. 20. MeBa.

3178   OAK, LYNDON. History of Garland, Maine. Dover: Observer Publishing, 1912. Pp. xii, 401.

GEORGETOWN (SAGADAHOC CO.)

3179   ALLEN, CHARLES EDWIN. "Light-keeper of old Seguin, a footnote to history." NEM, New Ser., 36 (1907), 700-702.
John Polereczky; served 1796-1802.

3180   CRANSHAW, FLORENCE F. A history of the first one hundred years of the Island Home Club of Five Islands, Maine. [Georgetown]: Island Home Club, 1972. Pp. 90, 7. Me.

3181   ETNIER, ELIZABETH. On Gilbert Head: Maine days. Boston: Little, Brown, 1937. Pp. 272.

3182   GILMAN, STANWOOD CUSHING and MARGARET COOK GILMAN. Georgetown on Arrowsic: the ancient dominions of Maine on the Kennebec, 1716-1966; 250th anniversary celebration. [Georgetown?, 1966]. Pp. 26.

3183   THAYER, HENRY OTIS. "Georgetown, Maine: the ancient and the modern." SJMH, 3 (1915-1916), 91-92.

SEE ALSO entry 1806.

GILEAD (OXFORD CO.)

3183A   CHAPMAN, GEORGE WHITEFIELD. Brief history of Gilead, and prose and poetic writings. 3rd ed., with additions. Portland, 1867. Pp. 139.

3184   "GILEAD and gold." BTJ, 18 (1905-1906), 313-314.

GLENBURN (PENOBSCOT CO.)

3185   BERRY, CLYDE G. and NAIDA J. GALLANT. The story of a town: Glenburn, 1822-1972. n.p., [1972]. Pp. 109.

GLENWOOD PLANTATION (AROOSTOOK CO.)

3186   No items located.

GORE A2 (PISCATAQUIS CO.)

3187   No items located.

GORHAM (CUMBERLAND CO.)

3188   BARKER, R. MILDRED. "History of Union Branch, Gorham, Maine, 1784-1819." Shaker Quarterly, 7 (1967), 64-82.
Shakers.

3189   COTTON, FRANCES MESERVE. "The old Hugh McLellan House." SJMH, 4 (1916-1917), 17-19.

3190   DOLE, SAMUEL THOMAS. "Little Falls, a chapter of local history." MeHSC, 2 Ser., 9 (1898), 197-206.

3191   EMERY, DANIEL C. History of Harmony Lodge, to which is added some notice of the Morgan excitement. Portland: Stephen Berry, 1870. Pp. 48.
Freemasons and antimasonry.

3192   FERRIS, LEONARD ZENAS. Sermon delivered before the society of the First Congregational Church ... at Gorham, Maine, September 24, 1877. Portland: Stephen Berry, 1877. Pp. 26. MBC.
A history of the church.

3193   GORHAM, ME. Bicentennial commemoration of the incorporation of the town of Gorham, Maine, 1764-1964. Portland: Bryant Pr., 1964. Pp. 18. Me.

3194   _____. Celebration of the one hundred and fiftieth anniversary of Gorham, Maine, May 26, 1886. Portland: B. Thurston, 1886. Pp. 133.
Addresses by Elijah Kellogg, John A. Waterman, George B. Emery, Edward Robie, C. W. Deering, and George L. Prentiss.

3195   "GORHAM, Maine." BTJ, 15 (1902-1903), 41-54.

3196   GORHAM SAVINGS BANK. Heritage one hundred, Gorham Savings Bank, Gorham, Maine, 1868-1968. [Gorham, 1968?]. Pp. 23. MeHi.

3197   "GORHAM State Normal School." Maine Teachers' Digest, 1 (1940-1941), 144-145, 162-163.
Now the University of Maine at Portland-Gorham.

3198   HUNTINGTON, HENRY STRONG. A farewell sermon; preached in the Congregational Church, Gorham, Maine, June 12, 1887. Portland: Brown Thurston, 1887. Pp. 21.
Includes an historical appendix.

3199 JOHNSON, WALTER H., comp. Bi-centennial history of Gorham, Maine, 1736-1936: an account of the anniversary celebration of the town. Westbrook: Henry S. Cobb, 1936. Pp. 171.

3200 LOMBARD, LUCINA HAYNES. "The Codman House." Pine Tree Magazine, 7 (1907), 338-339.

3201 _____. "Gorham, Maine, in the days of Gorham's first school teacher." SJMH, 7 (1919-1920), 29-34.

3202 _____. "Longfellow's vacations at Gorham." Pine Tree Magazine, 7 (1907), 21-27.

3203 McLELLAN, HUGH DAVIS. History of Gorham, Me. Katharine B. Lewis, comp. and ed. Portland: Smith & Sale, 1903. Pp. 860.

3204 MAINE. STATE TEACHERS COLLEGE, GORHAM. An account of the establishment of the State Normal School and of the exercises at the dedication of the new school building, Dec. 26, 1878. Portland: Daily Pr., 1879. Pp. 36.
    Now the University of Maine at Portland-Gorham.

3205 NASON, REUBEN. A valedictory address on relinquishing the charge of Gorham Academy, August 19, 1834. Portland: Mirror Office, 1834. Pp. 14.
    Includes a brief history of the academy.

3206 OAK, LYNDON. A sketch of the life of General James Irish of Gorham, Me., 1776-1863. Boston: Lee & Shepard, 1898. Pp. 70.

3207 PIERCE, JOSIAH. The centennial anniversary of the settlement of Gorham: an address delivered on May 26, 1836. Portland: Charles Day, 1836. Pp. 36.

3208 _____. A history of the town of Gorham, Maine. Portland: Foster & Cushing, 1862. Pp. iv, 239.

3209 ROMAINE, LAWRENCE B. "A country doctor's finances." CEAIA, 2 (1937-1944), 129-130.
    Joseph S. G. Hitchcock.

3210 SOCIETY OF COLONIAL WARS. MAINE. The fort at Gorhamtown, 1744-1764. n.p., 1930. Pp. 24. MBNEH.
    Historical address by Isaac W. Dyer.

    SEE ALSO entries 799, 1493, and 1508-1509.

GORHAM GORE (FRANKLIN CO.)

3211 No items located.

GOULDSBORO (HANCOCK CO.)

3212 "AN ACCOUNT of Gouldsborough, Maine." MeHist Mag, 7 (1891-1892), 67-71.

3213 BRAZER, ESTHER STEVENS. "The tinsmiths of Stevens Plains." Antiques, 35 (1939), 294-296; 36 (1939), 134-136.

3214 COLE, ERNEST H. "Last of its kind." Yankee, 30 (November, 1966), 76-78.
    Hunting match in 1900.

3215 DAUGHTERS OF LIBERTY. GOULDSBORO, ME. Historical researches of Gouldsboro, Maine. Gouldsboro, 1904. Pp. 108.

3216 HADLOCK, WENDELL STANWOOD. The Taft's Point shell mound at West Gouldsboro, Maine. [Bar Harbor: Robert Abbe Museum], 1939. Pp. 30.

3217 McKINNEY, STEPHEN N. "Don't give up the bell." Yankee, 37 (May, 1973), 84-87, 123-125.

3218 MERRIAM, ANN VAN NESS. Glimpses into other days of Prospect Harbor. [Prospect Harbor?]: Woman's Club of Prospect Harbor, [1964?]. Unpaged.

3219 RICH, LOUISE DICKINSON. The peninsula. (1958) Riverside, Conn.: Chatham Pr., 1971. Pp. 285.
    A republication of the 1958 edition with the addition of one new chapter.

3220 SMITH, WALTER BROWN. The Jones Cove shell heap at West Gouldsboro, Maine. Bar Harbor: Sherman Publishing, 1929. Pp. 28.

    SEE ALSO entry 1579.

GRAFTON TOWNSHIP (OXFORD CO.)

3221 FOBES, CHARLES BARTLETT. Grafton, Maine: a human and geographical study. Orono: Univ. Pr., 1951. Pp. v, 29.

3222 WOOD, RICHARD GEORGE. "Obituary for a township." Appalachia, 28 (1950-1951), 465-466.

GRAND FALLS PLANTATION (PENOBSCOT CO.)

3223 No items located.

GRAND ISLE (AROOSTOOK CO.)

3224 No items located.

GRAND LAKE STREAM PLANTATION (WASHINGTON CO.)

3225 ATKINSON, MINNIE. Hinckley Township: or, Grand Lake Stream Plantation, a sketch. Newburyport, Mass.: Newburyport Herald Pr., 1920. Pp. 122.

GRAY (CUMBERLAND CO.)

3226 BUTLER, BENJAMIN and NATALIE STURGES BUTLER. "The Mayall Woolen Mill: first in the United States." Down East, 17 (September, 1970), 29, 31-32, 35, 71, 74, 77.

3227 ST. JOHN, FREDERIC. "The birth of an industry." Maine's Own Magazine, 8 (April, 1930), 18.
    Woolen industry; author's name is a pseudonym.

3228 _____. "Gray, once New Boston." Sun Up, 8 (November, 1930), 18.
    Author's name is a pseudonym.

GREAT POND PLANTATION (HANCOCK CO.)

3229 No items located.

GREENBUSH (PENOBSCOT CO.)

3230 No items located.

GREENE (ANDROSCOGGIN CO.)

3231 MOWER, WALTER LINDLEY. History of the Old Baptist Church of Greene and read at the 140th anniversary. n.p., 1934. Pp. 7. Me.

3232 _____. Sesquicentennial history of the town of Greene, Androscoggin County, Maine, 1775 to 1900, with some matter extending to a later date. Auburn: Merrill & Webber, 1938. Pp. xiv, 578.

GREENFIELD (PENOBSCOT CO.)

3233 No items located.

GREENVILLE (PISCATAQUIS CO.)

3234 DIETZ, LEW. "100 years at the same old stand: D. T. Sanders & Son, a famous Maine store, celebrates its centennial." Down East, 4 (September, 1957), 32-34.

3235 "THE ELIZABETH House." The Northern, 6 (May, 1926), 7.
    Hotel.

3236 LANDER, DONNA and CATHERINE SKINNER. A brief history of Greenville, Maine and Mountain View Farm. n.p., [1971?]. Unpaged. MeBa.

3237 LORING, AMASA. "Early history of Greenville." The Northern, 6 (October, 1926), 3-5.

3238 SHAW, CHARLES D. "History of the Shaw family with a sketch of Milton G. Shaw of Greenville." PCHSC, 1 (1910), 424-433.

3239 _____. "Some facts relating to the early history of Greenville and Moosehead Lake." PCHSC, 1 (1910), 52-65.

3240 SMITH, EDMUND WARE. "Greenville, Maine." Pine Cone, 9 (Summer, 1953), 18-21.

3241 TRUE, EMMA J. History of Greenville, 1836-1936. Augusta: Augusta Pr., [1936]. Pp. 36. Me.

GREENWOOD (OXFORD CO.)

3242 No items located.

GRINDSTONE TOWNSHIP (PENOBSCOT CO.)

3243 No items located.

GUILFORD (PISCATAQUIS CO.)

3244 GUILFORD, ME. Guilford, Maine sesquicentennial. Milo: Milo Printing, 1966. Pp. 112. MBNEH.

3245 "GUILFORD centennial, 1816-1916." SJMH, 4 (1915-1916), 67-190.

3246 HUDSON, HENRY. "Some facts in regard to the early history of the town of Guilford." PCHSC, 1 (1910), 35-51.

3247 WADE, ABNER TURNER, L. H. WHITTIER, and W. L. BATES. History of Mount Kineo Lodge, No. 109, Free and Accepted Masons, Guilford, Maine, from its organization in 1861 to June, 1946. Guilford: Guilford Recorder Print, 1946. Pp. 185. Me.

    SEE ALSO entry 1782.

HALLOWELL (KENNEBEC CO.)

3248 ALLEN, WILLIAM, 1780-1873. "Now and then." MeHSC, 7 (1876), 267-287.

3249 BAKER, HENRY KNOX. The Hallowell book. Hallowell: Register Pr., 1902. Pp. 51.

3250 BOARDMAN, SAMUEL LANE. "Hallowell and its library." NEHGR, 34 (1880), 293-297.
Hubbard Free Library.

3251 CRANDALL, CHRISTINE. "Old Hallowell ... on the Kennebec." Down East, 9 (August, 1962), 32-35, 60-62, 64, 70.

3252 FREEMASONS. HALLOWELL, ME. ROYAL ARCH MASONS. History of Jerusalem Royal Arch Chapter, Hallowell, Maine. Hallowell: Masters & Livermore, 1876. Pp. 80

3253 FULLER, GEORGE. "Hallowell, the granite city of Maine." BTJ, 20 (1907-1908), 521-523, 525-526.

3254 "GOLDEN jubilee celebration at St. Matthew's Church, Hallowell." The North East, 38 (December, 1910), 3-4.

3255 GOLDSMITH, MARGARET O. "Two early homes in Hallowell, Maine." House Beautiful, 55 (1924), 361-364, 410, 412.
Vaughan House and Merrick House.

3256 HALLOWELL, ME. City Hall dedication and Hallowell reunion, with oration, poem, letters and register of visitors, Wednesday, July 12, 1899. Hallowell: Register Pr., 1899. Pp. 43.

3257 HALLOWELL SAVINGS INSTITUTION. The record of fifty years: Hallowell Savings Institution, 1854-1904. Portland: Lakeside Pr., [1904]. Pp. 32. Me.

3258 HUBBARD FREE LIBRARY, HALLOWELL, ME. Address and poem at the dedication of the Hallowell Public Library, March 9, 1880, with historical sketch. Portland: Hoyt, Foss & Donham, [1880]. Pp. 66.
Address is by Henry Vaughan Emmons; poem is by Emma Huntington Nason.

3259 HUNT, FITZ HERBERT L. A walking tour through Hallowell, Maine, in the late 1800's with "Bert" Hunt. Augusta: KJ Printing, 1966. Pp. 31.

3260 MAINE. INDUSTRIAL SCHOOL FOR GIRLS, HALLOWELL. By-laws and statutes ... of the Maine Industrial School for Girls at Hallowell [and] a historical sketch of its establishment.... Augusta: Sprague, Owen & Nash, 1875. Pp. 27. MeHi.

3261 MARSTON, DOROTHEA M. Old Hallowell on the Kennebec: the first ninety years, 1762 to 1852. [Hallowell?], 1962. 58 leaves. Me.

3262 NASON, EMMA HUNTINGTON. Old Hallowell on the Kennebec. Augusta: Burleigh & Flynt, 1909. Pp. 359.

3263 NORTON, EDWARD PREBLE. Legends and otherwise of Hallowell and Loudon Hill.... Augusta: Charles E. Nash & Son, 1923. Pp. 77. MeBa.

3264 PAGE, ANNIE FRAZIETTE. Historical sketch of the South Congregational Church of Hallowell. ... Hallowell: Register Pr., 1900. Pp. 43. MeBa.

3265 RIGBY, HAZEN F. "The Church in Maine's smallest city: the story of Saint Matthew's Parish, Hallowell." The Northeast, 75 (March, 1948), 14-17.

3266 SNELL, KATHERINE H. and VINCENT P. LEDEW. Historic Hallowell. [Augusta]: Kennebec Journal Print Shop, 1962. Pp. 112.

3267 VAUGHAN, WILLIAM WARREN. Hallowell memories. Hallowell: Priv. Print., 1913. Pp. 187.
Vaughan family.

3268 WATKINS, MALCOLM. "A regional collection of glass lamps." Antiques, 39 (1941), 249-250.

3269 WIGHT, CHARLES A. Doorways of Hallowell, with historical sketches. Augusta: Kennebec Journal, [1907]. Pp. 37. Me.

SEE ALSO entries 1637, 1650, and 3532.

HAMLIN PLANTATION (AROOSTOOK CO.)

3270 No items located.

HAMMOND PLANTATION (AROOSTOOK CO.)

3271 No items located.

HAMMOND TOWNSHIP (SOMERSET CO.)

3272 No items located.

HAMPDEN (PENOBSCOT CO.)

3273 CHAPMAN, HARRY J. "The Battle of Hampden." SJMH, 2 (1914-1915), 185-193.
September 3, 1814.

3274 COTTLE, LAURA BICKFORD. "My one-room schoolhouse." Down East, 18 (April, 1972), 24, 27-28, 30.

3275 HAMPDEN

3275 HAMPDEN, ME. FIRST CONGREGATIONAL CHURCH.
Manual of the First Congregational Church in
Hampden, Maine. Bangor: C. H. Glass, 1910.
MBNEH.
    Includes historical sketch.

3276 HAMPDEN HISTORICAL SOCIETY. Historical
sketches, Hampden, Maine, 1767-1976. Ellsworth: Ellsworth American, 1976. Pp. 172.
MeBa.

3277 HOLT, GEORGE D. "The Lawrence Silver Mining
Co., of Hampden, Penobscot County, Maine."
Maine Mining Journal, 2 (September 17, 1880),
183.

3278 MATHEWS, SAMUEL WORCESTER. History of Mystic
Lodge, No. 65, of Free and Accepted Masons,
Hampden, Maine, from March 1st, 1857 to
March 1st, 1875. Bangor: G. O. Bailey, 1875.
Pp. 27. [MePGLM].

3279 "TOWN of Hampden." BHistMag, 2 (1886-1887),
25-32.

HANCOCK (HANCOCK CO.)

3280 CRABTREE, ALFRED B. and HATTIE B. MARTIN.
Hancock, 1828-1928. Augusta: Kennebec
Journal, 1928. Pp. 90.

3281 CURRIER, ISABEL. "A castle in Maine." Down
East, 16 (October, 1969), 42-44, 49, 69, 72.
    Cuniculocus Castle, home of Altea and Neva
Austin.

3282 "THE FABULOUS 'cat castle.'" Yankee, 18
(March, 1954), 18-21.
    Home of Altea and Neva Austin.

    SEE ALSO entries 1569, 1579, and 1586.

HANOVER (OXFORD CO.)

3283 SEE entry 2289.

HARFORDS POINT TOWNSHIP (PISCATAQUIS CO.)

3284 No items located.

HARMONY (SOMERSET CO.)

3285 McLAUGHLIN, CHARLES CARROLL. Harmony's history, happenings, habits and humor ... to
1962. Skowhegan: Skowhegan Press, [1962?].
Pp. 96. Me.

HARPSWELL (CUMBERLAND CO.)

3286 ALEXANDER, WILLIAM T. Harpswell on Casco Bay:
its early history and shipbuilding. Portland: Print Shop, 1973. Pp. iii, 251.

3287 BAILEY, FRANK LINWOOD. Home folks of Harpswell and other poems. Plymouth, Mass.:
Rogers Print, 1961. Unpaged. MeHi.

3288 BAILEY ISLAND CHURCH. Bailey Island Church,
Bailey Island, Maine, 1885-1935. n.p. [1935].
Unpaged. MeHi.

3289 DOUGHTY, WILLIAM H. Historical sketch of
Orr's Island, with landscape descriptions.
Portland: Six Towns Times Print, 1899.
Pp. 53.

3290 HARPSWELL, ME. CONGREGATIONAL CHURCH. Sou-
venir of Elijah Kellogg Church. Franklin,
Mass.: Franklin Job Print, 1911. Unpaged.
MBC.

3291 JUST a peek at Orr's & Bailey Island, Maine.
Orr's Island: Orr's and Bailey Island Sports-
men's Club, [not before 1949]. Unpaged.
MeHi.

3292 LORING, AMASA. "A venerable tabernacle."
MHGR, 1 (1884), 85-86.
    Elijah Kellogg Church.

3293 MAGILL, ROBERT N. A short history of Damariscove Island. Walpole: Ira C. Darling Center,
1975. Pp. 5. MeP.

3294 MERRIAM, MRS. PELEG. "Historic old church at
Harpswell Center." Congregationalism in
Maine, 13 (1926), 27.
    Elijah Kellogg Church.

3295 MURPHY, THOMAS E. "Elijah's church: ye call
me chief and they still do." NEG, 9 (Spring,
1968), 12-22.
    Elijah Kellogg Church.

3296 O'CONNOR, THOMAS P. "Memento of Merryconeag."
Steamboat Bill, 27 (1970), 204-205.
    Fire aboard the Merryconeag at Orr's Island,
November 29, 1918.

3297 ROLLINS, RUTH. "One-of-a-kind: the cribstone
bridge." Down East, 22 (May, 1976), 58-59,
79.

3298 ROUX, WILLAN C. "Admiral Peary's quarter."
Yankee, 30 (August, 1966), 77-79, 102, 105-
106, 109.

3299 _____. "The bridge that divided a town."
Yankee, 30 (March, 1966), 68-69, 137-141.

3300 SINNETT, CHARLES NELSON. Historic Harpswell, Harpswell, Maine, its historic Congregational Church and famous ministers, 1758-1903. Haverhill, Mass.: C. C. Morse & Son, 1903. Pp. 19.

3301 THOMAS, MIRIAM STOVER. Harpswell in the American Revolution. n.p., [1976]. 18 leaves. MeU.

3302 _____. "South Harpswell's old tide mill." Down East, 19 (September, 1972), 21-23.

3303 THWING, ANNIE HAVEN. The story of Orr's Island, Maine. Boston: Geo. H. Ellis, 1925. Pp. 18.

3304 TODD, MARGARET and CHARLES TODD. Beautiful Harpswell: the Neck and its 45 island jewels. [Orr's Island?, 1967]. Pp. 58.

3305 WAUGAMAN, CHARLES A. "Harpswell's club for all seasons." Down East, 17 (June, 1971), 54-55, 77, 79-81. Harpswell Garden Club.

3306 WEST HARPSWELL BAPTIST CHURCH. One hundred years, 1836-1936, West Harpswell Baptist Church, West Harpswell, Maine. n.p., [1936]. Unpaged. Historical sketch by Mrs. Charles K. Durgan.

3307 WILL, RICHARD T. Digging up pre-history in southern coastal Maine. Tuscon, Ariz.: Alphagraphics, 1976. Pp. iv, 41. MeU.

SEE ALSO entry 2573.

HARRINGTON (WASHINGTON CO.)

3308 SEE entries 603, 1864-1865, and 1875.

HARRISON (CUMBERLAND CO.)

3309 MOULTON, ALPHONSO, HOWARD L. SAMPSON, and GRANVILLE FERNALD. Centennial history of Harrison, Maine, containing the centennial celebration of 1905, and historical and biographical matter. Portland: Southworth Printing, 1909. Pp. xii, 727.

3310 RIDLON, GIDEON TIBBETTS. Early settlers of Harrison, Maine, with an historical sketch of the settlement, progress and present condition of the town. Skowhegan: Kilby & Woodbury, 1877. Pp. 138.

3311 WARD, ERNEST E. My first sixty years in Harrison, Maine. Denmark: Cardinal Printing, 1967. Pp. 92.

HARTFORD (OXFORD CO.)

3312 No items located.

HARTLAND (SOMERSET CO.)

3313 HARTLAND, ME. 1820, Hartland, Maine, 1970. n.p., [1970]. Pp. 83. Me. Historical sketch by F. Wayne Libby.

HAYNESVILLE (AROOSTOOK CO.)

3314 "HISTORY of Haynesville." Liberty Bell, 1 (1934), 5-16. A publication of the Haynesville Junior High School; a copy is in the Maine State Library.

HEBRON (OXFORD CO.)

3315 BEARCE, ROGER M. and HAROLD E. HALL. A history of the Hebron Church, 1791-1966, the first 175 years. Hebron, 1966. Pp. 67. MWA.

3316 BONNEY, PERCIVAL. "William Barrows--John Tripp." MeHSC, 2 Ser., 3 (1892), 149-186.

3317 HEBRON, ME. BAPTIST CHURCH. Manual of the Baptist Church in Hebron, Maine, including its history, covenant, articles of faith, standing rules, and list of members' names, August, 1854. Portland: Brown Thurston, 1854. Pp. 24. MeBa.

3318 HEBRON ACADEMY. Hebron Academy: some thoughts on its history and its accomplishments, 1804-1954. [Hebron]: Record Pr., 1954. Unpaged.

3319 _____. Semi-centennial celebration of Hebron Academy, at Hebron, Maine, September 5, 1855. Paris: W. A. Pidgin, 1855. Pp. 39.

SEE ALSO entry 4049.

HERMON (PENOBSCOT CO.)

3320 HERMON, ME. Sesquicentennial souvenir and history of Hermon, Penobscot County, Maine, 1814-1964. n.p., [1964]. Pp. 36.

3321 HERMON, ME. HISTORICAL COMMITTEE. Centennial souvenir and history of Hermon, Penobscot County, Maine, 1814-1914. Frank A. Bishop, Roscoe W. Snow, and Annie Mayhew, comps. Carmel: Carmel Print, [1914]. Pp. 33.

3322 HERSEY

HERSEY (AROOSTOOK CO.)

3322   No items located.

HERSEYTOWN TOWNSHIP (PENOBSCOT CO.)

3323   DINGLEY, THEDA C. "Summit Farms of Maine."
        Sun Up, 2 (May, 1926), 11, 36-37.
            Dairy farm in the village of Davidson.

HIBBERTS GORE (LINCOLN CO.)

3324   No items located.

HIGHLAND PLANTATION (SOMERSET CO.)

3325   No items located.

HIRAM (OXFORD CO.)

3326   DUNN, CHARLES, JR. "Wadsworth Hall." Pine
        Tree Magazine, 7 (1907), 33-44.
            Estate of Peleg Wadsworth, Longfellow's
        grandfather.

3327   "EARLY history--Hiram, Maine." Maine Idler,
        1 (August, 1950), 7.

3328   HIRAM, ME. Official program ... one hun-
        dredth anniversary.... Cornish: Webb-Smith,
        [1914]. Pp. 34. MeHi.
            Includes history by Llewellyn Andrew Wads-
        worth.

3329   TEG, WILLIAM. History of Hiram. (1941)
        Sesquicentennial [i.e. rev. and enl.] ed.
        Cornish: Carbrook Pr., 1964. Pp. 137.

3330   WADSWORTH, LLEWELLYN ANDREW. "First settle-
        ment of Hiram, Me." Maine Genealogist and
        Biographer, 2 (1876-1877), 94-96.

        SEE ALSO entry 168.

HOBBSTOWN TOWNSHIP (SOMERSET CO.)

3331   No items located.

HODGDON (AROOSTOOK CO.)

3332   SCOTT, G. M. "W. H. Harding, potato barrel
        king of Aroostook." Down East, 22 (October,
        1975), 58-61.

HOLDEN (PENOBSCOT CO.)

3333   SEE entry 1762.

HOLEB TOWNSHIP (SOMERSET CO.)

3334   SEE entry 3377A.

HOLLIS (YORK CO.)

3335   LOMBARD, LUCINA HAYNES. "The first Baptist
        church in Maine." SJMH, 8 (1920), 34-35.

HOPE (KNOX CO.)

3336   HOPE, ME. Hope chronicle, census, history,
        statistics, business directory, etc. Union:
        Union Publishing, 1888. Pp. 32. MeHi.

        SEE ALSO entry 1833.

HOPKINS ACADEMY GRANT (PENOBSCOT CO.)

3337   No items located.

HOULTON (AROOSTOOK CO.)

3338   "AN ACCOUNT of Houlton, Me." BHistMag, 3
        (1887-1888), 14-15.

3339   BARNES, ANNA. "History of postal affairs in
        Houlton." Houlton Local Postal Guide, 1
        (January, 1901), 1-9.

3340   [BARNES, FRANCIS]. The story of Houlton from
        the public records, and from the experiences
        of its founders, their descendants, and asso-
        ciates to the present time.... Houlton:
        Will H. Smith, 1899. Unpaged.

3341   COTTON, PERCY G. "The faithful shepherding
        of God's flock: the record of the Church of
        the Good Shepherd, Houlton." The Northeast,
        74 (November, 1947), 4-6.

3342   HOULTON, ME. Houlton has its 150th birthday:
        souvenir program, sesquicentennial celebra-
        tion, August 17-24, 1957. Roland Atchison,
        comp. Houlton: Aroostook Print Shop, [1957].
        Unpaged.

3343   "HOULTON, the Aroostook capital." New North-
        east, 1 (1894), 35-49.

3344   "HOULTON--the gateway city to the garden of
        Maine." Sun Up, 3 (June, 1927), 27-30.

3345 [KENDALL, JOSEPH and GEORGE H. GILMAN].
History of the town of Houlton, (Maine),
from 1804 to 1883. By an old pioneer.
Haverhill, Mass.: C. C. Morse & Son, 1884.
Pp. 60.

3346 PUTNAM, AMOS. A history of Monument Lodge,
No. 96, 1858-1939. Houlton, [1939?].
Pp. 83. [MeHoC].
Freemasons.

3347 PUTNAM, CORA M. CARPENTER. The story of
Houlton. Portland: House of Falmouth,
1958. Pp. 423.

3348 [_____]. Supplement to [the] story of Houlton. n.p., [1969?]. Unpaged. [MeHoC].

3349 RICH, GEORGE B. "Ricker still pioneers."
Pine Cone, 7 (Spring, 1951), 7-11.
Ricker College.

3350 "RICKER Classical Institute and Junior College." Sun Up, 8 (October, 1930), 13, 31.
Now Ricker College.

3351 RICKER COLLEGE, HOULTON, ME. The RCI story,
Ricker Classical Institute, Houlton, Maine.
[Houlton, 1961?]. Pp. 8. [MeHoR].

3352 SALVATION ARMY, HOULTON, ME. 62nd anniversary, 1888-1950, Salvation Army Corps, Houlton, Maine. n.p., [1950?]. Unpaged.
[MeHoR].

3353 SHIRETOWN saga. [Houlton?, 1957?]. 38
leaves. [MeHoC].
Bicentennial pageant, August, 1957.

3354 SPAULDING, ROYAL CRAFTS. Autobiographical
sketch of Rev. Royal Crafts Spaulding, and
extracts from letters of himself, and of his
wife, Jerusha Bryant Spaulding. Francis
Barnes, ed. Houlton: W. H. Smith, 1891.
Pp. 53.

3355 THIBADEAU, WILLIAM JARVIS. The Irishman, a
factor in the development of Houlton; a
history of the Parish of St. Mary's; a word
about the Acadians of Madawaska. Augusta:
Kennebec Journal, [1910?]. Pp. 109. MBNEH.

SEE ALSO entries 50 and 1463.

HOWLAND (PENOBSCOT CO.)

3356 No items located.

HUDSON (PENOBSCOT CO.)

3357 No items located.

INDIAN ISLAND PENOBSCOT INDIAN RESERVATION (PENOBSCOT CO.)

3358 No items located.

INDIAN STREAM TOWNSHIP (SOMERSET CO.)

3359 No items located.

INDIAN TOWNSHIP STATE INDIAN RESERVATION (WASHINGTON CO.)

3360 No items located.

INDUSTRY (FRANKLIN CO.)

3361 ALLEN, WILLIAM, 1780-1873. History of Industry, Maine, from the first settlement in
1791. (1854) 2d ed., improved and enl.
Skowhegan: Smith & Emery, 1869. Pp. 48.

3362 HATCH, WILLIAM COLLINS. A history of the
town of Industry, Franklin County, Maine,
from the earliest settlement in 1787 down to
the present time, embracing the cessions of
New Sharon, New Vineyard, Anson and Stark; in
two parts, including the history and genealogy
of many of the leading families of the town.
Farmington: Knowlton & McLeary, 1893.
Pp. xiv, 862.

ISLAND FALLS (AROOSTOOK CO.)

3363 SAWYER, NINA G., comp. A history of Island
Falls, Maine, from its settlement in 1843 to
its centennial year 1972, and a collection of
historical sketches. [Island Falls, 1972].
Pp. 154.

ISLE AU HAUT (KNOX CO.)

3364 BATES, ARLO. "Isle au Haut." Outing, 6
(1885), 649-656.

3365 EUSTIS, ELIZABETH B. "Acadia's Isle au Haut
area." National Parks Magazine, 26 (January-
March, 1952), 14-17, 37-40.

3366 ISLE AU HAUT, ME. UNION CONGREGATIONAL
CHURCH. Union Congregational Church of Isle
au Haut, Maine, 1857-1957. Cambridge, Mass.:
Riverside Pr., 1957. Pp. 20.
The copy at the Maine State Library is
signed "Mary Hubbard French, author."

3367 ISLE AU HAUT

3367 "ISLE au Haute papers." BHistMag, 3 (1887-1888), 1-5.
Origin of the name.

3368 PRATT, CHARLES. Here on the island; being an account of a way of life several miles off the Maine coast. N.Y.: Harper & Row, 1974. Pp. 178.

SEE ALSO entries 611, 1561, 2834, 2836, and 2840-2842.

ISLESBORO (WALDO CO.)

3369 COOK, JOEL. An Islesboro sketch. [Boston]: Boston Photogravure, 1890. Pp. 36.

3370 DANIELS, CAROLINE T. LE FAVOR. Facts and fancies and repetitions about Dark Harbor, by one of the very oldest cottagers. Cambridge, Mass.: Cosmos Pr., 1935. Pp. 58.

3371 FARROW, JOHN PENDLETON. History of Islesborough, Maine. Bangor: T. W. Burr, 1893. Pp. xii, 313.

3372 HATCH, MARGARET TODD. "Islesboro's nabobs and neighbors." Down East, 10 (August, 1963), 32-36, 62, 65.
Social life and customs.

3373 HATCH, W. H. "Islesboro net makers." Down East, 15 (March, 1969), 42-43.
Fishing nets.

3374 KELLOGG, FREDERICK C. "God's rustic house at Islesboro: the chapel at Dark Harbor." The Northeast, 77 (July, 1950), 8.
Christ Chapel.

3375 "LONG Island--Islesboro." BHistMag, 1 (1885-1886), 167-172.

3376 ROGERS, DONALD. "The wreck of the 'Alice E. Clark.'" Down East, 21 (September, 1974), 23-24.
1909.

3377 ROLERSON, DARRELL A. "When Islesboro said 'whoa' to the horseless carriage." Down East, 14 (April, 1968), 44-47.

JACKMAN (SOMERSET CO.)

3377A JACKMAN BICENTENNIAL BOOK COMMITTEE. The history of the Moosehead Valley: Jackman, Moose River, Dennistown, Long Pond, Parlin Pond, Holeb, Skinner and Lowelltown. [Augusta]: KJ Printing, [1976]. Pp. 169. MeU.

3378 SPRAGUE, JOHN FRANCIS. "Jackman and the Moose River region." SJMH, 3 (1915-1916), 55-74.

JACKSON (WALDO CO.)

3379 MORTON, EVERETT E. Historical address of the town of Jackson, given at the one hundredth anniversary of Jackson as a plantation and of the Congregational Church, October 5-6, 1912. Waterville: Mail Publishing, 1912. Pp. 15. Me.

JAY (FRANKLIN CO.)

3380 CUSHMAN, HELEN CALDWELL. Horizons unlimited: a history of Jay. Livermore Falls: Livermore Falls Trust Company, 1967. Pp. 39.

3381 FOURNIER, PAUL J. "Little planes--big business." Flying, 65 (August, 1959), 46-47, 64-66.
Use of aircraft by Maine Woodlands Department of the International Paper Company, 1946-1959.

3382 LAWRENCE, BENJAMIN F. History of Jay, Franklin County, Maine. Boston: Griffith-Stillings Pr., 1912. Pp. vi, 93.

JEFFERSON (LINCOLN CO.)

3383 FREEMASONS. JEFFERSON, ME. RIVERSIDE LODGE. NO. 135. History of Riverside Lodge, Free and Accepted Masons, Jefferson, Maine. Waldoboro: Miller & Atwood, 1874. Pp. 15. [MePGLM].

3384 JEFFERSON, ME. Centennial celebration of the town of Jefferson, Lincoln County, Maine, U.S.A., August 21, 1907. Alberto A. Bennett, comp. Lewiston: Journal Printing, 1908. Pp. 61.

3385 RICHARDSON, CHARLES ALBERT, comp. Richardson letters: letters written to Albert Richardson from 1832 to 1881, with biographical sketches and a partial genealogy of the Richardson family. Jefferson, 1954 [i.e. 1955]. Pp. xii, 318.
Social life and customs.

JIM POND TOWNSHIP (FRANKLIN CO.)

3386 No items located.

JOHNSON MOUNTAIN TOWNSHIP (SOMERSET CO.)

3387 No items located.

JONESBORO (WASHINGTON CO.)

3388 SEE entry 1851.

JONESPORT (WASHINGTON CO.)

3389 BENSON, EARL M. "The promised land." Down
East, 2 (September, 1955), 21-23, 40-41.
George Jones Adams, founder of the Church
of the Messiah, led a group of Maine colonists
to the Holy Land in 1866 and started a colony
at Jaffa.

3390 DAVIS, HAROLD ARTHUR. "The Jaffa colonists
from Downeast." AmQ, 3 (1951), 344-356.

3391 DORSON, RICHARD M. "Collecting folklore in
Jonesport, Maine." American Philosophical
Society. Proceedings, 101 (1957), 270-289.

3392 EIDELBERG, SHLOMO. "The Adams colony in Jaffa (1866-1868)." Midstream, 3 (Summer, 1957),
52-61.

3393 GARDNER, GEORGE PEABODY. "Roque Island--home
anchorage." Down East, 6 (September, 1959),
20-24, 38-39.

3393A JONESPORT: a group of historical sketches
written in honor of the centennial. Machias:
Teague Publishing, [1932?]. Pp. 52. MeU.

3394 MONKS, JOHN PEABODY. "The history of Roque
Island, Maine." CSMP, 42 (1952-1956), 423-
472.

3395 _____. Roque Island, Maine. Diana Whitehill
Laing, ed. Boston: Colonial Society of Massachusetts, 1964. Pp. 51.

3395A NORTON, ALTON ACKLEY. Moosabec manavelins.
[Swarthmore?, Pa.], 1950. Pp. 140.

3396 PEARCE, GRACE NASH. "Bathed in light from
three lighthouses." Nautical Research Journal, 3 (June, 1951), 83-84.
Shipbuilding and the migration of George
Jones Adams and his followers to Palestine in
1866.

3396A SHAW, DAVID E. "Maine's Holy Land colonists."
Down East, 23 (January, 1977), 40-43.
Jaffa Colony.

SEE ALSO entries 467, 603, and 1840.

KATAHDIN IRON WORKS TOWNSHIP (PISCATAQUIS CO.)

3397 BROCKWAY, MARJORIE. "Katahdin Iron Works."
Down East, 8 (October, 1961), 20-25.

3398 EASTMAN, JOEL WEBB. "David Pingree's iron
works." EIHC, 103 (1967), 189-198.
Katahdin Iron Works Company.

3399 KOHN, CLYDE FREDERICK. "Katahdin Iron Works,
Maine: a study in population distribution."
Michigan Academy of Science, Arts, and Let-
ters. Papers, 25 (1939), 397-405.

3400 SAWYER, RALPH S. "Katahdin Iron Works." Sun
Up, 4 (September, 1927), 9, 52, 55.

3401 WORTHINGTON, J. W. "Katahdin Iron Works."
Appalachia, 22 (1938-1939), 346-355.

KENDUSKEAG (PENOBSCOT CO.)

3402 WINTERS, ERMA. A history of Kenduskeag,
Maine. Kenduskeag, 1966 [i.e. 1973]. Pp. 85.

KENNEBUNK (YORK CO.)

3403 BARRY, WILLIAM EDWARD. Chronicles of Kenne-
bunk, being scenes and episodes in an old
Maine village and vicinity. N.Y.: Redfield,
Kendrick, Odell, 1923. Pp. 86.

3404 _____. A stroll by a familiar river, comprising the colloquy of saunterers by its lower
course, and household words pertaining to its
early history. Kennebunk: Enterprise Pr.,
1911. 99 leaves.
Mousum River.

3405 _____. A stroll thro' the past, accompanied
by an invisible associate, and using an 18th-
century stage-route and river road, preceded
by a summary of the early ownerships and provincial governments of Maine, together with a
collection of historical data gathered in and
around Kennebunk village and sketches of
buildings which have long since disappeared.
Portland: Southworth Pr., 1933. Pp. vi, 93.

3406 BOURNE, EDWARD EMERSON, 1797-1873. Ancient
history of Kennebunk written in 1831. Kennebunk: Star Print, [1970]. Pp. 122. MeHi.

3407 BOURNE, EDWARD EMERSON, III and HARTLEY LORD,
II. Kennebunk folks. [Kennebunk]: Brick
Store Museum, 1967. Pp. 62.

3408 _____. Kennebunk in the nineties, and biographical sketches. Kennebunk: Brick Store
Museum, 1965. Pp. 80.

3409 BRYANT, SETH EMERY, comp. District of Kennebunk: a list of vessels built, from 1800 to
1873. Kennebunk, 1874. Pp. 12.

3410 DRAKE, J. H. "You are not invited." Yankee,
33 (June, 1969), 30-34.
The Wedding Cake House.

3411 KENNEBUNK

3411 FREEMAN, MELVILLE CHASE. "History of the First Congregational Parish Unitarian of Kennebunk." UHSP, 9 Pt. 2 (1952), 25-37.

3412 GILPATRIC, GEORGE A. and ALBERT W. MESERVE. History of York Lodge, No. 22, F. & A. M., from 1813 to 1913. Kennebunk: W. L. Watson, 1913. Pp. 183. MeHi.

3413 GILPATRIC, GEORGE A. Kennebunk history, not a history of Kennebunk but a few items in addition to and a sequel to "The Village of Kennebunk, Maine." Kennebunk: Star Print, 1939. Pp. 148. Me.

3414 _____. The village of Kennebunk, Maine: interesting facts from old documents and maps, and observations by the author. Kennebunk: Star Print, 1935. Pp. 79.

3415 KENNEBUNK, ME. BRICK STORE MUSEUM. In commemoration of the founding of the Brick Store Museum, twenty-fifth year, 1936-1961. [Kennebunk, 1961?]. Unpaged. MeHi.

3416 _____. Old family portraits of Kennebunk. Kennebunk, 1944. Unpaged.

3417 _____. Old houses of Kennebunk. Kennebunk, 1939. Unpaged.

3418 LEFFINGWELL, B. H. "Ye Olde Stagecoach Homestead, Kennebunk, Maine." Hobbies, 65 (June, 1960), 88-89.
Originally called Barnard's Inn; later known as Towles' Tavern and Frost Tavern.

3419 MESERVE, ALBERT W. A history of Murray Royal Arch Chapter, No. 33, holden at Kennebunk, Maine, 1869 to 1909. Portland: Stephen Berry, 1909. Pp. 87. MeBa.
Freemasons.

3420 POWERS, JESSIE D. O. "First Parish Church, Kennebunk, Maine." The Church Exchange, 6 (1898-1899), 69.

3421 REMICH, DANIEL. History of Kennebunk from its earliest settlement to 1890, including biographical sketches. Carrie E. Remich, ed. Portland: Lakeside Pr., 1911. Pp. viii, 542, xxxvi.

3422 SCHMIDT, HENRIETTA. Through the years. Thomas E. Bradbury, ed. Kennebunk: Star Pr., 1975. Pp. 94.

3423 THOMPSON, MARGARET JEFFERDS. Captain Nathaniel Lord Thompson of Kennebunk, Maine, and the ships he built, 1811-1889. Boston: Charles E. Lauriat, 1937. Pp. xix, 140.

3424 WALKER, ANDREW. Military and naval history of residents of Kennebunk, who enlisted during the late Civil War. Kennebunk, 1868. Pp. 24.

3425 WEST KENNEBUNK, ME. METHODIST CHURCH. One hundredth anniversary, 1868-1968. n.p., [1968?]. Unpaged. MeHi.

SEE ALSO entries 987, 1322, 1880, 1884, 1896, and 1898.

KENNEBUNKPORT (YORK CO.)

3426 ADAMS, ELEANOR. "Kennebunkport's little green man." Down East, 8 (September, 1961), 49.
Discovery of a copy of a Renaissance statue in Kennebunkport in 1924 and the theory of its origin.

3427 ADAMS, FRANK FORRESTAL. "A one time old Maine inn." Sun Up, 4 (September, 1927), 11, 54-55.
Luques House.

3428 BRADBURY, CHARLES. History of Kennebunk Port, from its first discovery by Bartholomew Gosnold, May 14, 1602 to 1837. (1837) Kennebunkport: Durrell Publications, 1967. Pp. 338.
This reprint edition contains indexes.

3429 BRADBURY, THOMAS E. "Arundel and the Revolution." Down East, 22 (September, 1975), 68.

3430 BROOKS, ANNIE PEABODY. Ropes' ends: traditions, legends and sketches of old Kennebunkport and vicinity. Kennebunkport, 1901. Pp. 236.

3431 BUTLER, JOYCE. "Abbott Graves, artist and citizen of Kennebunkport." Down East, 21 (January, 1975), 44-47.

3432 _____. The South Congregational Church, Kennebunkport, Maine: an architectural history. [Kennebunkport]: South Congregational Church, 1973. Pp. 8. MeHi.

3433 DOW, JOY WHEELER. Old-time dwellings in Kennebunk Port. Kennebunk: Star Print, 1926. Pp. 82.

3434 FREEMAN, MELVILLE CHASE. History of Cape Porpoise. Cape Porpoise, 1955. Pp. 107.

3435 FREEMASONS. KENNEBUNKPORT, ME. ARUNDEL LODGE, NO. 76. History of Arundel Lodge, No. 76, F. & A. M., Kennebunkport, Me., from 1854 to 1870. Portland: Stephen Berry, 1870. Pp. 28.

3436 _____. Supplementary history of Arundel Lodge, No. 76, Free and Accepted Masons, Kennebunkport, Me., from 1870 to 1890. Portland: Stephen Berry, 1894. Pp. 43. MeHi.

3437 HISTORICAL RECORDS SURVEY. MAINE. An inventory of the town archives of Kennebunkport. Portland, 1937. 8 leaves. Me.

3438 KENNEBUNKPORT, ME. ST. ANN'S CHURCH. St. Ann's Church, Kennebunkport, Maine, 1912. [Kennebunkport?, 1912]. Pp. 16.

3439 KENNEBUNKPORT, ME. 300TH ANNIVERSARY COMMITTEE. 300th anniversary Cape Porpoise, Arundel, Kennebunkport, 1653-1953. Kennebunkport: Star Print, [1953?]. Pp. 64.

3440 KNIGHT, HENRY F. "Cape Porpoise, old and new." MeHSC, 2 Ser., 6 (1895), 153-175.

3441 LOMBARD, LUCINA HAYNES. "Cape Porpoise days." Pine Tree Magazine, 7 (1907), 509-514.

3442 LOWRY, LOIS. "New life for the house Captain Lord built." Down East, 23 (November, 1976), 32-37.
          Nathaniel Lord.

3443 MacALISTER, LORIMER W. Chronicles of Cape Porpoise and Kennebunkport. Cape Porpoise: Atlantic Firemen's Educational Association, 1949. Unpaged. MeHi.

3444 MOWER, IRVING B. History of the Baptist Church, Kennebunkport. Biddeford: Times Book and Job Print, 1890. Pp. 17.

3445 WASHBURN, JENNIE M. "Kennebunkport--old and new." Pine Tree Magazine, 8 (1907), 21-30.

3446 WILLARD, LAWRENCE F. "The clock that D.S.T. begins." Yankee, 30 (April, 1966), 70-71, 155.
          Emmons Clock Farm.

     SEE ALSO entries 1880, 1896, and 1898.

KIBBY TOWNSHIP (FRANKLIN CO.)

3447 No items located.

KINEO TOWNSHIP (PISCATAQUIS CO.)

3448 FOBES, CHARLES BARTLETT. "Mt. Kineo, Maine." Appalachia, 36 (1966-1967), 521-527.

3449 MacDOUGALL, WALTER M. "Kineo." Down East, 22 (May, 1976), 62-67, 85-86, 89.

3450 SPRAGUE, JOHN FRANCIS. "Mount Kineo and the Maine summer resort industry." SJMH, 2 (1914-1915), 10-16.

KING & BARTLETT TOWNSHIP (SOMERSET CO.)

3451 No items located.

KINGFIELD (FRANKLIN CO.)

3452 ERICKSON, HAZEL CUSHMAN. I grew up on the narrow gauge. N.Y.: Carlton Pr., 1971. Pp. 48. [MeHoC].

3453 KINGFIELD, ME. Souvenir of historic Kingfield, 1816-1916. n.p., 1916. Pp. 20. MeHi.

3454 KINGFIELD, ME. SESQUICENTENNIAL COMMITTEE. Salute to Kingfield's past: Kingfield, Maine sesquicentennial, 1816-1966. n.p., [1966]. Pp. 80. Me.

3455 VOSE, JOSEPHINE. "The Kingfield rebellion." Down East, 9 (June, 1963), 77.
          Draft riot during the Civil War.

     SEE ALSO entry 1552.

KINGMAN TOWNSHIP (PENOBSCOT CO.)

3456 SEE entry 50.

KINGSBURY PLANTATION (PISCATAQUIS CO.)

3457 No items located.

KITTERY (YORK CO.)

3458 ALDEN, JOHN. "Portsmouth Naval Shipyard." United States Naval Institute. Proceedings, 90 (November, 1964), 89-105.
          Includes a list of vessels built there.

3459 ALLEN, NEAL WOODSIDE, JR. "A Maine witch." OTNE, 61 (1970-1971), 75-81.
          Sarah Keene.

3460 BAXTER, JAMES PHINNEY. "Piscataqua and the Pepperells." MeHSC, 2 Ser., 4 (1893), 426-430.

3460A BENNETT, JACOB. "George Savary Wasson and the dialect of Kittery Point, Maine." American Speech, 49 (1974), 54-66.

3461 BONAR, JAMES CHARLES. Canada greets Kittery. Kittery: Piscataqua Pr., 1947. Pp. 24.

3462 BROWN, JOHN HERBERT. Portsmouth Navy Yard, 1800, and her early commandants. N.Y.: Newcomen Society, 1974. Pp. 40.

3463 BURRAGE, HENRY SWEETSER. "The Baptist church in Kittery." MeHSC, 2 Ser., 9 (1898), 382-391.

3464 KITTERY

3464 COLBY, FRED M. "A day at old Kittery." Granite Mo, 2 (1879), 68-71.

3465 DENNETT, MARK. "Kittery in the olden time." Old Eliot, 8 (1908), 49-62.

3466 DRAKE, SAMUEL ADAMS. "The Pepperells of Kittery Point, Maine." Appleton's Journal, 11 (1874), 65-66.

3467 DUNN, CHARLES, JR. "Pepperell House." Pine Tree Magazine, 6 (1906-1907), 231-240.

3468 DUNNACK, HENRY ERNEST. A history of Fort McClary Memorial. Augusta: State Park Commission, [1955?]. Pp. 27. Me.

3469 DUTTON, JOHN G. History of the Second Christian Church of Kittery, Maine, organized May 25th, 1843. n.p., [1891?]. Pp. 8. MeB.

3470 FAIRCHILD, BYRON. Messrs. William Pepperell: merchants at Piscataqua. Ithaca: Cornell Univ. Pr., 1954. Pp. xi, 223.

3471 FENTRESS, WALTER E. H. 1775. 1875. Centennial history of the United States Navy Yard, at Portsmouth, N.H. Portsmouth, N.H.: O. M. Knight, 1876. Pp. 84.

3472 FROSST, GEORGE W. "Old Kittery." Old Eliot, 2 (1898), 21-23.
Origin of its name.

3473 FROST, JOHN ELDRIDGE. Colonial village. Kittery Point: Gundalow Club, [1948?]. Pp. 82.
Historic houses.

3474 FROST, JOSEPH WILLIAM PEPPERELL. "Pepperell Mansion, Kittery Point, Maine." Antiques, 89 (1966), 368-373.

3475 _____. Sir William Pepperrell, Bart., 1696-1759, His Britannic Majesty's obedient servant of Piscataqua. N.Y.: Newcomen Society in North America, 1951. Pp. 40.

3476 GEORGES, JUSTINE FLINT. "The house of the month." Shoreliner, 2 (December, 1951), 15-24.
Dennett House.

3477 HIGGINS, ROLAND W. "The Portsmouth Navy Yard." Shoreliner, 3 (July, 1952), 39-44.

3478 HILDRETH, HORACE A. The Pine Tree State salutes Kittery. Kittery: Piscataqua Pr., 1948. Pp. 16.

3479 KITTERY, ME. FIRST BAPTIST CHURCH. The First Baptist Church of Kittery Point, Maine. South Berwick: Chronicle Print Shop, 1973. Pp. 51. MeHi.
Includes a history of the church.

3480 KITTERY, ME. 300TH ANNIVERSARY PUBLICATION COMMITTEE. Old Kittery, 1647-1947; 300th anniversary. Kittery, 1947. Pp. 36.

3481 KITTERY BICENTENNIAL COMMITTEE. Kittery kaleidoscope. Somersworth, N.H.: New Hampshire Publishing, 1976. Pp. 76. MeHi.

3482 KITTERY COMMUNITY SERVICE ASSOCIATION. Kittery, ancient and modern. Kittery, 1925. Pp. 40.

3483 LIBBY, CHARLES THORNTON. "Naming of Kittery, Me." NEHGR, 71 (1917), 89-91.

3484 MERROW, JAMES. "Frisbee's Market." Yankee, 39 (August, 1975), 56-59, 100-102.

3485 MITCHELL, HORACE. "Eagles with feeling." Yankee, 29 (September, 1965), 28-30, 33.
Wooden eagles carved by John Haley Bellamy (1836-1914).

3486 _____. "Maine's oldest church." Down East, 10 (July, 1964), 36-37.
First Congregational Church.

3487 MITCHELL, JEANETTE GORDON. Kittery men & women in World War II. Kittery: Kittery Pr., 1947. Unpaged. MeHi.

3488 NEAGLE, MARJORIE SPILLER. "Appledore--Maine's house of entertainment." Down East, 9 (July, 1963), 34-37, 60.
Appledore Hotel on Appledore Island.

3489 "THE OLD Kittery Burying-Ground." MHGR, 8 (1895), 233-237.

3490 "THE OLD mill--Kittery." Old Eliot, 3 (1899), 104-107.
A grist mill built in 1706.

3491 PENROSE, CHARLES. Old Kittery, land of adventure, 1647, and Captain Francis Champernowne (1614-1687). N.Y.: Newcomen Society of England, American Branch, 1947. Pp. 40.

3492 PREBLE, GEORGE HENRY. History of the United States Navy Yard, Portsmouth, N.H. Washington: Govt. Print. Off., 1892. Pp. 219.

3493 REMICK, OLIVER PHILBRICK. "The gift of land for the first and only Episcopal Church in the towns of Kittery and Eliot." Old Eliot, 2 (1898), 141-145.
Granted by Jacob Remick, Jr.

3494 ROBIE, VIRGINIA. "Colonial pilgrimage, No. 3--Sir William Pepperell and his staircase." House Beautiful, 15 (1903-1904), 315-317.
Sparhawk House.

3495 RICHARDSON, HARRIET T. "John Bray House in Kittery, Maine." House Beautiful, 65 (1929), 704, 706, 708, 710, 712.

3496 ROLDE, NEIL. "The William Pepperell Mansion." Down East, 22 (May, 1976), 42-47.

3497 SAFFORD, MOSES A. "Historic homes of Kittery." MeHSC, 2 Ser., 5 (1894), 113-128, 387-407.

3498 _____. "Physicians of Kittery." Old Eliot, 7 (1906), 196-202.

3499 SAFFORD, VICTORIA. "John Haley Bellamy, the woodcarver of Kittery Point." Antiques, 27 (1935), 102-106.

3500 "A SKETCH of Kittery." MHGR, 9 (1898), 252-256.

3501 STACKPOLE, EVERETT SCHERMERHORN. Old Kittery and her families. Lewiston: Lewiston Journal, 1903. Pp. 822.

3502 SWEETSER, MARY CHISHOLM. "The legend of Appledore." NEG, 7 (Spring, 1966), 22-28.
Celia Thaxter, poetess.

3503 TRANI, EUGENE P. The Treaty of Portsmouth: an adventure in American diplomacy. Lexington: Univ. of Kentucky Pr., 1969. Pp. 194.

3504 VAUGHAN, DOROTHY M. "An afternoon at the Lady Pepperell Mansion." OTNE, 40 (1949-1950), 157-158.

3505 "WHEN Washington came to Maine." Sun Up, 10 (February, 1932), 52-53.
1789.

3506 WILSON, FRED ALLAN. The early history of the Wilson family of Kittery, Maine. Lynn, Mass.: J. Macfarlane, 1898. Pp. 98.

SEE ALSO entries 987, 1879, 1907, and 1911.

KNOX (WALDO CO.)

3507 No items located.

KOSSUTH TOWNSHIP (WASHINGTON CO.)

3508 No items located.

LAGRANGE (PENOBSCOT CO.)

3509 No items located.

LAKE VIEW PLANTATION (PISCATAQUIS CO.)

3510 No items located.

LAKEVILLE PLANTATION (PENOBSCOT CO.)

3511 No items located.

LAMBERT LAKE TOWNSHIP (WASHINGTON CO.)

3512 No items located.

LAMOINE (HANCOCK CO.)

3513 CHILDS, FRANCES SERGEANT. "Fontaine Leval, a French settlement on the Maine coast, 1791." AASP, New Ser., 51 (1941), 187-222.

3514 DOUGLAS, JOHN SHERMAN. The First Baptist Church, Lamoine, Maine.... n.p., [1932]. Pp. 22.

3515 "A FRENCH description of Frenchman's Bay, 1792." NEQ, 1 (1928), 396-410.
Unsuccessful settlement of Fontaine Leval, the present town of Lamoine.

3516 TALLMAN, RICHARD S. "James A. Herne and Lamoine, Maine." NEQ, 46 (1973), 94-105.
Playwright.

SEE ALSO entries 1569 and 1586.

LANG TOWNSHIP (FRANKLIN CO.)

3517 No items located.

LEBANON (YORK CO.)

3518 CHAMBERLAIN, GEORGE WALTER. The beginnings of Lebanon, Maine; for the York County tercentenary, West Lebanon, Maine, August 29, 1936. [West Lebanon, 1936]. Pp. 13.

3519 _____. Soldiers of the American Revolution, of Lebanon, Maine. Weymouth, Mass.: Weymouth & Braintree Publishing, 1897. Pp. 48.
Biographies.

3520 _____. "Studies on families surnamed Cowell, Door (Dore or Dorr) and Chamberlain of Lebanon, Maine." MeHSC, 2 Ser., 5 (1894), 306-311.

3521 LEBANON, ME. Town of Lebanon, York County, Maine, bicentennial observance, July 1-2-3-4. n.p., [1967]. Pp. 31. MBNEH.

3522 LEBANON HISTORICAL SOCIETY. This is Lebanon, Maine, 1765 to 1965. East Lebanon: Winifred Van Houten, [1965]. Pp. 20. MeHi.

3523 LEBANON

3523 SINNETT, CHARLES NELSON. Historic Lebanon: Lebanon, Maine, and the grand work of its Congregational Church in one hundred and thirty-eight years. Haverhill, Mass.: C. C. Morse & Son, 1903. Pp. 16.

LEE (PENOBSCOT CO.)

3524 HOUGHTON, VINAL A. The story of an old New England town: history of Lee, Maine. Wilton: Nelson Print, 1926. Pp. 248.

3525 HOUSE, C. J. "Soldiers from Lee, Penobscot County, in the War of the Rebellion." Maine Bugle, 1 (1894), 263-266.

LEEDS (ANDROSCOGGIN CO.)

3526 STINCHFIELD, JOHN CLARK. History of the town of Leeds, Androscoggin County, Maine, from its settlement June 10, 1780. Lewiston: Lewiston Journal, 1901. Pp. viii, 419.

LEVANT (PENOBSCOT CO.)

3527 LEVANT, ME. Levant, Maine, sesquicentennial celebration, August 3, 1963. n.p., [1963]. Pp. 63. MeBa.

LEWISTON (ANDROSCOGGIN CO.)

3528 "ANGLICANS coming to America want their Church: the story of Trinity Parish, Lewiston, Maine." The Northeast, 76 (March, 1949), 14-16.

3529 ANNETT, JOHN B. "Chemistry at Bates." Bates College Bulletin, 46 (May 1, 1949), 2-3.

3530 ANTHONY, ALFRED WILLIAMS. Bates College and its background: a review of origins and causes. Philadelphia: Judson Pr., 1936. Pp. 284.

3531 BARBER, WILLIAM H. "Bates College in the eighties." Bates Alumnus, 19 (March, 1939), 11-14, (June, 1939), 3-4.

3532 BECKFORD, WILLIAM HALE. Leading business men of Lewiston, Augusta and vicinity, embracing, also, Auburn, Gardiner, Waterville, Oakland, Dexter, Fairfield, Skowhegan, Hallowell, Richmond, Bath, Brunswick, Freeport, Canton, Buckfield, Mechanic Falls, South Paris, Norway, Farmington and Winthrop, with an historical sketch of each place. Boston: Mercantile Publishing, 1889. Pp. 360.

3533 BISCHOFF, CARL H. "Lewiston, a changing city." Sun Up, 8 (September, 1930), 6-8, 28.

3534 BUKER, MARGARET. "The Irish in Lewiston, Maine: a search for security on the urban frontier, 1850-1880." MeHSQ, 13 (Special, 1973), 3-25.

3535 CALLAHAN, GEORGE A. History of King Hiram's Chapter, No. 9, of Royal Arch Masons, Lewiston, Maine, date of precedence, Nov. 28, 1854. Lewiston, 1885. Pp. 61. MeHi.

3536 CHASE, CLARENCE AUGUSTINE. "Lewiston and Bates College." NEM, New Ser., 13 (1895-1896), 513-532.

3537 DAVIES, WALLACE EVANS. "A collectivist experiment Down East: Bradford Peck and the Coöperative Association of America." NEQ, 20 (1947), 471-491. 1899-1912.

3538 EATON, MABEL. "Bates College Library." MeLAB, 7 (June, 1946), 1.

3539 EATON, MIRIAM. "Oh tempora, oh mores." Bates College Bulletin, 54 (May, 1957), 6-8. Bates College.

3540 EMERSON, R. E. "Distinct[ive]ly different." Sun Up, 2 (December, 1925), 50-51. Bates Street Shirts.

3541 GOULD, SAMUEL B. "The lighter side." Bates Alumnus, 16 (November, 1935), 3-8, 13. Social life at Bates College.

3542 HALLOCK, LEAVITT HOMAN. Manual of Pine Street Congregational Church, Lewiston, Maine, with historical sketch.... Lewiston: Journal Print Shop, 1909. Pp. 20. Me.

3543 JAKEMAN, ADELBERT M. "Athletics at Bates in history and story: football from Briggs to Morey." Bates Alumnus, 15 (November, 1934), 2-7.

3544 _____. "Hockey and winter sports at Bates." Bates Alumnus, 16 (February, 1936), 3-8.

3545 _____. "Men's Athletic Association." Bates Alumnus, 17 (February, 1937), 3-6. Bates College.

3546 _____. "Sixty-five years of baseball." Bates Alumnus, 15 (May, 1935), 2-11. Bates College.

3547 _____. "Sixty years of track and field sports." Bates Alumnus, 15 (February, 1935), 3-11. Bates College.

3548 _____. "Tennis at Bates." Bates Alumnus, 16 (May, 1936), 11-14, 18.

3549 KENDALL, RAYMOND. "Twenty-one years of summer school at Bates." Bates Alumnus, 20
(June, 1940), 10, 22.

3550 KIRK, GENEVA. "The story of Lewiston."
Maine Townsman, 37 (September, 1975), 10-12.

3551 LEAMON, JAMES S. Historic Lewiston: a textile city in transition. [Lewiston]: Lewiston Historical Commission, 1976. Pp. vii,
60. MeHi.

3552 LEWISTON, ME. BOARD OF TRADE. Official manual of the Lewiston Board of Trade, containing portraits of officers, constitution, list
of members, history, views, etc. [Lewiston],
1912. Pp. 91. MeBa.

3553 LEWISTON, ME. MANUFACTURERS AND MECHANICS
LIBRARY ASSOCIATION. A brief history of the
Manufacturers and Mechanics Library Associa-
tion of Lewiston, Me.; with constitution and
by-laws. Lewiston: Journal Office, 1897.
Pp. 15.

3554 LEWISTON, ME. PAROISSE SAINT-PIERRE ET SAINT-
PAUL. Album souvenir du 75ᵉ anniversaire de
la Paroisse Saint-Pierre et Saint-Paul de
Lewiston, Maine. n.p., [1946?]. Pp. 88.
Me.

3555 _____. Paroisse Canadienne-Française de Lewiston (Maine), album historique. [Lewiston]:
Les Pères Dominicains, 1899. Pp. 107. MBC.

3556 LEWISTON, ME. SAINTE MARIE. Vingt-cinquième
anniversaire de la Paroisse Sainte-Marie,
1907-1932. Lewiston, 1932. Pp. 48.

3557 LEWISTON, ME. TRINITY CHURCH. A brief history of Trinity Parish, Lewiston, Maine,
1854-1903; to which are appended list of
communicants, baptisms, confirmations, marriages and burials since the organization of
the parish.... Lewiston: Haswell Pr., 1902.
Pp. 89. MeBa.

3558 LEWISTON HISTORICAL COMMISSION. Lewiston
school names. [Lewiston], 1971. 26 leaves.
MeHi.
Biographies of persons after whom the
schools were named.

3559 LEWISTON WEEKLY JOURNAL. A historical sketch
of the Lewiston Weekly Journal and Daily
Evening Journal.... Lewiston, 1887. Pp. 11.
MeU.

3560 "MANUFACTURERS National Bank, Lewiston, Me."
Bankers Magazine, 93 (1916), 449-453.

3561 MICHAUD, CHARLOTTE, ADELARD JANELLE, and
JAMES S. LEAMON. Historic Lewiston: Franco-
American origins. [Lewiston]: Lewiston His-
torical Commission, 1974. Pp. 47. MeU.

3562 MICHAUD, CHARLOTTE. "Maine's Franco-Americans: Lewiston." Maine History News, 7
(July, 1972), 8-9, 12, 14-16.

3563 PACKARD, BERTRAM EVERETT. History of the
Polymnian Society of Bates College. Auburn:
Merrill & Webber, 1899. Pp. 46. MeHi.

3564 PECK, BRADFORD. The world a department store:
a story of life under a coöperative system.
Lewiston, 1900. Pp. xv, 311.
Coöperative Association of America.

3565 PHILLIPS, CHARLES FRANKLIN. Bates College in
Maine: enduring strength and scholarship.
N.Y.: Newcomen Society, 1952. Pp. 24.

3566 RAMSDELL, HARRIET J. "In the beginning, Hathorn was the College." Bates College Bulletin, 70 (Winter, 1973), 1-6.
Hathorn Hall, Bates College.

3567 READE, JOHN L. "The Bates Alumni Association." Bates Alumnus, 6 (May, 1926), 17-18.

3568 RICKER, GEORGE S. "College sports in the
sixties." Bates Alumnus, 11 (May, 1931),
17.
Bates College.

3569 ROUNDY, RODNEY W. "Pine Street's one hundred
years." MeCP, 41 (November 15, 1954), 10.
Pine Street Congregational Church.

3570 ROWE, HARRY W. "The College Club, 1891-1932."
Bates Alumnus, 12 (May, 1932), 13-15.
Bates College.

3571 SAWYER, WILLIAM H. "Biology at Bates." Bates
College Bulletin, 54 (January 15, 1957), 6-7,
33.

3572 _____. "Our campus trees." Bates Alumnus,
14 (November, 1933), 1-7.

3573 STANTON BIRD CLUB, LEWISTON, ME. Fifty years
with the Stanton Bird Club, 1919-1969, anniversary booklet. Dorothy P. Webber and Shirley Clifford Hoy, eds. n.p. [1969?]. Unpaged. MeU.

3574 STONE, ELEANOR BAILEY. "Bates College--her
past, present, and future." Sun Up, 3 (February, 1927), 9, 12, 22.

3575 _____. "Bates College, pioneer in international debating." Sun Up, 5 (February, 1928),
10-11, 20-21.

3576 THOMAS, HOWARD E. "Forty years of intercollegiate debating." Bates Alumnus, 16 (May,
1936), 9-10.
Bates College.

3577 TURNER, AUGUSTUS R. Souvenir program of the one hundredth anniversary of the city of Lewiston, giving an historical sketch with incidents relating to the growth of the city, its principal business firms, scenery, etc. ... July fourth, 1895. Auburn: Merrill & Webber, 1895. Pp. 120.

SEE ALSO entries 556, 1422, 1424, 1426-1427, 1431-1432, 1434, and 4561.

LEXINGTON TOWNSHIP (SOMERSET CO.)

3578 No items located.

LIBERTY (WALDO CO.)

3579 FREEMASONS. LIBERTY, ME. LIBERTY LODGE, NO. 111. History of Liberty Lodge, No. 111, Montville, Maine, originally, now Liberty, Maine, from Nov. 8, 1861, to Jan. 1, 1890, with by-laws of lodge and appendix. Belfast: George W. Burgess, 1891. Pp. 40. [MePGLM].

3580 FREEMASONS. LIBERTY, ME. ST. GEORGES CHAPTER, NO. 45. History of St. Georges Chapter, No. 45, Liberty, Maine, from March 10th, 1881, to Jan. 1st, 1890, with by-laws of chapter and appendix. Belfast: George W. Burgess, 1892. Pp. 30. [MePGLM].
Signed: George W. Berry, Edwin A. Porter, A. P. Cargill, Committee on History.

3581 HURWITZ, ALFRED. The history of Liberty, Maine, 1827-1975. Liberty: Liberty Historical Society, 1975. Pp. 93. Me.

3582 LIBERTY, ME. HISTORICAL COMMITTEE. The town of Liberty: its history and geography. Thorndike: Newell White, 1927. Pp. 120.

LILY BAY TOWNSHIP (PISCATAQUIS CO.)

3583 No items located.

LIMERICK (YORK CO.)

3584 FREEMAN, CHARLES. "An account of Limerick." MeHSC, 1 (1831), 245-253.

3585 ILSLEY, GEORGE BOARDMAN. 1796-1896. Historical sermon and centennial poem at the one hundredth anniversary of the Limerick Baptist Church. Portland: Thurston Print, 1896. Pp. 11.
Poem is by Mrs. S. E. Ilsley.

3586 LAMPREY, LOUISE. History of Limerick. Cornish: Chester V. Small, [1927?]. Pp. 20.

3587 TAYLOR, LINDA MAULE. Limerick historical notes. Limerick: The Town, 1975. Pp. 127. Me.

LIMESTONE (AROOSTOOK CO.)

3588 GIBBS, GEORGE C. "The diamond jubilee of the Advent, Limestone." The Northeast, 74 (November, 1947), 7.
Church of the Advent.

3589 LIMESTONE, ME. Limestone centennial, 100th celebration, 1869-1969: the review of a century. n.p., [1970]. Unpaged. Me.

LIMINGTON (YORK CO.)

3590 CHICK, OLIVE M. A history of Limington Academy, 1848-1948. Cornish: Webb-Smith, 1948. Pp. 47. MeHi.

3591 LIMINGTON, ME. Limington sesquicentennial, 1798-1948. n.p., [1948]. Pp. 24. MeHi.

3592 LIMINGTON, ME. CONGREGATIONAL CHURCH. Manual of the Congregational Church, Limington, York County, Maine, containing history.... Portland: Southworth Bros., 1893. Pp. 32. MBNEH.

3593 TAYLOR, ROBERT L. History of Limington, Maine, 1668-1900. Norway: Oxford Hills Pr., 1975. Pp. ii, 211. Me.

LINCOLN (PENOBSCOT CO.)

3594 BAILEY, MAY MURRAY EDWARDS. The history of Methodism in Lincoln, including a sketch of all the ministers who have been sent here to labor for their Lord, 1836-1954. Old Town: Penobscot Times, [1954]. Pp. 44.

3595 _____. History of Trans Alpine, the southernmost part of the town of Lincoln, Maine, beyond the Alps. Lincoln, 1950. Pp. 109.

3596 FELLOWS, DANA WILLIS. History of the town of Lincoln, Penobscot County, Maine, 1822-1928. Lewiston: Dingley Pr., 1929. Pp. 436.

3597 GOODWIN, KATHRYN. Personal glimpses of the early settlers of Lincoln, Maine. n.p., 1970. Pp. 79. MeU.
Biographies.

3598 NELSON, JEREMY. "Notes on Lincoln, Maine." BHistMag, 1 (1885-1886), 89-91.

SEE ALSO entry 50.

LINCOLN PLANTATION (OXFORD CO.)

3599 WILSONS MILLS, ME. SESQUICENTENNIAL BOOKLET COMMITTEE. History of Wilsons Mills, Maine and the Magalloway settlements. Wilsons Mills: The Town, 1975. Pp. 285. Me.

LINCOLNVILLE (WALDO CO.)

3600 DAVIS, WILL R. Village Down East: sketches of village life on the northeast coast of New England, before "gas-buggies" came, by John Wallace, from conversations with Zackary Adams, Duck Trap Cove, Maine. Brattleboro, Vt.: Stephen Daye Pr., 1943. Pp. 184.

3601 MEARA, EMMETT and NANCY MEARA. "Lincolnville Volunteer Fire Department." Down East, 18 (May, 1972), 60-61.

SEE ALSO entries 1833 and 4612.

LINNEUS (AROOSTOOK CO.)

3602 No items located.

LISBON (ANDROSCOGGIN CO.)

3603 GOULD, RALPH ERNEST. Yankee boyhood: my adventures on a Maine farm seventy years ago. N.Y.: Norton, 1950. Pp. 251.

3604 HUDSON, MRS. D. E. "Lisbon annals: reminiscences of the Catholic history of Lisbon, Me., from the beginning in 1874." MeCathHM, 3 (September, 1914), 40-42.

3605 PLUMMER, FRANCIS W. Lisbon: the history of a small Maine town. Charles W. Plummer, ed. Lewiston: Twin City Printery, 1970. Pp. 225.

3606 "SAINT Matthew's celebrates its fortieth anniversary." The Northeast, 73 (November, 1946), 6-7, 12.

LITCHFIELD (KENNEBEC CO.)

3607 LITCHFIELD, ME. History of Litchfield and an account of its centennial celebration, 1895. Augusta: Kennebec Journal Print, 1897. Pp. 548.

3608 LITCHFIELD, ME. BICENTENNIAL COMMITTEE. Litchfield yesterdays. Litchfield, 1976. Pp. 61. MeU.

3609 SMITH, ASA P. History of the Congregational Church of Litchfield, Maine, written for its centennial celebration, June 15, 1911. n.p., [1911?]. Unpaged. MeHi.

3610 SPRINGER, ISAAC W., CYRUS KENDRICK, and J. E. CHASE. History of Morning Star Lodge No. 41, Free and Accepted Masons, Litchfield Corners, Me. Gardiner: H. K. Morrell and Son, 1884. Pp. 21. [MePGLM].

3611 THURSTON, DAVID. "Sketch of the half century history of the Congregational Church in Litchfield, Maine." CongQ, 4 (1862), 253-258.

LITTLE SQUAW TOWNSHIP (PISCATAQUIS CO.)

3612 No items located.

LITTLE W TOWNSHIP (SOMERSET CO.)

3613 No items located.

LITTLETON (AROOSTOOK CO.)

3614 No items located.

LIVERMORE (ANDROSCOGGIN CO.)

3615 FREEMASONS. LIVERMORE, ME. ORIENTAL STAR LODGE, NO. 21. History of Oriental Star Lodge, Livermore, Maine, from February 21, 1871 to January 1, 1881. Lewiston: Geo. A. Callahan, 1882. Pp. 20. MeHi.

3616 _____. History of Oriental Star Lodge, No. 21, Livermore, Me. Lewiston: Geo. A. Callahan, 1873. Pp. 34. MeHi.

3617 _____. History of Oriental Star Lodge, No. 21, Livermore, Me., from September, 1881 to January 15, 1892. Lewiston: Geo. A. Callahan, 1892. Pp. 13. MeHi.

3618 HUNT, GAILLARD, comp. Israel, Elihu and Cadwallader Washburn: a chapter in American biography. N.Y.: Macmillan, 1925. Pp. vi, 397.

3619 MONROE, IRA THOMPSON. History of the town of Livermore, Androscoggin County, Maine, from its inception in 1735 and its grant of land in 1772 to its organization and incorporation in 1795 up to the present time, 1928. Lewiston: Lewiston Journal Printshop, 1928. Pp. 275.

3620 STURTEVANT, REGINALD H. A history of Livermore, Maine. Lewiston: Twin City Printery, 1970. Pp. 256.

3621 _____. "Seven sons." Down East, 2 (June, 1956), 20-24, 38-39.
Algernon, Elihu, Cadwallader, Israel, Charles, William D. and Samuel Washburn; sons of Israel and Martha Washburn.

3622 WASHBURN, ISRAEL, 1813-1883. Notes, historical, descriptive, and personal, of Livermore, in Androscoggin (formerly in Oxford) County, Maine.... Portland: Bailey & Noyes, 1874. Pp. 169.

3623 WASHBURN, LILIAN. My seven sons: the true and amazing story of the seven famous Washburn brothers, as told by the old grandsire, Israel, Sr., and transcribed by his granddaughter, Lilian Washburn. Portland: Falmouth Publishing, 1940. Pp. 143.

3624 WASHBURN, REUEL. History of Oriental Star Lodge, No. 21, Livermore, Maine. Portland: Ira Berry & Son, 1862. Pp. 12. MH.

LIVERMORE FALLS (ANDROSCOGGIN CO.)

3625 LIVERMORE FALLS, ME. FIRST BAPTIST CHURCH. First Baptist Church, Livermore Falls, Maine, 1811-1911, centenary exercise, November 19-23, 1911. Livermore Falls: Advertiser, [1911?]. Pp. 33. MeHi.
Includes history by Charlotte H. Sturtevant.

3626 LIVERMORE FALLS TRUST COMPANY. Fiftieth anniversary, Livermore Falls Trust Company, 1895-1945. n.p., [1945?]. Unpaged. MeHi.

3627 STURTEVANT, REGINALD H. "Livermore Falls--Maine's boom town." Down East, 12 (March, 1966), 6-10, 56-57, 60, 62.

LOBSTER TOWNSHIP (PISCATAQUIS CO.)

3628 No items located.

LONG A TOWNSHIP (PENOBSCOT CO.)

3629 No items located.

LONG ISLAND PLANTATION (HANCOCK CO.)

3630 No items located.

LONG POND TOWNSHIP (SOMERSET CO.)

3631 SEE entry 3377A.

LOVELL (OXFORD CO.)

3632 LE BARON, WILLIAM B. Historical record of West Lovell. Arthur P. Stone, ed. n.p., [1946?]. 30 leaves. MBNEH.
Originally written in 1899.

3633 MOORE, PAULINE WINCHELL. Blueberries and pusley weed, the story of Lovell, Maine. Kennebunk: Star Press, 1970. Pp. 260, vii, ix. Me.

3634 PAISLEY, EVA COCHRAN WILSON. Sanctuary: a finding of life. N.Y.: E. P. Dutton, 1940. Pp. 253.

LOWELL (PENOBSCOT CO.)

3635 No items located.

LOWELLTOWN TOWNSHIP (OXFORD CO.)

3636 SEE entry 3377A.

LOWER CUPSUPTIC TOWNSHIP (OXFORD CO.)

3637 No items located.

LOWER ENCHANTED TOWNSHIP (SOMERSET CO.)

3638 No items located.

LUBEC (WASHINGTON CO.)

3639 ADAMS, FRANKLIN P., SR. "Notes on the maritime history of Lubec, Maine." AmNep, 24 (1964), 38-60.

3640 DRUMMOND, R. R. "The centennial of Lubec, Maine." Penn Germania, New Ser., 2 (1913), 215-216.

3641 GREET, WILLIAM CABELL. "A record from Lubec, Maine and remarks on the coastal type." American Speech, 6 (1931), 397-403.

3642 HALLET, RICHARD. "The great Quoddy gold hoax: one of the greatest swindles of the age." Down East, 1 (Winter, 1955), 18-20.
Perpetrated by Prescott Ford Jernegan and Charles Fisher in 1898.

3643 JOHNSON, RYERSON. 200 years of Lubec history, 1776-1976. [Lubec]: Lubec Historical Society, [1976]. Pp. 145. MeU.

3644 LYFORD, ELMORE B. "There is such a place as Baileys Mistake!" Yankee, 32 (March, 1968), 162-163.

3645 McGREGOR, JAMES. History of Washington Lodge, No. 37, Free and Accepted Masons, Lubec, Maine, 1822, 1890. Portland: E. W. Brown and J. B. Neagle, 1892. Pp. 99.
   Includes a brief sketch of the history of the town.

3646 MASON, JOHN. "The great sea-water swindle." Yankee, 29 (February, 1965), 56-59, 110-112.
   Prescott Ford Jernegan and the Electrolytic Marine Salts Co., 1897.

3647 SMYTH, LAWRENCE T. "When the Cambridge was lost." Steamboat Bill, 16 (1959), 15-16.
   Shipwreck on Old Man Ledge off Allen's Island, February 9, 1886.

   SEE ALSO entries 603, 1840, 1852 and 1859.

LUDLOW (AROOSTOOK CO.)

3648 No items located.

LYMAN (YORK CO.)

3649 LYMAN, ME. FIRST CONGREGATIONAL CHURCH. Programme of the dedication services of the Congregational Church, Lyman, Dec. 2, 1882. n.p., 1882. Pp. 8. MBC.

LYNCHTOWN TOWNSHIP (OXFORD CO.)

3650 HEYWOOD, DANIEL E. Diary of Daniel E. Heywood, a Parmachenee guide at Camp Caribou, Parmachenee Lake, Oxford County, Maine, fall of 1890. Bristol, N.H.: R. W. Musgrove, 1891. Pp. 101.

3651 MOSES, GEORGE H. "John Danforth and Camp Caribou." Granite Mo, 19 (1895), 315-320.
   Sportsmen's camp, established in 1870s on Parmachenee Lake.

MACHIAS (WASHINGTON CO.)

3652 BEAM, LURA ELLA. A Maine hamlet. N.Y.: W. Funk, 1957. Pp. 236.

3653 CHURCHILL, EDWIN A. "The historiography of the 'Margaretta' affair, or, how not to let the facts interfere with a good story." MeHSQ, 15 (1975-1976), 60-74.
   1775.

3654 COMAN, EDWIN TRUMAN and HELEN MARILLA GIBBS. Time, tide, and timber: a century of Pope & Talbot. Stanford, Calif.: Stanford Univ. Pr., 1949. Pp. xvi, 480.
   Lumber.

3655 DAUGHTERS OF THE AMERICAN REVOLUTION. MAINE. HANNAH WESTON CHAPTER, MACHIAS. Naval battle at Machias, June 12, 1775. Machias: Sanborn Publishing, [19--?]. Unpaged.

3656 _____. The story of Hannah Weston and her part in the first naval engagement of the Revolution, June 12, 1775. Machias, 1925. 12 leaves.

3657 DIETZ, LEW. "Long-log drive." Down East, 2 (April, 1956), 24-28.

3658 DONWORTH, GRACE. "Burnham Tavern, ancient hostelry at Machias." DARMag, 69 (1935), 35.

3659 DRISKO, GEORGE WASHINGTON. Narrative of the town of Machias, the old and the new, the early and the late. Machias: The Republican, 1904. Pp. 589.

3660 GARDNER, FRANK A. "State schooner Diligent." MassMag, 3 (1910), 40-46.

3661 HARDING, HENRY FISKE. Memorial address on the occasion of the centennial anniversary of the formation of Centre Street Congregational Church, at Machias, Me.; together with a brief history of the Congregational Sabbath School to September, 1884. Machias: C. O. Furbush, 1884. Pp. ix, 70.

3662 HARVEY, D. C. "Machias and the invasion of Nova Scotia." Canadian Historical Association. Report, (1932), 17-28.
   1776-1777.

3663 HAWES, HILDRETH GILMAN. The Bellamy treasure: the pirates of the Whydah in the Gulf of Maine. Augusta: Augusta Pr., 1940. Pp. 71.

3664 JONES, STEPHEN. "Historical account of Machias." MeHSQ, 15 (1975-1976), 44-56.
   Margaretta affair of 1775; written in 1822.

3665 LENHART, JOHN M. "Two Revolutionary chaplains in government employ (1780-1784)." CathHist Rev, 23 (1937-1938), 446-466.
   Father Frederick de Bourges and Father Juniper Berthiaume were sent to Maine by the Provincial Council of Massachusetts to give spiritual aid to Catholic Indians who sided with the Americans.

3666   MACHIAS, ME. Memorial of the centennial anniversary of the settlement of Machias. Machias: C. O. Furbush, 1863. Pp. 179
        Joseph Williamson attributes authorship to William Bartlett Smith who is the author of the "historical sketch."

3667   "MACHIAS one hundred years ago." MeHistMag, 9 (1894-1895), 153-157.

3668   NATIONAL ARCHIVES PROJECT. Ship registers and enrollments of Machias, Maine, 1780-1930. Rockland, 1942. 2v.

3669   "NOTES about Machias with some account of its first settlers." MeHistMag, 8 (1893), 70-85.

3670   O'BRIEN, JOHN. "Exertions of the O'Brien family of Machias, Maine in the American Revolution." MeHSC, 2 (1847), 242-249.

3671   OXTON, BEULAH SYLVESTER. "The first naval battle of the American Revolution." Maine's Own Magazine, 8 (May and June, 1930), 12-13, 32.

3672   PAGEANT of Machias Valley ... the celebration of the one hundred and fiftieth anniversary of the founding of Machias.... Machias: Machias Republican Pr., 1913. Pp. 28. MeU.

3673   PARKER, FOXHALL ALEXANDER. "The first seafight of the Revolution." MagAmHist, 1 (1877), 209-221.

3674   POPE, CHARLES HENRY. "Machias in the Revolution." MeHSC, 2 Ser., 6 (1895), 121-138.

3675   POTTER, GAIL M. "The Lexington of the seas." NEG, 10 (Spring, 1969), 50-57.
        First naval battle of the Revolution, June, 1775.

3676   SELIGMANN, HERBERT J. "From eastern Maine, 1823." Down East, 3 (June, 1957), 26-27, 48-49.
        "Eastern Star," a newspaper.

3677   _____. "Washington County's capital--Machias." Down East, 4 (July, 1958), 26-32, 52-54.

3678   SHERMAN, ANDREW MAGOUN. The O'Briens of Machias, Me., patriots of the American Revolution: their services to the cause of liberty. A paper read before the American-Irish Historical Society at its annual gathering in New York City, January 12, 1904; together with a sketch of the clan O'Brien by Thomas Hamilton Murray. Boston: For the Society, 1904. Pp. 87.

3679   SMITH, M. E. C. "Machias in the Revolution and afterward." NEM, New Ser., 12 (1895), 673-688.

3680   SPRAGUE, JOHN FRANCIS. "The Lexington of the seas." SJMH, 1 (1913-1914), 157-164, 175-184.
        Margaretta affair.

3681   TALBOT, GEORGE FOSTER. "The capture of the Margaretta: the first naval battle of the Revolution." MeHSC, 2 Ser., 2 (1891), 1-17.

3682   _____. "The first naval battle of the Revolution at Machias, Maine, June 11, 1775." BHistMag, 3 (1887-1888), 161-167.

3683   "WASHINGTON State Normal School." Maine Teachers' Digest, 2 (1941-1942), 124-125, 135-136.
        Now the University of Maine at Machias.

        SEE ALSO entries 603, 799, 1840, and 1851.

MACHIASPORT (WASHINGTON CO.)

3684   SEE entries 603, 1840, and 1863.

MACWAHOC PLANTATION (AROOSTOOK CO.)

3685   No items located.

MADAWASKA (AROOSTOOK CO.)

3686   ALBERT, JULIE D. Madawaska centennial, 1869-1969. n.p., [1969?]. Pp. 152.

3687   _____. St. David Parish: centennial, 1871-1971. Madawaska: St. John Valley Times, [1971]. Pp. 72.

3688   ALBERT, THOMAS. Histoire du Madawaska d'après les recherches historiques de Patrick Therriault et les notes manuscrites de Prudent L. Mercure. Quebec: Imprimerie franciscaine missionaire, 1920. Pp. xxiii, 448.
        A photocopy of a typescript translation by Marie Antoinette Page is at the University of Maine at Orono.

3689   COLLINS, CHARLES W. The Acadians of Madawaska, Maine. Boston: Thomas A. Whalen, 1902. Pp. 66.

3690   DEANE, JOHN GILMORE and EDWARD KAVANAGH. "State of the Madawaska and Aroostook settlements in 1831." New Brunswick Historical Society. Collections, 3 (1907-1914), 344-484.
        Edited by William O. Raymond.

3691   LUCEY, WILLIAM LEO. "Madawaska on the River St. John: New England's last frontier." American Catholic Historical Society of Philadelphia. Records, 60 (1949), 147-164.

3692   MELVIN, CHARLOTTE LENENTINE. Madawaska, a
        chapter in Maine-New Brunswick relations.
        Madawaska: St. John Valley Publishing, 1975.
        Pp. vii, 86, xxvi.

3693   STEWART, RONALD E. "Madawaska." Pine Cone,
        6 (Winter, 1950-1951), 32-35.

        SEE ALSO entries 1437 and 3355.

MADISON (SOMERSET CO.)

3694   CAIL, HAROLD L. "Lakewood--Maine's state
        theatre." Down East, 14 (July, 1968), 48-51.

3695   CLARK, EMMA FOLSOM, WILLIAM CASSIDY, and VIO-
        LET CASSIDY. History of Madison. Madison,
        1962. Pp. 370.

3696   OBLAK, JOHN BYRON. Bringing Broadway to
        Maine; the history of Lakewood, Lakewood,
        Maine. Terre Haute, Ind.: Moore-Langen,
        1971. Pp. 213. MeHi.

MADRID (FRANKLIN CO.)

3697   SWIFT, JOSIAH SPOONER. "Saddleback in 1839,
        the account of an ascent." Appalachia, New
        Ser., 11, (December, 1945), 490-503.
            Edited by Benton L. Hatch.

        SEE ALSO entry 1419.

MAGALLOWAY PLANTATION (OXFORD CO.)

3698   BENNETT, GERTRUDE ALLINSON. "A Magalloway
        schoolmarm never goes home." Down East, 12
        (October, 1965), 35, 39-41, 44-45.
            Reminiscences of the author.

MANCHESTER (KENNEBEC CO.)

3699   MANCHESTER, ME. BICENTENNIAL COMMITTEE.
        Stories about the town of Manchester and its
        people. Augusta: J. S. McCarthy, 1975.
        Pp. ix, 152. Me.
            Includes two errata slips.

3700   SHUTE, ALBERTA VAN HORN. A year and a day on
        the farm. North Manchester: Balm O' Gilead
        Pr., 1972. Pp. 206. MeP.
            Social life and customs.

MAPLETON (AROOSTOOK CO.)

3701   No items located.

MARIAVILLE (HANCOCK CO.)

3702   No items located.

MARION TOWNSHIP (WASHINGTON CO.)

3703   No items located.

MARS HILL (AROOSTOOK CO.)

3704   MARS HILL, ME. CENTENNIAL BOOKLET COMMITTEE.
        Mars Hill, Maine, centennial, 1867-1967.
        n.p., [1967]. Unpaged. Me.

3705   TWEEDIE, GLADYS SYLVESTER. Mars Hill, typical
        Aroostook town. Presque Isle: Northern
        Printers, 1952. Pp. 74.

MARSHFIELD (WASHINGTON CO.)

3706   No items located.

MASARDIS (AROOSTOOK CO.)

3707   No items located.

MASON TOWNSHIP (OXFORD CO.)

3708   No items located.

MASSACHUSETTS GORE (FRANKLIN CO.)

3709   No items located.

MATINICUS ISLE PLANTATION (KNOX CO.)

3710   CONDON, VESTA. "An island store one hundred
        years ago." OTNE, 32 (1941-1942), 52-56.

3711   EMMONS, CELIA PHILBROOK. Highlights of life
        on Matinicus Island. Westbrook: H. S. Cobb,
        1960. Pp. 32. Me.

3712   FILLMORE, ROBERT B., comp. Gems of the
        ocean. Rockland: Opinion Print, 1914.
        Pp. 38.

3713   LONG, CHARLES ALBERT EUGENE. Matinicus Isle:
        its story and its people. [Lewiston]: Lew-
        iston Journal Printshop, 1926. Pp. 235.

3714   "THE STORY of Matinicus Isle." MeHistMag,
       7 (1891-1892), 113-118.

3715   YOUNG, HAZEL. "Matinicus Island." Down
       East, 13 (August, 1966), 44-46.

MATTAMISCONTIS TOWNSHIP (PENOBSCOT CO.)

3716   No items located.

MATTAWAMKEAG (PENOBSCOT CO.)

3717   SMITH, GEORGE W., CHARLES F. PLUMLY, and JOHN
       E. CLARK. History of Mount Horeb Royal Arch
       Chapter, No. 49, Mattawamkeag, Maine from
       its organization to February, 1910. Port-
       land: Stephen Berry, 1910. Pp. 89. MeHi.
       Freemasons.

3718   SMITH, GEORGE W. History of Pine Tree Lodge,
       No. 172, Free and Accepted Masons, Mattawam-
       keag, Penobscot County, Maine, from January 1,
       1892 to January 1, 1908. Portland: Stephen
       Berry, 1908. Pp. 90. MeHi.

3719   _____. History of Pine Tree Lodge, No. 172,
       Free and Accepted Masons, Mattawamkeag, Pen-
       obscot County, Maine, from the date of its
       institution in 1873 to Jan. 1, 1892. Port-
       land: Stephen Berry, 1892. Pp. 81. MeBa.

       SEE ALSO entry 50.

MAXFIELD (PENOBSCOT CO.)

3720   No items located.

MAYFIELD TOWNSHIP (SOMERSET CO.)

3721   No items located.

MECHANIC FALLS (ANDROSCOGGIN CO.)

3722   PENNEY, JOHN W. "Mechanic Falls, past and
       present." BTJ, 18 (1905-1906), 349-351.

3723   WATERMAN, CHARLES ELMER. Historical sketch
       of the town of Mechanic Falls. Mechanic
       Falls: Ledger Publishing, 1894. Pp. 55.

       SEE ALSO entry 3532.

MEDDYBEMPS (WASHINGTON CO.)

3724   No items located.

MEDFORD (PISCATAQUIS CO.)

3725   PATRONS OF HUSBANDRY. MAINE STATE GRANGE.
       COLD BROOK GRANGE, NO. 436. Medford notes,
       1808-1958. Medford, [1958]. 78 leaves.

MEDWAY (PENOBSCOT CO.)

3726   BEATHEM, HAROLD C. History and genealogy of
       Medway Maine, compiled by the Medway Beathems
       for the centennial anniversary, 1875-1975.
       n.p., [1975]. Pp. 263. MeU.

MERCER (SOMERSET CO.)

3727   SEE entry 1419.

MERRILL (ARROSTOOK CO.)

3728   No items located.

MERRILL STRIP (FRANKLIN CO.)

3729   No items located.

MEXICO (OXFORD CO.)

3730   SEE entry 2868.

MILBRIDGE (WASHINGTON CO.)

3731   ANDERSON, MAIZIE FREEMAN. "Keeper of the
       light." Down East, 16 (August, 1969), 58-60.
       Petit Manan Light.

3732   BENSON, EARL M. "Down East emporium." Down
       East, 3 (October, 1956), 20-21, 34-35.
       General store and trading post owned by
       Joseph Wallace.

3733   "MILBRIDGE, Maine." MeHistMag, 9 (1894-1895),
       223-226.

3734   SAWYER, FRANKLIN. History of Pleiades Lodge,
       No. 173, Free and Accepted Masons, Milbridge,
       Maine, from its organization, July, 1874 to
       July, 1892. Portland: Stephen Berry, 1892.
       Pp. 40. MeBa.

3735   SAWYER, PHILIP, et al. Milbridge, 1848-1948,
       centennial program. n.p., [1948]. Pp. 96.
       MeHi.

       SEE ALSO entries 1840 and 1864.

MILFORD (PENOBSCOT CO.)

3736 MILFORD BICENTENNIAL COMMITTEE. History of Milford, about its origin, growth and its people from 1800. [Milford], 1976. Pp. 90. MeU.

SEE ALSO entry 1733.

MILLINOCKET (PENOBSCOT CO.)

3737 "THE DEVELOPMENT of Millinocket." Maine. Bureau of Industrial and Labor Statistics. Annual Report, 17 (1903), 150-174.

3738 EBERT, HERMAN. "Year by year at Millinocket: the record of Saint Andrew's Parish." The Northeast, 77 (November, 1950), 6-9.

3739 LAVERTY, DOROTHY BOWLER. Millinocket: magic city of Maine's wilderness. Freeport: Bond Wheelwright, 1973. Pp. xviii, 110.

3740 MILLINOCKET, ME. Millinocket, Maine, 50th anniversary, 1901-1951. n.p., [1951?]. Pp. 32. Me.

3741 REILLY, M. W. "St. Martin of Tours, Millinocket." MeCathHM, 2 (January, 1914), 23-26.

MILO (PISCATAQUIS CO.)

3742 KENISTON, FRANK WALTER. Biographies of Milo, Maine. Auburn: Merrill & Webber, 1945. Pp. xiv, 148.

3743 WEST, RETHEL C. History of Milo, 1802-1923. ... Dover-Foxcroft: F. D. Barrows, 1923. Pp. 78. MeBa.

MILTON TOWNSHIP (OXFORD CO.)

3744 BENNETT, RANDY L. "Mount Zircon, noon tide spring." Down East, 20 (May, 1974), 40-43. Spring with curative powers.

MINOT (ANDROSCOGGIN CO.)

3745 MINOT, ME. Historical resumé of the town of Minot. n.p., [1962?]. Unpaged. Me.

3746 NOYES, CROSBY STUART. The crown of New England: the grand old town of Minot, Maine; an address delivered at the celebration of the centennial anniversary of the town of Minot, Maine, held at West Minot, August seventh, nineteen hundred and two. Washington, D.C.: Judd & Detweiler, 1904. Pp. 32.

3747 SHAUB, BENJAMIN MARTIN. "Garnet locality of Minot." Rocks and Minerals, 32 (May-June, 1957), 227-234.

3748 "WILLIAM Ladd." MeLB, 12 (1926-1927), 98-105.
Includes a history of Minot and list of Ladd's writings.

SEE ALSO entry 1425.

MISERY GORE (SOMERSET CO.)

3749 No items located.

MISERY TOWNSHIP (SOMERSET CO.)

3750 No items located.

MOLUNKUS TOWNSHIP (AROOSTOOK CO.)

3751 ATKINSON, MINNIE. "The Molunkus House." SJMH, 13 (1925), 82-90. Hotel.

MONHEGAN PLANTATION (LINCOLN CO.)

3752 ASHLEY, ALTA. The Monhegan ice pond. n.p., [1969?]. Unpaged. Me.

3753 BURTON, CLARA R. "Monhegan shipwrecks." Down East, 13 (June, 1966), 52-57.

3754 ELLSWORTH, WOLCOTT WEBSTER. Monhegan Island Maine: brief description of the "Sentinel of New England." Hartford, Conn.: Case, Lockwood & Brainard, 1912. Pp. 13.

3755 FULLER, ANNE. "Monhegan, the fortunate island." Down East, 7 (June, 1961), 30-34, 64-65.

3756 GOSS, ELBRIDGE HENRY. "Something about Monhegan." MagAmHist, 12 (1884), 266-274.

3757 HAMLIN, AUGUSTUS CHOATE. "Supposed Runic inscriptions." American Association for the Advancement of Science. Proceedings, 10 Pt. 2, (1856), 214-216. Manana Island.

3758 HOLMES, H. R. "Monhegan Island." Granite Mo, 44 (1912), 147-149.

3759 "THE ISLAND of Monhegan." BHistMag, 3 (1887-1888), 141-145.

3760 MONHEGAN PLANTATION

3760 JENKS, WILLIAM. "On an inscription on a rock in the island of Mananas." American Academy of Arts and Sciences. Proceedings, 2 (1848-1852), 267.

3761 JENNEY, CHARLES FRANCIS. The fortunate island of Monhegan: a historical monograph. (1922) 2d ed. with additions. New Bedford, Mass.: Reynolds Printing, 1927. Pp. 78.
Originally appeared in AASP, New Ser., 31 (1922), 299-358.

3762 "A LEGEND of Monhegan." Maine Monthly Magazine, 1 (1836-1837), 202-204.

3763 "MONHEGAN Island, Maine." BTJ, 6 (1893-1894), 144.

3764 PETTENGILL, A. G. "Monhegan, historical and picturesque." NEM, New Ser., 19 (1898-1899), 65-81.

3765 PROPER, IDA SEDGWICK. Monhegan, the cradle of New England. Portland: Southworth Pr., 1930. Pp. xvii, 275.

3766 RAWLINGS, CHARLES. "Lobster town: Monhegan Island, Maine." Saturday Evening Post, 226 (August 15, 1953), 32-33, 74-77.

SEE ALSO entries 611, 962, 1712, and 2425.

MONMOUTH (KENNEBEC CO.)

3767 BARTER, J. MALCOLM. "Maine business profile: Chick Orchards." Down East, 11 (March, 1965), 38.
Includes history of the orchard.

3768 BRANIN, M. LELYN. "The Saffords: skilled earthenware potters of Monmouth, Maine." Spinning Wheel, 29 (January-February, 1973), 14-16.

3769 COCHRANE, HARRY HAYMAN. History of Monmouth and Wales. East Winthrop: Banner, 1894. 2v.

3770 HOOPER, EUNICE. "Beautiful Monmouth." Sun Up, 10 (August, 1932), 7, 22, 24.

3771 SOUTHARD, IRENE H. "The Custon Free Public Library." MeLAB, 16 (August, 1955), 10-11.

3772 TREAT, HARRY M. "Man failure!" Trains, 15 (March, 1955), 48-51.
Collision on the Maine Central Railroad in 1906.

MONROE (WALDO CO.)

3773 No items located.

MONSON (PISCATAQUIS CO.)

3773A ANDREWS, RICHARD L. "Old 2 x 6." Trains & Travel, 13 (May, 1953), 28-30.
Monson Railroad, 1883-1953.

3774 BUKER, H. W. "Mining slate in Maine." BTJ, 25 (1912-1913), 6-8.

3774A CRITTENDEN, HENRY TEMPLE. "The Monson Railroad." RLHSB, No. 57 (1942), 87-93.

3775 HAYNES, GEORGE HENRY. The Switzerland of Maine, short sketch of beautiful Monson, the discovery of slate and the use and growth of the Monson Maine Slate Company. Boston: Monson Maine Slate Co., 1889. Pp. 32. MeHi.

3776 HUSSEY, NELSON. "The 'two by six' railroad of Monson, Maine." Down East, 13 (March, 1967), 38-41.
Monson Railroad Co.

3777 MONSON, ME. Semi-centennial address of Chas. Davison, poems by W. S. Knowlton and T. N. Lord, etc., Monson, April 22, 1872. Portland: Hoyt, Fogg & Breed, 1872. Pp. 36.

3778 REED, JEANNE BROWN, ALTHEA HAGGSTOM FRENCH, and ELIZABETH EMANUELSON DAVIS. Monson, Maine, history, 1822-1972. Monson, 1972. Pp. 219. MeU.

3779 SPRAGUE, JOHN FRANCIS. History of Doric Lodge, No. 149, of Free and Accepted Masons, Monson, Maine, from A.D. 1868 to A.D. 1901. ... Guilford: Recorder Publishing, 1902. Pp. 40, 26.
"A continuation of the history of Doric Lodge from A.D. 1887 to A.D. 1901"; 26 pp. at end.

3780 _____. "Monson, Maine." BHistMag, 3 (1887-1888), 97-98.

MONTICELLO (AROOSTOOK CO.)

3781 No items located.

MONTVILLE (WALDO CO.)

3782 HALLDALE SCHOOL, MONTVILLE, ME. A brief history of the town of Montville. [Montville?, 1947]. Pp. 7. Me.

MOOSE RIVER (SOMERSET CO.)

3783 SEE entry 3377A.

MORO PLANTATION (AROOSTOOK CO.)

3784   No items located.

MORRILL (WALDO CO.)

3785   MORRILL MEETING HOUSE SOCIETY. An historical
sketch of the "Meeting house at Morrill,
Maine" 1848-1948. n.p., [1948?]. Unpaged.
MBNEH.

3786   ROBINSON, TIMOTHY WEYMOUTH. History of the
town of Morrill in the county of Waldo and
State of Maine. Belfast: City Job Print,
1944-1957. 2v.
   Volume one was edited by Theoda Mears
Morse; volume two, published by the Morrill
Historical Society, is genealogical.

MOSCOW (SOMERSET CO.)

3787   MOSCOW HISTORY COMMITTEE. Makers of Moscow.
Skowhegan: Independent-Reporter Pr., 1966.
Pp. xii, 66.

MT. ABRAM TOWNSHIP (FRANKLIN CO.)

3788   No items located.

MOUNT CHASE PLANTATION (PENOBSCOT CO.)

3789   SEE entry 1833.

MOUNT DESERT (HANCOCK CO.)

3790   BUTCHER, RUSSELL D. "The Jordan Pond House."
Down East, 16 (July, 1970), 52-55, 114-116.

3791   DAVISSON, JEAN. "Somesville summer party,
1855." Down East, 7 (August, 1960), 32-34,
58.

3792   HAMOR, EBEN M. History of Mt. Desert Lodge,
No. 140, of Free and Accepted Masons, Mt.
Desert, Maine, from February 14, 1867 to
February 14, 1871. Portland: S. Berry,
1871. Pp. 14. MB.

3793   HAMOR, JAMES E. History of Mount Desert
Lodge, No. 140, Free and Accepted Masons, at
Mount Desert, Maine, from February 14, 1871
to February 14, 1892. Bar Harbor: Maine
Coast Cottager Office, 1892. Pp. 16. MeHi.

3794   MEREDITH, IRVING. "Twenty-five years of Echo
Lake Camp." Appalachia, 26 (1946-1947),
320-325.
   An Appalachian Mountain Club camp.

3795   NORTHEAST HARBOR, ME. UNION CHURCH. Fiftieth anniversary of the Union Church, Northeast
Harbor, Me., ... July 16th, 1939. n.p.,
[1939]. Unpaged. MeBa.

3796   "A SUCCESSOR of the Apostles founds a parish."
The Northeast, 75 (November, 1948), 14-18.
   St. Mary's-by-the-Sea, Northeast Harbor.

3797   [VAUGHAN, WILLIAM WARREN]. Northeast Harbor:
reminiscences. By an old summer resident.
[Hallowell]: White & Horn, 1930. Pp. 86.

3798   WILLISTON, BELVIN THOMAS. "Records of the
First Church of Mount Desert, Maine, 1792-
1867." NEHGR, 73 (1919), 279-291.

   SEE ALSO entries 1587 and 1617.

MT. KATAHDIN TOWNSHIP (PISCATAQUIS CO.)

3799   AVERY, MYRON HALBURTON. "Forest fires at
Mount Katahdin." The Northern, 8 (June,
1928), 3-4.
   1795-1923.

3800   _____. "Katahdin, its history." In the
Maine Woods, (1939), 18-25.

3801   _____. "The Keep path and its successors:
the history of Katahdin from the east and
north." Appalachia, 17 (1928-1929), 132-147,
224-237.

3802   BAXTER, PERCIVAL PROCTOR. Greatest mountain:
Katahdin's wilderness ... with a historical
essay by Judith A. and John W. Hakola. San
Francisco: Scrimshaw Pr., 1972. Pp. 21.

3803   BOWDITCH, HENRY INGERSOLL. "A trip to Katahdin in 1856." Appalachia, New Ser., 24
(1958-1959), 145-162, 331-348.

3804   DE LASKI, JOHN. "Glacial actions on Mount
Katahdin." American Journal of Science, 103
(1872), 27-31.

3805   ECKSTORM, FANNIE HARDY. "The Katahdin legends." Appalachia, 16 (1924-1926), 39-52.

3806   LEAVITT, HAROLD WALTER. Katahdin skylines.
Orono: Univ. of Maine Pr., 1970. Pp. xx, 99.

3807   MERRILL, LUCIUS H. "Ktaadn." Bangor Historical Society. Proceedings, (1914-1915), 19-30.

3808   NITKIN, NATHANIEL. "Wild, the mountain of
Thoreau." NEG, 9 (Fall, 1967), 35-43.
   Mount Katahdin.

3809 MT. KATAHDIN TOWNSHIP

3809 SMITH, EDWARD STAPLES COUSENS and MYRON HAL-
BURTON AVERY. An annotated bibliography of
Katahdin, with corrigenda and 1937 supplement. Washington: Appalachian Trail Conference, 1950. Pp. iii, 75, 4. Me.

3810 SMITH, EDWARD STAPLES COUSENS. "Larrabee and
'the backwoods expedition.'" Appalachia, 19
(1926), 284-290.
    William C. Larrabee at Mount Katahdin in
1837.

3811 ____ and PHILIP W. K. SWEET. "Rock Creep
on Mt. Ktaadn, Maine." GeogRev, 14 (1924),
388-393.

3812 SMITH, MARION WHITNEY. Katahdin fantasies:
stories based on old Indian legends. Millinocket: Millinocket Pr., 1953. Pp. 44.

3813 ____. "Katahdin legend." Down East, 2
(February-March, 1956), 15-16.
    Legend of Pamola, evil spirit of Mount
Katahdin.

3814 SPRAGUE, JOHN FRANCIS. "Pamola." SJMH, 10
(1922), 215-220.
    Evil spirit of Mount Katahdin in Indian
folklore.

3815 VOSE, PRESCOTT H. "Katahdin in '94." Appalachia, 27 (1948-1949), 334-339.

3816 WING, GEORGE CURTIS. "Mount Ktaadn sometimes
Mount Katahdin." SJMH, 10 (1922), 115-136.

3817 WITHERLE, GEORGE H. Explorations west and
northwest of Katahdin in the late nineteenth
century. 2d ed. [Augusta]: Reprinted by
Maine Appalachian Trail Club, 1950. ii, 57
leaves.

MOUNT VERNON (KENNEBEC CO.)

3818 BLAKE, GEORGE H. Echoes in the silence: the
memorials in the First Baptist Church of
Mount Vernon with essential references to
the history of town and church. n.p.,
[1967?]. Pp. 23. Me.

MOXIE GORE (SOMERSET CO.)

3819 No items located.

NAPLES (CUMBERLAND CO.)

3820 DINGLEY, ROBERT JORDAN. A mini-history of
Naples, Maine.... Naples: Naples Historical
Society, [1970?]. Unpaged. MeHi.

3821 NAPLES, ME. Souvenir program, Naples centennial, 1834-1934, August 10-11-12. n.p.,
[1934]. Unpaged. MeHi.
    Includes a brief historical sketch.

3822 NAPLES, ME. CHURCH OF GOOD FELLOWSHIP.
Souvenir calendar, Church of Good Fellowship,
Naples, Maine, services of rededication,
August 12, 1934. n.p., [1934]. Unpaged.
MeHi.

NASHVILLE PLANTATION (AROOSTOOK CO.)

3823 No items located.

NESOURDNAHUNK TOWNSHIP (PISCATAQUIS CO.)

3824 No items located.

NEW CANADA PLANTATION (AROOSTOOK CO.)

3825 No items located.

NEW GLOUCESTER (CUMBERLAND CO.)

3826 CARR, FRANCES. "The New Gloucester Shaker
school and its teachers." Shaker Quarterly,
1 (1961), 16-20.

3827 ____. "The Tamar fruit compound: a Maine
Shaker industry." Shaker Quarterly, 2
(1962), 39-41.
    The Shaker Tamar Laxative.

3828 DAY, DAVID. Born in a blockhouse: the re-
ligious heritage of New Gloucester, Maine.
Lewiston: Central Maine Pr., 1965. Pp. 88.
MBC.

3829 FERRANTI, FRANK T. "A Shaker experience."
New England Social Studies Bulletin, 32
(1974-1975), 17-23.

3830 GODING, GEORGE HENRY. History of Cumberland
Lodge, No. 12, F. & A. M., New Gloucester,
Me., from April 7, 1873 to December 31, 1900.
Lewiston: Lewiston Journal, 1901. Pp. [49]-
113. MeHi.
    Pagination continued from Moses Plummer's
history for 1803 to 1873, entry 3846.

3831 HUTCHINSON, GLORIA. "The Shakers of Sabbathday Lake." Down East, 18 (October, 1971),
38-41, 66-67, 70, 75, 77.

3832 JOHNSON, THEODORE ELLIOT, ed. "The diary of
a Maine Shaker boy: Delmer Wilson--1887."
Shaker Quarterly, 8 (1968), 3-22.

3833 McCOOL, ELSIE A. "A brief history of the Central Dwelling, Sabbathday Lake." Shaker Quarterly, 1 (1961), 71-76.

3834 _____. "A brief history of the Shaker Mills, Sabbathday Lake, Maine." Shaker Quarterly, 3 (1963), 99-102.

3835 _____. "Gleanings from Sabbathday Lake church journals, 1872-1884." Shaker Quarterly, 6 (1966), 103-112, 124-134.

3836 _____. "Shaker woven poplar work." Shaker Quarterly, 2 (1962), 55-59.
Baskets and boxes.

3837 MAYBERRY, STEPHEN PHINNEY. "Historical sketches in New Gloucester." MHGR, 1 (1884), 107-109.

3838 NEW GLOUCESTER, ME. The bicentennial of New Gloucester, being an account of the celebration of the two hundredth anniversary of the coming of the first settlers, 1739-1939. [New Gloucester]: New Gloucester, Maine, Historical Society, 1945. Pp. 38. MeHi.

3839 _____. The New Gloucester book, account of the 150th anniversary celebration of the incorporation of the town, with a comprehensive review of the history of the town by Florence Hunt Nelson. Auburn: Webber, 1925. Pp. 187. MBNEH.

3840 _____. The New Gloucester centennial, September 7, 1874. Thomas Hawes Haskell, comp. Portland: Hoyt, Fogg & Donham, 1875. Pp. 139.

3841 PARSONS, ISAAC. "An account of New Gloucester." MeHSC, 2 (1847), 151-164.

3842 PÉLADEAU, MARIUS B. "The Shakers of Maine." Antiques, 107 (1975), 1144-1153.
Furniture.

3843 PENNEY, JOHN W. "Records of the proprietors of New Gloucester and reminiscences of some of the early settlers." MeHSC, 2 Ser., 8 (1897), 263-288.
Eighteenth century.

3844 PHILBROOK, ELEANOR. "A brief history of the Shaker post office [in] Sabbathday Lake, Maine." Shaker Quarterly, 4 (1964), 38-40.

3845 _____. "Home thoughs from Sabbathday Lake." Shaker Quarterly, 1 (1961), 77-79.

3846 PLUMMER, MOSES. History of Cumberland Lodge, No. 12, of Free and Accepted Masons, of New Gloucester, Me., from 1803 to 1873. Portland: Stephen Berry, 1873. Pp. 48. MB.
For continuation, see entry 3830.

3847 ROGERS, C. TALBOT. "The people called Shakers." Down East, 4 (October, 1957), 20-23.

3848 ROUNDS, JOHN. The Baptist Church in New Gloucester: an historical discourse preached at the re-opening of the Baptist meeting-house in New Gloucester, Sunday, August 16, 1857. Portland: J. B. Foster, 1857. Pp. 16. Me.

3849 SMITH, DAVID CLAYTON. "William A. Drew and the Maine Shakers." Shaker Quarterly, 7 (1967), 24-32.
Newspaper promotion of Shaker grape crops.

3850 WILLIAMS, STEPHEN GUION. Chosen land: the Sabbathday Lake Shakers. Boston: Godine, 1975. Unpaged.

SEE ALSO entry 1509.

NEW LIMERICK (AROOSTOOK CO.)

3851 No items located.

NEW PORTLAND (SOMERSET CO.)

3852 CURRIER, ALICE C. "Maine's oldest wire bridge." Yankee, 23 (September, 1959), 58.
Completed in 1842.

3853 LIBBY, STEVE. "Maine's fool bridge still standing after 126 years." Maine Dig, 4 (Winter, 1970), 60-61.

3854 LUCE-WHEELER, JANICE. "Colonel Morse's 'fool bridge.'" Down East, 23 (November, 1976), 42-43, 64.
F. B. Morse.

NEW SHARON (FRANKLIN CO.)

3855 PERRY, ANGELA H. "Maine's unique racquet factory." Down East, 13 (March, 1967), 42-44, 66-69.
Tennis racquets; C. A. Thompson Company.

SEE ALSO entries 1419 and 3362.

NEW SWEDEN (AROOSTOOK CO.)

3856 "ANNIVERSARY of the Congregational Church in New Sweden." MeCP, 24 (February, 1937), 8-9.

3857 MALMQUIST, MARIE. Lapptäcke. n.p., 1928-1929. 2v.
In Swedish.

3858 NEW SWEDEN

3858 MELVIN, CHARLOTTE LENENTINE. "The first hundred years in New Sweden." Swedish Pioneer Historical Quarterly, 21 (1970), 233-247.

3859 MILLGÅRD, PER-OLOF. "Letters from New Sweden, Maine." Swedish Pioneer Historical Quarterly, 26 (1975), 104-111.

3860 NEW SWEDEN, ME. Celebration of the decennial anniversary of the founding of New Sweden, Maine, July 23, 1880. Portland: B. Thurston, 1881. Pp. 87.
Historical oration by William W. Thomas, Jr.

3861 _____. Ninety years in New Sweden, 1870-1960. Caribou: Pride Printing, [1960?]. Unpaged. MeHi.

3862 _____. One hundred years in New Sweden. [Caribou: Pride Printing, 1970]. Unpaged. MeHi.

3863 _____. Souvenir of the 40th anniversary of the founding of New Sweden, Maine, June 25, 1910. n.p., 1910. Unpaged. MeHi.

3864 _____. The story of New Sweden as told at the quarter centennial celebration of the founding of the Swedish colony in the woods of Maine, June 25, 1895. Stanley J. Estes, ed. Portland: Loring, Short & Harmon, 1896. Pp. 134.
Oration by William W. Thomas, Jr.

3865 NORBERG, GARD E. "Stout-hearted Swedes took root in Maine." American Swedish Monthly, 42 (December, 1947), 22-23, 37-40.

3866 SETTERDAHL, LILLY. "A visit to New Sweden, Maine: reminiscences of an era." Swedish Pioneer Historical Quarterly, 26 (1975), 92-103.

3867 STAPLES, LINNEA STADIG. "New Sweden, Maine--its birth and settlement." National Historical Magazine, 73 (August, 1939), 77-79.

3868 SWANSON, EVADENE BURRIS. "Swedish colony in the Maine woods." Swedish Pioneer Historical Quarterly, 17 (1966), 3-21.

3869 THOMAS, WILLIAM WIDGERY, b. 1839. "The story of New Sweden." MeHSC, 2 Ser., 7 (1896), 53-85, 113-151.

3870 WIEDEN, CLIFFORD and MARGUERITE WIEDEN. "The beginnings of a New Sweden in Maine." American Swedish Historical Foundation. Yearbook, (1946), 85-96.

3871 WILSON, CHARLES G. "New Sweden." Down East, 5 (October, 1958), 31-33.

SEE ALSO entries 799, 1216, 1448, and 1456.

NEW VINEYARD (FRANKLIN CO.)

3872 BUTLER, BENJAMIN, NATALIE STURGES BUTLER, and DONALD W. McKEEN. Zephaniah builds a schoolhouse--among other things. Farmington: Knowlton & McLeary, 1975. Pp. 101. MBNEH.

3873 ST. JOHN, FREDERIC. "The deserted village of Maine." Sun Up, 8 (July, 1930), 12.
Author's name is a pseudonym.

SEE ALSO entry 3362.

NEWBURGH (PENOBSCOT CO.)

3874 No items located.

NEWCASTLE (LINCOLN CO.)

3875 CUSHMAN, DAVID QUIMBY. "Ancient settlement of Sheepscott." MeHSC, 4 (1856), 209-233.

3876 FLYE, WILLIAM L. "A brief history of the First Congregational Parish in Newcastle." MeCP, 25 (March, 1938), 8-9, 20.

3877 GILDERSLEEVE, NELSON. "An active summer and winter ministry at lovely St. Andrew's Church at Newcastle." The Northeast, 76 (July, 1949), 13-16.

3878 JOHNSON, SAMUEL and WILLIAM WILLIS. "Account of an ancient settlement on Sheepscot River." MeHSC, 2 (1847), 229-237.

3879 LARRABEE, GEORGE H. A souvenir of Lincoln Academy, Newcastle, Maine. Portland: Lakeside Pr., [1898]. Pp. 46. MeHi.
Includes historical sketch.

3880 LUCEY, WILLIAM LEO. "Two Irish merchants of New England." NEQ, 14 (1941), 633-645.
James Kavanagh and Matthew Cottrill.

3881 NEWCASTLE, ME. Newcastle, Maine, program, committees, together with an historical sketch on the observance of the 200th anniversary of its incorporation, June 19-21, 1953. Damariscotta: News Print Shop, [1953]. Pp. 29. Me.

3882 NEWCASTLE, ME. SECOND CONGREGATIONAL CHURCH. Manual and history, together with a history of the First Congregational Church in Newcastle. ... Newcastle, 1917. Pp. 55. MeB.
History is by Oscar William Peterson.

SEE ALSO entries 644, 1678, 1683-1684, 1709, and 4589.

NEWFIELD (YORK CO.)

3883 BACHELER, GILBERT H. An historical sketch of the Congregational Church, West Newfield, Maine, presented at the centennial anniversary, September 29th, 1901. Norwich, Conn.: The Bulletin Company, 1901. Pp. 16.

NEWPORT (PENOBSCOT CO.)

3884 FRIEND, GILMAN N. Newport sesquicentennial, 1814-1964. [Newport, 1964]. Unpaged. Me.

3885 MITCHELL, WILLIAM H. A brief history of Newport, Maine, 1814-1914. Newport: A. W. Lander, 1914. Pp. 55.

3886 "THE NEWPORT centennial." MeCP, 1 (September, 1937), 8-9.
High Street Union Church.

NEWRY (OXFORD CO.)

3887 WIGHT, CARRIE. Newry, Maine, 1805-1955. Bethel: Oxford County Citizen, 1955. Pp. 37. Me.

NOBLEBORO (LINCOLN CO.)

3888 WHITTEMORE, EDWIN CAREY. History of the First Baptist Church of Nobleboro, Maine, 1793-1893. Portland: Brown Thurston, 1893. Pp. 19. Me.

SEE ALSO entries 1678 and 1708.

NORRIDGEWOCK (SOMERSET CO.)

3889 ALLEN, WILLIAM, 1780-1873. The history of Norridgewock: comprising memorials of the aboriginal inhabitants and Jesuit missionaries, hardships of the pioneers, biographical notices of the early settlers, and ecclesiastical sketches. Norridgewock: E. J. Peet, 1849. Pp. 252.

3890 _____. "Statistics of Norridgewock." MeHSC, 7 (1876), 288-289.
Mortality, 1849-1867.

3891 "THE ATTACK on Norridgewock." Down East, 11 (September, 1964), 25, 48.
British raiders destroyed village of Norridgewock and mission of Sebastian Rasles, 1724.

3892 CUMMINGS, EPHRAIM CHAMBERLAIN. "The mission of Father Rasles." MeHSC, 2 Ser., 4 (1893), 146-169, 265-301, 404-410.

3893 ECKSTORM, FANNIE HARDY. "The attack on Norridgewock." NEQ, 7 (1934), 541-578.
Jesuit missionary Sebastian Rasles killed by British raiders in 1724; see also entry 3896.

3894 GOYAU, GEORGES. "Le P. Sébastien Racle." Revue Histoire des Missions, 1 (September, 1924), 161-197.
Jesuit missionary among the Norridgewock Indians.

3895 HEFFERNAN, JOHN PAUL. "Silent bell." Down East, 11 (September, 1964), 24, 26-27.
Father Sebastian Rasles.

3896 MORRISON, KENNETH M. "Sebastian Racle and Norridgewock, 1724: the Eckstorm conspiracy thesis reconsidered." MeHSQ, 14 (1974-1975), 76-97.
See also entry 3893.

3897 O'DWYER, GEORGE FRANCIS. "Sebastian Râle and the Puritans." Catholic World, 112 (1920-1921), 45-51.

3898 SPRAGUE, JOHN FRANCIS. Sebastian Ralé: a Maine tragedy of the eighteenth century. Boston: Heintzemann Pr., 1906. Pp. 162.

3899 TRIPP, ALTA E. "Norrigewock's corn factories." Down East, 13 (October, 1966), 37.
Canning; Burnham and Morrill and the G. S. and F. E. Jewett Company.

3900 VARNEY, LLOYD H. "Epilogue at Old Point." MeArchSocB, No. 2 ([October, 1964]), 17.
Catholic mission.

3901 WILLIAMSON, JOSEPH. "A memorial of Father Rale." MeHSC, 2 Ser., 9 (1898), 137-141.

3902 WOOD, HENRIETTA DANFORTH. Early days of Norridgewock. Freeport: Freeport Pr., 1933. Pp. 124. MeHi.

SEE ALSO entries 171, 799, and 1816.

NORTH BERWICK (YORK CO.)

3903 BUFFAM, SAMUEL. Historical sketch of North Berwick. n.p., [1931?]. Pp. 35.

3904 HAYES, CHARLES F. Historical sketch of the Baptist Church at North Berwick, Me., 1768-1894. North Berwick: Journal Print, 1894. Pp. 12. MeHi.

3905 HUSSEY, PHILIP W., JR. The Hussey manufacturers, 1835-1960. North Berwick, 1960. Pp. 72. MeHi.
   Physical education facilities.

3906 NORTH BERWICK BICENTENNIAL COMMITTEE. A pictoral [sic] history of North Berwick, Maine. [North Berwick], 1976. Pp. 47. MeU.

3907 PERRY, JOSEPHA M. "Samuel Snow, tanner and cordwainer." BBHS, 19 (1945), 183-193.

3908 ST. JOHN, FREDERIC. "The Morrills of Bonneg Beg." Sun Up, 8 (September, 1930), 15, 22.
   Author's name is a pseudonym.

3909 WEBBER, LAURANCE E. "From plowshares to bleachers: the Hussey Manufacturing Company of North Berwick, Maine." Down East, 17 (March, 1971), 62-65.
   Agricultural equipment prior to 1915; gymnasium seating since that date.

3910 WORTH, EDMUND. Centennial discourse delivered on the one hundredth anniversary of the organization of the Baptist Church of North Berwick, Me., September 10th, 1868. Biddeford: J. E. Butler, 1868. Pp. 32. MB.

NORTH HAVEN (KNOX CO.)

3911 BEVERIDGE, NORWOOD P. The North Island: early times to yesterday. North Haven, 1976. Pp. 75. MeU.

3912 BOUSFIELD, LILLIE SNOWDEN, ed. Our island town, by our townspeople and friends. Bar Harbor: Bar Harbor Times Publishing, 1941. Pp. 136.

3913 BREKKE, RAGNHILD. "Norminde: Norway comes to Maine." Down East, 6 (September, 1959), 27-29, 45-46.

   SEE ALSO entry 1656.

NORTH YARMOUTH (CUMBERLAND CO.)

3914 BANKS, CHARLES EDWARD. "The militia of North Yarmouth in early times." Old Times, 7 (1883), 1064-1067.

3915 _____. "North Yarmouth ministers." Old Times, 5 (1881), 649-653.

3916 _____. "The old planters of Westcustogo." Old Times, 4 (1880), 437-443.

3917 BUXTON, PHEBE M. "N. Yarmouth & Falmouth Social Library." Old Times, 3 (1879), 427-429.

3918 DRINKWATER, NICHOLAS. "Corrections to article on the old church." Old Times, 3 (1879), 316-318.
   See entry 3924.

3919 "FIRST Universalist Society of North Yarmouth, Maine." Old Times, 1 (1877), 56-57.

3920 NO ENTRY.

3921 HUMPHREY, JAMES J. "Vessels [built at North Yarmouth and Yarmouth, Maine, 1825-1879]." Old Times, 5 (1881), 743-748.
   Arranged chronologically.

3922 LORING, AMASA. "The four judges of North Yarmouth." MeHSC, 2 Ser., 1 (1890), 57-77.
   John Lewis, Jonas Mason, David Mitchell, and Jeremiah Powell.

3923 _____. "Historical sketch of the Loring family; those who were early residents of North Yarmouth, Maine." Old Times, 6 (1882), 875-886, 924-937.

3924 MASON, ELLEN. "The old meeting-house of North Yarmouth, Maine." Old Times, 2 (1878), 175-191.
   See also entry 3918.

3925 MERRILL, H. AUGUSTUS. "Hero of Westcustogo." SJMH, 3 (1915-1916), 148-150.
   Captain Walter Gendell; shot during skirmish with Indians.

3926 NORTH YARMOUTH, ME. FIRST CHURCH. Confession of faith and covenant, of the First Church in North Yarmouth, Me. with a catalogue of its members, and brief historical notices. ... Portland: Mirror Office, 1848. Pp. 64. MeBa.

3927 "NORTH Yarmouth books." Old Times, 4 (1880), 447-448; 5 (1881), 638-640.

3928 "THE POST Office." Old Times, 1 (1877), 66-67.

3929 RICH, MARSHALL NYE. "Early churches of Maine." BTJ, 5 (1892-1893), 171-172.
   Relates to the First Congregational Church in North Yarmouth; a shorter version appeared in "Old Times" in 1877.

3930 _____. "The North-west Religious Society of North Yarmouth, Maine." Old Times, 1 (1877), 22-27, 86.

3931 _____. "Shipping interest of North Yarmouth, Maine." Old Times, 1 (1877), 49-51.

3932 "THE RING Homestead." BTJ, 5 (1892-1893), 45.

3933 RUSSELL, EDWARD. "History of North Yarmouth." MeHSC, 2 (1847), 165-188.

3934 SARGENT, WILLIAM MITCHELL. "The old church." Old Times, 4 (1880), 453-465.
First Congregational Church.

3935 SEABURY, SAMUEL DORRANCE. "North Yarmouth Academy." Old Times, 2 (1878), 271-274.

3936 STOCKBRIDGE, JOSEPH. "North Yarmouth." Old Times, 5 (1881), 607-611.

3937 TRUE, NATHANIEL TUCKERMAN. "North Yarmouth Academy." Old Times, 8 (1884), 1128-1130.

SEE ALSO entries 1521-1522 and 1524.

NORTH YARMOUTH ACADEMY GRANT (AROOSTOOK CO.)

3938 No items located.

NORTHEAST CARRY TOWNSHIP (PISCATAQUIS CO.)

3939 No items located.

NORTHFIELD (WASHINGTON CO.)

3940 No items located.

NORTHPORT (WALDO CO.)

3941 SEE entry 1833.

NORWAY (OXFORD CO.)

3942 BEAL, EZRA FLUENT. Journal of Ezra F. Beal: diary kept by a distinguished son of Norway; published serially in the Norway Advertiser, Norway, Maine. Don C. Seitz, ed. [N.Y.?], 1926. Pp. 50.

3943 KIMBALL, MERTON L. "Secret fraternities of Norway." BTJ, 17 (1904-1905), 285-287.

3944 LAPHAM, WILLIAM BERRY. Centennial history of Norway, Oxford County, Maine, 1786-1886, including an account of the early grants and purchases, sketches of the grantees, early settlers, and prominent residents, etc., with genealogical registers, and an appendix. Portland: Brown Thurston, 1886. Pp. xvi, 659.

3945 LYFORD, ELMORE B. "What a way to rob a bank!" Yankee, 31 (September, 1967), 92-93, 157-159.
Norway Savings Bank, September 22, 1867.

3946 NORWAY, ME. Norway, Maine, sesquicentennial, 1786-1936, a program of events and brief historical outline of the town. Norway: Advertiser-Democrat, [1936?]. Pp. 32. MeU.

3947 NORWAY HISTORICAL SOCIETY. Norway salutes our country's bicentennial celebration, 1776-1976. Norway, 1976. Pp. 24. Me.
A town history.

3948 NORWAY JUNIOR HIGH SCHOOL. Booklet of Norway past and present. [Norway, 1942]. Unpaged. Me.

3949 NOYES, DAVID. The history of Norway; comprising a minute account of its first settlement, town officers, the annual expenditures of the town, with other statistical matter; interspersed with historical sketches, narrative and anecdote, and occasional remarks by the author. Norway, 1852. Pp. v, 215.

3950 _____. "Norway settlers." MHGR, 9 (1898), 303-308, 328-333, 361-366.

3951 PACKARD, HARRY A. "Norway--a town of unparalleled beauty." Sun Up, 3 (March, 1927), 5-9.

3952 _____. "Something of Norway before the fire." BTJ, 17 (1904-1905), 281-282.

3953 PIKE, CLIFFORD L. Norway centennial poem, delivered on the occasion of the centennial celebration of the settlement of Norway, Maine, Sept. 8th, 1886.... Norway, 1886. Pp. 23.

3954 SMITH, HOWARD DANIEL. History of Oxford Lodge, No. 18, Free and Accepted Masons, Norway, Maine, from date of charter, September 14, 1807, to December, 1909. Norway: Advertiser Book and Job Print, 1910. Pp. 185.

3955 WHITMAN, CHARLES FOSTER. A history of Norway, Maine, from the earliest settlements to the close of the year 1922. Lewiston: Lewiston Journal Printshop, 1924. Pp. 581.

3956 _____. "Norway, Maine, Revolutionary soldiers." DARMag, 47 (1915), 37, 184-186.

3957 WHITMAN, VIC. "The Weary Club." Down East, 18 (August, 1971), 53, 124-130.
Men's club.

3958 WILLIAMS, MYRON R. "When life was young." NEG, 5 (Fall, 1963), 43-52.
Charles Asbury Stevens and glimpses of Norway, 1866-1870.

3959 WRIGHT, WALTER W. "Norway, Maine." Norwegian-American Studies and Records, 15 (1949), 219-222.
Origin of the name.

SEE ALSO entries 1718, 1729, and 3532.

NO. 14 PLANTATION (WASHINGTON CO.)

3960   No items located.

NO. 21 PLANTATION (WASHINGTON CO.)

3961   No items located.

OAKFIELD (AROOSTOOK CO.)

3962   OAKFIELD COMMUNITY HIGH SCHOOL. CLASS OF
        1957. The story of Oakfield. Oakfield,
        [1957]. 2v. Me.
            Text on rectos only.

OAKLAND (KENNEBEC CO.)

3963   BENSON, LOUISE M. "Oakland, Maine." Sun Up,
        2 (April, 1926), 33-34, 36, 38, 41, 43-44,
        46-47.

3964   BROWN, HAROLD F. "Music on Lake Messalonskee."
        Down East, 17 (September, 1970), 52-55.
            New England Music Camp.

3965   GILMAN, JOHN WESLEY. History of Drummond R. A.
        Chapter, No. 27, West Waterville, Maine, from
        its organization to September, 1876. Portland:
        Stephen Berry, 1877. Pp. 38.
            Freemasons.

3966   KEBABIAN, JOHN S. "A visit to the Peavey fac-
        tory site, Oakland, Maine." CEAIA, 21 (1968),
        62-63.
            Peavey Manufacturing Co.; lumbering tools.

3967   "THE OLD axe shop in Oakland." Down East, 15
        (June, 1969), 40-43.
            Emerson & Stevens Manufacturing Co., Inc.

3968   SMALL, ABNER RANDALL. History of Messalonskee
        Lodge, West Waterville, from its organization
        to the year 1870. Portland: Stephen Berry,
        1871. Pp. 48. MeBa.
            Freemasons.

        SEE ALSO entries 1421, 3532, and 5041.

OLD ORCHARD BEACH (YORK CO.)

3969   "THE CHURCH at work in the playground of two
        nations: a missionary enterprise at St.
        John's, Old Orchard Beach." The Northeast,
        75 (July, 1948), 5-7, 9.

3970   FAIRFIELD, ROY P. "The Old Orchard 'set-off.'"
        NEQ, 27 (1954), 227-242.
            Development of the ocean resort area.

3971   GARDNER, RALPH D. "By the beautiful sea: a
        tale of Old Orchard, 1886." NEG, 16 (Summer,
        1974), 3-10.
            Horatio Alger's visit in 1886.

3972   GRAVES, SARAH BRIDGE. "1800 feet of bad
        luck." Yankee, 21 (March, 1957), 34-37, 78-
        81.
            Steel pier.

3973   JAKEMAN, ADELBERT M. The story of Ocean Park:
        an informal seventy-fifth anniversary history,
        1881-1956. Ocean Park: Ocean Park Associa-
        tion, 1956. Pp. 121.

3974   LOCKE, JOHN STAPLES. Historical sketches of
        Old Orchard and the shores of Saco Bay: Bid-
        deford Pool, Old Orchard Beach, Pine Point,
        Prout's Neck. (1880) Enl. ed. Boston: Chas.
        H. Woodman, 1884. Pp. 103.
            Varies only slightly from first edition,
        which has the title "Shores of Saco Bay."

3975   _____. Old Orchard Beach, Maine. Portland:
        G. W. Morris, 1900. Pp. 81.

3976   _____. Old Orchard, Maine. Boston: Graves,
        Locke, 1879. Pp. 48.

3977   PEVERLY, ELAINE M. and WILLIAM HELLEN McLIN.
        The dummy. [Sanford]: Wilson's Printers,
        1973. Pp. 48. MeP.
            Old Orchard Beach branch of the Boston &
        Maine Railroad.

3978   ST. MARGARET'S CHURCH, OLD ORCHARD BEACH, ME.
        Golden anniversary souvenir brochure, 1926-
        1976. Biddeford: Atlantic Coastal Printing,
        [1976?]. Unpaged. MeU.

        SEE ALSO entries 1880, 1904, 4232, and 4287.

OLD TOWN (PENOBSCOT CO.)

3979   GARY, HOBART JUDE. "In the ship mending their
        nets: an evaluation of Saint James, Old
        Town." The Northeast, 76 (November, 1949),
        7-10.

3980   NORTON, DAVID. Sketches of the town of Old
        Town, Penobscot County, Maine, from its ear-
        liest settlement, to 1879; with biographical
        sketches. Bangor: S. G. Robinson, 1881.
        Pp. 152.

3981   OLD TOWN, ME. Old Town, Maine, the first
        125 years, 1840-1965. n.p., [1965?]. Un-
        paged. MeU.

3982   PARENT-TEACHERS CLUB, STILLWATER, ME. A his-
        tory of Stillwater, Maine. [Stillwater],
        1952. Unpaged. Me.

3983 [PORTER, JOSEPH WHITCOMB]. "John Marsh, Jr., owner of the Orono island that bears his name." SJMH, 2 (1914-1915), 202-205.
Author attribution by the editor.

3984 ROTARY INTERNATIONAL, OLD TOWN, ME. Rotary Club of Old Town, Maine, a history, 1927-1944. n.p., [1944?]. Pp. 18. MeBa.

3985 SMITH, NICHOLAS N. The transition from wigwams to frame houses by the Old Town, Maine, Penobscot and Woodstock, New Brunswick, Malecite. n.p., 1971. 11 leaves. MeHi.

SEE ALSO entries 1750, 2082, and 4031.

ORIENT (AROOSTOOK CO.)

3986 No items located.

ORLAND (HANCOCK CO.)

3987 CHASE, FREEMAN HERSEY. History of Rising Sun Lodge, No. 71, of Free and Accepted Masons, Orland, Me., from A.D. 1852 to 1874. Portland: Stephen Berry, 1874. Pp. 35. MeBa.

3988 HARRIMAN, DANIEL. "Settlement of Orland." BHistMag, 1 (1885-1886), 54-55.

3989 MARDEN, GEORGE NATHANIEL. Sermon preached at the Congregational Church in Orland, October 28th, 1866. Ellsworth: N. K. Sawyer, 1867. Pp. 13. MB.
Includes an ecclesiastical history of the town.

ORNEVILLE TOWNSHIP (PISCATAQUIS CO.)

3990 SPRAGUE, JOHN FRANCIS. "General John Parker Boyd and Judge Henry Orne, the original proprietors of the town of Orneville." SJMH, 1 (1913-1914), 43-47, 131-136.

ORONO (PENOBSCOT CO.)

3991 ALPHA TAU OMEGA. BETA UPSILON CHAPTER. UNIVERSITY OF MAINE. Alpha Tau Omega: a history of Beta Upsilon Chapter, 1891-1971. [Orono?, 1971?]. 56 leaves. MeU.

3992 "ARREST and trial of Joseph Inman of Orono, for murder in 1801." BHistMag, 3 (1887-1888), 54-56.

3993 ASHMAN, ROBERT I. "Forestry at Maine." Maine Alumnus, 34 (February, 1953), 4-6, 12.

3994 BARKER, FLORENCE E. "A land boom in Maine one hundred years ago." Sun Up, 10 (June, 1932), 24.

3995 BOARDMAN, SAMUEL LANE. "Historical sketch of the State College." Maine. Board of Agriculture. Annual Report of the Secretary, 21 (1876), 208-220.

3996 "THE BOOKSTORE." Maine Alumnus, 30 (April, 1949), 7, 14.
University of Maine Bookstore.

3997 BURNHAM, JOHN. "The story of an outing club." Maine Alumnus, 47 (July, 1966), 22-25.
Maine Outing Club.

3998 CHAMBERLAIN, GEORGE WALTER. "The University of Maine." Americana, 5 (1910), 1-15.

3999 "THE 'COBURN Cadets'--a history of Maine's Military Department." Maine Alumnus, 19 (January, 1938), 5, 8.

4000 "CO-EDS of the seventies." Maine Alumnus, 26 (April, 1945), 5.
University of Maine.

4001 DAY, CLARENCE ALBERT. Historical sketch of Orono: the Orono sesquicentennial program celebrating the 150th anniversary of the incorporation of Orono, June 14, 15, 16, 1806-1956. n.p., [1956]. Pp. 108.

4002 _____. Twenty-five years of service. Orono: Univ. of Maine, 1937. Pp. 31. MeBa.
Agricultural Extension Service at the University of Maine.

4003 "THE DEPARTMENT of Mechanical Engineering." Maine Alumnus, 26 (April, 1945), 3-4.
University of Maine.

4004 ELLIOTT, LLOYD HARTMAN. Unique patterns in progress: the University of Maine and the pulp and paper industry. N.Y.: Newcomen Society in North America, 1964. Pp. 24.

4005 EVANS, WESTON S. "100 years at the U. of M." Down East, 11 (November, 1964), 24-28, 45-46.

4006 FERNALD, MERRITT CALDWELL. History of Maine State College and the University of Maine. Orono: Univ. of Maine, 1916. Pp. 450.

4007 _____. "The Maine State College of Agriculture and the Mechanic Arts." NEM, 5 (1886-1887), 546-557.

4008 "FIJI fiftieth." Maine Alumnus, 31 (December, 1949), 4.
Phi Gamma Delta Fraternity, University of Maine.

4009 "FOOTBALL in 1892." Maine Alumnus, 24 (November, 1942), 7.
University of Maine.

4010 ORONO

4010   HARVEY, KINGDON. "The development of Maine's
        state university." Maine's Own Magazine, 8
        (May and June, 1930), 4-5, 28-29.

4011   HASKELL, EDWIN J. "Recollections of the good
        old days." Maine Alumnus, 47 (November,
        1965), 5-6.
            University of Maine.

4012   HAUCK, ARTHUR ANDREW. Maine's university and
        the land-grant tradition. N.Y.: Newcomen
        Society in North America, 1954. Pp. 28.

4013   LAMBE, EMERSON P. "Memories of a student at
        Maine during 1903-07." Maine Alumnus, 38
        (February, 1957), 14.

4014   MAINE. AGRICULTURAL EXPERIMENT STATION,
        ORONO. Exercises at the twenty-fifth anni-
        versary of the Maine Agricultural Experiment
        Station held at the University of Maine,
        March 9, 1910; and a brief historical sketch
        of the station. n.p., [1910]. Pp. 38.

4015   MAINE. UNIVERSITY. Commemorative exercises
        for the seventy-fifth anniversary of the
        founding of the University, February 25 and
        26, 1940. [Orono?, 1940]. Pp. 49.

4016   _____. Dedication of Coburn Hall, June 26,
        1888. Augusta: Burleigh & Flynt, 1888.
        Pp. 71. MeBa.
            Historical address by Lyndon Oak.

4017   _____. Pride in the past, faith in the fu-
        ture, 1865-1965, University of Maine. Orono,
        1965. Pp. 32.

4018   MAINE. UNIVERSITY. COLLEGE OF AGRICULTURE.
        50th anniversary, Farm and Home Week ...
        April 1-4, 1957. [Orono?], 1957. Pp. 20.
        MeBa.

4019   MAINE. UNIVERSITY. COLLEGE OF AGRICULTURE.
        EXTENSION DEPARTMENT. 50 years with the Co-
        operative Extension Service in Maine. Orono,
        1962. Pp. 36.

4020   "MAINE Masque theatre enters second half cen-
        tury." Maine Alumnus, 37 (May, 1956), 10-11.
            University of Maine.

4021   ORONO, ME. Centennial celebration, and dedi-
        cation of Town Hall, Orono, Maine, March 3,
        1874.... Portland: Bailey & Noyes, 1874.
        Pp. 168.

4022   ORONO, Maine: a bicentennial view. n.p.,
        1976. Pp. 80. MeU.

4023   "THE PROPER study of mankind." Maine Alumnus,
        20 (February, 1939), 5-12.
            The Department of Psychology at the Univer-
        sity of Maine.

4024   SMITH, DAVID CLAYTON. "Forest history re-
        search and writing at the University of
        Maine." Forest History, 12 (July, 1968),
        27-31.
            1903-1968.

4025   STEVENS, JAMES STACY. "Librarians past and
        present." Maine Alumnus, 20 (April, 1939),
        8.
            University of Maine.

4026   _____. Meteorological conditions at Orono,
        Maine. Orono, 1907. Pp. 52.
            Includes historical tables.

4027   _____. "The summer session, a historical
        sketch." Maine Alumnus, 18 (April, 1937),
        4.
            University of Maine.

4028   STEWART, ALICE ROSE. "A woman's place."
        Maine Alumnus, 53 (April-May, 1972), 3-4.
            Women at the University of Maine.

4029   STEWART, PHYLLIS and CLARENCE ALBERT DAY. A
        history of the Orono Methodist Church. n.p.,
        [1960]. 15 leaves. MeU.

4030   "THREE quarters of a century." Maine Alum-
        nus, 25 (January, 1944), 4-5.
            University of Maine.

4031   TURNER, PERCIE HOPKINS. The first forty
        years of the Orono-Old Town Branch of the
        American Association of University Women,
        1924-1964. [Orono?, 1964?]. 12 leaves. MeU.

4032   _____. Phi Beta Kappa: the Delta of Maine,
        1923-1973. Orono, 1972. Pp. 33. MeU.
            University of Maine.

4033   "WHERE quality is the watchword." Maine
        Alumnus, 22 (March, 1941), 4-5.
            University Press.

4034   WHITE, THOMAS R. "Maine Masque: 60 years of
        drama." Maine Alumnus, 47 (January, 1966),
        6-9.
            University of Maine.

        SEE ALSO entries 1733, 1750, and 2082.

ORRINGTON (PENOBSCOT CO.)

4035   PORTER, JOSEPH WHITCOMB. "An address deliv-
        ered at the centennial celebration of the in-
        corporation of the town of Orrington, June
        28, 1888." MeHistMag, 7 (1891-1892), 183-
        202.

        SEE ALSO entries 1752 and 1762.

OSBORN PLANTATION (HANCOCK CO.)

4036   No items located.

OTIS (HANCOCK CO.)

4037   No items located.

OTISFIELD (CUMBERLAND CO.)

4038   HOLDEN, CHARLES F. "A sketch of the life of David Ray, and the early history of the town of Otisfield, county of Cumberland." SJMH, 9 (1921), 14-19.

4039   LABBIE, EDITH. "One thing's certain: the world is flat." Yankee, 39 (February, 1975), 72-77.
       Joseph White Holden (1816-1900).

4040   ROBINSON, ERNEST W. "Old meeting house." Sun Up, 9 (December, 1931), 5, 37.
       Bell Hill Church.

4041   SPURR, WILLIAM SAMUEL. A history of Otisfield, Cumberland County, Maine from the original grant to the close of the year 1944. Oxford: W. S. Spurr, 1959. Pp. 661.

OWLS HEAD (KNOX CO.)

4042   BROOKS, ALFRED A. "The boats of Ash Point, Maine." AmNep, 2 (1942), 307-323.
       Boat building.

4043   LEWIS, GRACE HEGGAR. "A summer cottage of long ago." Down East, 3 (September, 1956), 16-19.

4044   "OWL'S Head." Down East, 16 (April, 1970), 56-57.
       Owl's Head Light.

4045   SNOW, EDWARD ROWE. "The frozen couple of Owl's Head." Yankee, 20 (December, 1956), 32-35.
       Lydia Dyer and Richard Ingraham in a shipwreck on December 22, 1850.

OXBOW PLANTATION (AROOSTOOK CO.)

4046   No items located.

OXBOW TOWNSHIP (OXFORD CO.)

4047   No items located.

OXFORD (OXFORD CO.)

4048   ABBOTT, MORETON. "Biography of a house." Yankee, 28 (June, 1964), 78-79, 116-121.
       Oxford Spring House, a hotel.

4049   KING, MARQUIS FAYETTE, comp. Annals of Oxford, Maine, from its incorporation, February 27, 1829, to 1850; prefaced by a brief account of the settlement of Shepardsfield Plantation, now Hebron and Oxford, and supplemented with genealogical notes from the earliest records of both towns and other sources. Portland, 1903. Pp. xii, 298.

4050   WATERMAN, CHARLES ELMER. "Welchville and some of its early families." SJMH, 5 (1917-1918), 16-22, 147-154.

PALERMO (WALDO CO.)

4051   DOWE, MILTON E. History, town of Palermo, incorporated 1804. Palermo, 1954. Pp. 51.

4052   GOODWIN, ALLEN. A history of the early settlement of Palermo, Me. Belfast: Age Publishing, 1896. Pp. 34.

4053   HOWARD, MILLARD A. An introduction to the early history of Palermo, Maine. n.p., [1976]. Pp. 64. Me.

PALMYRA (SOMERSET CO.)

4054   PALMYRA, ME. Sesquicentennial, Palmyra, Maine, 1807-1957. [Pittsfield]: Pittsfield Advertiser, 1957. Pp. 20. Me.

PARIS (OXFORD CO.)

4055   HAMLIN, AUGUSTUS CHOATE. The history of Mount Mica of Maine, U. S. A. and its wonderful deposits of matchless tourmalines. Bangor: A. C. Hamlin, 1895. Pp. 72.

4056   KING, ABEL CHARLES THOMAS, GEORGE ADAM WILSON, and F. H. SKILLINGS. History of Paris Lodge, No. 94, of Free and Accepted Masons, situated at South Paris, Me. Portland: Berry, 1872. Pp. 26.

4057   KING, ABEL CHARLES THOMAS, ALBERT WARD WALKER, and HORATIO WOODBURY. History of Paris Lodge, No. 94, Free and Accepted Masons, situated at South Paris, Me. South Paris: Oxford Democrat, 1902. Pp. 55. Me.

4058   LABBIE, EDITH. Paris Hill, Olympus of Maine. Down East, 21 (July, 1975), 68-71.
       A village.

4059 LAPHAM, WILLIAM BERRY. After fifty years: semi-centennial of the Oxford Democrat; history of the paper from the first issue, with sketches of its editors, publishers, etc. Paris: Oxford Democrat Office, 1886. Pp. 35.

4060 _____ and SILAS PACKARD MAXIM. History of Paris, Maine, from its settlement to 1880, with a history of the grants of 1736 & 1771, together with personal sketches, a copious genealogical register and an appendix. Paris, 1884. Pp. 816.
Historical address by Horatio King.

4061 MORTON, AGNES L. "South Paris, a well-known industrial center." Sun Up, 3 (March, 1927), 11-13.

4062 PARIS, ME. FIRST BAPTIST CHURCH. Centennial of the First Baptist Church in Paris, Maine; observed October 1st, 1891. Paris: Oxford Democrat Office, 1892. Pp. 85.
Historical discourse by Hiram C. Estes.

4063 SOUTH PARIS, ME. FIRST CONGREGATIONAL CHURCH. 150 years, 1812-1962, First Congregational Church, South Paris, Maine. n.p., [1962]. Pp. 28. MBC.
Historical sketch by Earle R. Clifford.

4064 TUBBY, JOSIAH T. "Old granite gaol, South Paris, Maine, built in 1822." OTNE, 36 (1945-1946), 12-13.

4065 WATERMAN, CHARLES ELMER. A city on a hill (Paris Hill) with high lights that hit it. Auburn: Merrill & Webber, 1931. Pp. 102.

4066 WILSON, GEORGE ADAM. "Paris, the shire town of Oxford County." BTJ, 18 (1905-1906), 370-372.

SEE ALSO entries 1718 and 1727.

PARKERTOWN TOWNSHIP (OXFORD CO.)

4067 No items located.

PARKMAN (PISCATAQUIS CO.)

4068 McKUSICK, VICTOR A. "Parkman, Maine, a frontier settlement." OTNE, 49 (1958-1959), 41-48.

4069 STORMS, ROGER C. History of Parkman: mainstream democracy in Parkman, Maine, 1794-1969. Freeport: Dingley Pr., 1969. Pp. 108.

SEE ALSO entry 1782.

PARLIN POND TOWNSHIP (SOMERSET CO.)

4070 SEE entry 3377A.

PARMACHENEE TOWNSHIP (OXFORD CO.)

4071 No items located.

PARSONSFIELD (YORK CO.)

4072 DEARBORN, JEREMIAH WADLEIGH, ed. A history of the first century of the town of Parsonsfield, Maine; incorporated Aug. 29, 1785, and celebrated with impressive ceremonies at North Parsonsfield, August 29, 1885. Portland: Brown Thurston, 1888. Pp. xiv, 499.

4073 KEZAR FALLS, ME. RIVERSIDE METHODIST EPISCOPAL CHURCH. Centennial anniversary program and historical sketch ... September 6th and 7th, 1933. Cornish: Webb-Smith, [1933]. Pp. 31. MeHi.
History by Ina Stanley Emery.

4074 PARSONSFIELD SEMINARY. Parsonsfield Seminary, first hundred years, 1832-1932. n.p., [1932?]. Pp. 44. MBNEH.

PASSADUMKEAG (PENOBSCOT CO.)

4075 HADLOCK, WENDELL STANWOOD and THEODORE STERN. "Passadumkeag, a Red Paint cemetery, thirty five years after Moorehead." American Antiquity, 14 (October, 1948), 98-103.
For Moorehead's 1913 study, see entry 901.

4076 SNOW, DEAN R. A summary of excavation at the Hathaway site in Passadumkeag, Maine, 1912, 1947, and 1968. [Orono]: Department of Anthropology, Univ. of Maine, 1969. Pp. v, 106.

PATTEN (PENOBSCOT CO.)

4077 BENJAMIN, CHARLES H. A hill town in New England. Altadena, Calif., 1929. 45 leaves. MeU.

4078 OLSEN, IRENE A. The history of Patten Academy, 1847-1947. Bangor: Furbush-Roberts, [1947?]. Pp. 157. MeU.

PEMBROKE (WASHINGTON CO.)

4079   CAMPBELL, B. A. History of Crescent Lodge, No. 78, Free and Accepted Masons, Pembroke, Me., from 1880 to December 31, 1890. Part III. Portland: Stephen Berry, 1893. Pp. 55. MeBa.
        A continuation of works by John E. Walker and John C. Campbell; see entries 4080 and 4082.

4080   CAMPBELL, JOHN C. History of Crescent Lodge, No. 78, Free and Accepted Masons, Pembroke, Maine, from 1870 to December 31, 1880. Portland: Stephen Berry, 1882. Pp. 21-40. MeBa.
        Pagination continued from a work by John E. Walker; see entry 4082.

4081   FREEMASONS. PEMBROKE, ME. CRESCENT ROYAL ARCH CHAPTER, NO. 26. History of Crescent Royal Arch Chapter, No. 26, Pembroke, Maine. Portland: Stephen Berry, 1876. Pp. 27. MeBa.

4082   WALKER, JOHN E. History of Crescent Lodge, No. 78, Free and Accepted Masons, Pembroke, Me., from 1854 to 1870. Portland: Stephen Berry, 1872. Pp. 20. MeBa.
        Continued by entries 4079 and 4080.

        SEE ALSO entry 603.

PENOBSCOT (HANCOCK CO.)

4083   "AN ACCOUNT of the First Congregational Church and Parish in the town of Penobscot, Maine." BHistMag, 3 (1887-1888), 145-149.

4084   MONTGOMERY, JOB HERRICK. Address of J. H. Montgomery, Esq., at the centennial celebration of the town of Penobscot, Sept. 14, 1887. Camden: Herald Print, 1887. Unpaged. MeHi.

4085   MOORE, RILLA LEACH. Mill Creek, Penobscot, Maine. n.p., 1967. Pp. 54. MeU.
        Town history.

4086   WARDWELL, HOSEA B. "Early settlement of the town of Penobscot, Me." BHistMag, 5 (1889-1890), 96-100.

4087   _____. "The early settlers of the town of Penobscot." MeHistMag, 7 (1891-1892), 25-26.
        Banks family.

4088   _____. History of Rising Star Lodge, of Free and Accepted Masons, Penobscot, Maine, from August 4, 1875, to March 1, 1884. Portland: Stephen Berry, 1884. Pp. 12. MeBa.

4089   _____. History of Rising Star Lodge, of Free and Accepted Masons, Penobscot, Maine, from March 1, 1884, to December 31, 1890. Orland: R. P. Harriman, 1891. Pp. 15. MeHi.

        SEE ALSO entries 1597 and 1621.

PERHAM (AROOSTOOK CO.)

4090   No items located.

PERKINS TOWNSHIP (FRANKLIN CO.)

4091   No items located.

PERKINS TOWNSHIP (SAGADAHOC CO.)

4092   BARROWS, JOHN STUART. "A legend of Swan Island." NEM, New Ser., 19 (1898-1899), 606-608.

        SEE ALSO entry 1677.

PERRY (WASHINGTON CO.)

4093   COOKE, LE BARON P. "A picturesque tribe of New England Indians." National Magazine, 38 (1913), 437-438.
        Passamaquoddy.

4094   NO ENTRY.

4095   SESQUICENTENNIAL, 1818-1968; historical souvenir book, Perry, Maine. n.p., [1968]. Unpaged.

        SEE ALSO entry 603.

PERU (OXFORD CO.)

4096   TURNER, HOLLIS. The history of Peru, in the county of Oxford and State of Maine, from 1789 to 1911: residents and genealogies of their families, also a part of Franklin plan. Augusta: Maine Farmer Publishing, 1912. Pp. 313.

4097   VAUGHN, MARY SEARLES. A history of the town of Peru, Maine. Rumford: Rumford Publishing, 1971. Pp. 124.

PHILLIPS (FRANKLIN CO.)

4098 PEASE, ALBERT. Sketches of the history of Phillips, Maine. Phillips: Phillips Historical Society, 1962. Pp. 56. MBNEH.

4099 WHITNEY, WENDELL. History of Phillips, history contest conducted by Phillips High School, 1933. n.p., [1933?]. 25, 9A leaves. MBNEH.

SEE ALSO entry 1419.

PHIPPSBURG (SAGADAHOC CO.)

4100 BALLARD, EDWARD, ed. Memorial volume of the Popham celebration, August 29, 1862; commemorative of the planting of the Popham Colony on the peninsula of Sabino, August 19, O.S., 1607, establishing the title of England to the continent. Portland: Bailey & Noyes, 1863. Pp. xiv, 368.

4101 BANKS, CHARLES EDWARD. "New documents relating to the Popham Expedition, 1607." AASP, New Ser., 39 (1929), 307-334.

4102 BAXTER, JAMES PHINNEY. The chief actors in the Sagadahoc drama: an address delivered at the tercentenary celebration of the landing of the Northern Virginia colony at the mouth of the Sagadahoc, August 29, 1907. n.p., 1907. Pp. 10.

4103 BOURNE, EDWARD EMERSON, 1797-1873. An address on the character of the colony founded by George Popham, at the mouth of the Kennebec River August 19th, (O.S.) 1607; delivered in Bath, on the two hundred and fifty-seventh anniversary of that event. Portland: B. Thurston, 1864. Pp. 60.

4104 _____. "First Christian worship in New England." HistMag, 2 Ser., 2 (1867), 1-3.
Popham Colony; answer to article in "Congregational Quarterly" by David Q. Cushman; see entry 4106.

4105 _____. "The Popham celebration." HistMag, 9 (1865), 358-361.

4106 CUSHMAN, DAVID QUIMBY. "First Christian worship in New England." CongQ, 9 (1867), 21-24.
Popham Colony; see also entries 4104 and 4111 for comments on this article.

4107 DAVIES, JAMES. A relation of a voyage to Sagadahoc; now first printed from the original manuscript in the Lambeth Palace Library. B. F. De Costa, ed. Cambridge, Mass.: John Wilson & Son, 1880. Pp. 43.

4108 DE COSTA, BENJAMIN FRANKLIN. "The Sagadahoc Colony." MHSP, 18 (1880-1881), 82-117.

4109 _____. "The two hundred and seventy-fifth anniversary of the landing at the Kennebec." MagAmHist, 8 (1882), 555-561.
Popham Colony.

4110 DUNNACK, HENRY ERNEST. A history of Fort Popham Memorial. Augusta: State Park Commission, [1955?]. Pp. 28. Me.

4111 "THE FIRST Christian worship in New England." CongQ, 9 (1867), 275-276.
Popham Colony; in answer to David Q. Cushman's article, entry 4106; signed "B."

4112 FOLSOM, GEORGE. Address delivered on the site of the Popham Colony, near the mouth of the Kennebec, in New England, before the Maine Historical Society, on the 28th August, 1863. Ventnor, Isle of Wight: Fletcher Moor, 1866. Pp. 34.

4113 GILMAN, STANWOOD CUSHING and MARGARET COOK GILMAN. Phippsburg on the Kennebec, 1606-1964. [Phippsburg?], 1964. Pp. 32.

4114 _____. Small Point: the Cape of Many Islands, 1667-1965. [Phippsburg?, 1965?]. Pp. 62.

4115 HILL, WINFIELD SCOTT. The site of Fort Saint George, erected by Captain George Popham, in 1607. Read before the [Kennebec Natural History and Antiquarian] Society, July 23, 1891. [Augusta, 1891?]. Pp. 4.

4116 LAPHAM, WILLIAM BERRY, comp. Popham Beach as a summer resort, with a sketch of Popham Colony and the ancient Province of Sabino. Augusta: Maine Farmer Job Print, 1888. Pp. 15.

4117 "A LETTER from George Popham, president of the Sagadahock Colony, to King James I, dated December 13, 1607." MeHSC, 5 (1857), 343-360.

4118 McKEEN, JOHN. "Some account of the early settlements at Sagadahock and on the Androscoggin River; with the suggestion that the exploration by Popham's Colony was up the Androscoggin River and not the Kennebec." MeHSC, 3 (1853), 311-324.

4119 MAINE HISTORICAL SOCIETY. Tercentenary of the landing of the Popham Colony at the mouth of the Kennebec River, August 29, 1907. Portland: Maine Historical Society, 1907. Pp. 58.

4120 PATTERSON, JAMES WILLIS. Responsibilities of the founders of republics: an address on the peninsula of Sabino, on the two-hundred and fifty-eighth anniversary of the planting of Popham Colony, Aug. 29, 1865. Boston: John K. Wiggin, 1865. Pp. 38.

4121 PERKINS, JAMES E. and JANE PERHAM STEVENS. One man's world, Popham Beach, Maine. Freeport: Bond Wheelwright, 1974. Pp. xii, 131.

4122 PHIPPSBURG CONGREGATIONAL CHURCH. 200th anniversary of the organization of the Phippsburg Congregational Church, 1765-1965. [Phippsburg,?, 1965]. Unpaged. MBC.

4123 PHIPPSBURG HISTORICAL SOCIETY. Phippsburg, fair to the wind. Lewiston: Twin City Printery, 1964. Pp. 108, xvii.

4124 "THE PLYMOUTH Company and the settlement of Maine in New England." Devon and Cornwall Notes and Queries, 18 (1934-1935), 134-138.
        Popham Colony.

4125 POOR, JOHN ALFRED. The first colonization of New-England: an address, delivered at the erection of a monumental stone in the walls of Fort Popham, August 29th, 1862, commemorative of the planting of the Popham Colony on the peninsula of Sabino, August 19th, O.S. 1607, establishing the title of England to the continent. N.Y.: A. D. F. Randolph, 1863. Pp. iv, 58.

4126 THE POPHAM colony: a discussion of its historical claims, with a bibliography of the subject. Boston: J. K. Wiggin and Lunt, 1866. Pp. 72.
        A discussion between W. F. Poole, Edward Ballard, and Frederic Kidder; reprinted from the Boston Daily Advertiser, April 11-July 28, 1866.

4127 "POPHAM: first Christian worship in New England." HistMag, 2 Ser., 5 (1869), 113-115.

4127A PRESTON, RICHARD ARTHUR. "Sir Ferdinando Gorges--little-known colonizer." American History Illustrated, 4 (June, 1969), 33-38.
        Popham Colony.

4128 REED, PARKER McCOBB. "Reed family." MHGR, 5 (1888), 129-134.

4129 ROWSE, A. L. "New England in the earliest days." Am Heritage, 10 (August, 1959), 23-29.
        Popham Colony.

4130 SEWALL, RUFUS KING. "Popham's town of Fort St. George." MeHSC, 7 (1876), 291-322.

4131 THAYER, HENRY OTIS. "Notes concerning Ancient Augusta at Small Point." MeHSC, 2 Ser., 3 (1892), 424-430.

4132 _____. "The Popham Colony once more." SJMH, 4 (1916-1917), 253-254.

4133 _____, ed. The Sagadahoc Colony: comprising the relation of a voyage into New England (Lambeth ms.). Portland: The Gorges Society, 1892. Pp. xi, 276.
        Includes a bibliography.

4134 THORNTON, JOHN WINGATE. Colonial schemes of Popham and Gorges: speech at the Fort Popham celebration, August 29, 1862, under the auspices of the Maine Historical Society. Boston: E. L. Balch, 1863. Pp. 20.

4135 VONDEL, JOSEPH LEMAN. "Sagadahoc Colony." Pine Tree Magazine, 7 (1907), 535-544.

4136 WHEELER, HENRY WARREN. "Ancient Augusta." MeHSC, 2 Ser., 3 (1892), 233-246.
        A settlement which existed from 1716-1721.

4137 WILSON, JOSEPH KENNARD. "The door-step of New England." NEM, New Ser., 27 (1902-1903), 3-14.

SEE ALSO entry 4613.

PIERCE POND TOWNSHIP (SOMERSET CO.)

4138 No items located.

PITTSFIELD (SOMERSET CO.)

4139 COOK, SANGER MILLS. Pittsfield on the Sebasticook. Bangor: Furbush-Roberts, 1966. Pp. 191.

4140 MAINE CENTRAL INSTITUTE, PITTSFIELD, ME. History of the alumni et alumnae ... 1869-1877, by Blanche Robinson Getchell of '90; 1878-1886, by Flora Addie Boyd of '91; 1887-1896 by Kate Wright Eldridge of '91. Portland: Lakeside Pr., 1897. Pp. 104.

4141 PITTSFIELD GRAMMAR SCHOOL. Pittsfield past and present. Patricia Buxton and Lawrence Hallee, eds. [Pittsfield], 1948. 51 leaves. Me.

4142 WHITTEN, ALBION. History of Meridian Lodge, No. 125, Free and Accepted Masons. Pittsfield, Maine, from its organization, 1864, to 1878. Portland: Stephen Berry, 1878. Pp. 31. MeBa.

PITTSTON (KENNEBEC CO.)

4143 PITTSTON, ME. Vital records of Pittston, Maine, to the year 1892. Henry Sewall Webster and Asbury Coke Stilphen, eds. Gardiner: Reporter-Journal Pr., 1911. Pp. 387.

SEE ALSO entries 1633, 1649, and 1937.

PITTSTON ACADEMY GRANT (SOMERSET CO.)

4144   No items located.

PLEASANT POINT STATE INDIAN RESERVATION (WASHINGTON CO.)

4145   No items located.

PLEASANT RIDGE PLANTATION (SOMERSET CO.)

4146   No items located.

PLYMOUTH (PENOBSCOT CO.)

4147   No items located.

PLYMOUTH TOWNSHIP (SOMERSET CO.)

4148   No items located.

POLAND (ANDROSCOGGIN CO.)

4149   BENNETT, MARY E., ed. Poland: past and present, 1795-1970; published in commemoration of the 175th anniversary of Poland, Maine. Poland: Poland Anniversary Committee, 1970. Pp. 106.
    Errata slip inserted.

4150   GILLIS, CHARLES E. "Great Scott! What a hotel!" Yankee, 22 (October, 1958), 56-59, 102-103.
    Poland Spring House.

4151   LOVERING, FRANK W. "Poland water and the Ricker saga." Down East, 8 (July, 1962), 28-31.
    Resort at Poland Spring.

4152   POLAND, ME. Souvenir programme of Poland's centennial celebration held at Poland, Maine, Wednesday, September Eleventh, 1895. n.p., 1895. Unpaged. MeHi.
    Includes historical sketch by Charles E. Waterman.

4153   POLAND Spring centennial: a souvenir. N.Y.: A. H. Kellogg, 1895. Pp. 88.

4154   POOLE, HENRY A. and GEORGE W. POOLE. History of Poland ... embracing a period of over a century. Mechanic Falls: Poole Bros., 1890. Pp. vi, 145.

4155   RICKER, ALVAN BOLSTER. Poland centennial, September 11, 1895. N.Y.: A. H. Kellogg, 1896. Pp. 117.

4156   RICKER, HIRAM, & SONS, INC. Poland Mineral Spring Water, the story of its history and its marvellous curative properties. South Poland, 1891. Pp. 80. Me.

4157   _____. Poland Spring: the early history of this wonderful spring, its growth and development illustrated. South Poland, 1917. Unpaged.

4158   ROBBINS, MEL. Poland Spring: an informal history. [Poland Spring?], 1975. Pp. 24. MeU.
    Poland Spring House, hotel.

4159   VINCENT, PAL. The Moses bottle. Poland Spring: Palabra Shop, 1969. Pp. 58.
    Poland Spring Mineral Water.

    SEE ALSO entry 1425.

PORTAGE LAKE (AROOSTOOK CO.)

4160   No items located.

PORTER (OXFORD CO.)

4161   MOULTON, THOMAS. Porter, as a portion of Maine: its settlement, etc. Portland: Hoyt, Fogg & Donham, 1879. Pp. 96.

4162   TEG, WILLIAM. History of Porter. Kezar Falls: Parsonsfield-Porter Historical Society, 1957. Pp. xiv, 315.

PORTLAND (CUMBERLAND CO.)

4163   ACKERMAN, JOHN H. "Boynton's dream engine." Yankee, 31 (November, 1967), 170-173.
    E. Moody Boynton and his monorail locomotive.

4164   ALBION, ROBERT GREENHALGH. ["The port of Portland, Maine."] Ships and the Sea, 4 (August, 1954), 22, 44-48, 50.

4165   ANDERSON, ALBERT E. History of St. Alban Commandery, No. 8, Knights Templar. [Portland, 1942]. Pp. 39. MeHi.

4166   ANDREWS, DELMONT. "The people's hospital." Pine Cone, 3 (Autumn, 1947), 12-15.
    Maine General Hospital.

4167 ANTHOENSEN, FRED. Types and bookmaking, containing notes on the books printed at the Southworth-Anthoensen Press, and a bibliographical catalogue by Ruth A. Chaplin, with specimens of its work, types, borders, etc. Portland: Southworth-Anthoensen Pr., 1943. Pp. x, 170.

4168 ARMSTRONG, F. C. "Portland, Me., Longfellow's 'beautiful town.'" Chamber's Journal, 87 (February, 1910), 78-80.

4169 BACON, GEORGE FOX. Portland, its representative business men and its points of interest. Newark, N.J.: Glenwood Publishing, 1891. Pp. 200.

4170 BAKER, FLORENCE E. "Maine's first ice business." Sun Up, 10 (April, 1932), 17.
David Robinson, 1822.

4171 BAKER, RICHARD L. Historical synopsis of economic development in Portland, Maine. Portland, 1959. 100 leaves. MeP.

4172 BAKER, WILLIAM J. "Anglo-American relations in miniature: the Prince of Wales in Portland, Maine, 1860." NEQ, 45 (1972), 559-568.

4173 BAND, BENJAMIN. Portland Jewry, its growth and development. Portland: Jewish Historical Society, 1955. Pp. 117.

4174 _____ and JULES KREMS. Portland Jewry, supplement one. Portland: Jewish Historical Society, 1961. Pp. iii, 32. MeHi.

4175 BANGS, ELLA MATTHEWS. "An historic mansion." NEM, New Ser., 27 (1902-1903), 695-713.
Wadsworth-Longfellow House.

4176 _____. The story of the Woman's Literary Union of Portland, Maine. n.p., 1920. Unpaged. MeHi.

4177 BANKS, CHARLES EDWARD. "The destruction of Falmouth in 1775 and the responsibility therefor." MeHSC, 2 Ser., 5 (1894), 408-421.

4178 BASHFORD, JAMES WHITFORD. Outline history of Chestnut Street Methodist Episcopal Church, and directory of members. Portland: James S. Staples, 1887. Pp. 44. MeHi.

4178A BAXTER, JAMES PHINNEY. "New Casco Fort." MeHSC, 2 Ser., 9 (1898), 438-447.
Built in 1705.

4179 _____. The park system of Portland. Portland, 1905. Pp. 16.

4180 _____. "The story of Portland." NEM, New Ser., 13 (1895-1896), 349-370.

4181 BECKFORD, WILLIAM HALE and GEORGE W. RICHARDSON. Leading business men of Portland and vicinity; embracing Saco, Biddeford, Saccarappa and Deering. Boston: Mercantile Publishing, 1887. Pp. 228.

4182 "A 'BEETHOVEN Society' of 1819." MagHist, 7 (1908), 248-249.

4183 BENNETT, ERNEST NATHANIEL. "A temperance town." Nineteenth Century, 61 (1907), 87-96.

4184 BERRY, IRA. Sketch of the history of the Beethoven Musical Society, of Portland, Maine, 1819-1825. Portland: Stephen Berry, 1888. Pp. 48.

4185 BERRY, STEPHEN. History of Ancient Land-mark Lodge, No. 17, Free and Accepted Masons, Portland, Maine, from its organization in 1806 to 1880, inclusive. Portland, 1883. Pp. 204.

4186 _____. History of Mt. Vernon Chapter, No. 1, of Royal Arch Masons, Portland, Maine, from 1805 to 1878. Portland, 1879. Pp. 81. MeBa.

4187 _____. History of Portland Commandery, No. 2, of Knights Templar, including that of King Darius Council from 1805 to 1821, and of Maine Encampment No. 1, from 1821 till 1855, when its charter was given to Templars in the valley of the Kennebec. Portland, 1882. Pp. 139. MeBa.

4188 BIBLE SOCIETY OF MAINE. Act of incorporation and by-laws of the Bible Society of Maine with the by-laws of the trustees and a brief history of the society. Portland: Southworth Bros., 1896. Pp. 24. MeHi.

4189 BRANIN, M. LELYN. "The Dodge Pottery in Portland, Maine." OTNE, 59 (1968-1969), 75-84.

4190 _____. "The Lamson & Swasey Pottery in Portland, Maine." OTNE, 61 (1970-1971), 66-74.

4191 _____. "The Orcutt & Crafts Pottery in Portland, Maine." OTNE, 60 (1969-1970), 94-103.

4192 _____. "The Winslow Pottery in Portland." OTNE, 61 (1970-1971), 95-104.

4193 [BRINKLER, ALFRED]. "America's oldest music club celebrates golden jubilee; Rossini Club of Portland, Me., passes fiftieth anniversary." Musical America, 33 (February 5, 1921), 33.
Author attribution by the Bangor Public Library; signed with initials.

4194 PORTLAND

4194 _____. The Cathedral Church of Saint Luke, Portland, Maine: a history of its first century. Portland: House of Falmouth, 1967. Pp. 86.

4195 BURNHAM, EDITH. "Portland Observatory, or, the old brown tower." Americana, 4 (1909), 747-753.

4196 "THE BURNING of Falmouth, now Portland, Maine, Oct. 18, 1775." American Monthly Magazine, 11 (1838), 543-549.
Signed: G. F.

4197 BURRAGE, THOMAS J. "The Portland Charitable Dispensary and the Portland tuberculosis class." Maine Medical Association. Journal, 34 (1943), 174-176, 188.

4198 BURTON, ALFRED M. History of Atlantic Lodge, No. 81, Free and Accepted Masons, Portland, Me., from May 3, 1855, to Dec. 21, 1870. Portland: S. Berry, 1871. Pp. 31.

4199 CAIL, HAROLD L. "Famous American theatres." Theatre Arts, 40 (September, 1956), 69.
Jefferson Theatre.

4200 CALDERWOOD, CORNELIA L. The story of Victoria Mansion. [Portland]: Victoria Society of Maine Women, 1953. Pp. 15. MeHi.

4201 CAMMETT, STEPHEN. "The Longfellow town-- Portland, Maine." Putnam's Monthly and the Critic, 1 (1906-1907), 648-657.

4202 CARNES, JOSHUA A. A trip to Portland, with a descriptive view of the harbor, islands and scenery from the observatory on Munjoy Hill, also a graphic description of a week's rambles at Cape Elizabeth, Casco Bay.... Boston: Hill & Libbey, 1858. Pp. vi, 134.

4203 CHAMBERLAIN, MARY L. "Thanksgiving Day, 1898." Down East, 10 (November, 1963), 38-41.

4204 CHAPLIN, RUTH A. "The Anthoensen Press and the 'Gentlemen of the peaceful apple orchard.'" Print, 8 (February-March, 1954), 17-24.

4205 CHAPMAN, LEONARD BOND. "Land titles in Monument Square, Portland." MeHSC, 2 Ser., 3 (1892), 281-291.

4206 _____. "The mast industry of old Falmouth." MeHSC, 2 Ser., 7 (1896), 390-404.

4207 CHEVERUS HIGH SCHOOL, PORTLAND, ME. Cheverus High School, 50th anniversary, 1917-1967. Andrew J. Sedensky and James M. Keegan, eds. [Portland, 1967]. Pp. 40. MeHi.

4208 "THE CHILDREN'S Theatre of Portland, Maine." Maine Teachers' Digest, 4 (1943-1944), 12, 43.

4209 CHISHOLM, HUGH JOSEPH, b. 1886. A man in the paper industry, Hugh J. Chisholm (1847-1912). N.Y.: Newcomen Society in North America, 1952. Pp. 28.

4210 CHURCHILL, EDWIN A. "Merchants and commerce in Falmouth, (1740-1775)." MeHSN, 9 (1969-1970), 93-104.

4211 CLARK, CORNELIUS EDWARDS. "The building of the church," a sermon preached in the Woodfords Congregational Church, Portland, Maine, April 12, 1942. n.p., [1942?]. Unpaged. MeHi.

4212 "COMMERCIAL Portland, past and present." BTJ, 23 (1910-1911), 311-313, 315.

4213 CUMMINGS, GEORGE O. "Maine General Hospital: an historical sketch." Maine Medical Association. Journal, 51 (1960), 267-272, 279.

4214 CUMMINGS, OSMOND RICHARD. "Portland Railroad." Transportation, 11 (April, 1957), 1-42; 12 (January, 1959), 1-34.
Street railroad.

4215 CURRIER, ISABEL. "Tate House--Portland's historic landmark." Down East, 18 (July, 1972), 60-63.

4216 DALTON, ASA. A sermon on the history and principles of St. Stephen's Parish, Portland, Maine; preached July 4th, 1886.... Portland: B. Thurston, 1886. Pp. 20.

4217 DANA, EDWARD F. A bibliographical catalog: twenty-one years of the Anthoensen Press, 1947-1967.... Portland: Anthoensen Press, 1971. Pp. 75. MeHi.

4218 DANA, ISRAEL THORNDIKE. History of the Portland School for Medical Instruction: an address at the dedication of the new school rooms, and the opening of the eighteenth annual course, 17th of June, 1874, with remarks of Israel Washburn [and others]. Portland: Stephen Berry, 1874. Pp. 33.

4219 [DAVIS, DANIEL]. "The proceedings of two conventions, held at Portland, to consider the expediency of a separate government in the District of Maine." MHSC, 4 (1795), 25-40.
Both conventions held on September 6, 1786.

4220 DEANE, LLEWELLYN. Some reminiscences suggested by the semi-centennial celebration, October, 1881, of High Street Church, Portland, Maine.... [Washington, D.C., 1882]. Pp. 13.

4221 DEERING HIGH SCHOOL. Stroudwater sketches. n.p., 1938. Unpaged. MeHi.

4222 "THE DEERING Mansion in Portland, Maine." Sun Up, 2 (April, 1926), 11, 31.

4223 DIAMOND ISLAND ASSOCIATION. Great Diamond Island, Portland, Maine, 8000 B.C. to 1972 A.D. n.p., [1972]. Unpaged. MeHi.

4224 DORR, SUSAN ELVA. "Portland's oldest church." Cathedral Age, 23 (Summer, 1948), 26-27.
First Parish Church.

4225 DOW, EDWARD FRENCH and ORREN CHALMER HORMELL. City manager government in Portland, Maine. Orono: Univ. Pr., 1940. Pp. v, 119.

4226 DOW, STERLING THAYER. "The origin of the Portland, Maine Post Office." Mekeel's Weekly Stamp News, 67 (September 2, 1946), 191-192.

4227 DRISCOLL, JOSEPH A. and CARLETON POTTER SMALL. Preble Chapel in Portland, Maine, 1851-1951. n.p., [1951]. Unpaged. MBNEH.

4228 DRUMMOND, JOSIAH HAYDEN. History of Portland Lodge, No. 1, Free and Accepted Masons, Portland, Maine, from its organization (1769) to 1880. Portland: The Lodge, 1881. Pp. iv, 340.

4229 EDWARDS, GEORGE THORNTON. "'Highfield,' one of Longfellow's favorite haunts." Pine Tree Magazine, 7 (1907), 28-31.
Home of Alexander W. Longfellow.

4230 _____. The youthful haunts of Longfellow. Portland: G. T. Edwards, 1907. Pp. xxix, 205.

4231 ELDEN, ALFRED OWEN. "The Tate House, Stroudwater, Portland, Maine." OTNE, 26 (1935-1936), 138-140.

4232 ELWELL, EDWARD HENRY. Portland and vicinity, an illustrated souvenir and all-the-year-round guide to the city of Portland, with sketches of Old Orchard Beach, Cushing and Peak's Islands, and other famous resorts in the vicinity of Portland. (1876) [3d ed.]. Robert Grieve, ed. Portland: Loring, Short & Harmon, [1888?]. Pp. 162.

4233 _____. The schools of Portland, from the earliest times to the centennial year of the town, 1886. Portland: W. M. Marks, 1888. Pp. 37.

4234 EMERY, CARL S. Forest City (Portland, Maine). Portland, 1948. Pp. 149. MeP.

4235 FALES, MARTHA GANDY. "Benjamin Ilsley, cabinetmaker in federal Portland." Antiques, 105 (1974), 1066-1067.

4236 "FAREWELL to a birthplace." Yankee, 19 (November, 1955), 48.
Henry Wadsworth Longfellow; demolished in 1955.

4237 FEMALE ORPHAN ASYLUM OF PORTLAND. Semi-centennial report of the managers of the Female Orphan Asylum of Portland, October, 1878. Portland: Stephen Berry, 1878. Pp. 38. MeHi.
Includes historical sketch.

4238 FIRE service of Portland, a souvenir containing an account of the service from leather bucket times to the present fire department. Portland: Portland Firemen's Relief Association, 1888. Pp. 64. MB.

4239 "FIRST Baptist Church, Portland, Me." American Baptist Memorial, 13 (1854), 334-335.

4240 "THE FIRST printer in Maine." American Historical Record, 1 (1872), 331.
Benjamin Titcomb.

4241 FOBES, CHARLES BARTLETT. "The White Mountain Club of Portland, Maine, 1873-1884." Appalachia, 30 (1954-1955), 381-395.
Mountaineering society.

4242 FOBES, CHARLES S. "Changes in the commerce of Portland for half a century." BTJ, 16 (1903-1904), 314-316.

4243 "FORT McKinley and eleven years of C.M.T.C." Sun Up, 9 (May, 1931), 6-7.
Citizens' Military Training Camp.

4244 FRATERNITY CLUB, PORTLAND, ME. The book of the Fraternity Club, 1874-1924; issued in commemoration of the fiftieth anniversary of the organization of the club. Portland, 1925. Pp. 170.

4245 FREEMAN, FREDERIC WILLIAM. Mother Goose comes to Portland. Portland: Southworth Printing, 1918. Unpaged.
Caricatures and cartoons.

4246 FREEMASONS. PORTLAND, ME. ATLANTIC LODGE, NO. 81. 100th anniversary souvenir program and history of Atlantic Lodge, No. 81, A. F. and A. M., May 4 and 5, 1955. n.p., [1955?]. Pp. 45. MeP.

4247 FREEMASONS. PORTLAND, ME. PORTLAND LODGE, NO. 1. The one hundred and twenty fifth anniversary of Portland Lodge, No. 1, of Free and Accepted Masons, Portland, Maine, March 22, 1887. [Portland]: Published by the Committee, 1887. Pp. 33. MeBa.

4248 FREEMASONS. PORTLAND, ME. ROYAL AND SELECT MASTERS. PORTLAND COUNCIL. Historical sketch and by-laws of Portland Council of Royal and Select Masters. Portland: Stephen Berry, 1897. Pp. 48. MeHi.

4249 FRELLICK, ARLETTE F. Landmarks of Peaks Island, Maine. [Portland?], Temple V. Robinson, 1953. Unpaged. Me.

4250 PORTLAND

4250 FRENEAU, PETER. "When Longfellow was a Portland lad." CCJM, 27 (1914-1915), 439-443.

4251 THE GANNETTS: William Howard Gannett, Guy
Patterson Gannett. Portland: Southworth-
Anthoensen Pr., 1946. Pp. 16.
    Newspaper publishers.

4252 GILLESPIE, CHARLES BANCROFT. Portland past
and present. Portland: Evening Express,
1899. Pp. 236.

4253 GIVEN, CHARLES S. "The Portland Company."
RLHSB, No. 9 (1925), 6-14.
    Locomotive builders.

4254 GODFREY, EDWARDS. "Law and Maine." Maine
Alumnus, 46 (February-March, 1965), 8-9.
    University of Maine Law School.

4255 GOMME, LAWRENCE. "The 'Pirate of Portland'--
Thomas Bird Mosher." Maine Dig, 1 (Summer,
1967), 105-106; 2 (Winter, 1968), 90-93.

4256 GOODBAR, OCTAVIA WALTON. "The canal that
started a bank." Made in America Monthly,
12 (August, 1948), 8-9.
    Cumberland and Oxford Canal and the Canal
National Bank.

4257 GOODWIN, SHIRLEY B. 60th anniversary, Trinity
Episcopal Church, 1891 to 1951. [Portland?,
1951]. Pp. 66. Me.

4258 GOOLD, NATHAN. "Falmouth Neck in the Revolution." MeHSC, 2 Ser., 8 (1897), 66-95, 143-
169.

4259 _____. A history of Peaks Island and its
people; also a short history of House Island,
Portland, Maine. Portland: Lakeside Pr.,
1897. Pp. 84.

4260 _____. The Wadsworth-Longfellow House, Portland, Maine. Portland, 1969. Pp. 43.
    Revised by the Maine Historical Society from
the original 1908 publication.

4261 GOOLD, WILLIAM. "The burning of Falmouth (now
Portland), Maine, by a British squadron, in
1775." NEHGR, 27 (1873), 256-266.

4262 _____. "History of the Cumberland County
buildings in Portland." MeHSC, 2 Ser., 9
(1898), 292-308.

4263 _____. "John Taber & Son of Portland, and
their paper money." MeHSC, 2 Ser., 9 (1898),
128-132.
    1804.

4264 _____. Portland in the past; with historical
notes of old Falmouth. Portland: B. Thurston, 1886. Pp. 543.

4265 GOULD, WILLIAM EDWARD. "Portland banks."
MeHSC, 2 Ser., 4 (1893), 89-108.

4266 GRAND ARMY OF THE REPUBLIC. DEPARTMENT OF
MAINE. BOSWORTH POST, NO. 2, PORTLAND. Portland soldiers and sailors: a brief sketch of
the part they took in the War of the Rebellion; published for sale at the fair held in
Portland, June 2-7, 1884, in aid of the Soldiers and Sailors Monument. Portland: B.
Thurston, 1884. Pp. 56.

4267 GRANT, GEORGE FREDERICK. History of Deering
Lodge, No. 183, Free and Accepted Masons,
Portland, Maine, from the organization of the
lodge, April 2d, 1879, to February 11th, 1924.
[Portland]: Smith and Sale, 1924. Pp. viii,
203.

4268 GREATER PORTLAND LANDMARKS, INCORPORATED.
Portland. Architecture text, Patricia McGraw
Pancoast. History text, Josephine H. Detmer.
Portland, 1972. Pp. 236.

4269 GUIDE book for Portland and vicinity, to
which is appended a summary history of Portland, by Hon. Wm. Willis, with maps and six-
teen illustrations. Portland: B. Thurston
and J. F. Richardson, 1859. Pp. 104.

4270 HALE, AGNES BURKE. "The poets sang of Portland, Maine." Holiday, 12 (November, 1952),
79-83, 85-86.

4271 HALE, ROBERT. "Cushing's Island: a memoir."
Down East, 19 (September, 1972), 62-65, 80-82.

4272 _____ and AGNES BURKE HALE. Cushing's Island:
two memoirs. n.p., [1971?]. Pp. 62. MeHi.

4273 HALPERT, HAROLD KARL, ed. Temple Beth El,
dedication journal, 1950. 5711. Portland:
Maine Printing, 1950. Unpaged. MeHi.
    Includes a history of the temple.

4274 HAMBURGER, PHILIP PAUL. "Notes for a gazetteer: Portland, Maine." New Yorker, 36
(October 8, 1960), 177-179.
    Social life and customs.

4275 HAMLEN, JAMES HOPKINSON. J. H. Hamlen & Son,
Inc. 1846-1926. [Portland], 1926. Pp. iv,
14.
    Lumber.

4276 HAMMEL, MARGARET F. "F. M. O'Brien, Portland's antiquarian bookseller." American
Book Collector, 24 (October, 1973), 11-14.

4277 _____. "Victoriana." Down East, 20 (September, 1973), 55-59.
    Victoria Mansion.

4278 HATCH, BENTON LE ROY. A check list of the publications of Thomas Bird Mosher of Portland, Maine, MDCCCXCI [to] MDCCCXXIII ... with a biographical essay by Ray Nash. [Northampton, Mass.]: Gehenna Pr. for the Univ. of Massachusetts Pr., 1966. Pp. 211.

4279 HATCH, FRANCIS WHITING. "The 'Rebs' invade Portland Harbor." Yankee, 18 (July, 1954), 38-39.
    1863.

4280 HAYES, CHARLES WELLS. Twenty years of the second episcopate of Maine, an address in St. Luke's Cathedral, Portland, January 23, 1887. Westfield, N.Y.: Church Kalendar Pr., 1887. Pp. 25. MeHi.

4281 HEBERT, RICHARD A. "The making of Maine: the Burnham & Morrill Company." Pine Cone, 3 (Spring, 1947), 36-41.
    Food production and canning.

4282 HILTON, JOHN J. "Portland Harbor's Fort Gorges." Down East, 19 (June, 1973), 68-71.
    Built in 1864.

4283 "HISTORY of banking in Portland." CCJM, 29 (1916-1917), 303, 305, 307.

4284 HOLT, ERASTUS EUGENE. "The Portland Medical Club--1876 and 1902." JMS, 9 (1902-1903), 46-56.

4285 HOLVERSON, JOHN and WILLIAM DAVID BARRY. The McLellan-Sweat House, 1800: a brief guide. Portland: Portland Museum of Art, 1974. Pp. 12. MeHi.

4286 "THE HOUSE of a 'broad arrow' mast agent." Yankee, 29 (April, 1965), 72-73, 115-118.
    Tate House.

4287 HULL, JOHN THOMAS. Hand-book of Portland, Old Orchard, Cape Elizabeth and Casco Bay.... Portland: Southworth Bros., 1888. Pp. 246.

4288 _____. The siege and capture of Fort Loyall, destruction of Falmouth, May 20, 1690 (O. S.): a paper read before the Maine Genealogical Society, June 2, 1885. Portland: Owen, Strout, 1885. Pp. 116.

4289 ILSLEY, CHARLES PARKER. Centennials of Portland. 1675, 1775, 1875 and 1975. Somerville, Mass.: George B. King, 1876. Pp. 56.

4290 "AN INTRODUCTION to the State Street Church in Portland, Maine." MeCP, 51 (April 15, 1964), 3, 26.

4291 JACKSON, CHARLES E. "Maine Charitable Mechanic Association." Pine Tree Magazine, 7 (1907), 515-523.

4292 JACKSON, GEORGE STUYVESANT. A Maine heritage: the history of the Union Mutual Life Insurance Company. Portland, 1964. Pp. 221.

4293 JOHNSON, ALMON L. History of Atlantic Lodge, No. 81, Free and Accepted Masons, Portland, Me., from its organization May 3, 1855, to December 20, 1911, inclusive. Portland: Stephen Berry, 1912. Pp. 189. MeHi.

4294 JOHNSON, ARTHUR MENZIES. "Confederate raid on Portland Harbor." Down East, 7 (July, 1961), 52-54, 62-64.
    1863.

4295 JOHNSON, MARY KELLOGG. Longfellow's early home. Boston: H. H. Carter, 1905. Pp. 54.

4296 JOHNSON, THEODORE ELLIOT. "The great 'Portland meetings' of 1872." Shaker Quarterly, 12 (1972), 121-137.

4297 JONES, HERBERT GRANVILLE. Old Portland town. Portland: Machigonne Pr., 1938. Pp. 127.

4298 _____. When Dickens came to Portland. Portland: Machigonne Pr., 1938. Pp. 7. MeP.

4299 JONES, MARTHA YORK. "The Portland Glass Works." Antiques, 24 (1933), 56-57.

4300 KING, HENRY MELVILLE. Church of my boyhood: an address delivered at the seventy-fifth anniversary of the Free Street Baptist Church, Portland, Maine, Oct. 23, 1911. Providence, R.I.: F. H. Townsend, 1912. Pp. 16.

4301 LANE, CARLETON G. A Maine heritage: a brief history of Union Mutual Life Insurance Company, 1848-1968. N.Y.: Newcomen Society in North America, 1968. Pp. 28.

4302 "THE LAW of riot; the Portland riot." Monthly Law Report, New Ser., 8 (1855), 361-386.
    The Maine Historical Society attributes authorship to Charles Stewart Daveis.

4303 LEARY, PETER, JR. "The ancient defenses of Portland." MeHSC, 2 Ser., 7 (1896), 1-22.
    Fortifications.

4304 LEE, RUTH WEBB. "The tree of life and its sundry fruits." Antiques, 26 (1934), 141-143.
    Portland Glass.

4305 LINK, EUGENE P., ed. "Papers of the Republican Society of Portland, 1794-1796." NEQ, 16 (1943), 299-316.

4306 LINNELL, WILLIAM SHEPHERD. Asa W. H. Clapp (1805-1891), John A. Poor (1808-1871), General Neal Dow (1804-1897) and others: a short history of the Portland Gas Light Company. N.Y.: Newcomen Society in North America, 1950. Pp. 32.

4307 PORTLAND

4307　LONGFELLOW, SAMUEL. "The old Portland Academy: Longfellow's 'fitting school.'" NEQ, 18 (1945), 247-251.

4308　LONGFELLOW STATUE ASSOCIATION, PORTLAND, ME. Exercises at the unveiling of the statue of Henry Wadsworth Longfellow, Portland, Maine, Sept. 29, 1888. Portland: Brown, Thurston, 1888. Pp. 41.
　　　Oration by Charles F. Libby.

4309　LORING, PRENTISS. "Portland, past and present." BTJ, 5 (1892-1893), 360-362.

4310　LOTHROP, HARRY WOODWARD. The boys of eighty-five. n.p., n.d. Unpaged. MeHi.
　　　Reminiscences.

4311　LOWELL, CARRIE THOMPSON, comp. Impressions in and about Portland, Maine. Portland: A. W. Lowell, 1910. Pp. 46.

4312　MacDOUGALL, WALTER M. "The Portland Company: wood burning locomotives to atomic reactors." Down East, 10 (March, 1964), 46-50, 52-53.

4313　McELWAIN, HAROLD A. "Effective ministry in Portland's East End." The Northeast, 76 (January, 1949), 14-18.
　　　Saint Paul's Church.

4314　MacKAY, CONSTANCE D'ARCY. The historical pageant of Portland, Maine, produced on the Eastern Promenade as a free civic celebration of the Fourth of July, 1913. Portland: Southworth Print, 1913. Pp. 47.

4315　"THE McLELLAN-Sweat House at the Portland Museum of Art." Down East, 20 (June, 1974), 62-64.

4316　MacMILLAN, DONALD BAXTER. Portland Observatory, rededication address, Portland, Maine, Flag Day, June the fourteenth, 1939. n.p., [1939?]. Pp. 15. MeHi.

4317　McPHARLIN, PAUL. "The Anthoensen Press: printing for its true purpose." Publishers' Weekly, 153 (March 6, 1948), 1249-1254, 1256, 1258.

4318　MacVANE, LOUIS. "Winds of Portland." Sun Up, 9 (March, 1931), 14.
　　　Windmills.

4319　MacWILLIAMS, JAMES DONALD. A time for men. Lewiston: Twin City Printery, 1967. Pp. 161.
　　　Portland in 1866.

4320　MAINE. DIRECTORS OF PORT OF PORTLAND. Port of Portland, State of Maine, and its hinterland; being an orderly listing of all port and terminal facilities, including wharfage, depth of water, width of channels, towing, bunkering, lighterage, stevedoring, storage, bulk and general cargo handling equipment,

dry docks and ship repairs, port charges, administration and laws, etc. Clarence P. Day and William E. Meyer, eds. Portland, 1923. Pp. 89.

4321　"A MAINE boast." Sun Up, 2 (September, 1925), 12-13, 37, 40.
　　　Visits of famous musicians to Portland; signed "The Stroller," a local impresario.

4322　MAINE CHARITABLE MECHANIC ASSOCIATION. Constitution and history of the Maine Charitable Mechanic Association.... Portland: Bryant Pr., 1965. Pp. 101, 18. Me.

4323　_____. Constitution, instituted January 16, 1815, and incorporated June 14, 1815, with a historical sketch. Portland: Stephen Berry, 1896. Pp. 110.

4324　MAINE GENERAL HOSPITAL, PORTLAND. A sketch of the Maine General Hospital. Portland: Stephen Berry, 1872. Pp. 16.

4325　MAINE HISTORICAL SOCIETY. Centennial of the Maine Historical Society, April 11, 1922.... Portland, 1922. Pp. 51.

4326　MAINE SAVINGS BANK. 1859-1959. Portland, 1959. Pp. 32.

4327　[MANNING, PRENTICE CHENEY]. The semi-centennial anniversary of the Free Street Baptist Church, Portland, Me., September 26-27, 1886. Portland: Brown Thurston, 1887. Pp. viii, 88. MeHi.
　　　Author attribution by Joseph Williamson.

4328　MARSH, PHILIP M. "Maine's first newspaper editor: Thomas Wait." NEQ, 28 (1955), 519-534.
　　　Falmouth Gazette.

4329　MARSH, SCARBORO. "Cushing's Island." Pine Tree Magazine, 5 (1906), 564-571.

4330　"MEMORABLE events of the Catholic Church in Portland." MeCathHM, 8 (1919-1928), 9-11.
　　　1605-1869.

4331　MERRILL, PAUL E. Forty-six years a truckman: the story of Merrill Transport Company. N.Y.: Newcomen Society in North America, 1975. Pp. 26.

4332　MILLIKEN, TOMLINSON CO., PORTLAND. A history of the Milliken, Tomlinson Company, Portland, Maine. [Portland, 1965?]. Unpaged. MeHi.
　　　Grocers.

4333　MOLLOY, ANNE. "The Portland Stove Foundry." Down East, 13 (January, 1967), 28-29, 48-50.

4334　MORELAND, JAMES. "The theatre in Portland in the eighteenth century." NEQ, 11 (1938), 331-342.

4335 MORRILL, CHARLES S. "B & M," what two young Maine men founded 80 years ago! N.Y.: Newcomen Society in North America, 1950. Pp. 24.
Burnham and Morrill, food packagers.

4336 MOULTON, AUGUSTUS FREEDOM. Portland by the sea: an historical treatise. Augusta: Katahdin Publishing, 1926. Pp. 243.

4337 MOULTON, DAVID E. "History of the organization of the Portland Water District." New England Water Works Association. Journal, 43 (1929), 359-363.

4338 NEAL, JOHN. Account of the great conflagration in Portland, July 4th and 5th, 1866; and a new business guide giving removals, changes in business, etc. Portland: Starbird & Twitchell, 1866. Pp. 64, viii.

4339 _____. Portland illustrated. Portland: W. S. Jones, 1874. Pp. 160.

4340 NEALEY, ROBERT W. "Reminiscences of a Portland boyhood." Down East, 5 (May, 1959), 16-23.

4341 NELSON, BRUCE D. Portland: a collection of nineteenth-century engravings. Portland: Greater Portland Landmarks, 1976. 38 unnumbered leaves. MeU.

4342 NEW YORK INDUSTRIAL RECORDER. Portland, Maine, at the beginning of the 20th century, rapidly becoming the greatest mercantile centre in New England; showing its superior advantages on account of its shipping facilities and natural resources, with reviews of the leading business concerns who have helped to place it in its present proud position.... N.Y., 1900. Pp. 40.

4343 NEWTON, ROGER HALE. Victoria Mansion, Portland, Maine, an ante-bellum gem just rescued from wanton destruction. n.p., n.d. 3 leaves. MeBa.

4344 NICHOLS, ICHABOD. A discourse delivered at the dedication of the stone church, of the First Parish in Portland, February 9th, 1826; with an appendix containing a memoir of the parish. Portland: James Adams, Jr., 1826. Pp. 24.

4345 NICOLET, C. C. "Venture in independence." Outlook and Independent, 154 (April 16, 1930), 606-608, 636.
The Evening News.

4346 NOBLE, ROBERT E. "A glimpse of Portland, Maine, and its environs." Canadian Magazine, 5 (1895), 189-196.

4347 NORWOOD, LESLIE E. "Portland Head Light." SJMH, 11 (1923), 167-169.
First lighthouse on the Atlantic coast.

4348 _____. "Portland Observatory." SJMH, 12 (1924), 20-22.

4349 NOYES, EDWARD A. "History of banking in Portland." BTJ, 26 (1913-1914), 933, 935-937.

4350 "THE OLD church." Old Times, 2 (1878), 144-146.
Casco Street Baptist Church.

4351 "THE OLD Log Cabin Club of Portland." BTJ, 25 (1912-1913), 479.

4352 OLIPHANT, H. D. "Portland's finest eighty-two years ago." Sun Up, 9 (October, 1931), 20, 39.
Police department.

4353 "ONE HUNDRED years on Munjoy Hill." MeCP, 45 (March 15, 1958), 3.
St. Lawrence Congregational Church.

4354 OSGOOD, E. S. "Portland--its early romance and history." Sun Up, 3 (August, 1927), 7-10.

4355 OUR National Guard, historical sketch of Co's A.B.E.L., (2nd Battalion), 1st Reg. Inf., and Signal Corps, N.G.S.M. Portland: Southworth Bros, [1896?]. Unpaged. MeHi.

4356 "OVER one-hundred years in business." Maine's Own Magazine, 7 (January, 1929), 21, 31.
Byron Greenough and Company; men's clothing.

4357 OWEN, FRED K. "The Longfellows of Portland, Maine." SJMH, 10 (1922), 208-215.

4358 OWEN, MOSES. Ballads of Portland. Portland: W. S. Jones, 1874. Pp. 160.
Businessmen.

4359 PAIGE, EMELINE K. "Westbrook Junior College." Pine Cone, 6 (Winter, 1950-1951), 21-27.

4360 "A PARISH renaissance.' MeCathHM, 5 (December, 1915), 32-37.
St. Joseph's Church.

4361 "THE PASSING of a Portland industry." BTJ, 19 (1906-1907), 409-410.
Zenas Thompson & Brother, carriages.

4362 PAYSON, (H.M.) & CO. H. M. Payson & Co., partnership for 100 years, 1854-1954. n.p., [1954]. Pp. 24. MeHi.
Brokers.

4363 PEABODY, ELLEN ADAMS. Woolson School, home of the Girls' High School, Portland, Me., 1850-1863. n.p., 1903. Pp. 15. MeHi.

4364   PERKINS, DAVID PAGE. History of the Portland Society of the New Jerusalem, with a list of the secretaries, ministers, and members. Portland: Printed for the Society, 1883. Pp. 52. Me.

4365   PERKINS, JOHN CARROLL. "The First Parish in Portland." The Church Exchange, 4 (1896-1897), 66-67.
        First Parish Church.

4366   _____. How the First Parish became Unitarian ... historical sermon ... May 7, 1899. Portland: Stephen Berry, 1900. Pp. 22. MBC.

4367   _____. "Rev. Thomas Smith, D.D., and his First Parish of Falmouth, now Portland." MeHSC, 3 Ser., 1 (1904), 288-315.

4368   _____. Some old papers recently found in the stone tower of the First Parish Church of Portland; read before the Maine Historical Society, January 25, 1894. [Portland, 1894]. Pp. 30.

4369   PERRY, GEORGE SESSIONS. "The cities of America: Portland, Maine." Saturday Evening Post, 219 (July 13, 1946), 14-15, 64, 67, 69, 71.

4370   PERRY, WILLIAM STEVENS. A century of episcopacy in Portland: a sketch of the history of the Episcopal Church in Portland, Maine, from the organization of St. Paul's Church, Falmouth, November 4, 1763, to the present time. Portland, 1863. Pp. 16.

4371   PETERSON, ROGER C. "Fire, fog, and storm." The Quarterdeck, 2 (Winter, 1972), 7-9.
        Shipwrecks.

4372   PETTENGILL, BERTHA F. Sixty years with the Family Welfare Society. Portland: Portland Family Welfare Society, [1939]. Pp. 18. MeHi.

4373   PICTORIAL history, harbor defenses of Portland. Atlanta, Ga.: Army-Navy Publishers, 1941. Pp. 98. MeHi.

4374   PITMAN, LINWOOD T. One hundred years at Woodfords Congregational Church, United Church of Christ, Portland, Maine, 1872-1972. [Portland?], 1972. Pp. 61. MeHi.

4375   PORTER, CHARLES F. A brief history of works erected for the defense of Portland, Maine. Washington: Press of the [Army] Engineer School, 1904. Pp. 10.

4376   PORTLAND, ME. Centennial celebration: an account of the municipal celebration of the hundredth anniversary of the incorporation of the town of Portland, July 4th, 5th and 6th, 1886. John T. Hull, ed. Portland: Owen, Strout, 1886. Pp. 379.

4377   _____. City of Portland, Maine; the dedication of Lincoln Park being the public exercises held in the Payson Memorial Church and at Lincoln Park, February 12, 1909, in observance of the one hundredth anniversary of the birth of Abraham Lincoln. Portland: Smith & Sale, 1909. Pp. 35.
        Includes a brief history of Portland.

4378   _____. Exercises at dedication of the new City Hall and Memorial Organ, Portland, Maine, August 22, 1912; full text of the addresses delivered on that occasion, and a brief review of municipal action following the burning of the old City Hall, January 24, 1908. Portland: Southworth Printing, 1912. Pp. 79.

4379   PORTLAND, ME. BOARD OF TRADE. History of the Board of Trade of Portland, Maine; what it has originated and accomplished since its organization, constitution and by-laws, original and present membership.... Portland: Ford & Rich, 1887. Pp. 104.

4380   PORTLAND, ME. CHESTNUT STREET METHODIST EPISCOPAL CHURCH. Sesquicentennial program of the Chestnut Street Methodist Church, Portland, Maine, November 11 to 18, 1945; historical data.... Portland: Forest City Printing, 1945. Pp. 76. MeHi.

4381   _____. 1795-1895. Centennial of Chestnut Street Methodist Episcopal Church, Portland, Maine, November 7 to 10, 1895; a complete report of all proceedings. Portland: Thurston Print, 1896. Pp. 146.

4382   PORTLAND, ME. CITY PLANNING BOARD. Historic places in Portland. Portland, 1964. ii, 15 leaves. Me.

4383   PORTLAND, ME. FIRST BAPTIST CHURCH. Directory of the occupants of the pews ... April 1st, 1871, with historical notes ... from its origin to the present time. Portland: Ford & Perry, 1871. Pp. 16. MeHi.

4384   _____. One hundred and fifty golden years for Jesus Christ, being a history of the First Baptist Church, Portland, Maine. Portland, 1951. Pp. 55. MeHi.

4385   _____. The one hundredth anniversary, First Baptist Church of Portland, Maine; organized July twenty-fourth, MDCCCI.... Portland: Lefavor-Tower, [1901?]. Pp. 81.

4386   PORTLAND, ME. FIRST PARISH CHURCH. Baptisms and admission from the records of First Church in Falmouth, now Portland, Maine; with appendix of historical notes. Marquis F. King, comp. Portland: Maine Genealogical Society, 1898. Pp. 219.
        Appendix of historical notes concerns Portland and vicinity.

4387 _____. Bicentennial celebration commemorating the completion of two hundred years of worship on the present site, 425 Congress Street, July 20, 1941. n.p., 1941. Unpaged. Me.

4388 _____. The fiftieth anniversary of the dedication of the meeting house of the First Parish, Portland, Maine, February 8, 1826. [Portland]: Stephen Berry, 1876. Pp. 32.
Address by Thomas Hill.

4389 _____. Seventy-fifth anniversary of the dedication of the stone meetinghouse, First Parish, February 8, 1826--February 8, 1901. Portland, 1901. Pp. 91.

4390 PORTLAND, ME. FIRST UNIVERSALIST SOCIETY. Fiftieth anniversary of the First Universalist Society, Portland, Maine, Tuesday, April 18, 1871. Portland: Ford & Perry, 1871. Pp. 47. MBNEH.

4391 _____. Twenty-fifth anniversary of the dedication of the church, Feb. 13, 1890. [Portland, 1890]. Pp. 24.

4392 PORTLAND, ME. FREE STREET BAPTIST CHURCH. Catalogue of members of the Free Street Baptist Church, Portland, Me.; with historic notes, covenant, and by-laws. Portland: Thurston, 1886. Pp. 81.

4393 _____. Declaration of faith, with the church covenant, and list of members of the Free Street Baptist Church, Portland. Portland: Charles Day, 1837. Pp. 16. MeHi.
Includes a brief history of the church.

4394 _____. Directory of the Free St. Baptist Church, Portland, Maine. Portland: Brown Thurston, 1889. Pp. 47. MeHi.
Includes history.

4395 _____. The semi-centennial anniversary of the Free Street Baptist Church, Portland, Me. September, 26, 27, 1886. Portland: B. Thurston, 1887. Pp. 88. MeBa.

4396 PORTLAND, ME. HIGH STREET CONGREGATIONAL CHURCH. Services at the semi-centennial of High Street Church, Portland. Portland: Brown Thurston, [1881?]. Pp. 87.

4397 PORTLAND, ME. HOLY TRINITY HELLENIC ORTHODOX CHURCH. Golden jubilee, 1974; Holy Trinity Hellenic Orthodox Church. Portland, 1975. Pp. 138. MeP.

4398 PORTLAND, ME. HOUSING AUTHORITY. COMMISSION. Sagamore Village, 1943-1963, twenty years of progress. Portland, 1963. Unpaged. MeP.
Housing project.

4399 PORTLAND, ME. POLICE DEPARTMENT. The police manual, a manual containing historical sketches, aims and activities of the Portland Police Department, 1786 to 1925. Portland: Welch Printing, [1925]. Unpaged. MeHi.
History by Lawrence C. Dame.

4400 PORTLAND, ME. PUBLIC LIBRARY. Dedicatory exercises of the Baxter Building to the uses of the Portland Public Library and Maine Historical Society, Thursday, Feb. 21, 1889. Auburn: Lakeside Pr., 1889. Pp. 35.
Includes a history of the library by Edwin A. Noyes.

4401 _____. Portland Public Library and its predecessors, 1763-1949. Grace Trappan, comp. Portland, [1941?]. 15, 12 leaves. MeP.

4402 PORTLAND, ME. RENEWAL AUTHORITY. Portland renewal: a decade of planning progress, 1951-1961. [Portland, 1962]. Unpaged.

4403 PORTLAND, ME. ST. DOMINIC'S PARISH. Souvenir history of St. Dominic's Parish: twenty-fifth anniversary of the ordination of Rt. Rev. Monsignor Edward F. Hurley, at Portland, Maine, Nov. 1, 2, and 3, 1909. Portland: Printwell Printing, 1909. Pp. 138.

4404 _____. Souvenir program of the one hundredth anniversary of the founding of St. Dominic's Parish, Portland, Maine, October 7-8-9, 1930. Portland: Coughlin Pr., [1930?]. Unpaged. MBC.

4405 PORTLAND, ME. SAINT STEPHEN'S CHURCH. A book commemorating the one hundred and fiftieth anniversary of Saint Stephen's Church, Portland, Maine; the first Episcopal parish organized in the State of Maine. [Portland: Printwell Printing, 1913?]. Unpaged.

4406 _____. 185th anniversary of old St. Stephens, 1763-1948. n.p., [1948?]. Unpaged. MeP.

4407 PORTLAND, ME. SECOND PARISH CHURCH. History and manual of the Second Parish Church, Portland, Maine.... Portland: Smith & Sale, 1912. Pp. 42. MBC.

4408 _____. A history and manual of the Second Parish Church of Portland, Me., with a list of members. Portland: Smith & Sale, 1898. Pp. 71.

4409 PORTLAND, ME. STAPLES SCHOOL. The reunion of Master Franklin Staples' school boys, April 19, 1901. Nathan Goold, ed. Portland: Lakeside Pr., 1901. Pp. 70.

4410 PORTLAND, ME. STATE STREET CHURCH. Manual, State Street Congregational Church, with a brief historical sketch. Portland, 1904. Pp. 74. Me.

4411 _____. State Street Church, Portland, Maine, 1852-1902: services in commemoration of the organization of the church, March seventeenth, 1852, and of the dedication of its house of worship on June second, 1852, held in the church June 1st and 2d, 1902. Boston: Thomas Todd, [1902]. Pp. 140.

4412 PORTLAND, ME. STEVENS AVENUE CONGREGATIONAL CHURCH. The seventy-fifth anniversary of the Stevens Avenue Congregational Church, (United Church of Christ), 1886-1961. n.p., [1961]. Pp. 24. MBC.

4413 PORTLAND, ME. WILLISTON CHURCH. Tenth anniversary memorial and directory of Williston Church, 1873-1883. Portland: B. Thurston, [1883]. Pp. 40.
Includes historical sermon by Frank E. Clark.

4414 _____. Twentieth anniversary of Williston Church, Portland, Me., 1873-1893. Portland, 1893. Pp. 53.

4415 PORTLAND, ME. WOODFORDS CONGREGATIONAL CHURCH. 50th anniversary, 1872-1922, Woodfords Congregational Church, Portland, Maine. n.p., [1922]. Unpaged. MeHi.

4416 _____. Manual of the Woodfords Congregational Church, Portland, Maine, with historical sketch. n.p., 1929. Pp. 17. MeHi.

4417 "PORTLAND." Maine Central, 3 (1895-1896), 58, 60, 62, 64, 66.

4418 PORTLAND BENEVOLENT SOCIETY. Portland Benevolent Society, 1803-1903; exercises in recognition of the Society's centennial, held in the First Parish Church, Portland, Maine, February 15, 1903. Portland: Stephen Berry, 1903. Pp. 36.

4419 PORTLAND CADETS. Portland Cadets' semicentennial, Congress Square Hotel, Portland, Maine, January 3, 1920. n.p., [1919?]. Unpaged. MeHi.
Includes a history by J. H. Dow.

4420 "PORTLAND Custom House and its collectors." BTJ, 12 (1899-1900), 38.

4421 PORTLAND MARINE SOCIETY. Exercises at the centennial celebration of the Portland Marine Society, February 27th, 1896. Portland: William M. Marks, 1896. Pp. 50. Me.

4422 PORTLAND MEDICAL CLUB. Anniversary exercises, 1876-1902. History and statistics by Erastus Eugene Holt. Portland: Marks Printing House, 1903. Pp. 15. MeP.

4423 "PORTLAND newspapers and printers of fifty years ago." BTJ, 14 (1901-1902), 232.

4424 "PORTLAND Observatory." BTJ, 12 (1899-1900), 82.

4425 "PORTLAND painters." Portland Magazine, 1 (1834-1835), 121-123, 147-149, 243-246.
Charles Codman, Frederic Mellen, and Joseph T. Harris.

4426 PORTLAND postal guide together with an historical sketch of postal affairs in Portland. ... [Portland]: Macdonald Bros., 1900. Pp. 38. MeHi.

4427 PORTLAND ROSSINI CLUB. Golden anniversary of the Portland Rossini Club, Portland, Frye Hall, January 21st, 1921. n.p., [1921?]. Pp. 32. MeHi.
Includes a history of the club.

4428 _____. 100th anniversary of the Portland Rossini Club, Portland, Maine, Frye Hall, 2:30 P.M., February fourteenth, 1971. n.p., [1971?]. Unpaged. MeHi.

4429 PORTLAND SAVINGS BANK. Portland Savings Bank: the first century, 1852-1952. Portland: Anthoensen Pr., 1952. Pp. 25. Me.

4430 _____. The story of fifty years of the Portland Savings Bank, 1852-1902. Portland, [1902]. Pp. 31.

4431 "THE PORTLAND Society of Natural History; from 1866 to 1869." Portland Society of Natural History. Proceedings, 1 Pt. 2 (1869), 193-203.

4432 "PORTLAND--the metropolis of Maine." CCJM, 28 (1915-1916), 95-99, 101-103, 105.

4433 PORTLAND WATER DISTRICT. Over a century of water service, 1869-1972. [Portland, 1972]. Pp. 24. MeP.

4434 _____. Portland Water Company, water supply, rates, rules, and regulations, with a sketch of its history, charter, &c., &c. Portland: William M. Marks, 1881. Pp. 55. MeHi.
History is by Dennis W. Clark.

4435 PORTLAND YACHT CLUB. Portland Yacht Club, 1869-1963. n.p., [1963?]. Pp. 124. Me.

4436 "THE PORTLAND Y.M.C.A. is fifty years old." BTJ, 16 (1903-1904), 232.

4437 POTTER, NELLIE. "The Longfellow Garden." Sun Up, 8 (July, 1930), 4-5.

4438 _____. The Longfellow Garden of yesterday and today. (1924) 3d ed. Portland: Longfellow Garden Club, 1926. Pp. 44.

4439 RAND, EMILY K. The Portland Rossini Club, Portland, Maine, 1871-1896. Portland: Stephen Berry, [1896?]. Pp. 41. MeHi.

4440 READ, JAMES N. and WILLIAM H. SMITH. A synopsis of the history of Eastern Star Encampment, No. 2, I.O.O.F., from its organization, April 10, 1844, up to July 1, 1875. Portland: Spaulding & Drinkwater, 1875. Pp. 21. MeHi.

4441 "RECORD of harbor work done here since 1836." BTJ, 15 (1902-1903), 142.

4442 [RICH, MARSHALL NYE]. "Collectors of customs at Portland, Maine." BTJ, 15 (1902-1903), 140.
    Signed M. N. R.; attribution is by the editor.

4443 _____. "Portland, the metropolis of Maine." National Magazine, 15 (1901-1902), 712-717.

4444 "RISE and progress of the city of Portland." BTJ, 11 (1898-1899), 237-239.

4445 ROCKWOOD, CHARLES M. "Portland 1920." NEM, New Ser., 42 (1910), 531-544.

4446 ROLLINS, SARAH R. Early years at the Maine General Hospital. Portland, 1941. Pp. 23. MeHi.

4447 ROUNDY, RODNEY W. "State Street centennial." MeCP, 39 (April 15, 1952), 14-15.
    State Street Congregational Church.

4448 ROWE, MARIAN BRADFORD. "History of the Maine Historical Society." New England Social Studies Bulletin, 11 (October, 1953), 20-27.
    Also appeared in MeLAB, 14 (November, 1953), 3-7.

4449 _____. "Woodfords Congregational Church." MeCP, 50 (April 15, 1963), 31.

4450 ROWELL, GEORGE SMITH. "Maine's first newspaper." MeLB, 6 (1916-1917), 50-52.
    Falmouth Gazette.

4451 ROWLAND, ELIZABETH McLELLAN GOULD. Story of the Girls' High School of Portland, Maine, 1850-1863. Lee, Mass.: Valley Gleaner, 1897. Pp. 46. MeHi.

4452 RUGG, HENRY W. "Ancient Land-Mark Lodge." FR, 12 (1882-1883), 273-274.
    Freemasons.

4453 "ST. JOSEPH'S Academy." MeCathHM, 2 (April, 1914), 21-26.

4454 "ST. PAUL'S,--St. Stephen's,--St. Luke's: the background of Portland's oldest parishes." The Northeast, 76 (May, 1949), 9-12.

4455 SARGENT, RUTH. "Summer stock--where it all began." Down East, 22 (July, 1976), 86-87.
    Greenwood Garden Theater, Peaks Island.

4456 SARGENT, WILLIAM MITCHELL. An historical sketch, guide book, and prospectus of Cushing's Island, Casco Bay, coast of Maine. N.Y.: American Photo-engraving, 1886. Pp. 100.

4457 SEARS, DONALD A. "Libraries and reading habits in early Portland (1763-1836)." MeHSN, 12 (1972-1973), 151-164.

4458 _____. "Portland's early experiments in adult education." MeHSN, 10 (1970-1971), 11-20.
    1820s to 1840s.

4459 SHAILER, WILLIAM HOSMER. A discourse preached on the occasion of the seventy-fifth anniversary of the First Baptist Church in Portland, July 23, 1876. Portland: B. Thurston, 1876. Pp. 24. Me.

4460 SHARPE, PHILIP B. "The Portland Auto Show of 1907." Maine's Own Magazine, 8 (January, 1930), 8, 31-32.

4461 SHETTLEWORTH, EARLE G., JR. A history of the Heseltine School. Portland, 1966. 16 leaves. MeHi.
    Demolished in 1962.

4462 _____ and JOHN E. PANCOAST. Portland historic resources inventory. Augusta: Maine Historic Preservation Commission, 1976. 98 leaves. MeHi.

4463 SHETTLEWORTH, EARLE G., JR. "Portland, Maine, engravers of the 1820s." OTNE, 61 (1970-1971), 59-65, 105-110.

4464 _____. "The Radford brothers, Portland cabinetmakers of the Federal period." Antiques, 106 (1974), 285-289.

4464A SILLIMAN, VINCENT BROWN. "An early Unitarian Society in Portland, Maine." UHSP, 2 Pt. 1, (1931), 31-36.
    Unitarian Society of the town of Portland.

4465 _____. "Portland, Biddeford and early American Unitarianism." The Maine Unitarian, (Spring, 1946), [24-37].

4466 SILLS, CHARLES MORTON. Historical sketch of St. Luke's Parish, Portland, Me., delivered ... July 4th, 1886. Portland: B. Thurston, 1886. Pp. 16. MeHi.

4467 "SISTERS of Mercy, fifty years in Portland." MeCathHM, 8 (1919-1928), 89-106.

4468 "SIXTIETH anniversary, Portland Board of Trade." BTJ, 26 (1913-1914), 891-893, 895, 897, 899-901, 903.

4469 PORTLAND

4469 "SIXTY years in Woodfords: the history of
Trinity Parish." The Northeast, 79 (January,
1952), 3-9.

4470 SLEEPER, FRANK. "Portland, Maine." Sun Life
Review, 23 (October-November, 1966), 6-9.

4471 SMALL, CARLETON POTTER. "Church bells." The
Maine Unitarian, (Spring, 1946), [10-11].

4472 _____, ed. The diaconate of the First Parish
Church in Portland, Maine. n.p., 1944.
Pp. 40. MeHi.

4473 _____. Notes on music in the First Parish,
Portland, Maine, 1740-1942. Portland: Fred
L. Tower, [1942?]. Pp. 20. MB.

4474 _____. The sextons, bells, and ringers of
the First Parish Church of Portland. Portland: Fred L. Tower, 1943. Pp. 36. MBNEH.

4475 SMITH, ALONZO W. "Portland's parks and prom-
enades." BTJ, 19 (1906-1907), 455, 457, 459,
461.

4476 SMITH, ELMER J. "Good spirit and hard work
further God's work: a short history of St.
Peter's East Deering." The Northeast, 76
(September, 1949), 7-9.

4477 SMITH, FRANCIS ORMOND JONATHAN. A statement
of facts, concerning the history and manage-
ment of the Portland Gas Light Company....
[Portland, 1852]. Pp. 20.

4478 SMITH, JOSEPH COBURN. "Portland Camera Club:
75 years of photographic fun in Maine."
Down East, 20 (March, 1974), 41, 76-77.

4479 SMITH, MASON PHILIP. "Tate House in Stroudwater, Maine." Antiques, 84 (1963), 172-174.

4480 SMITH, THOMAS. Journals of the Rev. Thomas
Smith, and the Rev. Samuel Deane, pastors of
the First Church in Portland; with notes and
biographical notices, and a summary history of
Portland. (1821) 2d ed. William Willis, ed.
Portland: Joseph S. Bailey, 1849. Pp. vi,
483.
First edition was edited by Samuel Freeman.

4481 SOCIETY OF COLONIAL WARS. MAINE. Fort New
Casco.... n.p., 1929. Pp. 24. Me.
Includes historical address by Clarence
Hale.

4482 "SOMETHING of Portland's history." BTJ, 27
(1914-1915), 53, 55, 57, 59.

4483 SPEAR, PEARL S. The old sailor's story of
his life, written by himself. Portland:
Southworth Bros., 1888. Pp. 133.

4484 STANSBURY, HELEN. "The Victoria Mansion."
Down East, 2 (May, 1956), 20-25.

4485 STERLING, ROBERT THAYER. "The Portland Head
Light." Yankee, 2 (March, 1936), 23-24.

4486 STEWART, KATHERINE WALLACE. Peaks Island--as
it was; a memory-tour of the island--in its
heyday. Portland: H. S. Kinsman, 1962. 25
leaves. MeP.

4487 THE STORY of the landing of Capt. Moodey and
his soldiers on Falmouth Neck (Portland) in
June 1716. [Portland]: Southworth Printing,
1916. Pp. 15. MeHi.

4488 STRATTON, ARTHUR. "The Anthoenson Press, 105
Middle Street, Portland 6, Maine." BA, 21
(February, 1947), 2-6.

4489 STUART, JESSIE. A short history of Little
Diamond Island. [Portland?], 1961. 20, 3
leaves. Me.

4490 SWAN, FRANK HERBERT. Portland glass. (1949)
Rev. and enl. by Marion Dana. Des Moines:
Wallace-Homestead, [1969?]. Pp. xiii, 106.

4491 _____. Portland Glass Company. Providence,
R.I.: Roger Williams Pr., 1939. Pp. 127.

4492 THOMAN, RICHARD S. "Portland, Maine: an
economic-urban appraisal." Economic Geography, 27 (1951), 349-367.

4493 THOMAS, WILLIAM WIDGERY, 1873-1946. 115th
anniversary; being a brief history of the
Canal National Bank of Portland. Portland:
Canal National Bank, [1941]. Unpaged. MeHi.

4494 THOMPSON, FLORENCE WHITTLESEY. "Early
churches in Portland." SJMH, 9 (1921), 81-83.

4495 THOMPSON, WINFIELD MARTIN. "A Confederate
raid." The Rudder, 16 (1905), 130-136, 243-
250.
An 1863 attack on the revenue cutter 'Caleb
Cushing.'

4496 THURSTON, NORMAN W. "Cape Steam was built on
old dry dock site." Exciter, 43 (November,
1961), 6-7, 16.

4497 THWING, EDWARD PAYSON. "Portland churches."
CongQ, 16 (1874), 259-263.
Limited to Congregational churches.

4498 TOBIE, WALTER E. "According to their lights,
MGH--O.S." Maine Medical Association. Jour-
nal, 36 (1945), 23-29.
Maine General Hospital.

4499 TODD, ALDEN. A spark lighted in Portland:
the record of the National Board of Fire Underwriters. N.Y.: McGraw-Hill, 1966.
Pp. 231.
The Board was established as a result of
the Portland fire of 1866.

4500 TODD, JOHN M. A sketch of the life of John M. Todd (sixty-two years in a barber shop) and reminiscences of his customers. Portland: W. W. Roberts, 1906. Pp. vii, 322.
Social life and customs.

4501 TREFETHEN, JESSIE B. A history of Brackett Memorial Church. n.p., [1961]. Pp. 9. MeHi.

4502 _____. Trefethen, the family and the landing. Portland: House of Falmouth, 1960. Pp. 61.

4503 TREMBLAY, WILFRID. "A trip through the Portland organ." Maine's Own Magazine, 7 (September, 1929), 11, 43, 46.

4504 TRUE, LATHAM. Ten years of the Kotzschmar Club.... Portland: Kotzschmar Club, 1910. Pp. 28. MeHi.
Musical society.

4505 U. S. ENGINEER DEPARTMENT. BOARD OF ENGINEERS FOR RIVERS AND HARBORS. The port of Portland, Maine. Washington: Govt. Print. Off., 1937. Pp. x, 125.

4506 VAN TRUMP, JAMES D. and ARTHUR P. ZIEGLER, JR. "Thomas Bird Mosher: publisher and pirate." Book Collector, 11 (1962), 295-312.

4507 VERRILL, ROBINSON. Story of the firm of Verrill, Dana, Walker, Philbrick & Whitehouse, 1862-1962. Rockland: Seth Low Pr., 1962. Pp. 77.
Law firm.

4508 VIRGIN, HARRY R. "The Constitutional Convention of 1819." MeHSC, 3 Ser., 2 (1906), 416-464.

4509 "THE WADSWORTH-Longfellow House and its distinguished occupants." BTJ, 15 (1902-1903), 240-241.

4510 WALZ, WILLIAM EMMANUEL. "Our law school: its origin, its life, and its work." Maine Law Review, 6 (1912-1913), 309-317.
University of Maine, Portland-Gorham; the school was located in Bangor when this article was published.

4511 WARREN, JOHN C. "The burning of Falmouth." Pine Tree Magazine, 7 (1907), 152-157.

4512 _____. "Portland privateers of the past." Pine Tree Magazine, 6 (1906-1907), 296-299.
War of 1812.

4513 WEISS, HARRY B. "Twelve toy books of the past mid-century." American Book Collector, 1 (1932), 91-93.
Bailey & Noyes, printers.

4514 WENTWORTH, HOWARD L., JR. History of the Portland Marine Society. n.p., [1969?]. 21 leaves. MeHi.

4515 "WEST Congregational Chapel, Portland, Me." CongQ, 6 (1864), 134-137.

4516 WESTBROOK JUNIOR COLLEGE, PORTLAND, ME. 125th anniversary celebration, 1831-1956. n.p., [1956]. Unpaged. MeP.

4517 WESTON, ISAAC. "The theater in Portland; sixty years ago." Northern Monthly, 1 (1864), 387-389.

4518 WEYGAND, JAMES LAMAR. "The Yellow Kid Press." American Book Collector, 19 (March, 1969), 26-27.

4519 "THE WHARVES of Portland, Maine." BTJ, 25 (1912-1913), 179, 181-182.

4520 WHEELER, WILLIAM A. The Maine Central Railroad, 1847-1947. [Portland]: Maine Central Railroad Company, 1947. Pp. 23. MeBa.

4521 "WHEN Lafayette came to Portland." Sun Up, 9 (June, 1931), 29.
1825.

4522 WILLARD, BENJAMIN J. Captain Ben's book: a record of the things which happened to Capt. Benjamin J. Willard, pilot and stevedore, during some sixty years on sea and land, as related by himself. Portland: Lakeside Pr., 1895. Pp. 204.
Seafaring life.

4523 NO ENTRY.

4524 WILLIS, WILLIAM. The history of Portland; a facsimile of the 1865 ed. with a new foreword by Gerald Morris. 2d ed., rev. and enl. Somersworth, N.H.: New Hampshire Publishing, 1972. Pp. xiii, 928.
First edition was published in two volumes, 1831-1833.

4525 _____. "Introductory address before the Maine Historical Society, February 2, 1855, at Augusta." MeHSC, 4 (1856), 3-28.
History of the Society.

4526 _____. "The Maine Historical Society." HistMag, 2 Ser., 3 (1868), 13-17.

4527 _____. "Old Falmouth in 1749." SJMH, 2 (1914-1915), 87-88.

4528 WOOD, ELSIE. "The Portland Public Library." Pine Cone, 6 (Autumn, 1950), 13-17.

4529 "WRECKING of the Annie C. MacGuire." Sun Up, 2 (June, 1925), 10, 25, 27.
An 1886 shipwreck.

4530 WRITERS' PROGRAM. MAINE. Portland city guide. Portland: Forest City Printing, 1940. Pp. xlv, 337.

4531 NO ENTRY.

4532   YERXA, DONALD A. "The burning of Falmouth, 1775: a case study of British imperial pacification." MeHSQ, 14 (1974-1975), 119-160.

4533   YOUNG MEN'S REPUBLICAN CLUB, PORTLAND, ME. Young Men's Republican Club, its history, by laws, committee rules, list of officers, list of members, etc. Portland: Brown Thurston, 1890. Pp. 52. MeHi.

    SEE ALSO entries 168, 799, 1483, 1487, 1492, 1512, 1514, and 1534.

POWNAL (CUMBERLAND CO.)

4534   BRITT, BENJAMIN H. The ranger's history of Bradbury Mt. State Park, Pownal, Maine. [Freeport]: Freeport Pr., [1942?]. Pp. 15. Me.

4535   LATHAM, ETTIE J. History of the town of Pownal written for its centennial, Sept. 2, 1908. Lewiston: Lewiston Journal, 1908. Pp. 40.

4536   TRUE, NATHANIEL TUCKERMAN. "The Merrill Road, Pownal, Maine." Old Times, 4 (1880), 589-591.

4537   ———. "Peculiar people." Old Times, 3 (1879), 417-422.
    Biographies.

4538   ———. "Sketch of the pioneers of the Merrill Road, Pownal, Maine." Old Times, 8 (1884), 1135-1138.

PRENTISS PLANTATION (PENOBSCOT CO.)

4539   No items located.

PRENTISS TOWNSHIP (SOMERSET CO.)

4540   No items located.

PRESQUE ISLE (AROOSTOOK CO.)

4541   BARTER, J. MALCOLM. "The horse John R. Braden." Down East, 21 (October, 1974), 46-47, 65.

4542   CARTER, BERTHA. "Not bear, nor all potatoes. ..." Maine Teachers' Digest, 2 (1941-1942), 84-85, 88.
    Aroostook State Normal School, now University of Maine at Presque Isle.

4543   DUNN, CHARLES, JR. Cloudman Hill heritage. Northampton, Mass.: Marion E. Dodd, 1939. Pp. 37. MeHi.

4544   FLIGHT of the snowgoose, a history of the Presque Isle USO. n.p., [1946?]. Variously leaved. [MePriT].
    United Service Organization.

4545   LAMOREAU, MRS. PAUL DAVID. History, 1865-1965, Congregational Church, Presque Isle, Maine. n.p., [1965]. Pp. 52. MBC.

4546   PATTEN, ROLAND TAYLOR. 1783-1931, important data in the history of Presque Isle. Presque Isle: Star-Herald, [1932]. Unpaged. Me.

4547   PRESQUE ISLE CIVIC ROUNDTABLE, INC. Presque Isle centurama, 1859-1959. Edith Fairweather, ed. n.p., [1959]. Unpaged. Me.

4548   ROLFE, DAVID. "Presque Isle: city with a spirit." Down East, 5 (July, 1959), 42-45.

4549   TAYLOR, STANLEY R., C. RAYMOND WARD, and A. ERNEST SMITH. History of Trinity Lodge, No. 130, Presque Isle, Maine, from July 28, 1865 to December 31, 1954. n.p., [1955?]. Pp. 118. MeU.
    Freemasons.

4550   WELSH, STANLEY. "A Christian harvest in agricultural Aroostook: Saint John's Parish, Presque Isle." The Northeast, 77 (May, 1950), 12-14.

4551   [WHITE, MYRTLE T. M.]. Presque Isle, 1820-1920. [Presque Isle: Star Herald Publishing, 1920]. Unpaged. MeHi.
    Authorship and imprint from a newspaper clipping mounted in a copy at the Maine Historical Society.

    SEE ALSO entry 50.

PRINCETON (WASHINGTON CO.)

4552   BELMORE, BRUCE WEATHERBY. Early Princeton, Maine. Princeton, 1945. Pp. 219.

4553   FREEMASONS. PRINCETON, ME. LEWY'S ISLAND LODGE, NO. 138. History of Lewy's Island Lodge, No. 138, of Free and Accepted Masons, Princeton, Maine, from 1866 to [1890]. Portland: Stephen Berry, 1870-1893. 3v. MeBa.

    SEE ALSO entry 1840.

PROSPECT (WALDO CO.)

4554   DUNNACK, HENRY ERNEST. A history of Fort Knox State Park. Augusta: State Park Commission, [1960?]. Pp. 22. Me.

RAINBOW TOWNSHIP (PISCATAQUIS CO.)

4555   No items located.

RANDOLPH (KENNEBEC CO.)

4556   RANDOLPH, ME. 75th anniversary celebration, town of Randolph, Maine, August 9, 10, and 11, 1962. Gardiner: Knight Printing, 1962. Unpaged. MeP.

SEE ALSO entries 1624, 1629, and 1648-1649.

RANGELEY (FRANKLIN CO.)

4557   GOLDER, ARTHUR L. "The Rangeley Lakes." NEM, New Ser., 22 (1900), 565-586.

4558   HAINES, ZENAS THOMPSON and BARBARA A. BRUCE, eds. Squire Rangeley's township, the early days--1837 to 1849. Rangeley: Highland Publishers, 1970. Pp. 72. Me.

4559   HOAR, JOEL SHERMAN. Pioneer days of Rangeley, Maine. Rangeley, 1928. Pp. 46.

4560   LAMBERT, SAMUEL W., JR. The Oquossoc Angling Association, 1870-1970. Meriden, Conn.: Meriden Gravure, 1970. Pp. 84. MeHi.

4561   WILLARD, LAWRENCE F. "Boobytown." Yankee, 28 (November, 1964), 94-97, 137-138, 141-143. Shipment of Lewiston's poor to Rangeley in 1850.

RANGELEY PLANTATION (FRANKLIN CO.)

4562   No items located.

RAYMOND (CUMBERLAND CO.)

4563   DINGLEY, THEDA C. "Hawthorne's boyhood in Raymond, Maine." Sun Up, 8 (October, 1930), 24-25.

4564   DOLLEY, MIRA L. 150th anniversary, town of Raymond, Maine, 1803-1953. n.p., 1953. Pp. 24. Me.

4565   KNIGHT, ERNEST HARMON. The origin and history of Raymondtown. Norway: Oxford Hills Pr., 1974. Pp. v, 106. Me.

4566   RAYMOND, ME. 150th anniversary, town of Raymond, Maine, 1803-1953. Raymond, 1953. Pp. 24. MeP.

SEE ALSO entries 1508 and 1514.

READFIELD (KENNEBEC CO.)

4567   FRENCH, EDWIN RUTHVEN. History of Maine Wesleyan Seminary. Portland: Smith & Sale, 1919. Pp. 42.

4568   GREENE, JONAS. The crown won but not worn; or, M. Louise Greene, a student of five years at Kent's Hill, Me. Boston, 1868. Pp. iv, 162.

4569   KENT'S HILL SCHOOL, READFIELD, ME. Kent's Hill, 1824-1974, sesquicentennial. n.p., [1974?]. Pp. 36. MeU.

4570   "MAINE Wesleyan Seminary." American Quarterly Register, 2 (1829-1830), 110-112.

4571   "MAINE Wesleyan Seminary and Female Collegiate Institute." Maine Teacher and School Officer, 4 (1861-1862), 65-68.

4572   NEWTON, JOHN O. and OSCAR E. YOUNG. Kent's Hill and its makers. Farmington: Knowlton & McLeary, 1947. Pp. 228. Kent's Hill School.

4573   PAGE, MARY SCHULTZE. Reflections of Readfield. Farmington: Knowlton & McLeary, 1975. Pp. 56. Me.

REDINGTON TOWNSHIP (FRANKLIN CO.)

4574   No items located.

REED PLANTATION (AROOSTOOK CO.)

4575   No items located.

RICHARDSONTOWN TOWNSHIP (OXFORD CO.)

4576   No items located.

RICHMOND (SAGADAHOC CO.)

4577   FERRISS, LLOYD. "Richmond, 1823-1973." Down East, 19 (April, 1973), 44-49.

4578   FLEMING, JOHN DALY. Richmond on the Kennebec. Compiled from the manuscripts of Walter H. Sturtevant and Ruie L. Curtis.... Richmond: Richmond Historical Committee, 1966. Pp. viii, 198.

4579   LIBBY, ABIAL. History of Richmond Lodge, No. 63, of Free and Accepted Masons, from January 1st, 1850, to January 10th, 1886. Richmond: Ray Thompson, 1886. Pp. 34. Me.

4580   RICHARDS, CHARLES W. A historical almanac,
        1888, containing historical matter concerning
        the town of Richmond, collected from town
        records and other sources, and arranged by
        months, under each date.... Richmond: Bee
        Steam Job Print, 1887. Unpaged.

4581   RICHMOND HISTORICAL AND CULTURAL SOCIETY.
        Richmond, a long view, 1823-1973: pictorial
        supplement to "Richmond on the Kennebec."
        Richmond, 1973. Unpaged. Me.

4582   STURTEVANT, WALTER HENRY. Old Richmond on
        the Kennebec, a history. Richmond, 1938.
        Unpaged. MeHi.
            A prospectus for a work which was "to be
        published in the summer of 1938" but which
        never appeared; includes a brief historical
        synopsis.

4583   THAYER, HENRY OTIS. "Fort Richmond, Maine."
        MeHSC, 2 Ser., 5 (1894), 129-160.

        SEE ALSO entry 3532.

RILEY TOWNSHIP (OXFORD CO.)

4584   No items located.

RIPLEY (SOMERSET CO.)

4585   No items located.

ROBBINSTON (WASHINGTON CO.)

4586   KEENE, F. W. "Maine's only counterfeiters."
        Yankee, 7 (November, 1941), 18, 37.
            1829-1831.

4587   YOUNG, NORMA. "Murder at Moneymaker Lake."
        Down East, 5 (June, 1959), 39, 55.
            Ebenezer Ball, counterfeiter, killed deputy
        John Tileston Downes; trial held in Castine.

        SEE ALSO entries 2705 and 2745.

ROCKLAND (KNOX CO.)

4588   AVERILL, ALBERT E. "A Maine boy at sea in
        the eighties." AmNep, 10 (1950), 203-219.
            Lime-coasting fleet of schooners.

4589   BACON, GEORGE FOX. Rockland, Belfast and vi-
        cinity: its representative business men and
        its points of interest, embracing Rockland,
        Belfast, Camden, Rockport, Bucksport, Ells-
        worth, Thomaston, Waldoboro', Warren, Damar-
        iscotta, Wiscasset, Newcastle. Newark, N.J.:
        Glenwood Publishing, 1892. Pp. 176.

4590   BOWEN, ROGER. "Lucy's gift to Rockland."
        Yankee, 31 (June, 1967), 140-148, 150-151.
            Home of Lucy Farnsworth, now a museum.

4591   DIETZ, LEW. "The great Rockland bank rob-
        bery." Down East, 17 (April, 1971), 40-43,
        61-62.
            1870.

4592   DRINKWATER, NORMAN, JR. "The stone age of
        Dix Island." Down East, 10 (September, 1963),
        43-47.
            Granite industry.

4593   DUNTON, ALVIN ROBBINS. The true story of the
        Hart-Meservey murder trial, in which light is
        thrown upon dark deeds, incompetency, and per-
        fidy; and crime fastened upon those whose po-
        sition, if not manhood, should have commanded
        honest dealing. Boston, 1882. Pp. 309.
            Murder occurred in 1877.

4594   FINCH, GRANT E. and GEORGE F. HOWE. "The lime
        industry at Rockland, Maine." Economic Geog-
        raphy, 6 (1930), 389-397.

4595   FORBES-ROBERTSON, DIANA. "The Dermot sisters
        of Rockland, Maine." Down East, 11 (Septem-
        ber, 1964), 16-21, 42-43.

4596   HAVILAND, THOMAS P. "Rockland's ring-tailed
        Fourth." Yankee, 28 (July, 1964), 62-63, 85-
        87.
            Fourth of July, 1914.

4597   HEALEY, EDITH P. "Fire in the white city."
        NEG, 10 (Summer, 1968), 31-36.
            Fire in a lime-processing factory in March,
        1896; also includes accounts of other lime
        firm fires.

4598   HEBERT, RICHARD A. "Rockland." Pine Cone, 2
        (Autumn, 1946), 14-19.

4599   MEARA, EMMETT. "It breaks a feller's heart."
        Yankee, 36 (April, 1972), 38-46.
            Samoset Hotel.

4600   MERRILL, DAPHNE WINSLOW. "Rockland--lime city
        U.S.A." Down East, 17 (November, 1970), 40-
        44, 62-63.

4601   NEWBERT, ALBERT H. History of Aurora Lodge,
        No. 50, F. & A. M., from the date of its
        charter July 18, 1826 to July 19, 1926. Rock-
        land: Bald Mountain Pr., [1926]. Pp. 228.
        MeHi.

4602   RAWLINGS, CHARLES. "Mystery of Lucy Farns-
        worth." Saturday Evening Post, 225 (May 2,
        1953), 32-33, 102-104.
            Farnsworth Art Museum.

4603   "A ROCK of the faith in Peterland: milestones
        of St. Peter's Parish, Rockland." The North-
        east, 77 (January, 1950), 11-15.

4604 "ROCKLAND, Maine." BTJ, 3 (1890-1891), 274-275.
Signed: Winkle.

4605 ["ROCKLAND, Maine."] BTJ, 22 (1909-1910), 213-257.

4606 ROTARY INTERNATIONAL, ROCKLAND, ME. Rotary Club of Rockland, Maine, a history, 1924-1944. n.p., [1944?]. Pp. 15. MeBa.

4607 SHAFTER, TOBY. "The fleshpots of Maine: portrait of a Down-East Jewish community." Commentary, 7 (January, 1949), 60-67.

4608 _____. "The well-kept synagogue." Midstream, 2 (Winter, 1956), 4, 109.

4609 TRIPP, O. H. Our fine law library. n.p., [1922?]. Pp. 4. Me.
Knox County Bar and Library Association.

4610 VOGT, PETER S. "The Farnsworth House, Rockland." Down East, 20 (May, 1974), 66-67.

4611 WASSON, GEORGE SAVARY. "The old Rockland, Maine lime trade." OTNE, 21 (1930-1931), 156-167.

SEE ALSO entries 20, 1659-1660, 1666, 1673, and 2082.

ROCKPORT (KNOX CO.)

4612 CARLSON, SHIRLEE CONNORS. Rockport, Camden, Lincolnville, 1776-1976, the life and times of its people. [Camden]: Town Crier, 1975. Pp. 99. MeU.

4613 CRAMER, MARY MEEKER and ISABEL CURRIER. "Spite House." Down East, 7 (September, 1960), 24-29, 48.
Moved from Phippsburg in 1925.

4614 DIETZ, LEW. "Goose River portrait." Down East, 10 (October, 1963), 16-19, 22-23.
Goose River is the former name of Rockport.

4615 WALL, ARTHUR W. "Boyhood sailing days at Rockport." Down East, 21 (January, 1975), 50-53, 70, 72-73.

4616 _____. "Lime kilns of Rockport." Down East, 15 (May, 1969), 32-35, 54-55.

SEE ALSO entries 1653, 1659, 1666, 1668, 1671, 1673, 2082, 2641, and 4589.

ROCKWOOD STRIP (SOMERSET CO.)

4617 No items located.

ROME (KENNEBEC CO.)

4618 No items located.

ROQUE BLUFFS (WASHINGTON CO.)

4619 No items located.

ROXBURY (OXFORD CO.)

4620 No items located.

RUMFORD (OXFORD CO.)

4621 "THE DEVELOPMENT of Rumford Falls." Maine. Bureau of Industrial and Labor Statistics. Annual Report, 16 (1902), 116-154.

4622 FREEMASONS. RUMFORD, ME. BLAZING STAR LODGE, NO. 30. History of Blazing Star Lodge, Number Thirty, Free and Accepted Masons from 1819 to 1919. James B. Stevenson, comp. Auburn: Merrill & Webber, [1920?]. Pp. 169. MeU.

4623 GOULD, DANIEL. History of Rumford in 1826. Randy L. Bennett and Peter A. McKenna, eds. Rumford: Pennycook Pr., 1975. Pp. 79. MeHi.

4624 LAPHAM, WILLIAM BERRY. History of Rumford, Oxford County, Maine, from its first settlement in 1779, to the present time. Augusta: Maine Farmer, 1890. Pp. xv, 432.

4625 LEANE, JOHN J. A history of Rumford, Maine, 1774-1972. Rumford: Rumford Publishing, 1972. Pp. 160.

4626 _____. The Oxford story: a history of the Oxford Paper Company, 1847-1958. [Rumford]: Oxford Paper, 1958. Unpaged.

4627 MARTIN, GEORGE A. "Churches of Rumford Falls." BTJ, 18 (1905-1906), 597-598.

4628 TAYLOR, PEARL. "What happened on August 2, exactly fifty years ago." Yankee, 37 (August, 1973), 146-149.
Fire at the Oxford Paper Company.

4629 "A 'WELFARE' institution on a novel plan." American Review of Reviews, 45 (1912), 325-328.
Rumford Mechanics' Institute.

RUSSELL POND TOWNSHIP (SOMERSET CO.)

4630 No items located.

SABATTUS (ANDROSCOGGIN CO.)

4631   No items located.

SACO (YORK CO.)

4632   BEATTY, HAZEL. "Three hundred years for the faith: the history of Trinity Parish, Saco." The Northeast, 77 (March, 1950), 14-17.

4633   COGSWELL, JONATHAN. "A topographical and historical sketch of Saco, county of York, District of Maine." MHSC, 2 Ser., 4 (1816), 184-189.

4634   DEERING, FRANK CUTTER. The proprietors of Saco and a brief sketch of the years following the first settlement of the town, also a little about an old bank in Saco, Maine. Saco: York National Bank, 1931. Pp. 59.

4635   DUNN, CHARLES, JR. "The mansion of Col. Thomas Cutts." Pine Tree Magazine, 6 (1906-1907), 332-339.

4636   DWIGHT, EDWARD STRONG. An address delivered in Saco, Oct. 12, 1862, on the one hundredth anniversary of the organization of the First Church in Saco, Me. Saco: William Noyes, 1862. Pp. 27.

4637   FAIRFIELD, ROY P. "Labor conditions at the old York: 1831-1900." NEQ, 30 (1957), 166-180.
        York Manufacturing Company; textiles.

4638   _____. Sands, spindles, and steeples. Portland: House of Falmouth, 1956. Pp. xi, 461.

4639   FREY, LUELLA A. An historical paper: First Parish Congregational Church, Saco, Maine. Biddeford: Biddeford Journal, [1912?]. Pp. 15.

4640   LOMBARD, LUCINA HAYNES. "Saco block-house." Pine Tree Magazine, 7 (1907), 133-139.

4641   LORD, ELVIRA M. First Parish Congregational Church, Saco, Maine and its leadership (a 200th anniversary memoir), 1762-1962. n.p., [1962]. Pp. 44. MBC.

4642   MELCHER, BURDUS REDFORD. York Institute: something of its past, present, and future. Saco: Biddeford Journal, 1884. Pp. 24.
        Technical education.

4643   MOLLOY, ANNE. "Since 1872--the Saco Company, the firm a wooden water pump created." Down East, 19 (November, 1972), 58-59.
        Wooden products; primarily spools.

4644   NATIONAL ARCHIVES PROJECT. Ship registers and enrollments of Saco, Maine, 1791-1915. Rockland, 1942. xiii, 108 leaves.

4645   OWEN, DANIEL EDWARD. Old times in Saco: a brief monograph on local events.... Saco: Biddeford Times Print, 1891. Pp. viii, 172.

4646   SACO, ME. Saco's tercentenary program, Saco, Maine, June 22 to July 4. n.p., [1931]. Pp. 22. MeHi.

4647   SACO, ME. FIRST PARISH CONGREGATIONAL CHURCH. Manual of the First Congregational Church in Saco, Maine, 1886. Biddeford: Daily Times Print, 1886. Pp. 76. MeHi.
        Contains historical sketch.

4648   _____. Manual of the First Parish Congregational Church in Saco, Maine, 1903. Saco: W. L. Streeter, 1903. Pp. 67.
        Includes chronological list of members, 1762-1903.

4649   "THE SECOND Parish in Saco." The Church Exchange, 4 (1896-1897), 10-11.

4650   SUTTON, KATHARINE AUGUSTA and ROBERT FRANCIS NEEDHAM. Universalists at Ferry Beach: a history. Boston: Universalist Publishing, 1948. Pp. 137.

4651   "TRINITY Church, Saco." The North East, 37 (September, 1909), 3-5; 38 (September, 1910), 5.

       SEE ALSO entries 556, 799, 1265, 1881, 1890, 1893, 1901, 1904, and 4181.

ST. AGATHA (AROOSTOOK CO.)

4652   ST. AGATHA PARISH. St. Agatha diamond jubilee, 1889-1964. n.p., 1964. Pp. 76.

4653   "ST. AGATHA'S Church, St. Agatha, Aroostook County." MeCathHM, 3 (November, 1914), 19-20.

ST. ALBANS (SOMERSET CO.)

4654   No items located.

ST. CROIX TOWNSHIP (AROOSTOOK CO.)

4655   No items located.

ST. FRANCIS (AROOSTOOK CO.)

4656   ST. FRANCIS, ME. BICENTENNIAL COMMITTEE. Memories. Madawaska: St. John Valley Printers, 1976. Pp. 38. [MeMaHi].

ST. GEORGE (KNOX CO.)

4657 ALLEN, ELMER E. History of Eureka Lodge at St. George, Maine, from 1870-1909. Rockland: Courier-Gazette, 1909. Pp. 44. MeBa.
Freemasons.

4658 MERRIAM, KENDALL A. "Wreck of the concrete steamer 'Polias.'" Down East, 17 (April, 1971), 50-52, 57.
At old Cilley Ledge on February 6, 1920.

4659 MESERVEY, ROY E. Coaster days, shipping in the town of St. George, Maine. Christopher Fahy, ed. [St. George], 1976. Pp. 33. MeU.

4660 MILLER, FRANK BURTON. Soldiers and sailors of the plantation of lower St. Georges, Maine, who served in the war for American independence. Rockland, 1931. Pp. 66.

4661 NEESON, MARGARET GRAHAM. On solid granite: the story of St. George's Church, its village, priests, and people. Long Cove: St. George's Episcopal Chapel, 1974. Pp. 154.

4662 ST. GEORGE chronicles, containing an historical sketch from 1605 to 1932, together with names, ages and dates of birth; a complete business directory. Joseph T. Simmons and Mabelle Andrews Rose, comps. Augusta: C. E. Nash & Son, 1932. Pp. 78.

SEE ALSO entry 5003.

ST. JOHN PLANTATION (AROOSTOOK CO.)

4663 No items located.

ST. JOHN TOWNSHIP (SOMERSET CO.)

4664 No items located.

SALEM TOWNSHIP (FRANKLIN CO.)

4665 OUR first old home day at Salem, Maine, August seventeenth, 1904. Boston: D. C. Heath, 1905. Pp. xvi, 227.
A town history.

SANDBAR TRACT (SOMERSET CO.)

4666 No items located.

SANDWICH ACADEMY GRANT (SOMERSET CO.)

4667 No items located.

SANDY BAY TOWNSHIP (SOMERSET CO.)

4668 No items located.

SANDY RIVER PLANTATION (FRANKLIN CO.)

4669 No items located.

SANFORD (YORK CO.)

4670 BETCHER, J. A. "Churches of Sanford and Springvale." BTJ, 21 (1908-1909), 399-402.

4671 BLAGDEN, CHARLES W. "The secret societies of Sanford and Springvale." BTJ, 21 (1908-1909), 404-406.
Differs slightly from following article.

4672 _____. "Secret societies of Sanford and Springvale." BTJ, 27 (1914-1915), 213, 215-216.
Differs slightly from previous entry.

4673 CHADBOURNE, BENJAMIN F. "The story of the Goodwill industries." BTJ, 21 (1908-1909), 375-377, 379, 381, 383, 385.
Sanford Mills, textiles.

4674 COLBY, D. W. "Schools of Springvale and Sanford." BTJ, 21 (1908-1909), 393, 395-396.

4675 DAVIS, W. E. "'Velmo'--its history and manufacture." Maine Association of Engineers. Journal, No. 11 (April, 1930), 30-38.
Sanford Mills.

4676 EMERY, EDWIN. The history of Sanford, Maine, 1661-1900. William Morrell Emery, ed. Fall River, Mass.: William M. Emery, 1901. Pp. xvi, 537.

4677 FLINT, GEORGE B., JR. "Goodall-Sanford Mills." Shoreliner, 2 (August, 1951), 50-59.
Textiles.

4678 GAY, ROGER CROWELL. Nasson College, 1912-1957: a modern parable of the mustard seed. N.Y.: Newcomen Society in North America, 1958. Pp. 24.

4679 GILE, HUGH. "Springvale and Sanford: past, present, and future." BTJ, 21 (1908-1909), 357, 359, 361, 363, 365, 367, 369, 371.

4680 HEBERT, RICHARD A. "The making of Maine: Goodall-Sanford industries." Pine Cone, 1 (Spring, 1945), 23-27.
Woolen and worsted.

4681 HERRICK, MARY DARRAH. "Nasson College Library." MeLAB, 7 (June, 1946), 4-5.

4682 McKINLEY, ALAN R. "With hands and hearts reaching heavenward: a brief historical survey of St. George's, Sanford." The Northeast, 77 (July, 1950), 12-17.

4683 "NORTH Parish Congregational Church of Sanford celebrates 175th anniversary." MeCP, 49 (January 15, 1962), 4-5.

4684 PHILBROOK, EUGENE S. "Churches of Sanford and Springvale." BTJ, 27 (1914-1915), 197, 199, 201.

4685 PROSSER, ALBERT L. A history of North Parish Congregational Church of Sanford, Maine, 1786-1961. n.p., [1961]. Pp. 134. MBC. Errata sheet inserted.

4686 SANFORD HISTORICAL COMMITTEE. Sanford, Maine: a bicentennial history; published in commemoration of the anniversary of the incorporation of the town in 1768. Albert L. Prosser, ed. Sanford, 1968. Pp. x, 504.

4687 "SANFORD, Maine." Sun Up, 2 (January, 1926), 28-29, 31-32.

4688 "SANFORD, Maine's largest town." BTJ, 27 (1914-1915), 185, 187, 189, 191, 193, 195.

4689 SEEMAN, BERNARD. "The town that refused to die." Coronet, 39 (January, 1956), 65-69. Industry.

4690 SMITH, ISAAC A. "Schools of Sanford and Springvale." BTJ, 27 (1914-1915), 204-205.

4691 STONE, HENRY J., ed. The Messenger, devoted to interests of the Congregational Church, at Sanford, Me., containing a history of the great fire of 1878.... Portland: Stephen Berry, 1879. Pp. 16. MeHi.

4692 WARD, ELMER L. A healthy tradition: the colorful romance of the horse blanket, the Angora goat, and Goodall-Sanford, Inc. N.Y.: Newcomen Society in North America, 1951. Pp. 32.

SANGERVILLE (PISCATAQUIS CO.)

4693 KNOWLTON, WILLIAM SMITH. Sangerville, centennial poem.... Augusta, [1914]. Pp. 24.

4694 SANGERVILLE, ME. 150th anniversary, Sangerville sesquicentennial, 1814-1964. n.p., [1964]. Unpaged. Me.

4695 "SANGERVILLE centennial: 1814-1914." SJMH, 2 (1914-1915), 103-182.

SEE ALSO entry 1782.

SAPLING TOWNSHIP (SOMERSET CO.)

4696 No items located.

SCARBOROUGH (CUMBERLAND CO.)

4697 BEAM, PHILIP C. Winslow Homer at Prout's Neck. Boston: Little, Brown, 1966. Pp. xxii, 282.

4698 CHAPMAN, LEONARD BOND. Monograph on the Southgate family of Scarborough, Maine, their ancestors and descendants. Portland: H. W. Bryant, 1907. Pp. viii, 60.

4699 HOLLAND, RUPERT SARGENT. The story of Prouts Neck. Prouts Neck: Prouts Neck Association, 1924. Pp. 67.

4700 HUTCHINSON, GLORIA. "Atlantic House, a summer refuge." Down East, 21 (June, 1975), 50-55. Hotel.

4701 LEAMON, JAMES S. "The Stamp Act crisis in Maine: the case of Scarborough." MeHSN, 11 (1971-1972), 74-93.

4702 LIBBEY, DOROTHY SHAW. Scarborough becomes a town. Portland: Bond Wheelwright, 1955. Pp. 282.

4703 MOULTON, AUGUSTUS FREEDOM. Grandfather tales of Scarborough. Augusta: Katahdin Publishing, 1925. Pp. 209.

4704 _____. Old Prouts Neck. Portland: Marks Printing, 1924. Pp. 123.

4705 _____. "The settlement of Scarborough." MeHSC, 2 Ser., 6 (1895), 415-440.

4706 MOULTON, FRED E. History of the organization of the Universalist Church at Scarborough and South Buxton, Maine. n.p., [1939?]. 7 leaves. MeHi.

4707 PINES and surf, Higgins Beach, Maine. n.p., n.d. Pp. 13. MeHi.

4708 PROUTS NECK ASSOCIATION. Prouts then and now, 1888-1970. Prouts Neck, 1971. Pp. 96.

4709 SCARBOROUGH, ME. Scarborough, Maine, 300th anniversary, 1658-1958. n.p., [1958]. Pp. 71. MeHi.

4710 SCARBOROUGH PUBLIC LIBRARY. FRIENDS. History of Scarborough. [Scarborough, 1973]. 26 leaves.

4711 SOCIETY OF COLONIAL WARS. MAINE. The Scottow stockade fort located on Black Point, Scarborough, Maine, 1681-1690. n.p., 1931. Pp. 16. MBNEH.

4712 SOUTHGATE, WILLIAM SCOTT. "The history of Scarborough from 1633-1783." MeHSC, 3 (1853), 9-237.

4713 THORNTON, JOHN WINGATE. "Formation and early records of the church in Scarborough, Me." CongQ, 8 (1867), 188-194.
First Parish Congregational Church.

4714 _____. "The Kings of Scarborough and New York." HistMag, 2 Ser., 5 (1869), 50-51.
King family.

4715 VAN RENSSELAER, MRS. J. K. "The Kings of Owascoag." American Historical Register, 1 (1894-1895), 461-463.
King family.

4716 WARREN, JOHN C. "The attack on Black Point Garrison." Pine Tree Magazine, 8 (1907), 31-33.
King Philip's War.

SEE ALSO entry 1265.

SEARSMONT (WALDO CO.)

4717 CUNNINGHAM, CHARLES M. and OTIS D. WILSON. History of Quantabacook Lodge, No. 129, Free and Accepted Masons, Searsmont, Me., from 1871 to 1881. Belfast: George W. Burgess, 1881. Pp. 18. [MePGLM].

4718 CUNNINGHAM, CHARLES M., WILLIAM S. COX, and W. H. WOODCOCK. History of Quantabacook Lodge of Free and Accepted Masons, Searsmont, Maine, from 1865 to 1871. Belfast: George W. Burgess, 1871. Pp. 18. [MePGLM].

4719 GARBUS, BETTY. "The Robbins family mill at Searsmont." Down East, 23 (November, 1976), 48-51, 69.
Sawmill.

4720 WHITING, BARTLETT J. "Incident at Quantabacook, March, 1764." NEQ, 20 (1947), 169-196.
Hunting rights controversy with the Indians.

SEARSPORT (WALDO CO.)

4721 APPLEBEE, ROBERT B. Sailing ship history. Searsport: Penobscot Marine Museum, 1956. Pp. 14. MeBa.
Ships built in Searsport.

4722 BLACK, FREDERICK FRASIER, comp. Searsport sea captains: a collection of photographs with brief biographical sketches, including the

ships they commanded. Searsport: Penobscot Marine Museum, 1960. Pp. 226.

4723 CARVER, CLIFFORD NICKELS. John Carver (1799-1867) builder of wooden ships upon the Penobscot Bay! N.Y.: Newcomen Society in North America, 1957. Pp. 32.

4724 EASTMAN, JOEL WEBB. A history of Sears Island, Searsport, Maine. [Searsport]: Searsport Historical Society, 1976. Pp. 72. MeHi.

4725 KUHNERT, DALE WILLIAM. "Searsport: seaport to superport." Down East, 20 (November, 1973), 28-35, 67-68.

4726 SEARSPORT, ME. FIRST CONGREGATIONAL CHURCH. Congregational centennial at Searsport, Maine, 1815-1915. Portland: Southworth Printing, 1916. Pp. 77. MBC.

4727 SEARSPORT, ME. 125TH ANNIVERSARY COMMITTEE. 125th anniversary, Searsport, Maine, 1845-1970. n.p., [1970]. Unpaged. Me.

4728 SEARSPORT HISTORICAL SOCIETY. Around our town, Volume 1, 1967. Searsport, 1967. 130 leaves. MeHi.
No more published.

4729 SULLIVAN, J. H. Searsport ships and captains, a list of ships commanded by Searsport men, 1834-1927 [and a list of] vessels built in Searsport. [Searsport?], 1927. Broadside, 19 x 12 inches. MeU.

4730 THURSTON, STEPHEN. Semi-centennial: a sermon on the fiftieth anniversary of the organization of the First Congregational Church in Searsport ... delivered October 4th, 1865. Portland: Brown Thurston, 1866. Pp. 24. MeBa.

SEBAGO (CUMBERLAND CO.)

4731 MESERVE FRED L., comp. Centennial history of Sebago, Maine, 1826-1926; containing the centennial celebration of 1926, and historical matter. [Sebago?, 1926]. Pp. 54.

4732 NASON, LAWRENCE. Two stories from Sebago history. n.p., [1957?]. Unpaged. MeHi.
Potter Academy and the Spaulding Memorial Library.

SEBEC (PISCATAQUIS CO.)

4733 CUSHING, WAINWRIGHT. "Early history of the town of Sebec." PCHSC, 1 (1910), 10-34.

SEBOEIS PLANTATION (PENOBSCOT CO.)

4734   No items located.

SEBOOMOOK TOWNSHIP (SOMERSET CO.)

4735   No items located.

SEDGWICK (HANCOCK CO.)

4736   "ACCOUNT of the Baptist Church lately constituted at Sedgwick, District of Maine." Massachusetts Baptist Missionary Magazine, 1 (1803), 124-127, 144-146.

4737   FREEMASONS. SEDGWICK, ME. EGGEMOGGIN LODGE. History of Eggemoggin Lodge of Free and Accepted Masons, Sedgwick, Me., 1872. Ellsworth: N. K. Sawyer & Son, 1872. Pp. 15. MeHi.

4738   LEE, JOHN R. "Maine Lake Ice Company." Down East, 17 (March, 1971), 44-47.

4739   LOVETT, ROBERT WOODBERRY. "Storekeeping in a Maine seacoast town: records of the W. G. Sargent Company." BBHS, 27 (1953), 121-123. 1834-1927.

4740   NEESE, ABBY SARGENT. Sargentville: historical reminiscences. Rockland: Courier-Gazette, 1975. Pp. 50.

4741   SEDGWICK, ME. BICENTENNIAL COMMITTEE. Sedgwick, Maine, bicentennial, 1763-1963, August 2-3-4. n.p., 1963. Pp. 88. Me.

4742   SEDGWICK, ME. FIRST BAPTIST CHURCH. Centennial of the First Baptist Church, Sedgwick, Maine, June 11-18, 1905; two historical papers: I. Historical sketch of the town of Sedgwick by Rev. Arthur Warren Smith; II. Rev. Daniel Merrill, A.M.--an appreciation by Samuel P. Merrill. n.p., [1905]. Pp. 64.

4743   "SEDGWICK and settlers." MeHistMag, 8 (1893), 16-17.
     Includes ecclesiastical history.

4744   "SEDGWICK Public Library--its history and dedication." MeLB, 16 (1930-1931), 43-44.

4745   STRAND, MARK. The Sargeantville notebook. Providence, R.I.: Burning Deck, 1973. Unpaged.

SEE ALSO entry 1561.

SEVEN PONDS TOWNSHIP (FRANKLIN CO.)

4746   No items located.

SHAPLEIGH (YORK CO.)

4747   LORING, AMASA. A history of Shapleigh. Portland: B. Thurston, 1854. Pp. 40.

4748   VON KRUMREIG, EDWARD LUDWIG. An historical address of the First Baptist Church of Shapleigh, Maine. n.p., [1903]. Pp. 66. MeHi.

SHAWTOWN TOWNSHIP (PISCATAQUIS CO.)

4749   No items located.

SHERMAN (AROOSTOOK CO.)

4750   SHERMAN MILLS, ME. WASHBURN MEMORIAL CHURCH. History of the Washburn Memorial Church, Sherman Mills, Maine, and the program of the centennial observance, August 13 to 20, 1961. n.p., [1961]. Pp. 15. MBC.

SHIRLEY (PISCATAQUIS CO.)

4751   "THE SHIRLEY House at Shirley Corner, Maine." SJMH, 4 (1916-1917), 53.

SIDNEY (KENNEBEC CO.)

4752   SEE entry 1645.

SILVER RIDGE TOWNSHIP (AROOSTOOK CO.)

4753   No items located.

SKINNER TOWNSHIP (FRANKLIN CO.)

4754   SEE entry 3377A.

SKOWHEGAN (SOMERSET CO.)

4755   ANDERSON, THOMAS H. and FRANK A. NOLIN. History of Somerset Lodge, No. 34, Free and Accepted Masons, Skowhegan, Me., from January 1, 1875 to December 31, 1889. Skowhegan: J. O. Smith, 1891. Pp. 36.

4756   COBURN, LOUISE HELEN. History of the Skowhegan Woman's Club, read at the birthday dinner of the Skowhegan Woman's Club held at Lakewood, September 21, 1932 during the annual meeting of the Maine Federation of Women's Clubs. n.p., [1932]. Unpaged.

4757   _____. The passage of the Arnold Expedition through Skowhegan. Skowhegan, 1922. Pp. 24.

4758   _____. Skowhegan on the Kennebec. Skowhegan: Independent-Reporter Pr., 1941. 2v.

4759   DANFORTH, EDWARD F. Skowhegan lawyers, 1803-1927. Hinckley: Good Will Publishing, 1927. Pp. 58. Me.

4760   DIETZ, LEW. "The Skowhegan School of Painting and Sculpture." Down East, 16 (June, 1970), 40-43, 70, 72.

4761   DOWNER, ALAN S. "The Down East screamer." NEQ, 42 (1969), 181-200.
        Amos Angier Mann; journalist.

4762   ESTES, WILLIAM ROSCOE GREENE. History of Somerset Chapter, No. 15, Royal Arch Masons, Skowhegan, Maine, from 1863 to 1910. [Skowhegan]: Independent Reporter, 1910. Pp. 98. MeB.

4763   _____. History of Somerset Lodge, No. 34, of Free and Accepted Masons, Skowhegan, Me., from June 27, 1820, to January 1, 1875. Portland: Berry, 1875. Pp. 66.

4764   FIRST NATIONAL BANK OF SKOWHEGAN. A century of service, 1825-1925. [Skowhegan, 1925?]. Pp. 95. MH-BA.

4765   FOLSOM, EMMA B. "Historical church that has become an armory." Sun Up, 10 (March, 1932), 17.
        First Baptist Church.

4766   LAWRENCE, FRED F. "Progressive and beautiful Skowhegan." BTJ, 23 (1910-1911), 221-223, 225, 227.

4767   MERRILL, J. N. "Preventive medicine in Skowhegan." JMS, 2 (1895-1896), 647-649.

4768   NASH, HARRIET A. "A type of Bloomfield." NEM, New Ser., 20 (1899), 472-480.
        Social life and customs.

4769   PERKINS, DEFOREST H. "The schools and school system of Skowhegan." BTJ, 23 (1910-1911), 247-249.

4770   SKOWHEGAN, ME. 1724-1926, important data in the history of Skowhegan. [Skowhegan]: Independent-Reporter, [1926]. Unpaged. Me.

4771   "SKOWHEGAN." BTJ, 3 (1890-1891), 267-272.

        SEE ALSO entries 1816 and 3532.

SMITHFIELD (SOMERSET CO.)

4772   No items located.

SMYRNA (AROOSTOOK CO.)

4773   No items located.

SOLDIERTOWN TOWNSHIP (PENOBSCOT CO.)

4774   No items located.

SOLDIERTOWN TOWNSHIP (SOMERSET CO.)

4775   No items located.

SOLON (SOMERSET CO.)

4776   CUMMINGS, MILDRED H. South Solon: the story of a meeting house. [Solon]: South Solon Historical Society, 1959. Pp. 54.

4777   DAVIS, ISAAC FRANKLIN. A history of Solon, Maine. n.p., [1973?]. Pp. 77. Me.

4778   DIETZ, LEW. "The South Solon Meeting House." Down East, 3 (November, 1956-January, 1957), 21-23.

4779   RUSSELL, CHARLOTTE M. Scenes from Solon's history. [Solon]: Rusmer-linc, [1959]. 35 leaves.

4780   SOLON, ME. SESQUICENTENNIAL HISTORY COMMITTEE. Sketches from Solon's history. n.p., 1959. Pp. 95.

SOMERVILLE (LINCOLN CO.)

4781   No items located.

SOPER MOUNTAIN TOWNSHIP (PISCATAQUIS CO.)

4782   No items located.

SORRENTO (HANCOCK CO.)

4783   CHAFFEE, ZECHARIAH. Sorrento, Maine. Providence, R.I.: Livermore & Knight, 1911. Unpaged.

4784   LEWIS, LAWRENCE. Torna a Sorrento, 1938-1973. Worcester, Mass.: Commonwealth Pr., 1973. Pp. 74. MeBa.
        In English.

        SEE ALSO entry 1588.

SOUTH BERWICK (YORK CO.)

4785   BAER, ANNIE WENTWORTH. "Captain Nathan Lord's house." Granite Mo, 59 (1927), 201-206.

4786   BERWICK ACADEMY, SOUTH BERWICK, ME. A memorial of the 100th anniversary of the founding of Berwick Academy, July 1, 1891. Sarah Orne Jewett, ed. Cambridge, Mass.: Riverside Pr., 1891. Pp. xv, 118.
        Historical address by John Lord.

4787   _____. 175th anniversary sampler: a collection of essays by alumni and friends of Berwick Academy. Jean M. Goodwin, ed. South Berwick, 1966. Pp. vi, 100.

4788   BROWN, FRANK CHOUTEAU. "Interior details and furnishings of the Sarah Orne Jewett dwelling, built by John Haggins in 1774 at South Berwick, Maine." Pencil Points, 21 (1940), 115-130.

4789   CARROLL, GLADYS HASTY. "Schooling in the early nineteen hundreds." NEG, 14 (Fall, 1972), 15-23.

4790   DONAHUE, MARIE. "Hamilton House on the Piscataqua." Down East, 22 (October, 1975), 36-39, 65-66.

4791   _____. "Maine's oldest private academy." Down East, 13 (October, 1966), 26-29, 40-42.
        Berwick Academy.

4792   "GENERAL Lafayette in Maine." MHGR, 4 (1887), 229-235.
        1815.

4793   GEORGES, JUSTINE FLINT. "Mementos of a great lady." Shoreliner, 1 (September, 1950), 10-13.
        Sarah Orne Jewett House.

4794   HAMBLEN, ABIGAIL ANN. "Beloved village." Down East, 2 (August, 1955), 33, 45.

4795   HAWTHORNE, HILDEGARDE. "A garden of romance: Mrs. Tyson's, at Hamilton House, South Berwick, Maine." Century, 80 (1910), 778-786.
        Emily D. Tyson.

4796   HENNESSY, WILLIAM G. "The house of Hamilton." Shoreliner, 3 (July, 1952), 9-16.
        Jonathan Hamilton.

4797   HILTON, FANNIE MULLOY. Memories of a little country church or a brief history of the South Berwick & Wells Christian Church. South Berwick: Chronicle Print Shop, 1969. Pp. 54. Me.

4798   JEWETT, SARAH ORNE. Letters. (1956) Richard Cary, ed. Enl. and rev. ed. Waterville: Colby College Pr., 1967. Pp. viii, 186.

4799   KENISTON, AMANDA M. A history of the South Berwick Village Baptist Church from 1823 to 1926. n.p., [1926]. Pp. 14. MeHi.

4800   KINGSBURY, EDITH. "Hamilton House: historic landmark in South Berwick, Maine." House Beautiful, 65 (1929), 782-787, 874, 876.

4801   LEWIS, GEORGE. Address delivered by Rev. George Lewis, D.D., Wednesday, June 4th, 1902, at the two hundredth anniversary of the founding of the Congregational Church in South Berwick, Maine. South Berwick: Independent Pr., 1902. Pp. 30.

4802   RICKER, JENNIE DE R. South Berwick, Me., pages from the past. n.p., [1936?]. Pp. 17. MB.

4803   SCATES, JOHN CLARK. "Records of the First Church of Berwick (South Berwick), Me." NEHGR, 82 (1928), 71-98, 204-218, 312-333, 500-511; 83 (1929), 9-20, 147-156.

4804   SHELTON, LOUISE. "The garden at Hamilton House." American Homes and Gardens, 6 (1909), 422-425.

4805   SLOAN, ALEX. "South Berwick Church." Congregationalism in Maine, 13 (1926), 27-29.

4806   SOUTH BERWICK, ME. FIRST PARISH CHURCH. A brief history of the First Parish Church, South Berwick, Maine, 1702-1952. n.p., [1952]. Unpaged. MBC.

4807   STACKPOLE, EVERETT SCHERMERHORN. "The first permanent settlement in Maine." SJMH, 14 (1926), 190-215.
        Great Works.

4808   TRAFTON, BURTON W. F., JR. "Hamilton House, South Berwick, Maine." Antiques, 77 (1960), 486-489.

4809   _____. "Hamilton House, South Berwick, Maine." OTNE, 48 (1957-1958), 57-64.
        Differs from previous entry.

SEE ALSO entries 1322 and 1911.

SOUTH BRISTOL (LINCOLN CO.)

4810   GAMAGE, NELSON W. A short history of South Bristol, Maine. [South Bristol: Everett W. Gamage, 1953?]. Pp. 49.
        Even numbered pages are on rectos.

SEE ALSO entry 1706.

SOUTH PORTLAND (CUMBERLAND CO.)

4810A FREEMASONS. CAPE ELIZABETH, ME. HIRAM LODGE, NO. 180. History of Hiram Lodge, No. 180, Free and Accepted Masons, Cape Elizabeth, Maine, and a full abstract from the records from its organization, November, 1875 to November 10, 1891. Stephen Scamman, comp. Portland: Smith & Sale, 1892. Pp. 107.
Due to a boundary change, the lodge is now in South Portland.

4811 FREEMASONS. SOUTH PORTLAND, ME. HIRAM LODGE, NO. 180. History of Hiram Lodge, No. 180, F. & A. M., South Portland, Maine, 1876-1976. n.p., [1976]. Pp. 224. MeHi.

4812 JONES, HERBERT GRANVILLE. Portland ships are good ships: the building of thirty British and 236 liberty ships by the New England Shipbuilding Corporation, South Portland, Maine. Portland: Machigonne Pr., 1945. Pp. ix, 60.

4813 LEAGUE OF WOMEN VOTERS OF SOUTH PORTLAND. MAINE. South Portland, Maine, a brief history. Portland: Maine Printers, 1960. Unpaged. MeP.

4814 _____. South Portland, Me., an All-American city. South Portland, 1971. Pp. 69.
Includes historical sketch.

4815 PRIDE TRAINING SCHOOL, SOUTH PORTLAND, ME. Pride Training School for retarded children: report on ten years' progress. n.p., [1960]. Pp. 52. MeP.

4816 SLEEPER, FRANK. "South Portland: Maine's fastest growing industrial city." Down East, 13 (March, 1967), 8-12, 15-16, 60.

4817 SOUTH PORTLAND, ME. Centennial program, old home day celebration, city of So. Portland, Maine, Saturday, August 21, 1920. n.p., [1920]. Unpaged. MeHi.
Includes a brief history of the city.

4818 SOUTH PORTLAND, ME. CHURCH OF THE NAZARENE. 50th anniversary, South Portland Church of the Nazarene. n.p., [1950]. Unpaged. MeP.
Includes history by Ada F. MacDonald.

4819 SOUTH PORTLAND, ME. 50TH ANNIVERSARY COMMITTEE. Souvenir program, 50th anniversary, city of South Portland, Maine, August 28-29, 1948. n.p., [1948]. Pp. 36. MeHi.
Includes history by Rosella A. Loveitt.

4820 SOUTH PORTLAND, ME. FIRST CONGREGATIONAL CHURCH. Historical address, sermon, poem and hymn read at the one hundred and seventy-fifth anniversary of the First Congregational Church and Parish (Old North Church) of South Portland and Cape Elizabeth, celebrated August 14-16, 1909, in the church, Meeting House Hill, 1734-1909. Portland: Southworth Printing, 1909. Pp. 34.
Historical address by Fritz H. Jordan.

4821 SOUTH PORTLAND, ME. FIRST METHODIST CHURCH. First Methodist Church, Church Street, (Brown's Hill), South Portland, Maine, 150th anniversary, 1803-1953, souvenir history and church directory. n.p., 1953. Unpaged. MBNEH.
History is by Wilson L. Lyon.

SEE ALSO entries 1487 and 1512.

SOUTH THOMASTON (KNOX CO.)

4822 CLARKE, WINFIELD S. History of Knox Lodge, No. 189, F. & A. M., from its organization, October 4, 1884, to January 31, 1910. Rockland: Opinion Pr., 1910. Pp. 49.

4823 NEESON, MARGARET GRAHAM. "The favored rock." Down East, 22 (September, 1975), 58-59, 82-83.
On Spruce Head Island and called "Date Rock."

SEE ALSO entry 1660.

SOUTHPORT (LINCOLN CO.)

4824 LEPPER, RUTH RHOADS. A pictorial history of Southport. West Southport: Ruth Lepper Gardner, 1976. Unpaged. MeU.

4825 "MAINE claims the only existing autograph library in the world." Sun Up, 3 (August, 1927), 33, 56.
All books are autographed by either the author or the donor.

4826 MERRILL, JOHN P. and SUZANNE MERRILL, eds. Squirrel Island, Maine: the first hundred years. Freeport: Bond Wheelwright, 1973. Pp. 66.

4827 MERRILL, SAMUEL PEARCE. Souvenir of Squirrel Island. Waterville: E. A. Pierce, 1895. Pp. 31. MeU.

4828 SOUTHPORT HISTORY COMMITTEE. Historical gleanings from Cape Newagen, Townsend, Southport. Boothbay Harbor: Harbor Print Shop, 1976. Pp. 96. Me.

4829 SQUIRREL ISLAND, ME. LIBRARY. Squirrelana. Squirrel Island, 1954. Unpaged.

4830 WHEELER, EDITH H. "Squirrel Island's first hundred years." Down East, 17 (July, 1971), 52-55, 81, 83.

SEE ALSO entries 1681-1682 and 1689-1690.

SOUTHWEST HARBOR (HANCOCK CO.)

4831   BARTER, J. MALCOLM. "Henry R. Hinckley & Co. --Maine builder of fiberglass sail yachts." Down East, 14 (April, 1968), 28-33.

4832   THE CLAREMONT Hotel--my story, 1884-1964. n.p., [1964?]. Pp. 7. MeU.

4833   PARKER, JESSE L. Recollections of Southwest Harbor, Maine, 1885-1894. n.p., 1955. 49 leaves. MeU.

4834   STEWART, ALICE ROSE. "Russians in Maine." Down East, 8 (September, 1961), 44-47, 54. Visit of the 'Cimbria' in 1878.

SEE ALSO entries 1587 and 1617.

SPENCER BAY TOWNSHIP (PISCATAQUIS CO.)

4835   No items located.

SPRINGFIELD (PENOBSCOT CO.)

4836   BRADBURY, OSGOOD NATHAN. History of Forrest Lodge, No. 148, of Free and Accepted Masons, of Springfield, Maine, from July 4, A.D. 1868, to December 31, A.D. 1869. Portland: Stephen Berry, 1872. Pp. 15. MeBa.

SQUAPAN TOWNSHIP (AROOSTOOK CO.)

4837   No items located.

SQUARETOWN TOWNSHIP (SOMERSET CO.)

4838   No items located.

STACYVILLE (PENOBSCOT CO.)

4839   No items located.

STANDISH (CUMBERLAND CO.)

4840   DINGLEY, ROBERT JORDAN. Boating in the Switzerland of America ... the Sebago-Long Lake Waterway, the Songo River Line. [Naples]: Naples Historical Society, [1970?]. Unpaged. MeHi.

4841   DRUMMOND, JOSIAH HAYDEN. History of Standish Lodge, No. 70, Free and Accepted Masons, Standish, Me., from June 10, 1852, to Oct. 1, 1874. Portland: Harmon, Paine, 1874. Pp. 38.

4842   STANDISH OLD HOME ASSOCIATION. The record of the first observance of Old Home Day ... on Thursday, August 9th, 1900.... Portland: Tucker Printing, 1900. Pp. 35. MeHi.

4843   USHER, HELEN, et al. Facts about Standish. Standish: Hartford Printing, 1922. Pp. 16. Me.

SEE ALSO entry 1494.

STARKS (SOMERSET CO.)

4844   SEE entries 1419, 1816, and 3362.

STETSON (PENOBSCOT CO.)

4845   DANIELS, LILLA WOOD. History of Stetson, Maine, 1800-1931. Bangor: Furbush Printing, [1931?]. Pp. 66.

STETSONTOWN TOWNSHIP (FRANKLIN CO.)

4846   No items located.

STEUBEN (WASHINGTON CO.)

4847   COBLENS, GLENORE ORRIS. All Souls by the Sea, Petit Manan Point, Maine: the history of a little church. Cherryfield: Narraguagus Printing, 1972. Pp. 14.

4848   HARRIS, HERBERT. History of Ionic Lodge, of Free and Accepted Masons, Steuben, Maine, from its organization, in 1806, to its close in 1813. Portland: The Grand Lodge, 1894. Pp. 23.

SEE ALSO entries 1855 and 1864.

STOCKHOLM (AROOSTOOK CO.)

4849   STOCKHOLM, ME. Town of Stockholm, Maine-- 90th anniversary, 1881-1971. n.p., [1971?]. Pp. 56. [MeHoR]. Includes history by Fritz Anderson.

SEE ALSO entry 1456.

STOCKTON SPRINGS (WALDO CO.)

4850   CAREY, ROGER. "Fort Pownall." Down East, 19 (October, 1972), 54-56, 61.

4851 ELLIS, ALICE V. The story of Stockton Springs, Maine. [Stockton Springs]: Historical Committee of Stockton Springs, 1955. Pp. 223.

4852 HICHBORN, FAUSTINA. Historical sketch of Stockton Springs. Herbert C. Libby, ed. Waterville: Central Maine Publishing, 1908. Pp. 133.

4853 PIKE, RICHARD. "Building and occupancy of Fort Pownall." NEHGR, 14 (1860), 4-10.

4854 PORTER, JOSEPH WHITCOMB. "The expedition to Penobscot and the erection of Fort Pownal." MeHistMag, 7 (1891-1892), 61-65.

STONEHAM (OXFORD CO.)

4855 No items located.

STONINGTON (HANCOCK CO.)

4856 CURRIER, ISABEL. "The granite-bound town of Stonington." Down East, 13 (November, 1966), 16-21, 46, 48.

4857 _____. "A Maine quarry's fabulous feat." Down East, 14 (May, 1968), 22-25, 48-49.
The Rockefeller Bowl, the largest object to be cut from a single piece of granite anywhere in the United States.

SEE ALSO entries 1553, 1561, 2834-2836, and 2840-2843.

STOW (OXFORD CO.)

4858 No items located.

STRONG (FRANKLIN CO.)

4859 BUTLER, NATALIE STURGES and BENJAMIN BUTLER. Souvenir program, Republican centennial celebration, 1854-1954, Strong, Maine, August 7, 1954. n.p., [1954]. Unpaged. MeHi.
Includes a brief history of the town by Christine Richardson.

SEE ALSO entry 1419.

SUGARLOAF TOWNSHIP (FRANKLIN CO.)

4860 No items located.

SULLIVAN (HANCOCK CO.)

4861 GALLISON, WILLIAM W., EDWIN F. CLAPHAM, and SETH A. JOHNSON. History of David A. Hooper Lodge, No. 201, West Sullivan, Maine from the founding of the lodge to January 1, 1935. Ellsworth: American Print, 1935. Pp. 30. Me.

4862 SARGENT, WINTHROP. Colonel Paul Dudley Sargent, 1745-1827. [Philadelphia?, 1920]. Pp. 46.

SEE ALSO entries 1579 and 1588.

SUMMIT TOWNSHIP (PENOBSCOT CO.)

4863 No items located.

SUMNER (OXFORD CO.)

4864 SUMNER, ME. Centennial history of the town of Sumner, Me., 1798-1898. West Sumner: Charles E. Handy, Jr., 1899. Pp. 202, xxx.

SURRY (HANCOCK CO.)

4865 DODGE, ERNEST STANLEY. "The last days of coasting on Union River Bay." AmNep, 9 (1949), 169-179.
Ships and shipping.

4866 SURRY, ME. Surry's centennial souvenir, 1903. Ellsworth: Campbell Publishing, 1903. Unpaged. MBNEH.

SEE ALSO entry 1578.

SWANS ISLAND (HANCOCK CO.)

4867 "BURNT Coat or Swan's Island and other islands contiguous thereto." BHistMag, 3 (1887-1888), 21-26.

4868 SMALL, HERMAN WESLEY. A history of Swan's Island, Maine. Ellsworth: Hancock Publishing, 1898. Pp. 244.

4869 WESTBROOK, PERRY DICKIE. Biography of an island. N.Y.: T. Yoseloff, 1958. Pp. 224.

SWANVILLE (WALDO CO.)

4870 No items located.

SWEDEN (OXFORD CO.)

4871   No items located.

T3 INDIAN PURCHASE (PENOBSCOT CO.)

4872   No items located.

T4 INDIAN PURCHASE (PENOBSCOT CO.)

4873   No items located.

TALMADGE (WASHINGTON CO.)

4874   No items located.

TAUNTON & RAYNHAM ACADEMY GRANT (SOMERSET CO.)

4875   No items located.

TEMPLE (FRANKLIN CO.)

4876   SEE entry 1419.

THOMASTON (KNOX CO.)

4877   AYERS, BLANCHE WALDO. "The Knox memorial." DARMag, 56 (1922), 293-295.
        Montpelier.

4878   CILLEY, JONATHAN PRINCE. "The Burtons of Thomaston." Maine Bugle, 5 (1898), 200-212.
        Burton family.

4879   DEMERS, MABEL GOULD. "Doorways and beyond: Montpelier." Pine Cone, 6 (Summer, 1950), 25-30.

4880   DUNNACK, HENRY ERNEST. "General Henry Knox, American patriot." DARMag, 59 (1925), 354-357.
        Primarily concerned with Montpelier, Knox's home.

4881   ELKINS, L. WHITNEY. "Montpelier: the old mansion home at Thomaston, Maine where General Knox lived during the Revolution." Sun Up, 3 (August, 1926), 66, 69, 71, 74.

4882   FIELDS, J. E. "The mistress of Montpelier." DARMag, 87 (1953), 525-528.
        Lucy Knox.

4883   FOWLER, HENRY THATCHER. General Knox and his home in Maine: Montpelier. Rockland: Courier-Gazette Pr., 1931. Pp. 26.

4884   FREEMASONS. THOMASTON, ME. ORIENT LODGE, NO. 15. History of Orient Lodge, No. 15, of F. & A. Masons, located at Thomaston. Sanford: Jas. H. Goodall, 1895. Pp. 38. MeHi.

4885   GREEN, SAMUEL M. "The architecture of Thomaston, Maine." SocArchHistJ, 10 (December, 1951), 24-32.

4886   GRIFFITHS, THOMAS MORGAN. Major General Henry Knox and the last heirs to Montpelier. Arthur Morgan Griffiths, ed. Monmouth: Monmouth Pr., 1965. Pp. 130.

4887   HIGGINSON, MARY P. THACHER. "Two ancient landmarks." Scribner's Monthly Magazine, 9 (1874-1875), 615-618.
        Montpelier in Thomaston and the Cornwallis House, Camden, South Carolina.

4888   HUSSEY, MRS. LEROY FOGG. "Montpelier." DARMag, 83 (1949), 579-580.
        Home of Henry Knox.

4889   KARL, ALICE W. "The new Montpelier." Sun Up, 9 (July, 1931), 4, 28.
        The present Montpelier is a reproduction of the home built by General Knox in 1793.

4890   LEFFINGWELL, B. H. "Montpelier, the home of General Henry Knox at Thomaston, Me." Hobbies, 65 (August, 1960), 58-59.

4891   LETTERS to Christopher Prince, 1855-1865. Journals of Eliza Prince, 1859-1860. Arthur Spear, ed. Middletown, N.Y.: Whitlock Pr., 1969. Pp. ix, 215.

4892   LINDLEY, E. MARGUERITE. "Montpelier: historic home of Major-General Henry Knox." MagAmHist, 16 (1886), 121-132.

4893   MILES, CARLTON E. "Beautiful Montpelier, the rebuilt Knox home." Sun Up, 10 (May, 1932), 12-13, 17.

4894   "'MONTPELIER,' once the residence of Gen'l Knox at Thomaston, Me." BTJ, 6 (1893-1894), 241-242.

4895   NEALLEY, EDWARD BOWDOIN. "Oration delivered at the centennial celebration of the incorporation of the town of Thomaston, July 4, 1877." MeHistMag, 8 (1893), 121-137.

4896   PACKARD, AUBIGNE LERMOND. A town that went to sea. Portland: Falmouth Publishing, 1950. Pp. viii, 416.

4897   PARKER, W. J. LEWIS. "Sails, ships & cargoes: Dunn & Elliot of Thomaston, Maine." Down East, 17 (March, 1971), 48-52, 77, 80, 85-86, 90-91, 93.

4898 PORTER, JOSEPH WHITCOMB. "An abstract of the history of the Maine State Prison, 1822–1886." BHistMag, 6 (1890–1891), appendix, 1–15.

4899 _____. "An abstract of the history of the Maine State Prison to the present time, 1882." Maine State Prison. Annual Report, (1882), 45 pages of appendix at end.
This **article** is more detailed than the above entry.

4900 PRINCE, HEZEKIAH. Journals of Hezekiah Prince, Jr., 1822–1828. Arthur Spear, ed. N.Y.: Crown Publishers, 1965. Pp. xxii, 448.

4901 ROBBINS, ALLAN L. Information regarding the Maine State Prison, Thomaston, 1824–1953. Thomaston, [1953]. Pp. 55. MeBa.

4902 STARRETT, LEWIS FREDERICK. General Henry Knox: his family, his manor, his manor house, and his guests; a paper read before the 12mo Club, Rockland, Maine, March 3, 1902. Rockland: Huston's Bookstore, 1902. Pp. 34.

4903 STIMPSON, MARY STOYELL. "Thomaston––the home of Knox." NEM, New Ser., 29 (1903–1904), 730–740.

4904 TEETERS, NEGLEY K. "Early days of the Maine State Prison at Thomaston." Journal of Criminal Law and Criminology, 38 (July–August, 1947), 104–108.

4905 THOMASTON CONGREGATIONAL CHURCH. The 150th anniversary of the Thomaston Congregational Church, Thomaston, Maine, 1809–1959. n.p., [1959]. Unpaged. MBC.

4906 THOMASTON HISTORICAL SOCIETY. Tall ships, white houses, and elms: Thomaston, Maine, 1870–1900. Thomaston, 1976. Pp. 154. Me.
Pictorial history.

4907 WILLIAMS, HARRIET R. "Montpelier, the Maine home of Major General Henry Knox." DARMag, 98 (1964), 582–585.

SEE ALSO entries 1659–1660, 1663, 1666, 1753, 2082, and 4589.

THORNDIKE (WALDO CO.)

4908 THORNDIKE, ME. A brief history of Thorndike, Maine, 1819–1919. Thorndike: Newell White, 1919. Pp. 29. MBNEH.

4909 _____. Sesquicentennial celebration, town of Thorndike, county of Waldo, State of Maine, August 9, 10, 1969. n.p., [1969]. Pp. 36. Me.

THORNDIKE TOWNSHIP (SOMERSET CO.)

4910 No items located.

TIM POND TOWNSHIP (FRANKLIN CO.)

4911 No items located.

TOMHEGAN TOWNSHIP (SOMERSET CO.)

4912 No items located.

TOPSFIELD (WASHINGTON CO.)

4913 No items located.

TOPSHAM (SAGADAHOC CO.)

4914 SMALL, CHARLES H. The state seal. Pillsbury's soliloquy. When I was a lad; or The second Jackson, M.D.... Topsham, 1880. Pp. 8.

4915 SMITH, LINCOLN. "Leadership in local government––the New England town." Social Science, 29 (June, 1954), 147–157.

4916 TOPSHAM, ME. Topsham, Maine: 200th anniversary, July 17, 18, 19, 1964. [Brunswick: Brunswick Publishing, 1964]. Pp. 37.

4917 WILSON, ADAM. Historical discourse, delivered before the Baptist church in Topsham, at the close of the first half-century of their history, September 2, 1865. Waterville: Maxham & Wing's Print, 1866. Pp. 15. MB.

SEE ALSO entries 1315 and 2573.

TOWNSHIP C (OXFORD CO.)

4918 No items located.

TOWNSHIP D (FRANKLIN CO.)

4919 No items located.

TOWNSHIP E (FRANKLIN CO.)

4920 No items located.

TOWNSHIP 6 (FRANKLIN CO.)

4921   No items located.

TREMONT (HANCOCK CO.)

4922   COUSINS, EDGAR M. The Mt. Desert Congregational Church, Tremont, Maine: historical
sermon and notes. n.p., [1895]. Pp. 29.

4923   "HISTORY of McKinley and town of Tremont on
Mount Desert Island." SJMH, 10 (1922), 233-
235.
    McKinley is a village in Tremont.

4924   KEENE, WILLIAM R. History of Tremont Lodge,
No. 77, of Free and Accepted Masons, Tremont,
Maine, from 1881 to 1891, inclusive. Ells-
worth: Campbell's Job Print, 1891. Pp. 21.
[MePGLM].

4925   LURVEY, C. H. History of Tremont Lodge, No.
77, of Free and Accepted Masons, Tremont,
Maine, from 1871 to 1881. Ellsworth: Campbell Bros., 1881. Pp. 26. [MePGLM].

4926   TARR, ANDREW. History of Tremont Lodge, No.
77, of Free and Accepted Masons, Tremont,
Me., from 1854 to 1871. Portland: Stephen
Berry, 1874. Pp. 19. MeHi.

SEE ALSO entry 1587.

TRENTON (HANCOCK CO.)

4927   "REVIVAL in Trenton, Maine." The Sabbath
School Treasury, 6 (1833), 32.

SEE ALSO entries 1569 and 1579.

TRESCOTT TOWNSHIP (WASHINGTON CO.)

4928   No items located.

TROUT BROOK TOWNSHIP (PASCATAQUIS CO.)

4929   No items located.

TROY (WALDO CO.)

4930   No items located.

TURNER (ANDROSCOGGIN CO.)

4931   FRENCH, WILLIAM RILEY. A history of Turner,
Maine, from its settlement to 1886. Portland: Hoyt, Fogg & Donham, 1887. Pp. viii,
312.
    Manuscript indices by Ethel P. Hall and
Margaret Z. Garrett are at the Maine Historical Society.

4932   GILBERT, WASHINGTON. Address ... delivered at
the centennial celebration of the town of
Turner, July 7th, 1886. Portland: B. Thurston, 1886. Pp. 16. MeHi.

4933   HALE, CLARENCE. "Turner, Maine, centennial,
November 23, 1923." SJMH, 12 (1924), 149-158.

4934   RICH, CAROLINE WEBSTER D. STOCKBRIDGE. Poem
written for the centennial celebration of the
town of Turner, Maine. Portland: B. Thurston, 1886. Pp. 14.

SEE ALSO entries 405 and 549.

UNION (KNOX CO.)

4935   MATTHEWS, EDWARDS A. Horse and buggy days:
a brief history of Union, Maine. Belfast:
Kelley Pr., 1950. Pp. 381.

4936   NASH, CHESTER and PATRICIA KAHN. 200 years
in Union: a pictorial history of Union,
Maine. [Union]: Union Historical Society,
1974. Pp. 95. MeU.

4937   SIBLEY, JOHN LANGDON. A history of the town
of Union, in the county of Lincoln, Maine, to
the middle of the nineteenth century; with a
family register of the settlers before the
year 1800, and of their descendants. Boston:
Benjamin B. Mussey, 1851. Pp. ix, 540.

4938   UNION, ME. A brief story and census of Union.
Union: G. H. Cameron & J. R. Meservey, 1929.
Unpaged. MeHi.

4939   _____. Union register: census, history,
statistics, business directory.... Union:
Union Publishing, 1888. Pp. 31. MeHi.

4940   UNION WEEKLY TIMES. Union, past and present:
an illustrated history of the town of Union,
Maine, from earliest times to date. Union,
1895. Pp. 96.

UNITY (WALDO CO.)

4941   MURCH, EDMUND. A brief history of the town of
Unity, written and read ... at a meeting of
Harvest Moon Grange, Thorndike, 1892. Belfast:
G. W. Burgess, 1893. Pp. 18.

4942 TABER, JAMES R. History of Unity, Maine. Augusta: Maine Farmer Pr., 1916. Pp. 144.

4943 UNITY, ME. BICENTENNIAL BOOKLET COMMITTEE. Unity today, 1975-76. n.p., [1976]. Pp. 48. Me.

4944 UNITY SESQUICENTENNIAL SOCIETY. Sesquicentennial of the town of Unity, Maine, 1804-1954. n.p., [1954]. Pp. 26. Me.

4945 VICKERY, JAMES BERRY, III. A history of the town of Unity, Maine. Manchester: Falmouth Publishing, 1954. Pp. 254.
An enlargement of the author's master's thesis at the University of Maine.

UNITY TOWNSHIP (KENNEBEC CO.)

4946 No items located.

UPPER CUPSUPTIC TOWNSHIP (OXFORD CO.)

4947 No items located.

UPPER ENCHANTED TOWNSHIP (SOMERSET CO.)

4948 No items located.

UPPER MOLUNKUS TOWNSHIP (AROOSTOOK CO.)

4949 No items located.

UPTON (OXFORD CO.)

4950 HEYWOOD, CHARLES ERROL. History of Upton, Maine. Norway: Oxford Hills Pr., 1973. Pp. 14.

VAN BUREN (AROOSTOOK CO.)

4951 DUNN, CLAIRE MARY DEVEAU. There need never be discouragement. [Madawaska: Valley Publishing, 1972?]. Pp. 177. MeU.
Deveau family.

4952 PELLETIER, MARTINE. "In God we trust": Van Buren, Maine. Madawaska: St. John Valley Printers, 1976. Pp. 132. [MeMaHi].

4953 VAN BUREN, ME. PAROISSE ST. BRUNO. Album-souvenir du centenaire de la fondation de la Paroisse St. Bruno, Van Buren, Maine, 1838-1938. n.p., [1938]. Pp. 103. MBC.

VANCEBORO (WASHINGTON CO.)

4954 LOW, ELIZABETH ARMSTRONG. "The bridge over the River St. Croix." Down East, 20 (March, 1974), 66-67.
Attempt by a German spy, Werner Horn, to blow up the bridge during World War I.

VASSALBORO (KENNEBEC CO.)

4955 "HISTORY of the Vassalboro Free Public Library." MeLAB, 20 (August, 1959), 13-14.

4956 MANSON, RAYMOND RUSSELL and ELSIA HOLWAY BURLEIGH. First seventy years of Oak Grove Seminary. [Vassalboro]: Vassalboro Historical Society, 1965. Pp. 38.

4957 MARTIN, DON. "East Vassalboro's old water mill still going strong." Down East, 18 (November, 1971), 38-41.

4958 MASSE, HERMAN CHARLES. History of the old water power grist and saw mill at East Vassalboro, Maine, 1797-1971; owned and operated by the Masse family since 1912.... n.p., [1971]. 15 leaves.

4959 ROBBINS, ALMA PIERCE. The history of Vassalborough, Maine. [Vassalboro?, 1971?]. Pp. 62.

4960 WRIGHT, LAURIE ROBESON. "Maine Quakers with E.S.P." Maine Dig, 1 (Summer, 1967), 83-84.

SEE ALSO entry 1645.

VEAZIE (PENOBSCOT CO.)

4961 TODD, HELEN HATHORNE. Veazie in review.... [Veazie]: Ladies Aid Society of the Veazie Congregational Church, 1953. Pp. 10. MeU.

VEAZIE GORE (PENOBSCOT CO.)

4962 No items located.

VERONA (HANCOCK CO.)

4963 "Orphan's Island." MeHistMag, 8 (1893), 67-68.

VIENNA (KENNEBEC CO.)

4964 BRADLEY, IRVING R. History of Vienna, Maine from 1782 to 1952 ... as given on town's 150th anniversary. n.p., [1952?]. Unpaged. Me.

VINALHAVEN (KNOX CO.)

4965 CALDERWOOD, IVAN E. Days of Uncle Dave's fish house: Vinalhaven seafarers are re-called. Rockland: Courier-Gazette, 1969. Pp. 274.

4966 _____. The saga of Hod. Rockland: Courier Gazette, 1971. Pp. 197. MeP.
Social life and customs.

4967 _____. Sequel ... days of Uncle Dave's fish house: Vinalhaven seafarers are recalled. Rockland: Courier-Gazette, 1972. Pp. 266.

4968 CUMMINGS, MILDRED H. "When granite was king on Vinalhaven." Down East, 17 (September, 1970), 42-47.

4969 FLAGG, PALUEL JOSEPH. Maine holiday. N.Y.: Chad-Ohre Pr., 1947. Pp. 27. Me.

4969A GRINDLE, ROGER LEE. "Bodwell Blue: the story of Vinalhaven's granite industry." MeHSQ, 16 (1976-1977), 51-112.

4970 "LIFE and death of an island." Down East, 3 (February-March, 1957), 14-17, 29.
Hurricane Island.

4971 MASON, JOHN. "The wreck of the 'Royal Tar.'" Yankee, 29 (October, 1965), 85, 110-113.
1836.

4972 VINALHAVEN, ME. CENTENNIAL COMMITTEE. A brief historical sketch of the town of Vinal-haven, from its earliest known settlement; prepared by order of the town, on the occa-sion of its one hundredth anniversary. (1889) Rockland: Star Job Print., 1900. Pp. 84.
Present edition continued to 1900 by Albra J. Vinal.

4973 WINSLOW, SIDNEY L. Fish scales and stone chips. Portland: Machigonne Press, 1952. Pp. 256. Me.

SEE ALSO entry 1656.

WADE (AROOSTOOK CO.)

4974 No items located.

WAITE (WASHINGTON CO.)

4975 No items located.

WALDO (WALDO CO.)

4976 No items located.

WALDOBORO (LINCOLN CO.)

4977 BARTER, J. MALCOLM. "Waldoboro." Down East, 11 (June, 1965), 37-39, 49-50, 52.

4978 BROWN, GILBERT PATTEN. "New England's oldest Lutheran church." The Pennsylvania German, 11 (1910), 731-733.

4979 GROSS, ESTHER. Waldoborough, 1773-1973: 200 anniversary, a pictorial history. Waldoboro: Waldoboro Bicentennial Committee, 1973. Pp. 96.

4980 JORDAN, JOHN WOOLF. "A historical sketch of the Moravian Mission at Broad Bay, Maine, 1760-1770." Moravian HST, 4 (1891-1895), 1-12.

4981 KEENE, JESSIE L. History of Waldoboro Vil-lage Methodist Church, Waldoboro, Maine. n.p., 1957. Pp. 12. MeHi.

4982 LOCKE, JOHN LYMBURNER. "Translation of Gen. Waldo's circular--1753." MeHSC, 6 (1859), 319-332.
Includes an introduction; Samuel Waldo.

4983 McVICAR, C. WARNER, ed. Waldoboro's history: brief history of a beautiful Downeast town on Maine's midcoast. Waldoboro: Waldoboro His-torical Society, 1971. Pp. 16. Me.

4984 MILLER, FRANK BURTON. The Miller family: an address delivered before the Miller Family Re-union Association of North Waldoboro, Maine, September 7, 1904. Rockland: Caslon Pr. Print, 1909. Pp. 47.

4985 _____. "The Waldoboro Millers." MHGR, 8 (1895), 238-241.
Miller family.

4986 MILLER, SAMUEL LLEWELLYN. History of the town of Waldoboro, Maine. Wiscasset: Emer-son, 1910. Pp. 281.

4987 "A MORAVIAN colony in Maine." MeHSC, 2 Ser., 2 (1891), 333.

4988 PAYNE, FREDERICK G. 200th anniversary, Old German Church and meetinghouse. Waldoboro: Ladies Auxiliary and the Trustees of the Ger-man Protestant Society, [1972?]. Unpaged. Me.

4989 PITCHER, FRED A. Sketch of Waldoboro, Maine. [Boston?]: Waldoboro Club of Boston, n.d. Pp. 35. MBNEH.

4990 POHLMAN, HENRY N. The German colony and Lu-theran Church in Maine: an address delivered before the Historical Society of the Lutheran Church, at its meeting in Washington, D.C., May 14th, 1869.... Gettysburg, Pa.: J. E. Wible, 1869. Pp. 24.

4991 "THE REED Mansion in Waldoboro as a source of history." Sun Up, 9 (July, 1931), 5.

4992 ROGGENBAUER, JOSEF. "Über die schweren Anfänge einer deutschen Siedlung in Neu-England aus der Mitte des 18. Jahrhunderts." Institut für Auslandsbeziehungen. Stuttgart. Zeitschrift für Kulturaustausch, 19 (1969), 297-302.
    Title in English: Difficult beginnings of a mid-eighteenth-century German settlement in New England; a copy is in the Special Collections Department, University of Maine at Orono.

4993 STAHL, JASPER JACOB. "Diary of a Moravian missionary at Broad Bay, Maine, in 1760." NEQ, 12 (1939), 747-759.
    George Soelle.

4994 _____. History of old Broad Bay and Waldoboro. Portland: Bond Wheelwright, 1956. 2v.

4995 THOMPSON, GARRETT W. "The Germans in Maine." SJMH, 5 (1917-1918), 3-7, 140-146.
    "To be continued," but no more appeared.

4996 WALDOBORO, ME. The centennial celebration of the incorporation of Waldoboro', Maine, July 4, 1873. Bangor: B. A. Burr, 1873. Pp. 52.

4997 WALDOBORO folks. [Boston]: Waldoboro-Boston Club, 1917. Pp. 35. MeHi.

4998 WALDOBORO HIGH SCHOOL. Waldoboro. [Waldoboro, 1934]. Pp. 42. Me.

4999 WILLIAMSON, WILLIAM DURKEE. "Lutherans." American Quarterly Register, 13 (1840-1841), 162-169.
    German settlers at Waldoboro.

    SEE ALSO entries 1216, 1282, 1706, 4589, and 5003.

WALES (ANDROSCOGGIN CO.)

5000 SEE entry 3769.

WALLAGRASS PLANTATION (AROOSTOOK CO.)

5001 No items located.

WALTHAM (HANCOCK CO.)

5002 SOME history of the town of Waltham and the Jordan family. n.p., [1966]. v.p. Me.

WARREN (KNOX CO.)

5003 EATON, CYRUS. Annals of the town of Warren, in Knox County, Maine, with the early history of St. George's, Broad Bay, and the neighboring settlements on the Waldo Patent. (1851) Emily Eaton, ed. 2d ed. Hallowell: Masters & Livermore, 1877. Pp. xvi, 680.
    For index, see entry 5010.

5004 FROM Warren to the sea, 1827-1852: letters of the Counce and McCallum families. Bertha K. Drewett and Arthur Spear, eds. Middletown, N.Y.: Whitlock Pr., 1970. Pp. xix, 203.

5005 GOULD, EDWARD KALLOCH. Historical address; delivered August 30, 1936 at bi-centennial of the town of Warren, Maine. [Rockland, 1936]. Pp. 19.

5006 MOODY, LINWOOD W. "Warren Depot." Down East, 16 (October, 1969), 50-51, 53-55.
    History of the village of Warren Depot.

5007 PORTER, LILLIAN RUSSELL. Bicentennial pageant, Warren, Maine, 1736-1936. n.p., 1972. Pp. 18. MeU.

5008 REIMS, GORDON A. "Waterway in the wilderness." NEG, 17 (Fall, 1975), 32-38.
    Georges River Canal.

5009 WARREN, ME. Warren history.... Union: Union Publishing, 1888. Pp. 44. MBNEH.

5010 WARREN HISTORICAL SOCIETY. Index [to] Annals of Warren, 1605-1876. n.p., [1970?]. Pp. 47. Me.
    See entry 5003.

    SEE ALSO entries 1659, 1666, and 4589.

WASHBURN (AROOSTOOK CO.)

5011 WASHBURN, ME. Washburn, one hundred years of progress. n.p., [1961]. Pp. 39. Me.

WASHINGTON (KNOX CO.)

5012 WALWORTH, ARTHUR CLARENCE. The Medomak way: the story of the first fifty years of an American summer camp for boys. Lancaster, N.H.: Bisbee Pr., 1953. Pp. 116.

5013 WASHINGTON, ME. HISTORICAL COMMITTEE. Sesquicentennial celebration, Washington, Maine, 1811-1961. n.p., [1961]. Unpaged. Me.

WASHINGTON TOWNSHIP (FRANKLIN CO.)

5014   No items located.

WATERBORO (YORK CO.)

5015   HAMILTON, SAMUEL KING. The Hamiltons of
Waterborough (York County, Maine), their ancestors and descendants ... 912-1912. Boston: Murray and Emery, 1912. Pp. xiii, 407.
        Contains an account of the Massabesick
Plantation and the town of Waterboro.

5016   KNIGHTS, ERNEST G. "The accursed brook."
Yankee, 20 (March, 1956), 48-50.
        Thomas Hanson's smelt brook.

5017   _____. Waterboro, York County, Maine, 1768-
1955. n.p., 1955. Unpaged. Me.

5018   SMITH, MRS. H. A. "God of all creation
faithfully worshipped: Church of St. Stephen
the Martyr, Waterboro Center." The Northeast, 79 (July, 1952), 4.

WATERFORD (OXFORD CO.)

5019   DOUGLASS, JOHN ABBOT. A discourse delivered
before the Congregational Church and Society
of Waterford, Me., Nov. 7th, 1871, at the
semi-centennial anniversary of the settlement
of the pastor. Bridgton: News Pr., [1871].
Pp. 15.

5020   FREEMASONS. WATERFORD, ME. MT. TIRE'M
LODGE, NO. 132. Mt. Tire'm Lodge, No. 132,
Free and Accepted Masons, Waterford, Me.
Norway: Oxford County Advertiser, 1893.
Pp. 32. MeHi.

5021   GAGE, THOMAS HOVEY, ed. Notes on the history
of Waterford, Maine. Worcester, Mass., 1913.
Pp. 87.

5022   RIPLEY, LINCOLN. "A description and history
of Waterford, in the county of York." MHSC,
9 (1804), 137-147.

5023   WATERFORD, ME. The history of Waterford, Oxford County, Maine, comprising historical address, by Henry P. Warren; record of families,
by Rev. William Warren, D.D.; centennial proceedings, by Samuel Warren. Portland: Hoyt,
Fogg & Donham, 1879. Pp. vi, 371.

WATERVILLE (KENNEBEC CO.)

5024   BANGS, ISAAC SPARROW. Military history of
Waterville, Maine, including the names and
record, so far as known, of all soldiers from
Waterville, in the several wars of the
republic; a portion of the records of the
Waterville Monument Association, and a sketch
of W. S. Heath Post, No. 14, G. A. R. Augusta: Kennebec Journal Print, 1902. Pp. 75.

5025   "BASEBALL at Colby." Colby Alumnus, 1 (1911-
1912), 124-125.

5026   BIXLER, JULIUS SEELYE. Colby College (1813-
1953): a venture of faith. N.Y.: Newcomen
Society in North America, 1953. Pp. 32.

5027   _____. "To grasp the budding growth--nettle
and all." Colby Alumnus, 63 (Fall, 1973),
17-32, (Winter, 1974), 13-28.
        Colby College, 1942-1959.

5028   BUISSON, EMMA. Lettres de Mère Marie du Sacré-
Coeur, fondatrice des Ursulines de Waterville,
Maine, Etats Unis; précédées d'une notice
biographique par U. T. R. Québec: L'Action
sociale limitée, 1917. Pp. 238.

5029   BURRAGE, HENRY SWEETSER. "The beginnings of
Waterville College, now Colby University."
MeHSC, 2 Ser., 4 (1893), 124-145.

5030   CHAMPLIN, JAMES TIFT. A historical discourse
delivered at the fiftieth anniversary of Colby University, August 2d, 1870. Waterville,
1870. Pp. 30.

5031   CHAPMAN, ALFRED KING. "Contrasts in curricu-
lum." Colby Alumnus, 51 (Fall, 1961), 7-9.
        Colby College.

5032   CHIPMAN, CHARLES PHILLIPS. The formative
period in Colby's history. Waterville, 1912.
Pp. 29.

5033   "COBURN Classical Institute." BTJ, 19 (1906-
1907), 313-317.

5034   "COBURN Classical Institute, Waterville,
Maine." BTJ, 23 (1910-1911), 629, 631.

5035   COLBY COLLEGE, WATERVILLE, ME. General catalogue of officers, graduates and former students of Colby College. Charles P. Chipman,
ed. Centennial ed., 1820-1920. Waterville,
1920. Pp. 470.

5036   _____. The history of Colby College. By
Ernest Cummings Marriner. Waterville, 1963.
Pp. 659.

5037   _____. Twelve years of transition, 1942-1954;
report of the president of Colby College.
Waterville, 1954. Pp. 16. MeP.
        The president was Julius S. Bixler.

5038   "THE COLBY College Press: an anniversary report." ColbLibQ, 4 (1955-1958), 6-16.

5039   "COLBY in the old days." Colby Alumnus, 1
(1911-1912), 112-116.

5040 "COLBY'S first football team." Colby Alumnus, 26 (October, 1936), 2.

5041 CUMMINGS, OSMOND RICHARD. "Waterville, Fairfield and Oakland Railway Company." Transportation Bulletin, No. 72 (April-December, 1965), 1-40.

5042 CUSTOM and practice in medical care: a comparative study of two hospitals in Arbroath, Scotland, U.K., and Waterville, Maine, U.S.A. by J. Simpson et al. N.Y.: Oxford Univ. Pr., 1968. Pp. 119.
   Thayer Hospital.

5043 DUNN, REUBEN WESLEY. "The early days of baseball." Colby Alumnus, 15 (1925-1926), 49-50.
   Colby College.

5044 DYER, RICHARD NYE. "Colby on Mayflower Hill." Down East, 4 (May, 1958), 20-23.

5045 ELKS, BENEVOLENT AND PROTECTIVE ORDER OF, WATERVILLE, ME., WATERVILLE LODGE, NO. 905. Waterville Lodge 905, fiftieth anniversary, 1904-1954, souvenir program. n.p., [1954]. Unpaged. MeHi.
   Includes a history of the lodge by Ernest C. Simpson.

5046 "FOOTBALL at Colby." Colby Alumnus, 2 (1912-1913), 36-38.

5047 FOSS, H. WARREN. "Colby in the 90's." Colby Alumnus, 39 (February, 1950), 10, 12, 24.

5048 _____. "The gay nineties--the golden age." Colby Alumnus, 33 (April, 1944), 5-6.
   Colby College.

5049 FRYE, ROBIE G. "A diary in 1878." Colby Alumnus, 22 (1932-1933), 188-190.
   Colby College.

5050 GIVEEN, CLEMENT MARTIN, ed. A chronology of municipal history and election statistics, Waterville, Maine, 1771-1908. Augusta: Maine Farmer Pr., 1908. Pp. 278.

5051 _____. "Waterville as a railroad center." BTJ, 23 (1910-1911), 588-589, 591, 603.

5052 "A GREAT manufacturing institution." BTJ, 26 (1913-1914), 786-788.
   Lockwood Company, textiles.

5053 HALL, JON F., ed. Old Waterville: a picture book. Waterville: Waterville Historical Society, [1976?]. Unpaged. MeU.

5054 HALL, OLIVER A. "Some early Colby ball players." Colby Alumnus, 32 (May, 1943), 9-10, (July, 1943), 10-13.
   Baseball.

5055 HARTHORN, DREW THOMPSON. "Coburn Classical Institute." Colby Alumnus, 15 (1925-1926), 116-120.

5056 HATCH, BENTON LE ROY. A preliminary check list of Waterville, Maine, imprints through 1850. Waterville: Colby College Library, 1952. Pp. 23.

5057 HAYNES, GEORGE HENRY. Souvenir of Waterville, the university city of Maine. N.Y.: Kellogg, 1898. Pp. 32.

5058 HERRICK, MARY DARRAH and NIXON ORWIN RUSH. "Early literary societies and their libraries in Colby College, 1824-1878." College and Research Libraries, 6 (1944), 58-63.

5059 HERRICK, MARY DARRAH. "Forerunners of Colby fraternities." Colby Alumnus, 31 (March, 1942), 6-8.
   Literary societies.

5060 _____. "Two Colby clubs of the 80s." Colby Alumnus, 34 (May, 1947), 9.
   Munchausen Club and the Anti-Lingo League.

5061 HILL, J. F. "Brief account of the Waterville Clinical Society." JMS, 1 (1894-1895), 52.

5062 "HISTORY of Waterville Lodge, No. 33, of Maine." New England Freemason, 1 (1874), 393-401.

5063 JOHNSON, FRANKLIN WINSLOW. Exercises in celebration of the seventy-fifth anniversary of the opening of the Coburn Classical Institute, Waterville, Maine, June 19-25, 1904. Portland, 1904. Pp. 73.

5064 JORDAN, ARCHER. "Football in the nineties." Colby Alumnus, 2 (1912-1913), 38-40.
   Colby College.

5065 KING, GEORGE MELLEN PRENTISS. "Memories of Waterville College, 1853-1857." Colby Alumnus, 3 (1913-1914), 29-32.

5066 KNIGHT, JOHN T. "Maine's newest parish: the history of Saint Mark's Church, Waterville." The Northeast, 75 (September, 1948), 12-17.

5067 KNOWLTON, WILLIAM SMITH. "Some reminiscences." Colby Alumnus, 15 (1925-1926), 152-153.
   Colby College.

5068 LIBBY, HERBERT CARLYLE. "An historical address." Colby Alumnus, 21 (1931-1932), 61-75.
   Colby College.

5069 _____. "The public schools of Waterville, Maine." BTJ, 23 (1910-1911), 599, 601, 603.

5070 WATERVILLE

5070 "LOOKING backward fifty years." Colby Alumnus, 37 (May, 1948), 10-11.
Colby College in 1898.

5071 "THE MAN in the Hathaway shirt." Pine Cone,
8 (Winter, 1952-1953), 3-7.
C. F. Hathaway Shirt Company.

5072 MARRINER, ERNEST CUMMINGS. "A century of
achievement." Colby Alumnus, 37 (July,
1948), 8-12.
Colby Alumni Association.

5073 _____. "Money is not all." Colby Alumnus,
50 (Spring, 1961), 7-9.
Colby Alumni Association.

5074 _____. "Room and board in shillings." Colby
Alumnus, 60 (Winter, 1971), 20-21.
Colby in the 1830s.

5075 _____. "Some pointers from Colby's past."
Colby Alumnus, 52 (Spring, 1963), 2-6.

5076 _____. "The tradition of scholarship at Colby." Colby Alumnus, 48 (Summer, 1959), 20-
24.

5077 MOORE, KATRINA. "Waterville, Kennebec Valley
town." Down East, 6 (October, 1959), 22-26,
42-43.

5078 OWEN, FRED K. "Colby fifty years ago." Colby Alumnus, 26 (March, 1937), 13-14.

5079 PAINE, ALBERT WARE. "Recollections of the
early days." Colby Alumnus, 35 (April,
1946), 8-9.
Colby College as recalled in 1902 by an
alumnus of 1832.

5080 _____. "One hundred years ago." Colby Alumnus, 22 (1932-1933), 18-20.
Colby College, 1826-1832; written in 1895.

5081 PHI BETA KAPPA. MAINE BETA, COLBY COLLEGE.
Handbook of the Beta Chapter of Maine, Colby
College. J. William Black, comp. Water-
ville, 1901. Pp. 39. Me.

5082 PHILBRICK, MINNIE LAMBERT SMITH. Centennial
history of the First Baptist Church of Waterville, Maine. Waterville: Frank B. Philbrick, 1925. Pp. 129.
1818-1918.

5083 POTTLE, FREDERICK A. "Colby's second half-
century." Colby Alumnus, 34 (March, 1945),
7-9, (April, 1945), 7-10.

5084 PREBLE, FRED MYRON. The educational abbey of
Maine Baptists. Waterville, [1904?]. Pp. 32.
Colby College.

5085 RAMSDELL, T. J. "Colby in the 80's." Colby
Alumnus, 39 (April, 1950), 4, 15.

5086 REDINGTON, FRANK. "Waterville, the city of
progress." BTJ, 23 (1910-1911), 571-573,
575, 577, 579, 581, 583-584.

5087 REID, DICK. "Fifty years of Colby football."
Colby Alumnus, 32 (November, 1942), 11-14.

5088 RUSH, NIXON ORWIN. "Historical sketch of the
Colby library." Colby Alumnus, 28 (November-
December, 1938), 3-4.

5089 _____. "Maine's first circulating library."
MeLAB, 3 (August, 1942), 13-14.
Waterville Circulating Library, 1826.

5090 ["SIGNIFICANT moments in Colby history."]
Colby Alumnus, 64 (Spring, 1975), entire
issue.

5091 SKINNER, JOSEPH O. History of Waterville
Lodge, No. 33, of Free and Accepted Masons,
of Waterville, Me., from its foundation to
1874. Portland: Stephen Berry, 1874.
Pp. 104. MeBa.

5092 SMALL, ALBION WOODBURY. "Colby University."
NEM, 6 (1887-1888), 309-320.

5093 SMITH, JOSEPH COBURN. "The good old days and
now." Colby Alumnus, 20 (1930-1931), 226-
230.
Colby College, 1920-1930.

5094 _____. "150 honorable years." Colby Alumnus, 50 (Spring, 1961), 11-12.
Colby College.

5095 SMITH, WILLIAM A. "The Congregational Church
of Waterville." MeCP, 30 (May, 1943), 6-8.

5096 SOULE, BERTHA LOUISE. "Colby in the eighties." Colby Alumnus, 43 (April, 1954), 6-10.

5097 "A TWENTIETH birthday for the 'Colby Library
Quarterly.'" Colby Alumnus, 53 (Fall, 1963),
11-12.

5098 LES URSULINES à Waterville, précis historique,
1888-1913. Waterville: Elm City Publishing,
[1913]. Pp. 23. MBC.

5099 WATERVILLE, ME. Waterville centennial, 1802-
1902, June 22-23-24, the official programme.
Waterville: W. M. Ladd, [1902]. Pp. 36.
MeHi.

5100 WATERVILLE, ME. FIRST BAPTIST CHURCH. Cen-
tenary, 1818-1918, First Baptist Church,
Waterville, Maine. n.p., [1918]. Pp. 15.
MeHi.
Includes brief historical sketch by Minnie
Lambert Smith Philbrick.

5101 _____. A history of the First Baptist Church,
Waterville, Maine, articles of faith, church
government, and list of present members.
Portland: B. Thurston, 1872. Pp. 32. MeHi.

5102 "WATERVILLE claims one of the oldest banks in Maine." Sun Up, 4 (September, 1927), 36.
Ticonic National Bank.

5103 "WATERVILLE, Maine." BTJ, 3 (1890-1891), 329-335.

5104 WATERVILLE PUBLIC LIBRARY. The fiftieth anniversary, 1896-1946: historical facts covering the half century.... [Waterville?, 1946]. Pp. 21. Me.

5105 _____. Waterville Public Library, souvenir program of the fiftieth anniversary of the dedication of the library building, 1905-1955. n.p., [1955?]. Unpaged. MeU.
Includes brief history.

5106 "WATERVILLE Public Library, 1896-1946." MeLAB, 8 (February, 1947), 5-6.

5107 "THE WATERVILLE Street Railway group." Railroad Magazine, 47 (November, 1948), 82-87.

5108 "WATERVILLE, the heart of Maine." Sun Up, 3 (March, 1927), 19-20, 22, 26.

5109 "WATERVILLE'S modern public library." BTJ, 26 (1913-1914), 783.
Includes history.

5110 WEBER, CARL J. "Lowell's visit to Waterville." Colby Alumnus, 25 (May, 1936), 10.
1853.

5111 WHITE, CLARENCE H. Historical address delivered by Dr. Clarence H. White, on the occasion of the centennial celebration of the First Congregational Church, Waterville, Maine, October 21, 1928. n.p., [1928?]. Pp. 20. Me.

5112 _____. "Linking the old and new Colby." Colby Alumnus, 31 (October, 1941), 5-6.
Colby College architecture.

5113 WHITTEMORE, EDWIN CAREY, ed. The centennial history of Waterville, Kennebec County, Maine including the oration, the historical address and the poem presented at the celebration of the centennial anniversary of the incorporation of the town, June 23d, 1902. Waterville: Executive Committee of the Centennial Celebration, 1902. Pp. vii, 592.

5114 _____. "The churches of Waterville." BTJ, 23 (1910-1911), 621-622.

5115 _____. Colby College, 1820-1925: an account of its beginnings, progress and service. Waterville: The Trustees of Colby College, 1927. Pp. x, 276.

5116 _____. "The development of Colby College." Sun Up, 8 (November, 1930), 12-15.

5117 _____. "A new chapter in Colby history." Sun Up, 8 (December, 1930), 3, 31.

SEE ALSO entries 1421, 1639, and 3532.

WAYNE (KENNEBEC CO.)

5118 BRYANT, JUDSON B. A historical sketch of the Baptist Church of Wayne, Maine, read at the centennial exercises of the church, August 10, 1894. Portland: Brown Thurston, 1894. Pp. 17. MeHi.

5119 JOHNSON, JENNIE THORNE. "Picturesque 'Pocasset.'" Pine Tree Magazine, 7 (1907), 437-442.

5120 PERKINS, JACK. Illustrated history of Wayne, Maine; being a contemporary and past history of a small New England town. Wayne, 1968. Pp. 242.

5121 WALTON, GEORGE W., ed. History of the town of Wayne, Kennebec County, Maine, from its settlement to 1898. Augusta: Maine Farmer Publishing, 1898. Pp. iv, 354.

5122 WAYNE, ME. Centennial celebration of the town of Wayne, Kennebec County, Maine, August 18, 1898. Augusta: Maine Farmer Job Print, 1899. Pp. 38. Me.

WEBBERTOWN TOWNSHIP (AROOSTOOK CO.)

5123 No items located.

WEBSTER PLANTATION (PENOBSCOT CO.)

5124 No items located.

WELD (FRANKLIN CO.)

5125 CURRIER, GEORGE F. "One hundred fiftieth anniversary at Weld." MeCP, 46 (September 15, 1959), 9.
First Congregational Church.

5126 FOSTER, E. J. "Early settlers of Weld." MHGR, 1 (1884), 119-123, 172-179; 2 (1885), 38-44, 94-99, 181-186, 240-243.

5127 ODLIN, JOHN W. Weld, Maine. Milford, N.H.: Cabinet Pr., [1940?]. Unpaged. MeHi.

5128 WELD, ME. Weld sesquicentennial, 1816-1966, history and program. n.p., [1966]. Pp. 24. Me.

WELLINGTON (PISCATAQUIS CO.)

5129   No items located.

WELLS (YORK CO.)

5130   CUSHING, JAMES ROYAL. Historical discourse; delivered Oct. 29, 1851, at the one hundred and fiftieth anniversary of the organization of the First Congregational Church, (the second in the state), in Wells, Maine. Portland, 1851. Pp. 22.

5131   DEAN, JOHN. A narrative of the shipwreck of the Nottingham Galley, in her voyage from England to Boston; with an account of the miraculous escape of the captain and his crew, on a rock called Boone-Island, the hardships they endured there, and their happy deliverance. Mason Philip Smith, ed. Portland: Provincial Pr., 1968. Pp. 23.

5132   "THE FIRST Congregational Church of Wells." Congregationalism in Maine, 13 (1926), 29-30.

5133   FRYER, ROBERT. "Lessons at Ogunquit." National Theatre Conference Bulletin, 9 (October, 1947), 10-19.
   Ogunquit Playhouse.

5134   HUBBARD, JEREMIAH and JONATHAN GREENLEAF. "An account of Wells." MeHSC, 1 (1831), 255-268.

5135   PERKINS, ESSELYN GILMAN. History of Ogunquit Village, with many interesting facts of more recent interest. Portland: Falmouth Publishing, 1951. Pp. 66.

5136   _____. A new history of Ogunquit, Maine. n.p., 1974. Pp. vi, 64. Me.

5137   _____. Wells: the frontier town of Maine. Ogunquit, 1970-1971. 2v.

5138   STEELE, WILLIAM. "Ogunquit Playhouse." Down East, 20 (July, 1974), 82-85.

5139   WELLS, ME. Programme of the celebration of the 250th anniversary of the town of Wells, Maine, August 26th, 1903. Kennebunk: Eastern Star Print, 1903. Pp. 11. Me.
   Includes historical sketch by William M. Tripp.

5140   WELLS, ME. 300TH ANNIVERSARY COMMITTEE. 300th anniversary, Wells, Maine, 1653-1953. n.p., [1953]. Pp. 60. Me.

   SEE ALSO entries 1322, 1884, and 5320.

WESLEY (WASHINGTON CO.)

5141   No items located.

WEST BATH (SAGADAHOC CO.)

5142   "REMINISCENCES of a former resident of New Meadows." PejHSC, 1 Pt. 1 (1889), 46-53.

WEST FORKS PLANTATION (SOMERSET CO.)

5143   No items located.

WEST GARDINER (KENNEBEC CO.)

5144   LYFORD, ELMORE B. "The only house of its kind?" Yankee, 33 (May, 1969), 40-43.
   An octagon house.

5145   MARTIN, BUD. West Gardiner's hundred years. Augusta: Kennebec Journal, 1950. Pp. 73. Me.

   SEE ALSO entries 1633 and 1649.

WEST MIDDLESEX CANAL GRANT (SOMERSET CO.)

5146   No items located.

WEST PARIS (OXFORD CO.)

5147   HAMMOND, GEORGE WARREN, et al. History of Granite Lodge, No. 182, Free and Accepted Masons, West Paris, Me., from its organization, September 16, 1878 to 1895. Portland: Stephen Berry, 1895. Pp. 24. MeBa.

5148   "HISTORY in West Paris." Sun Up, 9 (March, 1931), 24.

5149   MORTON, AGNES L. "West Paris, Maine." Sun Up, 3 (March, 1927), 14-16.

WESTBROOK (CUMBERLAND CO.)

5150   BURROUGHS, ADELINE R. "Westbrook, the paper city." Sun Up, 5 (December, 1927), 10-11.

5151   CHAPMAN, LEONARD BOND. "The first occupancy by Europeans of Saccarappa Falls on the Presumpscot River, now Westbrook." MeHSC, 2 Ser., 10 (1899), 282-300.

5152 "THE CITY of Westbrook." BTJ, 13 (1900-1901), 73–88.

5153 COBB, OLIVER A. "A city of flourishing lodges." BTJ, 19 (1906-1907), 710–711.

5154 CUMBERLAND MILLS, ME. WARREN CONGREGATIONAL CHURCH. Manual of Warren Church of Cumberland Mills, Maine. Cumberland Mills: Henry S. Cobb, 1911. Pp. 91. MeHi.
Includes history.

5155 [DESJARDINS, PHILIPPE E.]. Jubilee, a chronicle, 1899-1949. Lewiston: Echo Publishing, [1950]. Pp. 52. MBC.
St. Hyacinth Parish; in English and French.

5156 ILSLEY, GEORGE BOARDMAN. "Westbrook, a city of churches." BTJ, 19 (1906-1907), 700–704.

5157 LEWIS, JOHN R. An early history of Pride's Corner Congregational Church, 1968. Pp. 69. Me.

5158 MILLIONS, JEAN. Warren Congregational Church, 1869-1969. n.p., [1969]. Pp. 65. MeHi.

5159 ODD FELLOWS. INDEPENDENT ORDER OF. WESTBROOK, ME., SACCARAPPA LODGE, NO. 11. 100th anniversary, Saccarappa Lodge, No. 11, I.O.O.F., Westbrook, Maine, May 22, 1944. [Westbrook]: H. S. Cobb, [1944]. Pp. 36. MeHi.

5160 RAND, LEROY H. "History of Westbrook." Westbrook Board of Trade Enterprise, 1 (June, 1911), 34, 36, (September, 1911), 34, 36, (January, 1912), 24, 26, 28, 30, 32.

5161 RAY, ISABEL T. Historical pageant of Westbrook, 1820-1920. Westbrook: H. S. Cobb, [1920]. Pp. 19. MeHi.

5162 _____. History of Westbrook Congregational Church, 1832-1932. One hundred years of service. [Westbrook]: H. S. Cobb, 1932. Pp. 22. MeHi.

5163 ROWE, ERNEST RAY, comp. Highlights of Westbrook history. Marian B. Rowe, ed. [Westbrook]: Westbrook Woman's Club, 1952. Pp. 237.

5164 STONE, KENNETH G. "The Dana Mills—a Bowdoin institution." BA, 16 (1941-1942), 19–21.
Cotton; many Bowdoin Alumni have been associated with the firm.

5165 "THREE quarters of a century." MeCP, 31 (November, 1944), 6, 41.
Warren Congregational Church.

5166 WARREN, S. D. CO. A history of the S. D. Warren Company, 1854-1954. Westbrook, 1954. Pp. vi, 120. MH-BA.
Paper.

5167 WESTBROOK, ME. Official program of the commemorative exercises of the one hundredth anniversary of the town of Stroudwater, name changed to Westbrook, June 9th, 1814.... Westbrook: H. S. Cobb, 1914. Pp. 40. MeHi.
Includes history by Leroy H. Rand.

5168 WESTBROOK, ME. CHAMBER OF COMMERCE. Who's who in Westbrook, Maine in 1964. Westbrook: Wiggin Pr., 1964. 25 leaves. Me.

5169 "WESTBROOK." BTJ, 4 (1891-1892), 104–110.

5170 WESTBROOK, Maine. Westbrook: Rich Bros., [1923?]. Unpaged. MeHi.
Includes history by Isabel T. Ray.

5171 WESTBROOK CONGREGATIONAL CHURCH. Jubilee year, 125th anniversary of the Westbrook Congregational Church, January 17-18-20, 1957. [Westbrook]: Wiggin Pr., [1957?]. Pp. 20. MBC.
Includes a chronology of the church.

SEE ALSO entries 1483, 1492, and 1512.

WESTFIELD (AROOSTOOK CO.)

5172 No items located.

WESTMANLAND PLANTATION (AROOSTOOK CO.)

5173 SEE entry 1456.

WESTON (AROOSTOOK CO.)

5174 No items located.

WESTPORT (LINCOLN CO.)

5175 No items located.

WHITEFIELD (LINCOLN CO.)

5176 KEALY, JOHN E. "An ancient country rectory." America, 42 (1930), 520–521.
Roman Catholic rectory erected in the nineteenth century.

5177 WATERS, HENRY C. A history of the town of Whitefield, Maine. Elizabeth Hardwick, ed. n.p., 1959. 10 leaves. Me.

5178 WHITEFIELD, ME. Sesquicentennial celebration, 1809-1959, Whitefield, Maine. n.p., 1959. Unpaged. Me.

WHITING (WASHINGTON CO.)

5179 FORSLUND, GLADYS HALL. History of Whiting, Maine. Calais: Advertiser Publishing, 1975. Pp. 94. Me.

WHITNEYVILLE (WASHINGTON CO.)

5180 SEE entry 1863.

WILLIAMSBURG TOWNSHIP (PISCATAQUIS CO.)

5181 No items located.

WILLIMANTIC (PISCATAQUIS CO.)

5182 PACKARD, MARLBOROUGH. A history of Packard's Camps, 1894-1916. D'Arcy Van Bokkelen and Elizabeth R. Cawley, eds. n.p., 1974. Pp. 30. MeU.

WILTON (FRANKLIN CO.)

5183 ADAMO, RUTH. A history of the town of Wilton. Rumford: Rumford Publishing, 1971. Pp. 60.

5184 BASS, STREETER. G. H. Bass Company, 1876-1976. n.p., 1976. Unpaged. MeU.
    Shoes.

5185 BEAN, DEARBORN GORHAM. The history of Wilton Lodge, No. 156, of Free and Accepted Masons, Wilton, Maine, from its organization to September 15th, 1880. Farmington: Knowlton & McLeary, 1880. Pp. 14. [MePGLM].

5186 GIFFORD, ROY. "Wilton, Maine." Sun Up, 3 (June, 1926), 51-52, 54.

5187 [HEBERT, RICHARD A.] "The making of Maine: G. H. Bass & Co." Pine Cone, 1 (Autumn, 1945), 30-34.
    Shoes.

5188 NOTTAGE, W. A. The history of Wilton Lodge, No. 156, of Free and Accepted Masons, Wilton, Maine, from September, 1880, to September, 1890. Farmington: Knowlton, McLeary, 1890. Pp. 13. [MePGLM].

5189 "SETTLEMENT of Wilton, Maine." Maine Genealogist and Biographer, 3 (1877-1878), 107-109.

5190 WILTON, ME. FIRST CONGREGATIONAL CHURCH. Manual of the First Congregational Church in Wilton, Maine. Wilton: J. W. Nelson, 1912. Pp. 28. MeHi.
    Historical sketch by Mary E. Eaton.

5191 _____. Manual of the First Congregational Church in Wilton, Maine, containing a brief historical sketch.... Wilton: R. A. Carver, 1888. Pp. 20.
    A copy is held by the church.

SEE ALSO entry 1419.

WINDHAM (CUMBERLAND CO.)

5192 BODGE, GEORGE MADISON. "New Marblehead, now Windham, Maine: grant, survey and settlement of the township." MHGR, 4 (1887), 35-47, 98-104, 197-203, 248-256; 5 (1888), 44-52, 90-105, 178-183, 225-233; 6 (1889), 270-275; 7 (1893), 108-115, 156-165, 210-218; 8 (1895), 8-18, 108-114, 168-174; 9 (1898), 22-29, 53-61, 103-108, 138-143, 167-173, 214-221, 333-340.

5193 DOLE, FREDERICK HOWARD. Sketches of the history of Windham, Maine, 1734-1935: the story of a typical New England town. Westbrook: H. S. Cobb, 1935. Pp. 155.

5194 DOLE, PHOEBE. An historical poem about Windham, Maine. [Windham]: Windham Historical Society, 1970. Unpaged. MeHi.

5195 DOLE, SAMUEL THOMAS. "Ancient Naguamqueeg." MeHSC, 2 Ser., 7 (1896), 405-412.

5196 _____. "Early schools in New Marblehead, now Windham." MeHSC, 2 Ser., 9 (1898), 391-403.

5197 _____. Historical address delivered at the one hundred and fiftieth anniversary of the Congregational Church at Windham Hill, December 14, 1893. Portland: Libby & Smith, [1894?]. Pp. 10.

5198 _____. "The meeting-house war in New Marblehead." MeHSC, 2 Ser., 10 (1899), 175-185.
    Controversy as to the location of the meeting-house.

5199 _____. "An old time burial ground." MeHSC, 3 Ser., 2 (1906), 245-260.

5200 _____. Windham in the past. Frederick Howard Dole, ed. Auburn: Merrill & Webber, 1916. Pp. 611.

5201 DUMONT, EMMA L. Heritage "76" soldiers of the American Revolution, Windham, Maine. Windham: Windham Historical Society, 1975. Pp. 114. MeHi.

5202 ELDER, ISAAC L. and CHARLES JONES. History of Presumpscot Lodge, No. 127 of F. and A. M., at North Windham, Maine from 1864 to 1880. Portland: Dresser, McLellan, 1882. Pp. 32. MeHi.

5203 GOOLD, NATHAN. "Stephen Manchester, the slayer of the Indian chief Polin, at New Marblehead, now Windham, Maine, in 1756, and a soldier of the Revolution, with his ancestry." MeHSC, 2 Ser., 8 (1897), 313-330.

5204 _____. Windham, Maine, in the war of the Revolution, 1775-1783. Portland: H. W. Bryant, 1900. Pp. 16.

5205 GOOLD, WILLIAM. "Thomas Chute, the first settler of Windham, Maine, and his descendants." MeHSC, 2 Ser., 7 (1896), 412-423.

5206 SMITH, THOMAS LAURENS. A historical address, delivered on the Fourth of July, 1839, at the centennial anniversary, of the settlement of Windham. Portland: Arthur Shirley, 1840. Pp. 32.

5207 _____. History of the town of Windham. Portland: Hoyt & Fogg, 1873. Pp. 104.

5208 SPILLER, NELLIE D. "The Parson Smith homestead, South Windham, Maine." OTNE, 48 (1957-1958), 48-56.
      Peter Thatcher Smith.

5209 WINDHAM, ME. BICENTENNIAL BOOKLET COMMITTEE. Windham 1976. [Windham, 1976]. Pp. 107. MeHi.

5210 WINDHAM, ME. BICENTENNIAL COMMITTEE. Report of the Windham Bicentennial Committee, July 30, 1938 together with a copy of the historical address by Frederick H. Dole. Auburn: Merrill & Webber, [1938]. Pp. 37. Me.

5211 "WINDHAM, Maine." American Pioneer, 2 (1843), 42-45.

SEE ALSO entries 1493-1494.

WINDSOR (KENNEBEC CO.)

5212 MILLETT, MARGARET, SHIRLEY DEWAR, and DAVID SWEARINGEN, comps. History of Windsor, Maine, 1822-1972. n.p., [1972]. Pp. 50. Me.

WINN (PENOBSCOT CO.)

5213 COOPER, ARTHUR M. "The 75th anniversary of St. Thomas, Winn, and the rural Church in America." The Northeast, 71 (October, 1944), 5-7.

5214 REILLY, M. W. "Parish of the Sacred Heart, Winn, Maine." MeCathHM, 2 (March, 1914), 7-14.

5215 WINN, ME. ST. THOMAS' CHURCH. Centennial, St. Thomas' Church, Episcopal, Winn, Maine, 1868-1968. n.p., [1968]. Unpaged. MeHi.

SEE ALSO entry 50.

WINSLOW (KENNEBEC CO.)

5216 FISHER, CARLETON EDWARD. History of Fort Halifax. Winthrop: Courier-Gazette, 1972. Pp. 28.

5217 GOOLD, WILLIAM. "Fort Halifax: its projectors, builders and garrison." MeHSC, 8 (1881), 199-289.

5218 STEWART, ARTHUR W. "Fort Halifax, 1754." SJMH, 9 (1921), 132-134.

5219 WILSON, CHARLES B. "Indian relics and encampments in Maine." American Antiquarian and Oriental Journal, 5 (1883), 181-183.

5220 WINSLOW, ME. 200th anniversary, 1771-1971. n.p., [1971]. Pp. 76. Me.

5221 WIXSON, MRS. ELDWIN A., SR. "Fort Halifax in the State of Maine." DARMag, 92 (1958), 558, 561.

SEE ALSO entry 1639.

WINTER HARBOR (HANCOCK CO.)

5222 CLEAVES, SAMUEL W. "Historical sketch of Iron Bound Island, Frenchman's Bay." MeHist Mag, 8 (1893), 168-172.

5223 HAHN, NATHALIE WHITE. A history of Winter Harbor, Maine. n.p., 1974. Pp. 92. Me.

5224 HASKINS, STURGIS. "The Winter Harbor 21s." Down East, 23 (September, 1976), 48-51.
      Winter Harbor Yacht Club.

5225 RICH, LOUISE DICKINSON. "All this and fishing, too!" Outdoor Life, 128 (August, 1961), 44-46, 100-103.
      Schoodic Point.

5226 SMALLIDGE, ALLAN L. "Winter Harbor's one time elegance." Down East, 18 (September, 1971), 46-50, 103-104, 108, 112.

WINTERPORT (WALDO CO.)

5227 ATWOOD, CHARLES FRANCIS. History of Howard Lodge, No. 69, Free and Accepted Masons, Winterport, Maine, for the decade from 1879 to 1890. Bangor: Benjamin Burr, 1890. Pp. 11. [MePGLM].

5228 LITTLEFIELD, ADA DOUGLAS. An old river town; being a history of Winterport, (old Frankfort), Maine. N.Y.: Calkins, 1907. Pp. xiii, 249.

5229 MANTER, EZRA. History of Howard Lodge, No. 69, of Free and Accepted Masons, Winterport, Maine, from its organization, A.D. 1851, to January 1, 1870. Portland: Berry, 1874. Pp. 21.

5230 _____. History of Howard Lodge of Free and Accepted Masons, Winterport, Me., continued from the end of the year 1869, at which time the former history closed. Bangor: Samuel Smith & Son, 1881. Pp. 10. [MePGLM].

5231 MORGAN, SETH H. History of Howard Lodge, No. 69, Free and Accepted Masons, Winterport, Maine, for the decade from 1910 to 1920. Winterport: Lougee, [1920?]. Pp. 28. MeHi.

5232 REILLY, M. W. "St. Gabriel's Parish, Winterport." MeCathHM, 2 (June, 1914), 12-23.

5233 WILLIAMSON, JOSEPH. "Albert Livingston Kelly and Webster Kelly, of Winterport (Frankfort), Maine." BHistMag, 4 (1888-1889), 230-233.

5234 WINTERPORT, ME. 100th anniversary, town of Winterport ... July 3-July 9, 1960. William K. Dunham and Philip D. Sherwood, eds. Belfast: Eastern Illustrating and Publishing, [1960?]. Unpaged. MeU.

SEE ALSO entry 3091.

WINTERVILLE PLANTATION (AROOSTOOK CO.)

5235 No items located.

WINTHROP (KENNEBEC CO.)

5236 BRAGDON, CHARLES R. "Oilcloth pioneers in Maine." Interchemical Review, 5 (Winter, 1946-1947), 102-109.
Wadsworth & Woodman.

5237 PARLIN, W. HARRISON. Reminiscences of East Winthrop. East Winthrop: Banner Publishing, 1891. Pp. 98. MBNEH.

5238 STACKPOLE, EVERETT SCHERMERHORN. History of Winthrop, Maine. Auburn: Merrill & Webber, 1925. Pp. 741.

5239 THURSTON, DAVID. A brief history of Winthrop, from 1764 to October 1855. Portland: Brown Thurston, 1855. Pp. xi, 247.

5240 TOWLE ACADEMY, WINTHROP, ME. Reunion of students at Towle Academy, Winthrop, Maine ... Thursday and Friday, July 30-31, 1908. Portland: Smith & Sale, 1909. Pp. 80. MeHi.

5241 WINTHROP, ME. An account of the centennial celebration at Winthrop, Me., May 20, 1871, embracing the historic address and poem in full.... Augusta: Sprague, Owen & Nash, 1871. Pp. 69.
Address is by Samuel P. Benson and poem is by John W. May.

5242 WINTHROP, ME. CONGREGATIONAL CHURCH. Centennial of the Congregational Church in Winthrop, Maine, September 4, 1876. Portland: B. Thurston, 1876. Pp. 24. MeHi.
Address by Thomas Newman Lord.

5243 WINTHROP, ME. WINTHROP BICENTENNIAL COMMITTEE. Winthrop, 1771-1971. Charles I. Foster, ed. Augusta: Kennebec Journal, 1971. Pp. 138. Me.

5244 "THE WOOLWORTH Farms at Winthrop." Down East, 9 (October, 1962), 20-23, 44.

5245 YORK, LOTTIE E. "Winthrop, the playground of central Maine." Sun Up, 3 (April, 1927), 38-40, 42-43, 45-46, 48.

SEE ALSO entry 3532.

WISCASSET (LINCOLN CO.)

5246 BRADFORD, ALDEN. "A description of Wiscasset and of the river Sheepscot." MHSC, 7 (1797), 163-171.

5247 BRIGGS, MAUD FULLER SMITH. Wiscasset, the home of my ancestors and the place of my birth. n.p., [194-?]. Pp. 26.

5248 CHASE, FANNIE SCOTT. Wiscasset in Pownalborough: a history of the shire town and the salient historical features of the territory between the Sheepscot and Kennebec Rivers. (1941) 2d ed., rev. Wiscasset, 1967. Pp. xvi, 546.

5249 ERSKINE, AMY ALBEE. "Governor Smith mansion, Wiscasset historic home." Sun Up, 10 (June, 1932), 11, 36.
Samuel E. Smith.

5250 FEMALE CHARITABLE SOCIETY OF WISCASSET. Centenary of the Female Charitable Society of Wiscasset, 1805-1905. Wiscasset: Emerson, [1905?]. Pp. 32. MBNEH.

5251 GOLDSMITH, MARGARET O. "Some old houses in Wiscasset, Maine." Architectural Forum, 45 (1926), 265-272.

5252 HUTCHINSON, GLORIA. "Wiscasset's Musical Wonder House." Down East, 23 (August, 1976), 52-55, 96-97.

5253 LOWNDES, MARION. "Yankee mansion." House and Garden, 77 (June, 1940), 40, 66, 69.
Lee-Payson-Smith House.

5254 MacFARLANE, MRS. JOHN. "Our church in a New England village, St. Philip's Parish in Wiscasset." The Northeast, 77 (September, 1950), 8-10.

5255 MAST, ALAN. "Castle Tucker, the house on Windmill Hill." Down East, 22 (August, 1975), 58-63, 91.

5256 _____. "The great house on Main Street." Down East, 20 (July, 1974), 58-63.
Nickels-Sortwell House.

5257 MOODY, ROBERT EARLE. "The Lincoln County Court House." OTNE, 56 (1965-1966), 61-62.

5258 NORMAN-WILCOX, GREGOR. "Jane Gove, her rug." Antiques, 35 (1939), 182-183.

5259 PACKARD, ALPHEUS SPRING. Address delivered on the occasion of the centennial celebration of the Congregational Church at Wiscasset, Aug. 6th, 1873. Wiscasset: Joseph Wood, 1873. Pp. 27.

5260 PATTERSON, WILLIAM DAVIS. An architectural monograph: Wiscasset, Maine. N.Y.: R. F. Whitehead, 1926. Pp. 4.

5261 _____. "A contribution to the history of Lincoln Lodge of F. & A. M. of Wiscasset." MeHistMag, 8 (1893), 25-36.

5262 _____. "The old house of Timothy Langdon in Wiscasset, 1771-1891." MeHistMag, 7 (1891-1892), 108-111.

5263 NO ENTRY.

5264 PATTERSON, WILLIAM DAVIS. Old Wiscasset. (1931) Revised by J. B. Doggett. Augusta: Augusta Pr., 1951. Pp. 51. Me.

5265 _____. Wiscasset in early days: historical notes pertaining to the old town on the Sheepscot River. Bath: The Times Co., 1929. Pp. 32.

5266 PINKHAM, CHARLES E. "The old Lincoln County jail." Down East, 2 (August, 1955), 28-29, 37.

5267 SEE, ANNA PHILLIPS. "A grandmother among women's clubs." DARMag, 54 (1920), 285-292.
Female Charitable Society of Wiscasset.

5268 SEWALL, RUFUS KING. History of Lincoln Lodge, at Wiscasset. Portland: Bailey & Noyes, 1863. Pp. 54.
Freemasons.

5269 _____. History of Lincoln Lodge, supplemental, from A.D. 1862, to A.D. 1870, inclusive. Portland: S. Berry, 1871. Pp. 59-68.
Pagination continued from previous entry.

5270 _____. Wiscasset Point: the old meeting house and interesting incidents connected with its history. Wiscasset: Chas. E. Emerson, 1883. Pp. 18. Me.

5271 "THE STORY of a century." Wiscasset Fire Society. Proceedings, (January 22, 1901), 7-38.
Wiscasset Fire Society.

5272 THAYER, HENRY OTIS. "The Indians' administration of justice: the sequel to the Wiscasset tragedy." MeHSC, 2 Ser., 10 (1899), 185-211.
Attack on Indians on December 2, 1749.

5273 _____. "A page of Indian history: the Wiscasset tragedy." MeHSC, 2 Ser., 10 (1899), 81-103.
Attack on Indians on December 2, 1749.

5274 WHITTEMORE, MARGARET. "America's first woman's club." Yankee, 19 (November, 1955), 32-33.
Female Charitable Society of Wiscasset, 1805.

5275 "WISCASSET ... the town that has made its past live." Down East, 6 (August, 1959), 28-31.

5276 WRENN, TONY P. "Documenting an 1824 court house: Lincoln County, Wiscasset, Maine." Pioneer America, 3 (1971), 3-18.

SEE ALSO entries 801, 1153, 1322, 1677, 1704, and 1937.

WOODLAND (AROOSTOOK CO.)

5277 WOODLAND, ME. Woodland, Maine, 50 years of progress, 1906-1956. n.p., [1956?]. Pp. 32. MeU.

WOODSTOCK (OXFORD CO.)

5278 BACON, RALPH M. The old village of Woodstock, Maine, 1808--1840-50. Bryant Pond: Woodstock Chamber of Commerce, 1970. Pp. 10. MeHi.

5279 CHASE, A. MONT. Reunion of the teachers and scholars of Woodstock, held at Bryant's Pond, October 9, 1890. Bryant's Pond, 1891. Pp. 113. MeHi.

5280 LAPHAM, WILLIAM BERRY. History of Woodstock, Me., with family sketches and an appendix. Portland: Stephen Berry, 1882. Pp. 315.

5281 [PERHAM, SIDNEY]. Recollections of the Chase School House, Woodstock, burned on the night of Jan. 26, 1883. Paris: Oxford Democrat, 1883. Unpaged. MeHi.
    Author attribution by Joseph Williamson.

5282 WHITNEY, STEPHEN T. "To reach the operator--turn the crank." Yankee, 38 (January, 1974), 58-63, 119.
    Bryant Pond Telephone Company.

WOODVILLE (PENOBSCOT CO.)

5283 No items located.

WOOLWICH (SAGADAHOC CO.)

5284 JEWELL, MARGARET H. "The Corliss Pottery at Woolwich, Maine." OTNE, 22 (1931-1932), 180-183.

5285 MONTSWEAG FREE BAPTIST CHURCH. Sesquicentennial of beginnings, 1780-1930. n.p., [1930]. Pp. 31. MeHi.

    SEE ALSO entry 1808.

WYMAN TOWNSHIP (FRANKLIN CO.)

5286 No items located.

YARMOUTH (CUMBERLAND CO.)

5287 BARROWS, JOHN HENRY. History of the First Baptist Church, Yarmouth, Maine, centennial discourse, June 16, 1897. n.p., [1897]. Pp. 16. MeHi.

5288 CURTIS, JOSEPH R. and NICHOLAS DRINKWATER. History of Casco Lodge, No. 36, Free and Accepted Masons, Yarmouth, Maine, from A.D. 1821 to 1870. Portland: Berry, 1870. Pp. 54.

5289 DRINKWATER, NICHOLAS. "History of Cumberland Royal Arch Chapter, No. 35, Yarmouth, Maine." Old Times, 3 (1879), 361-364.
    Freemasons.

5290 GARNISS, GEORGE W. Profiles of Yarmouth heritage. Yarmouth: Yarmouth Historical Society, 1967. Pp. v, 69. MeHi.

5291 "GETTING acquainted with Yarmouth, Maine." CCJM, 28 (1915-1916), 339, 341-343, 345-347.

5291A GURNEY, LEWIS. "Casco Lodge of Free and Accepted Masons, North Yarmouth, Maine." Old Times, 1 (1877), 57-58.
    The lodge is in Yarmouth despite the title.

5292 HAMMOND, GEORGE WARREN. A mill-built dwelling house. Boston: Parkhill, 1892. Pp. 27.

5293 HUMPHREY, WASHINGTON I. Origin and progress of the Baptist church in Yarmouth, Maine. Portland: B. Thurston, 1861. Pp. 26. MeHi.

5294 KASTER, KATHERINE PRESCOTT. Cousins and Littlejohn's Islands, 1645-1893. Portland: Loring Printing, [1942?]. Pp. iv, 128.

5295 PLUMMER, EDWARD CLARENCE. Reminiscences of a Yarmouth schoolboy. Portland: Marks Printing, 1926. Pp. 263.

5296 ROGERS, ORVILLE F. Grandma's island and grandma's ocean. [New Haven, Conn.], 1970. 33 leaves. MeHi.
    Littlejohn's Island.

5297 ROWE, WILLIAM HUTCHINSON. History of Casco Lodge, No. 36, 1821-1950. n.p., [1950?]. Unpaged. MeHi.
    Freemasons.

5298 _____. The Yarmouth poets. n.p., [1914?]. Unpaged. MeHi.
    Includes biographical sketches.

5299 "TOWN of Yarmouth, Maine: its rise, progress, and prosperity." BTJ, 13 (1900-1901), 9-20.

5300 YARMOUTH, ME. FIRST CONGREGATIONAL CHURCH. Exercises of the 150th anniversary of the First Church in Yarmouth, Me. 1730-1880. Portland: William M. Marks, 1881. Pp. 52. MeHi.
    Historical sermon by J. Torrey.

5301 _____. Second manual of the First Congregational Church in Yarmouth, Maine.... Portland: B. Thurston, 1878. Pp. 27. MBNEH.
    Includes historical sketch.

5302 "YARMOUTH." BTJ, 3 (1890-1891), 234-240.

5303 "YARMOUTH Corner." Old Times 5, (1881), 753-760; 6 (1882), 797-801, 946-952; 8 (1884), 1130-1133.
"To be continued," but periodical ceased publication.

SEE ALSO entries 440, 1521-1522, and 1524.

YORK (YORK CO.)

5304 BAER, ANNIE WENTWORTH. "Stories of an ancient city by the sea." Granite Mo, 11 (1888), 143-148, 188-192.

5305 BANKS, CHARLES EDWARD. History of York, Maine, successively known as Bristol (1632), Agamenticus (1641), Gorgeana (1642), and York (1652), with contributions on topography and land titles by Angevine W. Gowen. Boston: Calkins Pr., 1931-1935. 2v.
The title page states "in three volumes," but the third volume was never published.

5306 _____. "The Weare family of York, Maine." MHGR, 7 (1893), 90-99.

5307 BARDWELL, JOHN D. The York Militia Company, 1642-1972. York, 1972. Pp. 57. MeHi.

5308 BAXTER, JAMES PHINNEY. Agamenticus, Bristol, Gorgeana, York: an oration delivered by the Hon. James Phinney Baxter ... in York, Maine, on the two hundred and fiftieth anniversary of the town; together with a brief history of York and a descriptive account of the celebration of this anniversary, with a complete index of names and historic events August 5, 1902. York: Old York Historical and Improvement Society, 1904. Pp. 136.
Historical sketch by Frank D. Marshall.

5309 _____. Christopher Levett, of York, the pioneer colonist in Casco Bay. Portland: The Gorges Society, 1893. Pp. xii, 166.

5310 BOUVÉ, PAULINE CARRINGTON. "Old York, a forgotten seaport." NEM, New Ser., 26 (1902), 679-696.

5311 BRAGDON, KATHERINE. The York and Boston Tea Parties. [York]: Society for the Preservation of Historic Landmarks in York County, 1970. Unpaged. Me.

5312 CADWALADER, CAROLINE, ELIZABETH S. WINTON, and MARION P. HOSMER, eds. York, Maine, then and now. York: Old Gaol Museum Committee and the Old York Historical and Improvement Society, 1976. Pp. 97. MeHi.

5313 CATALOGUE of the relics and curiosities in the old gaol, York, Maine. York Corner: York Courant Printing House, 1901. Pp. 71 MeHi.
Includes a history of the prison.

5314 EMERY, GEORGE ALEXANDER. Ancient city of Georgeana and modern town of York (Maine), from its earliest settlement to the present time; also its beaches and summer resorts. Boston, 1873. Pp. xii, 192.

5315 ERNST, GEORGE. New England miniature: a history of York, Maine. Freeport: Bond Wheelwright, 1961. Pp. 284.

5316 FREEMASONS. YORK, ME. ST. ASPINQUID LODGE, NO. 198. History of Saint Aspinquid Lodge, No. 198, A. F. and A. M., York Village, Maine, 1892-1912. York Village: York Publishing, 1912. Pp. 62. Me.

5317 GOOLD, NATHAN. "Capt. Johnson Moulton's company; the first to leave the District of Maine in the Revolution." MeHSC, 2 Ser., 10 (1899), 300-308.

5318 HAYES, ADA. "The Clan McIntire." Shoreliner, 2 (October, 1951), 14-19.

5319 HUTCHINSON, GLORIA. "The house beside the Burying Ground." Down East, 21 (May, 1975), 36-39, 68-71.
Emerson-Wilcox House.

5320 _____. "Jefferds Tavern." Down East, 21 (October, 1974), 36-39, 68, 72, 74.
Built in Wells in 1754 and moved to York in 1939.

5321 JAMES, DONALD GRANT. This is my York. Albert Boulanger, ed. Haverhill, Mass.: B. & J. Yankee Guides, [1947?]. Pp. 39. MeHi.

5322 LABRIE, ROSE CUSHING. "Fifty years of faith." Shoreliner, 2 (August, 1951), 42-43.
Star of the Sea Church.

5323 _____. Sentinel of the sea, Nubble Light: a history of Cape Neddick Light Station. [Hampton, N.H.]: Hampshire Publishing, 1958. Unpaged.

5324 LITTLE, ELIZABETH N. "Nor' east by east." Newton, Mass., 1885. 13 leaves.

5325 MARSHALL, EDWARD WALKER. Old York, proud symbol of colonial Maine, 1652-1952. N.Y.: Newcomen Society in North America, 1952. Pp. 24.

5326 MARSHALL, FRANK DENNETT. An address before Old York Chapter, Daughters of the American Revolution, May 13, 1938, at the unveiling of tablet which marks the site of the first church in York, Maine, 1636-1667. n.p., 1938. Pp. 15. MeHi.

5327 MARSHALL, NATHANIEL GRANT. An address delivered at the dedication of the new Town Hall in York, Maine, on Monday evening, February 23, 1874. Portsmouth, N.H.: Journal Steam Pr., 1874. Pp. 31.

5328 YORK

5328 MARTIN, STELLA. "The captive of York." Graham's Magazine, 35 (1849), 113-120.
Amy Wakefield, 1692.

5329 MOODY, EDWARD C. Handbook history of the town of York, from early times to the present. Augusta: York Publishing, [1914]. Pp. 251.

5330 MOODY, THOMAS. Diary of Thomas Moody, campaign of 1760 of the French and Indian War. P. M. Woodwell, ed. South Berwick: Chronicle Print Shop, 1976. Pp. 56.

5331 NO ENTRY.

5332 NICHOLSON, NETTIE. "Candlemas Day in York, Maine, 1692." Ancestry: Quarterly Bulletin of the Palm Beach County Genealogical Society, 3 (April, 1968), 13-16.
Indian raid.

5333 "THE OLD gaol at York." Sun Up, 5 (August, 1928), 10-13.
Prison.

5334 PATTERSON, HELEN B. and PHILLIP DANA ORCUTT. "The saving of Sewall's Bridge." OTNE, 24 (1933-1934), 100-103.
Saved from demolition.

5335 PERKINS, ELIZABETH B. "An old village school at York, Maine." OTNE, 35 (1944-1945), 63-66.

5336 _____. "Sabby Day at York, Maine, 1750-1951." Shoreliner, 2 (July, 1951), 50-51.
First Parish Church.

5337 PREBLE, GEORGE HENRY. "The Garrison houses of York, Maine." NEHGR, 28 (1874), 268-272.

5338 REPPLIER, AGNES. "Where all roads lead." Harper's Magazine, 145 (1922), 501-512.

5339 REYNOLDS, JAMIE. York as Agamenticus, Bristol and Gorgeana. [York]: Society for the Preservation of Historic Landmarks in York County, 1969. Unpaged. Me.

5340 ROLDE, NEIL. York is living history. Brunswick: Harpswell Pr., 1975. Pp. 88. Me.

5341 SARGENT, WILLIAM MITCHELL. "The division of the 12,000 acres among the patentees at Agamenticus." MeHSC, 2 Ser., 2 (1891), 319-327.

5342 _____. "A topographical surmise: locating the houses of Gorges and Godfrey at York, Me." MeHSC, 2 Ser., 1 (1890), 133-135.

5343 SAWYER, RUFUS MORRILL. "Agamenticus, Georgiana, or York, Maine." CongQ, 8 (1866), 141-149, 267-276.

5344 SHAW, JUSTIN HENRY. "'Agamenticus majestic.'" SJMH, 11 (1923), 71-84.
Legend of "Saint" Aspenquid.

5345 SHERMAN, ARTHUR J. "Midsummer paradise." NEM, New Ser., 40 (1909), 485-495.

5346 STAR OF THE SEA CHURCH, YORK BEACH, ME. Golden jubilee, Star of the Sea Church, 1901-1951. n.p., [1951?]. Pp. 60. MeU.

5347 SYLVESTER, HERBERT MILTON. Ye romance of old York. Boston: Stanhope Pr., 1916. Pp. 427.
Also published in 1909 as volume two of the author's "Maine pioneer settlements."

5348 VAUGHAN, DOROTHY M. "The Sayward-Barrell House on York River, York Harbor, Maine." OTNE, 29 (1938-1939), 15-19.

5349 WARBURTON, SYBIL. The silent watcher; or, York as seen from Agamenticus, giving a glimpse into its past history as the city of Gorgeana, with a few suggestive pictures of the town at the present time. Boston: Heintzemann Pr., 1897. Pp. 70.

5350 WEBBER, LAURANCE E. "Maine's colonial warehouse on the York River." Down East, 19 (October, 1972), 62-63.
John Hancock stored contraband goods there during Revolution.

5351 WIGHTMAN, IDA MAY. The Indian massacre at York, Maine, January 25, 1691-2. [Newton?, N.H., 1917?]. Pp. 8.

5352 WILLOUGHBY, MALCOLM F. "The last of the 'Empire Knight.'" Down East, 21 (April, 1975), 20-21, 23-27.
A 1944 shipwreck off Boon Island Ledge.

5353 WINN, RALPH H. Legends of Cape Neddick. Freeport: Bond Wheelwright, 1964. Pp. xi, 99.

5354 _____. "Old Cape Neddick." Shoreliner, 3 (July, 1952), 56-58.
Cape Neddick House, hotel.

5355 YORK TERCENTENARY COMMITTEE. Three hundredth anniversary, 1652-1952, town of York, Maine. n.p., 1952. Unpaged. MeHi.

SEE ALSO entries 801, 962, and 987.

Supplementary Bibliographies and Guides

It is assumed that the user of this bibliography is familiar with such basic reference works as Constance M. Winchell's Guide to Reference Books. Bibliographies and guides relating to Maine subjects and places appear in the text proper. Listed below are a few additional subject bibliographies and guides to related materials which are either partially or wholly excluded from the bibliography, and which have geographical access.

ARNDT, KARL JOHN RICHARD and MAY E. OLSON. German-American newspapers and periodicals, 1732-1955: history and bibliography. 2d rev. ed. N.Y.: Johnson Reprint Corp., 1965. Pp. 810.
    Reprint of 1961 edition with the addition of an appendix.

BRIGHAM, CLARENCE SAUNDERS. History and bibliography of American newspapers, 1690-1820. Worcester: American Antiquarian Society, 1947. 2v.

_____. Additions and corrections. In the Proceedings of the American Antiquarian Society for April 1961 and reprinted separately.

COMPREHENSIVE DISSERTATION INDEX, 1861-1972. Ann Arbor, Mich.: Xerox University Microfilms, 1973. 37v.
    Volume 28, "History," has access under Maine locales.

_____. SUPPLEMENT. Ann Arbor, Mich.: Xerox University Microfilms, 1974-.

DICKINSON, ARTHUR TAYLOR. American historical fiction. 3d. ed. N.Y.: Scarecrow Pr., 1971. Pp. 380.

DICTIONARY OF AMERICAN BIOGRAPHY. Allen Johnson and Dumas Malone, eds. N.Y.: Charles Scribner's Sons, 1928-1937. 20v and index.
    Includes birthplace index and subject access under "Maine."

_____. SUPPLEMENTS 1-4. N.Y.: Charles Scribner's Sons, 1944-1974.
    Edited by Harris E. Starr, Robert L. Schuyler, Edward T. James, and John A. Garraty. Together, the entire set covers persons deceased as of December 1950.

DISSERTATION ABSTRACTS INTERNATIONAL. Ann Arbor, Mich.: University Microfilms, 1938-.
    Covers dissertations written since 1935. Volumes 1-11 have title "Microfilm Abstracts" and volumes 12-29 have title "Dissertation Abstracts." Indexes in each volume provide geographical access.

DORNBUSCH, CHARLES EMIL. Military bibliography of the Civil War. N.Y.: New York Public Library, 1971-1972. 3v.
    Volume one is a reprint of the 1961-1962 edition published as: Regimental publications and personal narratives of the Civil War.

DRAKE, MILTON. Almanacs of the United States. N.Y.: Scarecrow Pr., 1962. 2v.
    Covers 1639-1850.

EDWARDS, EVERETT EUGENE. A bibliography of the history of agriculture in the United States. Washington: Govt. Print. Off., 1930. Pp. iv, 307.

FORBES, HARRIETTE MERRIFIELD. New England diaries, 1602–1800: a descriptive catalog of diaries, orderly books, and journals. Topsfield, Mass.: Priv. Print., 1923. Pp. viii, 439.

GOHDES, CLARENCE H. Literature and theater of the United States and regions of the U. S. A.: an historical bibliography. Durham, N.C.: Duke Univ. Pr., 1967. Pp. ix, 275.

GREGORY, WINIFRED, ed. American newspapers, 1821–1936: a union list of files available in the United States and Canada. N.Y.: H. W. Wilson, 1937. Pp. 791.

GRIFFIN, APPLETON PRENTISS CLARK. Bibliography of American historical societies. 2d. ed. rev. and enl. Washington: Govt. Print. Off., 1907. Pp. 1374
    Issued as volume two of the annual report of the American Historical Association for 1905.

GUERRA, FRANCISCO. American medical bibliography, 1639–1783. N.Y.: Lathrop C. Harper, 1962. Pp. 885.

HAYWOOD, CHARLES. A bibliography of North American folklore and folksong. N.Y.: Greenberg, 1951. Pp. xxx, 1292.

KUEHL, WARREN F. Dissertations in history, and index to dissertations completed in history departments of United States and Canadian universities. Lexington: Univ. of Kentucky Pr., 1965–1972. 2v.
    Covers 1873–1970.

LARSON, HENRIETTA MELIA. Guide to business history: materials for the study of American business history.... Cambridge: Harvard Univ. Pr., 1948. Pp. 1181.

LE GEAR, CLARA EGLI. United States atlases: a list of national, state, county, city, and regional atlases in the Library of Congress. Washington: Govt. Print. Off., 1950–1953. 2v.

LOVETT, ROBERT WOODBERRY. American economic and business history information sources: an annotated bibliography of recent works pertaining to economic, business, agricultural and labor history, and the history of science and technology for the United States and Canada. Detroit: Gale Research, 1971. Pp. 323.

MILLER, GENEVIEVE. Bibliography of the history of medicine in the United States and Canada, 1939–1960. Baltimore: John Hopkins Univ., 1964. Pp. xvi, 428.
    Includes a section on local history arranged geographically.

NATIONAL CYCLOPEDIA OF AMERICAN BIOGRAPHY. N.Y.: White, 1892–.
    Volume 56 is 1975.

_____. CURRENT SERIES. N.Y.: White, 1930–.
    Volumes A–L have appeared as of 1977.

_____. REVISED INDEX. H. A. Harvey and Raymond D. McGill, comps. N.Y.: James T. White, 1971. Pp. 537.
    Subject index to events and institutions under "Maine."

ROOS, FRANK JOHN. Bibliography of early American architecture: writings on architecture constructed before 1860 in eastern and central United States. Urbana: Univ. of Illinois Pr., 1968. Pp. 389.

SCHLEBECKER, JOHN T. Bibliography of books and pamphlets on the history of agriculture in the United States, 1607–1907. Santa Barbara, Calif.: Clio Pr., 1969. Pp. 183.

SPEAR, DOROTHEA N. Bibliography of American directories through 1860. Worcester, Mass.: American Antiquarian Society, 1961. Pp. 389.
    Business, city, and county directories arranged by place. Many large libraries have in microform the directories listed herein.

STRATMAN, CARL J. Bibliography of the American theater excluding New York City. Chicago: Loyola Univ. Pr., 1965. Pp. x, 397.

TANSELLE, GEORGE THOMAS. Guide to the study of United States imprints. Cambridge: Harvard Univ. Pr., 1971. 2v.

Index

In using the index, a reader interested in a particular town or civil division as it relates to a subject should remember that he can locate entries for that town or civil division under subject headings if he keeps in mind the inclusive entry numbers for that locale.

Abagadusset, former name of Bowdoinham
Abbot, Edward, 1
Abbot, Herman, 2255
Abbot, Me., 1782, 1914
Abbot Mills, locality in Rumford
Abbott, Herman, see Abbot, Herman
Abbott, Jacob, 3046
Abbott, John Stevens Cabot, 2
Abbott, Moreton, 3045, 4048
Abbott, Samuel, 3046
Abbott, former name of Abbot
Abbott School, Farmington, Me., 3046
Abbottstown, former name of Temple
Abenakee Club, Biddeford, Me., 2292
Abnaki Indians, 3, 83, 279, 619, 855, 859, 1030,
    1073, 1160, 1164, 1182, 1309-1310, 1386, 1633,
    1816
Abolition of slavery, see Slavery
Academies, see Private schools
Acadia, 680, 1029, 2271
Acadia, locality in Connor Township
Acadia National Park, 1555-1556, 1558, 1560, 1563,
    1571-1573, 1605, 1615, 5225
Acadians, 39, 441, 1460, 1471, 3355, 3689
Achorn, Edgar Oakes, 2463
Ackerman, John H., 4163
Acme (ship), 2210
Acton, Me., 1915-1916
Actors and actresses, 2594, 5138
Actresses, see Actors and actresses
Adamo, Ruth, 5183
Adams, Eleanor, 3426
Adams, Frank Forrestal, 3427
Adams, George Jones, 3389-3390, 3392, 3396-3396A
Adams, George Moulton, 2685
Adams, Ephraim Douglass, 4
Adams, Franklin P., Sr., 3639
Adams, John, 1371-1372
Adams, Jonathan Edwards, 5
Adams, Sarah B., 1623
Adams, Silas, 2358
Adams, Solomon, 3055
Adams, William Cushing, 5, 2044
Adams, Zackary, 3600
Adams family (Solomon Adams), 3055
Adams family (William Adams, 1689?-1761), 5
Adams, former name of Adamstown Township
Adams, former name of Crawford
Adams, locality in Lake View Plantation
Adams Corner, locality in Kennebunkport
Adamstown Township, 1917

Addison, Me., 549, 1865
Admiralty Village, locality in Kittery
Adult education, see Education of adults
Advent Campground, locality in Mechanic Falls
Advent Christian churches, see Churches, Advent
    Christian
Agamenticus, former name of York
Agamenticus, locality in South Berwick
Agamenticus Village, locality in York
Agricultural education, 3153, 3174
Agricultural Experiment Station, Orono, see Maine.
    Agricultural Experiment Station, Orono
Agricultural extension work, 299, 533, 549, 783,
    1829, 4002, 4018-4019
Agricultural machinery, 3905, 3909
Agricultural societies, 957, 1545, 1900, 2958
Agriculture, 102, 118, 300; 124, 297-298, 579, 756,
    816, 870-871, 874, 1474, 1625-1626, 1834, 1838,
    1878, 2881, 3849, 3916, 4014, 4072
Ahlin, John Howard, 6
Ahlurmehsic, former name of Verona
Albany Township, 1919-1920
Albert, J. Wilfrid, 2280
Albert, Julie D., 1437, 3686-3687
Albert, Thomas, 3688
Albert Edward (1841-1910), Prince of Wales, see
    Edward VII, King of Great Britain
Albion, Robert Greenhalgh, 7-8, 4164
Albion, Me., 1645, 1921
Alden, John, 3458
Alder Brook Township, 1922
Alder Stream Township, 1923
Aldrich, Peleg Emory, 8
Alewive, locality in Kennebunk
Alexander, De Alva Stanwood, 10
Alexander, William T., 3286
Alexander family, 10
Alexander, Me., 1924
Alexander Island, locality in Perkins Township
Alfred, Me., 1925-1934
Alger, Horatio, 3971
Algonquian Indians, 678, 1160
Alice E. Clark (ship), 3376
All Souls by the Sea Church, Steuben, 4847
All Souls Church (Unitarian), Augusta, 1972, 2023
All Souls Congregational Church, Bangor, 2143
Allagash Plantation, 1935-1935A
Allagash River, 161, 322, 1446-1447, 1459,
    1470
Allan, George Hayward, 646
Allan, John, 645-646, 2924

Allan family, 646
Allen, C. F. H., 11-12
Allen, Charles Edwin, 13-15, 1677, 2885-2889, 3179
Allen, (E. C.) Co., Augusta, 2009
Allen, Elmer E., 4657
Allen, Frederic, 16
Allen, James P., 17-19
Allen, Joseph, Jr., 20
Allen, Joshua, 1971
Allen, Mildred Sellers, 2834
Allen, Neal Woodside, Jr., 738, 3459
Allen, Stephen, 21
Allen, William (1780-1873), 22-23, 2464, 3060,
    3248, 3361, 3889-3890
Allen, William (1784-1868), 24, 1384, 2568
Allen's Island, 3647
Allens Mills, locality in Industry
Allis, Frederick Scouller, 25
Allison, Roland, 2835
Almond, former name of Orneville Township
Alna, Me., 1677, 1704, 1706, 1936-1939
Alna Lodge, Freemasons, Damariscotta, 2822, 2824-
    2825
Alna Meeting House, 1706
Alpha Tau Omega. Beta Upsilon Chapter. University
    of Maine at Orono, 3991
Alton, Me., 1940
Alva, former name of Blaine
American Association of University Women, 651, 942,
    4031
American Chemical Society, Maine Section, 850
American Party, 3021A
Ames, Agnes H., 1762
Ames, Mrs. Edward W., see Ames, Agnes H.
Ames, John Wallace, 2359
Ames, Madge E., 746
Ames, Nathaniel P., 3120
Amestown, former name of Sangerville
Amherst, Me., 1941
Amity, Me., 1942
Amity Lodge, Freemasons, Camden, 2646
Amory, Thomas Coffin, 27
Anastas, Peter, 28
Ancient Augusta, 4114, 4131, 4136
Ancient Land-mark Lodge, Freemasons, Portland,
    4185, 4452
Anderson, Albert E., 4165
Anderson, Fritz, 4849
Anderson, Maizie Freeman, 3731
Anderson, Miriam Sylvia, 30
Anderson, Thomas H., 4755
Andover, Me., 1943
Andover North Surplus, Me., 1944
Andover West Surplus, Me., 1945
Andrews, Delmont, 4166
Andrews, L. A., 31
Andrews, Ralph, 1877
Andrews, Richard L., 1624, 3773A
Androscoggin County, 555, 1422-1436
Androscoggin lakes, 1
Androscoggin River, 665, 1293, 1296, 1726, 2572
Androscoggin Valley, 1238
Angibaut, Pierre, 305
Anglican churches, see Churches, Episcopal
Annett, John B., 3529
Annie C. MacGuire (ship), 4529
Annsborough, former name of Deblois

Annsburgh, former name of Deblois
Anson, Me., 1946-1947, 3362
Anson Academy, 1946
Anthoensen, Fred, 4167
Anthoensen Press, Portland, 4203, 4217, 4317, 4488
Anthony, Alfred Williams, 3530
Anti-Lingo League, Colby College, 5060
Antimasonic party, 3191
Antiques, 694
Antislavery, see Slavery
Antoinette, Marie, 2941, 2948-2949, 2951
Appalachian Mountain Club, 3794
Apple industry, 869, 3767
Applebee, Robert B., 2198, 4721
Appledore Hotel, Kittery, 3488
Appledore Island, 3488, 3502
Appleton, Daniel Fuller, 33
Appleton, Frederick Hunt, 2089
Appleton, James, 33
Appleton, Jesse, 2568
Appleton, Moses, 1639
Appleton, Me., 1948
Appleton Township, 1949
Araseeket, former name of Freeport
Archaeology, 161, 902, 1066, 1162, 1177, 1180-1181,
    1785, 2398, 3007, 3155, 4076
Archer, Gleason Leonard, 34-35
Archers Corners, locality in Amherst
Architecture, 251, 485, 819, 967, 1281, 2010, 2260,
    2267, 2554, 2556, 4268, 5112, 5257, 5276
Architecture, colonial, 573, 707, 987, 1114, 1281,
    5260
Architecture, domestic, 26, 92, 476, 573, 644, 707,
    987, 114, 1281, 1322, 1701, 1883, 1980, 1982,
    2015, 2182, 2199, 2262, 2302, 2334, 2340, 2345,
    2421, 2501, 2556, 2644, 2732, 2782-2783, 2785-
    2786, 2820, 3001, 3012, 3017-3018, 3035, 3269,
    3474, 3494-3495, 4043, 4215, 4231, 4277, 4462,
    4479, 4484, 4610, 4613, 4788, 4800, 4808-4809,
    4885, 4888, 4892, 5251, 5256, 5260, 5292, 5348
Architecture, ecclesiastical, see Church architec-
    ture
Archives, 769; 579-580, 615, 819, 1062, 3437
Archon Lodge, Freemasons, East Dixmont, 2870
Areys Corners, locality in Hampden
Argyle Township, 1733
Armories, 4765
Armstrong, F. C., 4168
Armstrong, Lebbeus, 37
Arnold, Benedict, 15, 24, 113, 132, 170, 239, 257,
    538, 566, 571, 589, 600, 648, 719, 724, 801, 844,
    864, 866, 882, 924, 949, 1051, 1154-1155, 1230,
    1276, 1329, 4756
Arnold, Frank B., 2867
Arnold Corner, locality in Newburgh
Arnold's expedition, see Canadian invasion (1775-
    1776)
Arnolds Landing, locality in Solon
Aroostook County, 108, 207, 1251, 1437-1479, 2673
Aroostook State Teachers College, see University of
    Maine at Presque Isle
Aroostook Valley Railroad Company, 1445
Aroostook War (1839), 38, 203, 327, 610, 623, 713,
    749, 988, 1208, 1220
Arosaguntacook Indians, 1238

Arrowscag, former name of Arrowsic
Arrowseag, former name of Arrowsic
Arrowsic, Me., 1951
Arsenals, 2020
Arsenault, Bona, 39
Art, 40, 250, 355, 586, 852, 865, 1065, 1201, 4315
Art education, see Art-study and teaching
Art-study and teaching, 4760
Arthur, Robert, 41
Artillery, coast, 4373
Artists, 42-43, 249, 252, 295, 389, 776, 787, 828, 1106, 1224, 1298, 2154, 2341, 3431, 4425, 4463, 4697
Arundel, Me., 1952
Arundel, former name of Kennebunkport
Arundel Lodge, Freemasons, Kennebunkport, 3435-3436
Ash Point, Me., 4042
Ashburton, Alexander Baring, Lord, 4, 58, 283, 432-433, 461, 624-625, 716, 880, 1346
Ashby, Thompson Eldridge, 2465-2466
Ashdale, locality in Phippsburg
Asheville, locality in Gouldsboro
Ashland, Me., 1953
Ashley, Alta, 3752
Ashman, Robert I., 3993
Ashville, locality in Sullivan
Askwith, alternate name of Taunton & Raynham Academy Grant
Aspenquid, "Saint," 5344
Asticou, locality in Mount Desert
Astral (ship), 2210
Astronomy, 720
Asylums, see Hospitals
Atchison, Roland, 3342
Athearns Corner, locality in Hope
Athenaean Society, Bowdoin College, 2479, 2536
Athens, Me., 1954-1956
Athens Victory Club, 1954
Atkinson, Minnie, 3225, 3751
Atkinson, Me., 1957
Atlantic, locality in Swans Island
Atlantic and St. Lawrence Railway, 45, 87, 983
Atlantic House, Scarborough, 4700
Atlantic Lodge, Freemasons, Portland, 4198, 4246, 4293
Atlantic Shore Line Railway, 280
Atlas (ship), 2210
Atlases, historical, 248, 826
Attean Township, 1958
Attwood, Stanley Bearce, 46
Atwood, Charles Francis, 5227
Auburn, Me., 1422, 1424, 1426-1427, 1431-1432, 1434, 1959-1970, 3532
Auburn, Me. Elm Street Universalist Parish, 1959
Augusta, Me., 143, 556, 1637, 1650, 1971-2035, 3532
Augusta, Me. All Souls Church (Unitarian), 1972, 2023
Augusta, Me. Sesquicentennial Committee, 1973
Augusta, Me. South Parish Congregational Church, 1974-1975
Augusta, Ancient, see Ancient Augusta
Augusta Savings Bank, 1976-1977
Augusta State Hospital, see Maine State Hospital, Augusta
Augusta Yacht Club, 2035
Aurora, Me., 2036

Aurora Lodge, Freemasons, Rockland, 4601
Austin, Altea, 3281-3282
Austin, Harry B., 47, 1537
Austin, Neva, 3281-3282
Authors, 1193; 329, 835, 876A, 900, 1397, 1575
Autographs, 4825
Automobile driver education, 537
Automobile industry and trade, 326
Automobiles, 2189, 3377, 4460
Avenues, see Thoroughfares
Averill, Albert E., 4588
Averill, Esther C., 2941
Avery, Myron Halburton, 1768, 3799-3801, 3809
Avezac de Castera-Macaya, Marie Armand Pascal d', 656
Avila, Lilian, 48
Avon, locality in Phillips
Avon, Me., 1419
Axe industry, 1168, 3967
Ayers, Blanche Waldo, 4877
Ayers, locality in Pembroke

B & M, see Burnham and Morrill
Babb, Cyrus Cates, 49, 75-76
Bachelder, Peter Dow, 1480
Bacheler, Gilbert H., 3883
Bachiler, Stephen, 1075
Back Abbot Road, locality in Abbot
Back Narrows, locality in Boothbay
Back River, locality in Boothbay
Back Settlement, locality in Mattawamkeag
Back Settlement, locality in St. Francis
Back Street, locality in Northfield
Bacon, George Fox, 50, 1840, 2047, 4169, 4589
Bacon, Ralph M., 5278
Baer, Annie Wentworth, 1878, 4785, 5304
Bagaduce Expedition, see Penobscot Expedition (1779)
Bagley, Marion Miller, 51-53
Bagley, locality in Troy
Bailey, Albert W., 2038
Bailey, Dudley Perkins, 54
Bailey, Frank Linwood, 3287
Bailey, Jacob Whitman, 1439
Bailey, Louise C., 2199
Bailey, May Murray Edwards, 3594-3595
Bailey family, 2038
Bailey and Noyes, Portland, 4513
Bailey Corner, locality in Pittston
Bailey Island, 3288, 3291
Bailey Island Church, Harpswell, 3288
Baileys Mistake, Me., 3644
Baileyville, Me., 2038-2040
Baileyville, locality in Winthrop
Baker, Florence E., 4170
Baker, Henry Knox, 3249
Baker, Orville Dewey, 55
Baker, Richard L., 4171
Baker, Richard W., 1729
Baker, William Avery, 56-57, 2200
Baker, William J., 4172
Baker family, 431
Baker Corner, locality in Windham
Baker Island, locality in Cranberry Isles
Bakers and bakeries, 1965
Bakerstown, Me., 1425
Bakerstown, former name of Moscow

Bald Head, locality in York

Bald Hill, locality in Wells

Bald Hill Cove, locality in Winterport

Bald Mountain, locality in Dedham

Bald Mountain, locality in Rangeley

Bald Mountain Township, 2041

Baldwin, Angie R., 2443

Baldwin, J. R., 58

Baldwin, Sidney, 2351

Baldwin, Me., 2042

Baldwin Corners, locality in Tremont

Ball, Ebenezer, 2705, 2745, 4587

Ball, Wilbur I., 1919

Ballard, Edward, 59-60, 1802, 1979, 4100, 4126

Ballard, Martha Moore, 2016

Ballard, William, 2686

Ballstown, former name of Jefferson

Ballstown, former name of Whitefield

Banasiak, Chester F., 61

Bancroft, Me., 2043

Band, Benjamin, 4173-4174

Bangor, Me., 171, 1736, 1751, 1761, 2044-2164, 4510

Bangor, Me. Board of Trade, 2050

Bangor, Me. Central Congregational Chruch, 2051, 2086, 2101

Bangor, Me. Chamber of Commerce, 2052

Bangor, Me. Congregation Beth Israel, 2053

Bangor, Me. First Baptist Church, 2054

Bangor, Me. First Congregational Church, 2055, 2102, 2152

Bangor, Me. First Methodist Episcopal Church, 2056

Bangor, Me. First Universalist Church, 2057

Bangor, Me. Hammond Street Congregational Church, 2058, 2126

Bangor, Me. Public Library, 61A, 2105, 2144

Bangor, Me. St. George Greek Orthodox Church, 2060

Bangor, Me. St. John's Catholic Church, 2061

Bangor, Me. St. Mary's Catholic Church, 2062-2063

Bangor, Me. Second Baptist Church, 2064

Bangor, Me. Water Department, 2065, 2118

Bangor and Aroostook Railroad, 61B-61C, 660, 1290, 1351, 1355, 1390, 1439A

Bangor and Piscataquis Canal and Railroad Company, 1732, 1734-1735

Bangor Children's Home, 2069

Bangor City Hall, 2091

Bangor Daily News, 2070

Bangor District Nursing Association, 2088

Bangor Female Orphan Asylum, 2069

Bangor Fire Department, 2150

Bangor Hebrew Community Center, 2071

Bangor Hebrew School, 2072

Bangor Historical Society, 2073

Bangor House, 2074

Bangor Hydro-Electric Company, 2108

Bangor Jeffersonian, 2158

Bangor Mechanic Association, 2076

Bangor, Old Town and Milford Railroad, 1763

Bangor Public Library, see Bangor, Me. Public Library.

Bangor Railway and Electric Company, 2108

Bangor Savings Bank, 2077

Bangor Street Railway, 2111

Bangor Theological Seminary, 2044, 2079, 2092, 2096, 2136-2138, 2140, 2162

Bangor Water Department, see Bangor, Me. Water Department

Bangs, Ella Matthews, 799, 4175-4176

Bangs, Isaac Sparrow, 5024

Bangs Beach, locality in Sidney

Banks, Charles Edward, 62-65, 436, 2394, 3914-3916, 4101, 4177, 5305-5306

Banks, Elias, 1961

Banks, Ronald Fillmore, 66-70, 693, 826

Banks family, 4087

Banks and banking, 54, 171, 197, 482, 534, 824, 879, 1086, 1227, 1976-1977, 2077, 2133, 2208, 2287, 2715, 3020, 3063, 3163, 3196, 3257, 3560, 3626, 3945, 4256, 4265, 4283, 4326, 4349, 4429-4430, 4493, 4591, 4634, 4764, 5102

Bapst, John, 3019

Baptist Church, Cornish, 2798

Baptist Church, Freeport, 3096

Baptist Church, Greene, 3231

Baptist Church, Hebron, 3317

Baptist Church, Kennebunkport, 3444

Baptist Church, Kittery, 3463

Baptist Church, New Gloucester, 3848

Baptist Church, North Berwick, 3904, 3910

Baptist Church, Sedgwick, 4736

Baptist Church, Topsham, 4917

Baptist Church, Wayne, 5118

Baptist churches, see Churches, Baptist

Baptists, 155, 263, 582, 878, 1044, 1105, 1130, 1692, 1716, 1989, 5084

Bar Harbor, Me., 20, 171, 603, 1587, 1589, 2165-2194

Bar Harbor Lodge, Freemasons, 2177

Bar Harbor Village Library, 2166

Bar Mills, locality in Buxton and Hollis

Barber, William H., 3531

Bardwell, John D., 5307

Baring, Alexander, see Ashburton, Alexander Baring, Lord

Baring Plantation, 2195

Barker, Mrs. Burleigh, 5220

Barker, Fen. G., 1803

Barker, Florence E., 3994

Barker, Fred Coshin, 1713

Barker, Lewis A., 71

Barker, R. Mildred, 1926, 3188, 3850

Barkerville, locality in Lewiston

Barlow, Mrs. James E., 72

Barnard Corner, locality in Barnard Plantation

Barnard Plantation, 2196

Barnard's Inn, Kennebunk, 3418

Barnards Township No. 1, former name of Madison

Barnes, Anna, 1440, 3339

Barnes, Charles P., 73

Barnes, Francis, 3340, 3354

Barnjum, locality in Mt. Abram Township

Barr, Annie L., 74

Barrels, see Coopers and Cooperage

Barretts Siding, locality in Caribou

Barrettstown, former name of Appleton

Barrettstown, former name of Hope

Barron, Earl T., 1962

Barron Corner, locality in Madison

Barron Memorial Congregational Church, Dexter, Me., 2857

Barrows, Harold Kilbrith, 75-76
Barrows, John Henry, 5287
Barrows, John Stuart, 3121-3122, 4092
Barrows, Lucius D., 829
Barrows, William, 3316
Barry Phillips, 77
Barry, William David, 4285
Barry, William Edward, 3403-3405
Barstow, James S., 3148
Barter, J. Malcolm, 78, 1553, 2758, 3767, 4541,
    4831, 4977
Barters Island, locality in Boothbay
Bartlet, William Stoodley, 2201
Bartlett, Arthur, 79, 3097
Bartlett, Arthur C., 80
Bartlett, Charles H., 1730
Bartlett, Edmund Hobart, 1731
Bartlett, Ralph Sylvester, 1879
Bartlettboro, locality in Stoneham
Barwise, Mark A., 2081
Baseball, 737, 2453, 2534, 3546, 5025, 5043, 5054
Basford, Chester Ellsworth, 2279
Bashaba (Indian), 453, 605
Bashford, James Whitford, 4178
Basin, locality in Addison
Basin Mills, locality in Orono
Basin Point, locality in Harpswell
Basket making, 277, 3836
Basketball, 737
Bass (G. H.) Company, Wilton, 5184, 5187
Bass, Streeter, 5184
Bass Harbor, locality in Tremont
Bassett, Norman L., 1980
Batchelder, Samuel Francis, 2687
Batchelders Crossing, locality in Litchfield
Batchelders Grant, Me., 2197
Bateman, Luther C., 81, 1422
Bates, Arlo, 2470, 3364
Bates, Horatio D., 5113
Bates, James, 2004
Bates, W. L., 3247
Bates Alumni Association, 3567
Bates College, 3529-3531, 3536, 3538-3539, 3541,
    3543-3549, 3563, 3565-3568, 3570-3572, 3574-3576
Bates Manufacturing Company, Lewiston, Me., 82, 556
Bates Street Shirt Company, Lewiston, 3540
Batesville, locality in Moro Plantation
Bath, Me., 259, 286, 923, 1153, 1806, 1808, 2198-
    2250, 3532
Bath, Me. Centennial Committee, 2202
Bath, Me. Central Congregational Church, 2203
Bath, Me. Winter Street Congregational Church,
    2204-2205, 2250
Bath Academy Grant, former name of Eustis
Bath History Club of 1935, 2206
Bath Independent, 2248
Bath Iron Works, 2207, 2212, 2216, 2241
Bath National Bank, 2208
Baxter (H. C.) and Brother, Brunswick, 2532
Baxter, James Phinney, 83-89, 803, 805, 1481, 2655,
    3460, 4102, 4178A-4180, 4400, 5308-5309
Baxter, Percival Proctor, 3802
Baxter, Sylvester, 90
Baxtree, Carthwheel, pseud., see McLaughlin, Peter J.
Bay Point, locality in Georgetown
Bay View, locality in Saco

Bayley, William Shirley, 91
Baymeath, Bar Harbor, 2169
Bayside, locality in Ellsworth and Trenton
Bayside, locality in Northport
Bayview Estates, locality in Raymond
Bayville, locality in Boothbay Harbor
Beacon Corner, locality in Kennebunkport
Beacons, see Lighthouses
Beal, Ezra Fluent, 3942
Beals, Me., 2251-2252
Beam, Lura Ella, 3652
Beam, Philip C., 4697
Bean, Dearborn Gorham, 5185
Bean, Eva E., 799
Bean, Eva Marion, 2285
Bean (L. L.), Inc., Freeport, 3097-3100, 3108
Bean, Leon Leonwood, 3098
Beane, C. H., 3149
Beans Corner, locality in Jay
Beans Corner, locality in Montville
Beans Mill, locality in Corinth
Bear Brook, locality in New Gloucester
Bear Island, locality in Cranberry Isles
Bearce, Roger M., 3315
Beard, Frank A., 92
Beard, George Miller, 1769
Beasley, Katherine A., 2873
Beathem, Harold C., 3726
Beattie Township, 2253
Beatty, Hazel, 4632
Beaver Dam, locality in Berwick
Beaver Hill, former name of Freedom
Beaver Hill, locality in Freedom
Beaverdam, locality in North Berwick
Beck, Horace Palmer, 93-95
Beck, Joseph T., 1981
Beckford, William Hale, 1880, 2082, 3532, 4181
Beddington, Me., 2254
Beebe, Richard W., 3123
Beech Hill, locality in Freeport
Beech Hill, locality in Mount Desert
Beech Hill, locality in Wayne
Beech Ridge, locality in North Berwick
Beech Ridge, locality in Sebago
Beech Ridge, locality in York
Beechland, locality in Franklin
Beechwood, locality in Glenburn
Beedy, Helen Coffin, 96
Beethoven Musical Society, Portland, 4182, 4184
Belanger Settlement, locality in Wallagrass Planta-
    tion
Belfast, Me., 2273; 707, 2082, 2255-2272, 4589
Belfast, Me. Congregational Church. Ladies' Circle,
    2257
Belfast, Me. North Church, 2258
Belfast Academy, 2272
Belfast Academy Grant, former name of Ludlow
Belfast Academy Grant, former name of New Limerick
Belfast and Moosehead Lake Railroad, 96A, 284, 711
Belfast Free Library, 2260
Belgards Corner, locality in Montville
Belgrade, Me., 2274-2276
Belgrade Lakes, locality in Belgrade
Bell Hill Church, Otisfield, 4040
Bell Hill Meeting House, Me., 4040
Bellamy, John Haley, 3485, 3499

Bellamy, Samuel, 3663
Bellgrade, former name of Belgrade
Bells, 685, 703, 2097, 3217, 4471, 4474
Belmont, Me., 2277
Belmore, Bruce Weatherby, 4552
Belvedere, locality in Crystal
Bemis, locality in Rangeley Plantation
Benedicta, Me., 2278
Benjamin, Asher, 3018
Benjamin, Charles H., 4077
Benner Corner, locality in Waldoboro
Bennett, Alberto A., 3384
Bennett, Ernest Nathaniel, 4183
Bennett, Gertrude Allinson, 3698
Bennett, Jacob, 3460A
Bennett, Mary E., 4149
Bennett, Randy L., 97, 3744, 4623
Bennett, Wells, 2262
Bensen, Richard A., 3099
Benson, Earl M., 3389, 3732
Benson, Louise M., 3963
Benson, Samuel Page, 5241
Benton, Me., 1421, 2279
Benton, Me. 100th Year Historical Survey Committee, 2279
Berean Baptist Church, Brunswick, Me., 2467, 2521
Berchen, William, 98
Berlin, alternate name of Township Six
Bernard, Francis, 1611
Bernard, John, 1608
Bernard, locality in Tremont
Bernardstown, former name of Cornville
Bernardstown plus Mile-and-a-Half Strip, former name of Madison
Berry, Clyde G., 3185
Berry, George Stillman, 2818
Berry, George W., 3580
Berry, Ira, 4184
Berry Stephen, 4185-4187
Berry Mills, locality in Carthage
Berrys Corner, locality in Garland
Berthiaume, Juniper, 3665
Berube, Jose Hyacinthe, 3086
Berwick, Me., 1911, 2280-2284
Berwick Academy. South Berwick, 4786-4787, 4791
Berwick Academy Grant, former name of Athens
Beston, Elizabeth Coatsworth, see Coatsworth, Elizabeth Jane
Beston, Henry, 99-100
Betcher, J. A., 4670
Beth Israel Congregation, Bangor, see Congregation Beth Israel, Bangor
Bethel, Me., 2285-2291
Bethel Savings Bank, 2287
Beveridge, Norwood P., 1652, 3911
Biard, Pierre, 1556, 1565, 1606, 1609
Bible Society of Maine, 523, 4188
Bibliographies, 7-8, 49, 57, 69, 101-102, 118, 144-145, 173, 215-216, 218, 221, 300, 345, 428, 492, 518, 543-545, 554, 598-599, 627, 629-630, 681, 687, 744-745, 752, 760, 769, 773, 775, 784, 804, 807, 821, 932-934, 936, 959, 1047, 1096, 1140, 1142, 1144, 1192-1193, 1247A, 1261, 1303, 1311, 1366, 1382, 1400, 1417, 1590, 1646, 1741, 1789, 1986, 2059, 2273, 2610, 3809, 3927, 4126, 4133
Bickford, Cora Belle, 799, 2310

Bickford, Gail H., 3124-3125
Bicknell, Henry S., 103
Biddeford, Me., 799, 1265, 1881, 1890, 1893, 1901, 2292-2311, 4181, 4465
Biddeford, Me. First Universalist Church, 2293
Biddeford, Me. Paroisse St. Joseph, 2294
Biddeford, Me. Public Library, 2295-2296, 2303
Biddeford, Me. Second Congregational Church, 2297, 2308
Biddeford and Saco Railroad, 1890
Biddeford Pool, Me., 3974
Big Island, locality in Seven Ponds Township
Big Lake Camp Ground, locality in No. 21 Plantation
Big Six Township, 2312
Big Squaw Township, 2313
Big Ten Township, 2314
Big Twenty Township, 2315
Big W Township, 2316
Bigelow, locality in Sugarloaf Township
Bigelow Township, 2317
Billias, George Athan, 104
Bingham, Millicent Todd, 2369
Bingham, William, 22, 25, 443, 1222
Bingham, Me., 2318-2319
Bingham, former name of Mariaville
Bingham, former name of Solon
Bingham Purchase, 22, 25, 443, 1222
Bingo, locality in Waite
Biography, collected, 21, 42-43, 50, 74, 96, 105-111, 126, 128, 138, 162, 177-178, 206, 210, 240, 326, 347, 377, 389, 398, 422-423, 446, 474, 495-496, 524, 546, 557, 587, 666, 690, 787, 800, 828, 831, 867, 910, 919, 948, 958, 960, 979, 986, 991, 1008, 1044-1045, 1146, 1187, 1204, 1206, 1235, 1237, 1248, 1272, 1345, 1347, 1359-1360, 1377, 1383-1384, 1387, 1428, 1482, 1485, 1506, 1524, 1584, 1593, 1597, 1610, 1634, 1741, 1750, 1758, 1765, 1782, 1797, 1840, 1864, 1880, 1882, 1886, 1897, 1907, 1909, 1957, 2003, 2018, 2027, 2047, 2082, 2104, 2120, 2131, 2154, 2236, 2248, 2326, 2332, 2348, 2376, 2384, 2442, 2463, 2476, 2506, 2519, 2586, 2594, 2780, 2837, 2839, 2854, 2880, 2910, 2924, 2967-2968, 2983, 2991, 2998, 3024, 3069, 3081, 3123, 3156, 3169, 3232, 3238, 3309, 3363, 3416, 3421, 3424, 3487, 3498, 3519, 3532, 3558, 3594, 3597, 3622, 3669, 3695, 3742, 3837, 3889, 3915-3916, 3944, 3950, 3956, 3980, 4060, 4072, 4128, 4155, 4169, 4181, 4357, 4537-4538, 4589, 4595, 4660, 4662, 4676, 4722, 4868, 5126, 5168, 5205, 5233, 5298, 5305, 5307
Biology-study and teaching, 3571
Biondi, Arnold S., 112
Birch Harbor, locality in Gouldsboro
Birch Island, locality in Harpswell
Birch Knolls, locality in Cape Elizabeth
Birch Point, locality in West Bath
Birch Stream, former name of Argyle Township
Bird, Harrison, 113
Births, see Vital records
Bisbee, Ernest Emerson, 114
Bisbeetown, locality in Waterford
Bischoff, Carl H., 3533
Bishop, Frank A., 3321
Bishop, William Henry, 115-116
Bishop, locality in Caribou
Bixler, Julius Seelye, 5026-5027, 5037

Black, Frederick Frasier, 4722
Black, J. William, 5081
Black Corner, locality in Sedgwick
Black Mansion, Ellsworth, 2994, 3000-3001, 3011-3012, 3018, 3021
Black Mountain, locality in Sweden
Black Point, former name of Prouts Neck
Black Point, locality in Scarborough
Black Point and Blue Point, former name of Scarborough
Blacks, 920, 1094
Blackstone family, 2823
Blackstone, locality in Westmanland Plantation
Blackstrap, locality in Falmouth
Blackwell Corner, locality in Madison
Blagden, Charles W., 4671-4672
Blaine, James Gillespie, 632, 1414, 1982, 2003, 2014-2015
Blaine, Me., 2320
Blaine House, Augusta, 1980, 1982, 2003, 2015
Blair Hill, locality in Greenville
Blaisdell, Carl E., 2159
Blaisdell Corners, locality in Lebanon
Blaisdelltown, former name of Exeter
Blake, George H., 3818
Blake Gore, Me., 2321
Blakes Corner, locality in Lisbon
Blakesburg, former name of Bradford
Blamey Corners, locality in Weld
Blanchard, Charles, 2323
Blanchard, Douglas, 2083
Blanchard, Edward P., 2322-2323
Blanchard family, 2322
Blanchard Corner, locality in Charlotte
Blanchard Plantation, 2322-2323
Blanding, Edward Mitchell, 117, 2051, 2073, 2084-2087
Blanding, Ina Potter, 2088
Blanding, William F., 867
Blank, John S., III, 2167
Blanket Lane, locality in Prospect
Blankets, 4692
Blazing Star Lodge, Freemasons, Rumford, 4622
Bliss, Charles Edmund, 2089
Bliss, Francis F., 2469
Bliss, George, 4996
Bloomfield, Me., 1816, 4768
Bloomingborough, former name of Monmouth
Blount, Edward F., 1963
Blue Hill, Me., 207, 1581, 2324-2345
Blue Hill, Me. Congregational Church, 2325
Blue Hill Academy, 2324, 2328
Blue Hill Academy Grant, former name of Centerville
Blue Hill Troupe, New York, 2327
Blue Point, locality in Scarborough
Blueberry industry, 743, 1847
Bluehill, former name of Blue Hill
Boardman, Harold Sherburne, 781
Boardman, Samuel Lane, 118-120, 1625-1626, 1770, 1983, 2089, 3250, 3995
Boards of trade, 117, 3552, 4468
Boatbuilding, 2639
Boats and boating, 1885, 2639, 2809, 4042
Bodge, George Madison, 5192
Bog Brook, former name of Hebron
Bog Corner, locality in Palmyra

Bog Road, locality in Gilead
Bogues Corner, locality in Waldoboro
Bokkelen, D'Arcy Van, see Van Bokkelen, D'Arcy
Bolsters Mills, locality in Harrison and Otisfield
Bolté, Mary, 2890
Bolton, Charles Edward, 121
Bolton, Charles Knowles, 121
Bonar, James Charles, 3461
Bond Brook, Me., 2025
Bonds Corners, locality in Corinna
Bonney, Percival, 3316
Bonny Eagle, locality in Standish
Bonnyeagle, locality in Hollis
Book clubs, 2110
Booker, Mabel Libby, 2762
Booksellers and bookselling, 3996, 4255, 4276
Boone, Florence E., 2613
Boone Island, 5131, 5352
Boothbay, Me., 1681-1682, 1689-1690, 2346-2350
Boothbay Harbor, Me., 1681-1682, 1689-1690, 2351-2354
Boothby, Maude Lougee, 4074
Boothby Park, locality in Saco
Boots and shoes, 817, 3160, 3907, 5184, 5187
Borns, Harold W., Jr., 123, 1255
Boston, former name of Gray
Boston, Mass., 56
Boston and Bangor Steamship Company, 2090
Boston and Maine Railroad, 124, 2954, 3977
Boston Tea Party, 5311
Bostwick, former name of Newry
Bottles, 4159
Boulanger, Albert, 5321
Boundaries, see Northeast Boundary
Boundary, locality in Bridgewater
Bourges, Frederick de, 3665
Bourne, Edward Emerson (1797-1873), 1883-1884, 3406, 4103-4106, 4127
Bourne, Edward Emerson, Jr. (b. 1831), 1884
Bourne, Edward Emerson, III, 3407-3408
Bourne, Miriam, 2688
Bourne, Russell, 2688-2689
Bourque, Bruce J., 125, 826
Bousfield, Lillie Snowden, 3912
Bouton, Nathaniel, 3145
Bouvé, Pauline Carrington, 5310
Bowdens Point, locality in Prospect
Bowditch, Henry Ingersoll, 3803
Bowditch, Horace E., 1627
Bowdoin, Me., 2355
Bowdoin, former name of Ellsworth
Bowdoin Alumni Association of Boston, 2480
Bowdoin College, 2463, 2469-2478, 2483-2489, 2499-2500, 2503, 2506, 2509-2513, 2516-2519, 2523-2524, 2526, 2530-2531, 2533-2534, 2536-2540, 2543-2547, 2550, 2552, 2554-2561, 2568-2569, 2571, 2577, 2579-2582, 5164
Bowdoin College. Athenaean Society, 2479
Bowdoin College. Masque and Gown, 2481
Bowdoin College. Music Department, 2482
Bowdoin College Grant, former name of Abbot
Bowdoin College Grant, former name of Dixmont
Bowdoin College Grant, former name of Etna
Bowdoin College Grant, former name of Guilford
Bowdoin College Grant, former name of Sebec
Bowdoin College Grant East, 2356

Bowdoin College Grant West, 2357
Bowdoin Medical School, 2471, 2476-2477, 2550, 2571
Bowdoinham, Me., 2358-2361
Bowdoinham, Me. Bicentennial Historical Booklet
    Committee, 2360
Bowdoinham Association (Baptists), 1132
Bowen, Howard Lancaster, 1811
Bowen, Mrs. Joseph T., 2169
Bowen, Roger, 4590
Bowerbank, Me., 2362
Bowie Hill, locality in Durham
Bowler, Ernest C., 126-128, 1714
Bowles, Ella Shannon, 1984
Bowling, 737
Bowmantown Township, 2363
Bowtown Township, 2364
Box making, 2468, 3836
Boxer (ship), 1680, 1691, 1703, 1710
Boxing, 737
Boyd, Charles H., 1842
Boyd, Flora Addie, 4140
Boyd, John Parker, 3990
Boyd, former name of Plymouth Township
Boyd Lake, locality in Orneville Township
Boyds, former name of Orneville Township
Boyer, Kenneth J., 2486-2487
Boyle, James, 129
Boynton, E. Moody, 4163
Brackett, George Emerson, 130, 1832
Brackett, Lucy B., 1538
Brackett, Muriel, 1915
Brackett Memorial Church, Portland, 4501
Bradbury, A. W., 4996
Bradbury, Charles, 3428
Bradbury, James Ware, 131
Bradbury, Osgood Nathan, 4836
Bradbury, Thomas E., 3422, 3429
Bradbury, locality in St. Francis
Bradbury Mountain State Park, Pownal, 4534
Bradburys, locality in Fort Kent
Braden, John R., see John R. Braden (horse), 4541
Bradford, Alden, 5246
Bradford, Charles, 132
Bradford, Dana, 2654
Bradford, E. Alice, 2858
Bradford, Peter Amory, 133
Bradford, Me., 1733
Bradlee, Charles W., 1927
Bradley, Caleb, 203
Bradley, Irving R., 4964
Bradley, Me., 2366
Bradman, Arthur, 134, 916
Bradstreet Township, 2367
Braeburn, locality in York
Bragdon, Charles R., 5236
Bragdon, Katherine, 5311
Bragdon, Roger, 2210
Branch, locality in Columbia
Branch Mills, locality in China and Palermo
Branin, M. Lelyn, 1628, 3768, 4189-4192
Brassard, Francis, 1441
Brassua Township, 2368
Brault, Gérard J., 135, 2488-2489
Bray, Israel Riggs, 3095
Bray, John, 3495
Brazer, Esther Stevens, 136, 3213

Brekke, Ragnhild, 3913
Bremen, Me., 1693, 2369-2370
Brennan, locality in Mapleton
Brentwood, locality in Cape Elizabeth
Brettuns Mills, locality in Livermore
Brewer, Me., 1736, 1752, 1761-1762, 2047, 2082,
    2371-2375
Brewer, Me. First Congregational Church, 2371
Brewer Church, 2372
Brick Store Museum, Kennebunk, 3415-3416
Brick trade, 2461
Brickett, George Edmund, 137
Bridges, Moody, 2383
Bridges family, 2383
Bridges, 370, 695, 710, 795, 839, 1493, 1822, 1824,
    2245, 2962, 3143, 3297, 3299, 3852-2854, 4954,
    5334
Bridges Town, former name of Wellington
Bridgestown, former name of Troy
Bridgeton, former name of Bridgton
Bridgewater, Me., 2376
Bridgewater and Portland Academy Grants, former
    name of Bridgewater
Bridgham, David Lyle, 102
Bridgton, Me., 2377-2391
Bridgton, Me. First Congregational Church, 2377-
    2378
Bridgton, former name of Troy
Bridgton Academy, North Bridgton, 2379, 2390
Bridgton Academy Grant, former name of Maxfield
Bridgton & Harrison Railway, 1488, 1516, 2386, 3311
Bridgton and Saco River Railroad, 862, 2387
Briggs, Maud Fuller Smith, 5247
Briggs Corner, locality in Freedom
Brighams Cove, locality in West Bath
Brighton, locality in Portland
Brighton Plantation, 2392
Brightwater, locality in Phippsburg
Brimstone Corner, locality in Paris
Brinkler, Alfred, 4193-4194
Bristol, Me., 286, 799, 1683, 1693, 1708, 1712,
    2398-2438, 4100
Bristol, former name of York
Bristol High School, 2395
Britt, Benjamin H., 4534
Brixham Lower Corners, locality in York
Brixham Upper Corners, locality in York
Broad Cove, locality in Bremen
Broad Cove, locality in Cape Elizabeth
Broadbay, former name of Waldoboro
Brockway, Marjorie, 3397
Brokers, 4362
Brook Haven, locality in Windham
Brookes, George S., 1554
Brookfield, former name of Anson
Brooklin, Me., 1561, 1589, 2439-2441
Brooklin Centennial Committee, 2439
Brooks, Alfred A., 4042
Brooks, Annie Peabody, 3430
Brooks, Noah, 2690
Brooks, Me., 2442
Brooksville, Me., 1581, 1597, 1621, 2443-2447
Brooksville Historical Society, 2443
Brookton Township, 2448
Brown, C. Donald, 2919
Brown, David A., 3038

Brown, Everett S., 141
Brown, Frank Chouteau, 1936, 4788
Brown, Gilbert Patten, 4978
Brown, Harold F., 3964
Brown, Herbert Ross, 2472
Brown, Hester P., 801
Brown, John Herbert, 3462
Brown, John Marshall, 142-143, 2570
Brown, Lenard E., 1555-1556
Brown, Philip Greely, 144
Brown Corner, locality in Limestone
Brown Corner, locality in Prospect
Brown Neighborhood, locality in Wilton
Browne, George Waldo, 3146
Brownfield, Me., 2449-2451
Brownfield, Me. Congregational Church, 2449
Browns Corner, locality in Canaan
Browns Corner, locality in West Gardiner
Brownsfield, former name of Brownfield
Browntown, locality in Jefferson
Brownville, Me., 2452-2462
Bruce, Barbara A., 4558
Brummitt, Howard, 2039, 2614
Bruneau, Charles G. E. M., 2490
Brunet, Henri, 1314
Brunswick, Me., 259, 516, 2463-2582, 3532
Brunswick, Me. Bicentennial Committee, 2493
Brunswick, Me. Church of St. John the Baptist, 2494
Brunswick, Me. First Parish Congregational Church,
    2465-2466, 2495-2498
Brunswick Convention, 2464, 2502
Brunswick Naval Air Station, locality in Brunswick
Bryant, George W., 5147
Bryant, H. W., firm, bookseller, Portland, Me.,
    145
Bryant, Judson B., 5118
Bryant, Seth Emery, 3409, 3435
Basin, locality in Addison
Bryant Pond, Me., 5282
Bryant Pond Telephone Company, 5282
Bryant Ridge, locality in Burlington
Bryants Corner, locality in Belfast
Buck, Jonathan, 2590
Buck, Rufus, 2586-2587
Buck family, 2586
Buckfield, Me., 2583-2585, 3532
Buckley Road, locality in Bridgewater
Bucknam, Samuel, 2781
Bucks Harbor, former name of Machiasport
Bucks Harbor, locality in Machiasport
Bucks Mills, locality in Bucksport
Bucksport, Me., 2082, 2586-2598, 4589
Bucksport, Me. Elm Street Congregational Church,
    2589
Buckstown, former name of Bucksport
Buckstown Island, former name of Verona
Bucktown, former name of Buckfield
Buettell, Roger B., 2168
Buffalo, locality in Portage Lake
Buffam Hill, locality in Wells
Buffum, Samuel, 3903
Bugbee, locality in Washburn
Buildings (see also Architecture), 573, 1114, 2267,
    2556, 4262
Buisson, Emma, 5028
Buker, H. W., 3774

Buker, Margaret, 3534
Bulfinch, Charles, 2010
Bull, Dixey, 2394, 2409
Bunganuc Landing, locality in Brunswick
Bunker Hill, locality in Jefferson
Bunkers Harbor, locality in Gouldsboro
Burbank, alternate name of Northeast Carry Township
Burdin Corner, locality in Wellington
Burgess, George, 146
Burgess, J. H., 666
Burial grounds, see Cemeteries
Burkettville, locality in Appleton
Burleigh, Albert A., 1351
Burleigh, Elsia Holway, 4956
Burlington, Me., 2599
Burnham, Edith, 4195
Burnham, Edward P., 426
Burnham, Horace M., 148
Burnham, John, 3997
Burnham, Philip E., 2499
Burnham, Me., 2600
Burnham and Morrill Company, 3899, 4281, 4335
Burnham Tavern, Machias, 3658
Burnt Coat, Me., 4867
Burrage, Henry Sweetser, 148-160, 690, 803, 876,
    1061, 1184, 2396-2397, 3463, 5029
Burrage, Thomas J., 4197
Burroughs, Adeline R., 5150
Burroughs, George, 1486
Burt, Frank H., 1557
Burton, Alfred E., 2500
Burton, Alfred M., 4198
Burton, Clara R., 3753
Burton family, 4878
Burton Corner, locality in Pittsfield
Bushnell, D. I., Jr., 901
Businessmen (see also Merchants), 50, 867, 1840,
    1880, 2047, 2082, 2120, 2248, 3532, 4169, 4181,
    4358, 4589
Busses, 677
Bustins Island, Me., 3107, 3111
Butcher, Russell D., 1558, 3790
Butler, Benjamin, 1985, 2763, 3047-3053, 3060, 3226,
    3872, 4859
Butler, Ellen Hamlin, 2064
Butler, Eva L., 161
Butler, Francis Gould, 3054
Butler, Joyce, 1885, 3431-3432
Butler, Mary A., 2955
Butler, Natalie Sturges, 1985, 2763, 3047-3053,
    3060, 3226, 3872, 4859
Butterfield, Chester F., 2920
Butterfield Landing, locality in Weston
Buttons Road, locality in Detroit
Butwin, David, 2921
Buxton, Henry James, 162
Buxton, Patricia, 4141
Buxton, Phebe M., 3917
Buxton, Philip W., 2592
Buxton, Me., 2610; 2298, 2601-2609
Buxton, Me. Proprietors, 2604
Buxton Congregational Church, 2608
Byers, Douglas S., 163, 3007
Byrne, Frank Loyola, 164
Byron, Me., 2611
Byron Greenough and Company, Portland, 4356

C Surplus, Me., 2612
Cabell, Royal Edwards, 1299
Cabot, John, 165, 656
Cabot, Sebastian, 656
Cadwalader, Caroline, 5312
Cail, Harold L., 3040, 3694, 4199
Calais, Me., 1840-1841, 1844, 1874, 2613-2630
Calais, Me. First Congregational Church, 2615-2616
Calais, Me. Ordinances, etc., 2617
Calais Street Railway, 2629
Calderwood, Cornelia L., 4200
Calderwood, Ivan E., 4965-4967
Caldwell, Augustine, 2956
Caldwell, Dabney W., 760
Caldwell Corner, locality in Oxford
Caleb Cushing (ship), 4495
Calef, John, 2691
Calhoun, John C., Jr., 166
Calhoun, Philo, 167
California, locality in Stockholm
Callahan, George A., 3535
Calliopean Baseball Team, 2453
Cambden, former name of Camden
Cambridge (ship), 3647
Cambridge, Me., 2631
Camden, Me., 707, 1653, 1666, 1671, 1673, 1833,
    2082, 2632-2650, 4589, 4612
California Road, locality in Limestone
Camden, Me. Chestnut Street Baptist Church, 2633,
    2636
Camden, Me. First Congregational Church, 2634, 2637
Camden Commandery, Knights Templar, 2649
Camden Herald Publishing Company, 1653
Camden Public Library, 2632
Came, Samuel McIntyre, 1931
Cameron Corner, locality in Lincolnville
Cammett, Stephen, 168, 4201
Camp, Helen B., 2398-2399
Camp Benson, locality in Newport
Camp Caribou, Lynchtown, 3650-3651
Camp Dry-Kye, locality in Ellsworth
Camp Ellis, Me., 1904
Camp Wyonegonic, Denmark, 2846
Campbell, B. A., 4079
Campbell, Charles E., 1193
Campbell, Edward Melvin, 1865
Campbell, Frederic L., 169-170
Campbell, Helen A., 2501
Campbell, John C., 4080
Campbell, Leroy A., 2636
Campbell, Thomas Joseph, 171, 2692
Campbell, W. E., 172
Campbell Circle, locality in Wells
The Campground, locality in Old Orchard Beach
Campo, Charles A., 173
Camps, 2846, 3650-3651, 3794, 3964, 5012
Canaan, Me., 1816, 2651-2653
Canaan, former name of Lincolnville
Canaan Academy Grant, former name of Coplin Planta-
    tion
Canadian Confederation, 1247
Canadian invasion (1775-1776), 15, 24, 113, 132,
    170, 239, 257, 538, 566, 571, 589, 600, 648,
    719, 724, 844, 864, 866, 882, 924, 949, 1051,
    1154-1155, 1230, 1276, 1329, 4757
Canadian Pacific Railroad, 2993

Canadians, 1211
Canal National Bank, Portland, 879, 4256, 4493
Canals, 228, 237, 333, 354, 508, 626, 670, 879,
    1507, 4256, 5008
Canavan, Frances Ebbs, 174
Candage, James, 2329
Candage, Rufus George Frederick, 2328-2332
Caniba Mill, locality in Van Buren
Canoes and canoeing, 505, 718, 1528
Canneries, see Food packaging industry
Canton, Me., 2654, 3532
Cape Cottage, locality in Cape Elizabeth
Cape Elizabeth, Me., 1265, 1483, 1487, 1492, 1512,
    1534, 2655-2666, 4202, 4287, 4820
Cape Elizabeth, Me. First Church of Christ, 2656
Cape Elizabeth High School, 2663
Cape Elizabeth Light, 2665
Cape Neddick, Me., 5353-5354
Cape Neddick House, York, 5354
Cape Neddick Light Station, York, 5323
Cape Newagen, Me., 4828
Cape Newagen, former name of Boothbay
Cape Porpoise, 3434, 3440-3441, 3443
Cape Rosier, locality in Brooksville
Cape Split, locality in Addison
Cape-Porpus, former name of Kennebunkport
Capitol Island, locality in Southport
Capitols, 1994, 2002, 2010, 2019, 2029
Capuchins, 176, 619, 680, 2700
Caratunk, Me. Congregational Church of Christ,
    2667
Caratunk, former name of Bingham
Caratunk, former name of Solon
Caratunk Plantation, 2667
Carberg, Warren C., 2444
Cardville, locality in Greenbush
Carey, Roger, 4850
Cargill, A. P., 3580
Caribou, Me., 50, 2668-2675
Caribou, Me. First Universalist Church, 2669, 2674
Caricatures and cartoons, 4245
Carles, Reginald E., 177-178
Carleton, John, 1273
Carleton, Osgood, 1143
Carlson, Shirlee Connors, 4612
Carlton Bridge, Bath, 2245
Carmel, Me., 2676
Carnes, Joshua A., 4202
Carr, Frances, 3826-3827
Carr, Joseph William, 179
Carr, Robert, 65
Carrabassett Lodge, Freemasons, Canaan, 2651
Carrabassett Valley, 2677
Carriage industry, 4361
Carritunk, former name of Caratunk
Carroll, Gladys Hasty, 4789
Carroll Plantation, 2678
Carrs Corner, locality in Palermo
Carrying Place Town Township, 2679
Carrying Place Township, 2680
Carson Siding, locality in Woodland
Carter, Bertha, 4542
Carter, Bertha Wheeler, 3026
Carter, George M., 2670
Carter, Robert Goldthwaite, 180
Carthage, Me., 2681

Cartland, John Henry, 2400-2402, 2419
Cartoons, see Caricatures and cartoons
Carver, Clifford Nickels, 4723
Carver, John (d. 1621), 1266
Carver, John (1799-1867), 4723
Carvers Corner, locality in Lincolnville
Carvers Harbor, locality in Vinalhaven
Cary, Austin, 181-184
Cary, Richard, 4798
Cary, Theodore, 1442
Cary Plantation, 2682
Carys Mills, locality in Houlton
Cascade, locality in Saco
Casco, Me., 2683-2684
Casco, former name of New Canada
Casco, former name of Portland
Casco Bay, 962, 1480-1481, 1486, 1495-1496, 1503,
    1510, 1512-1513, 1515, 1517, 1519, 1523, 1526,
    1528-1530, 1532, 3286, 4202, 4287, 4456, 5309
Casco Bay, former name of Falmouth
Casco Bay, former name of Portland
Casco Castle, Freeport, 3106
Casco Lodge, Freemasons, Yarmouth, 5288, 5291A,
    5297
Casco Street Baptist Church, Portland, 4350
Cash Corner, locality in South Portland
Cass Corner, locality in Cornville
Cassidy, Violet, 3695
Cassidy, William, 3695
Castiglioni, Luigi, 1226
Castine, Me., 707, 962, 1264, 1597, 1621, 2425,
    2685-2748, 4587
Castle Hill, Me., 2749
Castle Tucker, see Tucker Castle
Castner, Harold Webber, 1678-1679, 2403
Caswell Plantation, 2750
Caswells Corner, locality in Appleton
Caswells Corner, locality in Harpswell
Cathance, former name of Bowdoinham
Cathedral Church of Saint Luke, Portland, 4194,
    4280, 4454, 4466
Catholics, 19, 174, 185-188, 213, 260, 502, 618-
    619, 676, 680, 715, 886, 989, 1010, 1014, 1024,
    1109, 1113, 1186, 1328, 1337, 1402, 1441, 1694,
    2692, 2700, 2737, 3019, 3150, 3170, 3604, 3665,
    3900, 4330, 5176
Cattle industry, 120
Cawley, Elizabeth R., 5182
Cayford, John E., 2697
Cedar Breeze, locality in Glenburn
Cedar Grove, locality in Dresden
Cemeteries, 851, 1135-1136, 1165, 1389, 2027, 2129-
    2130, 3489, 4075, 5199
Center Belmont, locality in Belmont
Center Lebanon, locality in Lebanon
Center Lovell, locality in Lovell
Center Minot, locality in Minot
Center Montville, locality in Montville
Center Sidney, locality in Sidney
Center Vassalboro, locality in Vassalboro
Centerville, Me., 2751
Central Congregational Church, Bangor, 2051, 2086,
    2101
Central Congregational Church, Bath, 2203
Central Congregational Church, Eastport, 2922
Centre Street Congregational Church, Machias, 3661

Centreville, former name of Centerville
Ceramics, see Pottery
Chadbourne, Ava Harriet, 189-196
Chadbourne, Benjamin F., 4553, 4673
Chadbourne, H. H., 3435
Chadbourne, Paul Ansel, 2819
Chadbourne, Sumner J., 2869
Chadbourne, Walter Whitmore, 197
Chadwick, Edmund Alexander, 3151
Chadwick, Joseph, 198, 1559
Chadwick Survey, 364
Chafee, Zechariah, 4783
Chain of Ponds Township, 2752
Challenger (ship), 2221
Chamberlain, George Walter, 3126, 3518-3520, 3998
Chamberlain, John, 3126
Chamberlain, Joshua Lawrence, 199-200, 1118, 2625
Chamberlain, Mary L., 4203
Chamberlain, Samuel, 2782
Chamberlain family, 3520
Chamberlain, locality in Bristol
Champernowne, Francis, 3491
Champlain, Samuel de, 142, 362, 912, 1608, 1747,
    2625
Champlin, James Tift, 201, 5030
Chandler, Peleg, 1765
Chandler River, former name of Jonesboro
Chandlerville, former name of Detroit
Chandlerville, former name of Plymouth
Chaney, William H., 3021A
Chaplin, Ruth A., 4167, 4204
Chapman, Alfred King, 5031
Chapman, Carleton Abramson, 1560
Chapman, George Whitefield, 3183A
Chapman, Harry J., 2091, 3273
Chapman, Henry Leland, 2502-2503, 2549
Chapman, J. K., 202
Chapman, Leonard Bond, 203, 1483, 1913, 4205-4206,
    4698, 5151
Chapman, William Rogers, 1413
Chapman, Me., 2753
Charities, 1487, 2069, 2193, 2220, 2224, 3030-3034,
    4291, 4322-4323, 4372, 4514, 4629, 5250, 5267,
    5274
Charles Chase Corner, locality in Wells
Charleston Air Force Station, locality in Charleston
Charleston, Me., 2754
Charlestown, former name of Charleston
Charlotte, Me., 2755-2756
Charlotte, Me. Sesquicentennial Committee, 2755
Charters, 152
Chase, A. L., 2957
Chase, A. Mont, 5279
Chase, Albro Elmore, 1484
Chase, Benjamin Chapman, 2637
Chase, Clarence Augustine, 3536
Chase, Clifford G., 2195
Chase, Edith F., 2958
Chase, Edward Everett, 204
Chase, F. Halcyon, 2504
Chase, Fannie Scott, 5248
Chase, Freeman Hersey, 3987
Chase, George Davis, 179, 205
Chase, Halcyon, 2859
Chase, Henry, 206
Chase, J. E., 3610

Chase, Mary Ellen, 207-208
Chase, Solon, 1185
Chase, Virginia, 209, 2942-2945
Chase Corner, locality in Weld
Chase Mills, locality in East Machias
Chase School House, Woodstock, 5281
Chase Stream Township, 2757
Chases Mills, locality in Turner
Chases Pond, locality in York
Chatto, Clarence I., 1561, 1812
Chebeague Island, 2807, 2809
Chebeague Island Methodist Historical Society, 2807
Chelsea, Me., 1624, 1629, 1648, 2758-2759
Chemistry-study and teaching, 3529
Cherryfield, Me., 1840, 1864, 1875, 2760-2761
Chester, Me., 2762
Chester, former name of Chesterville
Chester and Wyman, former name of Chesterville
Chesterville, Me., 1419, 2763-2764
Chestnut Street Baptist Church, Camden, 2633, 2636
Chestnut Street Methodist Episcopal Church, Portland, 4178, 4380-4381
Chesuncook Lake, 1775
Chesuncook Township, 2765
Cheverus High School, Portland, Me., 4207
Chewleyville Corners, locality in Holden
Chi Phi Fraternity, Bowdoin College, 2511
Chi Psi Fraternity, Bowdoin College, 2531
Chick, Olive M., 3590
Chick Orchards, Monmouth, 3767
Chicopee, locality in Buxton
Chilcott, James C., 1562, 2995
Children, 2069, 2220, 2224, 4208, 4815
Children's literature, 835
Children's Theatre, Portland, 4208
Childs, Frances Sergeant, 3513
Chilman, C. William, 2169-2170
China, Me., 1645, 2766-2768
China, former name of Orrington
Chipman, Charles Phillips, 5032, 5035
Chisholm, Hugh Joseph (1847-1912), 211, 4209
Chisholm, Hugh Joseph (b. 1886), 4209
Chisholm, locality in Jay
Chittenden, Albert D., 212
Choate, Isaac Bassett, 287, 2391
Chouinard, Eva, 1443
Christ Chapel, Dark Harbor, 3374
Christ Church, Biddeford, 2304
Christ Church, Eastport, 2923, 2935
Christ Church, Gardiner, 3157, 3164, 3168
Christian, Sheldon, 1680, 2505
Christmas, 406, 430, 2628
Christmas Cove, locality in South Bristol
Church, Benjamin, 214, 217
Church and education, 562, 2568
Church architecture, 1581, 2412, 2509, 2799, 3432, 3833, 3924, 4350, 4885
Church history, 1417; 19, 146, 219-220, 489, 643, 819, 964, 1064, 1274, 1368, 1593, 1993, 5198
Church of Good Fellowship, Naples, 3822
Church of Our Father, Bar Harbor, 2171
Church of Our Holy Redeemer, Bar Harbor, 171
Church of St. John the Baptist, Brunswick, 2494
Church of St. Mary the Virgin, Falmouth Foreside, 3041
Church of St. Stephen the Martyr, Waterboro, 5018

Church of the Advent, Limestone, 3588
Church of the Good Shepherd, Houlton, 3341
Church of the New Jerusalem, see New Jerusalem Church
Churches (studies of several churches in a locale), 578, 794, 830, 1411, 1434, 1686, 2326, 2891, 2924, 3047, 3989, 4494, 4627, 4670, 4684, 4743, 5114, 5156, 5192
Churches, Advent Christian, 2966
Churches, Anglican, see Churches, Episcopal
Churches, Baptist, 151, 261, 274, 1130, 1132, 1508, 1536, 1595, 1644, 1716, 1780, 1790, 2054, 2064, 2183, 2467, 2521, 2633, 2636, 2798, 2869, 3072, 3096, 3231, 3306, 3315, 3317, 3335, 3444, 3463, 3479, 3514, 3585, 3625, 3785, 3818, 3848, 3888, 3904, 3910, 4062, 4239, 4300, 4327, 4350, 4383-4385, 4392-4395, 4459, 4736, 4742, 4748, 4765, 4799, 4917, 5082, 5100-5101, 5118, 5285, 5287, 5293
Churches, Christian, 4797
Churches, Congregational, 219-220, 223, 309-310, 350-351, 425, 950, 975, 1065, 1508, 1554, 1595, 1623, 1706, 1860, 1887, 1919-1920, 1933, 1936, 1939, 1964, 1967, 1974-1975, 2028, 2051, 2055, 2058, 2086, 2101-2102, 2126, 2143, 2152, 2203-2205, 2250, 2258, 2264, 2291, 2297, 2308, 2325, 2335, 2346, 2372, 2374, 2377-2378, 2449, 2465-2466, 2495-2498, 2589, 2608, 2615-2616, 2637, 2656, 2667, 2761, 2796, 2808, 2810, 2813, 2845, 2851, 2857, 2876, 2888, 2913, 2922, 2950, 2956-2957, 2963, 2969, 2981-2982, 3004, 3008, 3015, 3043, 3050, 3057-3058, 3074, 3101, 3123, 3133, 3141, 3161, 3177, 3192, 3198, 3264, 3275, 3288, 3290, 3292, 3294-3295, 3300, 3366, 3432, 3469, 3486, 3523, 3542, 3569, 3592, 3609, 3611, 3649, 3661, 3798, 3856, 3876, 3882-3883, 3886, 3918, 3924, 3926, 3929-3930, 3934, 4040, 4063, 4083, 4122, 4211, 4220, 4224, 4290, 4344, 4353, 4365-4368, 4374, 4386-4389, 4396, 4407-4408, 4410-4416, 4447, 4449, 4472-4474, 4480, 4497, 4515, 4546, 4636, 4639, 4641, 4647-4648, 4683, 4685, 4691, 4713, 4726, 4730, 4750, 4776, 4778, 4801, 4803, 4805-4806, 4820, 4905, 4922, 5019, 5095, 5111, 5125, 5130, 5132, 5154, 5158, 5162, 5165, 5190-5191, 5197, 5242, 5295, 5270, 5300-5301, 5336
Churches, Episcopal, 59, 278, 550, 941, 1006, 1153, 1962, 2032, 2039, 2145, 2151, 2171, 2185, 2304, 2307, 2524-2525, 2548, 2614, 2618, 2643, 2648, 2923, 2935, 3041, 3080, 3157, 3164, 3168, 3254, 3265, 3341, 3374, 3438, 3493, 3528, 3557, 3588, 3606, 3738, 3796, 3877, 3969, 3979, 4194, 4216, 4257, 4280, 4313, 4370, 4405-4406, 4454, 4466, 4469, 4476, 4550, 4603, 4632, 4651, 4661, 4682, 5018, 5066, 5213, 5215, 5254, 5326
Churches, Greek Orthodox, 2060, 4396
Churches, Lutheran, 1706, 4978, 4988, 4990, 4999
Churches, Methodist, 2807, 3172, 3425, 3594, 3822, 4029, 4501, 4806, 4821, 4981
Churches, Methodist Episcopal, 1016, 2030, 2056, 2249, 2626, 2865, 2955, 2972, 2979, 4073, 4178, 4380-4381
Churches, Moravian, 4980, 4987, 4993
Churches, nondenominational, 3795, 4847
Churches, Presbyterian, 1706, 4407-4408

Churches, Roman Catholic, 171, 715, 1978, 2061-2063, 2263, 2270, 2294, 2494, 3115, 3150, 3554-3556, 3687, 3741, 3978, 4360, 4403-4404, 4652-4653, 4953, 5155, 5214, 5232, 5322, 5346
Churches, Swedenborgian, see New Jerusalem Church
Churches, Unitarian, 290, 628, 1972, 2017, 2023, 2694, 3062, 3411, 3420, 4224, 4227, 4344, 4365-4368, 4386-4389, 4464A, 4471-4474, 4480, 4649
Churches, Universalist, 628, 970, 977, 1508, 1727, 1959, 1963, 2057, 2293, 2505, 2669, 2674, 2861, 3162, 3919, 4390-4391, 4706
Churchill, Edwin A., 215-216, 826, 1986, 3653, 4210
Churchill, Laurie, 2619
Chute, Thomas, 5205
Cider Hill, locality in York
Cilley, Jonathan, 2519
Cilley, Jonathan Prince, 218, 1655, 4878
Cimbria (ship), 4834
Cities and towns-planning, 601
Citizens Military Training Camp, Portland, 4243
The City, locality in Edgecomb
City halls (see also Town halls), 2000, 2091, 4378
City managers, 1391
City Point, locality in Belfast
Civil War (1861-1865), 218, 629-630, 775; 842, 1009, 1231, 1263, 1330, 1354, 1886, 2385, 2597, 2630, 2841, 2924, 2961, 3424, 3455, 3525, 4266, 4282, 5238
Civil War (1861-1865)-naval operations, 1842, 4279, 4294, 4495
Civilian Conservation Corps., 475
Civilian defense, 748, 1063
Clairvoyance, 2373
Clapham, Edwin F., 4861
Clapp, Asa W. H., 4306
Claremont Hotel, Southwest Harbor, 4832
Clark, Calvin Montague, 219-220, 2092
Clark, Charles E., 221-222
Clark, Cornelius Edwards, 223, 2264, 4211
Clark, Dennis W., 4434
Clark, Emma Folsom, 3695
Clark, Frank E., 4413
Clark, George Faber, 2698
Clark, Grace Wood, 3215
Clark, Isaac R., 1034
Clark, John E., 3717
Clark, Lewis E., 224
Clark District, locality in Prospect
Clark Island, locality in St. George
Clarke, Winfield S., 4822
Clarks Corner, locality in Liberty
Clarks Cove, locality in South Bristol
Clarks Mills, locality in Dayton and Hollis
Clason, O. B., 3152
Classen, H. George, 225
Clayton, Cathleen Sherman, 2172
Clayton, Tom, 2698
Clayton, W. Woodford, 1485, 1886
Cleaveland, Nehemiah, 2506, 2526
Cleaveland, Parker, 2507
Cleaves, Samuel W., 5222
Cleeve, George, 1075, 1481
Cleeves Neck, former name of Portland
Clepper, Henry Edward, 1715
Clergymen, 274, 350, 425, 446, 878, 1377, 1489, 1533, 1554, 1623, 2079, 2372, 3594, 3915

Cleveland, George Arthur, 226
Cliff Island, locality in Portland
Clifford, Angela Godfrey, 2093
Clifford, Earle R., 4063
Clifford, Harold Burton, 227, 1682
Clifford, Nathan, 1414
Clifford family, 2093
Clifton, Me., 2769
Clinton, Me., 799, 2770-2773
Clock and watch making, 423, 597, 1137, 3446
Clock Farm Corners, locality in Kennebunkport
Clothing trade, 3540, 4356, 5071
Cloudman, S. B., 228-229
Cloudman Hill, 4543
Clough, Annie L., 2333
Clough, Blanche Cole, 230-231
Clough House, see Marie Antoinette House, Edgecomb
Le Club Calumet, Inc., Augusta, 1987
Clubb, Henry Stephen, 232
Clubs, 353, 797-798, 800, 942, 1424, 1987, 2031, 2125, 2292, 2519, 2541, 3180, 3570, 3957, 4241, 4244, 4351, 4478, 4533, 4756, 5060, 5250, 5267, 5274
Cluff, Dohn A., 233
Coal Kiln Corners, locality in Scarborough
Coan, Leander Samuel, 2346
Coast artillery, see Artillery, coast
Coatsworth, Elizabeth Jane, 234-236
Cobb, David, 25
Cobb, Josiah F., 4820
Cobb, Miles, 644
Cobb, Oliver A., 5153
Cobb, Samuel, 1184
Cobbosecontee Stream, 3155
Cobbossee, former name of Gardiner
Cobbs Bridge, locality in New Gloucester
Coblens, Glenore Orris, 4847
Coburn, Louise Helen, 237-238, 2653, 4756-4758
Coburn, locality in Newport
Coburn Cadets, 3999
Coburn Classical Institute, Waterville, 5033-5034, 5055, 5063
Coburn Gore, Me., 2774
Coburn Steamboat Company, 1787
Cochrane, Harry Hayman, 3769
Cockhall, former name of Lyman
Codman, Charles, 4425
Codman, John, 239
Codman House, Gorham, 3200
Codyville Plantation, 2775
Coe, Harrie Badger, 240
Coe, Thomas U., 1748
Coffin, Charles, 2605
Coffin, Harold Wilhelm, 241, 2094
Coffin, Paul, 2610
Coffin, Robert Peter Tristram, 82, 242-247
Coffin District, locality in Harrington
Cogswell, Jonathan, 4633
Cohegan, former name of Skowhegan
Cohiggin, former name of Skowhegan
Cohigin, former name of Skowhegan
Coins, see Numismatics
Colborntown, former name of Orono
Colburn, Reuben, 801
Colby, D. W., 4674
Colby, Fred M., 3464

Colby, (George N.) & Co., 248
Colby Alumni Association, 5072-5073
Colby College, 249-250, 5025-5027, 5029-5032, 5035-
    5040, 5043-5044, 5046-5049, 5054, 5058-5060,
    5064-5065, 5067-5068, 5070, 5072-5076, 5078-
    5081, 5083-5085, 5090, 5092-5094, 5097, 5112,
    5115-5117
Colby College, Waterville, Me. Art Department, 251
Colby College, Waterville, Me. Art Museum, 252
Colby College Press, 5038
Colby Library Quarterly, 5097
Colby Siding, locality in Woodland
Colcord, Elmer D., 3156
Colcord, Lincoln, 1017
Cold Stream, former name of Enfield
Coldbrook Road, locality in Hermon
Cole, Aaron Burr, 2959
Cole, Albert, 2797
Cole, Alfred, 2584
Cole, Ernest H., 3214
Cole, Ichabod, 2960
Cole, John N., 253
Cole, Nan, 2173-2174
Cole, Sharon, 2620
Cole, William I., 254
Cole Corner, locality in Abbot
Coles Corner, locality in Winterport
Cole's Express, Bangor, Me., 255
Colesworthy, Daniel Clement, 1486
Collamore, Charles I., 2095
College Club, Bates College, 3570
College theatre, 2481, 4020, 4034,
Colleges, see Universities and colleges
Collegetown, former name of Dixmont
Collidge, Philip Tripp, 265-266
Collier, Sargent F., 256, 1563-1564, 2175
Collins, Charles W., 3689
Collins, George H., 1477
Collins, (S. W.) Co., Caribou, 2671
Collins, Samuel Wilson, Jr., 2672
Collins, W. E., 257
Collins family, 2672
Collinstown, locality in Appleton
Colony Ordinance, see Great Pond Ordinance
Columbia, Me., 1856, 2776-2780
Columbia Falls, Me., 1856, 2781-2786
Coman, Dale Rex, 1843
Coman, Edwin Truman, 3654
Comfort Magazine, 2024
Commerce, 699, 816, 1313, 4210-4211, 4242
Commercial travelers, 471
Commonwealth Shoe and Leather Company, Gardiner,
    3160
Communistic experiments, 3537
Composers, 1360
Comstock Township, 2787
Concord Township, 2788
Concordville, locality in York
Condeskeag, former name of Bangor
Condon, Vesta, 3710
Conflagrations, see Fires
Congdon, Isabelle, 259
Congregation Beth Israel, Bangor, 2053
Congregational Church, Albany, 1919-1920
Congregational Church, Alna, 1939
Congregational Church, Blue Hill, 2325, 2335

Congregational Church, Brownfield, 2449
Congregational Church, Cumberland, 2808, 2810, 2813
Congregational Church, Dennysville, 2851
Congregational Church, Dresden, 2888
Congregational Church, Edgecomb, 2950
Congregational Church, Garland, 3177
Congregational Church, Gorham, 3198
Congregational Church, Harpswell, see Elijah Kellogg
    Church, Harpswell
Congregational Church, Head Tide, 1936
Congregational Church, Jackson, 3379
Congregational Church, Lebanon, 3523
Congregational Church, Limington, 3592
Congregational Church, Litchfield, 3609, 3611
Congregational Church, New Sweden, 3856
Congregational Church, Presque Isle, 4545
Congregational Church, Sanford, 4691
Congregational Church, Waterford, 5019
Congregational Church, Waterville, 5095
Congregational Church, West Newfield, 3883
Congregational Church, Windham Hill, 5197
Congregational Church, Winthrop, 5242
Congregational Church, Wiscasset Point, 5259, 5270
Congregational Church of Christ, Caratunk, 2667
Congregational churches, see Churches, Congregational
Congregational Churches in Maine. York County Con-
    ference, 1887
Congregationalism, 5, 1489, 1533
Connolly, Donald F. X., 260
Connor Township, 2789
Connors Corner, locality in Liberty
Conservative Baptist Association of Maine, 261
Constitution (Maine), 739-740, 1123
Constitution (U. S.), 378, 382
Constitutional Convention (U. S.), 378, 382
Constitutional conventions (Maine), 4508
Convene, locality in Sebago
Conway House, Camden, 2644
Cook, Cara, 2380
Cook, Joel, 3369
Cook, Julia Anna, 262, 1888
Cook, Sanger Mills, 4139
Cook, Walter Leonard, 263, 2096
Cook Mills, locality in Casco
Cooke, Le Baron P., 4093
Cooks Corner, locality in Brunswick
Cooks Corner, locality in Troy
Cooks Corner, locality in Willimantic
Coolidge, Austin Jacobs, 264
Cooper, Arthur M., 5213
Cooper, John H., 3153
Cooper, Me., 2790
Cooperative Association of America, 3537, 3564
Cooperative societies, 3537, 3564
Coopers and cooperage, 3332
Coopers Corners, locality in Kennebunk
Coopers Mills, locality in Whitefield
Copeland, Melvin T., 2475
Coplin Plantation, 2791
Corbett, Ralph, 783
Corea, locality in Gouldsboro
Corey, Albert Bickmore, 267
Corinna, Me., 2792
Corinth, Me., 2793
Corinthian Chapter, Royal Arch Masons, Belfast, 2266
Cork, Me., 1807A, 1809

Corliss, Carlton Jonathan, 268
Corliss, Lewis H., 2381
Corliss Pottery, Woolwich, 5284
Cornish, Leslie C., 269, 1972
Cornish, Me., 2794-2798
Cornish Station, locality in Baldwin
Cornville, Me., 2799
Cornwall, L. Peter, 1539
Cornwallis House, Camden, South Carolina, 4887
Corsons Corner, locality in Athens
Costigan, locality in Milford
Costrell, Edwin, 270
Cote Corner, locality in Limestone
Cottle, Laura Bickford, 3274
Cotton, Frances Meserve, 3189
Cotton, Percy G., 3341
Cotton growing and manufacture, 5164
Cottrill, Matthew, 3880
Counce family, 5004
Council of Social Agencies, Portland, Me., 1487
Counterfeiting, 2705, 2745, 4587
Country life (see also Farm life and Outdoor life),
    349, 682, 896, 1910, 3181, 3603
Court records (see also Probate records), 738, 1688
Courts, 269, 279-381, 510, 524, 732, 738, 893, 928,
    1082-1083, 1302, 1316, 1364, 1383, 1385, 1506,
    2890, 2894, 2897, 5257, 5276
Cousens, Alice C., 2606
Cousins, Edgar M., 4922
Cousins Island, 5294
Cove Point Township, 2800
Covered Bridge, locality in Windham
Cowell family, 3520
Cox, William S., 4718
Cox Patent, 2801
Coxhall, former name of Lyman
Cozy Corners, locality in Wells
Crabtree, Alfred B., 3280
Craft unions, see Unions
Crafts, Martin, 4191
Craigie, Andrew, 1724
Cram, Hal, 271-273
Cram, Marshall, 2382
Cramer, Mary Meeker, 4613
Cranberry Isles, Me., 1570, 1587, 1617, 2802-2804
Crandall, Christine, 3251
Crane, Abijah Robinson, 274
Crane, J. R., 275, 2783
Cranes Corner, locality in Orland
Cranshaw, Florence F., 3180
Crawford, Me., 2805
Crediford, Annie Joyce, 1889
Crescent Beach, locality in Cape Elizabeth
Crescent Beach, locality in Owls Head
Crescent Chapter, Royal Arch Masons, Pembroke, 4081
Crescent Lake, locality in Casco
Crescent Lake Terrace, locality in Raymond
Crescent Lodge, Freemasons, Pembroke, 4079-4080,
    4082
Criehaven, Me., 3712
Crime and criminals, 1367, 1995, 2705, 2745, 3945,
    3992, 4586-4587, 4591, 4593
Criminal justice, administration of, 1367
Crittenden, Henry Temple, 276, 1488, 1540-1543,
    1629, 3774A
Crocker Turn, locality in Greenfield

Crockertown, alternate name of Sugarloaf Township
Crockery, see Pottery
Crockett, Fred E., 2638
Crockett, George B., 1716
Crockett, Marjorie, A., 2669
Crocketts Beach, locality in Owls Head
Crocketts Corner, locality in North Yarmouth
Crone, Alton H., 1656
Crosby, James Henry, 2055, 2097
Crosby, Jonah, 1957
Crosby, Ruth, 2288
Crosby, S. P., 1957
Crosby family, 1957
Crosbytown, former name of Etna
Cross, Harmon S., 3113
Cross Point, locality in Edgecomb
Cross Rock, locality in Allagash Plantation
Crossman Corner, locality in Durham
Crouseville, locality in Washburn
Crowe, Robert Watkins, 1391
Crowell, Marnie Reed, 277
Crowleys Junction, locality in Lewiston
Crumb, Lawrence N., 278
Crystal, Me., 2806
Culler, R. D., 2639
Cumberland, Me., 2807-2813
Cumberland and Oxford Canal, 228, 333, 354, 508,
    626, 879, 4256
Cumberland Association (Baptists), 1130, 1536
Cumberland Association of Congregational Ministers,
    1489, 1533
Cumberland Centre, Me. Congregational Church, 2808
2810, 2813
Cumberland Chapter, Royal Arch Masons, Yarmouth,
    5289
Cumberland County, 228, 333, 354, 508, 587, 626,
    879, 975, 978, 1045, 1409, 1480-1536, 2709, 4386
Cumberland County, Me. 200th Anniversary Committee,
    1490
Cumberland Lodge, Freemasons, New Gloucester, 3830,
    3846
Cumberland Lodge, Odd Fellows, Bridgton, 2389
Cumberland Mills, Me., 5154, 5158, 5165
Cumberland Mills, Me. Warren Congregational Church,
    5154, 5158, 5165
Cummings, Abbott Lowell, 2334
Cummings, Ephraim Chamberlain, 279, 1565, 2700, 3892
Cummings, George O., 4213
Cummings, Mildred H., 2640, 4776, 4968
Cummings, Osmond Richard, 280-282, 1657-1658, 1890,
    1988, 2508, 4214, 5041
Cummings, Randall Frederick, 1937
Cummings Crossing, locality in Berwick
Cummins, Robert, 2361
Cundys Harbor, locality in Harpswell
Cuniculocus Castle, Hancock, 3281-3282
Cunningham, Agnes H., 2996
Cunningham, Charles M., 4717-4718
Cunningham, Mrs. J. A., see Cunningham, Agnes H.
Cunningham Landing, locality in Orono
Curran, Jean Alonzo, 1134
Currency, see Money
Current, Richard N., 283
Currier, Alice C., 3852
Currier, George F., 5125
Currier, Isabel, 284, 2251, 3281, 4215, 4613, 4856-
    4857

Currier, Orlando, 3252
Curtis, Joseph R., 5288
Curtis, Kathryn B., 2601
Curtis, Kenneth M., 761
Curtis, Ruie L., 4578
Curtis, S. A., 3177
Curtis, Silas, 1989
Curtis Corner, locality in Leeds
Curvo, former name of Phillips
Cushanna, former name of Augusta
Cushena, former name of Augusta
Cushenac, former name of Augusta
Cushing, James Royal, 5130
Cushing, Wainwright, 4733
Cushing, Me., 1654, 4660
Cushing's Island, 4232, 4271-4272, 4329, 4456
Cushman, David Quimby, 285, 1683, 3875, 4104, 4106, 4127
Cushman, Helen Caldwell, 3380
Cushnoc, former name of Augusta
Custom houses, 2248, 4420
Customs administration, 1604, 4442
Custon Free Public Library, Monmouth, 3771
Cutler, Alexander Munro, 286
Cutler, Mrs. Lawrence, 2072
Cutler, Me., 962, 2815
Cutts, Thomas, 4635
Cyr, Kay, 3589
Cyr Plantation, 2816

Daggett, Athern P., 2509
Daggett, Windsor Pratt, 287
Daggette Ville, locality in Moscow
Daigle, Ronald J., 303
Daigle, former name of Fort Kent
Daigle, locality in New Canada
Daily Evening Journal, Lewiston, 3559
Dakin, Moses, 1833
Dale, Thomas Nelson, 288
Dallas, former name of Rangeley
Dallas, former name of Rangeley Plantation
Dallas Plantation, 2817
Dalton, Asa, 4216
Dalton, former name of Ashland
Damariscotta, Me., 1678, 1683-1684, 1708-1709, 2818-2826, 4589
Damariscotta Mills, locality in Nobleboro
Damariscove, Me., 2350
Damariscove Island, 3293
Damascus, locality in Carmel
Dame, Lawrence C., 4399
Dana, Edward F., 4217
Dana, Israel Thorndike, 4218
Dana, Marion, 4490
Dana, Samuel Trask, 289, 858
Dana, Woodbury Kidder, 5164
Dana Mills, Westbrook, 5164
Dane, Mary Elizabeth, 1928
Dane Corner, locality in Anson
Danforth, Edward F., 4759
Danforth, Florence Waugh, 799, 1813
Danforth, John S., 1713, 3651
Danforth, Me., 50, 2827
Danforth Point, Me., 2404
Danforth Point Trust, 2404
Daniels, Caroline T. Le Favor, 3370

Daniels, L. R., 290
Daniels, Lilla Wood, 4845
Danville, Me., 1961
Danville Corner, locality in Auburn
Dark Harbor, Me., 3370, 3374
Darrah, William C., 291
Dartmouth, former name of Newcastle
Date Rock, 4823
Daughters of Liberty. Gouldsboro, Me., 3215
Daughters of the American Revolution. Maine, 292-293
Daughters of the American Revolution. Maine. Hannah Weston Chapter, Machias, 3655-3656
Daveis, Charles Stewart, 542, 3127, 4302
Daveis, Edward Henry, 1302
Daviau, Jerome G., 294
Davidson, Jacqueline, 295
Davidson, Me., 3323
Davies, James, 4107, 4133
Davies, Wallace Evans, 3537
Davis, Albert H., 2997-2998, 3003
Davis, Andrew McFarland, 2281
Davis, B. H., 2874
Davis, Blynn Edwin, 2383-2384
Davis, Charles B., 427
Davis, Cyrus W., 1299
Davis, Daniel, 4219
Davis, Ebenezer, 542
Davis, Elizabeth Emanuelson, 3778
Davis, Gherardi, 296
Davis, Harold Arthur, 1844-1846, 3390
Davis, Isaac Franklin, 4777
Davis, Jefferson, 169, 2254
Davis, W. E., 4675
Davis, Will R., 3600
Davis Corner, locality in Waldoboro
Davis Grant, former name of Mason Township
Davis Island, locality in Edgecomb
Davis Township, 2828
Davison, Charles, 3777
Davisson, Jean, 3791
Davistown, former name of Montville
Day, Benjamin F., 2298
Day, Clarence Albert, 297-300, 1444, 1847-1848, 2776-2777, 4001-4002, 4029
Day, Clarence P., 4320
Day, David, 3828
Day, Holman Francis, 301
Day, Richard L., 1445
Days Academy Grant, 2829
Days Ferry, locality in Woolwich
Days Mill, locality in Arundel
Dayton, Me., 2830
Dayton, Me. Historical Committee, 2830
Dead Mans Cove, locality in Monhegan Plantation
Dead River, locality in Dallas Plantation
Dead River Company, Bangor, 2116
Dead River Township, 1821
Deadwater, former name of Orono
Dean, John, 5131
Dean Neighborhood, locality in West Paris
Deane, Charles, 302
Deane, John Gilmore, 3690
Deane, Joseph Augustus, 2999
Deane, Llewellyn, 4220
Deane, Samuel, 4480

Deantown Corner, locality in Lincolnville
Dearborn, Jeremiah Wadleigh, 4072
Dearborn, Vance E., 224, 303, 874
Dearborns Corner, locality in Garland
Deaths, see Mortality and Vital records
Debating, 3575-3576
Deblois, Me., 2832
Debsconeag Lakes, 1799
De Burians, Bangor, 2110
Decker Corner, locality in Clinton
De Costa, Benjamin Franklin, 304-307, 1566-1568, 4107-4109
Decrow, Gertrude, 308
Dedham, Me., 2833
Deeds, 1848, 1913
Deems, Mervin Monroe, 390-310
Deep Cove Shores, locality in Raymond
Deep Cut, locality in Brunswick
Deer, 61, 1232
Deer Hill, locality in Harrison
Deer Island, former name of Deer Isle
Deer Isle, Me., 1553, 1561, 2834-2844
Deer Isle, former name of Isle au Haut
Deering, C. W., 3194
Deering, Frank Cutter, 1893, 4634
Deering, Me., 1483, 1492, 1512, 4181
Deering High School, 4221
Deering Junction, locality in Portland
Deering Lodge, Freemasons, Portland, 4267
Deering Mansion, Portland, 4222
Deerpond, locality in Hollis
De Gregoire, Marie Thérèse, see Gregoire, Marie Thérèse de
Degregoire Park, locality in Bar Harbor
Delano Park, locality in Cape Elizabeth
Delano Park and Annex Association, Cape Elizabeth, Me., 2657
De Laski, John, 311, 3804
Delta Kappa Epsilon Fraternity, Bowdoin College, 2538, 2577
Demeritt, Dwight Burgess, 312
Demers, Mabel Gould, 1990, 3000, 3056, 4879
Democratic Party, 71, 662, 2034
Demography, see Population
De Monts, Pierre du Guast, see Monts, Pierre du Guast, sieur de
Denis, Michael J., 313
Dennicetown, former name of Dennistown
Dennis Corner, locality in Mount Vernon
Denmark, Me., 2845-2848
Denmark Congregational Church, 2845
Dennett, Mark, 3465
Dennett House, Kittery, 3476
Dennett's Wharf, Castine, 2714
Dennis, Alfred Lewis Pinneo, 805
Dennison Manufacturing Company, Brunswick, 2468
Dennistown Plantation, 3377A
Dennysville, Me., 1861, 2850-2854
Dennysville, Me. Congregational Church, 2851
Dentistry, 398
De Peyster, John Watts, 315-316
Depositors Corporation, 534
Derby, locality in Milo
Dermot, Gertrude, 4595
Dermot, Jessie, 4595
Dermot, Mary, 4595

Desert of Maine, Freeport, 3104
Desjardins, Philippe E., 316, 5155
Detmer, Josephine H., 4268
Detroit, Me., 2855
Deveau family, 4951
Devereaux Township, 2856
Devereux, Charlene, 2701
Devereux, Robert, see Essex, Robert Devereux, 2d Earl of
Dewar, Shirley, 5212
Dewey, locality in Harrington
Dexter, Frank Henry, 1891
Dexter, Henry Martyn, 214
Dexter, Me., 2857-2867, 3538
Dexter, Me. High School. Class of 1916, 2860
Dexter, Me. Universalist Church, 2861
Dexter Grammar School. Class of 1937, 2862
Deyo, Simeon L., 1634
Diamond Island Association, 4223
Dibner, Martin, 318
Dickens, Charles, 167, 4298
Dickey, William, 1440
Dickey, locality in Allagash Plantation
Dickeyville, former name of Frenchville
Dickson, Frederick Stoever, 421
Dickvale, locality in Peru
Dietz, Lew, 319-322, 1446-1447, 1659, 1935, 2347, 2641, 3100, 3234, 3657, 4591, 4614, 4760, 4778
Diligent (ship), 3660
Dillingham, Charles A., 323
Dillingham Point, locality in Camden
Dingley, Mrs. Edward N., 324
Dingley, Edward N., Jr., 324
Dingley, Nelson, 1414
Dingley, Nelson, Jr., 324-325, 1423
Dingley, Robert Jordan, 426, 1491, 2386, 3820, 4840
Dingley, Theda C., 3323, 4563
Diocese of Maine, 59, 1006
Diocese of Portland, 213
Dionne, former name of Frenchville
Dirigo Corner, locality in China
Disasters, see Earthquakes, Fires, and Floods
Dix Island, 4592
Dixfield, Me., 2868
Dixfield Bicentennial Committee, 2868
Dixie Corner, locality in St. Albans
Dixmont, Me., 2869-2871
Dixon, Joseph H., 327, 2961-2962
Dixon Corner, locality in Clinton
Dixtown, former name of Mexico
Dochet Island, 2621
Doctors, see Physicians
Dodd, Marion E., 329
Dodge, A. D., 2770
Dodge, Benjamin, 4189
Dodge, E. H., 1570
Dodge, Ernest Stanley, 505, 4865
Dodge, Reuben George Washington, 2335
Dodge, Stanley D., 330
Dodge Corner, locality in Burnham
Dodge Farm, Freeman, 3094
Dodge Pond, locality in Rangeley
Dodge Pottery, Portland, 4189
Dog Hill, locality in Unity
Dog Island Corner, locality in Belfast
Doggett, J. B., 5264

Doggett, Margaret F., 2946
Doggett Castle, Edgecomb, 2946
Dogtown, locality in Detroit and Palmyra
Dolby, locality in East Millinocket
Dole, Frederick Howard, 2510, 5193, 5200, 5210
Dole, Nathan Haskell, 331
Dole, Phoebe, 5194
Dole, Richard F., 332, 826, 1732, 1814
Dole, Samuel Thomas, 333, 1493-1494, 3190, 5195-
    5200
Dole Brook Township, 2872
Dolley, Mira L., 4564
Dolls, 3022
Dolly Corner, locality in Windham
Donahue, Marie, 4790-4791
Donnell, Albert, 2922
Donovan, Michael C., 334
Donworth, C. B., 2784
Donworth, Grace, 3658
Doolittle, Duane, 335
Door family, 3520
Doorways, 2732
Dore family, 3520
Doric Lodge, Freemasons, Monson, 3779
Dorman, locality in Harrington
Dorr, George Bucknam, 1118, 1563, 1571-1574
Dorr, Susan Elva, 4224
Dorr family, 3520
Dorsett, E. Lee, 336
Dorson, Richard M., 3391
Doucette, Earl, 2098
Doughty, William H., 3289
Douglas, Alice May, 2211
Douglas, John Sherman, 3514
Douglas Hill, locality in Sebago
Douglass, John Abbot, 5019
Dover, locality in Boothbay
Dover Bluff, locality in York
Dover South Mills, locality in Dover-Foxcroft
Dover-Foxcroft, Me., 2873-2884
Dover-Foxcroft Congregational Church, 2876
Dow, Edward French, 4225
Dow, Fred M., 337
Dow, George Francis, 1991
Dow, J. H., 4419
Dow, Joy Wheeler, 3433
Dow, Neal, 164, 232, 4306
Dow, Robert L., 338-340
Dow, Sterling Thayer, 341, 1992, 3039, 4226
Dow, locality in Caribou
Dow Corner, locality in St. Albans
Dow Corner, locality in Standish
Dow Field, Bangor, 2094
Dow Post, Veterans of Foreign Wars, Bangor, 2160
Dowe, Milton E., 4051
Downer, Alan S., 4761
Downes, John Tileston, 2705, 2745, 4587
Drake, J. H., 3410
Drake, Samuel Adams, 343, 962, 2702, 3466
Drakes Island, locality in Wells
Draper, Ruth L. W., 2852-2853
Dresden, Me., 1677, 1704, 1937, 2885-2897
Dresden Academy, 2892
Dresden Free High School, 2892
Dresser, David, 4553
Drew, William A., 3849

Drew Plantation, 2898
Drewett, Bertha K., 5004
Drinkwater, Nicholas, 3918, 5288-5289
Drinkwater, Norman, Jr., 4592
Driscoll, Joseph A., 4227
Drisko, Clarence H., 1856
Drisko, George Washington, 1850-1851, 3659
Drown, Edward S., 1993
Drown, Nahum S., 2298
Drug trade, 848
Druillettes, Gabriel, 143, 344, 619
Drummond, Josiah Hayden, 345-346, 4228, 4841
Drummond, R. R., 3640
Drummond Chapter, Royal Arch Masons, Oakland, 3965
Dry Mills, locality in Gray
Dryden, locality in Wilton
Dry-docks, 4496
Dubay, Guy, 3086
Duck Cove, locality in Tremont
Duck Trap Cove, 3600
Ducktrap, former name of Lincolnville
Ducktrap, former name of Northport
Ducktrap, locality in Lincolnville
Dukes County, Massachusetts, 64
Dudley Township, 2899
Dufour Landing, locality in Orono
Dumbarton, former name of Owls Head
Dumont, Emma L., 5201
Dunbar, Kendall M., 1630, 1685, 1804
Dunbar, Robert E., 2405, 2820
Duncan, Roger F., 3116
Dundee Acres, locality in Windham
Dunham, Rufus, 1406
Dunham, William K., 5234
Dunlap Lodge, Freemasons, Biddeford, 2298
Dunn, Charles, Jr., 3326, 3154, 3467, 4543, 4636
Dunn, Claire Mary Deveau, 4951
Dunn, Gerald C., 3155
Dunn, Martha Baker, 5113
Dunn, Reuben Wesley, 5043
Dunn, William Warren, 1495
Dunn and Eliot, Thomaston, 4897
Dunnack, Henry Ernest, 348-349, 774, 3468, 4110,
    4554, 4880
Dunning family, 960
Dunns, locality in North Yarmouth
Dunns Corner, locality in Mount Vernon
Dunntown, former name of Wade
Dunston, former name of Scarborough
Dunton, Alvin Robbins, 4593
Duren, Elnathan Freeman, 350, 1741
Duren, Gladys, 3029
Durepo, Mrs. Roger L., 3082
Durgan, Mrs. Charles K., 3306
Durgin, Benoni T., 3085
Durgintown, locality in Hiram
Durham, Mrs. J. C., 2265
Durham, Me., 2900-2901
Durin, Dea, 351
Durnbaugh, Jerry L., 3001
Durnin, Richard Gerry, 352
Durost, Lillian Mills, 353
Durrell, Janice, 1544
Dutch, 315-316
Dutton, John G., 3469
Dutton, former name of Glenburn

Du Wors, Richard E., 1852
Dwight, Edward Strong, 4636
Dyer, Isaac Watson, 354, 3210, 4244
Dyer, Lydia, 4045
Dyer, Richard Nye, 355, 5044
Dyer, Russell Glover, 2266-2267
Dyer, Walter A., 356
Dyer Brook, Me., 2902
Dyer Cove, locality in Harpswell
Dyer Township, 2903
Dyers Corner, locality in Brunswick

E Plantation, 2904
Eagle Island, 2838
Eagle Lake, Me., 2905
Eagle Lake Township, 2906
Earle, A. Gertrude, 1772
Earleys Landing, locality in Willimantic
Earnest Corner, locality in Garland
Earthquakes, 360
Earthy, John, 617
East Andover, former name of Andover
East Brewer, former name of Holden
East Butterfield, former name of Hartford
East Deering, Me., 4476
East Dixfield, locality in Dixfield and Wilton
East Dixmont, Me., 2869-2870
East Dover, locality in Dover-Foxcroft
East Eddington, Me., 2939
East Eliot, Me., 2955, 2972
East Eliot Methodist Episcopal Church, 2955, 2972
East End, locality in Portland
East Falmouth, former name of New Portland
East Half of No. 9 Greenwoods Survey and Orient
    Gore, former name of Orient
East Livermore, locality in Livermore Falls
East Machias, Me., 603, 2907-2911
East Maine Conference Seminary, Bucksport, 2597
East Middlesex Canal Grant, 2912
East Millinocket, Me., 2913-2915
East Millinocket, Me. First Congregational Church,
    2913
East Moxie Township, 2916
East New Portland, locality in New Portland
East Pond Road, locality in Jefferson
East Ridge, locality in Corinth
East Road Siding, locality in Fort Fairfield
East Sebago, Me., 4732
East Senebec, locality in Appleton
East Thomaston, former name of Rockland
East Vassalboro, Me., 4957-4958
East Winthrop, Me., 5237
Eastbrook, Me., 2917
Eastern Frontier Lodge, Freemasons, Fort Fairfield,
    3085
Eastern Gazette, Dexter, Me., 2863
Eastern Indians, War with (1722-1726), 1291, 3120,
    3124-3130, 3135, 3139-3140, 3144-3147, 3891, 3893
Eastern Ridge, locality in Northfield
Eastern Star (newspaper), Machias, 3676
Eastern Star Encampment, Odd Fellows, Portland,
    4440
Eastern State Normal School, Castine, 2703
Eastern Steamship Company, 657
Eastman, Joel Webb, 3398, 4724
Easton, Me., 549, 2918

Eastport, Me., 1071, 1840-1841, 1844, 1852, 1859,
    1874, 2919-2938
Eastport Fire Department, 2929
Eastport Sentinel, 2925
Easy Street, locality in Litchfield
Eaton, Cyrus, 1660, 5003, 5010
Eaton, Emily, 5003
Eaton, Estelle Foster, 5113
Eaton, Louis Woodbury, 361
Eaton, Mabel, 3538
Eaton, Mary E., 5190
Eaton, Miriam, 3539
Eaton, Thomas H., 2511
Eaton, locality in Danforth
Eaton Grant, 2673
Ebeeme, Me., 2456
Ebert, Herman, 3738
Echo Lake Camp, Mt. Desert, 3794
Eckstorm, Fannie Hardy, 77, 362-367, 1773, 1793,
    2373, 3128, 3805, 3893, 3896
Economic conditions (see also Poverty and Social
    conditions), 102, 543; 70, 549, 847, 946, 965,
    1046, 1074, 1307, 1352, 1415, 1576, 2881, 2921,
    4171, 4492
Eddington, Me., 1762, 2939-2940
Eddy, Jonathan, 1249, 2940
Eddy family, 2940
The Eddy, locality in Edgecomb
Eden, former name of Bar Harbor
Eden, locality in Bar Harbor
Edes, George V., 119
Edes, Peter, 2103, 2110
Edes Corner, locality in Guilford
Edes Falls, locality in Casco and Naples
Edgecomb, Me., 1937, 2941-2951
Edinburg, Me., 2952
Edmunds Township, 1861, 2953
Education, 30, 130, 189, 191, 196, 368, 466, 519,
    555, 602, 655, 683, 686, 750-751, 767, 816, 819,
    907, 1024, 1133, 1176, 1239, 1313, 1409, 1418,
    1457, 1631, 1743, 1811, 2242, 3465, 4060, 4233
Education, agricultural, see Agricultural education
Education of adults, 4458
Edward VII, King of Great Britain, 4172
Edwards, George Thornton, 369, 4229-4230
Edwards, Herbert, 1575
Edwards, Llewellyn Nathaniel, 370
Egery, Thomas N., 3086
Eggemoggin, locality in Deer Isle
Eggemoggin Lodge, Freemasons, Sedgwick, 4737
Egypt, locality in Franklin
Eidelberg, Shlomo, 3392
Eight Corners, locality in Scarborough
Elden, Alfred Owen, 1496, 2318, 4231
Elder, Isaac L., 5202
Elder Neighborhood, locality in New Portland
Eldridge, C. T., 2924
Eldridge, Kate Wright, 4140
Elections, 71, 141, 482, 501, 561, 848, 997, 1185,
    2014, 2318, 2430, 5050
Electric utilities, 1157-1158, 1857, 1869, 1872,
    2108
Electrolyte Marine Salts Company, Lubec, 3642, 3646
Elijah Kellogg Church, Harpswell, 3290, 3292, 3294-
    3295, 3300
Eliot, Charles William, 1576

Eliot, Samuel Atkins, 1577, 1616
Eliot, Me., 987, 1879, 1907, 1911, 2954-2992
Eliot, Me. Congregational Church, 2963
Eliot Academy, 2981, 2992
Eliot Historical Society, 2964
Eliot Social Library, 2977
Elizabeth Park, locality in Cape Elizabeth
Elkins, L. Whitney, 371-372, 4881
Elkinstown, former name of Dexter
Elks, Benevolent and Protective Order of, 5045
Ellingwood Corner, locality in Winterport
Elliot Landing, locality in Orono
Elliott, Lloyd Hartman, 4004
Elliott, Van Cortlandt, 2512
Elliottsville Plantation, 2993
Ellis, Alice V., 4851
Ellis, Caleb Holt, 3081
Ellis, Leola Chaplin, 2794-2795
Ellis Corner, locality in Corinna
Ellis Corner, locality in Madison
Ellsworth, Wolcott Webster, 3754
Ellsworth, Me., 603, 1569, 1578, 2082, 2994-3022,
    4589
Ellsworth, Me. First Congregational Church, 3004,
    3008, 3015
Elm Hill, locality in Paris
Elm Stream Township, 3023
Elm Street Congregational Church, Bucksport, 2589
Elm Street Universalist Parish, Auburn, 1959
Elmore, locality in St. George
Elms, locality in Wells
Elwell, Edward Henry, 2, 373, 1448, 1497, 1892,
    4232-4233
Embargo (1807-1809), 2222
Embden, Me., 3024
Emerson, Edward, 5319
Emerson, John Dolbeer, 1887
Emerson, R. E., 3540
Emerson, Ralph Waldo, 2122
Emerson, Walter Crane, 374-375
Emerson & Stevens Manufacturing Company, Oakland,
    3967
Emerson Corner, locality in Pittsfield
Emerson-Wilcox House, York, 5319
Emery, Carl S., 4234
Emery, Daniel C., 3191
Emery, Edwin, 4676
Emery, George Addison, 2299
Emery, George Alexander, 5314
Emery, George B., 3194
Emery, George Freeman, 376-378, 1302, 4060
Emery, Ina Stanley, 4073
Emery, Lucilius Alonzo, 379-383
Emery, Martha, 2833
Emery, William Morrell, 4676
Emery Corner, locality in Limerick
Emerys Bridge, locality in South Berwick
Emerys Mills, locality in Shapleigh
Emigration and immigration, 18, 303, 1216, 1471
Emmons, Celia Philbrook, 3711
Emmons, Henry Vaughan, 3258
Emmons Clock Farm, Kennebunkport, 3446
Emory Corner, locality in Buxton
Empire, locality in Poland
Empire Grove Campground, locality in Poland
Empire Knight (ship), 5352

Enfield, Me., 3025
Engineering-study and teaching, 2500, 4003
English, J. S., 3129
English, Thomas Dunn, 384
English language-provincialisms, 179, 205, 468,
    860-861, 903, 971-972, 1032, 3460A, 3641
Englishman River, former name of Addison
Enk, John C., 2838
Eno, Joel N., 385
Enterprise (schooner), 1680, 1691, 1703, 1705, 1710
Environmental protection, 480, 665, 980, 1074
Epidemics, see Hygiene, public
Episcopal churches, see Churches, Episcopal
Epping, Me., 2776
Epstein, Catherine, 2071
Epstein, Lucille, 2071
Erickson, Hazel Cushman, 3452
Ericsson, Leif, 1599
Ernst, George, 5315
Erskine, Amy Albee, 5249
Erskine, Robert J., 3156
Ervine, Annie M., 799
Eskew, Garnett Laidlaw, 2212
Esoteric Lodge, Freemasons, Ellsworth, 3009
Essex, Robert Devereux, 2d Earl of, 418
Estabrook Settlement, locality in Amity and Cary
    Plantation
Estcourt, locality in Big Twenty Township
Estes, Hiram Cushman, 4062
Estes, Stanley J., 3864
Estes, William Roscoe Greene, 4762-4763
Ethnocentrism, 1324
Etna, Me., 3026
Etnier, Elizabeth, 3181
Eugley Corner, locality in Waldoboro
Eureka Lodge, Freemasons, St. George, 4657
European and North American Railway, see Maine Cen-
    tral Railroad Company
European War (1914-1918), 270, 742, 870, 1813, 2463,
    4954, 5238
Eustis, Elizabeth B., 3365
Eustis, Me., 3027
Eustis Railroad, 1542
Evans, Elizabeth Edson Gibson, 2704
Evans, George, 1414
Evans, George Hill, 3130
Evans, Liston P., 1774, 2876
Evans, Ora L., 2876
Evans, Weston S., 4005
Evans Corner, locality in Waldo
Eveleth House, Greenville, 3235
Evening News, Portland, 4345
Everett, Charles Carroll, 2492
Everett, Edward, 445
Everson, Jennie G., 386
Exeter, Me., 3028
Experiment (ship), 2896

Factory system, 1353
Fahy, Christopher, 4659
Fairbanks, Me., 3053
Fairchild, Byron, 3470
Fairfax, former name of Albion
Fairfield, John, 390
Fairfield, Roy P., 3970, 4637-4638
Fairfield, Me., 1421, 3029-3036, 3532, 5041

Fairmount, locality in Fort Fairfield
Fairweather, Edith, 4547
Fales, Ione B., 801
Fales, Martha Gandy, 4235
Falmouth, Me., 1483, 1487, 1492, 1512, 3037-3043
Falmouth Congregational Church, 3043
Falmouth Foreside, Me., 3041
Falmouth Gazette, 4328, 4450
Falmouth Neck, 4258
Family Welfare Society, Portland, 4372
Farm life (see also Country life and Outdoor life), 2276
Farmingdale, Me., 1628, 1649, 3044
Farmington, Me., 1419, 3045-3071, 3532
Farmington, Me. First Congregational Church, 3057-3058
Farmington Historical Society, 3060
Farmington State Teachers College, see University of Maine at Farmington
Farms, 2302, 3236, 3323, 3446, 5244
Farnham, Mary Frances, 391
Farnsworth, Lucy, 4590, 4602, 4610
Farnsworth Art Museum, Rockland, 4590, 4602, 4610
Farnum, Dustin, 2594
Farnum, William, 2594
Farrell, Jack W., 1539
Farrer, Hiram P., 392
Farrington, Inez, 393-394
Farrow, John Pendleton, 3371
Farwells Corner, locality in Unity
Fassett, Frederick Gardiner, 395
Favor Tavern, Dover-Foxcroft, 2877
Favour, Edith, 396
Faxon, John, 1194
Fayette, Me., 3072-3073
Fayette Baptist Church, 3072
Federal Writers' Project. Maine, 397, 1994
Federation of Business and Professional Women's Clubs of Maine, 353
Felch Corner, locality in Limerick
Felicity Lodge, Freemasons, Bucksport, 2596
Fellows, Dana Willis, 398, 3596
Fellows, Raymond, 2100, 2705
Felt, Joseph Barlow, 399
Female Charitable Society of Wiscasset, 5250, 5267, 5274
Female Orphan Asylum of Portland, 4237
Fenians, 1844, 1874
Fenn, William Henry, 400
Fentress, Walter, E. H., 3471
Ferdinando, Simon, 304
Fernald, Bert. M., 4155
Fernald, Frank L., 2967
Fernald, Granville, 3309
Fernald, Merritt Caldwell, 1574, 4006-4007
Fernald, William Linwood, 2968
Fernald Law, 1157
Fernald Shore, locality in Lebanon
Ferranti, Frank T., 3829
Ferries, 1761, 1808
Ferris, Leonard Zenas, 3192
Ferriss, Lloyd, 4577
Ferry Beach, locality in Saco
Ferry Beach Park Association of Universalists, Saco, 4650
Ferry Village, locality in South Portland

Fertig, Ilonka, 1686
Fessenden, William Pitt, 1414
Fewkes, Jesse Walter, 401
Feylers Corner, locality in Waldoboro
Fickett, Peter C., 5147
Field, George Warren, 2101, 2258
Fields, J. E., 4882
Fields Meeting House, Eliot, 2969
Fillmore, Robert B., 1661-1662, 1687, 3712
Finance (see also Municipal finance), 614, 816
Finch, Grant E., 4594
Finley, Raymond Stevens, 1631
Finn Hall, locality in Monson
Finns, 321, 1652
Finntown, locality in Warren
Fire departments, 2150, 2929, 3601, 4238, 5271
Firearms, 312
Fires, 262, 289, 410, 413, 574, 759, 1888, 2194, 2268, 3106, 3296, 3799, 3952, 4196, 4261, 4319, 4338, 4499, 4511, 4532, 4597, 4628, 4691
First Baptist Church, Bangor, 2054
First Baptist Church, Kittery, 3479
First Baptist Church, Lamoine, 3514
First Baptist Church, Livermore Falls, 3625
First Baptist Church, Mount Vernon, 3818
First Baptist Church, Nobleboro, 3888
First Baptist Church, Paris, 4062
First Baptist Church, Portland, 4239, 4383-4385, 4459
First Baptist Church, Sedgwick, 4742
First Baptist Church, Shapleigh, 4748
First Baptist Church, Skowhegan, 4765
First Baptist Church, Waterville, 5082, 5100-5101
First Baptist Church, Yarmouth, 5287, 5293
First Church, Eliot, 2956-2957, 2963, 2982
First Church, Mt. Desert, 3798
First Church of Christ, Cape Elizabeth, 2656
First Congregational Church, Bangor, 2055, 2102, 2152
First Congregational Church, Belfast, 2258, 2264
First Congregational Church, Boothbay, 2346
First Congregational Church, Brewer, 2371, 2374
First Congregational Church, Bridgton, 2377-2378
First Congregational Church, Calais, 2615-2616
First Congregational Church, Camden, 2634, 2637
First Congregational Church, Cherryfield, 2761
First Congregational Church, East Millinocket, 2913
First Congregational Church, Ellsworth, 3004, 3008, 3015
First Congregational Church, Farmington, 3057-3058
First Congregational Church, Fryeburg, 3123, 3133, 3141
First Congregational Church, Gardiner, 3161
First Congregational Church, Gorham, 3192
First Congregational Church, Hampden, 3275
First Congregational Church, Kittery, 3486
First Congregational Church, Lyman, 3649
First Congregational Church, North Yarmouth, 3918, 3924, 3926, 3929, 3934
First Congregational Church, Penobscot, 4083
First Congregational Church, Searsport, 4726, 4730
First Congregational Church, South Paris, 4063
First Congregational Church, South Portland, 4820
First Congregational Church, Waterville, 5111
First Congregational Church, Weld, 5125
First Congregational Church, Wells, 5130, 5132

First Congregational Church, Wilton, 5190–5191
First Congregational Church, Yarmouth, 5300–5301
First Congregational Parish, Newcastle, 3876
First Congregational Parish Unitarian, Kennebunk, 3411
First Methodist Church, South Portland, 4821
First Methodist Episcopal Church, Bangor, 2056
First Methodist Episcopal Church, Calais, 2626
First National Bank, Fort Kent, 3087
First National Bank of Skowhegan, 4764
First Parish Church, Brunswick, 2465–2466, 2495–2498
First Parish Church, Kennebunk, 3420
First Parish Church, Portland, 4224, 4344, 4365–4368, 4386–4389, 4472–4474, 4480
First Parish Church, South Berwick, 4801, 4803, 4805–4806
First Parish Church, York, 5336
First Parish Church, Congregational, Freeport, 3101
First Parish Congregational Church, Brunswick, see First Parish Church, Brunswick
First Parish Congregational Church, Saco, 4636, 4639, 4641, 4647–4648
First Parish Congregational Church, Scarborough, 4713
First Parish of Falmouth, former name of Westbrook
First Unitarian Society, Farmington, 3062
First Universalist Church, Auburn, 1963
First Universalist Church, Bangor, 2057
First Universalist Church, Biddeford, 2293
First Universalist Church, Brunswick, 2505
First Universalist Church, Caribou, 2669, 2674
First Universalist Church, Gardiner, 3162
First Universalist Society, North Yarmouth, 3919
First Universalist Society, Portland, 4390–4391
Fish, E. S., 2440
Fish, John L., 1995
Fish Beach, locality in Monhegan Plantation
Fish Street, locality in Fryeburg
Fish Town, locality in Appleton
Fish Turn, locality in Liberty
Fisher, Carleton Edward, 2771, 5216
Fisher, Charles, 3642, 3646
Fisher, Charles E., 404, 1735
Fisher, Elijah, 405
Fisher, J. Alvin, 406
Fisher, Jonathan, 1578, 2334–2336, 2341, 2344–2345
Fisher, Lewis Beale, 2756
Fisheries, 47, 233, 294, 338–339, 407, 755, 915, 1268, 1715, 2083, 2803, 4973, 5016, 5225
Fishermen, 116
Fishing lodges, 4560
Fishing nets, 3373
Fiske, John Orr, 4100
Fitz, Grace E., 353
Five Corners, locality in Anson
Five Corners, locality in Greene
Five Corners, locality in Mechanic Falls
Five Corners, locality in North Berwick
Five Islands, Me., 3180
Five Islands, former name of Winn
Five Mile Corners, locality in Orland
Five Points, locality in Biddeford
Flagg, Charles Allcott, 2105
Flagg, Paluel Joseph, 4969
Flags, 539, 1705, 1842

Flagstaff Church, 3074
Flagstaff Township, 1821, 3074
Flanders Corner, locality in Waldoboro
Fleming, John Daly, 4578
Fletcher, Edward Garland, 2513
Fletcher, Lucille, 408–409
Flint, George B., Jr., 4677
Flint, J. P., 3063
Flintstown, former name of Baldwin
Flood, Ernest Cecil, 1736
Floods, 78, 3149
Flower, Eric S., 821
Flye, William L., 3876
Flye Point, locality in Brooklin
Flying Point, locality in Freeport
Flynt, Charles F., 1632
Fobes, Charles Bartlett, 410–416, 2337, 3221, 3448, 4241
Fobes, Charles S., 1498, 4242
Fogg, Charles H., 1450
Fogg, Clara Newhall, 2406
Fogg, W. Fred P., 417
Foggs Corner, locality in Greene
Folk songs, 77, 691, 920, 1022
Folklore, 93–95, 114, 308, 331, 401, 408, 467, 483, 650, 678–679, 819, 840, 873, 999, 1003, 1160, 1503, 2590, 2598, 3263, 3391, 3762, 3805, 3812–3814, 5344, 5353
Folsom, Emma B., 2799, 4765
Folsom, George, 153, 418–419, 1893, 4112
Fontaine Leval, 3513, 3515
Food, 1398
Food packaging industry, 2532, 3899, 4281, 4335
Football, 2518, 2555, 3543, 4009, 5040, 5046, 5064, 5087
Forbes, Arthur Elbridge, 1717
Forbes, Robert, 134, 916
Forbes family, 134, 916
Forbes District, locality in West Paris
Forbes-Robertson, Diana, 4595
Forbush, Ernest Howe, 1574
Forest City Township, 3075
Ford, Henry A., 1741
Forest Township, 3076
Forests and forestry, 7, 1140; 90, 181–183, 262, 265–266, 289, 410, 413, 475, 570, 574, 641, 664, 757–759, 785, 858, 1072, 1138, 1150, 1362–1363, 1405, 1888, 3799, 4024
Forests and forestry–study and teaching, 3993
Forestville, former name of Caribou
Foristall Corners, locality in York
The Forks Plantation, 3077
Forkstown Township, 3078
Forrest Lodge, Freemasons, Springfield, 4836
Forslund, Gladys Hall, 5179
Forsyth, William T., 760
Forsyth Township, 3079
Fort Baldwin, locality in Phippsburg
Fort Edgecomb, 2943, 2947–2947A
Fort Fairfield, Me., 50, 3080–3085
Fort Frederic, 2408
Fort George, 2716, 2727, 2734
Fort Gorges, 4282
Fort Gorhamtown, 3210
Fort Halifax, 5216–5218, 5221
Fort Hill, locality in Biddeford

Fort Hill, locality in Gorham
Fort Josselyn, 4711
Fort Kent, Me., 1437, 3086-3089
Fort Kent, Me. Centennial Book Committee, 3088
Fort Kent Pit, locality in Wallagrass Plantation
Fort Kent State College, see University of Maine
    at Fort Kent
Fort Knox State Park, 4554
Fort Loyall, 4288
Fort McClary Memorial, 3468
Fort McKinley, 4243
Fort Mary, 2305
Fort New Casco, 4178A, 4481
Fort Pemaquid, 2409
Fort Pentagoet, 2739
Fort Point, 198
Fort Popham Memorial, 4110
Fort Pownall, 198, 364, 4850, 4853-4854
Fort Richmond, 4583
Fort St. George, 2300, 2427, 4115, 4130
Fort Scottow, 4711
Fort Sullivan, 2931
Fort Western, 1986; 1991, 1996, 2022, 2033
Fort William Henry, 2405, 2407
Fort Williams, locality in Cape Elizabeth
Fortier, Moyse, 1007
Fortifications, 41, 774, 1275, 1483, 1712, 1986,
    1991, 1996, 2022, 2033, 2300, 2305, 2405, 2407,
    2409, 2413, 2427, 2716, 2727, 2739, 2931, 2943,
    2947-2947A, 3210, 3468, 4110, 4115, 4178A, 4282,
    4288, 4303, 4375, 4481, 4554, 4583, 4640, 4711,
    4716, 4850, 4853, 5216-5218, 5221, 5337
Fortunes Rocks, 2307
Foss, H. Warren, 5047-5048
Foss, Thomas, 1579
Fossett, Mildred B., 3157
Foster, Benjamin Browne, 420
Foster, Charles H., 420
Foster, Charles I., 5243
Foster, E. J., 5126
Foster, Elizabeth, 421
Foster Point, locality in West Bath
Fosters Corner, locality in Knox
Fosters Corner, locality in Windham
Four Corners, locality in Edgecomb
Four Corners, locality in Kennebunk
Four Corners, locality in Limestone
Fournier, Paul J., 3381
Fournier, locality in Madawaska
Fowler, Henry Thatcher, 4883
Fowler, William J., 2617
Fowler, William S., 3155
Fowler Township, 3090
Fox Islands, 1656
Fox Isle, former name of North Haven
Foxcroft, Joseph Ellery, 2879
Foxcroft, Me., see Dover-Foxcroft, Me.
Foxcroft, locality in Littleton
Foxcroft Academy, Dover-Foxcroft, 2883
Foxcroft Academy Grant, former name of Lincoln
Foxcroft Academy Grant, former name of Springfield
Framingham, locality in Littleton
Framingham Academy and Williams College Grants,
    former name of Littleton
Francisborough, former name of Cornish
Francistown, former name of Cornish

Franco-Americans, 17-18, 135, 316, 441, 502, 666,
    722, 1007, 1324, 1402, 1431, 1441, 1443, 1987,
    2294, 2301, 3554-3556, 3561-3562, 3687
Frankfort, Me., 1282, 3091
Frankfort, former name of Dresden
Franklin, Lynn, 422
Franklin, Me., 3092
Franklin and Megantic Railroad, 1542, 1550
Franklin County, 109, 555, 1025, 1537-1552
Franklin County Agricultural Society, 1545
Franklin Road, locality in Hancock
Fraternal organizations (see also Elks, Freemasons,
    Kiwanis, Odd Fellows, Rotary and United Fellow-
    ship), 426-427, 647, 654, 939, 981, 1034, 1172,
    1342, 1788, 1947, 1966, 2095, 2148, 2215, 2266,
    2269, 2298, 2338, 2381, 2389, 2441, 2596, 2646,
    2649, 2651, 2706, 2754, 2770, 2772-2773, 2778,
    2796, 2822, 2824-2825, 2844, 2867, 2870, 2907-
    2908, 2995, 2999, 3009, 3085, 3151, 3175, 3191,
    3247, 3252, 3278, 3346, 3383, 3412, 3419, 3435-
    3436, 3535, 3579-3580, 3610, 3615-3617, 3624,
    3645, 3717-3719, 3734, 3779, 3792-3793, 3846,
    3943, 3954, 3965, 3968, 3984, 3987, 4056-4057,
    4079-4080, 4088-4089, 4142, 4165, 4185-4186,
    4198, 4228, 4246-4248, 4267, 4293, 4440, 4452,
    4549, 4553, 4579, 4601, 4622, 4657, 4671-
    4672, 4717-4718, 4737, 4755, 4762-4763, 4810A-
    4811, 4822, 4836, 4841, 4848, 4861, 4884, 4924-
    4926, 5020, 5045, 5062, 5091, 5147, 5153, 5159,
    5185, 5188, 5202, 5227, 5229-5231, 5261, 5268-
    5269, 5288-5289, 5291A, 5297, 5316
Fraternities, see Greek letter societies
Fraternity Club, Portland, Me., 4244
Fredericks, Katherine M. E., 1688
Fredyma, James P., 423
Free Democratic Party, 1093
Free ports and zones, 133
Free Soil Party, 1093
Free Street Baptist Church, Portland, 4300, 4327,
    4392-4395
Free Will Baptist Meeting House, Augusta, 1989
Freedom, Me., 3093
Freeman, Charles, 424-425, 3584
Freeman, Frederic William, 4245
Freeman, Melville Chase, 3411, 3434
Freeman, Samuel, 4480
Freeman Township, 3094-3095
Freemasons, 426-427, 981, 1172, 1342, 1947, 1966,
    2095, 2177, 2215, 2266-2267, 2269, 2298, 2338,
    2381, 2441, 2596, 2646, 2649, 2651, 2654, 2706,
    2754, 2770, 2772-2773, 2778, 2796, 2822, 2824-
    2825, 2844, 2867, 2870, 2907-2908, 2995, 2999,
    3009, 3085, 3151, 3175, 3191, 3247, 3252, 3278,
    3346, 3383, 3412, 3419, 3435-3436, 3535, 3579-
    3580, 3610, 3615-3617, 3624, 3645, 3717-3719,
    3734, 3779, 3792-3793, 3830, 3846, 3954, 3965,
    3968, 3987, 4056-4057, 4079-4082, 4088-4089,
    4142, 4165, 4185-4187, 4198, 4228, 4246-4248,
    4267, 4293, 4452, 4549, 4553, 4579, 4601, 4622,
    4657, 4717-4718, 4737, 4755, 4762-4763, 4810A-
    4811, 4822, 4836, 4841, 4848, 4861, 4884, 4924-
    4926, 5020, 5062, 5091, 5147, 5185, 5188, 5202,
    5227, 5229-5231, 5261, 5268-5269, 5288-5289,
    5291A, 5297, 5316
Freeport, Me., 3096-3113, 3532
Freeport, Me. First Parish Church, Congregational,
    3101

Freeport Historical Society and Freeport Sesquicen-
  tennial Committee, 3102
Freetown, former name of Albion
Freetown, former name of Edgecomb
Freetown, former name of Monmouth
Freight and freightage, 255, 4331
Frellick, Arlette F., 4244
Fremont, former name of Easton
French, Althea Haggstom, 3778
French, Edwin Ruthven, 4567
French, Mary Hubbard, 3366
French, William Riley, 1959, 4931
French (nationality), 1573, 1577, 2527
French and Indian War (1755-1763), 1184, 5330
French Canadians, see Franco-Americans
French language, 48, 441, 1110, 2528-2529
French Settlement, locality in Old Town
French Settlement, locality in Skowhegan
Frenchboro, locality in Long Island Plantation
Frenchman's Bay, 1580, 1582-1583, 1602, 1604, 3515,
  5222
Frenchs Corner, locality in West Gardiner
Frenchtown Township, 3114
Frenchville, Me., 3115
Frenchville, Me. St. Luce Parish, 3115
Frenchville, locality in Ashland
Freneau, Peter, 4250
Frey, Luella A., 4639
Friend, Gilman N., 3884
Friends' Meeting House, South Durham, 2900
Friends, Society of, 1508, 2900, 4960
Friendship, Me., 1654, 3116-3119
Frisbee's Market, Kittery, 3484
Frosst, George W., 2969, 3472
Frost, Charles, 955
Frost, John, 2281
Frost, John Eldridge, 428, 3473
Frost, Joseph William Pepperell, 3474-3475
Frost family, 955
Frost Tavern, Kennebunk, 3418
Fry, Amelia, 858
Frye, Robie G., 5049
Frye, William P., 1414
Frye family, 2383
Frye, locality in Roxbury
Frye Tract, former name of Fryeburg
Fryeburg, Me., 3120-3147
Fryeburg Academy, 3132, 3142
Fryeburg Academy Grant, former name of Mason Town-
  ship
Fryeville, locality in Harrington
Fryer, Robert, 5133
Fuller, Anne, 3755
Fuller, G. Spencer, 2407
Fuller, George, 3253
Fuller, Henry Morrill, 429
Fuller, Melville Weston, 1414, 2470
Fuller, Nathan, 430
Fullers Corner, locality in Hartland
Fullonton, Joseph, 1916
Funnel, locality in Wayne
Furbish, John, 2514
Furbish family, 2970
Furbush, Mrs. C. G., 431
Furbush family, 2970
Furniture, 356, 548, 777, 3842, 4235, 4315, 4464,
  4788

Gag Corner, locality in Gorham
Gage, Thomas Hovey, 5021
Gagnon, Lana, 1775
Galeville, locality in Winthrop
Gallant, Naida J., 3185
Gallatin, Albert, 432
Gallison, William W., 4861
Gamage, Nelson W., 4810
Gambo, Me., 1493
Game protection, 631
Games, 396
Gannett, Guy Patterson, 4251
Gannett, William Howard, 4251
Gannett's Woods, 2001
Ganong, Susan Brittain, 2621
Ganong, William Francis, 433-435, 1737, 2621
Gantners Landing, locality in Herseytown Township
Garbus, Betty, 4719
Gardencrest, locality in Manchester
Gardens, see Horticulture
Gardiner, Harry Norman, 2373
Gardiner, Henry, 436
Gardiner, Robert Hallowell (1782-1864), 437-439,
  1384, 1805
Gardiner, Robert Hallowell (1809-1886), 437
Gardiner, Robert Hallowell (b. 1882), 437, 2893
Gardiner, William Tudor, 437
Gardiner family, 437, 3154
Gardiner, Me., 1221, 1628, 1633, 1637, 1642, 1649,
  3148-3175, 3532
Gardiner, Me. Board of Trade, 3159-3160
Gardiner, Me. First Congregational Church, 3161
Gardiner, Me. First Universalist Church, 3162
Gardiner Mills, 2887
Gardiner Savings Institution, 3163
Gardiner Lyceum, 3153, 3174
Gardinerston, former name of Pittston
Gardner, Frank A., 1499, 3660
Gardner, George Peabody, 3393
Gardner, Olive, 2622
Gardner, Ralph D., 3971
Garfield Plantation, 3176
Garland, Me., 3177-3178
Garland, Me. Congregational Church, 3177
Garland Tavern, Buxton, 2607
Garnet, 3747
Garniss, George W., 440, 5290
Garrett, Margaret Z., 4931
Gary, Hobart Jude, 3979
Gas manufacture and works, 4306, 4477
Gaspé District, Quebec, 256
Gatschet, Albert Samuel, 1853
Gauld, Joseph W., 2214
Gauvin, Marie Anne, 441
Gay, Maude C., 801
Gay, Roger Crowell, 4678
Gazetteers, 46, 313, 397, 553, 780, 1305
Geagan, Bill, 442
Gendell, Walter, 3925
Genealogy, 428
General Conference of Congregational Churches in
  Maine, see Maine Conference-United Church of
  Christ
A Gentleman from South Carolina, see Putnam, Henry
Gentners Corner, locality in Waldo
Geography, 118, 491, 634, 842-843, 3811

Geology, 49, 598, 760; 91, 123, 311, 370, 884, 1255, 1269, 1295, 1560, 1600, 2717, 3804
George Settlement, locality in Prospect
George Stevens Academy, Blue Hill, 2324
Georgeana, see Gorgeana
Georgeekeeg, former name of Thomaston
Georges, Justine Flint, 3476, 4793
Georges River Canal, 5008
George's Valley Railroad, 1667, 1676
Georgetown, Me., 1806, 3179-3183
Georgetown, locality in Columbia
German Meeting House, Waldoboro, 4978, 4988
Germans, 1018, 1216, 1282, 4990, 4992, 4995, 4999
Gerrish, Henry, 2455
Gerrish, Judson C., 2455
Gerrish Corner, locality in Troy
Gerrishville, locality in Winter Harbor
Gerry, former name of Windsor
Gerry, locality in Alton
Getchell, Blanche Robinson, 4140
Getchell, David R., 2765
Getchell, Ira E., 444
Getchell Corner, locality in Vassalboro
Getchells Corner, locality in Sanford
Ghent, locality in Searsmont
Gibbs, Alonzo, 2370
Gibbs, George C., 3588
Gibbs, Helen Marilla, 3654
Gibbs, Iris, 2370
Gibbs Mills, locality in Livermore
Gifford, Roy, 5186
Gilbert, Frank Y., 1500
Gilbert, Humphrey, 805
Gilbert, Washington, 4932
Gilbert Head, Me., 3181
Gilbertville, locality in Canton
Gildersleeve, Nelson, 3877
Gile, Hugh, 4679
Gilead, Me., 3183A-3184
Gill, George J., 445
Gillespie, Charles Bancroft, 4252
Gillett, Eliphalet, 446
Gillis, Charles E., 4150
Gilman, Charles, 2106
Gilman, George H., 1451, 3345
Gilman, John Wesley, 3965
Gilman, Margaret Cook, 447, 3182, 4113-4114
Gilman, Stanwood Cushing, 447, 3182, 4113-4114
Gilman, William S., 1452
Gilman Corner, locality in Sangerville
Gilman Mansion, Brunswick, 2501
Gilmore, Evelyn Langdon, 3164
Gilpatric, George A., 3412-3414
Girls' High School, Bangor, 2113
Girls' High School, Portland, 4363, 4451
Giveen, Clement Martin, 5050-5051
Given, Charles S., 448-450, 4253
Glantz Corner, locality in Windham
Glassware, 4299, 4304, 4490-4491
Gleason, Basil C., 2371
Glen Cove, locality in Rockport
Glenburn, Me., 3185
Glendon, locality in Nobleboro
Glenmere, locality in St. George
Glenwood Plantation, 3186
Glidden, Walter S., 2215

Globe, locality in Washington
Gluek, Alvin C., Jr., 1854
Goddard, Charles William, 1004
Goddard, Edward, 856
Goddard, Morrill, 1004
Godfrey, Edward, 436, 5342
Godfrey, Edward S., 4254
Godfrey, George Frederick, 2107
Godfrey, John Edwards, 451-455, 1741, 2048, 2707
Godfrey family, 2093
Goding, George Henry, 3830
Goffs Corner, locality in Dover-Foxcroft
Gold, 3642, 3646
Golden Ridge, former name of Sherman
Golden Ridge, locality in Sherman
Golder, Arthur L., 4557
Goldsboro, former name of Gouldsboro
Goldsmith, Margaret O., 2785, 3255, 5251
Goldthwait, Richard P., 2821
Goldthwait, Thomas, 180
Gomme, Lawrence, 4255
Good Will Home Association, Fairfield, 3030-3034
Good Will Record, Fairfield, 3032
Goodale Corner, locality in Orrington
Goodall, Thomas, 4692
Goodall Mills, see Sanford Mills
Goodbar, Octavia Walton, 4256
Goode, Ruth, 731
Goodell Corner, locality in Willimantic
Goodrich, locality in Fort Fairfield
Goodrich Corner, locality in Industry
Goodwin, Allen, 4052
Goodwin, Emma R., 457
Goodwin, Jean M., 4787
Goodwin, Kathryn, 3597
Goodwin, Shirley B., 4257
Goodwin, William Frederic, 458, 2604
Goodwin, locality in Fort Fairfield
Goodwin Corner, locality in Benton
Goodwin Corner, locality in Palmyra
Goodwins Mills, locality in Dayton and Lyman
Goold, Nathan, 1501, 1894, 2691, 2709, 2970-2971, 4258-4260, 4409, 5203-5204, 5317
Goold, William, 459, 5205, 5217
Goose River, former name of Rockport
Goose Rocks Beach, locality in Kennebunkport
Gordon, Adelbert W., 466
Gordon, Hugh Taylor, 461
Gordon, Irwin Leslie, 331
Gore, Christopher, 459
Gore A 2, 3187
Gore East of Brewer, former name of Clifton
Gorgeana, former name of York
Gorges, Ferdinando (1565?-1647), 88, 154, 302, 418, 429, 911, 982, 4100, 4127A, 4129, 4134, 5342
Gorges, Ferdinando (1630-1718), 88
Gorges, Raymond, 462
Gorges, Thomas, 88, 897-898
Gorges, William, 62
Gorges family, 88, 462
Gorham, Me., 799, 1493, 1508-1509, 3188-3210
Gorham Academy, 3205
Gorham Academy Grant plus Littles Grant and Dummer Academy Grant, former name of Woodstock
Gorham Gore, Me., 3211
Gorham Savings Bank, 3196

Gorham State College, see University of Maine at
  Portland-Gorham
Gorhamtown, former name of Gorham
Goshen, former name of Vienna
Goss, Elbridge Henry, 3756
Goss, John L., 4857
Goss, Leroy E., 464
Gould, Albert Trowbridge, 1663
Gould, Daniel, 4623
Gould, Edward Kalloch, 465, 2710, 5005
Gould, John, 466, 470, 3104
Gould, Ralph Ernest, 471-472, 3603
Gould, Samuel B., 3541
Gould, William, 4261-4264
Gould, William Edward, 4265
Gould Academy, Bethel, 2290
Gould Corner, locality in Cornville
Gould Landing, locality in Orono
Gouldsboro, Me., 1579, 3212-3220
Gove, Jane, 5258
Gove, William G., 473, 1815
Government publications, 604
Governors, 71, 177-178, 206, 474, 761, 1013, 2003
Gowen, Angevine W., 5305
Gower, Calvin W., 475
Goyau, Georges, 3894
Grace, Patrick W., 476
Grace Church, Bath, 1153
Grafton Township, 3221-3222
Graham, Edward Montrose, 2108
Graham, Elinor Mish, 477-479
Graham, Frank, 480
Graham, John R., 2108
Grand Army of the Republic. Department of Maine,
  481
Grand Army of the Republic. Department of Maine.
  Bosworth Post, No. 2, Portland, 4266
Grand Beach, locality in Old Orchard Beach and Scar-
  borough
Grand Falls Plantation, 3223
Grand Isle, Me., 3224
Grand Lake Stream Plantation, 3225
Grand Lodge of Maine, Freemasons, 426-427, 1172
Grange, see Patrons of Husbandry
Grange Corner, locality in Lincolnville
Granger, D. T., 2924
Granite industry and trade, 288, 696, 1618, 3105,
  3253, 4592, 4856-4857, 4968, 4969A, 4973
Granite Lodge, Freemasons, West Paris, 5147
Granite Point, locality in Biddeford
Grant, A. J., 2178
Grant, George Frederick, 4267
Grant, Manley, 2216
Grant, Philip A., Jr., 482
Grant, Rena V., 1453
Grant, Robert, 2179
Grant, Ulysses Simpson, 1371
Grant Isle, former name of Grand Isle
Grants, locality in Rangeley
Grants, locality in Stetsontown Township
Grants Turn, locality in Hope
Grapes, 3849
Graves, Abbott, 3431
Graves, Sarah Bridge, 3972
Graveyards, see Cemeteries
Gray, Roland Palmer, 483

Gray, Me., 3226-3228
Grays Corner, locality in Sedgwick
Grays Corner, locality in Wells
Grazier, John S., 1580
Great Diamond Island, 4223
Great East Pond, former name of Newport
Great Hill, locality in Kennebunk
Great Northern Paper Company, 317, 484
Great Pond, former name of Palermo
Great Pond Ordinance, 931, 1156, 1218
Great Pond Plantation, 3229
Great Salt Bay, 1678
Great Works, Me., 4807
Great Works, locality in New Portland
Great Works, locality in Old Town
Greater Portland Landmarks, Incorporated, 4268
Greek language-study and teaching, 2512
Greek letter societies, 2510-2511, 2531, 2538, 2577,
  3991, 4008
Greek Orthodox churches, see Churches, Greek Ortho-
  dox
Greeleys Landing, locality in Dover-Foxcroft
Greely Corner, locality in Palermo
Green, Fred C., 3006
Green, Samuel M., 250, 485, 1581, 4885
Green, former name of Belmont
Green, former name of Greene
Green, former name of Searsmont
Green Lake, locality in Dedham
Green Mountain Railway, 1557, 2180
Green Street Methodist Episcopal Church, Augusta,
  2030
Greenacre Lecture Course, Eliot, 2974
Greenan, John Thomas, 1855
Greenback Party, 71, 1185
Greenbie, Marjorie Latta Barstow, 2711
Greenbie, Sydney, 2711
Greenbush, Me., 3230
Greene, Charles Warren, 486
Greene, Francis Byron, 1689
Greene, Jonas, 4568
Greene, M. Louise, 4568
Greene, Marc T., 487, 2217
Greene, Nancy H., 1856
Greene, Me., 3231-3232
Greenfield, Me., 3233
Greening, W. E., 488
Greenland, former name of Bremen
Greenlaws Corner, locality in Northport
Greenleaf, Ebenezer, 916
Greenleaf, Jonathan, 489, 5134
Greenleaf, Moses, 490-491, 1145
Greenleaf Lodge, Freemasons, Cornish, 2796
Greenough, Byron, 4356
Greens Corner, locality in Troy
Greenstown, former name of Embden
Greenville, Me., 3234-3241
Greenwood, Me., 3242
Greenwood Garden Theater, Peak Island, 4455
Greers Corner, locality in Belmont
Greet, William Cabell, 3641
Gregoire, Marie Thérèse de, 1569
Gregory House, Calais, 2619
Grey Ghost (ship), 1057
Grieve, Robert, 4232
Griffin, Joseph, 492-493

Griffin, Ralph H., 494
Griffith, Frank Carlos, 495
Griffith, George Bancroft, 496
Griffiths, Arthur Morgan, 498, 4886
Griffiths, Thomas Morgan, 497-498, 4886
Grimes Mill, locality in Caribou
Grindle, Roger Lee, 449, 826, 4969A
Grindstone Neck, locality in Winter Harbor
Grindstone Township, 3243
Grinnell, Art, 1857
Grocers, 4332
Gross, Esther, 4979
Grossinger, Richard, 2803
Groton Academy Grant, former name of Hodgdon
Grove, locality in Cooper
Grover, Archer Lewis, 500, 631
Groveville, locality in Buxton
Grow, Mary M., 2766
Growstown, locality in Brunswick
Gruening, Ernest, 501
Guernsey, Thompson L., 2873
Guignard, Michael, 502, 2301
Guilford, Me., 1782, 3244-3247
Guinea Ridge, locality in Appleton
Guinea Road, locality in Biddeford
Gulf Hill, locality in York
Gulf of Maine, 142, 611, 3663
Gull Pond, locality in Dallas Plantation
Gun Point, locality in Harpswell
Gunpowder, 1493
Guns, see Firearms
Gunsmiths, 312
Guptill, Robert A., 2275
Gurnet, locality in Brunswick
Gurney, Lewis, 5291A
Gurneytown, locality in Appleton
Gushees Corner, locality in Appleton
Gutch, Robert, 1271
Gyles, John, 503, 1297
Gyles, Thomas, 1315

Haag, James J., 504
Hackelton, Maria W., 2408
Hackett Mills, locality in Minot
Hadley, Benjamin, L., 2177
Hadlock, Wendell Stanwood, 161, 505-507, 1582-1583, 2623, 2927, 3007, 3216, 4075
Haggerty, Michael, 508
Haggerty Ridge, locality in Littleton
Haggins, John, 4788
Hahn, Nathalie White, 5223
Haig, George Canterbury, 509
Haines, Zenas Thompson, 4558
Haines Corner, locality in Livermore Falls
Haines Landing, locality in Rangeley
Hakola, John W., 3802
Hakola, Judith A., 3802
Hale, Agnes Burke, 4270
Hale, Clarence, 510-511, 3008, 4933
Hale, Enoch, 3165
Hale, Eugene, 1414
Hale, Horatio Emmons, 512
Hale, Nathan, 513-514
Hale, Richard Walden, Jr., 515, 2180-2181
Hale, Robert, 516, 4271-4272
Hale, locality in Mexico

Hales Corner, locality in Troy
Haley, Adelaide, 2302
Haley, Mary Wilkes, 2194
Haley House, Biddeford, 2302
Haley Town, locality in Fryeburg
Halfway, locality in Old Orchard Beach
Halidon, locality in Westbrook
Halifax-Castine Expedition, 2712
Hall, Charles B., 517
Hall, Clarence, 4481
Hall, Drew Bert, 518
Hall, Edward A., 1545
Hall, Edward Winslow, 519
Hall, Ethel P., 4931
Hall, George O., 1231
Hall, Harold E., 3315
Hall, James A., 1684
Hall, Jon F., 5053
Hall, Joseph B., 763
Hall, Mabel Goodwin, 292
Hall, Oliver A., 5054
Hall, Robert E., 520
Hall Corner, locality in Windsor
Hall Quarry, locality in Mount Desert
Halldale, locality in Montville
Halldale School, Montville, 3782
Hallee, Lawrence, 4141
Hallet, Richard, 521-522, 1690, 2352, 2894, 3642
Hallock, Leavitt Homan, 523, 3542
Hallowell, Me., 1637, 1650, 3248-3269, 3532
Hallowell Academy Grant, former name of Harmony
Hallowell Court House, Me., 1992
Hallowell Hook, former name of Hallowell
Hallowell Public Library, see Hubbard Free Library, Hallowell
Hallowell Savings Institution, 3257
Halls Corner, locality in Belmont
Halls Corner, locality in Moro Plantation
Halls Mills, locality in Whiting
Halpert, Harold Karl, 4273
Hamblen, Abigail Ann, 4794
Hamburger, Philip Paul, 4274
Hamilton, Jonathan, 4790, 4796, 4800, 4804, 4808-4809
Hamilton, Samuel King, 5015
Hamilton family, 5015
Hamilton House, South Berwick, 4790, 4795-4796, 4800, 4804, 4808-4809
Hamilton Station, locality in Bar Harbor
Hamlen, Ewing W., 1997
Hamlen (J. H.) & Son, Portland, 4275
Hamlen, James Hopkinson, 4275
Hamlin, Augustus Choate, 3757, 4055
Hamlin, Charles, 524
Hamlin, Hannibal, 1414
Hamlin, Helen, 525, 1454
Hamlin Plantation, 3270
Hamm, Margherita Arlina, 526
Hammel, Margaret F., 2182, 4276-4277
Hammond, Anne W., 2515
Hammond, George Warren, 5147, 5292
Hammond, Richard, 1275
Hammond, Robert B., 1858
Hammond Plantation, 3271
Hammond Street Congregational Church, Bangor, 2058, 2126

Hammond Township, 3272
Hammond's Fort, 1275
Hammons, Everett, 2772
Hamor, Eben M., 3792
Hamor, H. E., 2183
Hamor, James E., 3793
Hampden, Me., 3273-3279
Hampden, Me. First Congregational Church, 3275
Hampden Academy Grant, former name of Weston
Hampden, Battle of, 3273
Hampden Historical Society, 3276
Hampton, former name of Aurora
Hance, Helen R., 527
Hancock, John, 5350
Hancock, Me., 1569, 1579, 1586, 3280-3282
Hancock, former name of Clinton
Hancock Association of Congregational Churches and
    Ministers, 1554
Hancock County, 108, 686, 966, 1553-1622
Hancock Lodge, Freemasons, Castine, 2706
Hanford Siding, locality in Perham
Hanks, Carlos C., 1691
Hannaford, Olive W., 2606
Hannan, Anne, 1455
Hannemann, Paul, 558
Hanover, Me., 2289
Hanover, former name of Eustis
Hanscom family, 2968
Hanson, John Wesley, 1633, 1816
Hanson, Thomas, 5016
Hanson Lake, locality in Mapleton
Happy Corner, locality in Kingsbury Plantation
Harbor, locality in Fryeburg
Harbor Point, locality in Winter Harbor
Harbors, 965, 4164, 4320, 4441, 4505
Harborside, locality in Brooksville
Harding, Anne Borden, 529
Harding, Henry Fiske, 3661
Harding, R. Brewster, 530
Harding, Wilbur Horatio, 3332
Harding, locality in Brunswick
Hardison, Grover M., 2673
Hardison family, 1453
Hardwick, Elizabeth, 5177
Hardy, locality in Lake View Plantation
Harfords Point Township, 3284
Harkness, O. A., 531
Harlow, Edwin Alphonso, 2656
Harmon Beach, locality in Standish
Harmons Corners, locality in Auburn
Harmony, Me., 3285
Harmony Lodge, Freemasons, Gorham, 3191
Harpswell, Me., 2573, 3286-3307
Harpswell, Me. Congregational Church, 3290
Harpswell Garden Club, 3305
Harraseeket, former name of Freeport
Harriman, Daniel, 3988
Harrimans Point, locality in Brooklin
Harrington, John M., 532
Harrington, Me., 603, 1864-1865, 1875
Harrington and Walpole, former name of Bristol
Harrington Meeting House, Bristol, 2412
Harris, Herbert, 2778, 2907, 4848
Harris, Joseph T., 4425
Harris, Louisa E., 2656
Harris, May Pashley, 533

Harris, Samuel, 2909
Harriseeket, former name of Freeport
Harrison, Mrs. Burton, see Harrison, Constance Cary
Harrison, Constance Cary, 2184
Harrison, O. M., 2939
Harrison, Me., 3309-3311
Harrytown, former name of Wilton
Hart, Nathan F., 4593
Hartford, Me., 3312
Harthorn, Drew Thompson, 5055
Hartland, Me., 3313
Harts Corners, locality in Holden
Harvey, D. C., 2712, 3662
Harvey, George A., 3133
Harvey, Kingdon, 4010
Harvey, locality in Monticello
Harwoods Corner, locality in Bowdoinham
Haselton, Wallace M., 534
Hasenfus, Nathaniel John, 535-536
Hasenfus, Robert, 539
Hasey Bus Company, 677
Haskell, Caleb, 538, 2843
Haskell, Charles B., 1776, 1817
Haskell, Edwin J., 4011
Haskell, Jessica J., 539, 799
Haskell, Loren E., 540
Haskell, Louis O., 1818
Haskell, Mary L., 1261
Haskell, Thomas Hawes, 3840
Haskell, William Edwin, 541
Haskell family, 2843
Haskell, former name of Greenville
Haskell Corner, locality in Auburn
Haskins, David Greene, Jr., 542
Haskins, Sturgis, 5224
Hasse, Adelaide Rosalia, 543-544
Hastings, Charles H., 2516
Hastings, Me., 2197
Hasty Corner, locality in Newport
Hatch, Benton Le Roy, 545, 1723, 3697, 4278, 5056
Hatch, Francis Whiting, 2593-2594, 2713-2715, 4279
Hatch, Frieda, 2716
Hatch, Louis Clinton, 546, 2517
Hatch, M. P., 2773
Hatch, Margaret Todd, 3372
Hatch, W. H., 3373
Hatch, William Collins, 3362
Hatchs Corner, locality in Dresden
Hathaway (C. F.) Shirt Company, Waterville, 5071
Hathaway, George E., 3166
Hathorn Hall, Bates College, 3566
Hauck, Arthur Andrew, 4012
Hauk, Zarah William, 2809
Haven, Herbert M. W., 547
Haven, locality in Brooklin
Haviland, Thomas P., 4596
Hawes, Charles T., 2518
Hawes, Hildreth Gilman, 548, 1998, 2409, 3663
Hawkes, Micajah Collins, 1194
Hawkins, Dexter Arnold, 2379
Hawthorne, Hildegarde, 4795
Hawthorne, Nathaniel, 497, 1514, 2499, 2519, 3138,
    4563
Hay, Donald Gordon, 549
Hay Brook, locality in Soldiertown Township
Hayden, Ralph Henry, 550, 2185

Hayden Corner, locality in Winslow
Hayes, Ada, 2972, 5319
Hayes, Charles F., 3904
Hayes, Charles Wells, 1777, 2879, 4280
Hayes, Roy, 3740
Hayford, Elbert D., 551
Hayford Corner, locality in Belfast
Haynes, Aaron, 1738
Haynes, George Henry, 552, 2864, 3105, 3775, 5057
Haynes, Williams, 1503
Haynesville, Me., 3314
Haystack, locality in Castle Hill
Hayward, John, 553
Hazelton, Louise, 554
Head of the Bay, locality in Owls Head
Head of the Tide, locality in Belfast
Head Tide, Me., 1936
Heads Corner, locality in Denmark
Healey, Edith P., 4597
Heals Corner, locality in Lincolnville
Health and Welfare, State Department of, 754
Healy, Richard Wyman, 555
Heath, locality in Saco
Heath Post, Grand Army of the Republic, Waterville, 5024
Hebert, Richard A., 556-557, 1718, 1859, 2109, 4281, 4598, 4680, 5187
Hebron, Me., 3315-3319, 4049
Hebron, Me. Baptist Church, 3317
Hebron Academy, 3318-3319
Hebron Church, 3315
Hecht, Arthur, 558-559
Hede, Richard, 1456
Heffernan, John Paul, 560-561, 2218, 3895
Helmreich, Ernst Christian, 562
Helmreich, Louise Roberts, 2465, 2520
Hempstead, Alfred Geer, 563-564, 1739-1740, 1778-1779
Henderson, Kenneth A., 565
Henderson, Ruth, 1999, 3106
Hendricks Harbor, locality in Southport
Hennessey, Mark William, 2219
Hennessey, Wilfrid A., 2110
Hennessy, William G., 4796
Henry, John Joseph, 566
Herbert, George, 1121
Hereditary societies, 292-293, 1188
Hermon, Me., 3320-3321
Hermon, Me. Historical Committee, 3321
Hermon Lodge, Freemasons, Gardiner, 3151, 3175
Herne, James A., 3516
Heron Island, locality in South Bristol
Herrick, Mary Darrah, 2303, 4681, 5058-5060
Herrick, Robert, 567
Herricks, locality in Brooksville
Herricks Corner, locality in Northport
Herring, Charles Macomber, 1780, 2521
Hersey, Samuel, 2144
Hersey, Me., 3322
Herseytown Township, 3323
Heseltine, Charles Dana, 568, 1664, 2111
Heseltine School, Portland, 4461
Heywood, Charles Errol, 4950
Heywood, Daniel E., 3650
Heywoodstown, former name of Canaan
Hibberts Gore, 3324

Hichborn, Faustina, 4852
Hicks Corner, locality in Garland
Higgins, Albert L., 1585
Higgins, Roland W., 3477
Higgins Beach, Me., 4707
Higgins Corner, locality in Lisbon
Higgins Corner, locality in Standish
Higginson, Mary P. Thacher, 4887
Higginsville, locality in Kenduskeag
High Head, locality in Harpswell
High Pasture, locality in York
High schools, 2113, 2663, 4207, 4363, 4451
High Street Congregational Church, Auburn, 1967
High Street Congregational Church, Portland, 4220, 4396
High Street Union Church, Newport, 3886
Highfield (house), Portland, 4229
Highland, locality in Warren
Highland Lake, locality in Westbrook
Highland Park, locality in Fryeburg
Highland Plantation, 3325
The Highlands, locality in Greenville
Highpine, locality in Wells
Hildreth, Horace A., 3478
Hildreths Mill, locality in Perkins Township
Hill, Henry Francis, Jr., 2000-2001
Hill, J. F., 5061
Hill, Mark Langdon, 2222
Hill, Thomas, 4388
Hill, Winfield Scott, 569, 4115
Hill family, 2975
Hill, former name of Winterville
Hills Beach, locality in Biddeford
Hills Corner, locality in Lincolnville
Hills Siding, locality in Littleton
Hillside, locality in Brunswick
Hillside, locality in Sebago
Hillside Congregational Church, Cornish, 2796
Hilton, Cecil Max, 570
Hilton, Fannie Mulloy, 4797
Hilton, Flora A., 1586
Hilton, John J., 4282
Hilton, William H., 2822
Hilton, Seaverns W., 571
Hinckley, George Walter, 3031-3033
Hinckley, Henry R. and Company, Southwest Harbor, 4831
Hinckley, Me., 3030-3034
Hinckley Township, former name of Grand Lake Stream Plantation
Hinckley's Corner, Me., 644
Hincks, Francis, 572
Hingham Academy Grant, former name of Codyville Plantation
Hinsdale, Burke Aaron, 1244
Hiram, Me., 168, 3326-3330
Hiram Lodge, Freemasons, South Portland, 4810A-4811
Historic American Buildings Survey, 573
Historic houses, see Houses, historic
Historical Records Survey. Maine, 577-581, 3437
Historical societies, 803, 1183, 1906, 2073, 4325, 4448, 4525-4526
History Committee of the Bingham Sesquicentennial, 2319
Hitchcock, Joseph S. G., 3209
Hitchcock, Pelatiah, 1765

Hoar, Jay S., 1546
Hoar, Joel Sherman, 4559
Hoar, John W., 4553
Hoar, Samuel O., 4553
Hobart, Isaac, 2953
Hobbs Crossing, locality in Wells
Hobbstown Township, 3331
Hockey, 3544
Hodgdon, Me., 3332
Hodges, Margaret B., 1487
Hodgkins, Theodore Roosevelt, 138
Hog Island, 2369
Holbrook, Stewart H., 2114-2115
Holden, Charles, 1504
Holden, Charles F., 4038
Holden, Joseph White, 4039
Holden, Theodore L., 1505
Holden, William Cross, 2683
Holden, Me., 1762
Holdentown, former name of Dennistown Plantation
Holdentown, former name of Moose River
Holeb Township, 3377A
Holiday Beach, locality in Owls Head
Holidays, 82, 406, 430, 2628, 4203, 4596
Holland, Rupert Sargent, 4699
Hollandville, locality in Limerick
Hollis, Me., 3335
Holman, W. O., 1692
Holman Grant, former name of Dixfield
Holmanstown, former name of Mexico
Holmes, H. R., 3758
Holmes, Herbert Edgar, 585
Holmes, former name of Grafton Township
Holmes Bay, locality in Machiasport
Holmes Mill, locality in Belfast
Holt, Anne Carroll Payson, 3041
Holt, Erastus Eugene, 4284, 4422
Holt, George D., 3277
Holverson, John, 4285
Holway Corner, locality in Fairfield
Holy Trinity Hellenic Orthodox Church, Portland,
    4396
Homeopathy, 961
Homer, Winslow, 4697
Honor societies, 2542, 2549, 4032, 5081
The Hook, former name of Hallowell
Hookers Corner, locality in Winthrop
Hooper, Eunice, 3770
Hooper Lodge, Freemasons, West Sullivan, 4861
Hoopes, Donelson F., 586
Hope, Me., 1833, 3336
Hopkins, James Dean, 587, 1506
Hopkins, Ruth, 3084
Hopkins Academy Grant, 3337
Horan, James F., 342
Horgan, Thomas Patrick, 1564
Hormell, Orren Chalmer, 588, 4225
Horn, Werner, 4954
Horne, Clifton, 3029
Horns Corner, locality in West Gardiner
Horns Hill, locality in Monhegan Plantation
Horse-racing, 271, 721, 1124, 2192, 4541
Horses, 1283, 4541
Horsman, Leander R., 4553
Horticultural societies, 3305
Horticulture, 4437-4438, 4795, 4804

Hosmer, George Lawrence, 2839
Hosmer, Marion P., 5312
Hosmer, Miriam, 3107
Hosmer Pond, locality in Camden
Hospitals, 1134, 1500, 1895, 2004, 2011-2012, 2758-
    2759, 4166, 4197, 4213, 4237, 4324, 4446, 4498,
    5042
Hotels, taverns, etc., 569, 705, 2074, 2190, 2592,
    2607, 2877, 3106, 3110, 3235, 3418, 3427, 3449,
    3488, 3658, 3751, 4048, 4150, 4158, 4599, 4700,
    4832, 5182, 5320, 5354
Hough, Franklin Benjamin, 2410-2411
Houghton, Lloyd E., 589
Houghton, Vinal A., 3524
Houghton, Mrs. William Addison, 590
Houghton family, 2247
Houghton, locality in Byron
Houghtonville, locality in Fort Fairfield
Houlton Academy Grant, former name of Westmanland
    Plantation
Houlton, Me., 50, 1463, 3338-3355
House, C. J., 3525
House Island, 4259
Household furnishings, 5258
Houses, historic, 26, 476, 644, 700, 702, 830, 900,
    917, 987, 1322, 1581, 1696, 1701, 1899, 1957,
    1980-1982, 1990, 2003, 2015, 2131, 2153, 2169,
    2182, 2199, 2262, 2265, 2302, 2334, 2340, 2344-
    2345, 2501, 2556, 2578, 2582, 2619, 2644, 2704,
    2732, 2782-2786, 2820, 2852-2853, 2941, 2946,
    2948-2949, 2951, 2971, 2990, 2994, 3000-3001,
    3011-3012, 3017-3018, 3021, 3035, 3052, 3056,
    3094, 3154, 3189, 3200, 3255, 3281-3282, 3326,
    3410, 3417, 3427, 3442, 3464, 3466-3467, 3473-
    3474, 3476, 3495-3497, 3504, 3790, 3932, 4043,
    4175, 4200, 4215, 4222, 4229, 4231, 4236, 4260,
    4268, 4277, 4285-4286, 4295, 4315, 4343, 4462,
    4479, 4484, 4509, 4538, 4590, 4610, 4613, 4635,
    4751, 4785, 4788, 4790, 4793, 4795-4796, 4800,
    4804, 4808-4809, 4877, 4879-4880, 4882-4883,
    4886-4890, 4892-4894, 4902-4903, 4907, 4991,
    5144, 5208, 5249, 5251, 5253, 5255-5256, 5262,
    5292, 5303, 5319, 5337, 5342, 5348
Housing, 4398
Houston Corner, locality in Detroit
Howard, Everett, 953
Howard, James, 940
Howard, Millard A., 4053
Howard, Prescott L., 591
Howard, former name of Willimantic
Howard Corner, locality in Sangerville
Howard Lodge, Freemasons, Winterport, 5227, 5229-
    5231
Howards Gore, former name of Hanover
Howardstown, former name of Canaan
Howe, George F., 4594
Howe Brook, locality in St. Croix Township
Howes Corner, locality in Turner
Howland, Me., 3356
Hows Corner, locality in Plymouth
Hoy, Shirley Clifford, 3573
Hoyt Neck, locality in Biddeford
Hoyttown, locality in Machias
Hubbard, Jeremiah, 5134
Hubbard, Lucius Lee, 545, 592
Hubbard Free Library, Hallowell, 3250, 3258

Hubbard Hall, Bowdoin College, 2579
Hubbardstown, former name of Newfield
Hubbardstown, former name of Shapleigh
Hubler, Harold A., 1563
Hudson, Mrs. D. E., 3604
Hudson, Henry, 3246
Hudson, Me., 3357
Hueston, Ethel Powelson, 593
Huff, Jean Keirstead, 1457
Huff Corner, locality in Wellington
Hugh McLellan House, Gorham, 3189
Huguenots, 13, 2889
Huise Corners, locality in Dixmont
Hull, John Thomas, 1492, 4287-4288, 4376
Hull's Cove, Me., 2170-2171, 2183
Hull's Cove Grammar School, Bar Harbor, 2170
Humiston, Fred S., 594-595
Humphrey, James J., 3921
Humphrey, Washington I., 5293
Hungry Hollow, locality in West Paris
Hunt, Fitz Herbert L., 3259
Hunt, Gaillard, 3618
Hunt, Harmon C., 597
Hunt, Harry Draper, 2003
Hunt, Isaac H., 2004
Hunter, John M. S., 1547
Hunter, Michael Reed, 2220
Hunting, 631, 1023, 1178, 1278, 1332, 1713, 1807,
    1867, 3214, 3650-3651, 4720
Huntington, Henry Strong, 3198
Huntington Mill, locality in Bradford
Huntressville, former name of Lowell
Hunts Corner, locality in Albany Township
Hurd, locality in Caribou
Hurd Corner, locality in Palmyra
Hurds Corner, locality in Ellsworth
Hurds Corner, locality in Northport
Hurds Ridge, former name of Burlington
Hurley, Edward F., 4403
Hurricane Island, 1656, 4970
Hurwitz, Alfred, 3581
Hussey, Arthur M., II, 598
Hussey, Mrs. Leroy Fogg, 4888
Hussey, Nelson, 3776
Hussey, Philip W., Jr., 3905
Hussey Manufacturing Company, North Berwick, 3905,
    3909
Huston, A. J., bookseller, Portland, 599
Huston, James A., 600
Hutchins, Arthur E., 601
Hutchins, Curtis Marshall, 2116
Hutchins Corner, locality in Wellington
Hutchinson, Gloria, 3831, 4700, 5252, 5319-5320
Hutchinson, Vernal R., 2840-2842
Hyde, William De Witt, 2909
Hyde, Zina, 2239
Hyde School, Bath, 2214
Hygiene, public, 139, 1134, 2962, 3165
Hylan, John Coffey, 602

Ice industry, 386, 2218, 3752, 4170, 4738
Ilsley, Benjamin, 4235
Ilsley, Charles Parker, 4289
Ilsley, George Boardman, 2064, 3585, 5156
Ilsley, Mrs. S. E., 3585
Independence, former name of Kingman Township

Indian Island Penobscot Indian Reservation, 3358
Indian Point, locality in Bar Harbor
Indian Point, locality in Georgetown
Indian River, locality in Addison and Jonesport
Indian Rock, Me., 4560
Indian Stream Township, 3359
Indian Township State Indian Reservation, 3360
Indian Township 3, alternate name of T3 Indian
    Purchase
Indian Township 4, alternate name of T4 Indian
    Purchase
Indians (see also specific tribes), 804, 807; 3, 28,
    35-36, 81, 83, 86, 95, 114, 125, 143, 147, 163,
    174, 187, 192-193, 214, 259, 277, 279, 302, 323,
    331, 357, 363, 365, 367, 398, 401, 408, 412, 435,
    453, 503, 505-507, 512, 526, 532, 575, 592, 605-
    607, 619, 635, 638, 645, 678-679, 704, 832, 840,
    842, 845, 851, 855-856, 863, 891, 901, 944, 955,
    994, 999-1003, 1020-1022, 1028, 1030, 1033, 1073,
    1078, 1103, 1108, 1135-1136, 1145, 1160, 1163-
    1165, 1168-1170, 1178-1179, 1181-1182, 1186,
    1197-1203, 1214, 1238, 1246, 1258, 1288, 1291,
    1293-1297, 1300-1301, 1309-1310, 1326-1327, 1357,
    1386, 1399, 1486, 1582-1583, 1599, 1712, 1773,
    1816, 1853, 1979, 2005, 2246, 2424, 2435, 2924,
    2973, 3120, 3124-3130, 3135, 3139-3140, 3144-
    3147, 3155, 3216, 3225, 3307, 3665, 3812-3814,
    3889, 3891-3894, 3896-3898, 3925, 3933, 3985,
    4075, 4093, 4720, 5192, 5211, 5219, 5272-5273,
    5328, 5332, 5351
Indians-government relations, 947, 1301, 1343
Indians-missions, 143, 176, 676, 680, 1109, 1113,
    1186, 2700
Industrial education, see Technical education
Industry, 102; 90, 294, 331, 816, 819, 1046, 1422,
    1625, 1637, 2141, 3159, 3737, 4342, 4621, 4689,
    4816
Industry, Me., 3361-3362
Industry, former name of Mercer
Ingalls Hill, locality in Bridgton
Ingersoll, Anna Josephine, 2974
Ingraham, Richard, 4045
Ingrahams Beach, locality in Owls Head
Inman, Joseph, 3992
Inns, see Hotels, taverns, etc.
Insurance, 639
Insurance companies, 4292, 4301
Intellectual life, 1369A
Interdenominational Commission of Maine, 1064
International Boundary Commission (U. S., Alaska,
    and Canada), 608-609
International Paper Company, 541, 3381, 4209
Intervale, locality in New Gloucester
Ionic Lodge, Freemasons, Steuben, 4848
Ira Berry Lodge, Freemasons, Blue Hill, 2338
Ireland, Genevieve R., 1305
Ireland Corner, locality in Windham
Irish, James, 3206
Irish, Maria M., 610, 799
Irish family, 3206
Irish (nationality), 502, 837, 937, 940, 1010,
    1402, 1807A, 3355, 3534, 3670, 3678, 3880
Iron Bound Island, 5222
Iron industry and trade, 3397-3398, 3400-3401
Isaacson, Dorris A., 819
Island Falls, Me., 3363

Island Home Club, Georgetown, 3180
Island of Lett, former name of Verona
Island Park, locality in Winthrop
Island Pond, locality in Harrison
Islandport, former name of Long Island
Isle au Haut, Me., 611, 1561, 2834, 2836, 2840-2842, 3364-3368
Isle au Haut, Me. Union Congregational Church, 3366
Isle of Springs, locality in Boothbay Harbor
Islesboro, Me., 3369-3377
Islesford, locality in Cranberry Isles
Italians, 659

Jack, Edward, 2719
Jackins Settlement, locality in Hodgdon
Jackman, Me., 3377A-3378
Jackman Bicentennial Book Committee, 3377A
Jackman Corner, locality in Sangerville
Jackson, Annette, 1458
Jackson, Charles E., 4291
Jackson, George Stuyvesant, 4292
Jackson, Herbert G., Jr., 1781
Jackson, Me., 3379
Jackson, former name of Eustis
Jackson, former name of Hudson
Jackson Brook, former name of Brookton Township
Jacksons Corner, locality in Sangerville
Jacksonville, locality in East Machias
Jaffa Colony, 3389-3390, 3392, 3396-3396A
Jails, see Prisons
Jakeman, Adelbert M., 3543-3548, 3973
James I, 4117
James, Donald Grant, 5321
James Kavanagh House, Damariscotta, 2820
Jameson's Tavern, Freeport, 3110
Janelle, Adelard, 3561
Jarvis Gore, former name of Clifton
Jay, Me., 3380-3382
Jed Prouty Tavern, Bucksport, 2592
Jefferds Tavern, York, 5320
Jefferson, Me., 3383-3385
Jefferson Theatre, Portland, 4199
Jeffries, David, 2232
Jellison, Constance Hanscom, 1941
Jemtland, locality in New Sweden
Jenkins, Richard W., 3161
Jenkins, Sue Perrigo, 2456
Jenks, E. A., 2457
Jenks, William, 3760
Jenney, Charles Francis, 3761
Jepson, Ada F., 1508
Jeremisquam, former name of Westport
Jeremy Squam Island, former name of Edgecomb
Jernegan, Prescott Ford, 3642, 3646
Jerusalem Chapter, Royal Arch Masons, Hallowell, 3252
Jerusalem Township, alternate name of Carrabassett Valley
Jesuits, 585, 619, 1606, 2700, 3019, 3889, 3894-3898, 3901
Jesup Memorial Library, Bar Harbor, 2166
Jewell, Margaret H., 612-613, 5284
Jewells Corner, locality in Monticello
Jewett, Fred Eugene, 614
Jewett (G. S. and F. E.) Company, Norridgewock, 3899

Jewett, Sarah Orne, 2282, 4786, 4788, 4793, 4798
Jewett, locality in South Berwick
Jews, 2053, 2071-2072, 4173-4174, 4607-4608
Jim Pond Township, 3386
John, Timothy, 2412
John Bray House, Kittery, 3495
John F. Hill Grange, Eliot, 2958
John R. Braden (horse), 4541
Johnson, Alfred, 2273, 2413
Johnson, Allen, 615
Johnson, Almon L., 4293
Johnson, Arthur Menzies, 4294
Johnson, E. F., 4100
Johnson, Franklin Winslow, 5063, 5113
Johnson, George W., 2651
Johnson, Jennie Thorne, 5119
Johnson, Lelia Ardell Clark, 1588
Johnson, Mary Kellog, 4295
Johnson, Ryerson, 3643
Johnson, Samuel, 3878
Johnson, Seth A., 4861
Johnson, Theodore Elliot, 616, 1509, 1929, 3832, 4296
Johnson, Walter H., 3199
Johnson Corner, locality in Bingham
Johnson Corner, locality in St. Albans
Johnson Mountain Township, 3387
Johnston, Donald P. 2118
Johnston, John, 617, 1693, 4100
Jonas (ship), 1580
Jonathan Fisher House, Blue Hill, 2334, 2345
Jones, Arnold H., 1665
Jones, Mrs. C. H., 1955
Jones, Carmita De Solms, 618-619, 1694
Jones, Charles, 5202
Jones, Clif, 2221
Jones, Erasmus Archibald, 3091
Jones, Herald A., 3117
Jones, Herbert Granville, 620-622, 1510-1511, 2005, 4297-4298, 4812
Jones, Howard, 623
Jones, John, 799
Jones, Joseph Rodney, 1938
Jones, Martha York, 4299
Jones, Rufus M., 2767
Jones, Stephen, 3664
Jones, Wilbur Devereux, 624-625
Jones, former name of Jonesboro
Jones Cove, Me., 3220
Jonesboro, Me., 1851
Jonesport, Me., 467, 603, 1840, 3389-3396A
Jonesport-Beals High School. American History Department, 2252
Jones, Eddy, 1805
Jordan, Alice M., 1347
Jordan, Archer, 5064
Jordan, Fritz H., 4389, 4820
Jordan, George, 3790
Jordan, John, 3790
Jordan, John Woolf, 4980
Jordan, Lucy H., 4820
Jordan, Nellie Woodbury, 626
Jordan, William Barnes, Jr., 546, 627-630, 2659
Jordan, William W., 4820
Jordan family, 5002
Jordan Mills, locality in Mattawamkeag

Jordan Pond House, Mt. Desert, 3790
Jorgensen, Frederick E., 631
Josselyn, John, 222
Josselyn Botanical Society, 72, 238, 653, 904, 1005
Josselyn's Point, 2985
Journalism, see Newspapers
Journalists, 979, 1008, 4328, 4761
Joy, Kenneth, 1896
Joy, former name of Troy
Joyville, locality in Ellsworth
Judges, 126, 210, 269, 377, 524, 893, 1385, 1387, 1741, 3922
Julian, George Washington, 632

Kadesquit, former name of Bangor
Kahn, Patricia, 4936
Kahn, Richard, 633
Kaler, James Otis, 634, 1512, 2414
Kalers Corner, locality in Waldoboro
Kamankeag, locality in Rangeley
Kansas, 1299
Kappa Sigma Fraternity, Bowdoin College, 2510
Karl, Alice W., 4889
Kaskake, former name of Portland
Kaster, Katherine Prescott, 5294
Katahdin Iron Works Township, 3397-3401
Katahdin, Mount, see Mount Katahdin
Katen Corner, locality in Corinna
Kavanagh, Edward, 3690
Kavanagh, James, 2820, 3880
Kay, David, 4038
Kealy, John E., 5176
Kearney, W. D., 635
Kebabian, John S., 3966
Kebo Valley, 2175
Keefe, Francis, 1897, 2975-2977
Keegan, James M., 4207
Keegan, locality in Van Buren
Keeler, Seth Harrison, 1860
Keene, Carter B., 636
Keene, F. W., 4586
Keene, Hiram A., 2865
Keene, Jessie L., 4981
Keene, Sarah, 3459
Keene, William R., 4924
Keenes Corner, locality in Leeds
Keens Mills, locality in Turner
Keith, Philip Edward, 1743
Kelley, Edith, 1935A
Kelley, Mary Carpenter, 1930
Kelley Hill Road, locality in Stacyville
Kelleyland, locality in Baileyville
Kelleys Point, locality in Jonesport
Kelliher, John T., 638
Kellogg, Elijah, 3194, 3290, 3292, 3294-3295, 3300
Kellogg, Frederick C., 3374
Kelly, Albert Livingston, 5233
Kelly, Francis R., 1964
Kelly, Richard D., Jr., 826
Kelly, Webster, 5233
Kenalclin, former name of Edmunds Township
Kendall, Joseph, 3345
Kendall, Raymond, 3549
Kendalls Corner, locality in Waldo
Kende, Berthold, 639
Kenderquit, former name of Bangor

Kendrick, Cyrus, 3610
Kenduskeag, Me., 3402
Kenduskeag, former name of Bangor
Kenduskeag, former name of Levant
Keniston, Amanda M., 4799
Keniston, Frank Walter, 1782, 2880, 3742
Kennard Corner, locality in Eliot
Kennebago, locality in Rangeley
Kennebago, locality in Stetsontown Township
Kennebago Lake, 2828
Kennebec (steamer), 487
Kennebec, former name of Manchester
Kennebec, locality in Machias
Kennebec and Wiscasset Railroad Company, 640
Kennebec Arsenal, 2020
Kennebec Association (Baptists), 1644
Kennebec Central Railroad Company, 1624, 1629, 1648
Kennebec Company, 2232
Kennebec Conference (Congregational), 1623
Kennebec County, 16, 1358, 1623-1650
Kennebec Indians, 1357
Kennebec Journal, 2006
Kennebec Log Driving Company, 320
Kennebec Patent, 158, 438, 641-643, 918, 966, 1252, 1266, 1633, 1649, 2018, 2033
Kennebec Point, locality in Georgetown
Kennebec Purchase, see Kennebec Patent
Kennebec River, 57, 75, 103, 143, 184, 237, 243, 320, 386, 439, 563, 569, 1223, 1271, 1273-1274, 1650, 1885, 1985, 2035, 2200, 2232, 2893
Kennebec Road, 488
Kennebec Valley, 13-14, 243, 447, 1027, 1210, 1357, 1646
Kennebunk, Me., 987, 1322, 1880, 1884, 1896, 1898, 3403-3425
Kennebunk, Me.   Brick Store Museum, 3415-3417
Kennebunk Port, former name of Kennebunkport
Kennebunk River, 1898A
Kennebunkport, Me., 1880, 1896, 1898, 3426-3446
Kennebunkport, Me.   St. Ann's Church, 3438
Kennebunkport, Me.   300th Anniversary Committee, 3439
Kennedy Corner, locality in Jefferson
Kennedys Corner, locality in Jay
Kennibonke, former name of Kennebunk
Kennibunck, former name of Kennebunk
Kents Hill, locality in Readfield
Kent's Hill School, Readfield, Me., 4567-4572
Kennedy, Ben F., 1513
Kerosene lamps, 3268
Kershaw, Gordon E., 641-643, 2895
Ketcham, former name of Riley Township
Ketchum, former name of Riley Township
Keune, Russell V., 644
Keyes, Charles Wesley, 1548
Keyes Corner, locality in Whitefield
Kezar Falls, Me., 4073
Kezar Falls, Me.   Riverside Methodist Episcopal Church, 4073
Kezar Falls, locality in Porter
Kezarville, locality in Durham
Kibby Township, 3447
Kidder, Frederic, 645-646, 3135, 4126
Kidney, Dorothy Boone, 1459
Kilby, Cyrus Hamlin, 647, 1820, 1861

Kilby, William Henry, 648, 2850, 2924-2926
Kilmarnock, former name of Medford
Kimball, A. S., 2379
Kimball, Amos, 2870
Kimball, Frank R., 2480
Kimball, Marion Reed, 1744
Kimball, Merton L., 3943
Kimballs Corner, locality in Buxton
Kineo Township, 3448-3450
King, Abel Charles Thomas, 4056-4057
King, Francis Plaisted, 91
King, George Mellen Prentiss, 5065
King, Henry Melville, 4300
King, Horatio, 4060
King, Marquis Fayette, 649, 4049, 4386
King, Richard, 4715
King, William, 801, 2222, 4100
King family, 1171, 4714-4715
King & Bartlett Township, 3451
King Darius Council, Knights Templar, 4187
King George's War (1744-1748), 156
King Hiram's Chapter, Royal Arch Masons, Lewiston, 3535
King Philip's War (1675-1676), 4716
King William's War (1689-1697), 214, 217, 503, 1297, 5328, 5332, 5351
The Kingdom, locality in Montville
Kingfield, Me., 1552, 3452-3455
Kingfield, Me. Sesquicentennial Committee, 3454
Kingfield and Dead River Railroad, 1542
Kingman Township, 50
Kings Mills, locality in Whitefield
Kingsbury, Edith, 4800
Kingsbury, Henry D., 1634
Kingsbury, Isaac W., 2927
Kingsbury Plantation, 3457
Kingsfield, former name of Winslow
Kingsley, Maud Elma, 2910
Kingville, former name of Troy
Kinney Nation, locality in Brookton Township
Kinney Shores, locality in Saco
Kinsmantown, former name of Athens
Kirk, Geneva, 3550
Kirkland, Edward Chase, 2522
Kirkland, former name of Hudson
Kirtley, Basil F., 650
Kitchen-middens, 340, 1012, 1300, 1517, 1582-1583, 1679, 2818-2819, 2821, 2826, 2835, 2927, 3216, 3220, 3307
Kittery, Me., 987, 1879, 1907, 1911, 3458-3506
Kittery, Me. First Baptist Church, 3479
Kittery, Me. 300th Anniversary Publication Committee, 3480
Kittery Bicentennial Committee, 3481
Kittery Burying-Ground, 3489
Kittery Community Service Association, 3482
Kiwanis Club, Auburn-Lewiston, Me., 1424
Klein, Elsa, 651
Knapps Square, former name of Brewer
Knickerbocker, Charles H., 2119
Knickerbocker, Frances Wentworth Cutler, 2119
Knight, Enoch, 652
Knight, Ernest Harmon, 4565
Knight, Henry F., 3440
Knight, John T., 5066
Knight, Russell W., 1505

Knight Corner, locality in Garland
Knights, Ernest, G., 5016-5017
Knights Corner, locality in Searsmont
Knights Landing, locality in Brownville
Knights of Labor, 1100
Knights Templars (Masonic), see Freemasons
Knightsville, locality in South Portland
Know-Nothing Party, see American Party
Knowles, Archie, 3040
Knowles Corner, locality in Moro Plantation
Knowlton, Clarence H., 653
Knowlton, David Hunter, 1549
Knowlton, Isaac Case, 2624
Knowlton, Newell R., 654
Knowlton, William Smith, 655, 3777, 4693, 5067
Knowlton Corner, locality in Damariscotta
Knowltons Corner, locality in Farmington
Knowltons Mills, locality in Sangerville
Knox, Henry, 443, 497, 801, 4877, 4880-4883, 4886, 4888-4890, 4892-4894, 4902-4903, 4907
Knox, Lucy, 4882
Knox, Me., 3507
Knox County, 107, 907, 1651-1676
Knox County Bar and Library Association, Rockland, 4609
Knox Hill Corner, locality in Corinna
Knox Lodge, Freemasons, South Thomaston, 4822
Knox Railroad, 1667, 1676
Kohl, Johann Georg, 306, 656
Kohn, Clyde Frederick, 2881, 3399
Kokadjo, locality in Frenchtown Township
Kolledgewidgwock, former name of Blue Hill
Kossuth Township, 3508
Kotzschmar Club, Portland, 4504
Koussinoc (trading post), 2005
Krems, Jules, 4174
Kuhnert, Dale William, 2268, 4725
Kurt, Franklin T., 657
Kynett, Harold Havelock, 2353
Kyper, Frank, 658

Labbie, Edith, 4039, 4058
Labby, locality in Wallagrass Plantation
Labor and laboring classes, 61B, 688, 746, 827, 1100, 1353, 4637
Labrie, Rose Cushing, 2415, 5322-5323
Lacognata, Angelo A., 659
Ladd, Horatio O., 2533
Ladd, Vaughn, 660
Ladd, William, 1425, 3748
Lady Pepperell Mansion, Kittery, 3504
Lafayette, Marie Joseph Paul Yves Roch Gilbert du Motier, Marquis de, 1128, 4521, 4792
Lagrange, Me., 3509
Laighton, Thomas, 3488
Laing, Diana Whitehill, 3395
Lake City, locality in Camden
Lake Messalonskee, 3964
Lake Moxie, locality in The Forks Plantation
Lake Parlin, locality in Parlin Pond Township
Lake Shore, locality in Sidney
Lake View Plantation, 3510
Lakes, 1, 331, 375, 411, 726, 780, 873, 1511, 1715, 1749, 1770, 1777, 1785, 1787, 1799, 4557
Lakeside Landing, locality in Glenburn
Lakeville Plantation, 3511

Lakewood, Me., 3694, 3696
Lakewood, locality in Ellsworth
Lakewood Summer Theater, Madison, 3694, 3696
Lakin Four Corners, locality in Stetson
Lamb, Frances A., 661
Lambe, Emerson P., 4013
Lambert, Samuel W., Jr., 4560
Lambert Lake Township, 3512
Lambs Corner, locality in Winslow
Lamoine, Me., 1569, 1586, 3513-3516
Lamoreau, Mrs. Paul David, 4545
Lamprey, Louise, 3586
Lamson, Rufus, 4190
Lamson and Swasey Pottery, Portland, 4190
Lancaster, Lane W., 662
Land, 140, 770-771, 929, 1011, 1020, 1474, 1838,
    2232, 2423, 2457, 2673, 3493, 3994
Land grants, 29, 35, 1020, 1075, 1569, 3944, 4060
Land of Nod, locality in Windham
Land titles, 990, 1080, 1649, 1848, 2081, 3086,
    4205, 5305, 5341
Lander, Donna, 3236
Lane, Carleton G., 4301
Lane, Fitz Hugh, 1106
Lang, Constance Rowe, 1695
Lang, John Wilson, 1834
Lang Township, 3517
Langdon, Timothy, 5262
Langford, Evelyn E., 2467
Langtown Mill, locality in Lang Township
Lapham, William Berry, 405, 663, 1589, 1635, 2289,
    3944, 4059-4060, 4116, 4624, 5280
Larcom, Lucy, 698
Larkin, Alice T., 2354
Larone, Me., 3036
Larrabee, George H., 3879
Larrabee, William Clark, 3810
Larrabee, locality in Machiasport
Larson, Edwin van Horn, 664
Latham, Ettie J., 4535
Laverty, Dorothy Bowler, 3739
Lavolta (ship), 3006
Law family, 2638
Law (see also Legislation), 345, 744-745; 33, 129,
    232, 328, 337, 383, 502, 692, 746, 763, 818, 825,
    892, 915, 931, 1122, 1156-1157, 1194, 1196, 1218,
    1353, 1383, 1403, 1688, 2232, 2617, 4302, 4701
Law firms, 4507
Law reports, digests, etc., 1082-1083, 1302, 1316
Law-study and teaching, 4254, 4510
Lawrance, William A., 665
Lawrence, Benjamin F., 3382
Lawrence, Charles D., 3035
Lawrence, Charles K. C., 2304
Lawrence, Fred F., 4766
Lawrence Silver Mining Company, Hampden, 3277
Lawry, locality in Friendship
Lawton, R. J., 666
Lawyers, 110, 126, 377, 587, 1025, 1212, 1295, 1345,
    1383, 1506, 1584, 1641, 1707, 1730, 1741, 1745,
    1760, 1765, 4072, 4507, 4759
Leach Hill, locality in Casco
League of Women Voters of Bangor, 2121
League of Women Voters of South Portland, 4813-4814
Leamon, James S., 668-669, 3551, 3561, 4701
Leane, John J., 3167, 4625-4626

Leary, Peter, Jr., 4303
Leathers Corner, locality in Hermon
Leavitt, Harold Walter, 670, 3806
Leavitt, Robert G., 4074
Leavittstown, former name of Parsonfield
Lebanon, Me., 3518-3523
Lebanon Historical Society, 3522
Le Baron, William B., 3632
Le Blant, Robert, 671
Ledew, Vincent P., 3266
Ledges, locality in Fort Kent
Le Duc, Thomas Harold André, 672
Lee, John R., 4738
Lee, Richard H., 673
Lee, Ruth Webb, 4304
Lee, Silas, 5255
Lee, William Storrs, 674-675
Lee, former name of Monroe
Lee, Me., 3524-3525
Lee-Payson-Smith House, Wiscasset, 5249, 5253
Leeds, Me., 3526
Leeds Junction, locality in Wales
Leffingwell, B. H., 3418, 4890
Legal education, see Law-study and teaching
Leger, Mary Celeste, 676
Leger, Paul A., 677
Legislation (see also Law), 33, 141, 368, 746, 1062,
    1353
Legislators, see Statesmen
Leicester Academy Grant, former name of Stetson
Leighs Mills, locality in South Berwick
Leighton, Levi, 2779-2780
Leighton, William, 2281
Leighton's Store, Epping, 2776
Leland, Charles Godfrey, 678-679
Lemont, Levi P., 1806
Lenentine, Charlotte, see Melvin, Charlotte Lenen-
    tine
Lenhart, John M., 680, 3665
Lepage (F. R.) Bakery, Auburn, 1965
Lepage, Regis A., 1965
Lepper, Ruth Rhoads, 4824
Lermond, Norman Wallace, 681
Levant, Me., 3527
Levaseur, Mrs. Alphy, 2816
Leveling, 849
Levett, Christopher, 5309
Levetts Corner, locality in Lincolnville
Levetts Corner, locality in Waldo
Lewis, Alonzo Freeman, 3136
Lewis, George, 4801
Lewis, Gerald E., 682
Lewis, Grace Heggar, 4043
Lewis, John, 3922
Lewis, John R., 5157
Lewis, Julia Tuttle, 2652
Lewis, Katherine B., 3203
Lewis, Lawrence, 4784
Lewis, Minnie Gertrude, 2377
Lewis, Susan M., 2452
Lewis family, 1855
Lewiston, Me., 556, 1422, 1424, 1426-1427, 1431-
    1432, 1434, 3528-3577, 4561
Lewiston, Me. Board of Trade, 3552
Lewiston, Me. Manufacturers and Mechanics Library
    Association, 3553

Lewiston, Me. Paroisse Saint-Pierre et Saint-Paul, 3554-3555
Lewiston, Me. Sainte Marie, 3556
Lewiston, Me. Trinity Church, 3528, 3557
Lewiston Historical Commission, 3558
Lewiston Junction, locality in Auburn
Lewiston Weekly Journal, 3559
Lewistown, former name of Lewiston
Lewy's Island Lodge, Freemasons, Princeton, 4553
Lexington Township, 3578
Libbey, Dorothy Shaw, 4702
Libby, Abial, 4579
Libby, Charles Freeman, 4308
Libby, Charles Thornton, 738, 3483
Libby, E. H., 957
Libby, F. Wayne, 3313
Libby, Herbert Carlyle, 4852, 5068-5069
Libby, Hilda, 2416
Libby, John E., 1969
Libby, Richard J., 683
Libby, Steve, 684, 3853
Libbytown, locality in Portland
Liberty, Me., 3579-3582
Liberty, Me. Historical Committee, 3582
Liberty Corner, locality in Denmark
Liberty Lodge, Freemasons, 3579
Librarians, 74, 4025
Libraries, 190, 838, 1068, 1270, 1347, 1932, 2007-
   2008, 2013, 2089, 2166, 2227-2230, 2260, 2486-
   2487, 2579, 2632, 2873, 2944, 2977, 3250, 3538,
   3553, 3771, 3917, 4400-4401, 4457, 4528, 4609,
   4681, 4732, 4744, 4825, 4955, 5058, 5088-5089,
   5104-5106, 5109
Library associations, 44
Ligertwood, Margaret, 2830
Lighthouses, 1243, 1480, 1496, 1596, 1602, 2415-
   2416, 2665, 3179, 3731, 4044, 4347, 4485, 5323
Lille, locality in Grand Isle
Lily Bay Township, 3583
Lime industry, 371, 499, 4588, 4594, 4597, 4600,
   4605, 4611, 4616
Limeburner, Grace M. Grindle, 2443, 2445
Limerick, Me., 3584-3587
Limerick Baptist Church, 3585
Limerick Mills, locality in Limerick
Limestone, Me., 3588-3589
Limington, Me., 3590-3593
Limington, Me. Congregational Church, 3592
Limington Academy, 3590
Lincoln, Charles Stuart Fessenden, 2524-2525
Lincoln, Edward Joshua, 2823
Lincoln, Enoch, 3137
Lincoln, J. J., 685
Lincoln family, 2853
Lincoln, former name of Thorndike
Lincoln, Me., 50, 3594-3598
Lincoln Academy, Newcastle, 3879
Lincoln Academy Grant, former name of Jefferson
Lincoln Baptist Association, 1692
Lincoln County, 16, 107, 907, 966, 1677-1712
Lincoln County Bicentenary Committee, 1696
Lincoln County Courthouse, Dresden, see Pownalborough
   Courthouse, Dresden
Lincoln County Court House, Wiscasset, 5257, 5276
Lincoln County Jail, 5266
Lincoln Lodge, Freemasons, Wiscasset, 5261, 5268-
   5269

Lincoln Mills, locality in Corinna
Lincoln Park, Portland, 4377
Lincoln Plantation, 3599
Lincolntown, former name of Garland
Lincolnvil, former name of Lincolnville
Lincolnville, Me., 1833, 3600-3601, 4612
Lincolnville Volunteer Fire Department, 3601
Lindley, E. Marguerite, 4892
Lindquist, Vernon R., 2122
Linekin, locality in Boothbay
Link, Eugene P., 4305
Linnell, William Shepherd, 4306
Linneus, Me., 3602
Linscott, Edward Lyon, 686
Liquor industry, 1408
Liquor laws, 33, 37, 232, 328, 1403
Lisbon, Me., 3603-3606
Lisbon Falls, Me., 3606
Litchfield, Me., 3607-3611
Litchfield, Me. Bicentennial Committee, 3608
Literary history, 167, 208, 254, 329, 497, 528, 674-
   675, 698, 885, 900, 913, 919, 956, 1397, 1514,
   2122, 2157, 2466, 2499, 2553, 3138, 3171, 3202,
   3971, 4229-4230, 4236, 4250, 4260, 4295, 4298,
   4307, 4357, 4563, 5110
Literary societies, 2146, 2479, 2530, 2536, 3563,
   4176, 5058-5059
Lithgow, Robert, 1272
Lithgow, William, 940, 1272
Lithgow Library and Reading Room, Augusta, 2008
Litoff, Hal, 688
Litoff, Judy Barrett, 688
Little, Dana A., 601
Little, Elizabeth N., 5324
Little, George Barker, 689
Little, George Thomas, 690, 2477, 2497, 2526
Little, Henry, 2595
Little Deer Island and Isles of Holt, former name
   of Deer Isle
Little Deer Isle, locality in Deer Isle
Little Diamond Island, 4489
Little Falls, Me., 3190
Little Falls, former name of Hollis
Little Falls, former name of Limington
Little Machias, locality in Cutler
Little Ossipee, former name of Limington
Little River, former name of Freeman Township
Little River, former name of Salem Township
Little River, locality in Lebanon
Little Squaw Mountain, former name of Little Squaw
   Township
Little Squaw Township, 3612
Little W Township, 3613
Littleborough, former name of Greene
Littleborough, former name of Leeds
Littlefield, Ada Douglas, 5228
Littlefield, Edith, 2830
Littlefield, Otis, 2338
Littlefield Corner, locality in Auburn
Littlejohn's Island, 5294, 5296
Littleton, Me., 3614
Livermore, Me., 3615-3624
Livermore Falls, Me., 3625-3627
Livermore Falls, Me. First Baptist Church, 3625
Livermore Falls Trust Company, 3626
Liverton, former name of Livermore

Lobster, see Fisheries
Lobster Cove, locality in Monhegan Plantation
Lobster Township, 3628
Local government, 504, 576, 581, 601, 768, 1213, 1391, 1731, 2563-2567, 4225, 4915
Locke, Herbert E., 692
Locke, John Lymburner, 2269, 2642, 4982
Locke, John Staples, 3974-3976
Locke, William Nash, 2527-2529
Locke Mills, locality in Greenwood
Locks Corner, locality in Mount Vernon
Lockwood Company, Waterville, 5052
Log Cabin Club, Portland, 4351
Logging, see Lumber trade
Lohnes, Barry J., 693
Lombard, Alvin Orlando, 591, 725
Lombard, Lucina Haynes, 694-705, 1427, 2607, 3200-3202, 3335, 3441, 4640
Long, Charles Albert Eugene, 3713
Long, Peirce, 2585
Long, Zadoc, 2585
Long family, 2585
Long A Township, 3629
Long Beach, locality in Sebago
Long Beach, locality in York
Long Cove, Me., 4661
Long Island, former name of Islesboro
Long Island, locality in Portland
Long Island Plantation, 3630
Long Pond Township, 3377A
Long Reach, former name of Bath
Long Ridge, locality in Burlington
Longfellow, Alexander W., 4229
Longfellow, Henry Wadsworth, 168, 1514, 3202, 3326, 4175, 4229-4230, 4236, 4250, 4260, 4295, 4307-4308, 4509
Longfellow, Samuel, 4307
Longfellow, Stephen, 1384
Longfellow family, 4357
Longfellow Garden, Portland, 4438
Longfellow Statue Association, Portland, 4308
Lookout, locality in Isle Au Haut
Loomis, Alfred Fullerton, 706
Loomis, Charles Dana, 707
Loon Lake, locality in Dallas Plantation and Rangeley
Lord, Arthur, 708
Lord, Elvira M., 4641
Lord, Hartley, II, 3407-3408
Lord, John, 4786
Lord, Nathan, 4785
Lord, Nathaniel, 3442
Lord, Thomas, 1581
Lord, Thomas Newman, 3777, 5242
Lord, Trueman C., 3009
Lord House, Kennebunkport, 3442
Lords Corner, locality in Thorndike
Loring, Amasa, 1783, 3237, 3292, 3922-3923, 4747
Loring, Philip Quincy, 709
Loring, Prentiss, 4309
Loring family, 3923
Loring Air Force Base, locality in Limestone
Lothrop, Harry Woodward, 4310
Loudon Hill, Me., 3263
Louds Island, 2433
Loudville, locality in Bristol

Love, Wilbur J., 2827
Loveitt, Rosella A., 4819
Lovejoy, David Sherman, 3138
Lovejoy, John, 1041
Lovejoy, Scott K., 710
Lovejoy family, 1041
Lovell, Solomon, 2710, 2721
Lovell family, 2721
Lovell, Me., 3632-3634
Lovering, Frank W., 711-712, 2673, 4151
Lovett, Robert Woodberry, 2009, 4739
Lovewell, John, 86, 3120, 3124-3130, 3135, 3138-3140, 3144-3147
Lovewell's War, see Eastern Indians, War with (1722-1726)
Low, Elizabeth Armstrong, 4954
Lowell, Carrie Thompson, 4311
Lowell, Charles, 1194
Lowell, James Russell, 803, 5110
Lowell, Mary Chandler, 2882
Lowell, W. L., 2417, 2947
Lowell, Me., 3635
Lowells Corner, locality in Windham
Lowelltown, locality in Beattie Township
Lowelltown Township, 3377A
Lowenthal, David, 713
Lower Cupsuptic Township, 3637
Lower Enchanted Township, 3638
Lower Gloucester, locality in New Gloucester
Lower Mill, locality in Madison
Lower Sandy River, former name of Starks
Lower Street, locality in Turner
Lowndes, Marion, 5253
Lowry, Lois, 1514, 2928, 3442
Lows Bridge, locality in Guilford
Lowtown, former name of Guilford
Loyalists, American, 14, 465, 1117, 1273, 1319, 2687, 2719, 2731, 2743-2744, 3665
Lubbock, Alfred Basil, 714
Lubec, Me., 603, 1840, 1852, 1859, 3639-3649
Lubeck, former name of Lubec
Luce-Wheeler, Janice, 3854
Lucerne in Maine, locality in Dedham
Luces Corner, locality in Washington
Lucey, William Leo, 715-716, 3691, 3880
Lucia Beach, locality in Owls Head
Lucky Landing, locality in Glenburn
Ludlow, Me., 3648
Lumber trade, 1140; 184, 275, 320, 361, 411, 456, 473, 531, 563-564, 591, 725, 727, 875, 927, 1058-1060, 1072, 1138-1139, 1141, 1149, 1151-1152, 1166, 1175, 1217, 1225, 1348, 1398, 1401, 1454, 1470, 1659, 1739-1740, 1746, 1768, 1792, 1815, 1862, 2078, 2114-2116, 2671-2672, 3654, 3657, 3966, 4275, 4719
Lund, Edgar P., 3038
Lund, Morten, 717
Lunds Corner, locality in No. 14 Plantation
Lunt, Dudley Cammett, 718
Lunt, Robert H., 2530
Luques House, Kennebunkport, 3427
Lurvey, C. H., 4925
Lutheran churches, see Churches, Lutheran
Lyceums, 3153, 3174
Lyford, Elmore B., 719, 3644, 3945, 5144
Lyford Corner, locality in St. Albans

Lygonia, former name of Albion
Lygonia Lodge, Freemasons, Ellsworth, 2995, 2999
Lyman, Frederick W., 112
Lyman, John, 2223
Lyman, Me., 3649
Lyman, Me. First Congregational Church, 3649
Lynchtown Township, 3650-3651
Lynchville, locality in Albany Township
Lyndon, former name of Caribou
Lynn, John A., 1747
Lyon, Wilson L., 4821
Lyons, Owen P., 4972

McAleer, Neil, 720
MacAlister, Lorimer W., 3443
McArthur Library, Biddeford, see Biddeford, Me.
  Public Library
McCallum family, 5004
McCarthy, Marcia, 721
McClintock, John Norris, 3140
McCool, Elsie A., 3833-3836
McCoy Crossing, locality in Vassalboro
McCrillis, Herbert O., 2418-2420
McCrillis, former name of Kingman Township
MacCrillis Corner, locality in Wilton
MacDonald, Ada F., 4818
MacDonald, Thomas L., 1821
MacDonald, William, 722-723
MacDougall, Walter M., 724-727, 1784, 1822-1824,
  2458, 2993, 3449, 4312
MacDuffie, Malcolm, 728
McElwain, Harold A., 4313
McFarlands Corner, locality in Montville
MacFarlane, Mrs. John, 5254
McGee, Thomas D'Arcy, 4100
McGorrill, Milton Morse, 2057
McGovern, James R., 2124
McGraw, locality in Caribou
McGregor, James, 3645
McGuire, Joseph Deakins, 1785
Machias, Me., 603, 799, 1840, 1851, 3652-3683
Machias Bay, 1839
Machiasport, Me., 603, 1840, 1863
Machiasport Historical Society, 1862
Machiasport Station, locality in East Machias
Machigonne, former name of Portland
McInnis, A. E., 2929
McIntire, Glenn R., 2531
McIntire family, 5318
McIntyre, Philip Willis, 867, 2385
Mack, James H., 2914
Mackamp, locality in Long Pond Township
Mackay, Constance D'Arcy, 4314
MacKay, Robert G., 1078
McKeen, Donald W., 3872
McKeen, John, 729, 4118
McKeen, Joseph, 2559, 2568
McKenna, Peter A., 4623
McKenney, Lewis Timothy, 730
McKenney family, 2684
Mackenzie, Gertrude, 731
McKeown, Judy, 2805
McKinley, Alan R., 4682
McKinley, Me., 4923
McKinney, Earle T., 2669
McKinney, Stephen N., 3217
Mackintosh, Newton, 5292

McKusick, Victor A., 4068
McKusick, Vincent L., 732
Mackworth Point, locality in Falmouth
McLanathan, Richard B. K., 2010
McLaughlin, Charles Carroll, 3285
McLaughlin, Peter J., 1515
McLean, James A., 733
McLellan, Hugh Davis, 3189, 3203
McLellan-Sweat House, Portland, 4285, 4315
McLeod, Andrew James, 4996
McLin, William Hellen, 734, 1904, 2386, 3977
Macmahan, locality in Georgetown
MacMillan, Donald Baxter, 4316
McMullan, Jean G., 2846
McMurtrie, Douglas Crawford, 735-736
McNally, locality in Winterville Plantation
McPharlin, Paul, 4317
McShea, locality in Fort Fairfield
MacVane, Louis, 4318
McVicar, C. Warner, 4983
Macwahoc Plantation, 3685
MacWilliams, Don, see MacWilliams, James Donald
MacWilliams, James Donald, 737, 4319
Macy, locality in Rangeley
Madakamigossek, former name of Camden
Madawasca, former name of Madawaska
Madawaska, Me., 1437, 3355, 3686-3693
Madawaska Training School, see University of Maine
  at Fort Kent
Madawaska War, see Aroostook War (1839)
Madison, Me., 3694-3696
Madrid, Me., 1419, 3697
Madrid Junction, locality in Phillips
Madrid Railroad, 1542
Magalloway Plantation, 3698
Magalloway River, 1713, 1723
Magazines, see Periodicals
Magic, 367
Magill, Robert N., 3293
Magnetism, terrestrial, 444
Main Street, Castine, 2725
Maine, former name of Clifton
Maine, 61A, 101, 145, 221, 518, 554, 599, 627, 687,
  752, 773, 821, 933, 936, 959, 1047, 1096, 1193,
  1261, 1303, 1366, 1382; 1-1421
Maine, separation from Massachusetts, see Massachu-
  setts, separation from
Maine (Colony), 738
Maine (District) Constitutional Convention (1819),
  739-740
Maine. Adjutant General's Office, 741-742
Maine. Agricultural Experiment Station, Orono, 743,
  4014
Maine. Attorney General, 744-745
Maine. Bureau of Labor and Industry, 746
Maine. Centennial Committee, 747
Maine. Civilian Defense Corps, 748
Maine. Council, 749
Maine. Department of Agriculture, 1189
Maine. Department of Education, 750-752
Maine. Department of Education and Cultural Ser-
  vices, 753
Maine. Department of Health and Welfare, 139, 754
Maine. Department of Sea and Shore Fisheries, 755
Maine. Development Commission. Agricultural Sur-
  vey Committee, 756

Maine. Directors of Port of Portland, 4320
Maine. Educational Department, see Maine. Department of Education
Maine. Forest Commissioner, 757-758
Maine. Forestry Department, 759
Maine. Geological Survey, 760
Maine. Governor, 1967-1974 (Kenneth M. Curtis), 761
Maine. Hydrographic Survey, 762
Maine. Industrial School for Girls, Hallowell, 3260
Maine. Laws, Statutes, etc., 763
Maine. Legislature. House of Representatives, 948, 1756, 1868
Maine. Legislature. Senate, 948, 1146, 1756, 1870
Maine. National Guard, 764-765
Maine. Office of State Commissioner of Education, 766-767
Maine. State Archives, 768-769
Maine. State Chamber of Commerce and Agricultural League, 770-771
Maine. State Highway Commission, 772
Maine. State Hospital, Augusta, 2004, 2011-2012
Maine. State Library, Augusta, 773-775, 2007, 2013
Maine. State Military and Naval Children's Home, 2220, 2224
Maine. State Museum, 776-777
Maine. State Planning Office, 778, 1590
Maine. State Police, 779
Maine. State Teachers College, Gorham, see University of Maine at Portland-Gorham
Maine. State Water Storage Commission, 780
Maine. University, 781, 4015-4017
Maine. University. College of Agriculture, 4018
Maine. University. College of Agriculture. Department of Animal Pathology, 782
Maine. University. College of Agriculture. Extension Department, 783, 4019
Maine. University. Department of History and Government, 784
Maine. University. Forestry Department, 785
Maine Antislavery Society, 1092
Maine Baptist Missionary Convention, 151
Maine Board of Osteopathic Examination and Registration, 212
Maine Broadcasting System, 789
Maine Central Institute, Pittsfield, 4139-4140
Maine Central Railroad Company, 11-12, 124, 332, 346, 404, 448, 450, 658, 673, 734, 790-793, 952, 976, 983, 1356, 2168, 3772, 4520
Maine Charitable Mechanic Association, 4291, 4322-4323
Maine Civilian Defense Corps, see Maine. Civilian Defense Corps
Maine Commandery, Knights Templar, 1342
Maine Conference, Methodist Episcopal Church, 1016
Maine Conference-United Church of Christ, 309, 350-351, 425, 950
Maine Conference of Unitarian Churches, 290
Maine Consumer Credit Code, 1196
Maine Dental Society, 398
Maine Driver Education Association, 537
Maine Educational Association, 583
Maine Encampment, Knights Templar, 4187
Maine Federation of Music Clubs, 796
Maine Federation of Women's Clubs, 797-801
Maine General Conference of Congregational Churches, see Maine Conference-United Church of Christ

Maine General Hospital, Portland, 4166, 4213, 4324, 4446, 4498
Maine Historic Preservation Commission, 802
Maine Historical Society, 803-806, 1384, 2625, 4119, 4325, 4400, 4448, 4525-4526
Maine Historical Society. Library, 807
Maine Infantry. 27th Regiment, 1009
Maine Insane Hospital, see Maine. State Hospital, Augusta
Maine Lake Ice Company, Sargentville, 4738
Maine League of Historical Societies and Museums, 819
Maine Library Association, 44
Maine Library Association. Bicentennial Committee, 821
Maine Literary and Theological Institute Grant, former name of Argyle Township
Maine Maritime Academy, Castine, 2699
Maine Masque, 4020, 4034
Maine Missionary Society, 220, 223, 310, 689, 1065
Maine Municipal Association, 576
Maine Music Festival, 1413
Maine Osteopathic Association, 822
Maine Outing Club, 3997
Maine Pedagogical Society, 823
Maine Potato Growers, Inc., 1444
Maine Savings Bank, Portland, 4326
Maine Seacoast Missionary Society, 888, 2193
Maine State Bar Association, 110, 825
Maine State Bicentennial Commission, 826
Maine State Board of Trade, 117
Maine State College, see University of Maine at Orono
Maine State Federated Labor Council, AFL-CIO, 827
Maine State Library, Augusta, see Maine. State Library, Augusta
Maine State Museum, see Maine. State Museum
Maine State Prison, Thomaston, 4898-4899, 4904
Maine Supreme Judicial Court, 732, 928, 1385
Maine Teachers' Association, 1069
Maine Turnpike, 829
Maine Universalist Convention, 977
Maine Wesleyan Seminary, see Kent's Hill School, Readfield
Maine Writers Research Club, 830-835
Mains, locality in Caribou
Mainstream, locality in Harmony
Major-bagaduce, former name of Penobscot
Malbons Mills, locality in Skowhegan
Malcolm, John, 2644
Malden Island, locality in Georgetown
Malecite Indians, 512, 840, 1297, 3985
Mallett, Richard Purington, 2533, 3065
Mallett, Wilbert Grant, 3066
Malmquist, Marie, 3857
Malta, former name of Windsor
Manana Island, 3757, 3760
Manchester, Stephen, 5203
Manchester family, 5203
Manchester, Me., 3699-3700
Manchester, Me. Bicentennial Committee, 3699
Manks Corner, locality in Waldoboro
Mann, Amos Angier, 4761
Manning, Prentice Cheney, 4327
Mansel, former name of Tremont
Manset, locality in Southwest Harbor
Mansfield, E. R., 1398

Mansfield, John Brainard, 264
Manson, Raymond Russell, 4956
Manson Corner, locality in Hartland
Manter, Ezra, 5229-5230
Mantor, Agnes P., 841
Manufacturers and Mechanics Library Association, Lewiston, 3553
Manufacturers National Bank, Lewiston, 3560
Manufacturing, see Industry
Manuscripts, 784
Maple, locality in Atkinson
Maple Grove, locality in Fort Fairfield
Maple Ridge, locality in Harrison
Mapleton, Me., 3701
Maplewood, locality in Newfield and Parsonsfield
Maps, 545, 1144; 1143
Maquoit, locality in Brunswick
Maranacook, locality in Winthrop
Marble, Albert Prescott, 842-843
Marblehead Academy Grant, former name of Exeter
Marden, George Nathaniel, 3989
Margaretta (ship), 799, 3653, 3655-3656, 3660, 3664, 3671, 3673-3675, 3679-3682
Margison Crossroad, locality in Woodland
Mariaville, Me., 3702
Mariaville North, former name of Amherst
Mariaville South, former name of Waltham
Marie Antoinette House, Edgecomb, 2941, 2948-2949, 2951
Marie du Sacré-Coeur, Mère, 5028
Marine Lodge, Freemasons, Deer Isle, 2844
Marine societies, 4421, 4514
Mariner, locality in Portland
Marion Township, 3703
Markets, 3484
Marks, Arthur E., 845
Marlboro, locality in Lamoine and Sorrento
Marple, Howard A., 1697
Marriages, see Vital Records
Marriner, Ernest Cummings, 846-848, 1636, 5036, 5072-5076
Marriners Corner, locality in Searsmont
Marrtown, locality in Georgetown
Mars Hill, Me., 3704-3705
Mars Hill, Me. Centennial Booklet Committee, 3704
Marsh, Helen Searles, 3067
Marsh, John, Jr., 799, 3983
Marsh, Philip M., 4328
Marsh, Scarboro, 4329
Marsh Bay, former name of Frankfort
Marsh Corner, locality in Palmyra
Marshall, Edward Walker, 5325
Marshall, Frank Dennett, 5308, 5326
Marshall, Katherine Eastman, 1899
Marshall, Nathaniel Grant, 5327
Marshall, Robert Bradford, 849
Marshall Gore, former name of Medford
Marshfield, Me., 3706
Marshville, locality in Harrington
Marston, Dorothea M., 3261
Marstons Corner, locality in Auburn
Martin, Bud, 5145
Martin, Clara Barnes, 1591
Martin, Don, 4957
Martin, Eleanor Dutton, 3034
Martin, Frederic Thurman, 850

Martin, George A., 4627
Martin, George Castor, 851
Martin, Hattie B., 3280
Martin, Kenneth R., 852
Martin, Robert, 1966
Martin, Stella, 5328
Martin, locality in Friendship
Martin Corner, locality in Madison
Martins Siding, locality in Van Buren
Martinsville, locality in St. George
Maryland, 851
Marytown, former name of Bremen
Masardis, Me., 3707
Mason, Alfred, 2519
Mason, Clara Arthur, 2924
Mason, Edward G., 2014
Mason, Ellen, 3924
Mason, John, 1080, 3646, 4971
Mason, Jonas, 3922
Mason, William Castein, 1748
Mason Township, 3708
Masons, see Freemasons
Masons Bay, locality in Jonesport
Masque and Gown, Bowdoin College, 2481
Massabesic, former name of Waterboro
Massachusetts, 201, 1379-1380
Massachusetts, separation from, 9, 68, 82, 520, 892, 1091, 1233, 1375, 2464, 2502, 3110, 4219, 4508
Massachusetts. General Court, 853
Massachusetts. General Court. House of Representatives, 1601, 1837, 2332
Massachusetts Bar Association, 854
Massachusetts Bay Colony, 529
Massachusetts Gore, 3709
Massachusetts Medical Society, 1195
Masse, Herman Charles, 4958
Masse family, 4957-4958
Mast, Alan, 5255-5256
Mast industry, 4206
Mast Landing, locality in Freeport
Masta, Henry Lorne, 855
Matawamkeag, former name of Mattawamkeag
Matchebiguatus, 708
Mathews, Samuel Worcester, 3278
Mathews Mill, locality in Berwick
Matinicus Isle Plantation, 3710-3715
Matinicus Rock, 3712
Mattamiscontis Township, 3716
Mattanawcook, former name of Lincoln
Mattawamkeag, Me., 50, 3717-3719
Matthews, Albert, 856-857
Matthews, Edwards A., 4935
Maunder, Elwood R., 858
Maurault, Joseph Pierre Anselme, 859
Maxcy, Josiah Smith, 3158, 3168
Maxey Mills, locality in Windsor
Maxfield, Ezra Kempton, 860-861
Maxfield, Me., 3720
Maxim, Silas Packard, 4060
May, John Walker, 5241
Mayall Woolen Mill, Gray, 3226
Mayberry, Stephen Phinney, 3837
Mayberry Hill, locality in Casco
Mayers, Clayton W., 1807, 2896
Mayfield Township, 3721
Maygog, locality in Appleton

Mayhew, Annie, 3321
Maynard, locality in Fort Fairfield
Mayors, 2049, 2248
Mayville, locality in Bethel
Mdamiguk, former name of Princeton
Mead, Edgar Thorn, Jr., 862, 1516, 2386-2387
Mead, Janet Cutler, see Mead, Mary Janet Cutler
Mead, Mary Janet Cutler, 286
Meadow Brook, locality in Phippsburg
Meadowville, locality in Mattawamkeag
Means, Edgar L., 2534
Meara, Emmett, 3601, 4599
Meara, Nancy, 3601
Mecadacut, former name of Owls Head
Mechanic Falls, Me., 3532, 3722-3723
Mechanic Savings Bank, Auburn, 1968
Mechanics (persons), 2076, 4291, 4322-4323
Mechisses, former name of East Machias
Medals, 1009
Meddybemps, Me., 3724
Medeiros, John, 2535
Mederwomkeag, former name of Mattawamkeag
Medford, Me., 3725
Medical School of Maine, see Bowdoin Medical School
Medical societies, 822, 1195, 1748, 4284, 4422, 5061
Medicine, 137, 147, 212, 925, 961, 1127, 1134, 1194,
    1339, 1378, 1639, 1769, 2159, 3744, 4767
Medicine-study and teaching, 633, 1237, 2471, 2477,
    2550, 2571, 4218
Medomak, locality in Bremen
Medomak Camp, Washington, 5012
Medomak Falls, former name of Waldoboro
Meduncook, former name of Friendship
Medunkook, former name of Friendship
Medway, Me., 3726
Mee Corners, locality in Newfield
Meeds, Melvil F. 2305
Meetinghouse Hill, locality in South Portland
Megeis, former name of Machias
Megunticook, former name of Camden
Meigs, Return Jonathan, 864
Melcher, Burdus Redford, 4642
Melita Club, Bangor, 2125
Mellen, Frederic, 4425
Mellen, Prentiss, 1384
Mellon, Gertrud A., 865
Melvin, Andrew Alonzo, 866
Melvin, Charlotte Lenentine, 227, 3692, 3858
Melvin, James, 866
Melvin Heights, locality in Camden
Memorial Hall, Bowdoin College, 2570
Mendenhall, Thomas Corwin, 868
Meniceag, former name of Harpswell
Meningitis, see Hygiene, public
Menotomy, locality in Fryeburg
Men's Athletic Association, Bates College, 3545
Mental retardation, 4815
Mercer, Me., 1419
Merchant, Charles Henry, 869-871
Merchant marine, 714, 2219
Merchants (see also Businessmen), 4210
Mercure, Prudent L., 3688
Meredith, Irving, 3794
Merepoint, locality in Brunswick
Mericoneeg, former name of Harpswell
Meridian Lodge, Freemasons, Pittsfield, 4142

Merk, Frederick, 872
Merriam, Ann Van Ness, 3218
Merriam, Kendall A., 4658
Merriam, Mrs. Peleg, 3294
Merrick, John, 3255
Merrick House, Hallowell, 3255
Merriconeague, former name of Harpswell
Merrill, B. B., 2808
Merrill, Daniel, 4742
Merrill, Daphne Winslow, 873, 1969, 4600
Merrill, Georgia Drew, 1428
Merrill, H. Augustus, 3925
Merrill, J. N., 4767
Merrill, John P., 4826
Merrill, Lucius H., 3807
Merrill, Paul E., 4331
Merrill, Samuel Pearce, 4742, 4827
Merrill, Suzanne, 4826
Merrill, Me., 3728
Merrill Corner, locality in Brownfield
Merrill Road, Pownal, 4536, 4538
Merrill Strip, 3729
Merrill Transport Company, Portland, 4331
Merrills Corner, locality in West Gardiner
Merriman, Edward A., 1825
Merrow, James, 3484
Merry, Charles Glidden, 2824-2825
Merry, Edwin D., 1938
Merryconeag (steamer), 3296
Merrymeeting Bay, 1807
Merrys Island, locality in Edgecomb
Meserve, Albert W., 3412, 3419
Meserve, Fred L., 4731
Meservey, Roy E., 4659
Meservey, Sarah H., 4593
Messalonskee Lodge, Freemasons, Oakland, 3968
Metawascah, former name of Madawaska
Meteorology, see Weather
Methodism, 21, 1736, 1927, 2920, 3594
Methodist Church, Gardiner, 3172
Methodist Church, West Kennebunk, 3425
Methodist Corner, locality in Durham
Methodist Episcopal Church, Dexter, 2865
Methodist Episcopal churches, see Churches, Method-
    ist Episcopal
Metzger, Homer B., 874
Mexico, Me., 2868
Meyer, William E., 4320
Mica, 4055
Michaud, A. J., 1460
Michaud, Charlotte, 3561-3562
Michener, Roger, 2536
Michigan Settlement, locality in Fort Kent
Micmac Indians, 678
Middle Intervale, locality in Bethel
Middle Township, former name of Strong
Milbridge, Me., 1840, 1864, 3731-3735
Miles, Carlton E., 3011, 4893
Miles Cobb Farm, Hinckley's Corner, 644
Miles Corner, locality in Palmyra
Milford, Me., 1733, 3736
Milford Bicentennial Committee, 3736
Miliken, Henry, 875
Military art and science-study and teaching, 3999
Military bases, 2094, 2931
Military intelligence, 241

Military Order of the Loyal Legion of the United
    States. Maine Commandery, 876
Military service, Compulsory, 3455
Military training camps, 4243
Militia, 229, 517, 733, 741-742, 749, 764-765,
    1354, 1499, 1501-1502, 1894, 2698, 2709, 2962,
    3914, 5307, 5317
Millard, Kera C., 2794-2795
Miller, Alan R., 876A
Miller, Alice M., 3012
Miller, C. S. S., 877
Miller, Frank Burton, 4660, 4984
Miller, Samuel Llewellyn, 1698, 4986
Miller, William B., 249
Miller family, 4984-4985
Miller Corner, locality in Acton
Miller Corner, locality in Palmyra
Millerites, 1219
Millet, Joshua, 878
Millett, Margaret, 5212
Millgård, Per-Olof, 3859
Milligan, D. Winfield, 2626
Milliken, Fred G., 2930
Milliken, James Alphonso, 1864, 2760
Milliken, Philip I., 879
Milliken Mills, locality in Old Orchard Beach
Milliken Road, locality in Bridgewater
Milliken, Tomlinson Co., Portland, 4332
Millinocket, Me., 3737-3741
Millinokett, former name of Millinocket
Millions, Jean, 5158
Mills, Dudley A., 880
Mills, Hiram Francis, 881
Mills, William Howard, 882
The Mills, locality in Springfield
Mills, 358, 883, 2142, 2887, 3302, 3490, 3834, 4719,
    4957-4958
Milltown, Me., 1840, 2624
Milltown, New Brunswick, 2624
Millvale, locality in Bucksport
Millville, locality in Camden
Milnokett, former name of Millinocket
Milo, Me., 3742-3743
Milton, former name of Orneville Township
Milton Township, 3744
Minchassett, former name of Wells
Mineral water, 4151, 4156, 4159
Mineralogy, 1721, 1724
Mines and mineral resources, 974, 3277
Mingo Springs, locality in Rangeley
Ministerial associations, 425, 1489, 1533, 1554
Ministers, see Clergymen
Minot, John Clair, 885, 2537-2539
Minot, Me., 1425, 3745-3748
Minturn, locality in Swans Island
Misery Gore, 3749
Misery Township, 3750
Missions, 223, 886, 888, 1337, 1556, 1606, 1694,
    2692, 3889, 3891-3892, 3900
Missouri Compromise, 899
Mitchell, David, 3922
Mitchell, Dorothy, 887
Mitchell, Edwin Valentine, 888-890
Mitchell, George O., 2596
Mitchell, Harry Edward, 1865
Mitchell, Horace, 3485-3486

Mitchell, Jeanette Gordon, 3487
Mitchell, Jonathan, 2709
Mitchell, William H., 3885
Mitchell, Wilmot Brookings, 2540-2541
Mitchell Corner, locality in Cornville
Mitchell Corner, locality in Troy
Moffett, Ross, 891
Moldenhauer, Joseph J., 1800
Molloy, Anne, 4333, 4643
Mollusca, 681
Molunkus House, 3751
Molunkus Township, 3751
Monarda, locality in Silver Ridge Township
Money, 4263
Monhegan Plantation, 611, 962, 1712, 2425, 3752-3766
Monk, Guy Maxwell, 2388
Monks, John Peabody, 3394-3395
Monmouth, Me., 3767-3772
Monmouth Academy Grant, former name of Detroit
Monmouth Academy Grant, former name of Ripley
Monroe, Ira Thompson, 3619
Monroe, James, 1371
Monroe, Me., 3773
Monson, Me., 3773A-3780
Monson Academy and Hebron Academy Grants, former
    name of Monson
Monson Junction, locality in Abbot
Monson Maine Slate Company, 3775
Monson Mill, locality in Fort Fairfield
Monson Railroad Company, 3773A, 3774A, 3776
Montague, Henry Burt, 892
Montawamkeag, former name of Mattawamkeag
Monteith Road, locality in Bridgewater
Monterey, former name of Mount Chase Plantation
Montgomery, Job Herrick, 893, 4084
Montgomery, former name of Troy
Montgomery and St. Bernard Chapter, Royal Arch
    Masons, Bath, 2215
Monticello, Me., 3781
Montpelier, Thomaston, 4877, 4879-4883, 4886-4890,
    4892-4894, 4902-4903, 4907
Montrésor, John, 1101
Monts, Pierre du Guast, sieur de, 403, 1118, 2623-
    2625, 4100
Montsweag, Me., 5285
Montsweag Free Baptist Church, 5285
Montville, Me., 3782
Montville, former name of Liberty
Monument Lodge, Freemasons, Houlton, 3346
Monument Square, Portland, 4205
Monuments (see also Statues), 1330, 1573, 2385,
    2590
Moodey, Samuel, 4487
Moody, Edward C., 5329
Moody, Linwood W., 894-895, 1550-1551, 1667-1668,
    5006
Moody, Ralph, 896
Moody, Robert Earle, 738, 897-898, 1893, 5257
Moody, Samuel, 5336
Moody, Thomas, 5330
Moody, locality in Corinna
Moody, locality in Wells
Moody Beach, locality in Wells
Moody Corner, locality in Brighton Plantation
Moody Point, locality in Wells
Moor, John Louder, 3013

Moore, Albert, 1947
Moore, Anne Carroll, 1347
Moore, Glover, 899
Moore, Katrina, 2015, 5077
Moore, Marjorie Ann, 900
Moore, Pauline Winchell, 3633
Moore, Rilla Leach, 4085
Moorehead, Warren King, 901-902, 2421, 4075
Moorestown, former name of Abbot
Moose Hill, locality in Livermore Falls
Moose Island, 2933
Moose Pond, locality in Bridgton
Moose River, Me., 3377A
Moosehead, locality in Big Squaw Township
Moosehead Lake, 143, 1770, 1773, 1784-1787, 1791, 1801, 3239
Moosehead Valley, 3377A
Moosehorn, locality in Abbot
Moosehorn, locality in Coburn Gore
Mooselookmeguntic, locality in Rangeley
Morancy, locality in Sullivan
Morang, Bruce, 1898
Moravian churches, see Churches, Moravian
Moreland, James, 4334
Morgan, Charles S., 1898A
Morgan, Seth H., 5231
Morgan Beach, locality in Enfield
Morison, Samuel Eliot, 903, 1592
Morning Star Lodge, Freemasons, Litchfield Corners, 3610
Moro Plantation, 3784
Morrell, Hiram Kelly, 3169
Morrell, Jennie May, 904
Morrill, Charles S., 4335
Morrill, John Adams, 1967
Morrill, Lot, 1414
Morrill, Philip, 547
Morrill family, 3908
Morrill, Me., 3785-3786
Morrill Meeting House Society, 3785
Morrills Corner, locality in Portland
Morrills Corner, locality in Windham
Morris, Edward Parmelee, 905
Morris, Gerald E., 826, 906, 4524
Morrison, Kenneth M., 3896
Morrison Corner, locality in Clinton
Morrisons Corner, locality in Sanford
Morse, Charles Wyman, 2218
Morse, F. B., 3852-3854
Morse, Frank Leander Staples, 907
Morse, Ivan, 3118
Morse, J. T. (steamer), 20
Morse, Theoda Mears, 3786
Morse Corners, locality in Corinna
Morse-Libby House, see Victoria Mansion, Portland
Mortality, 303, 1971, 3890
Morton, Agnes L., 4061, 5149
Morton, Andrew, 1765
Morton, Everett E., 3379
Moscow, Me., 3787
Moscow History Committee, 3787
Moseley, Emma, 908
Moses, George H., 3651
Mosher, Thomas Bird, 4255, 4278, 4506
Mosher Corner, locality in Pittsfield
Moshers Corner, locality in Gorham

Moulton, Alphonso, 3309
Moulton, Augustus Freedom, 803, 909-911, 1719, 4325, 4336, 4703-4705
Moulton, David E., 4337
Moulton, Fred E., 4706
Moulton, Johnson, 5317
Moulton, Thomas, 4161
Moulton, Warren J., 2126
Moultonborough, locality in Sanford
Mt. Abraham, former name of Mt. Abram Township
Mount Cadillac, 2180
Mt. Abram Township, 3788
Mount Chase Plantation, 1833
Mount Desert, Me., 1587, 1617, 3790-3798
Mount Desert Congregational Church, Tremont, 4922
Mt. Desert Ferry, locality in Hancock
Mount Desert Island, 1590; 307, 509, 611, 801, 962, 1071, 1555-1560, 1563-1577, 1585, 1587, 1589, 1591-1595, 1599-1600, 1605-1611, 1613-1618, 1620, 2175-2176, 4923
Mount Desert Larger Parish, 1595
Mt. Desert Lodge, Freemasons, 3792-3793
Mount Desert Rock, 1596
Mt. Hope Cemetery, Bangor, 2130
Mount Horeb Chapter, Royal Arch Masons, Mattawamkeag, 3717
Mount Humpback, 2254
Mount Hunger, locality in Edgecomb
Mount Katahdin, 3809; 3799-3817
Mt. Katahdin Township, 3799-3817
Mount Kineo, 3448-3450
Mount Kineo Lodge, Freemasons, Guilford, 3247
Mount Mica, 4055
Mt. Tire'm Lodge, Freemasons, Waterford, 5020
Mount Vernon, Me., 3818
Mount Vernon Chapter, Royal Arch Masons, Portland, 4186
Mount Zircon, 3744
Mountain View Farm, Greenville, 3236
Mountaineering societies, 3794, 3997, 4241
Mountains, 331, 408, 412, 2650, 2684, 3448-3449, 3697, 3799-3817
Mountainview, locality in Rangeley
Mountainview Park, locality in Cape Elizabeth
Mountainville, locality in Deer Isle
Mountfort, Anne, see Mountfort, Julia Ann Dyke
Mountfort, Julia Ann Dyke, 1699, 1899
Mousum, former name of Sanford
Mousum River, 3404
Moving picture theaters, see Theaters
Mowat, Henry, 2691
Mower, Ella J., 2866
Mower, Irving B., 3444
Mower, Walter Lindley, 3231-3232
Moxie Corner, locality in The Forks Plantation
Moxie Gore, 3819
Munchausen Club, Colby College, 5060
Municipal finance (see also Finance), 504, 588
Munjoy Hill, locality in Portland
Munjoys Neck, former name of Portland
Munn, Henry, 1517
Munsangan Stream, 161
Munson, Gorham Bert, 912-914, 2645, 2720
Murch, Edmund, 4941
Murch, Lucius H., 1835
Murchie, Guy, 1866

Murphy, Thomas E., 3295
Murphy Corner, locality in Woolwich
Murray, Dick, 1356
Murray, George M., 2439
Murray, John Chick, 1900
Murray, Thomas Hamilton, 3678
Murray Chapter, Royal Arch Masons, Kennebunk, 3419
Muscle Ridge, extinct township in Knox County
Muscongus, Me., 2430
Muscongus, former name of Bremen
Muscongus lands, 497, 2430, 4990, 5003
Museums, 2747, 3022, 3415, 4315, 4589
Music, 94, 366, 369, 401, 483, 691, 888, 908, 920,
    1360, 1413, 2469, 2482, 3045, 3049, 3964, 4072,
    4773
Musical instruments, 4503, 5252
Musical societies, 796, 3071, 4182, 4184, 4193,
    4427-4428, 4439, 4504
Musical Wonder House, Wiscasset, 5252
Musicians, 369, 1360, 4072, 4321
Myers, Denys Peter, 573
Myers, Edward A., 915
Mystic Lodge, Freemasons, Hampden, 3278

Nader, Ralph, 946
Naguamqueeg, Me., 5195
Nalagwemmenahan, former name of Verona
Names, geographical, 31, 46, 60, 192-195, 273, 365,
    376, 412, 592, 606, 857, 863, 945, 1070, 1076,
    1145, 1293, 1410, 1578, 1605, 1737, 1773, 1853,
    1905, 3367, 3472, 3483, 3959
Names, personal, 649, 1293, 1296
Nampscoscocke, former name of Wells
Naples, Me., 3820-3822
Naples, Me. Church of Good Fellowship, 3822
Narantsouac, former name of Norridgewock
Narragansett No. 1, former name of Buxton
Narragansett No. 7, former name of Gorham
Narraguagus, former name of Cherryfield
Narraguagus, former name of Harrington
Narraguagus Valley, 1864
Narrantsouack, former name of Norridgewock
Narrow gauge railroads, see Railroads
Nash, Charles Elventon, 739, 1975, 2016
Nash, Chester, 4936
Nash, Gilbert, 2721
Nash, Harriet A., 4768
Nash, Ray, 4278
Nash Corner, locality in Pittsfield
Nashville Plantation, 3823
Naskeag, former name of Sedgwick
Naskeag, locality in Brooklin
Naskeag Lodge, Freemasons, Brooklin, 2441
Naskeeg, former name of Sedgwick
Nason, Emma Huntington, 917-918, 3258, 3262
Nason, Lawrence, 4732
Nason, Reuben, 3109, 3205
Nason Beach, locality in Greene
Nasson College, Sanford, 4678, 4681
National Archives Project, 3668, 4644
National Board of Fire Underwriters, 4499
National Home for Disabled Volunteer Soldiers,
    Togus, 2758-2759
Nativism, 3021A
Natural history, 442, 1038, 1209, 1226, 1798, 2369,
    4431

Naurantsouac, former name of Norridgewock
Naval art and science, 1412
Nazarene churches, see Churches, Nazarene
Neagle, Marjorie Spiller, 3488
Neal, Ben, 1867
Neal, John, 287, 4338-4339
Nealey, Robert W., 4340
Nealeys Corner, locality in Hampden
Nealley, Edward Bowdoin, 4895
Needham, Robert Francis, 4650
Neese, Abby Sargent, 4740
Neeson, Margaret Graham, 4661, 4823
Negausseg, former name of Woolwich
Negroes, see Blacks
Neighborhood associations, 2657
Nelson, Bruce D., 4341
Nelson, Florence Hunt, 3839
Nelson, G. J., 2422
Nelson, Jeremy, 3598
Nemscossecke, former name of Wells
Neptune, John, 367, 1161
Nequasseag, former name of Woolwich
Nequasset, former name of Woolwich
Nequasset, locality in Woolwich
Nesourdnahunk Township, 3824
Nett, Bruce Owen, 921, 1551A,
Nevin, Doris, 2339
New Auburn, locality in Auburn
New Boston, former name of Dedham
New Boston, former name of Gray
New Boston, former name of Leeds
New Bowdoin, former name of Ellsworth
New Bristol, former name of Sullivan
New Brunswick, 202, 441, 645-646
New Canada Plantation, 3825
New Casco, former name of Falmouth
New Casco Fort, see Fort New Casco
New Charlestown, former name of Charleston
New Dartmouth, former name of Newcastle
New England Music Camp, Oakland, 3964
New England Telephone and Telegraph Company, 2128
New England Shipbuilding Corporation, South Portland,
    4812
New Gloucester, Me., 1509, 3826-3850
New Hampshire, 2728
New Harbor, Me., 2404
New Ireland, Me., 2687, 2731, 2743-2744
New Jersey, 851
New Jerusalem Church, 2239, 4364
New Jerusalem Church, Bath, 2239
New Limerick, Me., 3851
New Marblehead, former name of Windham
New Meadows, Me., 5142
New Merrymeeting, former name of Woolwich
New Milford, former name of Alna
New Ohio, former name of Corinth
New Pennacook, former name of Rumford
New Plymouth Colony, 529
New Portland, Me., 3852-3854
New Salem Academy Grant and Williams College Grant,
    former name of Houlton
New Sandwich, former name of Wayne
New Sharon, Me., 1419, 3362, 3855
New Somersetshire, 1358
New Suncook, former name of Lovell
New Sweden, Me., 799, 1216, 1448, 1456, 3856-3871

New Town, former name of Gray
New Vineyard, Me., 3362, 3872-3873
New Waterford, former name of Windsor
New Worcester, former name of Brewer
New Worcester, former name of Orrington
New York, 4714
New York Industrial Recorder, 4342
Newagen, locality in Southport
Newberg, former name of Newburgh
Newbert, Albert H., 4601
Newbert, E. E., 2017
Newburgh, Me., 3874
Newcastle, Me., 644, 1678, 1683-1684, 1709, 3875-
    3882, 4589
Newcastle, Me. Second Congregational Church, 3882
Newell, William Stark, 923
Newfield, Me., 3883
Newhall, Me., 1493
Newichawannock, former name of Berwick
Newman, Walter S., 1180
Newmarket, former name of Parsonsfield
Newport, Me., 3884-3886
Newport, former name of Blue Hill
Newry, Me., 3887
Newspapers, 492; 373, 395, 493, 713, 1097-1098,
    1407, 1423, 1429-1430, 1436, 1442, 1450-1452,
    1469, 1473, 1484, 1497, 1504, 1520, 1525, 1527,
    1531, 1535, 1538, 1547-1549, 1562, 1603, 1612,
    1622, 1627, 1630, 1632, 1635, 1638, 1640, 1643,
    1647, 1655, 1665, 1669-1670, 1672, 1675, 1685,
    1698, 1700, 1711, 1714, 1717, 1720, 1725, 1754-
    1755, 1757, 1774, 1776, 1795, 1803-1804, 1810,
    1817-1818, 1820, 1825, 1827-1828, 1831-1832,
    1835-1836, 1850, 1889, 1891-1892, 2149, 2158,
    2248, 2535, 2884, 2925, 2934, 3032, 3169, 3559,
    3676, 3849, 4059, 4251, 4328, 4345, 4423, 4450,
    4761
Newton, John C., 4572
Newton, Roger Hale, 4343
Newton Road, locality in Biddeford
Nicatow, former name of Medway
Nichols, Charles Joseph, 924, 1183
Nichols, George E., 925
Nichols, Ichabod, 1384, 4344
Nichols, L. Nelson, 926
Nicholson, Nettie, 5332
Nickels-Sortwell House, Wiscasset, 5256
Nickerson, Kermit S., 750
Nicolar, Joseph, 365
Nicolet, C. C., 4345
Nicolin, locality in Ellsworth
Nile, Le Roy, 1749, 2828
Niles, Margaret, 799
Nimscoscook, former name of Wells
Niscassett, former name of Wells
Nitkin, Nathaniel, 927, 3808
Nixon, Milton, A., 928
Nixon, Paul, 2542
Noble, Arthur, 940
Noble, John, 929, 2423
Noble, Robert E., 4346
Nobleboro, Me., 1678, 1708, 3888
Nobles Corner, locality in Norway
Noe, Sydney Philip, 2722
Nolin, Frank A., 4755
Nondenominational churches, see Churches, nondenomi-
    national

Norberg, Gard E., 3865
Norcross, locality in T3 Indian Purchase
Nordica, Lillian, 3045, 3056
Noridgewoc, former name of Norridgewock
Norigwok, former name of Norridgewock
Norland, locality in Livermore
Normal schools, see Teachers, training of
Norman-Wilcox, Gregor, 5258
Norridgewock, Me., 171, 1799, 1816, 3889-3902
Norridgewock Indians, 1030, 3889, 3891-3894, 3896-
    3898
Norridgewogg, former name of Norridgewock
Norrigeawok, former name of Norridgewock
Norris, Jane P., 1968
North, James William, 2018, 2543
North Anson, Me., 1947
North Bangor, former name of Veazie
North Berwick, Me., 3903-3910
North Berwick Bicentennial Committee, 3906
North Bridgton, Me., 2379, 2388, 2390
North Brownville, Me., 2461
North Chapel, locality in Arundel
North Church, Belfast, 2258
North Deering, locality in Portland
North Gray, Me., 3227
North Hancock, Me., 1579
North Haven, Me., 1656, 3911-3913
North Hill, former name of Brighton Plantation
North Island, 3911
North Lovell, Me., 3634
North New Portland, locality in New Portland
North Oak Hill, locality in Litchfield
North Parish Congregational Church, Sanford, 4683,
    4685
North Parish of Kittery, former name of Eliot
North Parish of Sanford, former name of Alfred
North Precinct of Pownalborough, former name of Alna
North Road, locality in Gilead
North Road, locality in Springfield
North Salem, former name of Salem
North Windham, Me., 5202
North Yarmouth, Me., 3927; 1521-1522, 1524, 3914-
    3937
North Yarmouth, Me. First Church, 3918, 3924, 3926
North Yarmouth Academy, 3935, 3937
North Yarmouth Academy Grant, 3938
North Yarmouth and Falmouth Social Library, North
    Yarmouth, 3917
Northeast Boundary, 544, 1247A; 4, 38, 58, 148, 157,
    159, 203, 225, 267; 283, 327, 334, 432-434, 445,
    461, 513-515, 542, 572, 608-610, 623-625, 672,
    713, 716, 749, 788, 853, 868, 872, 880, 930, 983,
    988, 1208, 1220, 1267, 1321, 1333, 1340, 1346,
    1393, 1866, 1871, 1876, 2924, 3690
Northeast Carry Township, 3939
Northeast Harbor, Me., 3795-3797
Northeast Harbor, Me. Union Church, 3795
Northeastern Boundary, see Northeast Boundary
Northern Maine Junction, locality in Hermon
Northern Star Lodge, Freemasons, North Anson, 1947
Northfield, Me., 3940
Northmen, 306, 585, 656, 1021, 1129, 1370, 2426
Northport, Me., 1833
Northwest Carry, former name of Seboomook
North-west Religious Society, North Yarmouth, 3930
Norton, Alton Ackley, 3395A

Norton, Arthur Herbert, 681
Norton, David, 1750, 3980
Norton, Edward Preble, 3263
Norton, Lillian see Nordica, Lillian
Nortons Corner, locality in Willimantic
Norumbega, 304, 455, 527, 1264, 1728, 1137, 1759, 2045, 2640
Norumbega, locality in Brooksville
Norumbega (castle), 2640
Norway, Me., 1718, 1729, 3532, 3942-3959
Norway Historical Society, 3947
Norway Junior High School, 3948
Norway Lake, locality in Norway
Norway Savings Bank, 3945
Norwegians, 3913
Norwood, Francis, 4100
Norwood, Leslie E., 931, 2660, 4347-4348
Norwood, Seth Wademere, 2442
Nottage, W. A., 5188
Nottingham (ship), 5131
Nova Scotia, 256, 357, 3662
Noyes, Benjamin Lake, 2843
Noyes, Crosby Stuart, 3746
Noyes, David, 3949-3950
Noyes, Edward A., 4349
Noyes, Edwin A., 4400
Noyes, Reginald Webb, 735, 932-934
Nubble, locality in York
Nubble Light, York, 5323
Nuclear reactors, 4312
Number Four, locality in Lovell
No. 5 West of Machias, former name of Harrington
No. 14 Plantation, 3960
No. 21 Plantation, 3961
Numismatics, 1534, 2666, 2722, 2741, 4587
Nurses and nursing, 2012, 2088
Nutter Corner, locality in St. Albans
Nutting, John, 2687
Nutting, Wallace, 935
Nye, Carol F., 2275
Nyes Corner, locality in Fairfield

Oak, Lyndon, 3178, 3206, 4016
Oak Grove Seminary, Vassalboro, 4956
Oak Hill, locality in Scarborough
Oak Hill, locality in Standish
Oak Hill, locality in Swanville
Oak Ledge, locality in Harpswell
Oak Point, former name of Trenton
Oak Ridge, locality in Biddeford and Kennebunkport
Oakdale, locality in Portland
Oakfield, Me., 3962
Oakfield Community High School. Class of 1957, 3962
Oakhurst, locality in Cape Elizabeth
Oakland, Me., 1421, 3532, 3963-3968, 5041
Oakland Park, locality in Rockport
Oaklands (house), Gardiner, 3154
Oakwood, locality in Burnham
Ober, Grace M., 2040
Obermann, Henry B., 3092
Oblak, John Byron, 3696
O'Brien, Francis Massey, 936, 4276
O'Brien, John, 3670
O'Brien, Michael Charles, 2089
O'Brien, Michael J., 937, 1807A
O'Brien family, 3670, 3678

Observatories, 4195, 4316, 4348, 4424
Ocean Park, Me., 3973
Ocean Point, locality in Boothbay
Oceanville, locality in Stonington
O'Connor, Thomas P., 3296
Odd Fellows, 647, 654, 939, 1788, 2389, 4440, 5159
Odlin, John W., 5127
O'Dwyer, George Francis, 940, 3897
Ogden, Marguerite, 941, 1006, 2661
Ogier, Jesse H., 1669, 1700
Ogunquit, Me., 5133, 5135-5136, 5138
Ogunquit Playhouse, Wells, 5133, 5138
Ohio, former name of Corinth
Oil-cloth, 5236
Olamon, former name of Greenfield
Olamon, locality in Greenbush
Old Casco, former name of Portland
Old Crow Indian Band, Farmington, 3071
Old Man Ledge, 3647
Old No. 5, former name of Waterford
Old Orchard Beach, Me., 1880, 1904, 3969-3978, 4232, 4287
Old Orchard Beach Railroad, 1904
An Old pioneer, 3345
Old Point, Me., 3900
Old South Church, Farmington, 3050
An Old summer resident, see Vaughan, William Warren
Old Town, Me., 1750, 2082, 3979-3985, 4031
Oldfields, locality in South Berwick
O'Leary, Wayne M., 102
Oliphant, Duncan, 1518
Oliphant, H. D., 4352
Olive Branch Lodge, Freemasons, Charleston, 2754
Oliver, Velma K., 942
Oliver Hill Corner, locality in Garland
Olmsted, Carolyn, 943
Olmsted, Margaret, 943
Olsen, Irene A., 4078
Onawa, Me., 2993
Onesqueak, locality in Gouldsboro
Opdycke, Leonard, 2186
Oquossoc, locality in Rangeley
Oquossoc Angling Association, Rangeley, 4560
Orangetown, former name of Whiting
Orantsoak, former name of Norridgewock
Orchard, William C., 944
Orcutt, Eleanzer, 4191
Orcutt, Phillip Dana, 5334
Orcutt and Crafts Pottery, Portland, 4191
Orffs Corner, locality in Waldoboro
Organs, 4503
Orient, Me., 3986
The Orient (newspaper), 2535
Orient Lodge, Freemasons, Thomaston, 4884
Oriental Lodge, Freemasons, Bridgton, 2381
Oriental Star Lodge, Freemasons, Livermore, 3615-3617, 3624
Orland, Me., 3987-3989
Orne, Henry, 3990
Orneville Township, 3990
Orono (Indian), 532
Orono, Me., 1733, 1750, 2082, 3991-4034
Orono Methodist Church, 4029
Orphan's Island, 4963
Orrington, Me., 1752, 1762, 4035
Orrington Church, Brewer, 2372

Orr's Island, 3289, 3291, 3296, 3303
Osborn, William C., 946
Osborn Plantation, 4036
Osgood, E. S., 4354
Ossipee, former name of Limington
Ossipee Mills, locality in Waterboro
Osteopathy, 212, 822
Otis, James, pseud., see Kaler, James Otis
Otis, Me., 4037
Otisfield, Me., 4038-4041
O'Toole, Francis J., 947
Otter Creek, locality in Mount Desert
Outdoor life (see also Country life and Farm life), 374, 718, 1458, 1798, 1801, 2456
The Outlet, locality in Manchester
Ovariotomy, 137
Owascoag, former name of Scarborough
Owen, Daniel Edward, 4645
Owen, Fred K., 4357, 5078
Owen, Henry Wilson, 2225-2226
Owen, Howard, 948, 1429, 1638
Owen, M. B., 949
Owen, Moses, 4358
Owls Head, Me., 4042-4045
Owl's Head Light, 4044
Oxbow Plantation, 4046
Oxbow Township, 4047
Oxford, Me., 4048-4050
Oxford, former name of Albany Township
Oxford and Hammond, former name of Lagrange
Oxford Baptist Association, 1716
Oxford County, 109, 228, 333, 354, 508, 602, 626, 879, 975, 1045, 1713-1727
Oxford Democrat, Paris, 4059
Oxford Lodge, Freemasons, Norway, 3954
Oxford Paper Company, 4209, 4626, 4628
Oxford Royal, former name of Livermore
Oxford Spring House, Oxford, 4048
Oxton, Beulah Sylvester, 799, 801, 1440, 3671
Oyster River Bog, 1659

Packard, Alpheus Spring, 565, 950, 2506, 2544-2545, 5259
Packard, Aubigne Lermond, 4896
Packard, Bertram Everett, 1221, 3563
Packard, Charlotte Mellen, 2546
Packard, F. H., 5147
Packard, George Thomas, 2547
Packard, Harry A., 3951-3952
Packard, Leonard O., 951
Packard, Marlborough, 5182
Packard Landing, locality in Willimantic
Packard Road, locality in Bridgewater
Page, Annie Fraziette, 3264
Page, Marie Antoinette, 3688
Page, Mary Schultze, 4573
Paige, Emeline K., 4359
Paine, Albert Ware, 1751, 2129, 2132, 5079-5080
Paine Corner, locality in Oxford
Paines Corner, locality in Winslow
Paisley, Eva Cochran Wilson, 3634
Palermo, Me., 4051-4053
Palmer, Mason Skinner, 2793
Palmer family, 2198
Palmyra, Me., 4054
Paltsits, Victor Hugo, 2424

Pamola, 3813-3814
Pancoast, John E., 4462
Pancoast, Patricia McGraw, 4268
Pantha Pond Beach, locality in Raymond
Pantha Pond Park, locality in Raymond
Panther Pines, locality in Raymond
Paper making and trade, 90, 182, 211, 317, 484, 541, 946, 1141, 1724, 1815, 2572, 3167, 3381, 4004, 4209, 4626, 4628, 5150, 5166
Parent, locality in Van Buren
Parent-Teachers Club, Stillwater, 3982
Paris, Me., 1718, 1727, 4055-4066
Paris, Me. First Baptist Church, 4062
Paris Hill, 4058, 4065
Paris Lodge, Freemasons, South Paris, 4056-4057
Parish of St. Mary's, Houlton, 3355
Parish of the Sacred Heart, Winn, 5214
Parish of Unity, former name of South Berwick
Park, Francis E., 952
Parker, Arlita Dodge, 2425-2426
Parker, Arthur T., 2480
Parker, Barrett, 2627
Parker, Foxhall Alexander, 3673
Parker, Freeman, 2888
Parker, Jessie L., 4833
Parker, Lester Ward, 953
Parker, Thomas, 3068
Parker, W. J. Lewis, 4897
Parker, William J., 954
Parker Head, locality in Phippsburg
Parkers Island, former name of Georgetown
Parkertown Township, 4067
Parkhurst, Frederick H., 2089
Parkman, Francis, 2290
Parkman, Samuel, 4068
Parkman, Me., 1782, 4068-4069
Parks, 1555, 1558, 1560, 1563, 1571-1573, 1605, 1615, 4179, 4377, 4475, 4534, 4554
Parlin, W. Harrison, 5237
Parlin Pond Township, 3377A
Parmachenee Lake, 1713, 1715, 3650-3651
Parmachenee Township, 4071
Paroisse St. Bruno, Van Buren, 4953
Paroisse St. Joseph, Biddeford, 2294
Paroisse Saint-Pierre et Saint-Paul, Lewiston, 3554-3555
Paroisse Sainte-Marie, Lewiston, 3556
Parris, Albion Keith, 1384
Parson Landing, locality in Dover-Foxcroft
Parsons, Charles Wesley, 4381
Parsons, Isaac, 3841
Parsons, James E., 2995
Parsons, Louis A., 2548
Parsons, Usher, 955, 1931
Parsons, Vesta M., 956
Parsons, Willis E., 1788, 2883
Parsons Creek, locality in Edgecomb
Parsons Memorial Library, Alfred, Me., 1932
Parsons Mill, locality in Auburn
Parsonsfield, Me., 4072-4074
Parsonsfield Seminary, 4074
Parsontown, former name of Parsonsfield
Partridge, Cora Presson, 2019
Partridge, F. S., 2233
Partridgetown, former name of Peru
Pascataway, Me., 1911

Passadumkeag, Me., 4075-4076
Passamaquoddy, former name of Eastport
Passamaquoddy Bay, 1853, 1857, 1869, 1871-1872, 1876, 2924
Passamaquoddy Bay Treaty, 1854
Passamaquoddy Indians, 401, 678-679, 840, 947, 999-1001, 1003, 1073, 1117, 1246, 1343, 2924, 3225, 4093
Patricktown, former name of Somerville
Patriotic societies, 292-293, 1188
Patrons of Husbandry, 957, 1900, 2958, 3725
Pattagumpus, former name of Medway
Pattangall, William Robinson, 958
Pattee Corner, locality in Monroe
Patten, Roland Taylor, 4546
Patten, Me., 4077-4078
Patten Academy, 4078
Patten Free Library, Bath, 2227-2230
Pattensborough, former name of Surry
Pattershall, Margaret S., 959
Patterson, Helen B., 5334
Patterson, James Willis, 4120
Patterson, Raymond S., 1639
Patterson, Samuel, 104
Patterson, William Davis, 960, 1701-1702, 2947A, 5260-5262, 5264-5265
Patterson Mill, locality in Warren
Paugus (Indian), 3129
Pauls, locality in Caribou
Pauls Corner, locality in Searsmont
Payne, Frederick G., 4988
Payne, William Elisha, 961
Payneton Place, locality in York
Payson (H. M.) & Co., Portland, 4362
Payson Corner, locality in Hope
Payson Memorial Church, Portland, 4407-4408
Pea Cove, locality in Old Town
Peabody, Ellen Adams, 4363
Peabody, Henry Greenwood, 962
Peabody, Marian L., 2187
Peabodys Patent, former name of Gilead
Peak Island, 4232, 4249, 4259, 4455, 4486, 4501-4502
Peaks, Joseph B., 963
Pearce, Grace Nash, 3396
Pearl, Cyril, 964
Pearsontown and Hobbstown, former name of Standish
Peary, Robert Edwin, 3298
Pease, Albert, 4098
Pease, Allen G., 761
Peat, 925
Peavey Manufacturing Company, Oakland, 3966
Peaveyville, locality in Lebanon
Peck, Bradford, 3537, 3564
Peck, Calvin, 3014
Peck, Henry Austin, 965
Pegwacket, former name of Fryeburg
Peirce, Charles, 966
Pejepscot, locality in Topsham
Péladeau, Marius B., 967, 2020, 3842
Pelletier, Lawrence Lee, 968
Pelletier, Martine, 4952
Pemaquid, 1683, 1693, 1712, 2393-2394, 2396-2403, 2406-2407, 2411, 2413-2414, 2416-2418, 2420-2422, 2424-2426, 2428-2429, 2431-2432, 2434, 2436-2438
Pemaquid Beach, locality in Bristol

Pemaquid Harbor, locality in Bristol
Pemaquid Light, Bristol, 2415-2416
Pemaquid Patent, 2423
Pemaquid Point, locality in Bristol
Pembroke, Me., 603, 4079-4082
Penley Corners, locality in Auburn
Pennamaquan, former name of Dennysville
Pennamaquan, former name of Pembroke
Pennellville, locality in Brunswick
Penney, John W., 3722, 3843
Penney, Minnie, 2276
Penney, Will, 2276
Penobscot, Me., 1597, 1621, 4083-4089
Penobscot Bay, 311, 465, 509, 657, 707, 943, 962, 969, 1043, 1071, 1117, 1241, 1334, 1350, 1833, 2838, 4723
Penobscot County, 1741; 1251, 1728-1765
Penobscot County Bar Association, 1730
Penobscot County Medical Association, 1748
Penobscot Expedition (1779), 2689, 2691, 2697-2698, 2709-2710, 2721, 2728, 2730, 2734-2735, 2742
Penobscot Indians, 28, 95, 323, 367, 512, 526, 678, 944, 1002, 1073, 1108, 1161, 1163, 1168-1169, 1179, 1197-1202, 1258, 3985
Penobscot Island, former name of Verona
Penobscot Lodge, Freemasons, Dexter, 2867
Penobscot Log Driving Company, 1739
Penobscot River, 29, 76, 258, 304, 358, 362, 451-452, 456, 505, 564-565, 912, 1166, 1229, 1334, 1350, 1728, 1733, 1737-1738, 1740, 1744, 1753, 1758, 2372
Penobscot River, former name of Penobscot
Penobscot Savings Bank, Bangor, 2133
Penobscot Valley, 365, 914
Penrose, Charles, 3491
Pentagoet, former name of Penobscot
Pepperell, Lady, see Lady Pepperell Mansion, Kittery
Pepperell, William (1646-1734), 3470, 3474, 3496
Pepperell, William (1696-1759), 1221, 1901, 3470, 3475, 3494
Pepperell family, 3460, 3465-3467
Pepperell Cove, locality in Kittery
Pepperell House, Kittery, 3467, 3474, 3496
Pepperell Manufacturing Company, 1901, 2306, 2311
Pepperrellborough, former name of Biddeford and Saco
Peppermint Corner, locality in Lisbon
Pequaket, former name of Fryeburg
Pequawket, former name of Fryeburg
Pequawket Indians, 86, 3120, 3124-3130, 3135, 3139-3140, 3144-3147
Perch Cove, locality in Orono
Percy and Small Company, Bath, 2243
Perham, David, 1752
Perham, Harold C., 970
Perham, Sidney, 5281
Perham, Me., 4090
Perham Junction, locality in Madrid
Periodicals, 173, 1142, 1646; 1312, 1338, 2024, 3169, 4423, 5097
Perkins, Anne E., 971-972
Perkins, David Page, 4364
Perkins, DeForest H., 4769
Perkins, Edward H., 973
Perkins, Elizabeth B., 5335-5336
Perkins, Esselyn Gilman, 1902, 5135-5137

Perkins, Jack, 5120
Perkins, James E., 4121
Perkins, John, 2688
Perkins, John Carroll, 4365-4368, 4389
Perkins, Lucius M., 1933
Perkins, Virginia Chase, 974
Perkins, locality in T4 Indian Purchase
Perkins Corner, locality in Kennebunkport
Perkins Homestead, Newcastle, 644
Perkins Street, Castine, 2724
Perkins Town, locality in Wells
Perkins Township (Franklin Co.), 4091
Perkins Township (Sagadahoc Co.), 1677, 4092
Perley, Jeremiah, 740
Perry, A., 2258
Perry, Adelaide E., 1598, 1903
Perry, Angela H., 3855
Perry, George Sessions, 2134, 4369
Perry, Josepha M., 3907
Perry, Trueman Summerfield, 975, 1920, 2379, 2808, 2810
Perry, Wilder Washington, 1670
Perry, William Stevens, 4370
Perry, Me., 603, 4093-4095
Perrys Corner, locality in Limerick
Peru, Me., 4096-4097
Peters, Bradley L., 976
Peters, Russell H., 2116
Peterson, Oscar William, 3882
Peterson, Roger C., 4371
Petit Manan Light, 3731
Petit Manan Point, 4847
Petroleum industry and trade, 133, 480, 1111
Pettengill, A. G., 3764
Pettengill, Bertha F., 4372
Peucinian Society, Bowdoin College, 2536
Peverly, Elaine M., 1904, 3977
Pewter, 1406
Phair, locality in Presque Isle
Phi Beta Kappa. Maine Alpha, Bowdoin College, 2542, 2549
Phi Beta Kappa. Maine Beta, Colby College, 5081
Phi Beta Kappa. Maine Delta, University of Maine at Orono, 4032
Phi Gamma Delta Fraternity. University of Maine at Orono, 4008
Philbrick, Mrs. Frank B., see Philbrick, Minnie Lambert Smith
Philbrick, Minnie Lambert Smith, 5082, 5100
Philbricks Corner, locality in Waldo
Philbrook, Eleanor, 3844-3845
Philbrook, Eugene S., 4684
Philips, David E., 2135
Phillips, Charles Franklin, 3565
Phillips, Jerrie K., 1748
Phillips, Me., 1419, 4098-4099
Phillips Academy and Dummer Academy Grants, former name of Greenwood
Phillips and Rangeley Railroad, 1542
Phillips Gore, former name of Hebron
Phillips Limerick Academy Grant, former name of New Limerick
Phillipsburg, former name of Hollis
Phillipstown, former name of Sanford
Philomathian Society, Bowdoin College, 2536
Philoon, James E., 977

Phinney, Edmund, 1499, 1501-1502
Phinney family, 799
Phipps Canada, former name of Jay
Phippsburg, Me., 4100-4137, 4613
Phippsburg Congregational Church, 4122
Phippsburg Historical Society, 4123
Phips, William, 1221, 4100
Phipsburg, former name of Phippsburg
Phoenix Lodge, Freemasons, Belfast, 2269
Photographers, 291
Photography, 4478
Physical education facilities, 3905, 3909
Physicians, 846, 1134, 1195, 1237, 1320, 2991, 3209, 3498, 4072, 4284
Pickard, Samuel Thomas, 1520
Picking, Sherwood, 1703
Pidgin, William Abner, 1430
Pierce, George Washington, 2519
Pierce, Harry H., 2021
Pierce, Josiah, 3207-3208
Pierce, May, 2910
Pierce, True P., 1651
Pierce, William C., 978
Pierce family, 2124
Pierce Pond Township, 4138
Piersontown and Hobbstown, former name of Standish
Piggwackett, former name of Fryeburg
Pigwacket fight (1725), 3120, 3124-3130, 3135, 3138-3140, 3144-3147
Pigwacket Indians, see Pequawket Indians
Pike, Clifford L., 3953
Pike, Manley, H., 55
Pike, Richard, 4853
Pike Corner, locality in Casco
Pilgrim Fathers, 918, 1985, 2702, 2707
Pilsbury, Charles Albert, 979, 1836
Pilsbury, William Hacket, 21
Pine Cliff, locality in Southport
Pine Corner, locality in Charlotte
Pine Hill, locality in York
Pine Point, Me., 3974
Pine Street Congregational Church, Lewiston, 3542, 3569
Pine Tree Lodge, Freemasons, Mattawamkeag, 3718-3719
Pingree, David, 3398
Pingree family, 1348
Pinehurst, locality in Fryeburg
Pineland, locality in New Gloucester
The Pines, locality in Wesley
Pingree Center, locality in Parkman
Pinkham, Charles E., 5266
Piper, Clara Collins, 2669, 2671
Pirates, 2394, 2409, 3663
Piscataqua, former name of Kittery
Piscataqua Pioneers, 1906
Piscataquis Baptist Association, 1780
Piscataquis County, 1789; 30, 108, 1766-1801
Piscataquis County Historical Society, Dover, Me., 1789
Piscataquis Observer, Dover, Me., 2884
Pishon Ferry, locality in Clinton
Pitcher, Donald T., 2948
Pitcher, Fred A., 4989
Pitman, Linwood T., 4374
Pitmans Corner, locality in Appleton

Pittman-Robertson Project, 61
Pittsfield, Me., 4139-4142
Pittsfield Grammar School, 4141
Pittston, Me., 1633, 1649, 1937, 4143
Pittston Academy Grant, 4144
Plaisted, locality in Eagle Lake
Plantation Number Thirty Three, alternate name of
    Great Pond Plantation
Playwrights, 3516
Pleasant Hill, locality in Falmouth
Pleasant Hill, locality in Freeport
Pleasant Hill, locality in Scarborough
Pleasant Point, Me., 4093
Pleasant Point, locality in Cushing
Pleasant Point State Indian Reservation, 4145
Pleasant Pond, locality in Caratunk Plantation
Pleasant Ridge, former name of Caswell Plantation
Pleasant Ridge Plantation, 4146
Pleasant River, 1843, 1848
Pleasant Vale Corner, locality in Corinna
Pleasant Valley, locality in Paris
Pleasantdale, locality in South Portland
Pleiades Lodge, Freemasons, Milbridge, 3734
Plough Patent, 1075, 1265
Plourde, H. Pauline, 2275
Plourde Mill, locality in Wallagrass Plantation
Plumly, Charles F., 3717
Plummer, Charles W., 3605
Plummer, Edward Clarence, 2226, 2231, 2244, 5295
Plummer, Francis W., 3605
Plummer, Moses, 3846
Plummer Corner, locality in Detroit
Plummers Mill, locality in Durham
Plymouth, Me., 4147
Plymouth Colony, see New Plymouth
Plymouth Company (1749-1816), 642, 918, 2018
Plymouth Gore, former name of Pittsfield
Plymouth Grant, former name of Fort Fairfield
Plymouth Patent, see Kennebec Patent
Plymouth Township, 4148
Pocasset, former name of Wayne
Pochasset, former name of Wayne
Poets, 496, 919, 3171, 3502, 5298
Pohl, Frederick J., 1599
Pohlman, Henry N., 4990
Poland, Me., 1425, 4149-4159
Poland Mineral Spring Water, 4151, 4156, 4159
Poland Spring, Me., 4150-4151, 4153, 4156-4159
Poland Spring House, 4150, 4158
Polands Corner, locality in Montville
Polereczky, John, 3179
Polias (steamer), 4658
Police departments, 779, 4352, 4399
Polin (Indian), 5203
Political parties (see also specific parties), 71,
    417, 662, 1048, 1093, 1185, 1317, 2034, 3021A,
    4305, 4533
Politicians, see Statesmen
Politics and government, 588, 723, 819, 968, 1054,
    1239, 1244, 1324, 1731, 1994, 2000, 2562, 2924,
    4225
Politics and government-colonial period, 516
Politics and government (1775-1865), 69; 378, 551,
    1094, 1365, 2034, 3021A, 4305, 4351
Politics and government (1865-1933), 55, 958, 1048,
    1185
Politics and government (1951-), 342, 1317, 1323

Polk, James Knox, 1371
Pollard, J. A., 980
Pollard, Ralph J., 981
Polymnian Society, Bates College, 3563
Pond, Enoch, 2136-2138
Pond Cover, locality in Cape Elizabeth
Pondicherry, Me., 2383
Pondstown, former name of Winthrop
Pondtown, former name of Winthrop
Poole, George W., 4154
Poole, Henry A., 4154
Poole, William Frederick, 4126
Pools Landing, locality in Edgecomb
Poor, John Alfred, 87, 153, 982-985, 4100, 4125,
    4306
Poor, Laura Elizabeth, 983
Poor family, 2124
Poors Mill, locality in Belfast
Pope, Alton, S., 1639
Pope, Charles Henry, 3674
Pope and Talbot, Inc., Machias, 3654
Popeville, locality in Windham
Popham, George, 4103, 4115, 4117, 4130, 4134
Popham family, 4133
Popham Beach, 4116, 4121
Popham Colony, 4126, 4133; 35, 982, 2425, 2427,
    2436, 4100-4110, 4112, 4115-4120, 4124-4127A,
    4129-4130, 4132-4135
Population, 303, 330, 415, 778, 816, 951, 1313, 3399
Port Clyde, locality in St. George
Port Royal, former name of Livermore
Port Watson, former name of Brooklin
Portage, locality in Portage Lake
Portage Lake, Me., 4160
Porter, Albert O., 1826
Porter, Allen, 1406
Porter, Charles F., 4375
Porter, Charles Greenleaf, 1105
Porter, Edwin A., 3580
Porter, Florence Collins, 986
Porter, Frederic Hutchinson, 987
Porter, Freeman, 1406
Porter, Georgia Pulsifer, 797
Porter, J. B., 2139
Porter, Joseph Whitcomb, 198, 988-991, 2089, 2140,
    2232, 2940, 3983, 4035, 4854, 4898-4899
Porter, Lillian Russell, 5007
Porter family, 991
Porter, Me., 4161-4162
Porter District, locality in West Paris
Porter Settlement, locality in Houlton
Porterfield, former name of Porter
Porterfield, locality in Porter
Porters Landing, locality in Freeport
Portland (ship), 209
Portland, Me., 168, 799, 1483, 1487, 1492, 1512,
    1514, 1534, 4163-4533
Portland, Me. Board of Trade, 4379
Portland, Me. Chestnut Street Methodist Episcopal
    Church, 4178, 4380-4381
Portland, Me. City Planning Board, 4382
Portland, Me. First Baptist Church, 4239, 4383-
    4385, 4459
Portland, Me. First Parish Church, 4224, 4344,
    4365-4368, 4386-4389, 4472-4474, 4480
Portland, Me. First Universalist Society, 4390-
    4391

Portland, Me. Free Street Baptist Church, 4300, 4327, 4392-4395
Portland, Me. High Street Congregational Church, 4396
Portland, Me. Holy Trinity Hellenic Orthodox Church, 4397
Portland, Me. Housing Authority Commission, 4398
Portland, Me. Police Department, 4352, 4399
Portland, Me. Public Library, 4400-4401, 4528
Portland, Me. Renewal Authority, 4402
Portland, Me. St. Dominic's Parish, 4403-4404
Portland, Me. Saint Stephen's Church, 4405-4406
Portland, Me. Second Parish Church, 4407-4408
Portland, Me. Staples School, 4409
Portland, Me. State Street Church, 4410-4411
Portland, Me. Stevens Avenue Congregational Church, 4412
Portland, Me. Williston Church, 4413-4414
Portland, Me. Woodfords Congregational Church, 4415-4416
Portland Academy, 4307
Portland Auto Show, 4460
Portland Benevolent Society, 4418
Portland Board of Trade, 4468
Portland Cadets, 4419
Portland Camera Club, 4478
Portland Charitable Dispensary, 4197
Portland Commandery, Knights Templar, 4187
Portland Company, 4253, 4312
Portland Council, Royal and Select Masters (Freemasons), 4248
Portland Custom House, 4420
Portland Dry Docks, 4496
Portland Family Welfare Society, 4372
Portland Fire Department, 4238
Portland Gas Light Company, 4306, 4477
Portland Glass Company, 4299, 4304, 4490-4491
Portland Head Light, 4347, 4485
Portland-Lewiston Interurban, 281
Portland Lodge, Freemasons, 4228, 4247
Portland Marine Society, 4421, 4514
Portland Medical Club, 4284, 4422
Portland Observatory, 4195, 4316, 4348, 4424
Portland Police Department, see Portland, Me. Police Department
Portland Public Library, see Portland, Me. Public Library
Portland Railroad, 4214
Portland Rossini Club, 4427-4428, 4439
Portland Savings Bank, 4429-4430
Portland School for Medical Instruction, 4218
Portland Society of Natural History, 4431
Portland Society of the New Jerusalem, 4364
Portland Stove Foundry, 4333
Portland Water District, 4337, 4433-4434
Portland Yacht Club, 4435
Portsmouth, Treaty of (1905), 3503
Portsmouth Naval Shipyard, Kittery, 3458, 3462, 3471, 3477, 3492
Postal cards, 530
Postal service, 341, 359, 469, 558-559, 636, 705, 1336, 1992, 2112, 2248, 2942, 3039, 3166, 3339, 3844, 3928, 4226, 4426

Postmarks, 341
Pot-8-O Club, Bowdoin College, 2519
Potato industry, 90, 1444, 1454, 1461, 1468, 1478-1479, 2670, 3332
Potter, Edward Wesley, 2141
Potter, Gail M., 3675
Potter, Joseph, 2142
Potter, Mark L., 2142
Potter, Nellie, 4437-4438
Potter Academy, Sebago, 4732
Pottery, 613, 1628, 3768, 4189-4192, 5284
Pottle, Frederick A., 5083
Pottle, George, 992
Poultry industry, 782
Poverty (see also Economic conditions and Social conditions), 2962, 4561
Powell, Jeremiah, 3922
Powers, Jessie D. O., 3420
Powers, W. A., 993
Powers Corner, locality in Easton
Pownal, Me., 4534-4538
Pownalborough, former name of what is now Alna, Dresden, and Wiscasset
Pownalborough Court House, Dresden, 2890, 2894, 2897
Prairie, locality in Brownville
Pratt, Charles, 3368
Pratt, F. H., 1790
Preble, Ebenezer, 2246
Preble, Fred Myron, 5084
Preble, George A., 2233
Preble, George Henry, 1705, 3492, 5337
Preble, William Pitt, 4344
Preble Chapel, Portland, 4227
Preble Corner, locality in Garland
Prentiss, George Lewis, 3194
Prentiss, Thomas Mellen, 995
Prentiss Plantation, 4539
Prentiss Township, 4540
Presbyterian churches, see Churches, Presbyterian
Presbyterianism, 424, 996, 1388
Prescott and Carrs, former name of Belgrade
Prescotts, former name of Belgrade
President's House, Bowdoin College, 2582
Presque Isle, Me., 50, 4541-4551
Presque Isle Civic Roundtable, Inc., 4547
Preston, Richard Arthur, 4127A
Preston, former name of Wells
Presumpscot, locality in Falmouth
Presumpscot Cove, locality in Windham
Presumpscot Lodge, Freemasons, North Windham, 5202
Presumpscot River, 1493, 1498, 5151
Presumpscot Union Parish, 1508
Pretty Marsh, locality in Mount Desert
Prices, 870-871, 874
Pride, locality in St. Croix Township
Pride Training School, South Portland, Me., 4815
Pride's Corner, Me., 5157
Prince, Christopher, 4891
Prince, Eliza, 4891
Prince, George, 998
Prince, Henry C., 1827
Prince, Hezekiah, 4900

Prince, J. Dyneley, 999-1003
Prince, Katherine H., 2550
Prince family, 4891
Prince Edward Island, 256
Princeton, Me., 1840, 4552-4553
Pring, Martin, 805
Printers, 119, 932, 2103, 4203, 4217, 4240, 4317, 4423, 4488, 4513, 4518
Printing, 492, 932, 934; 493, 735-736, 926, 1286, 2110, 4033, 4167, 5056
Pripet, locality in Islesboro
Prisons, 1742, 4064, 4898-4899, 4901, 4904, 5266, 5313, 5333
Private schools, 352, 1946, 1956, 2214, 2272, 2290, 2299, 2324, 2328, 2379, 2390, 2883, 2909-2910, 2981, 2992, 3132, 3142, 3205, 3318-3319, 3590, 3879, 3935, 3937, 4078, 4139-4140, 4307, 4453, 4567-4572, 4732, 4786-4787, 4791, 4956, 5033-5034, 5055, 5063, 5240
Privateering, 1015, 4512
Probate records (see also Court Records), 1081, 1463, 1702, 1912
Progressive Party (founded 1912), 1048
Prohibition (see also Temperance), 33, 80, 164, 232, 328, 337, 384, 522, 818, 1057, 1299, 1392, 1403
Proper, Ida Sedgwick, 3765
Prospect, Me., 4554
Prospect Harbor, Me., 3214, 3217-3218
Prosser, Albert L., 1005, 4685-4686
Protestant Episcopal Church in the U. S. A. Maine (Diocese), 1006
Protestant Episcopal churches, see Churches, Episcopal
Protestants, 19
Prouts Gore, former name of Freeport
Prouts Neck, 3974, 4697, 4699, 4704, 4708, 4711
Prouts Neck Association, 4708
Provost, Honorius, 1007
Psychology-study and teaching, 4023
Public health, see Hygiene, public
Public houses, see Hotels, Taverns, etc.
Public lands, 22, 25, 443, 758, 1222, 1401
Public opinion, 270
Public welfare, 584
Public works, 1253
Publishers and publishing, 1008, 2009, 4251, 4255, 4278, 4506, 5038
Puddle Dock, 1938
Pullen, Clarence, 1462
Pullen, John J., 1009
Pullorum, 782
Pulpit Harbor, locality in North Haven
Pumpkin Valley, locality in Bridgton
Pumpkintown, former name of Cornish
Pumpkinville, locality in Sullivan
Pungustook, former name of North Yarmouth
Purcell, Richard J., 1010
Purgatives, 3827
Purington, George Colby, 3069
Purington, William C., 1808
Puritans, 3897
Pushaw, locality in Old Town
Putnam, Amos, 3346
Putnam, Beecher, 1463
Putnam, Cora M. Carpenter, 3347-3348

Putnam, Frank Arthur, 1011
Putnam, Frederick Ward, 1012
Putnam, Henry, 2551
Putnam, former name of Washington

Quack, former name of York
Quaker Hill, locality in Unity
Quaker Meeting House, locality in Durham
Quaker Point, locality in West Bath
Quaker Ridge, locality in Casco
Quakers, see Friends, Society of
Quampeagan Landing, former name of South Berwick
Quantabacook, Me., 4720
Quantabacook Lodge, Freemasons, Searsmont, 4717-4718
Queen Acres, locality in Cape Elizabeth
Queen Anne's War (1703-1713), 86, 214, 217
Queenstown, former name of Embden
Quimby, locality in Winterville Plantation
Quimby Pond, locality in Rangeley
Quinby, George Washington, 1640
Quinn, Erland L., 2838
Quinn, William P., 2234
Quinn family, 2838
Quoddy Times, Eastport, 2934
Quoddy Village, locality in Eastport

Radcliffe, Jane E., 1013
Radford, Benjamin, 4464
Radford, Daniel, 4464
Radford, William, 4464
Radio broadcasting, 789
Rahill, Peter James, 1014
Railroads, 11-12, 45, 61B-61C, 87, 96A-97, 112, 124, 131, 204, 268, 276, 284, 332, 346, 404, 448-450, 469, 473, 568, 640, 658, 660, 670, 673, 711, 734, 790-793, 839, 848, 862, 894-895, 921, 952, 963, 976, 978, 983-985, 1284-1285, 1290, 1351, 1355-1356, 1361, 1390, 1394, 1488, 1537, 1539-1543, 1550-1552, 1557, 1624, 1629, 1648, 1667-1668, 1676, 1723, 1732, 1734-1735, 1763, 1808, 1814-1815, 1822-1824, 1826, 1863, 1904, 1921, 2168, 2180, 2386-2387, 2768, 2954, 2962, 2993, 3173, 3311, 3772, 3773A, 3774A, 3776, 3977, 4163, 4253, 4312, 4520, 5051
Rainbow Township, 4555
Raisz, Erwin Josephus, 1600
Ramsdell, Harriet J., 3566
Ramsdell, T. J., 5085
Rand, Edwin Holmes, 1015
Rand, Emily K., 4439
Rand, John A., 1431
Rand, Leroy H., 5160, 5167
Randall, Daniel Boody, 1016
Randel, William Peirce, 1905
Randolph, Me., 1624, 1629, 1648-1649, 4556
Rangeley, Me., 4557-4561
Rangeley Lakes, 421, 1749, 4557
Rangeley Plantation, 4562
Ranlett, Charles Everett, 1017
Ranlett, Frederick Jordan, 1017
Ranlett, Louis Felix, 1017, 2133, 2143-2144
Ranlett, Susan Alice, 1017
Rascohegan, former name of Georgetown
Rasles, Sebastian, 171, 279, 801, 1088, 1386, 3891-3898, 3901

Rattermann, Heinrich Armin, 1018
Rattlesnake Mountain, 2684
Rawlings, Charles, 1019, 3766, 4602
Ray, Mrs. Fabius Maximus, see Ray, Isabel T.
Ray, Isaac, 2004
Ray, Isabel T., 5161-5162, 5170
Ray, Roger Bray, 804, 807, 1020-1021, 2662
Ray Corner, locality in Knox
Raymond, John H., 2235
Raymond, William Odber, 1464, 3690
Raymond, Me., 1508, 1514, 4567-4573
Raymondton, former name of Raymond
Raymondtown, former name of Raymond
Rays Corner, locality in Greene
Rayville, locality in Otisfield
Razorville, locality in Washington
Reach, locality in Deer Isle
Read, James N., 4440
Read, Mary Salina, 1959
Reade, John, 1022
Reade, John L., 3567
Readfield, Me., 4567-4573
Readstown, former name of Strong
Record, Fred W., 1119
Records, locality in Carrabassett Valley
Rectories, 5176
Red Beach, locality in Calais
Red Bridge, locality in Oakfield
Red Eagle, Henry, 1791
Red Paint People, 163, 507, 638, 891, 901, 1078,
    1135-1136, 1165, 1170, 1178, 4075
Red Rock Corner, locality in Bar Harbor
Redden, John, 1024
Redding, locality in Sumner
Reddington, Asa, 1025, 1641
Redington, Frank, 5086
Redington Township, 4574
Redman, John B., 2999
Reed, Donald Winslow, 1026
Reed, Jeanne Brown, 3778
Reed, Parker McCobb, 1027, 2236, 4128
Reed, Thomas Brackett, 1414, 2552
Reed family, 4128
Reed Mansion, Waldoboro, 4991
Reed Plantation, 4575
Reedfield, former name of Readfield
Reeds, locality in Madrid
Reedstown, former name of Strong
Reeve, Samuel H., 2979
Referendum, 968
Reform schools, see Prisons
Reformatories, see Prisons
Reid, Dick, 5087
Reid, John G., 1029
Reilly, M. W., 3741, 5214, 5232
Reims, Gordan A., 5008
Religious societies, 523, 616, 689, 1335, 1509,
    1925-1926, 1929-1930, 3188, 3352, 3826-3829,
    3831-3836, 3842, 3844-3845, 3847, 3849-3850,
    4188, 4296
Remich, Carrie E., 3421
Remich, Daniel, 3421
Remick, Jacob, Jr., 3493
Remick, Oliver Philbrick, 1906-1907, 3493
Replogle, James, 644
Repplier, Agnes, 5338

Representative government and representation, 551
Republican Party, 71, 417, 4305, 4533
Republican Society, Portland, 4305
Resorts, 712, 2172, 2179, 2182, 2184, 2187-2188,
    2190-2191, 2704, 3449-3450, 3970, 4116, 4150-
    4151, 4153, 4156-4158, 5314
Retail trade, 472
Reuel Williams House, Augusta, 1990
Revenue, 1933
Revere, Paul, 685, 703, 2097, 2742
Revivals, 2637, 4927
Revolution, American, 215-216; 6, 14-15, 24, 113,
    132, 170, 180, 187, 239, 257, 347, 405, 465, 538,
    566, 571, 589, 600, 607, 645-646, 648, 669, 719,
    724, 799, 842, 844, 864, 866, 882, 924, 949,
    1015, 1028, 1051, 1088, 1103, 1117, 1154-1155,
    1211, 1230, 1273, 1276, 1319, 1329, 1499, 1501-
    1502, 1794, 1907, 2283, 2653, 2662, 2687, 2689,
    2691, 2697, 2709-2710, 2719, 2728, 2730, 2734-
    2735, 2742, 2840, 2842-2843, 2988, 3301, 3429,
    3519, 3653, 3655-3656, 3660, 3662, 3664-3665,
    3670-3671, 3673-3675, 3679-3682, 3956, 4177,
    4196, 4258, 4261, 4511, 4532, 4660, 4701, 4756,
    5201, 5204, 5238, 5311, 5317, 5350
Revolution, American-British forces, 1894, 2745
Revolution, American-naval operations, 465, 799,
    2689, 2691, 2697, 2728, 2730, 2734-2735, 2742,
    3653, 3655-3656, 3660, 3664, 3671, 3673-3675,
    3680-3682
Revolutionary Soldiers Grant, former name of Sol-
    diertown Township (Somerset Co.)
Reyher, Rebecca, 1031
Reynolds, Edward Clayton, 2663
Reynolds, Harris Walter, 2145
Reynolds, Horace, 1032
Reynolds, Jamie, 5339
Reynolds Corner, locality in Burnham
Rice, George Wharton, 2348
Rice, Marshall, 1033
Rice, W. A., 1034
Rice, William B., 1035
Rice Corner, locality in Durham
Rice Corner, locality in Solon
Rich, Caroline Webster D. Stockbridge, 4934
Rich, George B., 3349
Rich, Louise Dickinson, 1036-1040, 3219, 5225
Rich, Marshall Nye, 3929-3931, 4379, 4442-4443
Richards, Charles W., 4580
Richards, Helen M., 2553
Richards, John, 3164
Richards, Josephine, 1041
Richards, Laura Elizabeth Howe, 3171
Richards, Rosalind, 1642
Richards, former name of Aurora
Richardson, Albert, 3385
Richardson, Charles Albert, 3385
Richardson, Christine, 4859
Richardson, Mrs. Edwin A., 3110
Richardson, George B., 3111
Richardson, George W., 2082, 4181
Richardson, Harriet T., 3495
Richardson, Hobart Wood, 1042, 1913
Richardson, John Mitchell, 1043
Richardson family, 3385
Richardsontown Township, 4576
Richmond, Bernice, pseud., see Robinson, Bernice
    Nelke

Richmond, Me., 3532, 4577-4583
Richmond Historical and Cultural Society, 4581
Richmond Lodge, Freemasons, 4579
Richmond Mill, locality in Fayette
Richmond's Island, 1265, 1534, 2655, 2660-2661, 2666
Richtown, locality in Tremont
Richville, locality in Standish
Ricker, Alvan Bolster, 4155
Ricker, George S., 3568
Ricker, Hiram Jabez, 4151
Ricker, Hiram W., 4155
Ricker, Hiram and Sons, Poland, 4156-4157, 4159
Ricker, Jennie De R., 4802
Ricker, Joseph, 1044
Ricker College, 3349-3351
Rideout, Annie E., 2376
Riedel, Wesley U., 3142
The Ridge, locality in Bridgton
Ridge, locality in Lubec
Ridgewock, former name of Norridgewock
Ridlon, Gideon Tibbetts, 1045, 3310
Ridlonville, locality in Mexico
Ridlonville, locality in Sweden
Rigby, Hazen F., 3265
Riley, locality in Jay
Riley Township, 4584
Rinehart, Jonathan, 1046
Rinehart, Mary Roberts, 2188
Ring, Elizabeth, 784, 826, 1047-1049
Ring Hill, locality in Litchfield
Ring Homestead, North Yarmouth, 3932
Riots, 1231, 2593, 3455, 4302
Ripley, Lincoln, 5022
Ripley, Me., 4585
Rising Star Lodge, Masons, Penobscot, 4088-4089
Rising Sun Lodge, Freemasons, Orland, 3987
Rising Virtue Lodge, Freemasons, Bangor, 2095
River Road, locality in South Thomaston
River Townships 2 and 3, former name of Lincoln
River Township 4, former name of Winn
Rivers, 75-76, 103, 184, 237, 243, 258, 331, 334,
   370, 386, 439, 451-452, 456, 563-565, 665, 780,
   912, 1206, 1223, 1229, 1264, 1267, 1334, 1350,
   1419, 1439, 1446-1447, 1458A-1459, 1464, 1470,
   1491, 1498, 1578, 1663, 1723, 1726, 1728, 1737-
   1739, 1744, 1839, 1843, 1866, 1885, 2200, 2572,
   3404, 5151, 5246
Riverside, locality in Vassalboro
Riverside Lodge, Freemasons, Jefferson, 3383
Riverside Methodist Episcopal Church, Kezar Falls,
   4073
Riverton, locality in Portland
Roach Pond, alternate name of Frenchtown Township
Roads, see Thoroughfares
Robador (yacht), 2638
Robbins, Allan L., 4901
Robbins, Alma Pierce, 4959
Robbins, Chester W., 1754
Robbins, Linville W., 3172
Robbins, Mel, 4158
Robbins family, 4719
Robbinston, Me., 2705, 2745, 4586-4587
Roberts, Al, 3116
Roberts, Arthur J., 5113
Roberts, Charlotte, 2146

Roberts, Kenneth Lewis, 1050-1052
Roberts, Sadie, 2830
Roberts, locality in Caribou
Roberts Corner, locality in Buxton
Roberts Corner, locality in Parsonsfield
Roberts Mills, locality in Lyman
Robie, Edward, 3194
Robie, Virginia, 3494
Robin Hood, locality in Georgetown
Robinson, Bernice Nelke, 1602
Robinson, Clarence Cromwell, 1053
Robinson, Claude E., 1054
Robinson, D. A., 2147
Robinson, David, 4170
Robinson, Edwin Arlington, 3148
Robinson, Ernest W., 4040
Robinson, Grace Louise, 2427
Robinson, Reuel, 1671, 2646
Robinson, Timothy Weymouth, 3786
Robinson, William A., 1055
Robinson, locality in Blaine
Robyville, locality in Corinth
Rockabema, former name of Moro Plantation
Rockefeller Bowl, 4857
Rockland, Me., 20, 1659-1660, 1666, 1673, 2082,
   4588-4611
Rockland, Thomaston and St. George Railway, 1657-
   1658, 1664
Rockport, Me., 1653, 1659, 1666, 1668, 1671, 1673,
   2082, 2641, 4612-4616, 4589
Rockville, locality in Rockport
Rockwood, Charles M., 4445
Rockwood Strip, 4617
Rodger, William, 1056
Roerden, Chris, see Roerden, Harold H.
Roerden, Harold H., 2664
Rogers, C. Talbot, 2628, 3847
Rogers, Donald, 1057, 3376
Rogers, John, 2956, 2982
Rogers, Lore Alfred, 1058-1060, 1792
Rogers, Mary Elizabeth Barker, 1465
Rogers, Orville F., 5296
Rogers, Susannah Whipple, 2956
Rogers, William, 2223
Rogers Corner, locality in Troy
Roggenbauer, Josef, 4992
Rolde, Neil, 3496, 5340
Rolerson, Darrell A., 3377
Rolf, Charles, 4553
Rolfe, David, 4548
Rolfe, Eldred, 826
Rolfe, Fred P., 4553
Rollins, Frank W., 1603
Rollins, Ruth, 3297
Rollins, Sarah R., 4446
Rollins Mill, locality in Charleston
Rollins Mills, locality in Dixmont
Romaine, Lawrence B., 3209
Roman Catholic churches, see Churches, Roman
   Catholic
Roman Catholics, see Catholics
Rome, Me., 4618
Ronco, Edward, 1793
Roque Bluffs, Me., 4619
Roque Island, Me., 3393-3395
Rose, Mabelle, Andrews, 4662

Rosemont, locality in Portland
Rosier, James, 1061
Ross, Frank D., 2237
Ross, Leland A., 2867
Ross, Lillian, 468
Ross, Linwood, 1062
Ross Corner, locality in Shapleigh
Rossini Club, Portland, 4193
Rotary International, 2148, 3984, 4606
Round Pond, 286
Rounds, John, 3848
Roundy, Charles G., 1063
Roundy, John, 2329
Roundy, Rodney W., 1064-1065, 3074, 3569, 4447
Roux, Willan C., 3298-3299
Rowe, Ernest Ray, 5163
Rowe, Harry W., 3570
Rowe, Herbert W., 1755, 2149
Rowe, James Swett, 2150
Rowe, John Howland, 1066
Rowe, Marian Bradford, 4448-4449, 5163
Rowe, Mary-Louise, 2146
Rowe, William Hutchinson, 1067, 1521-1524, 5297-5298
Rowe Corner, locality in Newport
Rowell, George Smith, 4244, 4450
Rowes Corner, locality in Auburn
Rowing, 2516
Rowland, Elizabeth McLellan Gould, 4451
Rowse, A. L., 4129
Roxbury, Me., 4620
Roxbury Pond, locality in Roxbury
Roy, Lucienne C., 2726
Royal Junction, locality in Yarmouth
Royal Tar (ship), 4971
Royall, William F., 826
Royalls River, former name of North Yarmouth
Royallsborough, former name of Durham
Royalstown, former name of Durham
Rube, Burdock, pseud., see Harrison, O. M.
Rugg, Henry W., 4452
Ruggles, Thomas, 2782-2786
Rule, Glenn K., 1466
Rumford, Me., 4621-4629
Rumford Falls, Me., 4627
Rumford Falls and Rangeley Lakes Railroad, 97
Rumford Mechanics' Institute, 4629
Runic inscriptions, 3757, 3760
Rush, Nixon Orwin, 1068, 5058, 5088-5089
Russell, Carrie Page, 2460
Russell, Charlotte M., 4779
Russell, Edward, 3933
Russell, Walter E., 1069
Russell Pond Township, 4630
Russians, 4834
Rustfield, former name of Norway
Rutherford, Phillip R., 1070
Ryan, Allie, 1071

Sabattus, Me., 4631
Sabbathday Lake, 3831, 3833-3835, 3842, 3844-3845, 3850
Sabine, Lorenzo, 1072-1073, 2924, 2932-2933
Sabino, locality in West Bath
Saccarappa, Me., 4181
Saccarappa Falls, 5151

Saccarappa Lodge, Odd Fellows, Westbrook, 5159
Saco, Me., 556, 799, 1265, 1881, 1890, 1893, 1901, 1904, 4181, 4632, 4651
Saco, Me. First Parish Congregational Church, 4647-4648
Saco, locality in Columbia
Saco Bay, 3974
Saco Company, 4643
Saco East, former name of Biddeford
Saco Valley, 1045, 1411
Saddleback, locality in Dallas Plantation
Saddleback Mountain, 3697
Safford, Moses A., 3497-3498
Safford, Victoria, 3499
Safford Pottery, Monmouth, 3768
Sagadahoc Colony, see Popham Colony
Sagadahoc County, 107, 1409, 1802-1810
Sagadahoc Ferry, locality in Woolwich
Sagamore Village (housing project), 4398
Sailboat racing, 3117
Sails, 286
St. Agatha, Me., 4652-4653
St. Agatha Parish, 4652-4653
St. Alban Commandery, Knights Templar, Poland, 4165
St. Albans, Me., 4654
St. Andrew's Church, Newcastle, 3877
St. Andrew's Parish, Millinocket, 3738
St. Anne's Church, Calais, 2614, 2618
St. Ann's Church, Kennebunkport, 3438
St. Aspinquid Lodge, Freemasons, York, 5316
Saint Castin, Anselm, Baron de, 454
Saint Castin, Jean Vincent de l'Abadie, Baron de, 671, 1264, 2720
St. Croix, former name of Calais
St. Croix Commission, 159
St. Croix Indians, 435
St. Croix Island, 2621, 2627
St. Croix River, 334, 1267, 1866, 4954
St. Croix Township, 4655
St. Croix Valley, 1845-1846, 1862, 1873
St. David, locality in Madawaska
St. David Church, Madawaska, 3687
St. Dominic's Parish, Portland, 4403-4404
St. Francis, Me., 4656
St. Francis, Me. Bicentennial Committee, 4656
St. Francis of Assisi Church, Belfast, 2263, 2270
St. Gabriel's Parish, Winterport, 5232
St. George, Me., 4657-4662, 5003
St. George, former name of Cushing
St. George Greek Orthodox Church, Bangor, 2060
St. George Lowertown, former name of Thomaston
St. Georges Chapter, Freemasons, Liberty, 3580
St. George's Church, Long Cove, 4661
St. George's Church, Sanford, 4682
St. George's River, 1663
St. Hyacinth Parish, Westbrook, 5155
St. James Church, Old Town, 3979
St. John, Frederic, 1432, 1934, 2022, 2238, 2900, 2949, 3227-3228, 3873, 3908
St. John Plantation, 4663
St. John River, 1439, 1464
St. John the Baptist Parish, Brunswick, 2494
St. John Township, 4664
St. John's Catholic Church, Bangor, 171, 2061
St. John's Church, Bangor, 2145, 2151
St. John's Church, Old Orchard Beach, 3969

St. John's Parish, Presque Isle, 4550
St. Joseph Parish, Biddeford, see Paroisse St. Joseph, Biddeford
St. Joseph's Academy, Portland, 4453
St. Joseph's Church, Portland, 4360
St. Lawrence Congregational Church, Portland, 4353
St. Luce Parish, Frenchville, 3115
St. Luce Station, locality in Frenchville
St. Luke's Church, Baileyville, 2039
St. Luke's Church, see Cathedral Church of Saint Luke, Portland
St. Margaret's Church, Old Orchard Beach, Me., 3978
St. Mark's Church, Augusta, 2032
St. Mark's Church, Waterville, 5066
St. Martin of Tours Church, Millinocket, 3741
St. Mary's-by-the-Sea Church, Northeast Harbor, 3796
St. Mary's Catholic Church, Bangor, 2062-2063
St. Mary's Church, Augusta, 1978
St. Matthew's Church, Hallowell, 3254, 3265
St. Matthew's Church, Lisbon, 3606
St. Michael's Church, Auburn, 1962
St. Paul's Church, Brunswick, 2524-2525, 2548
St. Paul's Church, Fort Fairfield, 3080
St. Paul's Church, Portland, 4313, 4454
St. Peter's Church, East Deering, 4476
St. Peter's Parish, Rockland, 4603
St. Philip's by the Sea Church, Fortunes Rocks, 2307
St. Philip's Parish, Wiscasset, 5254
Saint Sauveur (colony), 1556, 1565, 1606, 1609, 1614
St. Saviour's Church, Bar Harbor, 2185
St. Stephen, New Brunswick, 2624
St. Stephen's Church, Portland, 4216, 4405-4406, 4454
St. Thomas' Church, Camden, 2643, 2648
St. Thomas' Church, Winn, 5213, 5215
Sale, Thomas D., 1525
Salem Township, 4665
Salisbury Cove, locality in Bar Harbor
Salmon Brook, former name of Washburn
Salmon Falls, locality in Buxton
Saltonstall, Richard, 1074
Salvation Army, Houlton, 3352
Samoset Hotel, Rockland, 4599
Sampson, Howard L., 3309
Samuels, Harriet Brockman, 1908
Sanborn, Emily Frances, 2910
Sanborn, Evelyn, 2847
Sanborn, Fred W., 1643, 1720
Sanborn, Lauren M., 3156
Sanborn, V. C., 1075
Sanborn Corner, locality in Palmyra
Sanborntown, former name of Cornville
Sand Hill, Me., 5219
Sand Hill Corner, locality in Somerville
Sandbar Tract, 4666
Sanders (D. T.) & Son, Greenville, 3234
Sanders family, 4862
Sanderson Corners, locality in Fayette
Sandford, William, 2152
Sands, Donald B., 1076
Sandwich Academy Grant, 4667
Sandy Bay, former name of Moose River
Sandy Bay Township, 4668
Sandy Beach, locality in Freeport

Sandy Beach, locality in Glenburn
Sandy Creek, locality in Bridgton
Sandy Point, former name of Prospect
Sandy Point, locality in Stockton Springs
Sandy River, 23, 1419
Sandy River, former name of Strong
Sandy River, locality in Norridgewock
Sandy River and Rangeley Lakes Railroad, 1537, 1539-1543, 1551-1552
Sandy River Lower Township, former name of Farmington
Sandy River Plantation, 4669
Sandy River Upper Township, former name of Avon
Sane, Perc, pseud., see Brown, Allen D.
Sanford, Lewis W., 2023
Sanford, Me., 4670-4692
Sanford, Everts & Co., 1433
Sanford Historical Committee, 4686
Sanford Mills, 4673, 4675, 4677, 4680, 4692
Sanger, David, 1077-1078
Sanger, Joseph, 1995
Sanger, Phoebe, 1995
Sangerville, Me., 1782, 4693-4695
Sapling, Township, 4696
Saponac, locality in Grand Falls Plantation
Sarah Orne Jewett House, South Berwick, 4788, 4793
Sargent, Charles F., 2608
Sargent, Paul, 1079
Sargent, Paul Dudley, 4862
Sargent, Ruth, 4455
Sargent (W. G.) Company, Sedgwick, 4739
Sargent, William, 4553
Sargent, William Mitchell, 1080-1081, 1913, 3934, 4456, 5341-5342
Sargent, Winthrop, 4862
Sargent family, 4862
Sargents Point, locality in Winter Harbor
Sargentville, Me., 4738-4740, 4745
Sarsfield, former name of Fort Fairfield
Sasanoa River, 1802
Savage, Albert Russell, 1082-1083
Savage, Richard A., 1084, 1604, 2189-2190
Sawmills, 275
Sawpit Corner, locality in Appleton
Sawtelle, William Otis, 1085, 1605-1611
Sawyer, Alden H., 1086
Sawyer, Edith A., 1706
Sawyer, Franklin, 3734
Sawyer, Nathaniel Knight, 1612
Sawyer, Nina G., 3363
Sawyer, Otis, 1509
Sawyer, Philip, 3735
Sawyer, Ralph S., 3400
Sawyer, Rufus Morrill, 5343
Sawyer, William H., 3571-3572
Sawyers Island, locality in Boothbay
Saylor, John P., 1869
Sayward, Dorothy Steward, 2024
Sayward-Barrell House, York Harbor, 5348
Saywards Corner, locality in Wells
Scamman, James, 1894
Scamman, Stephen, 4810A
Scammon, E. Parker, 1087-1089
Scammon, Jonathan Young, 1090
Scarborough, Me., 1265, 4697-4716
Scarborough Public Library. Friends, 4710

Scates, John Clark, 4803
Scates, Eva Winnifred, 3083
Schauffler, Robert Haven, 1613
Schenck High School, East Millinocket, 2915
Schmeckebier, L. F., 1091
Schmidt, Henrietta, 3422
Schneider, Stewart P., 1526
Schoodic Point, 5225
Schoodic Pond, former name of Lake View
Schoogun, former name of Skowhegan
Schools, 457, 751, 1010, 1133, 1176, 1245, 1254,
    1441, 1937, 2072, 2147, 2170, 2211, 2613, 2635,
    2805, 2915, 2924, 2945, 2962, 2980, 3066, 3274,
    3558, 3698, 3826, 4072, 4233, 4409, 4461, 4674,
    4690, 4769, 4789, 4815, 5069, 5196, 5279, 5281,
    5335
Schools, preparatory, see Private schools
Schott, Charles Anthony, 2507
Schouhegan, former name of Skowhegan
Schriver, Edward Oswald, 1092-1098
Schuyler, Montgomery, 2554
Scientific societies, 238, 653, 850, 904, 1005,
    3573, 4431
Scituate, locality in York
Scofield, John, 1099
Scohegan, former name of Skowhegan
Scohigin, former name of Skowhegan
Scontras, Charles Andrew, 1100
Scotch-Irish, 1388
Scotland, locality in Windham
Scotland, locality in York
Scott, G. M., 3332
Scott, Kenneth, 2728
Scottie, former name of Damariscotta
Scowhegan, former name of Skowhegan
Scows, 1938
Scribner, Caleb Warren, 1058, 1060
Scribner, Fred C., Jr., 2848
Scribners Mills, locality in Harrison
Scull, Gideon Delaplaine, 1101
Scunkhegon, former name of Skowhegan
Seabury, Samuel Dorrance, 3935
Seabury, locality in York
Seafaring life, 494, 594, 1017, 1067, 4483, 4522
Seal Cove, locality in Tremont
Seal Harbor, locality in Mount Desert
Seals (numismatics), 539, 906, 1102
Seamen, 702, 4722, 4729
Sears, Donald A., 4457-4458
Sears, George B., 2555
Sears Island, 4724
Searsmont, Me., 4717-4720
Searsport, Me., 4721-4730
Searsport, Me. First Congregational Church, 4726
Searsport, Me. 125th Anniversary Committee, 4727
Searsport Historical Society, 4728
Seaveys Corner, locality in Vienna
Seawall, locality in Southwest Harbor
Seaward Mills, locality in Vassalboro
Sebago, Me., 4731-4732
Sebago and Long Pond Steam Navigation Company, 1505
Sebago Lake, 1511, 4840
Sebago Lake, Songo River, and Bay of Naples Steam-
    boat Company, 1505
Sebasco, locality in Phippsburg
Sebasco Estates, locality in Phippsburg

Sebasticook, former name of Benton
Sebasticook, former name of Pittsfield
Sebasticook and Moosehead Railroad Company, 1814,
    1826
Sebasticook Lodge, Freemasons, Clinton, 2770, 2772-
    2773
Sebec, Me., 4733
Sebec Lake, 1777, 1781
Sebec Lake, locality in Willimantic
Seboeis Plantation, 4734
Seboomook Lake and St. John Railroad, 1815
Seboomook Township, 4735
Seccombe, Joseph, 503
Second Advent Church, Eliot, 2966
Second Baptist Church, Bangor, 2064
Second Christian Church, Kittery, 3469
Second Congregational Church, Biddeford, 2297, 2308
Second Congregational Church, Newcastle, 3882
Second Parish Church, Portland, 4407-4408
Second Parish Church, Saco, 4649
Second Parish of Georgetown, former name of Bath
Second Parish of Kittery, former name of Eliot
Sedensky, Andrew J., 4207
Sedgley, George Burbank, 3095
Sedgwick, Me., 1561, 4736-4745
Sedgwick, Me. Bicentennial Committee, 4741
Sedgwick, Me. First Baptist Church, 4742
Sedgwick Public Library, 4744
See, Anna Phillips, 5267
Seeman, Bernard, 4689
Segal, Henry H., 2053
Seguin (tugboat), 954, 2234
Seguin Island Light, 3179
Seitz, Don Carlos, 3942
Selden, locality in Weston
Seligmann, Herbert J., 1615, 2191, 2786, 3676-3677
Seminaries, theological, see Theology-study and
    teaching
Sennetts Corner, locality in Albion
Serette, David W., 4518
Sergeant, Joseph, 2232
Setterdahl, Lilly, 3866
Settlement at Kenduskeag Stream, former name of
    Bangor
Seven Mile Brook, former name of Embden
Seven Mile Brook, former name of New Portland
Seven Mile Brook Settlement, former name of Anson
Seven Ponds Township, 4746
Sewall, Arthur, & Company, Bath, 2219
Sewall, Dummer, 2763
Sewall, Frank, 2239
Sewall, Joseph, 2240
Sewall, Jotham Bradbury, 2570
Sewall, Oliver, 2764
Sewall, Rufus, 2950
Sewall, Rufus King, 1103-1104, 1707, 1939, 2428,
    2729, 2951, 4100, 4130, 5268-5270
Sewall, Samuel, 5334
Sewall, William Dunning, 2239
Sewall's Bridge, York, 5334
Sewing-equipment and supplies, 4643
Seymour, Richard, 4100
Shackford, John, 2924
Shackford, Samuel, 2924
Shadagee, former name of Phillips
Shady Nook, locality in Newfield

Shafter, Toby, 4607-4608
Shailer, William Hosmer, 1105, 1644, 4459
Shaker Village, locality in New Gloucester
Shakers, 616, 1335, 1509, 1925-1926, 1929-1930,
    3188, 3826-3829, 3831-3836, 3842, 3844-3845,
    3847, 3849-3850, 4296
Shakespeare Club, Bangor, 2146
Shamanism, 1161, 1198
Shapleigh, Charles A., 1909, 2981
Shapleigh, Me., 4747-4748
Shapleigh House, Eliot, 2971
Sharf, Frederic Alan, 1106
Sharp, locality in Monticello
Sharpe, Philip B., 4460
Shaub, Benjamin Martin, 3747
Shaughnessy, Jim, 1107
Shaw, Charles D., 3238-3239
Shaw, David E., 3396A
Shaw, Donald E., 2629
Shaw, Henry I., Jr., 2730
Shaw, Justin Henry, 5344
Shaw, Milton G., 3238
Shaw, Thomas, 287
Shaw family, 3238
Shaw, locality in Washburn
Shawmut, Me., 1421
Shaws Mill, locality in Gorham
Shawtown Township, 4749
Shay, Florence Nicola, 1108
Shea, John Gilmary, 344, 1109
Sheahan, Henry Beston, see Beston, Henry
Sheepscot, 1683
Sheepscot Great Pond, former name of Palermo
Sheepscot River, 2943, 3878, 5246
Sheldon, Edward Stevens, 1110
Shell-heaps, see Kitchen-middens
Shelton, Louise, 4804
Shenton, Edward H., 1111
Shepley, David, 2519
Sheppardsfield, former name of Hebron and Oxford
Sheppardstown, former name of Hebron
Sheppardstown, former name of Palmyra
Sheridan, former name of Caribou
Sheridan, locality in Ashland
Sherman, Andrew Magoun, 3678
Sherman, Arthur J., 5345
Sherman, Sylvia J., 347
Sherman, Me., 4750
Sherman Mills, Me. Washburn Memorial Church, 4750
Sherman Station, locality in Stacyville
Shermans Corner, locality in Belfast
Shermans Corner, locality in Liberty
Shermans Mill, locality in Appleton
Shermans Point, locality in Camden
Sherwood, Mary P., 1113
Sherwood, Philip D., 5234
Sherwood, R. H., 1113
Sherwood Forest, locality in Cape Elizabeth
Shettleworth, Earle G., Jr., 826, 1114, 2153, 3035,
    4461-4464
Shibles Corner, locality in Troy
Shiloh, locality in Durham
Shin Pond, locality in Mount Chase Plantation
Shipbuilding, 57; 275, 540, 923, 1067, 1115, 1190,
    1334, 1522-1523, 1708, 1846, 1858, 1898A, 1902,
    2200, 2207, 2212, 2216, 2219, 2223, 2225, 2231,
    2233, 2235, 2237, 2241, 2243-2244, 2247-2248,

2349, 2515, 2960, 2968, 3286, 3396, 3409, 3423,
    3423, 3458, 3462, 3464, 3471, 3477, 3492, 4206,
    4723, 4812, 4897, 5004, 5295
Shipman, William D., 2556
Shipping, 8, 1192; 954, 1043, 1334, 1523, 2167,
    2198, 2200, 2222, 2225, 2348, 2919, 3006, 3173,
    3639, 3668, 3931, 4320, 4588, 4644, 4659, 4739,
    4865, 4900
Ships (see also specific ships), 8, 57; 104, 714,
    728, 1031, 1115, 1263, 1289, 2210, 2221, 2231,
    2235, 2248, 2361, 2896, 3668, 3921, 4615, 4644,
    4721, 4729, 4865, 4897
Shipwrecks, 209, 661, 3376, 3647, 3753, 4045, 4371,
    4529, 4658, 4971, 5131, 5352
Shirley, Me., 4751
Shoes, see Boots and shoes
Shore Acres, locality in Cape Elizabeth
Shorey, Eula M., 2380
Shorey, Henry A., 1527, 2389
Shorey, locality in Dudley Township
Short, Vincent, 1115
Shriners, see Freemasons
Shurt, Abraham, 617
Shurt's Fort, see Fort William Henry
Shute, Alberta Van Horn, 1116, 2025-2026, 3700
Shuy Corner, locality in Livermore Falls
Siberia, locality in Stacyville
Sibley, John Langdon, 4936
Sibley Corner, locality in Freedom
Sidelinger, Lowell H., 1708
Sidney, Me., 1645
Siebert, Wilbur Henry, 1117
Sieur de Monts, Pierre du Guast, see Monts, Pierre
    du Guast, sieur de
Silber, Mark, 1119
Silhouettes, 953
Silliman, Vincent Brown, 4464A-4465
Sills, Charles Morton, 4466
Sills, Kenneth Charles Morton, 803, 2471, 2558-
    2559, 4325
Silsby, Herbert T., II, 826, 1121, 2036, 3002, 3015
    3016
Silsby, Samuel Schoppee, 1122-1123
Silver, 3277
Silver Ridge Township, 4753
Silvers Mills, locality in Dexter
Silversmithing, 423
Simmons, Franklin, 803
Simmons, Mildred, 1124
Simmons, Joseph Teel, 4662
Simonton Corners, locality in Rockport
Simpson, Mrs. A. L., see Simpson, Corelli C. W.
Simpson, Corelli C. W., 2154
Simpson, Dorothy, 1125
Simpson, Ernest C., 5045
Simpson, John, 5042
Simpson, Suellen, 1126
Simpson Corners, locality in Dixmont
Simpsons Corner, locality in Belfast
Simpsons Hill, locality in York
Sincock, Lora K., 2674
Sincock, W. E., 1127
Singers, 908, 3045, 3056
Sinnett, Charles Nelson, 3300, 3523
Sisterhoods, 213, 4467, 5028, 5098
Sisters of Mercy, 213, 4467

Six Mile Falls, locality in Bangor
Sixth Street Congregational Church, Auburn, 1964
Skillertown, former name of Byron
Skillings, F. H., 4056
Skillings family, 663
Skillings Corner, locality in Turner
Skilling's River, 1579
Skillingston, locality in Bethel
Skinner, Catherine, 3236
Skinner, Joseph O., 5091
Skinner, Ralph Burgess, 1434, 1969
Skinner, locality in Lowelltown Township
Skinner Township, 3377A
Skolfield, Alfred, 2578
Skolfield family, 2515
Skowhegan, Me., 1816, 3532, 4755-4771
Skowhegan Falls, former name of Skowhegan
Skowhegan School of Painting and Sculpture, 4760
Skowhegan Woman's Club, 4756
Slab City, locality in Lincolnville and Searsmont
Slab City, locality in Lovell
Slafter, Edmund Farwell, 1129
Slate, 2454, 2458, 3774-3775
Slattery, Charles Lewis, 2561
Slavery, 32, 104, 220, 624, 803, 1092-1093, 1095,
    1365, 1373
Sleeper, Francis H., 2011
Sleeper, Frank, 4470, 4816
Sloan, Alex, 4805
Sloops, 3116-3117
Small, Abner Randall, 3968
Small, Albion Keith Parris, 1130, 2054
Small, Albion Woodbury, 5092
Small, Carleton Potter, 1131, 4227, 4471-4474
Small, Charles H., 4914
Small, Edwin Sumner, 1132
Small, Herman Wesley, 2844, 4868
Small, Lauriston Ward, 2798
Small, William A., 1133
Small Point, Me., 4114, 4131
Small Point Beach, locality in Phippsburg
Small Point Harbor, 1979
Smallidge, Allan L., 5226
Smart Ridge, locality in Weston
Smarts Corner, locality in Troy
Smillie, Wilson George, 1134
Smith, A. Ernest, 4549
Smith, Alonzo W., 4475
Smith, Arthur Warren, 4742
Smith, Asa P., 3609
Smith, Benjamin Franklin, 560
Smith, Benjamin L., 1135-1136
Smith, C. Wilder, 746
Smith, Carolyn B., 1646
Smith, Charles W., 1137
Smith, David Clayton, 826, 1138-1141, 3173, 3849,
    4024
Smith, David Clifford, 560
Smith, Dorothy, 1142
Smith, Edgar Crosby, 1143-1146, 1435, 1794, 2027,
    2156, 2884
Smith, Edmund Ware, 3240
Smith, Edward Staples Cousens, 3809-3811
Smith, Elizabeth Oakes Prince, 1147
Smith, Elmer J., 4476
Smith, Francis, 560

Smith, Francis Ormond Jonathan, 4477
Smith, Frank K., 1757, 1795
Smith, George Otis, 75, 1148
Smith, George W., 3717-3719
Smith, George Warren, 560
Smith, Mrs. H. A., 5018
Smith, Howard Daniel, 3954
Smith, Isaac A., 4690
Smith, Joseph Coburn, 1149-1152, 4478, 5093-5094
Smith, Joseph Otis, 1828
Smith, Joseph S., 1153
Smith, Justin Harvey, 1154-1155
Smith, Lillian Clayton, 2653
Smith, Lincoln, 1156-1158, 1872, 2562-2567, 4915
Smith, M. E. C., 3679
Smith, Marion Jaques, 1159, 2242
Smith, Marion Whitney, 1160-1161, 3812-3813
Smith, Mary Elizabeth Oakes, 1410A
Smith, Mason Philip, 2630, 4479, 5131
Smith, Nicholas N., 1162-1165, 3985
Smith, Oscar L., 2754
Smith, Oscar S., 1166
Smith, Peter Thatcher, 5208
Smith, Roland, 1167
Smith, Samuel E., 5249
Smith, Seba, 876A, 1410A, 3144
Smith, Thomas, 4367, 4480
Smith, Thomas Laurens, 5206-5208, 5211
Smith, Walter Brown, 1168-1170, 3220
Smith, William A., 5095
Smith, William Bartlett, 3666
Smith, William H., 1171-1172, 4440
Smith family, 560
Smith Crossing, locality in Rumford
Smith Homestead, South Windham, 5208
Smithfield, Me., 4772
Smithfield, former name of Litchfield
Smithtown, former name of Freedom
Smithtown, former name of Litchfield
Smithville, locality in Steuben
Smuggling, 1057, 1173-1174, 1374
Smyrna, Me., 4773
Smyth, Egbert Coffin, 2470, 2568
Smyth, Lawrence T., 1175, 3647
Smyth, Mary Winslow, 77, 366
Snell, Katherine H., 3266
Snider, Rose, 2157
Snow, Benjamin Poor, 1887
Snow, Charles Augustus, 1176
Snow, Dean R., 1177-1182, 4076
Snow, Donald Francis, 2537
Snow, Edward Rowe, 1528, 4045
Snow, Ralph L., 2243
Snow, Roscoe W., 3321
Snow, Samuel, 3907
Snow, Walter A., 2446-2447
Snow Settlement, locality in Bridgewater
Snows, former name of Belgrade
Snows Corner, locality in Hermon
Snows Falls, locality in West Paris
Snowville, former name of Winn
Soap trade, 1930
Social conditions (see also Economic conditions and
    Poverty), 549, 1323, 1487, 1852

Social life and customs, 99-100, 116, 207, 230-231,
234-236, 245, 247, 301, 318-319, 393-394, 464,
466, 477-479, 494, 535-536, 549, 567, 611-612,
655, 712, 718, 731, 889, 905, 953, 993, 1019,
1039, 1050, 1099, 1116, 1119, 1148, 1207, 1236,
1250, 1420, 1466, 1674, 1746, 1910, 1957, 2169,
2172, 2175, 2179, 2184, 2187-2188, 2190-2191,
2288, 2318, 2339, 2342, 2499, 2640, 2704, 2803,
2828, 3067, 3181, 3368, 3372, 3385, 3450, 3600,
3652, 3700, 3791, 3845, 3970, 4150-4151, 4156-
4157, 4203, 4274, 4500, 4768, 4776, 4966, 5047,
5085, 5225
Society of Colonial Wars. Maine, 1183-1184, 3210,
4481, 4711
Society of Friends, see Friends, Society of
Society of Jesus, see Jesuits
Sodom, locality in Yarmouth
Soelle, George, 4993
Soldier Pond, locality in Wallagrass Plantation
Soldiers, 347, 1028, 1794, 2283, 2385, 3519, 3525,
3956, 5024, 5201
Soldiertown Township (Penobscot Co.), 4774
Soldiertown Township (Somerset Co.), 4775
Solon, Me., 4776-4780
Solon, Me. Sesquicentennial History Committee, 4780
Somerby, H. G., 418
Somerset Academy, Athens, 1956
Somerset Academy Grant, former name of Portage Lake
Somerset Chapter, Royal Arch Masons, Skowhegan, 4762
Somerset County, 108, 1025, 1358, 1811-1831
Somerset County Farm Bureau, 1829
Somerset Junction, locality in Misery Gore
Somerset Lodge, Freemasons, Skowhegan, 4755, 4763
Somerset Railroad, 1822-1824
Somerville, Me., 4781
Somes Sound, 1618
Somesville, Me., 1617, 3791
Songo Lock, locality in Naples
Songo River, 1491, 1505, 4840
Sons of the American Revolution. Maine Society,
1188
Soper Mountain Township, 4782
Sorrento, Me., 1588, 4783-4784
Sou heagan, former name of Skowhegan
Sou heavyon, former name of Skowhegan
Soule, Alfred Morton Gilmore, 1189
Soule, Bertha Louise, 5096
Soule, Phelps, 1190
Soule, William H., 1191
Sound, locality in Mount Desert
Sourdnahunk Dam and Improvement Company, 1778-1779
South Berwick, Me., 1322, 1911, 4785-4809
South Berwick, Me. First Parish Church, 4806
South Berwick and Wells Christian Church, 4797
South Berwick Village Baptist Church, 4799
South Bristol, Me., 1706, 4810
South Buxton, Me., 4706
South China, Me., 2767
South Congregational Church, Hallowell, 3264
South Dover, locality in Dover-Foxcroft
South Durham, Me., 2900
South Eliot, Me., 2979
South Eliot Methodist Episcopal Church, 2979
South Fox Island, former name of Vinalhaven
South Freeport, Me., 3112
South Harpswell, Me., 3302, 3307

South Oak Hill, locality in Litchfield
South Paris, Me., 1718, 3532, 4056-4057, 4060,
4063-4064
South Paris, Me. First Congregational Church,
4063
South Parish Congregational Church, Augusta, 1974-
1975, 1993, 2028
South Portland, Me., 1487, 1512, 4810A-4821
South Portland, Me. Church of the Nazarene, 4818
South Portland, Me. 50th Anniversary Committee,
4819
South Portland, Me. First Congregational Church,
4820
South Portland, Me. First Methodist Church, 4821
South Precinct of Pownalborough, former name of
Wiscasset
South Solon Meeting House, 4778
South Thomaston, Me., 1660, 4822-4823
South West Bend, locality in Durham
South Windham, Me., 5208
Southard, Eugenia M., 1193
Southard, Irene H., 3771
Souther, Samuel, 3131
Southgate, William Scott, 4712
Southgate family, 4698
Southport, Me., 1681-1682, 1689-1690, 4811-4821
Southport History Committee, 4828
Southwest Harbor, Me., 1587, 1617, 4831-4834
Sowadabscook, former name of Hampden
Spalding, James Alfred, 1194-1195
Spang Mills, locality in Lyman
Spanogle, John A., Jr., 1196
Sparhawk House, Kittery, 3494
Spaulding, Jerusha Barstow Bryant, 3354
Spaulding, Royal Crafts, 3354
Spaulding Memorial Library, Sebago, 4732
Spaulding Siding, locality in Perham
Spauldingtown, former name of Solon
Spear, Arthur, 4891, 4900, 5004
Spear, Pearl S., 4483
Spears Corner, locality in West Gardiner
Speck, Frank Gouldsmith, 1197-1203
Spencer, Wilbur Daniel, 1204-1206, 2283
Spencer family, 1205
Spencer Bay Township, 4835
Sperry, Willard Learoyd, 1207
Spiker, La Rue, 2192-2193, 2804
Spiller, Nellie D., 5208
Spinney, Mary L., 2984
Spirit leveling, see Leveling
Spite House, Rockport, 4613
Spooners Mills, locality in Dexter
Sporting goods, 2098, 3097-3100 3108, 3855
Sports, 737, 2453, 2485, 2518, 2534, 2555, 2580,
3543-3548, 3568, 3855, 4009, 4541, 5025, 5040,
5043, 5046, 5054, 5064, 5087
Spout Hill, locality in Prospect
Sprague, Charles A., 1647
Sprague, E. C., 4553
Sprague, Edwin, 1672
Sprague, John Francis, 1208-1223, 1759, 1789, 1796-
1797, 2158, 2731, 3378, 3450, 3680, 3779-3780,
3814, 3898, 3990
Sprague, Richard, 1224
Sprague, Richard W., 1467-1468
Sprague City, locality in Newfield

Sprague Corner, locality in Waldoboro
Sprague Mill, locality in Greene
Spragues Mill, locality in Corinna
Sprinchorn, Carl, 1224
Springer, Isaac W., 3610
Springer, John S., 1225
Springer Road, locality in Weston
Springfield, Me., 4836
Springs, 697
Springvale, Me., 4670-4672, 4674, 4678-4679, 4684, 4690
Spruce, Vivian, 3736
Spruce Head, locality in St. George
Spruce Head Island, 4823
Spruce Point, locality in Boothbay Harbor
Spruce Shores, locality in Boothbay
Sprucehead, locality in South Thomaston
Spurr, William Samuel, 4041
Spurrs Corner, locality in Otisfield
Spurwink, former name of Falmouth
Spurwink, locality in Cape Elizabeth
Squahegan, former name of Skowhegan
Squapan, locality in Ashland and Masardis
Squapan Township, 4837
Squaretown Township, 4838
Squhegan, former name of Skowhegan
Squirrel Island, 4826-4827, 4829-4830
Squirrel Island, Me. Library, 4829
Staack, F., 1226
Stackpole, Everett Birney, 1227
Stackpole, Everett Schermerhorn, 1228, 2901, 2985, 3501, 4807, 5238
Stackpole, John, 1228
Stacyville, Me., 4839
Stahl, Jasper Jacob, 4993-4994
Stamp acts, 4701
Standish, Me., 1494, 4840-4843
Standish Lodge, Freemasons, 4841
Standish Old Home Association, 4842
Stanley, George Francis Gilman, 1229-1230
Stanley, Ruel H., 1231
Stansbury, Helen, 4484
Stanton, Don C., 1232
Stanton Bird Club, Lewiston, 3573
Stanwood, Cordelia J., 2340, 2732, 3017
Stanwood, Edward, 1233
Stanwood, I. Augustus, 3167
Staples, Arthur Gray, 390, 1234-1236
Staples, Charles J., 2985
Staples, Franklin, 1237, 4409
Staples, Linnea Stadig, 3867
Staples family, 2986
Staples School, Portland, 4409
Star of the Sea Church, York Beach, 5322, 5346
Starbird, Charles Millard, 1238
Starbird Corner, locality in Bowdoin
Starbirds, locality in Dover-Foxcroft
Starboard, locality in Machiasport
Stark, former name of Starks
Starkey, Glenn Wendell, 1239
Starkey Corners, locality in Littleton
Starks, Me., 1419, 1816, 3362
Starr, John T., 1240
Starrett, Lewis Frederick, 4902
Start, Edwin A., 1241
State houses, see Capitols

State Military and Naval Children's Home. Bath, see Maine. State Military and Naval Children's Home
State Road, locality in Mapleton
State Street Congregational Church, Portland, 4290, 4410-4411, 4447
Statesmen, 128, 500, 948, 1146, 1248, 1601, 1837, 1868, 1870, 2049, 2332
Statues (see also Monuments), 1330, 3426, 4308
Steadman Landing, locality in Dover-Foxcroft
Steam navigation, 20, 56, 324, 487, 521, 595, 657, 728, 1035, 1043, 1071, 1084, 1115, 1491, 1495, 1505, 1526, 1695, 1744, 1777, 1781, 1784, 1787, 2091, 2218, 3296, 4658
Stearns, George W., 3740
Stearns, Joseph B., 2640
Stebbins, locality in Fort Fairfield
Steele, Thomas Sedgwick, 1798
Steele, William, 5138
Steep Falls, locality in Standish
Sterling, Robert Thayer, 1243, 4485
Sterling, former name of Fayette
Sterling, former name of Union
Sterlington, former name of Union
Stern, Theodore, 4075
Stetson, John Glidden, 2484
Stetson, William Wallace, 1244-1245
Stetson, Me., 4845
Stetsontown Township, 4846
Steuben, Me., 1855, 1864, 4847-4848
Stevens, Charles Asbury, 3958
Stevens, Ernest N., 2390
Stevens, James P., Jr., 2349
Stevens, James Stacy, 4025-4027
Stevens, Jane, 2203
Stevens, Jane Perham, 1721, 4121
Stevens, Neil E., 3174
Stevens, Susan MacCulloch, 1246
Stevens, Zachariah Brackett, 136
Stevens Avenue Congregational Church, Portland, 4412
Stevens Corner, locality in Lincolnville
Stevens Corner, locality in Newfield
Stevens Mill, locality in Auburn
Stevens Plains, Me., 3213
Stevenson, Edward Irenaeus, 2733
Stevenson, James B., 4622
Stevensville, locality in Fort Fairfield
Steventown, locality in Litchfield
Stewart, Alice Rose, 48, 826, 1247-1247A, 4028, 4834
Stewart, Arthur W., 5218
Stewart, John C., 1248
Stewart, Katherine Wallace, 4486
Stewart, Phyllis, 4029
Stewart, Ronald E., 3693
Stickney, Daniel, 1469
Stickney, Eliza Ann Gibson, 2450
Stickney Corner, locality in Washington
Stiles, Dan, pseud., see Haig, George Canterbury
Stillwater, Me., 3982
Stillwater, former name of Orono
Stilphen, Asbury Coke, 4143
Stimpson, Mary Stoyell, 1673, 3070, 4903
Stinchfield, John Clark, 3526

Stinchfield, Mary L., 799
Stockbridge, Joseph, 3936
Stockholm, Me., 1456, 4849
Stockton Springs, Me., 4850-4854
Stoddard, J. N., 3151
Stokesbury, James L., 1249
Stolle, John William, 1250
Stone, Arthur P., 3632
Stone, Edwin Martin, 1276
Stone, Eleanor Bailey, 3574-3575
Stone, Fanny, 2942
Stone, Henry J. 4691
Stone, Kenneth G., 5164
Stone, Thomas Treadwell, 1722
Stone cutting, 3747
Stoneham, Me., 4855
Stones Corner, locality in Jay
Stonington, Me., 1553, 1561, 2834-2836, 2840-2843,
    4856-4857
Stores, 2776, 2942, 3234, 3710, 3732, 4739
Stores Corner, locality in Bradford
Storm, Colton, 2734
Storms, Roger C., 1251, 4069
Stoves, 4333
Stow, Me., 4858
Stowe, Harriet Beecher, 2466, 2553
Strand, Mark, 4745
Stratton, Arthur, 4488
Stratton, locality in Eustis
Street, George Edward, 1616
Street railroads, 280-282, 387, 684, 1421, 1445,
    1664, 1657-1658, 1890, 1988, 2111, 2508, 2629,
    4214, 5041, 5107
Streets, see Thoroughfares
Stricklands, locality in Livermore Falls
Strikes and lockouts, 61B
Strong, Me., 1419, 4859
Stronghold, locality in St. Albans
Stroudwater, Me., 1512, 4221, 4231, 4286, 4479
Stroudwater, former name of Westbrook
Stuart, Jessie, 4489
Stuart, Richard Kenneth, 1253
Stuarts Corner, locality in Harrison
Stubbs, Albert Roscoe, 690
Stubbs, Marion Brainerd, 2030
Stuiver, Minze, 1255
Sturgeon Creek, former name of Eliot
Sturges, Florence M., 1709
Sturges, Walter Knight, 3018
Sturtevant, Charlotte H., 3625
Sturtevant, Lawrence M., 2276
Sturtevant, Reginald H., 3072, 3620-3621, 3627
Sturtevant, Walter Henry, 4578, 4582
Sudbury Canada, former name of Bethel
Sugar Hill, locality in Bridgewater
Sugar Town, locality in Moscow
Sugarloaf Township, 4860
Sullivan, J. H., 4729
Sullivan, James, 27, 1221, 1257-1259
Sullivan, Me., 1579, 1588, 4861-4862
Summer Harbor, locality in Winter Harbor
Summer schools, 3549, 4027
Summit, locality in York
Summit Farms, Davidson, 3323
Summit Hill, locality in Harrison
Summit Township, 4863

Sumner, Me., 4864
Sunday River, former name of Newry
Sunday schools, 3661, 4515
Sunkhaze, former name of Milford
Sunkhole, former name of Milford
Sunnebec, former name of Appleton
Sunset, locality in Deer Isle
Sunset Park, locality in South Portland
Sunshine, locality in Deer Isle
Supreme Judicial Court of Maine, 269
Surfside, locality in Old Orchard Beach
Surry, Me., 1578, 4865-4866
Surry Gore, former name of Ellsworth
Sutton, Katharine Augusta, 4650
Sutton Island, locality in Cranberry Isles
Svensen, Sara E., 799
Swan, Frank Herbert, 4490-4491
Swan, former name of Swanville
Swan Island, 4092
Swans Corner, locality in Bethel
Swans Island, Me., 4867-4869
Swans Tract, former name of Swanville
Swansfield, former name of Lyman
Swanson, Evadene Burris, 3868
Swanville, Me., 4870
Swasey, Eben, 4190
Swearingen, David, 5212
Sweat House, see McLellan-Sweat House, Portland
Sweden, Me., 4871
Sweden, locality in New Sweden
Swedenborgianism, see New Jerusalem Church
Swedes, 668, 1216, 1448, 1456, 3857-3871
Sweet, Philip W. K., 3811
Sweetser, Mary Chisholm, 3502
Sweetser, Mary E., 2811
Sweetser, Moses Foster, 1260
Sweetser, Phyllis Sturdivant, 2812
Swett, Clyde W., 1261
Swett, Sophia Miriam, 1262
Swift, Josiah Spooner, 3697
Switzer, David C., 1263
Sylvester, Herbert Milton, 1264-1265, 1529-1530,
    2429, 5347
Sylvester, Torrey A., 2735
Sylvester, former name of Turner
Sylvester Canada, former name of Turner
Sylvestertown, former name of Turner
Symmes, Thomas, 3128, 3135, 3145
Symonds, Joseph W., 4389
Synagogues, 2053, 4273

T3 Indian Purchase, 4872
T4 Indian Purchase, 4873
Taber, Daniel, 4263
Taber, James R., 4942
Taber, John and Son, Portland, 4263
Tacoma, locality in Monmouth
Taconic, former name of Waterville
Taft, Lewis A., 2430
Taft's Point, 3216
Takach, Steve, 2934
Talbot, Archie Lee, 1266
Talbot, George Foster, 1703, 2850, 2909, 3681-3682,
    4100
Talbot, Louisa, 3112
Talbot, Micah Jones, 2909

Talbot, Nina V. A., 801
Talcott, Daniel Smith, 2089
Talleyrand-Perigord, Charles Maurice de, 1607
Tallman, Julie I., 1267
Tallman, Richard S., 3516
Tallman, Ronald D., 1267
Tallwood, locality in Winthrop
Talmadge, Me., 4874
Tamar fruit compound, 3827
Tanner, Virginia, 2245
Tannery Loop, locality in Amherst
Tapley, Abbie L., 2443
Tapley family, 2444
Tarr, Andrew, 4926
Tarratine, locality in Taunton & Raynham Academy Grant
Tarratine Indians, 453
Tate, George, 4479
Tate House, Portland, 4215, 4231, 4286, 4479
Tatnic, locality in South Berwick and Wells
Tatterson, Estelle Morris, 2309
Taunton Academy Grant, former name of Embden
Taunton & Raynham Academy Grant, 4875
Taverns, see Hotels, taverns, etc.
Taxation, 129, 588, 1011, 1026
Taylor, Clyde C., 1268
Taylor, George H., 755
Taylor, Helen V., 1910
Taylor, Linda Maule, 3587
Taylor, Pearl, 4628
Taylor, Robert L., 3593
Taylor, Stanley R., 4549
Taylor Brothers Lumber Company, 591
Taylor City, locality in Parsonsfield
Taylortown, former name of Union
Teacher education, see Teachers, training of
Teachers, 1010, 2044, 2478, 3069, 3698
Teachers' associations, 583, 823, 1069
Teachers, training of, 2703, 3061, 3065, 3089,
    3197, 3204, 3683, 4542
Tebbetts, Leon Harold, 1269
Technical education, 1053, 3153, 3174, 3260, 4642
Teconnet, former name of Waterville
Teeters, Negley K., 4904
Teg, William, 2451, 3329, 4162
Telephone, 317, 2128, 5282
Television broadcasting, 789
Telos Cut, 1792
Temperance (see also Prohibition), 37, 202, 2164,
    2962, 3465, 4183
Temple, Robert, 1807A
Temple, Me., 1419
Temple Beth El, Portland, 4273
Temple Heights, locality in Northport
Temple Hill, locality in Harrison
Ten Thousand Acre Tract, locality in Chase Stream
    Township
Tenants Harbor, locality in St. George
Tenney, Helen, 1674
Tennis, 3548, 3855
Tewksbury, John Leslie, 2649
Textile industry, 556, 2311, 3226, 3551, 4637, 4673
    4675, 4677, 4680, 4692, 5052, 5164
Thanksgiving Day, 4203
Thatcher, George, 458
Thaxter, Celia, 3502
Thayer, Addison Sanford, 2471

Thayer, Henry Otis, 805, 1271-1275, 1710, 1809,
    2246, 2431-2432, 3183, 3592, 4131-4133, 4583,
    5272-5273
Thayer, Mildred N., 1761-1762
Thayer, Simeon, 1276
Thayer Hosptial, Waterville, 5042
Theater, 2327, 2915, 3694, 3696, 4208, 4334, 4455,
    4517, 5133, 5138
Theater, college, see College Theater
Theaters, 1546, 4199, 5138
Theological education, see Theology-study and teach-
    ing
Theology-study and teaching, 2044, 2079, 2092,
    2096, 2136-2138, 2140, 2162, 2597, 4074
Therriault, Patrick, 3688
Thibadeau, William Jarvis, 3355
Thielen, Benedict, 1277
Third Congregational Church, Eliot, 2981
Thoman, Richard S., 4492
Thomas, Elmer Erwin, 1278
Thomas, Howard,E., 3576
Thomas, Miriam Stover, 1279-1280, 3301-3302
Thomas, William Widgery (b. 1839), 3860, 3864, 3869
Thomas, William Widgery (1873-1946), 4493
Thomas Rod Company, Bangor, 2098
Thomas Ruggles House, Columbia Falls, 2782-2786
Thomaston, Me., 1659-1660, 1663, 1666, 1753, 2082,
    4589, 4877-4907
Thomaston Congregational Church, 4905
Thomaston Historical Society, 4906
Thompson, Benjamin, 799
Thompson (C. A.) Company, New Sharon, 3855
Thompson, Deborah, 1281
Thompson, Ernest, 2433
Thompson, Florence Whittlesey, 4494
Thompson, Garrett W., 1282, 4995
Thompson, John Wallace, 1283
Thompson, Margaret Jefferds, 3423
Thompson, Matthew R., 1911
Thompson, Nathaniel Lord, 3423
Thompson, Ralph E., 1911
Thompson, Winfield Martin, 1799, 2350, 4495
Thompson, Zenas, 4361
Thompson, locality in Palmyra
Thompson Corner, locality in Hartland
Thompson Corners, locality in Prentiss Plantation
Thompson Free Library, Dover-Foxcroft, 2873
Thompsonborough, former name of Lisbon
Thoreau, Henry David, 913, 956, 1179, 1800, 3808
Thorndike, Me., 4908-4909
Thorndike Township, 4910
Thornes Corner, locality in Lewiston
Thornton, John Wingate, 1259, 2434, 4134, 4713-4714
Thornton, Nellie C., 1617
Thornton, Mrs. Seth S., see Thornton, Nellie C.
Thornton Academy, Biddeford, 2299
Thornton Heights, locality in South Portland
Thoroughfares, 364, 488, 621, 701, 705, 772, 829,
    1079, 1766, 1981, 2132, 2724-2725, 2962, 2978,
    4536, 4538, 5303
Thurlow, Clinton F., 1284-1285, 1648, 2768
Thurston, Brown, 1286, 1531
Thurston, David, 3611, 5239
Thurston, Florence G., 3113
Thurston, Kate E. Barker, 4074
Thurston, Norman W., 4496

Thurston, Stephen, 2325, 4730
Thurstons Corner, locality in Freedom
Thwing, Annie Haven, 3303
Thwing, Edward Payson, 4497
Tibbetts, R. G., 2461-2462
Tibbetts, Mrs. Raymond R., 2291
Tibbettstown, locality in Columbia Falls
Ticonic, former name of Waterville
Ticonic, former name of Winslow
Ticonic National Bank, Waterville, 5102
Tidd, Marshall M., 1723
Tillson, George W. 2569
Tilton, Gilbert Wight, 1119
Tilton Corner, locality in Pittsfield
Tim Pond Township, 4911
Timber Point, locality in Biddeford
Tingley, J. Fred, 3740
Tinware, 136, 3213
Titcomb, Benjamin, 4240, 4450
Titcomb, Edward S., 1912
Titcomb, Joseph, 2570
Titcombtown, former name of Anson
Titcombtown, former name of Embden
Titus, Anson, 1287
Titus, Edward Kirk, 1288
Titus Corner, locality in Garland
Tobey, Ray, 3029
Tobie, Walter E., 2571, 4498
Tod, Giles M. S., 1289
Todd, Alan, 1290
Todd, Alden, 4499
Todd, Charles, 3304
Todd, Helen Hathorne, 4961
Todd, John M., 4500
Todd, Margaret, 3304
Todd, William, 1873
Todd family, 1873
Todds Corner, locality in Ripley
Togus, 1624, 1629, 1648, 2758-2759
Tolan, former name of Falmouth
Tomah, locality in Forest Township
Tomhegan Township, 4912
Toney, locality in Guilford
Tools, 1060, 1151, 3966
Toothaker, Eleanor A., 2871
Toothaker, Llewellyn P., 2871
Topsfield, Me., 4913
Topsham, Me., 1315, 2573, 4914-4917
Torrey, J., 5300
Tory Hill, locality in Buxton
Totman, Henrietta T., 801
Tourism, 1420
Tourmaline, 4055
Towle, Bernard L., 4074
Towle Academy, Winthrop, 5240
Towles Tavern, Kennebunk, 3418
Town and College Club, Brunswick, 2541
Town halls (see also City halls), 4021, 5327
Town Hill, Me., 2176
Town House, Eliot, 2981
Town House, locality in Albany Township
Town House, locality in Freedom
Town House Corner, locality in Swanville
Town meetings, see Local government
Town registers, 1311
Town Woods, locality in Wells

Townhouse Corner, locality in Lincolnville
Townhouse Corners, locality in Kennebunkport
Townsend, Me., 4828
Townsend, former name of Boothbay
Townshend, former name of Boothbay
Townshend, former name of Southport
Township C, 4918
Township D, 4919
Township E, 4920
Township 6, 4921
Townsley family, 1855
Toynbee, Arnold J., 1050
Towrook, former name of Lebanon
Towwoh, former name of Lebanon
Track-athletics, 2485, 2580, 3547
Tracy Corners, locality in Addison
Trade unions, see Unions
Trading posts, 708, 2005, 2702, 3732
Trafton, Burton W. F., Jr., 4808-4809
Trafton, John B., 3085
Trails, 112
Train wrecks, 2993, 3772
Trainors Corner, locality in Whitefield
Trani, Eugene P., 3503
Tranquil Lodge, Freemasons, Auburn, 1966
Trans Alpine, Me., 3595
Transportation, 272, 670, 727, 819, 1107, 1336,
  1475, 3377
Trap Corner, locality in West Paris
Trappan, Grace, 4401
Trask, Helen Brown, 986
Trask, William Blake, 1291
Travels, see Voyages and travels
Travis, Harold G., 1292
Treacy, Gerald C., 3019
Treadwell, former name of Carrabassett Valley
Treasurer (ship), 1580
Treasure-trove, 1513
Treat, Harry M., 3772
Treaties, 4, 58, 283, 432-433, 435, 461, 624-625,
  716, 880, 1214, 1340, 1346, 1854, 3503
Treats Tract, former name of Enfield
Treaty of Portsmouth, see Portsmouth, Treaty of
  (1905)
Treaty of Washington (1842), see Webster-Ashburton
  Treaty
Trees, 409, 3572
Trefethen, Jessie B., 4501-4502
Trefethen family, 4502
Trefethen, locality in Portland
Trelawny, Robert, 89
Tremblay, Wilfrid, 4503
Tremont, Me., 1587, 4922-4926
Tremont Lodge, Freemasons, 4924-4926
Trenton, Me., 1569, 1579, 4927
Trescott, Lemuel, 2924
Trescott Township, 4928
Trevett, locality in Boothbay
Trial (ship), 661
Trinity Church, Saco, 4651
Trinity Episcopal Church, Portland, 4257
Trinity Lodge, Freemasons, Presque Isle, 4549
Trinity Parish, Lewiston, 3528, 3557
Trinity Parish, Saco, 4632
Trinity Parish, Woodfords, 4469
Tripp, Alta E., 3899

Tripp, John, 3316
Tripp, O. H., 4609
Tripp, William M., 5139
Tripp Lake, locality in Poland
Trolleys, see Street railroads
Trott, Raymond H., 2247
Trout Brook Township, 4929
Troutdale, locality in The Forks Plantation
Trowbridge, Mason, Jr., 2159
Troy, Me., 4930
Truax, C. V., 1618
True, Charles Henry, 1354
True, Emma J., 3241
True, Mrs. Hilton W., 2031
True, Latham, 4504
True, Mabel L., 2196
True, Nathaniel Tuckerman, 1293-1296, 2286, 3937,
    4536-4538
Trueman, Stuart, 1297
Trues Town, former name of Shirley
Tryon, Sylvia, 2665
Tubby, Josiah T., 4064
Tucker, Richard H., 5255
Tucker Castle, Wiscasset, 5255
Tuell Town, locality in West Paris
Tunk Lake, locality in Sullivan
Tunley, Roul, 1298
Tupper, James, 2896
Turbatts Creek, locality in Kennebunkport
Tureen, Thomas N., 947
Turner, Augustus R., 3577
Turner, Clair Elsmere, 1561
Turner, Daniel, 2915
Turner, Hollis, 4096
Turner, Percie Hopkins, 4031-4032
Turner, Walter Frye, 2248
Turner, Me., 405, 549, 4931-4935
Turners Corner, locality in Bremen
Turners Corner, locality in Freedom
Turnpikes, see Thoroughfares
Tuscan Lodge, Freemasons, Columbia, 2778
Tweedie, Gladys Sylvester, 3705
Twelve Corners, locality in Fayette
Twelve Corners, locality in Madison
Twentyfivemile Pond, former name of Burnham
Twentyfivemile Pond, former name of Unity
Twin Allen Four Corners, locality in Stetson
Twin Bridges, locality in Harrison
Twin Brook, locality in Garland
Twinem, Joseph C., 760
Twitchell Corner, locality in Burnham
Two Trails, locality in Standish
Tyler, Samuel, 2449
Tyler Corner, locality in Oakland
Tylers Corner, locality in Windsor
Tyngtown, former name of Wilton
Type and type founding, 4167
Tyson, Emily D., 4795
Tyzzer, E. E., 1300

Underwood, Joseph H., 3073
Unemployment, 1046
Union, Me., 4935-4940
Union Church, East Dixmont, 2869
Union Church, Northeast Harbor, 3795
Union Conference (Congregationalists), 975

Union Congregational Church, Isle Au Haut, 3366
Union Falls, locality in Dayton
Union Mutual Life Insurance Company, Portland,
    4292, 4301
Union River, 1578
Union River, former name of Ellsworth
Union River Bay, 4865
Union Trust Company, Ellsworth, Me., 3020
Union Weekly Times, 4940
Unions, 1100
Unionville, locality in Steuben
Unitarian Church, Augusta, 2017
Unitarian Society, Castine, 2694
Unitarian Society of the Town of Portland, 4464A
Unitarianism, 1131, 4465
United Fellowship, 1034
United Service Organization, Presque Isle, 4544
U. S. Commission on Civil Rights. Maine Advisory
    Committee, 1301
U. S. District Court. Maine, 1302
U. S. Engineer Department. Board of Engineers for
    Rivers and Harbors, 4505
U. S. Infantry, 18th Continental Regiment, 1501
U. S. Infantry, 26th Regiment, Provincial Army,
    1499
U. S. Infantry, 31st Regiment of Foot, 1502
U. S. Library of Congress, 1303
U. S. Navy Yard, Portsmouth, see Portsmouth Naval
    Shipyard, Kittery
Unity, former name of New Sharon
Unity, Me., 4941-4945
Unity, Me. Bicentennial Booklet Committee, 4943
Unity Club, Augusta, 2031
Unity Sesquicentennial Society, 4944
Unity Township, 4946
Universalism, 970, 1287, 1772
Universalist Church, Dexter, 2861
Universalist Church, Scarborough, 4706
Universalist Society and Church, Norway and Paris,
    1727
Universalists, 4650
Universities and colleges, 66, 201, 519, 781, 816,
    1068, 1148, 2044, 2079-2080, 2092, 2096, 2136-
    2138, 2140, 2162, 2463, 2469-2489, 2499-2500,
    2503, 2506, 2509-2513, 2516-2519, 2523-2524,
    2526, 2530-2531, 2533-2537, 2542-2547, 2549,
    2552, 2554-2561, 2568-2571, 2577, 2579-2582,
    2699, 2703, 3061, 3065, 3069, 3089, 3197, 3204,
    3349-3351, 3529-3531, 3536, 3538-3539, 3541,
    3543-3549, 3563, 3565-3568, 3570-3572, 3574-
    3576, 3683, 3993, 3995-4000, 4002-4020, 4023-
    4025, 4027-4028, 4030, 4033-4034, 4074, 4218,
    4254, 4359, 4510, 4516, 4542, 4678, 5025-5027,
    5029-5032, 5035-5040, 5043-5044, 5046-5049,
    5054, 5058-5060, 5064-5065, 5067-5068, 5070,
    5072-5076, 5078-5081, 5083-5085, 5087-5088,
    5090, 5092-5094, 5097, 5112, 5115-5117
University Heights, locality in Orono
University of Maine at Farmington, 3061, 3065, 3069
University of Maine at Fort Kent, 3089
University of Maine at Machias, 3683
University of Maine at Orono, 66, 781, 785, 3991,
    3993, 3995-4000, 4002-4020, 4023-4025, 4027-4028,
    4030, 4032-4034
University of Maine at Portland-Gorham, 463, 3197,
    3204, 4254, 4510

University of Maine at Presque Isle, 4542
University Press, Orono, 4033
Upham, Frank Kidder, 2736
Upham, Samuel, 1765
Upham family, 2736
Upjohn, Samuel, 2032
Upper Cupsuptic Township, 4947
Upper Dam, locality in Richardsontown Township
Upper Drew, locality in Drew Plantation
Upper Enchanted Township, 4948
Upper Frenchville, Me., 3115
Upper Gloucester, locality in New Gloucester
Upper Molunkus Township, 4949
Upper Parish of Kittery, former name of Eliot
Upper Ridge, locality in Bridgton
Upper Street, locality in Turner
Uppertown, former name of Avon
Upton, Joshua Foy, 1810
Upton, Me., 4950
Urban renewal, 4402
Ursulines, 5028, 5098
Usher, Helen, 4843

Valleau, Steven L., 1470
Van Bokkelen, D'Arcy, 5182
Van Buren, Me., 4951-4953
Van Buren, Me. Paroisse St. Bruno, 4953
Van Burkells Township, former name of Waltham
Van Burketts Township, former name of Franklin
Van Burketts Township, former name of Waltham
Van Rensselaer, Mrs. J. K., 4715
Van Trump, James D., 4506
Vanceboro, Me., 4954
Varney, George Jones, 1304-1306
Varney, Lloyd H., 3900
Varney, Marianne, 2935
Varney Crossing, locality in North Berwick
Vassalboro, Me., 1645, 4955-4960
Vassalboro Free Public Library, 4955
Vaughan, Benjamin, 3255
Vaughan, Dorothy M., 3504, 5348
Vaughan, William Warren, 3267, 3797
Vaughan, Zephaniah Morton, 3872
Vaughan family, 3267
Vaughan House, Hallowell, 3255
Vaughanstown, former name of Harmony
Vaughantown, former name of Harmony
Vaughn, Mary Searles, 4097
Vaughn's Pond, 1678
Veazie, Carl E., 1307
Veazie, Me., 4961
Veazie Gore, 4962
Verona, Me., 4963
Verrill, Alpheus Hyatt, 1308
Verrill, Harry Mighels, 4507
Verrill, Robinson, 4507
Verrill, Dana, Walker, Philbrick, and Whitehouse,
   Portland, 4507
Vesey, Maxwell, 2936
Veterans of Foreign Wars of the United States.
   Maine. Norman N. Dow Post, Bangor, 2160
Vetromile, Eugene, 1309-1310
Viana, former name of Vienna
Vickery, James Berry, III, 1311-1312, 2161, 2375,
   4945
Vickerys Corner, locality in Belmont

Veterans' organizations, 481, 876, 5024
Victoria Mansion, Portland, 4200, 4277, 4343, 4484
Vienna, Me., 4964
Vigneras, Louis-André, 1314
Vikings, see Northmen
Villa Vaughn, locality in Orono
Vinal, Albra Josephine, 4972
Vinal Haven (steamer), 728
Vinalhaven, Me., 1656, 4965-4973
Vinalhaven, Me. Centennial Committee, 4972
Vincent, Pal, 4159
Vines, Richard, 4100
Vinton, John Adams, 1315, 2435
Violette, Augusta Genevieve, 3736
Violette, Lawrence A., 1471
Violette, Maurice, 1987
Violette, locality in Van Buren
Violette Settlement, locality in Fort Kent
Virgin, Harry R., 4508
Virgin, William Wirt, 1316
Virginia, locality in Rumford
Vital records, 303
Vocational rehabilitation, 753
Vogel, C. William, 3119
Vogt, Peter S., 4610
Von Krumreig, Edward Ludwig, 4748
Vondel, Joseph Leman, 2436, 4135
Vose, Clement E., 1317
Vose, Josephine, 3455
Vose, Peter Ebenezer, 2850, 2953
Vose, Prescott H., 3815
Vose, Z. Pope, 1675
Voyages and travels, 1400
Vroom, James, 1319, 1874

Wabenaki Indians, see Abnaki Indians
Wade, Abner Turner, 3247
Wade, Me., 4974
Wadsworth, Herbert E., 5236
Wadsworth, Llewellyn Andrew, 3328, 3330
Wadsworth, Peleg, 3326, 4175
Wadsworth, R. C., 1320
Wadsworth & Woodman, Winthrop, 5236
Wadsworth Hall, Hiram, 168, 3326
Wadsworth-Longfellow House, Portland, 168, 4175,
   4260, 4295, 4437-4438, 4509
Wages, 129
Wait, Thomas Baker, 4328, 4450
Waite, David S., 3540
Waite, Me., 4975
Wakefield, Amy, 5328
Waldo, Samuel, 497, 4982
Waldo, Me., 4976
Waldo County, 30, 107, 1832-1838
Waldoboro, Me., 1216, 1282, 1706, 4589, 4977-4999,
   5003
Waldoboro High School, 4998
Waldoboro Meeting House, 1706
Waldoboro Village Methodist Church, 4981
Waldron, C. W., 1321
Waldron, Holman Douglas, 1532
Wales, Me., 3769
Walker, Albert Ward, 4057
Walker, Andrew, 3424
Walker, Charles Howard, 1322
Walker, David Bradstreet, 1323-1324

Walker, Ernest George, 3024
Walker, Elinor Stevens, 1325
Walker, George R., 2159
Walker, Harold S., 1676, 1763
Walker, Howell, 1472
Walker, John, 304
Walker, John E., 4082
Walker, Raymond J., 1473
Walker, Willard, 1326-1327
Walker Corner, locality in Thorndike
Walkers Mill, locality in Bethel
Wall, Arthur W., 4615-4616
Wallace, Charlotte, 3042
Wallace, Donald, 3042
Wallace, John, see Davis, Will R.
Wallace, Joseph, 3732
Wallagrass Plantation, 5001
Wallston, locality in St. George
Walnut Hill, locality in North Yarmouth
Walpole, Me., 1706
Walpole, former name of Nobleboro
Walpole Meeting House, 1706
Walsh, Louis Sebastian, 1328, 2270, 2737
Waltham, Me., 5002
Walton, George W., 5121
Walton, Octavia, see Goodbar, Octavia Walton
Waltons Mills, locality in Cornville
Walworth, Arthur Clarence, 5012
Walz, William Emmanuel, 4510
War of 1812, 150, 693, 799, 842, 1121, 1173-1174,
    1229, 1341, 1680, 1691, 1703, 1705, 1710, 2397,
    2647, 2686, 2695, 2712, 2924, 2926, 2933, 2936,
    3273, 4512, 5238
Warburton, Sybil, 5349
Ward, C. Raymond, 4549
Ward, Elmer L., 4692
Ward, Ernest E., 3311
Ward, Julius Hammond, 1801
Ward, Kent, 1764
Ward Hill, locality in Madison
Ward Hill, locality in Troy
Wards Cove, locality in Standish
Wardtown, locality in Freeport
Wardwell, Hosea B., 4086-4089
Ware, Ashur, 1302
Ware, Joseph, 1329
Warehouses, 5350
Warner, Maurice J., 1330
Warren, Henry Pelt, 5023
Warren, John C., 4511-4512, 4716
Warren, Juliet Marion Stanley, 1331
Warren, (S. D.) Co., Westbrook, 5166
Warren, Samuel, 5023
Warren, William, 5023
Warren, Me., 1659, 1666, 4589, 5003-5010
Warren Academy Grant, former name of Katahdin Iron
    Works
Warren Congregational Church, Cumberland Mills,
    5154, 5158, 5165
Warren Depot, 5006
Warren Historical Society, 5010
Warren Lodge, Freemasons, East Machias, 2907-2908
Warrenstown, former name of Hartland
Warsaw, former name of Pittsfield
Warships, 2186
Washburn, Algernon Sidney, 3621, 3623
Washburn, Cadwallader Colden, 1414, 3618, 3621,
    3623

Washburn, Charles, 3621, 3623
Washburn, Elihu Benjamin, see Washburne, Elihu
    Benjamin
Washburn, Emory, 4100
Washburn, Fremont E., 1332
Washburn, Israel (1784-1826), 3621, 3623
Washburn, Israel (1813-1883), 1333, 1414, 3618,
    3621-3623, 4218
Washburn, Jennie M., 3445
Washburn, Lilian, 3623
Washburn, Martha, 3621
Washburn, Monty, see Washburn, Fremont E.
Washburn, Reuel, 3624
Washburn, Samuel, 3621, 3623
Washburn, W. H. H., 2654
Washburn, William D., 1414, 3621, 3623
Washburn family, 3621, 3623
Washburn, Me., 5011
Washburn Memorial Church, Sherman Mills, 4750
Washburne, Elihu Benjamin, 1414, 3618, 3621, 3623
Washington, George, 3505
Washington, Me., 5012-5013
Washington, Me. Historical Committee, 5013
Washington, former name of Belgrade
Washington, former name of Brooks
Washington, former name of Limerick
Washington, former name of Mount Vernon
Washington, former name of Newfield
Washington, Treaty of (1842), see Webster-Ashburton
    Treaty
Washington Academy, East Machias, 2909-2910
Washington Academy Grant, former name of Cherryfield
Washington Academy Grant, former name of Cutler
Washington County, 108, 686, 1251, 1839-1876
Washington County Conference of Congregational
    Churches, 1860
Washington Junction, locality in Hancock
Washington Lodge, Freemasons, Lubec, 3645
Washington State Teachers College, see University of
    Maine at Machias
Washington Township, 5014
Wassataquoik, 1768
Wasson, George Savary, 1334, 3460A, 4611
Wasson, Mildred, 3021
Wasson, Samuel, 1619
Water resources development, 294
Water supply, 75-76, 172, 762, 1234, 1396, 2065,
    2118, 3159, 4337, 4433-4434
Waterboro, Me., 5015-5018
Waterborough, former name of Waterboro
Waterford, Me., 5019-5023
Waterman, Charles Elmer, 1335-1336, 1436, 1724,
    3723, 4050, 4065, 4152
Waterman, John Anderson, 3194
Watermans Beach, locality in South Thomaston
Waters, Henry C., 5177
Waterville, Me., 1421, 1639, 3532, 5024-5117
Waterville, Me. First Baptist Church, 5099-5101
Waterville Academy, see Coburn Classical Institute,
    Waterville
Waterville Circulating Library, 5089
Waterville Classical Institute, see Coburn Classical
    Institute, Waterville
Waterville Clinical Society, 5061
Waterville College, see Colby College
Waterville Fairfield and Oakland Railway, 5041

Waterville Lodge, Elks, 5045
Waterville Lodge, Freemasons, 5062, 5091
Waterville Monument Association, 5024
Waterville Public Library, 5104-5106, 5109
Waterville Street Railway, 5107
Watkins, George Henry, 1725
Watkins, Lura Woodside, 1406
Watkins, Malcolm, 3268
Watson, Andrew Elwell, 1474, 1838
Watterson and Pray Purchase and Camden Grant, former
    name of Kingman
Watts, George B., 1337
Waugaman, Charles A., 3305
Waukeag, former name of Sullivan
Waukeag, locality in Hancock
Waverly, locality in Pittsfield
Wawenock Indians, 1203
Wawridgewick, former name of Norridgewock
The Wayfarer, pseud., see Porter, Joseph Whitcomb
Waymouth, George, 160, 175, 285, 302, 729, 806, 998,
    1061, 1318, 4100
Wayne, John Lakmord, 1338
Wayne, Me., 5118-5122
Weapons, see Firearms
Weare family, 5306
Weary Club, Norway, 3957
Weather, 414, 416, 1313, 1344, 2507, 2748, 4026
Webb, Nathan B., 2597
Webb District, locality in Columbia
Webb Hill, locality in Mattawamkeag
Webb Mills, locality in Casco
Webber, Dorothy P., 3573
Webber, John W., 2650
Webber, Laurance E., 3909, 5350
Webber, Samuel R., 1339
Webber Neighborhood, locality in Freedom
Webbertown Township, 5123
Weber, Carl J., 5110
Webhannet, former name of Wells
Webhannet, locality in Wells
Webster, Arthur Gordon, 1620
Webster, Daniel, 4, 58, 283, 432-433, 461, 624-625,
    632, 716, 1340, 1369, 2100, 3132, 3134
Webster, David W., Jr., 2706
Webster, Donald B., Jr., 1341
Webster, Henry Sewall, 1342, 1649, 3175, 4143
Webster, Millard D., 2284
Webster, alternate name of Sabbattus
Webster, locality in Orono
Webster-Ashburton Treaty, 4, 58, 283, 432-433, 461,
    624-625, 716, 880, 1340, 1346
Webster Corner, locality in Lisbon
Webster Corner, locality in Sabbattus
Webster Plantation, 5124
Wedding Cake House, Kennebunk, 3410
Weed, Ernest H., 2572
Weeks Corner, locality in Pittsfield
Weeks Mills, Me., 2768
Weeks Mills, locality in New Sharon
Weeksboro, locality in Dudley Township
Weiss, Harry B., 4513
Welchville, Me., 4050
Weld, Me., 5125-5128
Wellcome, Henry Solomon, 3095
Wellcome family, 3095
Wellington, Me., 5129

Wellington, former name of Monticello
Wells, Me., 1322, 1884, 5130-5140, 5320
Wells, Me. 300th Anniversary Committee, 5140
Welsh, David, 1343
Welsh, Stanley, 4550
Welsh (nationality), 2454
Wendell, Thomas, 3053
Wentworth, Bertrand Hebron, 1344
Wentworth, Howard L., Jr., 4514
Wentworth, John, 641
Wentworth Corners, locality in Cushing
Wescott, locality in Waterboro
Wesley, Me., 5141
Wesley Methodist-Episcopal Church, Bath, Me., 2249
Wesserunsett, former name of Canaan
West, Albert, 2897
West, Rethel C., 3743
West Bath, Me., 5142
West Bernardstown, former name of Cornville
West Bowdoinham, former name of Bowdoin
West Bowdoinham, former name of Lisbon
West Brooksville, Me., 1581
West Butterfield, former name of Sumner
West Butterfield Slip, former name of Sumner
West Congregational Chapel, Portland, 4515
West Dover, locality in Dover-Foxcroft
West Eden, Me., 2176
West Falmouth, former name of Freeman
West Forks Plantation, 5143
West Gardiner, Me., 1633, 1649, 5144-5145
West Gouldsboro, Me., 1579, 3216, 3220
West Harpswell, Me., 3306
West Harpswell Baptist Church, 3306
West Indian Township, former name of Woodville
West Kennebunk, Me., 3425
West Kennebunk, Me. Methodist Church, 3425
West Lovell, Me., 3632
West Machias, former name of Machias
West Middlesex Canal Grant, 5146
West Mills, locality in Industry
West New Portland, locality in New Portland
West Newfield, Me., 3883
West Paris, Me., 5147-5149
West Parish Congregational Church, Bethel, 2291
West Pittston, former name of Randolph
West Point, locality in Phippsburg
West Pond, former name of Rome
West Precinct of Pownalborough, former name of
    Dresden
West Road, locality in Bridgewater
West Seboeis, locality in Long A Township
West Senebec, locality in Appleton
West Sullivan, Me., 1579, 4861
West Waterville, former name of Oakland
Westbrook, Perry Dickie, 4869
Westbrook, Thomas, 258, 1291
Westbrook, Me., 1483, 1492, 1512, 5150-5171
Westbrook, Me. Chamber of Commerce, 5168
Westbrook, locality in Weld
Westbrook College, 4359, 4516
Westbrook Congregational Church, 5162, 5171
Westbrook Junior College, see Westbrook College
Westcustogo, former name of North Yarmouth
Westfield, Me., 5172
Westfield Academy Grant and Deerfield Academy Grant,
    former name of Westfield

Westford Academy Grant, former name of Linneus
Westmanland Plantation, 1456
Weston, Hannah Watts, 1851
Weston, Isaac, 1345, 1533, 2813, 4517
Weston, Jonathan Delesdernier, 2924, 2937
Weston family, 1851
Weston, Me., 5174
Westport, Me., 5175
Westquatagoe, former name of North Yarmouth
Weston, Nathan, 2033
Wetherell, Alice M., 1347
Wetmore Isle, former name of Verona
Weygand, James Lamar, 4518
Wetherbe, R. L., 1346
Weygandt, Cornelius, 2826
Weymouth, George, see Waymouth, George
Weymouth, Gorham N., 2310
Whaling, 336, 852
Wharves, 2575, 2714, 3972, 4519
Wheatland, Stephen, 1348
Wheelden, Mrs. L. B., 2164
Wheeler, Amos Dean, 4100
Wheeler, Edith H., 4830
Wheeler, George Augustus, 1621, 2573, 2706, 2738-2739
Wheeler, Henry Warren, 2573-2575, 4136
Wheeler, W. C., 265-266
Wheeler, William A., 2576, 4520
Wheelersborough, former name of Hampden
Whipple, George Chandler, 75
Whipple, Joseph, 1350
Whitcombs Corner, locality in Waldo
White, Bruce H. M., 2577
White, Clarence H., 5111-5113
White, Jessie Wing, 3044
White, John, 3146
White, John W., 1351, 1475
White, Myrtle T. M., 4551
White, Stella King, 2674
White, Thomas R., 4034
White, William, 2271
White Mountain Club, Portland, 4241
White Oak Hill, locality in Poland
White Rock, locality in Gorham
White School Corner, locality in Madison
Whitefield, Me., 5176-5178
Whitehead, Russell Fenimore, 707
Whiteoak Corner, locality in Warren
White's Bridge, 1494
Whites Bridge, locality in Standish
Whites Corner, locality in Montville
Whites Corner, locality in New Gloucester
Whites Corner, locality in Winterport
Whiteside, William B., 1352
Whitin, Ernest Stagg, 1353
Whiting, Bartlett J., 4720
Whiting, Me., 5179
Whitman, Charles, Foster, 2584, 3955-3956
Whitman, Vic, 3957
Whitman, William Edward Seaver, 1354, 2759
Whitmore, Allan R., 3021A
Whitney, Clinton, 1355-1356
Whitney, Seth Harding, 1357-1358
Whitney, Stephen T., 5282
Whitney, Wendell, 4099
Whitney Corner, locality in Warren

Whitney Corner, locality in Newburgh
Whitney Lodge, Freemasons, Canton, 2654
Whitneyville, Me., 1863
Whitneyville and Machiasport Railroad, 1863
Whittaker, Frederick W., 2162
Whittemore, Edwin Carey, 3888, 5113-5117
Whittemore, James O., 2598
Whittemore, Margaret, 5274
Whitten, Albion, 4142
Whittier, Charles, 2850-2851
Whittier, Henry Smith, 2911
Whittier, Isabel Mary Skolfield, 2578
Whittier, John Greenleaf, 698
Whittier, L. H., 3247
Widber, Mrs. J. O., 799, 801
Wieden, Clifford, 3870
Wieden, Marguerite, 3870
Wiggin, Edward, 1476-1477
Wiggin, Frances Turgeon, 1360
Wiggin, Ruby Crosby, 1361, 1921
Wight, Carrie, 3887
Wight, Charles A., 3269
Wight, Denham Bartlett, 1726
Wightman, Ida May, 5351
Wilcox Settlement, locality in Cary Plantation
Wild River Railroad, 473
Wilde, Oscar, 2157
Wilder, Elizabeth F., 865
Wilder, Gerald G., 2579
Wilder, Philip S., 2493, 2580-2582
Wilder Young Hill, locality in Freedom
Wildes District, locality in Kennebunkport
Wildwood, locality in St. Albans
Wildwood Park, locality in Cumberland
Wiley Corner, locality in Lincolnville
Wilkins, Austin Horatio, 1362-1363
Wilkins, Raymond S., 1364
Will, Richard T., 3307
Willard, Benjamin J., 4522
Willard, Lawrence F., 3446, 4561
Willard, locality in South Portland
Willardham, locality in St. George
Willey, A. S., 1875
Willey, Austin, 1365
Williams, Anson R., 2194
Williams, Harriet R., 4907
Williams, Henry Clay, 106
Williams, Margaret, 2194
Williams, Myron R., 3958
Williams, Nathaniel West, 2609
Williams, Reuel, 1990
Williams, Stephen Guion, 3850
Williams College Grant, former name of Garland
Williams College Grant, former name of Lee
Williamsburg Township, 5181
Williamson, Joseph, 1366-1374, 1578, 2034, 2272-2273, 2740-2745, 3901, 4523, 5233
Williamson, Robert B., 1375
Williamson, William Durkee, 1376-1377, 1765, 2163, 4999
Willimantic, Me., 5182
Willis, John Lemuel Murray, 1378-1380, 2959, 2987-2992
Willis, William, 656, 1381-1388, 1534, 2666, 3878, 4100, 4269, 4480, 4524-4527
Willis Corners, locality in Thomaston

Williston, Belvin Thomas, 3798
Williston Church, Portland, 4413-4414
Willoughby, Charles Clark, 1389
Willoughby, Malcolm F., 5352
Wills, see Probate records
Wilson, Adam, 4917
Wilson, Charles B., 5219
Wilson, Charles G., 1552, 3871
Wilson, Charles Morrow, 1390, 1478
Wilson, Delmer, 3832
Wilson, Ella M., 1479
Wilson, Fred Allan, 3506
Wilson, George Adam, 4056, 4060, 4066
Wilson, James, 1391
Wilson, John, 150
Wilson, Joseph Kennard, 4137
Wilson, Otis D., 4717
Wilson family, 3506
Wilson, former name of Elliottsville Plantation
Wilson Corner, locality in Ellsworth
Wilson District, locality in Harrington
Wilson Museum, Castine, Me., 2746-2747
Wilsons Mills, Me., 3599
Wilsons Mills, Me. Sesquicentennial Booklet Com-
    mittee, 3599
Wilton, Me., 1419, 5183-5191
Wilton, Me. First Congregational Church, 5190-5191
Wilton Lodge, Freemasons, 5185, 5188
Winchester, Alice, 2341
Windemere, locality in Unity
Windham, Me., 1493-1494, 5192-5211
Windham, Me. Bicentennial Booklet Committee, 5209
Windham, Me. Bicentennial Committee, 5210
Windmills, 4318
Windsor, Me., 5212
Windsorville, locality in Windsor
Wing, George Curtis, 1970, 3816
Wing, Henry A., 1392
Wings Mills, locality in Mount Vernon
Winkumpaugh Corners, locality in Ellsworth
Winn, Ralph H., 5353-5354
Winn, Me., 50, 5213-5215
Winn, Me. St. Thomas' Church, 5213, 5215
Winnecook, locality in Burnham
Winnegance, locality in Phippsburg
Winslow, Howard L., 3043
Winslow, John T., 4192
Winslow, Sidney L., 4973
Winslow, Will P., 3036
Winslow, Me., 1639, 5216-5221
Winslow Mills, locality in Waldoboro
Winslow Pottery, Portland, 4192
Winsor, Justin, 1329, 1393, 3147
Winter, Carl George, 1876
Winter, Francis, 1806
Winter Harbor, Me., 5222-5226
Winter Harbor Yacht Club, 5224
Winter Street Congregational Church, Bath, 2204-2205,
    2250
Winterport, Me., 3091, 5227-5234
Winters, Erma, 3402
Winterville Plantation, 5235
Winthrop, Me., 3532, 5236-5245
Winthrop, Me. Congregational Church, 5242
Winthrop, Me. Winthrop Bicentennial Committee, 5243
Winton, Elizabeth S., 5312

Wiscasset, Me., 801, 1153, 1322, 1677, 1704, 1937,
    5246-5276
Wiscasset and Quebec Railroad, 1394
Wiscasset Fire Society, 5271
Wiscasset, Waterville and Farmington Railroad, 276,
    921, 1285, 1361, 1921
Wish, Oscar R., 1535
Wiswall, Ichabod, 1271
Witchcraft, 848, 1395, 2984, 3459
Witham Corner, locality in Starks
Witherle, George H., 3817
Withington, Lothrop, 538
Wixson, Mrs. Eldwin A., Sr., 5221
Wohlfarth, J. B., 1396
Wolf's Neck, 3105
Woman's Christian Temperance Crusade, 2164
Woman's Literary Union, Portland, 4176
Women, 96, 189, 353, 651, 688, 797-798, 800, 908,
    942, 1397, 2164, 4000, 4028, 4031, 4176, 4237,
    4756, 5250, 5267, 5274
Wood, Beatrice Dawson, 75
Wood, Charles Dayton, 1398
Wood, Elsie, 4528
Wood, Esther E., 2342-2345
Wood, Ethel M., 1399
Wood, Henrietta Danforth, 3902
Wood, Jacob, 1727
Wood, Joseph, 1622, 1711, 1831
Wood, Lilla Eva, 2792
Wood, Richard George, 1400-1401, 3222
Wood, Solomon, 2391
Wood carving, 1031, 3485, 3499
Wood pulp, see Paper making and trade
Woodbridge Corner, locality in Sherman
Woodbury, Charles Levi, 1712
Woodbury, Horatio, 4057
Woodbury, Kenneth B., Jr., 1402
Woodbury, Nathan Franklin, 1403-1404
Woodcock, A. H., 4553
Woodcock, W. H., 4718
Woodfords, Me., 4211, 4374, 4415-4416, 4449, 4469
Woodfords Congregational Church, Portland, 4211,
    4374, 4415-4416, 4449
Woodland, Me. (Aroostook Co.), 5277
Woodland, Me. (Washington Co.), 2039-2040
Woodland Junction, locality in Baileyville
Woodlawn, see Black Mansion, Ellsworth
Woodman, Cyrus, 2610
Woodman, Harris S., 5236
Woodmans Mills, locality in Searsmont
Woodrowville, locality in Rumford
Woods, John B., 1405
Woodside, Charles L., 1406
Woodstock, Me., 5278-5282
Woodstock, New Brunswick, 3985
Woodville, Me., 5283
Woodwell, P. M., 5330
Woolen and worsted, 3226-3227, 4680
Wooley, Dion E., 1407
Woolsey, Sarah C., 962
Woolson School, Portland, 4363
Woolwich, Me., 1808, 5284
Woolworth Farms, Winthrop, 5244
World War (1939-1945), 241, 870, 1063, 2237, 3487,
    4373, 4544

World War I, see European War, 1914-1918
Worth, Edmund, 3910
Worthey, Mary G., 1408
Worthington, J. W., 3401
Wottens Mill, locality in Warren
Wray, Ruth Arline, 1409
Wrenn, Tony P., 5276
Wright, Abiel H., 1489
Wright, Frank V., 2480
Wright, Harold W., 1410
Wright, Laurie Robeson, 4960
Wright, T. C., 2654
Wright, Walter W., 3959
Writers' Program. Maine, 1650, 4530
Wyman, Drew T., 1536
Wyman, Mary Alice, 1410A
Wyman, former name of Vienna
Wyman, locality in Milbridge
Wyman Dam, locality in Moscow
Wyman Township, 5286
Wytopitlock, locality in Reed Plantation

Yacht clubs, 2035, 4435, 5224
Yachts and Yachting, 79, 166, 296, 2216, 2638, 4831
Yallalee, Bud, 3022
Yarmouth, Me., 440, 1521-1522, 1524, 5287-5303
Yarmouth, Me. First Congregational Church, 5300-5301
Yarmouthville, locality in Yarmouth
Yeaton, Polly, 3071
Yellow Kid Press, Portland, 4518
Yerxa, Donald A., 1412, 4532

York, Dick, 1413
York, Lottie E., 5245
York, Robert M., 1414-1418
York, Vincent, 1419
York, Me., 801, 962, 987, 5304-5355
York and Cumberland Railroad, 978
York Beach, Me., 5322, 5346
York County, 602, 978, 1045, 1877-1913
York Co., Me. Register of Deeds, 1913
York County Conference, 1887
York Harbor, Me., 5348
York Institute, Saco, 4642
York Lodge, Freemasons, Kennebunk, 3412
York Manufacturing Company, Saco, 4637
York Militia Company, 5307
York National Bank, Saco, 4634
York Tea Party, 5311
York Tercentenary Committee, 5355
Yorke, Dane, 1420, 2296, 2311
Young, Arthur H., 2437-2438
Young, Harold H., 1421
Young, Hazel, 3715
Young, Norma, 2938, 4587
Young, Oscar E., 4572
Young Men's Christian Association, Portland, 4436
Young Men's Republican Club, Portland, 4533
Youngs Corner, locality in Auburn
Youngtown, locality in Lincolnville

Zenas Thompson and Brother, Portland, 4361
Ziegler, Arthur P., Jr., 4506
Zion's Hill, Me., 2763

NEW BRUNSWICK

QUEBEC

AROOSTOOK

PISCATAQUIS

PENOBSCOT

N

Madawaska
St Agatha
Frenchville
Fort Kent
Grand Isle
Van Buren
Hamlin Plt
Caswell Plt
Cyr Plt
Connor Twp
Limestone
Caribou City
Fort Fairfield
Easton
Mars Hill
Blaine
Cox Patent
Bridgewater
Monticello
Littleton
Houlton
Hodgdon
Cary Plt
Amity
Orient
Weston
Danforth
Forest City Twp
Forest Twp
Brookton
Topsfield
Cordville
Lambert Lake Twp
Vanceboro
T3 R3 NBPP

St Francis
St John Plt
New Canada Plt
Wallagrass Plt
Eagle Lake
Winterville Plt
Portage Lake
Nashville Plt
Garfield Plt
Oxbow Plt
Ashland
Masardis
Stockholm
New Sweden
Woodland
Westmanland Plt
Perham
Wade
Castle Hill
Mapleton
Chapman
Westfield
E Plt
Presque Isle City

Stacyville
Patten
Mount Chase
Sherman
Crystal
Hersey
Dyer Brook
Merrill
Moro Plt
Smyrna
Oakfield
Island Falls
Dudley Twp
Webbertown Twp
Ludlow
New Limerick
Hammond Plt
Linneus
Glenwood Plt
Reed Plt
North Yarmouth Academy Grant
Macwahoc Plt
Kingman Twp
Drew Plt
Prentiss Plt
Webster Plt
Carroll Plt
Lakeville Plt
Winn
Chester
Woodville
Medway
East Millinocket
Millinocket
Indian Purchase
Grindstone Twp
Hopkins Academy Grant
Soldiertown Twp
Long A Twp
Mattawamkeag Twp
Benedicta
Silver Ridge
Upper Molunkus Twp
Molunkus Twp
Matta wamkeag Plt
Kossuth Plt
Carroll Plt
Topsfield

Big Twenty Twp
Allagash Plt
Big Ten Twp
Big Six Twp
Comstock Twp
Dole Brook Twp
Seboomook
Pittston Academy Grant
Plymouth Twp
Little W Twp
West Middlesex Canal Grant
Soldiertown Twp T2 R3
Brassua Twp
Tomhegan Twp
Rockwood Strip T1 R1
Misery Twp
Sapling Twp
Big Squaw Twp
Harfords Point Twp
Little Squaw Twp
Squaretown Twp
Chase Stream Twp
Misery Gore
Long Pond Twp
Parlin Pond Twp
Johnson Mountain Twp
Upper Enchanted Twp
Bald Mountain Twp T4 R3
Alder Brook Twp
Hammond Twp
West Forks Plt
Moxie Gore
Moose River
Jackman
Dennistown Plt
Attean Twp
Holeb Twp
Appleton Twp
Skinner Twp
Lowelltown Twp
Gorham Gore
Beattie Twp
Merrill Strip
Coburn Gore
Forsyth Gore
Blake Gore
Bradstreet Twp
T5 BKP WKR
T5 R7
T5 R6 BKP WKR
T4 R5 NBKP
Sandy Bay Twp
Hobbstown Twp
Prentiss Twp

Mt Katahdin Twp
Rainbow Twp
Frenchtown Twp
Shawtown Twp
Bowdoin College Grant East
Bowdoin College Grant West
Beaver Cove Plt
Greenville
Kineo Twp
Days Academy Grant
Spencer Bay Twp
Lily Bay Twp
Sandbar Tract
East Middlesex Canal Grant
Lobster Twp
Northeast Carry Twp
Little W Twp
Elm Stream Twp
Russell Pond Twp
St John Twp
Chesuncook Twp
Eagle Lake Twp
Super Mountain Twp
Trout Brook Twp
Nesourdnahunk Twp
Yaezie Gore
TA R11 WELS
TB R11 WELS
TB R10 WELS
Katahdin Iron Works Twp
T5 R9 NWP
T3 R9 NWP
Greenville

WELS